Advanced Financial Accounting

FOURTH EDITION

Richard Lewis MSc FCA

Pro-Vice-Chancellor of the Open University

David Pendrill BSc (Econ) MSc FCA ATII LTCL

Esmée Fairbairn Professor of Accounting and Financial Management,
University of Buckingham

PITMAN
PUBLISHING

PITMAN PUBLISHING
128 Long Acre, London WC2E 9AN

A Division of Pearson Professional Limited

First published in Great Britain 1981
Second edition 1985
Third edition 1991
Fourth edition first published in 1994

A CIP catalogue record for this book can be obtained from the British Library.

ISBN 0 273 60500 3

10 9 8 7 6 5 4 3 2

Typeset by Wyvern Typesetting Limited
Printed and bound in Great Britain by Page Bros, Norwich

The Publishers' policy is to use paper manufactured from sustainable forests.

CONTENTS

PREFACE

In the third edition of *Advanced Financial Accounting*, published in 1991, we explained the widespread changes which had been made to the system for setting and enforcing accounting standards in the United Kingdom. Since that time, the Accounting Standards Board has had a considerable impact on the form of financial statements, while the Financial Reporting Review Panel has begun to flex its muscles.

Two of the most important new standards of the ASB have been FRS 1 'Cash Flow Statements' and FRS 3 'Reporting Financial Performance'. FRS 1, which is discussed in Chapter 11, replaces the requirement for a Statement of Source and Application of Funds with a requirement for a more comprehensible Cash Flow Statement. FRS 3, discussed in Chapter 6, has made fundamental changes to the presentation of the profit and loss account and introduced a new primary statement, the Statement of Total Recognised Gains and Losses. As a consequence, financial statements of large companies are looking much more complicated than they ever did. Other important pronouncements have been FRS 4 'Capital Instruments' (*see* Chapter 5) and FRED 4 'Reporting and Substance of Transactions' (*see* Chapter 6), while the Discussion Paper 'Goodwill and Intangible Assets' (*see* Chapter 8) suggests that a solution in this controversial area is still a long way off.

While moving ahead with the issue of standards, the ASB has also been undertaking substantial work on its Statement of Principles, which will ultimately be published as a book. This is an attempt to build a conceptual framework to provide help in setting consistent accounting standards and in coping with new problems. We refer to the various discussion drafts and exposure drafts where relevant throughout the text.

In its Discussion Paper 'The role of valuation in financial reporting', published in March 1993, the ASB makes it clear that, although it recognises the serious limitations of the present modified historical cost accounting system, it proposes to continue to operate within that system. It makes the modest proposal that certain assets be revalued, namely properties, quoted investments and some stocks. Such an approach falls far short of the more full blooded accounting systems which we discuss in Part IV, Accounting and Price Changes, but is probably all that is politically acceptable in this era of low inflation.

As with the third edition, we have included in Appendix I questions from the professional examination papers of the Chartered Association of Certified Accountants and the ICAEW. This time we have also included questions taken from the Advanced Financial Accounting paper of the Chartered Institute of Management Accountants. We gratefully acknowledge the permission of these three bodies to reproduce their questions.

In order to help readers to check their understanding of topics, answers to certain questions are included in Appendix II. However, to keep the book to a reasonable size and to assist lecturers, answers to the remaining questions are contained in a separate solutions manual. We are very grateful to Brian Pain, Senior Lecturer in Accounting, the University of Luton, and John Blakemore, Visiting Lecturer in Accounting, the University of Luton, for all their work in providing these solutions.

We are grateful to our publisher, Pat Bond, for his encouragement and advice, and to our secretaries, Barbara Heaton and Jean Thompson for all their skill and hard work in turning our drafts into a final manuscript. As always, we are heavily indebted to our wives, Pamela and Louise, for allowing work on *Advanced Financial Accounting* to encroach so much upon our leisure time.

RWL
DP
July 1994

PART I

The framework of financial reporting

1. Introduction

One of the most difficult tasks facing an author is deciding how to start his book. An elegant epigram or an eye-catching sentence might well fix the attention of prospective readers or, more importantly, potential purchasers of the book, but such devices do not seem appropriate in this case. We feel that it would be best to start the book in a fashion which reflects its approach, i.e. we shall adopt a practical stance and start by discussing what we mean by the three words which constitute the title of the book – *Advanced Financial Accounting*. It will be convenient to start at the end of the title and then work back.

A number of definitions of accounting are available in the literature, and of these we will select the oft-quoted description provided by the Committee of the American Accounting Association (AAA), which was formed in order to prepare a statement of basic accounting theory. In its report, which was published in 1966, the Committee defined accounting as 'the process of identifying, measuring, and communicating economic information to permit informed judgments and decisions by users of the information'.[1] The Committee went on to point out that the concept of economics referred to in the definition 'holds that economics is concerned with any situation in which choice must be made involving scarce resources'.[2]

We feel that the definition is a useful one in that it focuses not on the accounting process itself but on the reasons why information is required. It is all too easy for accountants to become obsessed with the techniques of their craft and to forget that the application of these techniques is not an end in itself but merely a means to an end. In this book we shall constantly reiterate such questions as 'Why is this information required?' or 'How will this data be used?' We believe that a proper study of accounting must start with an examination of the needs of decision makers.

The distinction between financial and management accounting is a convenient one to make, but it must not be regarded as one which divides the two areas of study into water-tight compartments. It would be better if the phrases financial and management accounting were replaced by external and internal accounting as management accounting has financial implications while managers have more than a passing interest in financial accounting. However one describes the dichotomy, it is generally agreed that financial, or external, accounting is primarily concerned with the communication of information about an entity to those who do not share in its management, while management, or internal, accounting refers to the communication of information to the managers of the particular

---

1 *A statement of basic accounting theory*, AAA, New York, 1966, p. 1.
2 *Ibid.*, p. 1.

entity. Thus the American Financial Accounting Standards Board (FASB) has defined financial reporting as activities which are intended to serve 'the informational needs of external users who lack the authority to prescribe the financial information they want from an enterprise, and therefore must use the information that management communicates to them.'[3] This is a helpful definition which indicates that in this book we will be concerned with financial information that is given to users rather than information which is required by an individual or group of individuals who are in a position to enforce their request.

We should also make it clear that we shall concentrate on the question of accounting for limited companies. We, of course, recognise that there are many other forms of entity which are of importance, including nationalised industries, charities and central and local government and their associated agencies. Our reason for deciding to concentrate on the topic of limited companies is not because we do not think that the other forms of entity do not merit the concern of financial accountants, but it is because we recognise that, at least at present, most accounting courses are concerned with the private profit-seeking sector of the economy. More attention is now being paid to the problems of accounting for other forms of entity, and we hope that this work will soon be reflected in the content of accounting courses. In the meantime our readers will appreciate that many of the topics that will be discussed in the context of limited companies are of direct relevance to other forms of economic entity.

We should also provide some indication of the interpretation that should be placed on the adjective 'advanced' in the title of this book. It does not mean that the text will concentrate on detailed and complex manipulations of debits and credits, although we shall of course have to deal with such matters from time to time. In the context of this book, 'advanced' means that we shall concentrate on the identification, measurement and communication of economic information in the light of our acceptance of the view of the AAA that such information is required to help in decision making. Thus we shall concentrate on such questions as what information is relevant to decision makers, how the information is relevant to decision makers, how the information should be measured, and the manner in which it should be communicated. In so doing we shall describe and evaluate alternative approaches to the solution of accounting problems.

The definition of accounting which we quoted above stops at the 'communication' of information. However, it must be emphasised that the interpretation of information is a vital part of an accountant's work, and it is clear that this aspect must be regarded as being an integral part of the process of communication. It should be noted that the definition of accounting does not extend to decision making. Of course, many accountants do become involved in decision making, but when they do so they are performing a managerial rather than an accounting role. We would not for one moment wish to argue that accountants should not become involved in management, but it is essential to distinguish between accounting and decision making. It is important that information provided by accountants should be as free as possible from personal bias (*see* the discussion of the meaning of objectivity on page 18) but if the accountant does not keep the distinction between accounting and decision making clear in his own mind, there is a great danger that he might, possibly quite unconsciously, bias the information provided towards the decision which he would wish to see made.

The above discussion might suggest that we see the work of an accountant as being of

3 Statement of Financial Accounting Concepts (SFAC) 1, *Objectives of financial reporting by business enterprises*, FASB, Stamford, Conn., 1978, Para. 28.

a purely technical nature in which he or she is allowed little latitude for professional judgment. This is not the case, because we believe that the accountant must strive to find out and attempt to satisfy the information needs of decision makers and, as we shall show, this is no easy task.

ACCOUNTING THEORY

Academic accountants tend to bemoan the lack of generally accepted accounting theory. This is understandable because theory is the stock in trade of academics. Some 'practical' accountants are probably rather pleased that there is no generally agreed theory of accounting because some practical men are suspicious of theory and theorising as they believe that it gets in the way of 'real work'. However, those who take this view are probably ignorant of the role that theory can play in practical matters and do not realise that an absence of theory does give rise to many real and practical difficulties.

The description of accounting theory provided by Hendriksen shows clearly the practical uses of theory. Hendriksen defines accounting theory as 'logical reasoning in the form of a set of broad principles that (i) provide a general frame of reference by which accounting practice can be evaluated and (ii) guide the development of new practices and procedures'.[4] Expressed in this way, it is obvious that the function of theory is to assist in the resolution of practical problems. The existence of a theory would mean that we could say and explain why, given a number of assumptions, method X (perhaps current cost accounting) is to be preferred to method Y (say historical cost accounting).

There have been numerous attempts to construct a theory of accounting.[5] In the early stages of development an *inductive* approach was employed. Thus the practices of accountants were analysed in order to see whether patterns of consistent behaviour could be derived from the observations. If a general principle could be observed, then procedures which deviated from it could be castigated as being unsound. These first attempts were mainly directed towards the establishment of explanatory theories, i.e. theories which explained why certain rules were followed.

This approach failed for two main reasons. One is the difficulty of distinguishing consistent patterns of behaviour from a mass of procedures which had developed with the growth of accountancy and the problem of establishing any general set of explanatory statements. The second, and possibly more important, reason was that the approach did not help to improve accounting practice in any significant way. The approach only allowed the theorist to say 'what is' and not 'what ought to be'.

In response to these problems a different method of theory construction emerged in the 1950s. This method was normative in nature, i.e. it was directed towards the improvement of accounting practice. The method also included elements of the deductive approach, which essentially consists of the derivation of rules on the basis of logical reasoning from a basic set of objectives. The theories generally consisted of a mixture of deductive and inductive approaches, the latter being used to identify the basic objectives. These approaches to theory construction were extremely valuable in that they generated a number of books and papers which have had a profound effect on the development of accounting practice, in particular in the area of current value accounting.[6]

4 E. S. Hendriksen, *Accounting Theory*, 4th edn, R. D. Irwin, Homewood, Ill., 1982, p. 1.
5 Hendriksen, *op. cit.*, provides a detailed and authoritative description of these attempts.
6 Some of the more important developments are summarised in Chapter 15.

Attempts have been made to construct a general conceptual framework for accounting. The most ambitious attempt was that of the Financial Accounting Standards Board (FASB) in the USA, and, although this ran into difficulties and work on the project ceased in the mid-1980s, it has had considerable influence on accounting thought and developments in the USA and elsewhere.

One approach to the development of a framework is based on the suggestion that accounting theory should be developed by first identifying the users of accounts and then finding out what information they require. It is suggested that the framework would allow us to judge current accounting practice and to help guide the development of new procedures, i.e. satisfy the objectives of accounting theory which were specified by Hendriksen. This is an essentially practically oriented approach, and is the point which was made explicitly by Professor B Carsberg and his co-authors when they wrote, 'usefulness for specified purposes is the criterion by which the merits of accounting practice must finally be judged'.[7]

This approach has been endorsed by a number of significant British and international studies, including *The Corporate Report* (*see* page 8); the report of the Sandilands' Committee on Inflation Accounting[8]; the International Standards Committee publication *Framework for the Preparation and Presentation of Financial Statements*[9]; Professor David Solomons' report to the Research Board of the ICAEW *Guidelines for Financial Reporting Standards* (*see* page 10); *Making Corporate Reports Valuable*, a discussion document published by the Research Committee of the Institute of Chartered Accountants of Scotland (*see* Chapter 18) and the draft 'Statement of Principles' published by the Accounting Standards Board (ASB) (*see* page 13). A central feature of all these reports is the identification of user groups and a discussion of their needs.

The various stages in this approach, which has been termed a user decision-oriented approach, has been summarised by Arnold as follows:[10]

(a) Identify the various user groups and determine the information requirements of each group.
(b) Identify alternative accounting methods which might be employed for reporting to users.
(c) Specify ways of testing the extent to which the alternative accounting methods satisfy the needs of the different user groups.
(d) Using the methods developed in (c) above, select the best methods of reporting to each group paying regard to the costs of each alternative.
(e) Consider the extent to which the method selected in (d) can be combined in a general report.

Arnold points out that the outcome of the above procedure is unlikely to remain stable over time and that it will be necessary to repeat the process at regular intervals. One reason why this would be necessary is that users' understanding of accounting information may change, perhaps as a result of the introduction of new concepts in published financial accounts. Another possible reason may be social changes which might have an effect on

---

7 Carsberg *et al.*, 'The objectives of published accounting reports', *Accounting and Business Research*, Winter 1974.
8 *Report of the Inflation Accounting Committee*, Cmnd 6225, HMSO, London, 1975.
9 IASC *Framework for the preparation and presentations of financial statements*, London, 1989.
10 J. Arnold, 'Information requirements of shareholders', in *Current Issues in Accounting*, 2nd edn, B. Carsberg and T. Hope (eds), Philip Allan, Oxford, 1984.

the balance between the different user groups. Thus a method of accounting which might be considered suitable in an era when the objective of limited companies is the maximization of shareholders' wealth may well not prove to be acceptable in a period when the interests of employees of limited companies are given greater consideration.

The above approach is intuitively appealing, but it does beg a large number of questions, some of which will be considered later in the book. First, let us consider the way in which accountants should react if they believe that users are basing their decisions on the wrong data. Should they simply supply decision makers with the information for which they are asking, or should accountants supply them with the information for which they should be asking? For the management accountant, the problem is not a difficult one for he usually has a direct link with the decision maker and can supply the information for which he has been asked, but he can also tell the decision maker how, in the accountant's opinion, the decision-making process could be improved. The problem for the financial accountant is very much greater because there is nothing like the same direct link between the supplier and user of information and because of the impact of legal and other regulatory influences on financial accounting. This question must be considered as part of the broader issue of who should write the rules for financial accounting, and we shall consider this question in Chapter 2.

Another matter which merits further consideration is whether it is desirable that accountants should attempt to produce one 'all purpose' form of report, i.e. whether step (e) above is necessary. It may be that the information needs of the different user groups are so disparate that little will be gained by attempting to produce one form of accounting report. A related question is how intergroup conflicts of interests can be handled. An obvious example of such potential conflict is provided by the employee user group as they might well request information which the shareholder group might prefer them not to have. Less obvious perhaps, but equally important, is the question of intragroup conflict. It may very well be that the different user groups are by no means homogeneous and that within each group there might be found subgroups with different needs for information and with conflicting interests. To take an extreme example, a short-term creditor might not wish long-term creditors to be made aware of the unhealthy financial state of the particular company if that company is relying on the acquisition of long-term finance in order to pay off the short-term creditors.

The resolution of conflicts such as these means that some group or body will need to consider the costs and benefits in so far as they affect each group or subgroup and fix on a compromise. The obvious candidates for this role are the government and the accountancy profession. This is a controversial issue to which we shall return when reviewing the current position concerning the establishment of rules in the financial accounting area.

USER GROUPS

The approach to the construction of an accounting theory which we described above has only just started to develop. A number of attempts have been made to identify user groups but, as yet, little progress has been made in respect of the remaining steps.

The traditional view was that the most significant or, in the extreme case, the only user groups were those comprising the company's shareholders and creditors, and this view was dominant, until recent times, in the development of company law. Given this attitude, one should ask why the law requires the publication of financial accounts of limited companies, for it could be argued that shareholders and creditors only need invest in or lend to those companies which agree to provide them with the desired amount of information. The intervention of the State would seem to be an abrogation of the *laissez faire* principle upon which the development of company law was based.

There are perhaps a number of reasons, including the paternalistic attitude of governments which is exhibited by the desire to stop people making fools of themselves by investing in, say, gold mines in Dorking. But perhaps the most important factor is the belief founded in classical economic theory that under conditions of perfect competition the interests of society are best served if all individuals seek to maximize their own wealth. This point was elegantly made in 1850 by the Society for Promoting Christian Knowledge in its *Easy Lessons on Money Matters for the Use of Young People* when it wrote 'it is curious to observe how, through the wise and beneficent arrangement of Providence, men thus do a greatest service to the public when they are thinking of nothing but their gain'.[11]

One of the necessary conditions for perfect competition is perfect knowledge, and thus it is argued that in order for the 'wise and beneficent arrangement of Providence' to come to fruition, it is necessary among other things for shareholders to know where they will be able to earn the greatest returns; this can be brought about by the publication of financial accounts by limited companies. While the argument is an important one, justifying the existence of laws requiring the publication of accounting information, it must be admitted that most markets are not perfectly competitive and that the information supplied by financial accounts can in no way be described as supplying the participants of the markets with perfect knowledge.

Another factor which can be said to justify the State's role in the regulation of the publication of accounting information is the recognition of groups other than existing and potential shareholders with a legitimate interest in being informed of a company's financial performance. The recognition of other user groups whose interests needed to be considered was a major feature of *The Corporate Report*.

THE CORPORATE REPORT

In 1974 the Accounting Standards Committee (ASC) set up a working party to re-examine the scope and aims of published financial reports in the light of modern needs and conditions. The conclusion of the working party was published in June 1975 as a discussion document entitled *The Corporate Report*. This is an important document which did not perhaps receive the attention it deserved because its publication was followed closely by the arrival of the Sandilands report on inflation accounting which was considered to have greater immediate impact. The slow progress of accounting reform can be gauged by the observation that a report published in the mid-1970s is still of great relevance some 20 years later. All serious students of accounting should read *The Corporate Report* and we shall not attempt to summarise its conclusions here but shall confine ourselves to a discussion of the user groups which were identified by the report. The report listed seven user groups,[12] and these groups were:

11 A somewhat more modern exposition of this view which deals with its implications for financial accounting will be found in H. B. Rose, *Disclosure in company accounts*, Eaton Paper 1, Institute of Economic Affairs, London, 1965.

12 The Sandilands Committee produced a similar list.

1 The equity-investor group, which includes existing and potential shareholders as well as holders of convertible securities, options and warrants.
2 The loan-creditor group, existing and potential holders of debentures and loan stock as well as providers of short-term secured and secured loans.
3 The employee group, including existing, potential and past employees.
4 The analyst-adviser group. This group includes financial analysts and journalists, and other providers of advisory services such as credit-rating agencies.
5 The business-contact group, which includes customers, trade creditors and suppliers and competitors, business rivals and those interested in mergers, amalgamations and takeovers.
6 The government, including tax authorities, local authorities and those departments and agencies concerned with the supervision of commerce and industry.
7 The public. This is perhaps the most controversial group and includes, according to the authors of *The Corporate Report*, tax-payers, rate-payers, consumers and other special-interest groups such as political parties.

It might be said that of the above groups the analyst-adviser group does not constitute a separate group in so far as advisers act on behalf of one or more of the main user groups. The importance of the recognition of the analyst-adviser group relates to the way in which information is presented, because the existence of this group might justify the publication of information which would not be readily understood by the members of other groups unless such information could be interpreted for them by their advisers.

As mentioned earlier in the chapter, the identification of user groups is only the first stage in the development of accounting theory. The next step is the identification of their needs, but unfortunately we are still not clear about these despite the considerable attention that has been paid to the decision models employed by, in particular, shareholders. We will, in the course of this book, refer to the present state of knowledge in this area and should emphasise that any discussion of alternative accounting methods in such areas as depreciation, the treatment of foreign currency, etc., should be prefaced by consideration of the likely relevance of the information supplied to those who use the accounts.

FASB CONCEPTUAL FRAMEWORK PROJECT

In the United States the FASB was, from the mid-1970s to the mid-1980s, engaged in a major project to develop a 'conceptual framework' for accounting which it defined as 'a constitution, a coherent system of interrelated objectives and fundamentals that can lead to consistent standards and that prescribes the nature, function and limits of financial accounting and financial statements'.[13] While the FASB set itself the ambitious task of identifying a 'coherent system of interrelated objectives and fundamentals' in practice its approach was close to the user-oriented approach we have discussed above.

Thus with regard to financial reporting in business enterprises, the Board arrived at a number of initial conclusions which were published in November 1978 in the Statement of Financial Accounting Concepts (SFAC) 1, 'Objectives of financial reporting by business

---

13 *Scope and Implications of the Conceptual Framework Project*, FASB, Stamford, Conn., 1976, p. 2.

enterprises'. The conclusions have been summarised by Macve[14] as follows:

1 The users on whose decisions attention is focused are investors and creditors, but other users have similar needs.
2 The main factor of importance for the decision they have to take is the assessment of the amount, timing and uncertainty of the future cash flows of the business enterprises in which they are interested.
3 The primary focus of financial reporting is on the provision of measures of enterprise income together with information about enterprises' economic resources, obligations and owners' equity. Information about past cash flows is also useful, and so are explanations by management about the accounts.

While the main users were identified as investors and creditors many other user groups were identified in SFAC 1 which correspond fairly closely with those enumerated in *The Corporate Report*. The suggestion that the assessment of future cash flows is the major factor is, of course, well rooted in economic theory but still leaves open the question of the extent and the manner by which this need can be satisfied by the publication of financial reports. Based on its initial conclusion, much of the FASB's ambitious programme was concerned with how financial accounts could be constructed in such a way as to make them useful in helping investors, creditors and others assess the magnitude, timing and risk of future cash flows.

Unfortunately, it proved impossible to obtain general acceptance of the conclusions which flowed from this approach and work on the project ceased soon after the publication of SFAC 5, 'Recognition and measurement in financial statements of business enterprises' in December 1984.

GUIDELINES FOR FINANCIAL REPORTING STANDARDS

In this paper[15] prepared for the Research Board of the ICAEW and addressed to the ASC, Solomons made an important contribution to the debate on accounting reform. As the title of the paper suggests, Solomons set out to provide the ASC with a set of broad conceptual guidelines to aid it in the setting of standards. His view on the way in which conceptual underpinnings, whether described as a framework or by the less ambitious term guidelines, can best be summarised by reproducing a quotation described by Solomons as 'wise words from Canada':

... attempts to state conceptual frameworks are unlikely to result in great flashes of illumination that instantly resolve areas of controversy in financial reporting. It is only if standard-setters are prepared to take an explicit framework seriously and allow its influence to guide their

---

14 Richard Macve, *A Conceptual Framework for Financial Accounting and Reporting*, ICAEW, London, 1981, p. 55. In this report which was commissioned by the ASC, Professor Macve *inter alia* reviewed current literature and opinion in the UK, US and elsewhere on the possibility of developing an agreed conceptual framework. He provides a very useful summary of the work of the FASB as well as commenting on other endeavours including *The Corporate Report*. Macve's conclusion is that while the quest for a conceptual framework or general theory is important in identifying questions that need to be answered, it would be idle to hope that a framework could be developed that would give explicit guidance on practical problems.
15 David Solomons, *Guidelines for Financial Reporting Standards*, ICAEW, London, 1989.

resolution of individual issues that it will, little by little and from precedent to precedent, gain in power and utility.[16]

Solomons was a major contributor to the US conceptual framework project and thus it is not surprising that there are many similarities in the approaches advocated by the two reports. The approach of the Solomons report may be summarised as follows:

1 Needs of user groups

Identify the needs of those who use general purpose financial statements. His list of user groups is similar to, but more restricted, than those identified in *The Corporate Report*. Solomons lists four groups of prime users:

(a) present and potential investors;
(b) present and potential creditors (including suppliers);
(c) present and potential employees, and those who may act on their behalf, such as trade unions;
(d) present and potential customers who are or may be tied to a company by long-term supply contracts.

Solomons excludes governments and regulatory agencies from the list of users of general purpose reports as they have the power to be provided with information specific to their needs.

2 The nature of financial statements

Solomons argues that assets and liabilities are the basic elements of financial statements and that all other items comprising the financial statements, or sub-elements, are derived from changes in the basic elements. He identifies two schools of thought on the derivation of profit. One is the revenue and expense view, which regards the profit or loss for the period as being the difference between the revenue for the period and the expense of earning that revenue. The alternative view, espoused by Solomons, the asset and liability view, sees the profit or loss for the period as the difference between the excess of assets over liabilities at the end of the period and the excess at the beginning of the period, after adjusting for capital introduced and withdrawn.

The revenue and expense view allows, for example, the inclusion in the balance sheet of costs incurred in the period which are not deemed to relate to the revenue of the period while the asset and liability approach only allows assets and liabilities to be included which satisfy specified tests both for existence and recognition (*see* Chapter 6).

Solomons' arguments in favour of the asset and liability approach may be briefly summarised as follows:

(a) It is based on a more logical and consistent set of principles.
(b) It is more closely related to the measurement of wealth creation; the objective of profit-seeking enterprises.
(c) It preserves the integrity of the balance sheet and its value as a financial statement.

---

16 Ross M. Skinner, *Accounting Standards in Evolution*, Holt, Rinehart and Winston of Canada Ltd, 1987, p. 649, quoted by Solomons, *op. cit.*, p.8.

(d) It discourage artificial methods of 'smoothing income'.[17]

3 Desirable qualities of financial statements

Solomons, like a number of other authorities, believes that there are a number of qualities that need to be exhibited by financial reports if they are to be of value to users. We shall return to this subject later in the chapter.

4 Choice of accounting model

Finally, Solomons chooses an accounting model which he believes best serves the needs of users and which is derived from the asset and liability approach and reflects the desirable qualities referred to above. His choice is a model based on the maintenance of real financial capital with assets and liabilities measured by reference to their 'value to the business' (*see* Chapters 3, 15 and 16).

IASC FRAMEWORK

In 1989 the International Accounting Standards Committee published a paper called *Framework for the Preparation and Presentation of Financial Statements*, the purpose of which was to assist national and international standard setters, to help accountants with the treatment of items not yet covered by a standard and assist auditors form an opinion as to whether a set of financial statements comply with international standards.

The paper is structured in the same way as the Solomons' *Guidelines*, in that it starts with a discussion of user groups and their needs, the objectives of financial statements and the desirable characteristics of financial statements. It then goes on to deal with the definition, recognition and measurement of the elements of financial statements and a discussion of the various concepts of capital and capital maintenance.

At this point it is worth noting that its list of user groups is virtually identical to that contained in *The Corporate Report*, that is it includes the government and the public. However, it does give primacy to the needs of investors insofar that it states that 'As investors are providers of risk capital to the enterprise, the provision of financial statements that meet their needs will also meet most of the needs of other users that financial statements can satisfy'.[18]

The IASC adopt a similar position to Solomons on the desirability of only including in the balance sheet assets and liabilities which satisfy recognition criteria (*see* Chapter 6).

---

17 A spirited defence of the revenue and expense approach is provided by Ron Paterson, 'Primacy for the P & L Account', *Accountancy*, August 1990. Paterson argues that historical cost accounting should be regarded as a modification of cash flows accounting and that the function of the balance sheet is to pick up the effects of the reallocation made to the cash flows resulting from the application of the accruals and prudence concepts.

18 IASC, *Framework for the Preparation and Presentation of Financial Statements*, Para. 10.

THE ACCOUNTING STANDARDS BOARD'S STATEMENT OF PRINCIPLES

In 1991 the ASB initiated a period of consultation on its draft 'Statement of Principles' through the issue of a series of discussion drafts and exposure drafts which, because of the intention to publish a complete document, carry chapter numbers.

As at January 1994 the following drafts were in issue:

(a) Exposure Draft. 'The objective of financial statements and the qualitative characteristics of financial information' (Chapters 1 and 2)
(b) Discussion Draft. 'The elements of financial statements' (Chapter 3)
(c) Discussion Draft. 'The recognition of items in financial statements' (Chapter 4)
(d) Discussion Draft. 'Measurement in financial statements' (Chapter 5)
(e) Exposure Draft. 'Presentation of financial information' (Chapter 6).

We will deal in this chapter with the first of these exposure drafts, chapters 1 and 2 of the Statement of Principles; reference will be made to other draft chapters later in the book.

Chapters 1 and 2 follow closely the relevant sections of the IASC's 'Framework' paper; indeed, other than in a few cases where there is a difference in substance between the two documents, the ASB adopted the exact wording of the IASC paper subject only to some minor drafting changes.

DESIRABLE CHARACTERISTICS OF FINANCIAL ACCOUNTING REPORTS

The essentially pragmatic approach to theory construction which was described earlier in the chapter, and which has been in vogue for over 15 years, includes the identification of the desirable characteristics of financial accounting reports. The characteristics are, in the words of Solomons, 'the principal criteria that distinguish "good" accounting from "bad" accounting'.[19]

Most authorities are in broad agreement about the nature of the desirable characteristics, but unfortunately there is no consistency in the terminology used to describe them. The various reports referred to earlier in this chapter, as well as many other authors, all present their own list of characteristics, but in order not to swamp readers with a book of lists we shall present only three, those of:

(a) the FASB, as published in SFAC 2, Figure 1.1
(b) David Solomons from 'Guidelines for Financial Reporting Standards', Figure 1.2, and
(c) the ASB, which is based on the IASC, Figure 1.3.

Of these the FASB comes first both in time and importance insofar that the conceptual framework project was a major influence on the reports which followed.

The identification of the desirable characteristics can help in the development of a conceptual framework in that they can be used to test various alternative models or in the setting of specific accounting standards. Their value is diminished to the extent that the lists include potentially conflicting characteristics such as prudence and realism. The FASB

19 Solomons, *op. cit.*, p. 5.
20 SFAC 2 'Qualitative Characteristics of accounting information', FASB, Stamford, Conn., 1980.

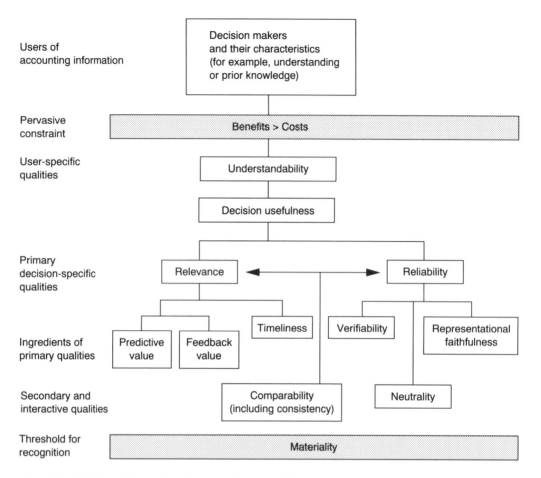

Fig. 1.1 FASB – a hierarchy of accounting qualities

hierarchy of characteristics is useful in this respect in that it distinguishes between the primary and secondary qualities.

The FASB list of characteristics is headed by usefulness for decision making, with relevance and reliability being regarded as the two primary qualities. Thus, subject to two overriding requirements, that the benefits exceed the costs and that the information is material, the more relevant and reliable the more desirable it is.

Solomons, who surprisingly does not refer to understandability, subsumes relevance within decision usefulness; he regards relevance as the prime characteristic: 'Relevance must come first, for if information is irrelevant, it does not matter what other qualities it has'.[21]

One of the differences between the IASC and the ASB is in the identification of the principal qualitative characteristics. The IASC listed four:

- Relevance
- Reliability

21 Solomons, *op. cit.*, p. 30.

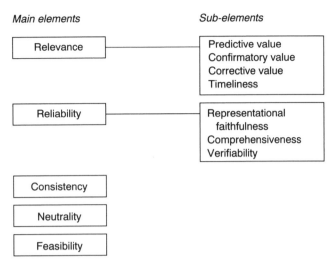

Note: materiality is regarded as setting a lower limit on the size of error, omission, etc below which a reasonable person's judgement would not be affected. Solomons therefore sees it as a different kind of characteristic of information from the others listed above.

Fig. 1.2 Solomons' 'Guidelines for Financial Accounting Standards'

- Understandability
- Comparability.

As can be seen in Figure 1.3 the ASB suggests that only the first two of these are principal characteristics; understandability and comparability are regarded as secondary characteristics. This view makes sense. Information which is reliable or relevant will be of some use even if lacking understandability and comparability, whilst understandable and comparable information which is neither relevant nor reliable would be of no use at all. But the absence of understandability and comparability from relevant and reliable information would greatly limit the usefulness of the information, hence they are important secondary characteristics.

We shall now briefly discuss some of the more important elements identified in the list, starting with the two elements, identified by both the FASB and ASB, as being primary – relevance and reliability.

Relevance

The ASB (and IASC) and Solomons argue that information is relevant to decision making if it has the capacity to help a decision maker:

- to form an expectation (predictive value);
- to confirm an expectation (confirmatory value);
- to revise an expectation (corrective value).

The definition looks both towards and backwards – some financial information is relevant because it helps make predictions about the future while some is relevant because of what it says about the past, but the past is past and so past information is only truly relevant if it helps users make future predictions.

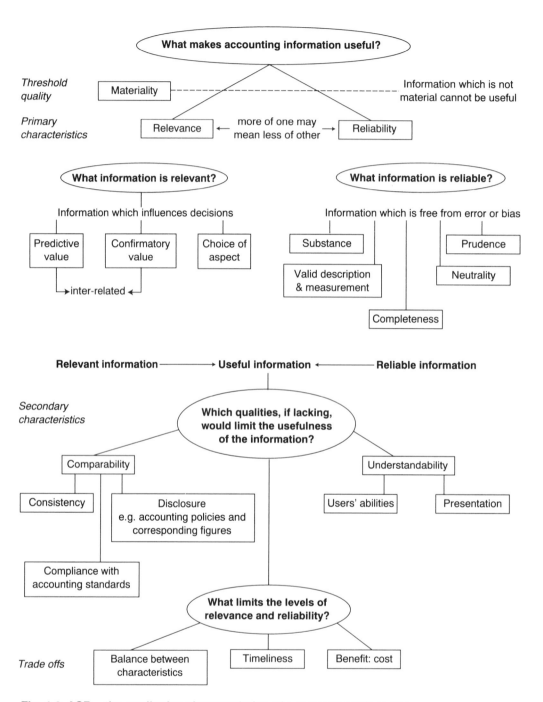

Fig. 1.3 ASB – the qualitative characteristics of accounting information

Timeliness is regarded as being related to relevance by all three authorities cited. Up-to-date information is more relevant than stale news and there are occasions when a rough estimate made quickly is more useful than a more protracted, more precise statement.

Thus, there may be a trade-off between relevance and reliability; the balancing of competing characteristics ultimately, as is pointed out by the IASC, is a matter of professional judgment.[22]

The use of the term 'choice of aspect' by the ASB in the sub-elements of the relevance characteristic needs some explanation. It is related to the 'valid description and measurement' aspect of the 'reliability' primary characteristic and represents another of the differences between the IASC and the ASB. The IASC took the view that 'faithful representation' was a sub-element of reliability. In other words, if information is to be reliable then it needs to present a valid description, free of error, of the transaction or event recorded. The ASB agrees that faithful representation does in the main relate to reliability but wishes to emphasise that the choice of what aspect of a transaction or event to report bears also on the *relevance* of the information. A simple example is the decision whether or not to report the change in market value of an asset. Thus, the ASB draft separates out as two elements of 'faithful representation', the 'choice of aspect' dimension, which aspect of a transaction or event to record, which supports relevance, and 'valid description and measurement' which supports reliability.

Reliability

Solomons describes the nature of reliable information neatly by stating that to be reliable information must:

- tell the truth and nothing but the truth – representational faithfulness
- tell the whole truth – comprehensiveness
- be of such a nature that users can be reasonably assured of its truthfulness – verifiability.

The IASC specifically includes the concept of 'substance over form' in its list while Solomons sees this concept as part of representational faithfulness. The notion of substance over form which requires that the accounting treatment of a transaction should reflect the commercial effect is an important issue to which we shall return in Chapter 6.

Verifiability is vital if users are to have confidence in the financial statements; normally the required assurance to users stems from the knowledge that the information has been verified by a qualified observer who is independent of the person responsible for the preparation of the statement.

The Corporate Report placed a special meaning on the element of reliability in that it suggested that 'information should be reliable in that users should be able to assess what degree of confidence may be reposed in it'.[23] The committee went on to state that the credibility of information is enhanced if it is independently verified but that there may be circumstances where it is useful for an entity to supply information which is not verifiable in this way.

Understandability

It is generally agreed that an essential quality of information presented in financial statements is that it is readily understandable by users. But what level of knowledge of accounting should be assumed of users?

22 IASC, *op. cit.*, Para. 45.
23 *The Corporate Report, op. cit.*, Para. 29. A similar point was made by the Sandilands Committee in their discussion of realism.

The ASB suggests that:

> ... users are assumed to have a reasonable knowledge of business and economic activities and accounting and a willingness to study the information with reasonable diligence.[24]

Yes, but what is reasonable?

The authors of *The Corporate Report*, who generally took a more liberal attitude to the needs of user groups such as employees and the general public, suggested a dual approach and stated that understandability:

> calls for the provision, in the clearest possible form, of all the information which the reasonably instructed reader can make use of and the parallel presentation of the main features for the use of the less sophisticated.[25]

The Corporate Report line of argument supports the production of simplified accounts as alternatives to the main financial statements (*see* Chapter 11). These simpler accounts are likely to be of even greater value if the ASB carries through its intentions which will result in more complex primary financial statements.

The ASB's policy is set out in the paragraph cited above:

> Information about complex matters that should be included in the financial statements because of its relevance to the economic decision-making needs of users should not be excluded merely on the grounds that it may be too difficult for certain users to understand.

The greater complexity of financial statements resulting from the need to comply with Financial Reporting Standards can already be seen; FRS 3 'Reporting Financial Performance' is a good example.

Neutrality (objectivity)

Both the FASB and the IASC regard neutrality or objectivity as a sub-element of reliability while Solomons sees it as a main element.

Most accountants appear to believe that objectivity is one of the most important of the desirable qualities. Unfortunately, it is not clear that all accountants attach the same meaning to the word. It is probably true that most accountants believe that objectivity is virtually synonymous with verifiability, i.e. that accounts should, so far as it is possible, be based on information which is capable of independent verification and should exclude items which depend on personal opinion or judgment. However, it is clear that the authors of the reports attached different meanings to the word objectivity. In *The Corporate Report* and the FASB's SFAC 2 (which uses the term neutrality) objectivity is defined as the avoidance of bias towards any particular user group. This point is made in *The Corporate Report*, where it is stated:

> The information presented should be objective or unbiased in that it should meet all proper user needs and neutral in that the perception of the measurer should not be biased towards the interest of any one user group. This implies the need for reporting standards which are themselves neutral as between competing interests.[26]

The difference between the 'traditional' (objectivity equals verifiability) and the more recent interpretation of objectivity is an extremely important one which might have a

24 ASB, draft 'Statement of Principles', Chapter 2, Para. 38.
25 *The Corporate Report*, *op. cit.*, p. 29.
26 *The Corporate Report*, *op. cit.*, p. 29.

considerable impact on the development of accounting practice. For example, in the past objectivity was claimed as the justification for the use of historical cost accounting as opposed to current value accounting on the grounds that the historical cost of an asset was more objective than its current value. However, to the extent that historical cost financial statements are conservative in that they understate the values of assets, it is likely that they will be biased in favour of potential shareholders at the expense of existing shareholders and could thus be said to fail the test of objectivity applied in *The Corporate Report* and SFAC 2.

The Sandilands Committee did not define objectivity in the same way as the others, but it did to some extent reject the traditional interpretation of objectivity. The Sandilands Committee accepted that it was highly desirable that accounts should be based on information which is capable of independent verification but went on to state that the principle should not be rigidly applied as it believed that an element of subjective judgment may be necessary if accounts are to show a true and fair view. The Sandilands Committee's conclusion was that:

> However, while objectivity for its own sake may not necessarily be desirable, the scope for the exercise of subjective judgment should be kept to reasonable levels. In general the principle should be not to exclude the exercise of subjective judgment provided it is made clear where and to what extent it has been used.[27]

The ASB (and IASC) take a slightly different line. They agree that neutrality means freedom from bias but relate this not to the need to balance the interests of different user groups but the need to ensure that the users are not unduly influenced in their decision making. Thus financial statements are not neutral 'if, by the selection or presentation of information, they influence the making of a decision or judgement in order to achieve a predetermined result or outcome'.[28]

Comparability and consistency

Comparability is seen to be vital because users of accounts will want to be able to compare a company's results both with the results achieved by that company in previous periods and with the results achieved by other companies. The first aspect is important because it helps users to form judgments about the progress of an entity while the importance of the second aspect stems from the need to compare various opportunities.

It is all very well to state that comparability is desirable, but it is not clear how comparability is best achieved. It is not necessarily true that the adoption of the same accounting policies by all companies will achieve comparability if it is found that an accounting policy which might be appropriate to the circumstances faced by one company is inappropriate in the case of another company facing different circumstances.

Consistency is included in both the Sandilands and SFAC 2 lists but reservations were expressed about excessive adherence to this feature. All other things being equal the consistent application of the selected accounting treatment over time is desirable in that it aids comparability, but when the needs of users change or better accounting techniques are developed then the accounting methods should also change. The Sandilands Committee emphasised the possible conflict between realism and consistency and stated

27 *The Sandilands Report, op. cit.*, p. 63.
28 ASB Statement of Principles, Chapter II (draft), Para.31.

that, in general, realism was the more important of the two. Similarly, in the SFAC 2 hierarchy of qualities, comparability (including consistency) is shown as being a second-order quality when compared with relevance and reliability.

While it is important to ensure that new methods are introduced when it is appropriate to do so, it is desirable in such cases to report the results using both the old and new methods for at least one year in order to aid comparability.

PRUDENCE – AN UNDESIRABLE CHARACTERISTIC?

Prudence is identified as a virtue by the ASB and IASC which state that preparers of accounting statements have to contend with many uncertainties which should, in its view, be recognised by the disclosure of their nature and extent and by the exercise of prudence in the preparation of the financial statements. Along traditional lines the ASB counsels against the overstatement of assets and income and the understatement of liabilities and expenses but recognises that deliberate over- and understatements would not be neutral and, therefore, not have the quality of reliability.[29]

A similar position is taken in SFAC 2 where it is declared that conservatism should be regarded as a 'prudent reaction to uncertainty to try and ensure that uncertainties and risks inherent in business situations are adequately considered and not be interpreted as the deliberate, consistent understatement of net assets and profits'.[30]

Solomons does not accept that prudence is a desirable characteristic, except insofar that estimates must be made with care. Both he and the authors of this book question the value of an approach which introduces a bias derived from the application of tests of different degrees of rigour in the estimation of the value of assets and expenses as compared with the estimation of liabilities and revenues; an approach which is given implicit support by the IASC. Solomons regards prudence as being a financial, not an accounting virtue.

Prudence, if interpreted as encouraging or permitting a systematic bias in accounting measurement, should not be regarded as a desirable characteristic. Neutrality, relevance and reliability are much surer guides for the development of accounting practice.

SUMMARY

We have in this chapter stressed the need for 'theory' to guide and underpin 'practice'. We have also, very briefly, pointed out that the attempts to formulate general theories have not yet proved to be successful and have suggested that less ambitious methods linked directly to the needs of users of accounts may prove to be more fruitful.

In the absence of any generally agreed theory of accounting, the identification of the desirable characteristics of accounting reports may be regarded as a necessary 'second best' solution and a possible set of characteristics derived from a number of important reports has been discussed.

We have reiterated the necessity to relate the provision of accounting information to the needs of the decision makers, and this point has influenced the way in which this book has been written. Some of the chapters, especially those related to interpretation and

29 ASB, *op. cit.*, Para. 32.
30 SFAC 2, 'Qualitative characteristics of accounting information', FASB, Stamford, Conn., 1980, Para. 95.

problems of valuation, directly address the way in which accounting information is used. Other chapters, such as those concerned with the problems of group accounts, place greater emphasis on technical accounting matters, but even then our discussion of the relative merits of different methods would be sterile if the needs of users were ignored.

The questions of who does and who should set the rules by which the accounting game is played are important and complex issues and these form the subject of the next chapter.

RECOMMENDED READING

E. S. Hendriksen, *Accounting Theory* 4th edn, R. D. Irwin, Homewood, Ill, 1982.

The Corporate Report, ASC, London, 1975.

Report of the Inflation Accounting Committee, Cmnd 6225, HMSO, London, 1975 (The Sandilands Report).

ICAS, *Making Corporate Reports Valuable*, Kogan Page, London, 1988.

D. Solomons, *Guidelines for Financial Reporting Standards*, ICAEW, London, 1989.

CHAPTER 2

Sources of authority

INTRODUCTION

UK Statute Law imposes a requirement for companies to prepare accounts and provides detailed rules on the contents of those accounts. The Companies Act 1981, which implemented the European Community Fourth Directive, substantially increased the minimum information to be disclosed, introduced prescribed formats for accounts and specified valuation rules which must be applied in preparing accounts. The legal rules are now contained in the Companies Act 1985, as amended by the Companies Act 1989.

The Stock Exchange increases the disclosure requirements for companies within its jurisdiction.

Statute law and the Stock Exchange rules do not specify completely how the various amounts disclosed in the accounts should be calculated. For this the accountant must turn to such sources of authority as accounting principles and conventions established over many years as well as recommendations and standards issued by relevant professional bodies.

This chapter looks at each of these sources of authority and concludes by looking briefly at the work of the International Accounting Standards Committee and the European Community.[1]

LEGISLATION

Background

The advent of the limited liability company by registration under general Act of Parliament in the mid-nineteenth century made possible the separation of management from ownership, which is such a dominant feature of business organisation today. With this separation came the need for directors to render accounts to shareholders to show the performance and financial position of the company. It followed that it was necessary to determine what should be included in such accounts and how they should be prepared.

It would have been possible for the law to have left the specification of the form and content of such accounts to be determined by contract between the shareholders and directors, or even to have left the directors to decide what information should be made available in the particular circumstances. However, the law initially flirted with the regulation of accounting disclosure in the period 1844–56 and then became permanently involved with regulating the contents of company accounts early in this century. The Companies Act 1929 increased the information which companies had to disclose while

---

1 Within the European Union, the company law harmonisation programme, with which we are concerned, is within the jurisdiction of the European Community.

extensive disclosure has been required since the Companies Act 1948.[2]

Before the Companies Act 1981, the accounting requirements of company law allowed companies considerable latitude. The directors were required to prepare accounts which showed a true and fair view and which contained the minimum information specified by the various Companies Acts. These accounts, together with the accompanying auditors' and directors' reports, had to be laid before the shareholders and filed with the Registrar of Companies within certain time limits. While the basic position is unchanged, substantial alterations were made by the Companies Act 1981.

The Companies Act 1981 was mainly concerned with the implementation of the EC Fourth Directive, a directive heavily influenced by the more prescriptive approach to accounting found in France and Germany. As a consequence, the Act was much more prescriptive than previous legislation in the UK. Although it still contained the overriding principle that accounts should give a true and fair view, it increased substantially the amount of information to be disclosed and reduced considerably the flexibility which companies previously enjoyed. Thus, whereas directors were previously able to choose the particular formats and valuation rules which seemed most appropriate in the circumstances, the Companies Act 1981 specified much more tightly the formats and valuation rules to be used.

The provisions of the Companies Act 1981 are now contained in the Companies Act 1985, which was a consolidating Act, but these in turn have been amended by the subsequent Companies Act 1989. The Companies Act 1989 implemented the EC Seventh Directive on consolidated accounts and the EC Eighth Directive on the regulation and qualification of auditors, although it dealt with many other matters as well.

The law requires that full accounts, including group accounts where appropriate, are sent to all shareholders and debenture holders of the company, although permission is given for a listed public company to send a summary financial statement to its shareholders.[3] The latter provision was intended to reduce the cost of sending full accounts to large numbers of relatively unsophisticated shareholders, particularly following the large privatisation issues of the 1980s. Full accounts have to be laid before the company in general meeting except that a private company may elect not to do so.[4] Such provisions are designed to ensure that shareholders and debenture holders receive financial information about companies, while recognising that it may not be necessary formally to present the accounts of a private company at a general meeting.

In addition to the above, companies are required to make their accounts available to the public by filing them with the Registrar of Companies within certain time limits, namely ten months after the end of the accounting year for a private company and seven months after the end of an accounting year for a public company. A lesser degree of accountability to the outside world is imposed on small and medium-sized companies which may file modified accounts. Thus, a small company need not deliver a profit and

---

2 Readers who wish to study this historical development of accounting further are referred to H. C. Edey, 'Company accounting in the nineteenth and twentieth centuries', in *The Evolution of Corporate Financial Reporting*, T. A. Lee and R. H. Parker (eds), Nelson, London, 1979, and J. R. Edwards, *A History of Financial Accounting*, Routledge, London, 1989: Chapters 9, 10 and 11 of the latter are particularly relevant.

3 Companies Act 1985, Sec. 251 (as inserted by Companies Act 1989, Sec. 15). This section was implemented by The Companies (Summary Financial Statement) Regulations 1990, SI 1990/515. See Chapter 11, pages 329 to 330.

4 Companies Act 1985, Sec. 252 (as inserted by Companies Act 1989, Sec. 16).

loss account and may file a summarised balance sheet and much abridged notes to the accounts while a medium-sized company may file a modified profit and loss account in which certain items are combined.[5]

The current position

The Companies Act 1985, as amended by the Companies Act 1989, requires that the accounts of a company give the information specified in Schedule 4 using one of the profit and loss account and balance sheet formats provided. However, compliance with this requirement is not sufficient to ensure compliance with the law for there is an overriding requirement that every balance sheet shall give a true and fair view of the state of affairs of the company and that every profit and loss account shall give a true and fair view of the profit or loss of the company for the financial year.[6]

Hence, having prepared the accounts containing the required disclosure, the accountant must then step back and decide whether or not the overall impression created is true and fair. If the accounts do not give such an impression, additional information must be provided. If the provision of additional information still does not result in a true and fair view, then the accounts must be changed, even if this means that they do not comply with the other statutory rules. Particulars of any departure, the reasons for it and its effect must be disclosed in the notes to the accounts.

The statutory requirements outlined above pose a number of problems for the accountant. Familiarity with the disclosure requirements of the Companies Acts is required as is knowledge of the valuation rules to apply in arriving at the figures to be disclosed. Also the accountant must be aware of what is meant by the words 'true and fair'. We will look at each of these three aspects in turn.

The first problem involves detailed knowledge of the Companies Acts and the various guides thereto and considerable practice in applying those rules in various circumstances. We assume that readers have already undertaken a course of study which has given them some knowledge of the requirements of the Companies Acts although, where relevant, we shall reproduce the statutory rules in later chapters.

The second problem involves the selection of valuation rules to apply in arriving at the various figures which appear in the set of accounts. This requires a considerable knowledge of accounting, which this book will help to provide.

Until the Companies Act 1981 accountants would have looked to accounting principles, conventions, recommendations and standards to help them with this task. Although, as we shall see, such sources are extremely important, certain basic accounting principles have now been incorporated into the law. Thus, the law requires that accounts should be prepared in accordance with five accounting principles:

1 Going concern.
2 Consistency.
3 Prudence.
4 Accruals.
5 Separate determination of each asset and liability.

5 Companies Act 1985, Sec. 246 (as inserted by Companies Act 1989, Sec. 13). For further details, *see* Companies Act 1985, Schedule 8.
6 Companies Act 1985, Sec. 226 (as inserted by Companies Act 1989, Sec. 4).

Statute law now requires that these principles must be applied unless there are special reasons for departing from them. Where such special reasons exist, a note to the accounts must state the details of the departure, the reason for it and its effect.[7] We shall discuss the first four of these principles later in this chapter and the fifth principle in Chapter 6.

The Act provides that companies may prepare their accounts using either historical cost accounting rules or alternative accounting rules.[8]

The alternative accounting rules are so framed to permit companies to use piecemeal revaluations in their historical cost accounts or to prepare current cost accounts as their main accounts, although in either case it is necessary to provide certain information to enable partial reconstruction of the historical cost accounts.

Some UK accountants are strongly opposed to the inclusion of such accounting principles and valuation rules in the law. They argue that it provides a straitjacket which may impede accounting development and two examples will illustrate their arguments.

In Chapter 1 (page 20) we have suggested that accountants should depart from the prudence convention and thereby remove the systematic bias which it produces in accounts. It has become much harder for accountants to effect such a departure now that the prudence convention has been enshrined in statute law.

The alternative accounting rules permit the preparation of current cost accounts as the company's main accounts. While this may have been the system of accounting which was in vogue when the Act was passed, this may not be the case in future years. The reference to current cost in the Act makes it more difficult for accounting to evolve.

When accounts have been prepared, the accountant must decide whether they show a true and fair view and, if not, in what respects they need to be altered. These words 'true and fair' were first introduced together in the Companies Act 1948, following the recommendations of the Cohen Committee.[9] They have never been defined by statute but, rather, their meaning has become established by usage. A good definition has been provided by G. A. Lee:[10]

> Today, 'the true and fair view' has become a term of art. It is generally understood to mean a presentation of accounts, drawn up according to accepted accounting principles, using accurate figures as far as possible, and reasonable estimates otherwise; and arranging them so as to show, within the limits of current accounting practice, as objective a picture as possible, free from wilful bias, distortion, manipulation or concealment of material facts.

So, in order to decide whether or not a set of accounts presents a true and fair view, it is necessary for the accountant to have recourse to a body of accounting principles which have developed over many years, wedded mainly to the historical cost basis of valuation.[11]

STOCK EXCHANGE RULES

Where companies are listed on the Stock Exchange or have shares which are dealt in on

7 Companies Act 1985, Schedule 4, Part II, Sec. A., Paras 9–15.
8 The historical cost accounting rules are contained in the Companies Act 1985, Schedule 4, Sec. B while the alternative accounting rules are contained in Schedule 4, Sec. C.
9 *Report of the Committee on Company Law Amendment*, Cmnd 6659, HMSO, London, 1945.
10 G. A. Lee, *Modern Financial Accounting*, 3rd edn, Nelson, London, 1981, p. 270.
11 For a fuller discussion of the term 'true and fair' readers are referred to David Flint, *A True and Fair View in Company Accounts*, Gee and Co., London, 1982.

the Unlisted Securities Market, they must comply with additional disclosure requirements laid down by the Stock Exchange. In the former case the requirements are contained in the Stock Exchange Listing Agreement which is to be found in the official publication *Admission of securities to listing* (the Yellow Book). In the latter case, they are set out in *The Stock Exchange unlisted securities market* (the Green Book).

The rules require the provision of both greater and more frequent information than that required by law and two examples will suffice to illustrate them.

First, listed companies are required to provide additional information in respect of certain creditors, namely, (i) bank loans and overdrafts and (ii) other borrowings of the company. Such companies must provide more detailed information than required by statute law and, in particular, must show the aggregate amounts payable:

(a) in 1 year or less, or on demand;
(b) between 1 and 2 years;
(c) between 2 and 5 years;
(d) in 5 years or more.[12]

This is a more detailed analysis than that required by statute law.[13]

Second, listed companies and those which have shares dealt in on the Unlisted Securities Market must prepare and publish an interim report which contains certain minimum information. In the former case, the report must be sent to shareholders and debenture holders or inserted as a paid advertisement in two leading newspapers while, in the latter case, the report must be circulated to shareholders or published in one newspaper. These exemplify the application of the desirable characteristic of timeliness which we have discussed in Chapter 1.

ACCOUNTING PRINCIPLES AND CONVENTIONS

Accounting concepts

We have seen how statute law requires companies to disclose a considerable amount of information and lays down broad principles which must usually be applied in arriving at the figures disclosed. We have also seen how this information is extended for companies subject to the rules of the Stock Exchange.

In order to prepare accounts complying with the law and, where appropriate, the Stock Exchange rules, an accountant must turn to what are referred to as generally accepted accounting principles or generally accepted accounting conventions. These were first developed during the latter part of the nineteenth century but have been the subject of continuous development as new situations have arisen.[14]

Many such principles or conventions could be listed, but a useful starting point would seem to be the fundamental accounting concepts of SSAP 2, 'Disclosure of accounting policies'. These are defined as 'the broad basic assumptions which underlie the periodic financial accounts of business enterprises'.[15]

Four concepts are listed and these are the same as the first four principles listed in the

---

12 Listing Agreement, Para. 10(1).
13 Companies Act 1985, Schedule 4, Para. 48.
14 *See* B. S. Yamey, 'The development of company accounting conventions', *Three Banks Review*, 1960.
15 SSAP 2, 'Disclosure of accounting policies', Para. 14.

Companies Act 1985. Users of the accounts may assume that the concepts have been applied in the preparation of a set of accounts unless warning is given to the contrary.

The four concepts are as follows:

(a) *Going concern*   Following the application of this concept, the accounts are drawn up on the basis that the enterprise will continue in operational existence for the foreseeable future. Thus, the accountant does not normally prepare the accounts to show what the various assets would realise on liquidation or on the assumption of a fundamental change in the nature of the business. It is assumed that the business will continue to do in the future the same sort of things that it has done in the past. If, of course, such continuation is not expected, then the going concern concept must not be applied. So if, for example, liquidation seems likely then the valuation of assets on the basis of sale values would be appropriate. The accountant must then give warning to the users that the usual going concern concept has not been applied.

(b) *Accruals*   While this is an easy concept to describe and, indeed, to apply in situations which are commonly encountered, its implementation sometimes gives rise to problems. Revenues and costs are not calculated on the basis of cash received or paid. Revenues are recognised when they are earned usually at the date of a transaction with a third party. Against such revenues are charged, not the expenditures of a particular period, but the costs of earning the revenue which has been recognised.

(c) *Consistency*   The consistency concept requires like items to be treated in the same manner both within one set of accounts and from one period to another.

Such a concept could easily prevent progress if applied too rigidly for, if a better accounting treatment than the existing method was discovered, it could never be applied because it would be inconsistent with the past! Obviously, it will be necessary to depart from this concept on occasions but then it is necessary to give warning that such departure has occurred and what the effect has been.

(d) *Prudence*   This concept requires that accountants do not take credit for revenue until it has been realised but do provide for all known liabilities. The intention of this asymmetrical approach is to introduce a bias which will tend to understate profit and undervalue assets. As we have argued in Chapter 1, although such a concept might at first sight be thought to benefit users, it may instead damage their interests. Thus, a shareholder may sell his shares at a low price because the accounts show low profits and low asset values. In addition we shall see that the failure of accountants to come to grips with changing prices results in the overstatement of profits in inflationary periods. In these circumstances adherence to historical cost-based measures has the very opposite effect to that which a prudence concept would seem to require.

It is, of course, possible to have a conflict between two of the above concepts, and SSAP 2 explicitly deals with the situation where a conflict exists between the accruals concept and the prudence concept. In such a case prudence is stated to prevail although, as we shall see, it has been difficult and indeed sometimes unreasonable for the standard setters to comply with this instruction in later Exposure Drafts and Standards.[16]

We have looked at the four fundamental accounting concepts listed in SSAP 2, although it is important to realise that other possible concepts could have been listed. Thus, in International Accounting Standard (IAS) 1, 'Disclosure of accounting policies', the International Accounting Standards Committee (IASC) lists only three fundamental

---

16 *See*, for example, the problem of accounting for foreign currency transactions discussed in Chapter 10.

accounting assumptions: going concern, consistency and accruals. Prudence, substance over form and materiality are then relegated to a secondary level as governing the selection and application of accounting policies.

Even though an accountant follows the four fundamental accounting concepts, he or she still has considerable flexibility in the way in which assets are valued and profit determined. There are, for example, many methods of depreciating fixed assets or of valuing stocks and work-in-progress; there are many ways of accounting for deferred taxation and for translating the accounts of overseas subsidiaries. From the numerous accounting bases available, an accountant must choose the appropriate policy to apply in the circumstances of the particular company.

As we have seen in Chapter 1, there are many different users of financial accounts and their needs for information may conflict: in addition, as we have seen in this chapter, we have no precise idea of what is meant by the words 'true and fair'. Add to this the fact that the valuation of any asset or liability by its very nature, even under the historical cost system, involves taking a view of the future, and it is not surprising that different accountants will arrive at different views of the same business reality and hence report different figures.

Recommendations and freedom of choice

In order to help their members to choose the appropriate accounting policies, the various professional bodies have issued recommendations on accounting principles. For example, the Institute of Chartered Accountants in England and Wales (ICAEW) issued 29 such recommendations between 1942 and 1969, and these provided guidance on all manner of accounting matters. These recommendations were persuasive rather than mandatory and often permitted a choice from various methods of accounting for a particular set of transactions.

To most accountants the existence of such flexible recommendations was useful. In the majority of cases they could be followed, but if their application was not appropriate in a particular set of circumstances an alternative treatment could be used. Most thoughtful accountants appreciated that there was a multitude of accepted accounting principles and that, if two or more accountants independently prepared accounts for the same company, it was unlikely that they would produce the same results.

A number of incidents in the late 1960s brought the existence of such flexibility to the attention of the general public and in 1968 Sir Frank Kearton, Chairman of Courtaulds and the Industrial Reorganisation Corporation, wrote to the President of the ICAEW to complain about 'the plethora of generally accepted accounting principles'. The problem was brought to a head in 1968 in connection with the GEC/AEI and Pergamon/Leasco affairs.[17]

On 11 September 1969 Professor Edward Stamp wrote a letter to *The Times* in which he was very critical of some aspects of the accountancy profession, in particular its lack of independence and its lack of a theoretical foundation for the preparation of accounts. His letter provoked an angry reaction from the accountancy profession in the person of Ronald Leach, President of the ICAEW. Suffice it to say that the criticism and ensuing debate led to the issue of a 'Statement of intent on accounting standards in the 1970s' by the ICAEW in 1969 and to the subsequent formation of the Accounting Standards Steering Committee.

17 These are dealt with in E. Stamp and C. Marley, *Accounting Principles and the City Code: the Case for Reform*, Butterworths, London, 1970.

STANDARDISATION
From 1970 to 1990

The 'Statement of intent on accounting standards in the 1970s' issued by the Council of the ICAEW in 1969 set out a plan to advance accounting standards along the following lines:

(a) narrowing the areas of differences and variety in accounting practice;
(b) disclosure of accounting bases;
(c) disclosure of departures from established definitive accounting standards;
(d) wider exposure for major new proposals on accounting standards;
(e) continuing programme for encouraging improved standards in legal and regulatory matters.

To this end, an Accounting Standards Steering Committee was set up by the Institute of Chartered Accountants in England and Wales, the Institute of Chartered Accountants of Scotland and the Institute of Chartered Accountants in Ireland. The Committee was later joined by representatives of the Association of Certified Accountants (now the Chartered Association of Certified Accountants) and the Institute of Cost and Management Accountants (now the Chartered Institute of Management Accountants) in 1971 and by representatives of the Chartered Institute of Public Finance and Accountancy in 1976. From 1 February 1976 its name was changed to the Accounting Standards Committee and it was reconstituted as a joint committee of the six member bodies acting through the Consultative Committee of Accountancy Bodies (CCAB).

Until 1982, the ASC consisted of more than 20 members, all of whom were qualified accountants. Membership of the committee was part-time and unpaid. The ASC had no power to issue standards in its own right but, once a standard had been set by the committee and approved and issued by the councils of the six CCAB members, individual members of the various professional accountancy bodies were required to comply with the standard. Thus, we had a body of professional accountants imposing rules above those required by the law of the land and attempting to enforce them through the constituent member bodies. Such a process was criticised on two counts.

First the people who can be expected to benefit from standards are the users of accounts. If such is the case, then it may be argued that these users should have a larger say in the formulation of standards. Indeed, accounting standards may have considerable impact on economic behaviour which some would argue should, in a democratic state, be taken into consideration by duly elected Members of Parliament.[18] To give an example, a standard requiring companies to write off all research and development expenditure as it is incurred may cause firms to stop undertaking research and development due to its adverse effects on the profit figure. This may have severe consequences for the progress and competitive position of the nation.

Second, for standards to be effective, it is essential that they are enforced. However, the law places the onus for preparing accounts clearly on the shoulders of directors and professional accountancy bodies have no authority over such directors unless the directors happen to be professional accountants. Even where professional accountants are involved, the ultimate penalty for non-compliance is disciplinary action against those members and the professional bodies appear to have been loath to take such action.

18 For an account of the effect of standard setting on economic behaviour *see* S. A. Zeff, 'The rise of "economic consequences"', *Journal of Accountancy*, December 1978.

The ASC was aware of these and other criticisms and a number of changes were made as a result of two papers: *Setting accounting standards: a consultative document*, known colloquially as the Watts Report after the then chairman of the ASC, Mr Tom Watts, published in 1978, and *Review of the standard setting process*, known as the McKinnon Report' after its chairman, published in 1983.

As a consequence of these reports, membership of the ASC was opened up to include non-accountants representing user groups and some new types of pronouncement were introduced. However, the Watts Report's recommendation that a panel be established to review non-compliance with accounting standards by listed companies was never acted upon.

The 1983 Review introduced the publication of two new types of statement, the Statement of Intent (SOI) and the Statement of Recommended Accounting Practice (SORP). While the SOI, a short public statement explaining how the ASC proposed to deal with a particular accounting matter, has been used very rarely, the SORP is a completely different type of statement issued on topics which are not of sufficient importance to warrant the issue of an accounting standard. These non-mandatory SORPs hark back to the earlier recommendations of the professional accountancy bodies. It was intended that such statements would be issued for matters which are of widespread application but not of fundamental importance, or for matters which are of limited application, in specific industries or particular areas of the public sector. In the case of statements of limited application, SORPs are prepared by the specific industry or areas of the public sector and then 'franked', that is approved, by the ASC or its successor.[19] In spite of the changes which were made, the ASC came under increasing criticism in the 1980s. Its lack of powers of enforcement became blatantly obvious in the context of SSAP 16 'Current Cost Accounting', when at one time only some 25 per cent of the companies to which it applied were actually complying with its provisions. In addition, the ASC faced enormous difficulties in developing standard practice for controversial areas such as accounting for business combinations and intangible assets.

A decline in the credibility of the ASC led to the establishment of the Dearing Committee, named after its chairman, Sir Ron Dearing, which produced its report *The Making of Accounting Standards* (the Dearing Report) in September 1988. This, in turn, has led to fundamental changes in the process of setting and enforcing accounting standards in the British Isles.

The current regime – structure

The Dearing Report took the view that standards should no longer be set by an inadequately financed ASC made up of part-time unpaid members, with only a small technical staff, and with no powers of ensuring compliance with its standards. It therefore recommended major changes.

In the view of the Dearing Report, effective standard setting required considerably more resources than had been available in the past. Given that a large constituency of users benefit from the existence of accounting standards, it was thought to be unreasonable for the process of standard setting to be financed wholly by the accountancy profession.

---

19 An example of the first type of SORP is SORP 2 'Accounting for Charities', issued in May 1988. Some examples of franked SORPs are those issued by the Oil Industry Accounting Committee and the Accounting Standards for Local Authority Group.

Dearing therefore recommended a large increase in the finance available and a sharing out of the cost of standard setting.

As a consequence of the Dearing Report, a Financial Reporting Council, drawn from a wide constituency of interests, has been set up to guide the standard setting process and to ensure that it is properly financed. Standards are set by a new body, the Accounting Standards Board, which has the power to issue standards in its own right. In addition a Financial Reporting Review Panel has been established to examine contentious departures from accounting standards by large companies.

An Urgent Issues Task Force has also been set up as a committee of the ASB to provide timely and authoritative interpretations on the application of standards. As a consequence the present structure is as shown in Figure 2.1.

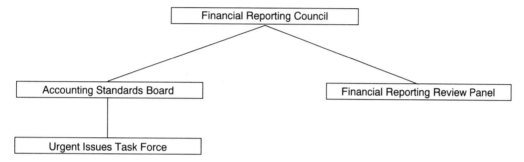

Fig. 2.1 Structure of the organisation for setting and enforcing accounting standards

The Accounting Standards Board is now a much smaller body than its predecessor, the ASC. It consists of not more than nine members with a full-time Chairman and Technical Director, supported by a much larger technical staff of approximately ten professional accountants, to permit a higher level of research. As recommended by the Dearing Report, it has the power to issue standards in its own right and, for this, a two-thirds majority is required.

The introduction of a Financial Reporting Review Panel was more revolutionary, although the establishment of such a body had been proposed in the Watts Report in 1978. It is a panel of some twenty members chaired by a QC. The function of the Review Panel is to examine the accounts of large companies to ensure that they give a true and fair view and comply with accounting standards.

Although the government chose not to give statutory backing to accounting standards, it introduced provisions which facilitate the operations of the Review Panel. The first of these is a requirement for directors of all large (but not small or medium-sized) companies to state in the notes to the accounts whether or not those accounts have been prepared in accordance with applicable accounting standards, drawing attention to material departures and explaining the reasons for them.[20] The second is the introduction of procedures for the revision of accounts which are considered to be defective. These include a procedure whereby accounts can be revised voluntarily by the directors and a procedure whereby the Secretary of State for Trade and Industry or other authorised persons are able

20 Companies Act 1985, Schedule 4, Part III, Para 36A.

to apply to the court for an order requiring the revision of a company's accounts.[21] The Financial Reporting Review Panel is an 'authorised person' under these provisions and concentrates on the accounts of public and large private companies.

The current regime – progress

One of the major problems which confronted the ASB, and indeed the ASC before, was the problem which we have discussed in Chapter 1, the lack of a conceptual framework for accounting. Not surprisingly, the ASB decided to try and develop its own Statement of Principles to provide a framework for standard setting. As we have seen in Chapter 1, a number of discussion drafts and exposure drafts have been issued and it is intended that these will be collected together and published as a book in due course.

While some people might argue that no standards should be set until the Statement of Principles has been finalised, it would have been quite impossible for the ASB to adopt such an approach. Indeed, it is becoming more widely recognised that the search for one conceptual framework is a search for the Holy Grail. Given the multiple users of accounts, there are probably many different conceptual frameworks, with a consequent implication for the adoption of multicolumn reporting.[22] If such is the case then we should not be under any illusion that the Statement of Principles will solve all the problems of accounting although, of course, it may enable us to remove some of the many inconsistencies which exist at present.

While work has been proceeding on the Statement of Principles, the ASB has continued its work on standard setting. It adopted the standards set by its predecessor, while recognising that some of these would need changing in due course, and proceeded to work towards the issue of its own standards. Two of the early standards of the ASB have changed the face of financial reporting quite considerably.

FRS1 'Cash Flow Statements' replaced the requirement for a 'Statement of Source and Application of Funds' with a requirement for a Cash Flow Statement.[23] FRS 3 'Reporting Financial Performance' has changed the face of the profit and loss account, introduced a requirement for a new primary statement 'Statement of Total Recognized Gains' and introduced notes on the historical cost profit or loss and a reconciliation of movements in shareholders' funds.[24]

As we shall see in Chapter 6, the profit and loss accounts appearing since FRS3 are much more complex than previously and it will undoubtedly take some time for users to be able to interpret these new statements adequately.

When we turn to more specific areas of accounting which previously posed problems for the ASC, the jury is still out. Although many well written, thorough discussion papers and exposure drafts have been issued, the ASB has still not produced standards on, for example, Acquisitions and Mergers and Goodwill. Indeed the Discussion Paper on 'Goodwill and Intangible Assets', published in December 1993, is a clear demonstration of how little help the Statement of Principles provides in resolving this particular issue. As we explain in Chapter 8, there appears to be no consensus on the way forward at the present time.

21 These provisions are contained in Companies Act 1985, Sections 245–245C.
22 *See* Chapter 18.
23 *See* Chapter 11.
24 *See* Chapter 6.

While the ASB has been working on these and other major issues, the Urgent Issues Task Force has been providing timely guidance on contemporary accounting problems. Its guidance is provided in the form of Abstracts and, at the end of December 1993, it had issued nine such abstracts.[25]

As explained above, the law now requires directors of large companies to state in the notes to accounts whether or not those accounts have been prepared in accordance with applicable standards, drawing attention to material departures and explaining reasons for them. This provision, introduced in 1989, is clearly set out so it came as something of a surprise and an indication of problems ahead when we learned that one of the first tasks undertaken by the Financial Reporting Review Panel in 1991 and 1992 was to write to the directors of some 240 companies who had failed to include the note required by law!

With regard to other apparent departures from the accounting requirements of the Companies Act, the Financial Reporting Review Panel does not systematically examine the accounts of all the companies within its ambit. Rather it acts only when something which appears to be wrong is drawn to its attention. Its references come from three broad sources: qualified audit reports or recorded non-compliance, cases referred by individuals or corporate bodies and press comment.

During the period up until November 1993, 123 companies were brought to the Panel's attention.[26] Some were not pursued beyond an initial examination but most were pursued with the directors concerned. By November 1993, the Review Panel had not considered it necessary to apply for a Court order for rectification of accounts, although a fund of approximately £2m has been established to finance such legal action. In cases where the companies were found to be at fault, the Panel has been able to reach voluntary agreement with the directors concerned, frequently requiring them to rectify errors in the next set of financial statements.

Advantages and disadvantages of standardisation

Before we examine briefly international standardisation, it is perhaps helpful if we review both the advantages and the disadvantages of standardising accounting practice for the process of standardisation is not without its critics.

Accounting may be described as the language of business. As with any communication, it is important that the preparers of a document and the users adopt the same language. Standards may be regarded as the generally accepted language.

When directors prepare accounts for their companies, they are not likely to be indifferent to the position shown by those accounts for, after all, they will be judged on the basis of the results disclosed. Thus, given many generally accepted accounting bases, the choice of a particular policy may not be free from bias. The establishment of accounting standards, with the consequent need to justify departures from them, limits the possibility of exercising such bias and strengthens the hands of the auditor.

---

25 Some examples of the topics covered are:
UITF Abstract 1 'Convertible bonds – Supplemental Interest/Premium', 24 July 1991,
UITF Abstract 3 'Treatment of goodwill on disposal of a business', 19 December 1991,
UITF Abstract 6 'Accounting for post-retirement benefits other than pensions', 9 November 1992, and
UITF Abstract 9 'Accounting for operations in hyper-inflationary economies', 9 June 1993.
26 *See* 'The State of Financial Reporting', FRC, Second Annual Review (November 1992) and Third Annual Review (November 1993).

In addition it is clear that the issue of exposure drafts and standards has provoked considerable thought and discussion among members of the accounting profession, which has made accounting an exciting area of study.

One of the most pertinent criticisms of the process of standardisation was made by Professor W. T. Baxter writing about recommendations on accounting principles in 1953[27], long before the Accounting Standards Steering Committee was formed. He argued that authoritative backing for one particular accounting treatment may have adverse effects. Although it may help practical men in their day-to-day work, in the longer run it may hinder experimentation and progress. An accountant or auditor may become loath to depart from a particular recommendation or standard and the educational process may become one of learning rules rather than searching for theories or truth. Indeed he argued that, if truth subsequently shows a recommendation or standard to have been wrong, then it may be hard for authoritative bodies to admit that they were wrong.

Both the ASC and the ASB have been well aware of these criticisms. Thus the 'Foreword to Accounting Standards', issued by the ASB in June 1993, makes it quite clear that the requirement to give a true and fair view may in exceptional circumstances require a departure from accounting standards and permits such a departure although particulars of the departure, the reasons for it and its financial effects must then be disclosed in the financial statements (Paras 18 and 19). It also recognises that the standards are not absolute but will require amendment as the business environment and accounting thought evolves (Para. 33).

INTERNATIONAL STANDARDISATION

Introduction

It seems reasonable to suggest that, if standards have merit within the boundaries of one country, there would be merit if they were applied more generally.

In a period in which investors based in one country choose between investments in many countries, a lack of comparability between accounts drawn up in different countries may well lead to incorrect decision taking and thereby to an inefficient allocation of scarce resources. As individual countries have pursued a policy of standardisation, so too a number of bodies have become concerned with international standardisation. Both the United Nations and the Organisation for Economic Co-operation and Development have studied and issued publications on the regulation of accounting.[28] As might be expected these bodies are mainly concerned with the regulation of disclosure by large multinational companies.

Two more general attempts at standardisation are relevant in the UK: those of the International Accounting Standards Committee (IASC) and of the European Community (EC). We first look at the work of the IASC and then consider the work of the EC in the final section of this chapter.

---

27 W. T. Baxter, 'Recommendations on accounting theory', in *Studies in Accounting Theory*, 2nd edn (W. T. Baxter and S. Davidson, eds), Sweet & Maxwell, London, 1962, pp. 414–27.

28 Examples are: *International Standards of Accounting and Reporting for Transnational Corporations*, UN, 1977, *Conclusions on Accounting and Reporting by Transnational Corporations*, UN, 1988 and *Guidelines for the Disclosure of Information by Multinationals*, OECD, 1976.

The International Accounting Standards Committee

Although the possibility of international standards has been debated since early this century, the most successful programme began with the formation of the IASC in 1973.

The founder members were drawn from professional accountancy bodies in the following countries: Australia, Canada, France, Germany, Japan, Mexico, the Netherlands, the UK, the Republic of Ireland and the USA. Since that time the professional accountancy bodies from more than 80 countries have been admitted to membership and these include developed countries, such as the Scandinavian countries, as well as many developing countries, including, for example, India, Nigeria and Trinidad and Tobago.

The objectives of the IASC as stated in the original 1973 agreement were:

> to formulate and publish in the public interest basic standards to be observed in the presentation of audited accounts and financial statements and to promote their worldwide acceptance and observance.

Under a revised agreement entered into in 1982 the reference to basic standards was removed and the revised objectives became:

(a) to formulate and publish in the public interest accounting standards to be observed in the presentation of financial statements and to promote their worldwide acceptance and observance, and

(b) to work generally for the improvement and harmonisation of regulations, accounting standards and procedures relating to the presentation of financial statements.

In order to achieve these objectives, members joining the IASC enter into the following undertaking:

> to support the work of IASC by publishing in their respective countries every International Accounting Standard approved for issue by the Board of IASC and by using their best endeavours:

(i) to ensure that published financial statements comply with International Accounting Standards in all material respects and disclose the fact of such compliance;

(ii) to persuade governments and standard-setting bodies that published financial statements should comply with International Accounting Standards in all material respects;

(iii) to persuade authorities controlling securities markets and the industrial and business community that published financial statements should comply with International Accounting Standards in all material respects and disclose the fact of such compliance;

(iv) to ensure that the auditors satisfy themselves that the financial statements comply with International Accounting Standards in all material respects;

(v) to foster acceptance and observance of International Accounting Standards internationally.

The undertaking emphasises the fact that the IASC has no direct power to implement or enforce its standards. Rather it must rely on its members to persuade the relevant institutions in their particular countries to adopt and enforce the standards.

Given the very different ways in which countries regulate accounting, in some countries this involves persuading the relevant standard-setting bodies to comply while, in other countries, it involves the much more difficult task of persuading the government that changes to the law are necessary.

Even before the IASC had been established, Irving Fantl identified three major barriers to international standardisation:[29]

29 I. L. Fantl, 'The case against international uniformity', *Management Accounting*, May 1971.

(a) differences in background and traditions of countries;
(b) differences in the needs of various economic environments;
(c) the challenge to the sovereignty of states in making and enforcing standards.

These are enormous problems for the IASC, although it has taken steps to try and overcome the barriers. Thus, it tries to work closely with the major standard-setting bodies to ensure that it is involved before a country's position becomes entrenched. In addition, like the ASB, it consults widely and has formed a consultative committee drawn from a number of international bodies including the International Association of Financial Executives Institutes, the International Confederation of Trade Unions and World Confederation of Labour and the World Bank.

What then has been the progress of the IASC?

By 1990 the IASC had issued 31 International Accounting Standards and these provided a set of inexpensive ready-made standards which could be adopted by those countries which had not developed their own mechanism for standard setting. While many of the International Accounting Standards covered topics on which a standard had already been set in the British Isles, this was not always the case. For example IAS 14 'Reporting financial information by segments' (1981) was published many years before the issue of SSAP 25 'Segmental reporting' (1990) and IAS 18 'Revenue recognition' (1982) dealt with a subject on which neither the ASC nor the ASB have issued a standard.

As might has been expected, the activities of the IASC attracted considerable criticism and, during the 1980s, it was accused of Anglo-Saxon domination and of issuing standards which were too flexible. It has taken action on both counts.

The Committee had its first non Anglo-Saxon Chairman, Georges Barthès of France, from 1987 to 1989 and although it had a US Chairman, Arthur Wyatt, between 1990 and 1992, a Japanese Chairman, Eiichi Shiratori, took over in 1993.

By the close of the 1980s, the IASC had recognised that it had reached a new phase in its work, and its emphasis changed from the production of new standards to the tightening of its existing standards. A revised International Accounting Standard number 7 'Cash Flow Accounting' was published in 1992 and a batch of ten standards were revised and issued in November 1993.

Under the guidance of its Secretary General, the IASC will undoubtedly continue to be a major force in the international harmonisation of accounting.

Harmonisation in the European Community

The use of Directives

When the European Economic Community was established by the Treaty of Rome on 25 March 1957 one of the objectives to be achieved by member states was 'the approximation of their respective national laws to the extent required for the common market to function in an orderly manner'.[30] To achieve this objective a number of programmes of law harmonisation have been undertaken. One of these is the company law harmonisation programme under the provisions of Article 54(3)(g) which calls for 'the co-ordination of the safeguards required from companies in the Member States, to protect the interests both of members and of third parties'.

---

30 Treaty of Rome, Article 3(h).

When the EC Commission has obtained agreement on a set of proposals on a particular topic, it places a Draft Directive before the Council of Ministers. If the Directive is adopted, governments of member states then have a specified period to enact legislation and incorporate the provisions of the Directive into their national law.

In practice, many countries were unable to keep to the timetable imposed by the early Directives and, for the Seventh Directive, the time limits set were much longer than for previous Directives. This was, however, to a large extent necessary to accommodate fundamental changes which have been required in some member states.[31]

While a number of Directives have been adopted, the two of most concern to accountants are the Fourth Directive on company accounts and the Seventh Directive on consolidated accounts.[32]

The former was adopted on 25 July 1978 and implemented in the UK by the Companies Act 1981. The latter was adopted on 13 June 1983 and implemented by the Companies Act 1989.

In this section of the chapter we look briefly at these two Directives.

The Fourth Directive

The original draft of the Fourth Directive was published in November 1971, some time before the UK became a member of the EC. Not surprisingly the draft was, as it still is, heavily influenced by the current law and practice in France and Germany. When the UK joined the EC in March 1973, it pressed for certain changes to the draft and, as a result, an amended draft was issued in February 1974. Although not all of the changes suggested by the UK were accepted, the requirement to give a 'true and fair view' was admitted as an overriding objective of accounts and the Directive was eventually adopted by the Council of Ministers on 27 July 1978.

As we have explained earlier in this chapter, the major changes prescribed by the Fourth Directive were as follows:

(a) limited companies have to adopt compulsory formats for both the balance sheet and the profit and loss account;
(b) defined methods of valuing assets, the so-called 'valuation rules' must be followed.

In addition, the Directive provided definitions of small and medium-sized companies and permitted member states to offer such companies exemptions from complying with certain requirements of the Directive.[33]

We have already seen how the provisions of the Fourth Directive have been implemented in the UK, but it is worth spending a little time looking at the impact of the Fourth Directive in the EC as a whole.

Given the very different accounting systems which exist in member countries, it is perhaps not surprising that it took some 10 years for the Fourth Directive to be adopted. Although this Directive undoubtedly moves the accounting requirements of the various countries closer together, there are two major factors which have limited its effectiveness in achieving harmonisation.

31 *See below.*
32 These directives may be found in the *Official Journal of the European Communities*. The text of the Fourth Directive is in Volume 21, L222, 14 August 1978, while the text of the Seventh Directive is in Volume L193/1, 18 July 1983.
33 Fourth Directive, Articles 11, 27 and 47.

First, as we have seen, the Directive contains an overriding requirement that accounts must give a 'true and fair view'. Although it is difficult to define such a term, accountants in the UK have long experience of working with it and are thoroughly familiar with what it means. In many EC countries the term is unknown and, although it has been translated and included in their respective national legislation, it is certainly not interpreted or applied in the same way in all of those countries as it is in the UK.

Second, in order to be able to obtain agreement, it was necessary to include a large number of options in the Fourth Directive and there are over 60 points on which EC countries were able to exercise a choice.[34] Member states had to decide whether or not to incorporate the particular options in their national legislation and could, in fact, even permit individual companies a choice from alternative treatments under the national legislation.

One example is the possible exemptions for small and medium-sized companies. Some countries, such as the UK, gave most of these while other countries did not. As a result, the information provided by small companies in different countries is not comparable.

A second example is that countries could adopt historical cost valuation rules or either permit or require the application of alternative accounting rules. In the UK the Companies Acts permit the use of such alternative accounting rules while other countries do not do so. Given the requirement for information to reconstruct historical cost accounts when alternative accounting rules are used, this means that many international comparisons are possible only on the basis of the historical cost figures.

A third example is provided by the possible choice of formats. The Directive provided two balance-sheet formats and four profit-and-loss-account formats. Although part of the choice was merely between a horizontal or a vertical format, there are differences between the information disclosed in the two pairs of profit-and-loss-account formats.

Member states could either impose one balance-sheet format and one profit-and-loss-account format on all companies or they could specify all formats and permit companies to choose between them. The UK Companies Acts have given the widest possible choice with the result that, even in the UK, different companies disclose somewhat different information. Other countries have been more rigid and, hence, there is a lack of comparability.

Even if all countries were to adopt the same formats, the inability to define terms with precision means that there is a superficial comparability only. For example, the profit-and-loss-account format of Article 25 requires the disclosure of, *inter alia*, cost of sales, distribution costs and administrative expenses. Even if we ignore the flexibility of the underlying valuation rules, it is highly likely that different companies will analyse similar expenses between these three categories in different ways and, hence, although the same descriptions are used, the figures are not comparable.

The above examples are not given to belittle the efforts which have been made to try and achieve harmonisation in the EC but rather to ensure that readers do not overestimate their impact.

The Seventh Directive

Although a proposed Seventh Directive was first issued in May 1976 and an amended proposal was issued in December 1978, it was not until June 1983 that the Seventh

---

34 T. R. Watts, ed., *Handbook on the EEC Fourth Directive*, ICAEW, London, 1979, p. 1.

Directive was actually adopted.[35] As with the Fourth Directive it has been a long and difficult task to reach agreement on when consolidated accounts should be prepared and what they should contain. This should not surprise us when it is realised that some EC countries had no legal requirement for consolidated accounts at all.[36] One of the major difficulties was defining the circumstances in which consolidated accounts should be required and a large part of the Directive was devoted to this problem.[37]

In the UK the basic legal position was that group accounts were required when one company owned more than half of the equity share capital in another company or had the legal power of control over that other company, irrespective of whether the investing company actually exercised that power. The proposed Directive was initially concerned to ensure that information was provided about concentrations of economic power and, as a consequence, consolidated accounts were required when companies were managed in practice by a 'central and unified management'. Ownership was only important to the extent that it led to a presumption that such central management might exist.

A criterion based on the existence of an economic unit is much more difficult to apply than one based on the legal power of control and accountants in the UK were relieved to find that the Directive came down in favour of a definition based on the existence of this legal power of control.[38]

Some other problems which had to be resolved in this connection were whether or not consolidated accounts should be required when an individual or partnership controls companies, whether consolidated accounts should be required for subgroup holding companies where the ultimate parent company is in another EC country or non-EC country and whether horizontal consolidations should be required for companies in the EC where, for example, two French companies are both under the control of a US company.[39]

The second part of the Directive is concerned with the preparation of consolidated accounts. As is the case for the accounts of individual companies, there is an overriding requirement that consolidated accounts give a 'true and fair view' as well as the requirement that they give the information specified by the Directive using the valuation rules and formats specified in the Fourth Directive as far as appropriate.

There is no doubt that the Seventh Directive has had a much greater impact on accounting in other EC countries than it has had in the British Isles, where many of its provisions were already established by existing law and accounting standards. However, this is not to say that it has had no impact at all in the British Isles. As in the case of the Fourth Directive, rules previously set by accounting standard are now a part of the law and the introduction of new definitions has widened the coverage of consolidated accounts to include certain off-balance-sheet finance schemes as well as certain partnerships and joint ventures. We deal with these topics in Chapters 6 and 9.

35 *Official Journal of the European Communities*, Volume L193/1, 18 July 1983.

36 Examples are Greece and Luxembourg.

37 Seventh Directive, Sec. 1, 'Conditions for the preparation of consolidated accounts' (Articles 1–15).

38 Seventh Directive, Sec. 1. As we shall see in Chapter 9 it is still possible for member states to require consolidated accounts where there is unified management but no legal power of control (Article 1, Para. 2).

39 Readers who wish to pursue these topics are referred to Chapter 9 and Sharon M. McKinnon, *Consolidated Accounts: The Seventh EEC Directive*, Alan D. H. Newham (ed.), AMSA, 1983: Chapter 15 is particularly relevant.

As in the case of the Fourth Directive, member states were given a large number of options in the Seventh Directive. The different ways in which they have exercised these options has inevitably limited the degree of harmonisation achieved.

RECOMMENDED READING

W. T. Baxter, 'Accounting standards – boon or curse?' *Accounting and Business Research*, ICAEW, Winter 1981.

M. Bromwich and A. G. Hopwood (eds), *Accounting Standard Setting: An International Perspective*, Pitman, London, 1983.

H. C. Edey, 'Accounting Standards in the British Isles', in *Studies in Accounting*, 3rd edn, W. T. Baxter and S. Davidson (eds), ICAEW, London, 1977.

R. Leach and E. Stamp (eds), *British Accounting Standards: The First Ten Years*, Woodhead–Faulkner, Cambridge, 1981.

The Making of Accounting Standards (The Dearing Report), ICAEW, London, 1988.

CHAPTER 3

What is profit?

The layman has no doubt about the way in which this question should be answered. Profit is the difference between the cost of providing goods or services and the revenue derived from their sale. If a greengrocer can sell for 5p an apple which cost him 3p, his profit must be 2p. Accountants also used to inhabit this seemingly comfortable world of simplicity, but they are now aware that such a world is not only uncomfortable but downright dangerous. We can perhaps agree that profit is the difference between cost and revenue, but there is more than one way of measuring cost. Historical cost – the cost of acquisition – is only one alternative, which may indeed be one of the least helpful for many purposes. Furthermore, it is not even obvious that we should measure the difference between costs and revenue in monetary terms – actual pounds – for another unit of measurement has been suggested; the purchasing power of pounds.

In order to answer the question 'what is profit?' it is perhaps best to start by considering the most useful of hypothetical examples in accounting theory – the barrow boy who trades for cash and rents his barrow.

Consider such a barrow boy whose only asset at the start of a day's trading is cash of £2000. Let us suppose that the barrow boy rents a barrow and a pitch for the day which together cost him £20. Let us further assume that he spends £80 in the wholesale market for a barrow-load of vegetables, all of which are sold for £130. The trader therefore ends the day with cash of £2030 and we can all agree that the profit for that day's trading is £30.[1] In other words we have taken the barrow boy's profit to be the increase in monetary wealth resulting from his trading activities.

Let us extend the illustration by supposing that the barrow boy has changed the style of his operation. He now owns his barrow and trades in household sundries of which he can maintain a stock. If we wish to continue to apply the same principle as before in calculating his profit, we would need to measure his assets at the beginning and the end of each day. Thus we would need to place a value on his stock and his barrow at these two points of time as well as counting his cash.

All this may appear to be very simple, but it is by no means trivial for the above argument contains one important implication, that profit represents an increase in wealth or 'well-offness', and one vital consequence, that in order to measure the increase in wealth it is necessary to attach values to the assets owned by the trader at the beginning and end of the period.

Let us now consider the implied definition of profit in a little more detail. The argument is that a trader makes a profit for a period if either he is better off at the end of the period than he was at the beginning (in that he owns assets with a greater monetary value) or would have been better off had he not consumed the profits. This essentially simple view was elegantly expressed by the eminent economist Sir John Hicks, who wrote that income

---

1 Actually this is not strictly true, for one might wish to impute a charge for the labour supplied by the barrow boy and would say that his profit is the excess of £30 over the imputed labour charge.

– the term which economists use to describe the equivalent, in personal terms, of the profit of a business enterprise – could be defined as 'the maximum value which [a man] can consume during a week and still expect to be as well off at the end of the week as he was at the beginning'.[2]

This definition cannot be applied exactly to a business enterprise since such an entity does not consume. The definition can, however, be modified to meet this point, as was done by the Sandilands Committee,[3] which defined a company's profit for a year by the following adaptation of Hicks' dictum: 'A company's profit for the year is the maximum value which the company can distribute during the year and still expect to be as well off at the end of the year as it was at the beginning'.[4]

The key questions that have to be answered in arriving at such a profit are 'How do we measure "well-offness" at the beginning and end of a period?' and 'How do we measure the change in "well-offness" from one date to another?'

This is not the end of the matter for we may wish to make a distinction between that part of the increase in 'well-offness' which is available for consumption and that which should not be so regarded. In traditional accounting practice a distinction is made between realised and unrealised profits such that only the former is normally available for distribution. Subsequently company legislation[5] introduced into statute law the concept of distributable profits and the legal aspects of the assessment of this element of profit will be discussed in the final section of this chapter.

Turning to our two questions, we will first examine the question of how we may measure 'well-offness' or 'wealth' of a business at a point in time. There are two approaches. First, the wealth of a business can be measured by reference to the expectation of future benefits; in other words the value of a business at a point of time is the present value of the expected future net cash flow to the firm. The second approach is to measure the wealth of a business by reference to the values of the individual assets of the business. Actually these two approaches can be linked by the recognition of an intangible asset, often called goodwill, which can be defined as the difference between the value of the business as a whole and the sum of the values of the individual assets less liabilities.

PRESENT-VALUE APPROACH

We will assume that readers are familiar with the principles and mechanics of discounted cash flow techniques.

The present-value approach is based on the assumption that the owner of a business is only interested in the pecuniary benefits that will accrue from its ownership ('I am only in it for the money'). Well-offness at any balance sheet date is then measured by the present value of the expected future net cash flows at that date and profit for the period is the difference between the present values at the beginning and end of the period after adjustment for injections and withdrawals.[6]

This requires some formidable problems of estimation of both cash flows and

---

2 J. R. Hicks, *Value and Capital*, 2nd edn, Oxford University Press, Oxford, 1948, p. 172.
3 *Report of the Inflation Accounting Committee*, Cmnd 6225, HMSO, London, 1975.
4 *Ibid.*, p. 29.
5 Companies Act, 1980 and 1981.
6 *See* T. A. Lee, *Income and Value Measurement*, 3rd edn, Van Nostrand Reinhold, Wokingham, 1985.

appropriate discount rates, but such estimates are made either explicitly or implicitly (usually the latter) when businesses or individual assets are bought and sold. The present-value approach is an important and useful one when applied to the valuation of shares for an entire business to determine whether their sale or purchase would be worthwhile at a given price, and the methods used for such purposes will be discussed in Chapter 14.

It may well be thought, however, that the problems of estimation are such as to render the approach unsuitable for the measurement of an entity's periodic profit on a regular basis specifically given the desirable characteristics of accounting systems discussed in Chapter 1. But there is a more fundamental objection to the use of this method for financial accounting in that it is agreed that the regular reporting of profits should not be based solely on future expectations. The present-value approach is, of course, based entirely on expectations of the future and depends on decisions involving the way in which assets will be employed. It is argued that one of the objectives of accounting is to aid decision making and it is hardly appropriate if the fundamental measure of profit is based on the assumption that all decisions have already been made. This point was made by Edwards and Bell, who wrote:

> A concept of profit which measures truly and realistically the extent to which past decisions have been right or wrong and thus aids in the formulation of new ones is required. And since rightness or wrongness, must, eventually, be checked in the market place, it is changes in market values of one kind or another which should dominate accounting objectives.[7]

This quotation provides a neat introduction to the asset by asset approach.

MEASUREMENT OF WEALTH BY REFERENCE TO THE VALUATION OF INDIVIDUAL ASSETS

In this section we shall discuss some of the different methods that may be used to value assets. We shall at this stage concentrate on the problems associated with the determination of an asset's value using the different bases and shall defer the question of the suitability of the different bases of asset valuation for profit measurement until later.

Historical cost

The historical cost of an asset can usually be determined with exactitude so long as the records showing the amount paid for the asset are still available. The matter, however, is not always that simple. The historical cost of a fixed asset purchased when new may well be known, but it will usually be impossible to say what proportion of the original total cost should be regarded as being applicable to that portion of the asset which remains unused at a point in time. For example, imagine that we are dealing with a 2-year-old car which cost £10 000 and which we expect to have a total life of 5 years – do we say that the historical cost of the unused portion of the car is three-fifths of £10 000, i.e. £6000? This is, of course, the class of question which is answered by the use of some more or less arbitrary method of depreciation. As we will show later, much the same sort of expedient is used in various forms of current-value accounting.

---

7 E. O. Edwards and P. W. Bell, *The Theory and Measurement of Business Income*, University of California Press, Stanford, Calif., 1961, p. 25.

Readers will be aware of the difficulties involved in the determination of historical cost of trading stock – whether stock should be valued on the basis of 'average', FIFO, etc. The problem is even more acute when trading stock involves work in progress and finished goods as the question of the extent to which overheads should be included in the stock figure must be considered. Similar problems arise when determining the cost of fixed assets which are constructed by a firm for its own use.

There is another class of assets for which it may be difficult to find the historical costs. These are assets which have been acquired through barter or exchange, a special case of which are assets which are purchased in exchange for shares in the purchasing company. In such instances it may be necessary to estimate the historical cost of the assets acquired. This is usually done by reference to the amount that would have been realised had the assets, which had been given in exchange, been sold for cash. In some cases it might prove to be extremely difficult to make the necessary estimates as there may not be a market in the assets concerned.

Yet further problems occur where a number of assets are purchased together, for example, where a company purchases the net assets of another company or unincorporated firm. For accounting purposes it is necessary to determine the historical cost of the individual assets and liabilities which have been acquired and this involves an allocation of the global price to the individual assets and liabilities which are separately identified in the accounting system. Any balancing figure represents the amount paid for all assets and liabilities not separately identified in the accounting system and is described as goodwill.[8] Such an allocation is made using 'fair values', which usually results in the individual assets being valued at their replacement cost and liabilities being valued at their face value.

The contents of this section may seem fairly obvious, but it is important to remember that the determination of an asset's historical cost is not always an easy task.

'Adjusted' historical cost

By 'adjusted' historical cost we mean the method whereby the historical cost of an asset is taken to be its original acquisition cost adjusted to account for changes in the value or purchasing power of money between the date of acquisition and the valuation date. This method of valuation forms the basis of current purchasing power accounting (*see* Chapter 15).

The practical difficulties of this approach include all those which were discussed in the preceding section on historical cost but to these must be added the problems involved in reflecting the changes in the value of money. This is done by using a price index, which is an attempt to measure the average change in prices over a period.

Great care must be taken when interpreting the figures produced by the adjusted historical cost approach. It must be remembered that this method does not attempt to revalue (i.e. state at current value) the assets; it is money and not the asset which is revalued. The adjusted historical cost method can be contrasted with those approaches under which assets are stated at their current values which are the subjects of the following sections.

8 Such an approach is also necessary when preparing consolidated accounts and this is discussed in Chapter 9.

Replacement cost

Replacement cost (RC) is often referred to as an entry value because it is the cost to the business of acquiring an asset. In crude terms it may be defined as the estimated amount that would have to be paid in order to replace the asset at the date of valuation.

This is a useful working definition, but it is crude as it begs a large number of questions, some of which will be discussed below.

The definition includes the word 'estimated' because the exercise is a hypothetical one in that the method is based on the question 'How much would it cost to replace this asset today?' Since the asset is not being replaced the answer has to be found from an examination of the circumstances prevailing in the market for the asset under review. If the asset is identical with those being traded in the market, the estimate may be reasonably objective. Thus, if the asset is a component which is still being manufactured and used by a business, its replacement cost may be found by reference to manufacturer's or supplier's price lists. However, even in this apparently straightforward case, there may still be difficulties in that the replacement cost may depend on the size of the order. Typically a customer placing a large order will pay a lower price per unit than someone buying in small lots. In some types of business the difference between the two sets of prices may be significant, as is evidenced by the different prices paid for food by large supermarkets and small grocery shops. This observation leads to the conclusion that in certain instances it will be necessary to add to the above definition of replacement cost that the estimate should assume that the owner of the asset would replace it in 'the normal course of business', in other words that the replacement would be made as part of the normal purchasing pattern of the business.

The difficulties inherent in the estimation of replacement cost loom very much larger when we turn our attention to assets which are not identical to those which are currently being traded in the market, including those which have been made obsolete by technological progress. A special, and very important, class of non-identical assets are used assets because all used assets will differ in some respect or other from other used assets of a similar type.

A more detailed discussion of the ways in which the replacement cost of assets, which are not identical with those traded in the market, are found will be provided later in the book, but it will be helpful if we indicate some of the possible approaches at this stage:

(a) *Gross/net replacement cost*   The most common approach, particularly if the asset has been the subject of little technological change, is to take the cost of a new asset (the gross replacement cost) and then deduct an estimate of depreciation; for example, if the asset is two years old and is expected to last for another three years then, using straight-line depreciation, the net replacement cost is 3/5th of the gross replacement cost.

(b) *Market comparison*   In the case of some used assets, such as motor vehicles, the asset might be valued by reference to the value of similar used assets. It may prove necessary to adjust the value found by direct comparison to account for any special features pertaining to the particular asset. Thus, the approach includes a subjective judgment element which is combined with the reasonably objective comparison with the market.

(c) *Replacement cost of inputs*   In certain cases, particularly fixed assets manufactured by the owner for his own use and work in progress and finished goods, it might be possible to determine an asset's replacement cost by reference to the current replacement cost of the various inputs used in the construction of the asset. Thus the necessary labour input could be costed at the wage rates prevailing at the valuation date with similar procedures being applied to the other inputs – raw materials, bought-in components and overheads.

Whilst in practice the focus of valuation is often the physical asset itself, we need to recognise that this is a proxy for that which is actually being valued – the services provided by the asset. The point is well made by the ASB in its discussion draft 'Measurement in Financial Statements' (the draft of Chapter 5 of the 'Statement of Principles') where a distinction is made between *reproduction cost*, the cost of acquiring an identical asset, and *replacement cost*, the lowest cost of acquiring identical services.

Take, as an example, a machine which is expected to operate for another 2000 hours. A new machine might have a life of 4000 hours and have operating costs which are less than those of the machine whose replacement cost we are seeking to estimate. In this case, the replacement cost of the old machine would be half the cost of the new machine less the present value of the savings in the operating costs. If there is a 'good market' in second-hand machines the replacement cost of used machines will approximate for this value but if this is not the case the replacement cost will be based on the cost of a new machine after adjusting for differences in capacity and operating costs.

Net realisable value

The net realisable value of an asset may be defined as the estimated amount that would be received from the sale of the asset less the anticipated costs that would be incurred in its disposal. It is sometimes called an exit value as it is the amount realisable when assets leave the firm.

One obvious problem with this definition is that the amount which would be realised on the disposal of an asset depends on the circumstances in which it is sold. It is likely that there would be a considerable difference between the proceeds that might be expected if the asset were disposed of in the normal way and the proceeds from a forced and hurried sale of the assets. Of course, it all depends on what is meant by the 'normal course of business', and while the phrase may be useful enough for many practical purposes it must be remembered that it is often not possible to think in terms of the two extreme cases of 'normal' and 'hurried' disposals. There may be all sorts of intermediate positions between these extremes. It can thus be seen that there may be a whole family of possible values based on selling prices which depend on the assumptions made about the conditions under which they are sold and that, particularly in the case of stock, great care must be taken when interpreting the phrase that the net realisable value of an asset is £x.

As was true for the replacement cost basis of valuation, the difficulties associated with the determination of an asset's net realisable value are less when the asset in question is identical, or very similar to, assets which are being traded in the market. In such circumstances the asset's net realisable value can be found by reference to the prevailing market price viewed from the point of view of a seller in the market. The replacement cost is, of course, related to the purchaser's viewpoint. If there is an active market the difference between an asset's replacement cost and its net realisable value may not be very great and will depend on the expenses and profit margins of traders in the particular type of asset.

The relationship of the business to the market will determine whether, in the case of that business, an asset's replacement cost exceeds its net realisable value or vice versa. It is likely that the barrow boy to whom reference was made earlier would find that the replacement cost of his barrow could be greater than its net realisable value, while the reverse is likely to hold for his vegetables. It is generally, but not universally, true that a business will find that the replacement costs of its fixed assets will exceed their net realisable values while in the case of trading stock the net realisable value will be the greater.

Generally the estimation of the net realisable value of a unique asset is even more difficult than the determination of such an asset's replacement cost. It may be possible to use a 'units of service' approach in that one could examine what the market is prepared to pay for the productive capacity of the asset being valued, but the process is likely to be more subjective. In the replacement cost case the owner is the potential purchaser and will base his valuation on his own estimate of the productive capacity of the asset, but in the net realisable value case the hypothetical purchaser will have to be convinced of the asset's productive capacity.

A further difficulty involved in the estimation of net realisable value is the last phrase in the definition – 'less the anticipated costs that would be incurred in its disposal'. This sting in the definition's tail can be extremely significant, especially in the case of work in progress, in relation to which the estimation of anticipated additional costs may be difficult and subjective.

Present value

It might be possible to apply the present-value approach to the valuation of individual assets. To do so would require the valuer to attach an estimated series of future cash flows to the individual asset and select an appropriate discount rate. This may be possible in the case of assets which are not used in combination with others, such as an office block which is rented out, but most assets are used in combination to generate revenue. Thus, a factory purchases raw materials which are processed by many machines to produce the finished goods which are sold to earn revenue. In such circumstances as these it would seem impossible to say what proportion of the total net cash flow should be assigned to a particular machine.

CAPITAL MAINTENANCE

Let us for a while ignore the practical problems associated with the valuation of assets at an instant in time and assume that one can generate a series of figures (depending on the basis of valuation selected) reflecting the market value of the bundle of assets which constitutes a business and hence, after making appropriate deduction for creditors[9], arrive at a series of figures showing the owners' equity or capital in the enterprise at an instant in time.

If this can be done, is the profit for a period found by simply deducting the value of the assets (less liabilities) at the start of the period from the corresponding value at the end of the period? In other words if, using the selected basis of valuation, the value of the assets at the time t_0 was £1000 and the value at the time t_1 £1500 is the profit for the period £500? The answer is, probably not.

---

9 The valuation of liabilities is an even less well developed subject than the valuation of assets but things are changing and more attention is now being paid to this topic. However, in order to focus on the principles underlying the concept of capital maintenance and its relationship to the measurement of profit we will defer the subject of the valuation of liabilities to later chapters.

We must remember that we have defined profit in terms of the amount that can be withdrawn or distributed while leaving the business as well-off at the end as it was at the beginning of the period. Now assume that in this simple example the valuation basis used is replacement cost and, for the sake of even more simplicity, that no capital has been introduced or withdrawn during the period and that the firm only holds one type of asset, the replacement cost of which has increased by 50 per cent. (Thus the company holds the same number of assets at the end as it did at the beginning of the period.) Let us also assume that prices in general have not increased over the period.

The question which has to be answered is how much could be distributed by way of a dividend at the end of the period without reducing its 'well-offness' below that which prevailed at the start of the period. It could be argued that £500 could be paid as that would leave the value of the assets constant. It could also be argued that nothing should be paid because in order to pay a dividend the company would have to reduce its holding of assets. If the latter view is accepted, it means that the whole of the increase in the value of the assets should be retained in the business in order to maintain its 'well-offness'. It will be seen that each of the approaches described in the simple example will be found in different accounting models, but at this stage we simply want to show that it is not sufficient to find the difference between values at two points in time. The profit figure will also depend on the amount which it is deemed necessary to retain in the business to maintain its 'well-offness', that is on the concept of *capital maintenance* which is selected. We shall describe the various approaches to capital maintenance in a little more detail below.

There are thus two choices to be made – the basis of asset valuation and the aspect of capital which is to be maintained. In theory each of the possible bases of valuation can be combined with any of the different concepts of capital maintenance with each combination yielding a different profit figure. In practice the two choices are not made independently of each other in that, as we will show, there are some combinations of asset value/capital maintenance which are mutually consistent and yield potentially helpful information while others appear not to provide useful information, usually because the two choices are made on the basis of an inconsistent approach to the question of the objectives served by the preparation of financial accounts.

We can summarise the argument thus far by stating that the profit figure depends on (a) the basis of valuation selected, and (b) the concept of capital maintenance used, and is found in the following way:

1 Find the difference between the value of the assets less liabilities at the beginning and end of the period after adjusting for capital introduced or withdrawn.
2 Decide how much of the difference (if any) needs to be retained in the business to maintain capital.
3 The residual is then the profit for the period.

We will now turn to more detailed examination of the possible ways of viewing the capital of the company (or of its owners) which is to be maintained. It will be helpful to categorise the various approaches to capital maintenance in the following way:

- Financial capital maintenance
  - Not adjusted for inflation (Money financial capital maintenance)
  - Adjusted for inflation (Real financial capital maintenance)

- Operating capital maintenance[10]
  - From the standpoint of the entity
  - From the standpoint of the equity shareholders' interest.

We shall deal with the above in turn.

Money financial capital maintenance

With money financial capital maintenance the bench mark used to decide whether a profit has been earned is the book value of the shareholders' interest at the start of the period.

If money capital is to be maintained then in the absence of capital injections or withdrawals[11] the profit for the period is the difference between the values of assets less liabilities at the start and end of the period with no further adjustment. Money financial capital maintenance is used in traditional historic cost accounting which is not to say that, as we will show in Example 3.1, it cannot be combined with other bases of asset valuation.

Real financial capital maintenance

With real financial capital maintenance (which is often referred to simply as real capital maintenance) the bench mark used to determine whether a profit has been made is the *purchasing power* of the equity shareholders' interest in the company at the start of the period. Thus, if the equity shareholders' interest in the company is £1000 at the start and the general price level increases by 15 per cent in the period under review, a profit will only arise if, on the selected basis, the value of the assets less liabilities, and hence the equity shareholders' interest[12] at the time, amounts to at least £1150.

Both the money financial capital and real financial capital maintenance approaches concentrate on the equity shareholders' interest in the company and are hence sometimes referred to as measures of profit based on *proprietary capital maintenance*.

Operating capital maintenance

The operating capital maintenance concept is less clear-cut than the financial capital maintenance approach. Broadly, it is concerned with the physical assets of the enterprise and suggests that capital is maintained if at the end of the period the company has the same level of assets as it had at the start. A very simple example of the operating capital approach is provided by the following example.

Suppose a business starts the period with £100 in cash, 20 widgets and 30 flanges and ends the period with £130 in cash, 25 widgets and 32 flanges. Then the profit for the period, using the operating capital maintenance approach, could be regarded as being:

Profit = £30 in cash + 5 widgets + 2 flanges.

---

10 In the draft Chapter 5 of the Statement of Principles 'Measurement in Financial Statement' the ASB uses slightly different terms; 'nominal money' rather than 'money financial' and 'physical capital' instead of 'operating capital'. We have not adopted those terms because, in our view, those used in this chapter both provide better descriptions and are more widely used in the literature.

11 In order to save repeating this phrase readers should, for the remainder of this section, continue to assume the absence of capital injections and withdrawals.

12 Preference shares being treated as liabilities for this purpose.

For certain purposes one could stop here, for the list of assets given above shows the increase in wealth achieved by that business over the period. To state profit in this way does provide a very clear picture of what has happened and shows in an extremely objective fashion the extent to which the business has grown in physical terms. Accountancy, however, is concerned with providing information stated in monetary terms.

In order to take this additional step it is necessary to select a basis of valuation, for this would then enable the accountant to place a single monetary value on the profit.

Let us assume that it is decided that replacement cost is the selected valuation basis and that the replacement costs at the end of the year are widgets £100 each and flanges £150 each. The profit for the period would then be stated as follows:

	£
Increase in cash	30
Increase in widgets, 5 x £100	500
Increase in flanges, 2 x £150	300
Profit	830

The above example is obviously simplistic in so far that companies hold a large number of different sorts of assets and, only in the most static of situations, will the assets held at the end of the year match those which are owned at the start of the period. However, the example does illustrate the sort of thinking which will be developed in later chapters.

The example was based on the variant of the operating capital maintenance measure which states that a company only makes a profit if it has replaced (or is in a position to replace) the assets which were held at the start of the period and which have been used up in the course of the period. A more sophisticated alternative would be to consider the output which is capable of being generated by the initial holding of assets and design an accounting model which would only disclose a figure for profit if the company is able to maintain the same level of output.

Most variants of the operating capital maintenance approach relate the determination of profit to the assets held by the business, i.e. look at the problem from the standpoint of the business. The operating capital approach is thus often referred to as an *entity measure of profit*. It is, however, possible to combine the operating capital maintenance concept with the proprietary approach. Thus, a profit based on an entity concept can be derived which can be adjusted to show the position from the point of view of the equity holders. If, for example, part of the assets are financed by long-term creditors, it might be assumed that part of the additional funds required, in a period of rising prices, to maintain the business's operating capital will also be contributed by the long-term creditors. Hence, the profit attributable to equity holders would be higher than the profit derived from the strict application of the entity concept. Assume that a company has the following opening balance sheet:

	£			£
Equity shareholders	60	Assets		
		10 items of stock at £10 each		100
Debentures	40			
	100			100

Stock is valued at its replacement cost and the proportion of debt finance in the capital structure (i.e. the gearing) is 40 per cent. For simplicity we will assume the debentures are interest free.

Assume that the company holds the stock for a period and then sells all 10 items for cash at £18 each so that the closing balance sheet includes just one asset, cash, of £180. In the period the replacement cost of stock has risen from £10 to £15 per unit.

If the operating capital maintenance concept is followed, then in order to maintain the operating capital of the entity an amount of £150, that is 10 items at the new replacement cost of £15, would be needed. Thus, the entity profit would be:

	£
Closing capital in cash	180
less Amount necessary to replace 10 items at £15	150
Entity profit	30

However, in order to maintain the operating capital of the equity shareholders' interest in the entity an amount of £90 rather than £150 would be needed. Shareholders were financing 60 per cent of the stock and 60 per cent of £150 is £90. Thus the proprietary profit would be:

Net assets at end of period:	£
Cash	180
less Debentures	40
Equity interest	140
Amount necessary to maintain the equity interest in entity	90
Profit attributable to equity shareholders	50

The additional £20 of profit may be described as a gearing gain and represents the profit which accrued to the shareholders because the company borrowed money and invested it in stock which rose in value. It is therefore 40 per cent of the increase in the replacement cost of stock: $40\% \times (150-100)$.

If the gearing gain were distributed, the operating capital of the entity would fall, unless the debentures were increased to maintain the original gearing ratio of 40 per cent.

An extended illustration is provided in Example 3.1, in which the combinations of three different bases of valuation and three different concepts of capital maintenance are shown.

EXAMPLE 3.1: DIFFERENT PROFIT CONCEPTS

In this example the three valuation bases used are historical cost (HC), replacement cost (RC) and net realisable value (NRV), and the three measures of capital maintenance are money financial capital, real financial capital and operating capital.

Suppose that a trader has an inventory consisting of 100 units at the start of the year (all of which were sold during the year) and 120 units at the end of the year, but has no other assets or liabilities.

Assume that the trader has neither withdrawn nor introduced capital during the period.

Suppose that the following prices prevailed:

Opening position (100 units)

Basis of valuation	Unit price £	Total capital £
Historical cost	1.00	100
Replacement cost	1.10	110
Net realisable value	1.15	115

Closing position (120 units)

Basis of valuation	Unit price £	Total capital £
Historical cost	1.50	180
Replacement cost	1.70	204
Net realisable value	1.80	216

In order to use the real financial capital approach it is necessary to know how a suitable general price index moved over the year. We will assume that an index moved as follows:

	Index
Beginning of the year and date on which the opening inventory was purchased	100
Date on which the closing inventory was purchased	118
End of year	120

(a) *Money financial capital*
The opening money financial capital depends on the selected basis of asset valuation and profit is the difference between the value of the assets at the end of the period and the corresponding figure for opening money capital.

Basis of valuation	Closing value of assets £	Opening money capital £	Profit £
Historical cost	180	100	80
Replacement cost	204	110	94
Net realisable value	216	115	101

(b) *Real financial capital*
   (i) *Historical cost*   The closing inventory of £180 (as measured by its historical cost) was acquired when the general price index was 118. The index has risen to 120 by the year end and thus the historical cost of inventory expressed in terms of pounds of year-end purchasing power is £180 x 120/118 = £183.

   Opening money capital based on historical cost was £100. The index stood at 100 at the beginning of the year and rose to 120 by the year end. Thus the real financial capital which has to be maintained is £100 x 120/100 = £120.

   The profit derived from the combination of historical valuation and real financial capital is hence £183 − £120 = £63 (expressed in 'year-end pounds').

(ii) *Replacement cost* As the replacement cost is a current value it is automatically expressed in year-end pounds and hence the closing value of inventory is £204.

Opening money capital using replacement cost was £110 which, expressed in year-end pounds, is equivalent to £132 (£110 x 120/100). The profit for this particular combination is thus £204 − £132 = £72.

(iii) *Net realisable value* The argument is similar to that which was used above and the profit derived from a net realisable value/real financial capital concept combination is calculated as follows:

	£
Closing inventory at net realisable value (automatically expressed in pounds of year-end purchasing power)	216
Opening money capital (based on net realisable value) restated in year-end pounds, £115 x 120/110	138
Profit	78

(c) *Operating capital*

In this simple example it can be seen that the wealth of the business has increased by 20 units and the only question is how the 20 units should be valued:

Basis of valuation		Profit £
Historical cost (using first in, first out)	20 x £1.50	30
Replacement cost	20 x £1.70	34
Net realisable value	20 x £1.80	36

The various profit figures are summarised in the following table:

	Capital maintenance concept		
Basis of valuation	Money financial £	Real financial £	Operating capital £
Historical cost	80	63	30
Replacement cost	94	72	34
Net realisable value	101	78	36

THE USEFULNESS OF DIFFERENT PROFIT MEASURES

In Example 3.1 nine different profit figures emerged. It is impossible to say that one of these is the 'correct' figure. They are all 'correct' in their own terms, although it may be argued that some of them are generally more useful than others. The different measures reflect reality in different ways. We will meet some of these measures later in this book in the context of the various proposals that have been made for accounting reform.

It might be useful if at this stage we examined a number (but by no means all) of the different objectives which are served by the preparation of financial accounts and consider which of the different profit measures would appear to be the more useful in each case.

We will first discuss the question of whether a business should be allowed to continue in existence. For simplicity we will assume that the business is a sole proprietorship. Consider the profit figure of £78 derived from the combination of the net realisable value asset valuation method and real financial capital maintenance. This figure shows the potential increase in purchasing power which accrued to the owner of the business by virtue of his decision not to liquidate the business at the beginning of the year. Had he taken that option, the owner would have received £115, which expressed in terms of year-end pounds amounts to £138, i.e. he could at the beginning of the year purchase an 'average' combination of goods and services amounting to £115 but it would cost £138 to purchase the same quantity of goods and services at the end of the year. By allowing the business to continue, the owner has increased his wealth by £78 in that should he liquidate the business at the end of the year he would release purchasing power amounting to £216. Now this analysis does not enable the owner to tell whether he was right to allow the business to continue in operation, but the figures do allow him to compare his increase in wealth with that which he would have achieved had he liquidated the business at the beginning of the year and invested his funds elsewhere. In the words of Edwards and Bell (*see* page 43) the owner has been able to check in the market place his decision not to wind up the business.

But, of course, the past is dead and it is current decisions which are important, the decision to be taken in this case being whether or not the business should be liquidated at the end of the year. It would be naive to assume that the figure of past profit can be expected to continue in the future. However, the decision maker has to start somewhere and most people find it easier to think in incremental terms. With this approach the decision maker might say: 'In the conditions which prevailed last year I made a profit of £x. I accept that next year there will be a number of changes in the circumstances facing the business, and I estimate that the effect of these changes will be to change my profit by £y'. It is clear that if this approach is adopted a profit figure related to the decision maker's objectives (in this case assumed to be the maximisation of his potential consumption) is a valuable input to the decision-making process.

Let us now consider the subject of taxation. A government might well take the view that a company should be able to maintain its productive capacity and that taxation should only be levied on any increase in the company's wealth as measured against that particular yardstick. In that case, one of the set of profit figures derived from the application of physical capital maintenance might be thought to be most suitable on the grounds that, to use the figures given in our example, if the company started the year with 100 units, then in order to maintain the productive capacity it should hold 100 units at the end of the year. The government would, if it took this view, wish to base its taxation levy on the physical increase of wealth of 20 units. Arguments for and against the use of one of the three members of the physical capital maintenance set could be deployed, but these will not be pursued at this stage. There are obviously severe practical difficulties in the use of the physical units approach where the company owns more than one type of asset and, as will be discussed later, other more practical methods have been suggested which would allow governments to apply a taxation policy which closely approximates to that postulated above.

Later in this book we will point out the limitations of the historical cost approach and, in fairness, we should now consider whether the profit derived from the traditional accounting system (historical cost asset values and money capital maintenance) could be said to be particularly apposite for any purpose. It is sometimes suggested that the traditional profit figure is of use in questions concerned with distribution policy, for, to quote Professor W. T. Baxter:

> The ordinary accounting concept has obvious merits; it is familiar and (inflation apart) cautious, and most of its figures are based on objective data; its widespread use has therefore been sensible where the decisions are about cash payments (e.g. tax and dividends), since it reduces the scope for bickering and the danger of paying out cash before the revenue has been realized.[13]

HOW DO WE CHOOSE?

We have identified nine different methods of measuring profit and pointed out that many other different methods are available. One possible way forward would be to include in a company's annual financial statements a list of different profit figures. However, if this is not considered practical, the question becomes which basis or bases is/are the most suitable for inclusion in published accounts. The reference to the plural 'bases', holds upon the possibility that it might be found desirable to include more than one profit concept in the published accounts.

A sensible approach to this question would be a consideration of the purposes for which a knowledge of a company's profits are used, which is in effect the consideration of the aims and objectives of published financial accounts. A very long list of such purposes can be provided, but it might be helpful if these were analysed under four different heads, i.e. control, consumption, taxation, valuation. It must, however, be recognised that the divisions between these heads are not watertight and that they share numerous common features.

THE LIMITATIONS OF HISTORICAL COST ACCOUNTING

Later chapters of the book deal with the subject of current purchasing power and current value accounting and will, by implication, highlight some of the deficiencies of the traditional form of accounting, i.e. historical cost basis of valuation and money financial capital maintenance.[14] It might, however, be helpful if by way of introduction we tested the traditional system against the objectives enumerated above.

Control

It is a widely held view that the prime objective of the preparation and publication of regular financial reporting is – so far as public limited companies are concerned – to provide a vehicle whereby the directors can account to the owners of the company on their *stewardship* of the resources entrusted to their charge. This involves providing

---

13 W. T. Baxter, *Accounting Values and Inflation*, McGraw-Hill, London, 1975, p. 23. It may be strange to quote the words of one of the foremost advocates of current value accounting in support of historical cost accounting. However, Professor Baxter, on whose work this section of the book is largely based, was seeking to show that different profit concepts may be useful for different purposes.

14 The weaknesses of the traditional accounting model are lucidly and concisely set out by the Accounting Standards Committee in *Accounting for the Effects of Changing Prices: a Handbook*, published in 1986 and by the Accounting Standards Board in its Discussion Paper 'The Role of Valuation in Financial Reporting' published in 1993. *See* Chapters 17 and 18.

shareholders with information about the progress of the company as well as details of the amounts paid to directors by way of remuneration. In theory shareholders can, when supplied with this information, take certain steps to remedy the position if the information suggests that all is not well. One mechanism that is available to shareholders is to effect a change in directors, but in practice it is rare for shareholders directly to oust directors because of the publication of unfavourable results. This end might be achieved by the indirect process of a takeover, in that shareholders might accept an offer for their shares on the grounds that they believe that the new management will be more effective than existing management. An individual shareholder can, of course, achieve similar ends by selling his shares but in so doing he must compare what he considers to be the value of the shares with the existing management with the current market price (*see* the section on valuation below).

The above discussion is based on the view that the directors need only account for their stewardship to their shareholders, but it has been suggested that the concept of stewardship should be extended – at least so far as large companies are concerned – to cover the need to report to the community at large. This view, propounded for example in *The Corporate Report*,[15] is based on the view that large companies control the use of significant proportions of a country's scarce resources and that consequently large companies should report to the community at large on the way in which the resources have been used. It will be realised that such a view does not attract the support of all businessmen and accountants, who might well be concerned with the nature of the control devices which might follow if this view were adopted. The pressure of public opinion might be an acceptable control device, but many would be concerned that this might not be regarded as being sufficiently strong and that recourse might be made to government intervention or 'interference' or, ultimately, nationalisation.

If stewardship is narrowly defined to cover simply the reporting by directors to shareholders of how they have used shareholders' funds, then it is possible to argue that historical cost accounting is reasonably adequate. An historical cost balance sheet lists the assets of the company and the claim by outsiders (liabilities) on the company; however it will not identify *all* the assets, as it will usually omit many intangible assets such as the skill and knowledge of the employees, degree of monopoly power, etc. The main point, however, is whether stewardship should be narrowly defined in the manner suggested above. If shareholders, and others, are to apply effective control they should be helped to form judgments about how well the directors have used the resources entrusted to them.

As we indicated earlier in the chapter there are a number of different possible approaches to the question of how one can measure how successful a company – and by implication its managers – has been over a period. At this stage it is perhaps sufficient to point out that historical cost accounting will not – except in the simplest of cases where a high proportion of a company's assets is made up of cash – be of much assistance. Historical cost accounts, in general, simply show the acquisition cost or the depreciated historical cost of a company's assets and not their current values, let alone the value of the company as a whole.

It is sometimes argued that even if historical cost accounts do not provide an absolute measure of success they can at least allow comparisons to be made between the quality of performance achieved by different companies. This statement is sometimes justified by

15 Scope and Aims Committee of the Accounting Standards Steering Committee, *The Corporate Report*, Accounting Standards Steering Committee, London, 1975.

arguments such as, 'Inflation affects all companies to more or less the same extent and therefore a comparison of profitability measured on a historical cost basis, e.g. rate of return on capital employed, enables a rough comparison to be made of relative success.'

Two points need to be made. The first concerns inflation. As will be shown, the problem is not just inflation – a general increase in prices or fall in the value of money – but includes the treatment of changes in relative prices. For, even in an inflation-free economy, there will be changes in individual prices. The limitations of historical cost accounting in the context of changes in relative prices can be seen by considering the following simple example.

Suppose that two companies start operations as commodity dealers, in an inflation-free environment, with £1000 each. Company A spent its £1000 on commodity A while Company B invested its £1000 in commodity B. Assume that neither company bought or sold any units during the period and that over the period the market value[16] of commodity A increased by 2 per cent and commodity B increased by 20 per cent. Historical cost accounts will not show that Company B performed better in the sense that it has chosen to invest in a commodity which experienced a greater increase in value.

The second point which should be made about the argument advanced above is that it is not true that inflation affects all companies to more or less the same extent. This point will be developed later when we will show that price changes (both general and relative) affect different companies in very different ways and that it is in fact the case that historical cost accounts are most unhelpful when it comes to the comparison of performance.

Consumption

Probably one of the most important uses of the profit figure is in determining the amount of any increment of wealth which is available for distribution and how it should be shared between the various groups entitled to share in such a distribution, i.e. the different classes of shareholders, the directors and employees (either directly through profit-sharing schemes or indirectly through wage claims) and the community through taxation. There are what might be called 'legal' and 'economic' aspects to this question. Company law requires that dividends may only be paid out of profits and tax law specifies the amount of taxation which has to be paid; however, subject to these constraints, plus any other legal limitations arising from such things as profit-sharing agreements, it is for the directors to make economic judgments about the level of dividends and, again subject to numerous institutional and possible legal constraints, the level of wages. Empirical evidence suggests that companies' dividends are related to the level of reported profit. It is also safe to suggest that sole traders and partners act in a similar fashion in that, when deciding on the level of their drawings, they will be influenced by the profits of their businesses.

The concept of capital maintenance based on historical cost accounting principles has, in periods of anything but modest price changes, proved to be a dangerous bench mark when used to assess the amount which a company can pay out by way of dividend or through taxation. For example, the maintenance of money financial capital is not, except in the simplest of cases, the same as the maintenance of the company's productive capacity. The point is an obvious one, for we could visualise a company which started business with

---

16 For simplicity we will ignore transaction costs and assume, in the case of both commodities, that there is no difference between the commodities' replacement costs and net realisable values.

£10 000 which it invested in 1000 units of stock. If the price of the stock increases and if the whole of the company's historical cost profit is taxed or consumed away, its money financial capital will be maintained, but it is clear that the company will have to reduce the physical quantity of stock.

It should be recognised that there is a great deal of difference between using the capital maintenance approach as a bench mark to measure profit and requiring companies to maintain their capital. Presumably distribution decisions should be made on the basis of consumption needs and perceived future investment opportunities inside and outside the company, and in many cases it would be sensible not to restrict distributions to profits. It is necessary that company law should attempt to provide a measure of protection to creditors, but this should not be done in an inflexible way.[17]

It will be argued in the following chapters that there is a need to devise a measure of profit that will provide a signal that if more than the amount of profit is consumed or taxed away then the substance of the business – however that may be defined – will be eroded. However, this is not to say that the substance of the business should never be reduced by way of dividend – in other words a partial liquidation of the business might in certain circumstances be beneficial to shareholders without being detrimental to the interests of creditors and employees.

Taxation

In Britain, as in many other countries, a company's tax charge is based on its accounting profit, although numerous adjustments might have to be made when computing the profit subject to taxation. The general rule is, however, clear – the higher the accounting profit, the higher, all other things being equal, the amount that will be paid in tax.

For reasons similar to those discussed in the above section on consumption, the traditional accounting system does not constitute a suitable basis for the computation of the taxation obligations of businesses. This view depends on the not unreasonable assumption that governments would wish companies to be at least able to maintain the substance of their businesses. As we have shown, it is possible for historical cost accounting to generate a profit figure even when there has been a decline in the productive capacity of the business or, in less extreme cases, the reported profit might far exceed the growth in the company's productive capacity. Thus the use of historical cost accounting as the basis for taxation means that in periods of rising prices the proportion of the increase in a company's wealth which is taken by taxation may be very much larger than that which is implied by the nominal rate of taxation. In extreme cases taxation might be payable even where there has been a decline in the productive capacity of the business.

The rapid and extreme inflation of the mid-1970s made governments and others very much aware of the inadequacy of historical cost accounting for the purposes of taxation. Special measures were enacted which allowed businesses some relief against taxation for the impact of increasing prices, namely stock appreciation relief and accelerated capital allowances. In contrast, financial accounting practice remained and remains essentially rooted in the traditional model of historical cost valuation combined with money financial capital maintenance, although as described later in this book, the debate on possible reforms continues.

---

17 Current legal practice regarding distributable profit is outlined in the final section of this chapter.

Valuation

The information contained in a company's accounts is a significant, but not the sole, input to decisions concerning the valuation of a business or of a share in a business. This subject will be discussed in detail in Chapter 14. At this stage it is perhaps sufficient to point out that the value of any asset, including a business or a share, depends on the economic benefits which are expected to flow to the asset's owner. It requires neither much space nor forceful argument to suggest that a knowledge of the historical cost of a company's assets will not be of much help in assessing the value of a company or of its shares. Indeed, it was never the view of accountants that historical cost accounts should be used in this way. However, this view has never fully been accepted by the users of accounts, who have, understandably from their point of view, believed that the information provided by a company's accounts should help them form judgments concerning valuation. In fact the case for accounting reform does not simply rest on the existence of inflation, which still appears to be a permanent feature of our economy, but on the recognition that the wish of users to be supplied with information which will help them assess the value of companies and shares therein is a legitimate demand and one which will be better served by accounts based on current value principles than by historical cost accounts.

SUMMARY

So far in this chapter, we have considered the meaning of profit and have shown that there are very many ways of measuring this elusive concept. These depend essentially on the choice made regarding the basis of asset valuation and the aspect of capital which is to be maintained. We have also discussed the limitations of historical cost accounting when tested against the more important purposes which a 'reasonable man' might expect financial accounts to serve. In the later chapters we will consider in some detail a number of the more important accounting models which have been developed and used in practice. But before doing so we will turn our attention briefly to the subject of distributable profits.

DISTRIBUTABLE PROFITS

Because the liability of its shareholders is limited to the amount which they have paid or agreed to pay in respect of their shares, creditors of a failed limited company will normally only have recourse to the assets of the company itself. The assets representing the share capital, and any other reserves which are treated as being similar to share capital, may be seen as a buffer or cushion which provides some protection to creditors in the event of a failure. If a company were permitted to use its assets to repay this 'permanent' capital, the buffer would be reduced or disappear entirely with the result that the creditors' position would be more risky.

While the law cannot prevent companies from reducing their 'permanent' capital by making losses, it does attempt to restrict the reduction of capital in other circumstances and, where a reduction of capital is permitted, it is strictly regulated. One way in which the law achieves its aim is by restricting payments of dividends to the distributable profits of the company. Another way is by the regulation of any transactions involving the purchase or redemption of a company's own shares and of any capital reduction or reorganisation schemes. We look at the former here and the latter in Chapter 12.

It has long been the case that dividends can only be paid out of profits but, surprisingly, until the passage of the Companies Act 1980, statute law offered no guidance on what constituted profits available for distribution. There were a number of leading cases, some of which were distinguished by their age rather than their economic rationale, which combined to produce some rather odd and confusing results.[18]

The implementation of the Second and Fourth EC Directives necessitated the inclusion of provisions relating to distributable profits in UK statute law and, as a result, the Companies Act 1985 contains the following definition

> ... a company's profits available for distribution are its accumulated, realized profits, so far as not previously utilized by distribution or capitalization, less its accumulated, realized losses, so far as not previously written off in a reduction or reorganization of capital duly made.[19]

The above represents the only legal requirement placed on private companies, but additional rules apply to public companies and investment companies.

A public company may not pay a dividend which would reduce the amount of its net assets below the aggregate of its called-up share capital plus its undistributable reserves.[20] For this purpose the Act defines undistributable reserves as:

(a) The share premium account.
(b) The capital redemption reserve.
(c) Excess of accumulated unrealised profits over accumulated unrealised losses (to the extent that these have not been previously capitalised or written off)
(d) Any other reserve which the company may not distribute.

Before turning to the special case of investment companies we will discuss the implications of the above for public and private companies. Note that no distinction is made between revenue and capital profits, both are distributable; the key element is whether the profits have been *realised*, a term which will be discussed in further detail below.

A private company may, legally, pay a dividend equal to the accumulated balance of realised profits less realised losses, irrespective of the existence of unrealised losses. In contrast, the effect of the 'net asset rule' or 'capital maintenance rule' imposed on public companies is to require such a company to cover any net unrealised losses.

Thus, suppose a company's balance sheet is as given below:

	£	£
Share capital		50
Share premium		25
Unrealised profits	20	
Unrealised losses	(35)	(15)
Realised profits less realised losses		40
Net assets		100

---

18 Interested readers are referred to E. A. French, 'Evolution of the Dividend Law of England', in *Studies in Accounting*, W. T. Baxter and S. Davidson (eds), ICAEW, London, 1977.
19 Companies Act 1985, Sec. 263(3).
20 Companies Act 1985, Sec. 264(1).

If the concern were a private company it could pay a dividend of £40, but if it were a public company the maximum possible dividend would, because of the net asset rule be restricted as follows:

	£	£
Net assets		100
less Share capital and undistributable reserves		
Share capital	50	
Share premium	25	
Excess of unrealised profits over unrealised losses[21]	0	75
Maximum dividend payable by public company		25

The effect of the net asset rule is to reduce the possible dividend by the net unrealised losses:

	£
Realised profits less realised losses	40
less excess of unrealised losses over unrealised profits	15
Maximum dividend	25

Given the general bias in accounting to treat all losses and provisions as being realised, it has to be recognised that unrealised losses are likely to be somewhat rare.

An investment company is a listed public company whose business consists of investing its funds in securities with the intention of spreading the risk and giving its shareholders the benefits of the results of its management of funds. Such a company can, if it satisfies a number of conditions,[22] including a prohibition on the distribution of capital profits, give notice to the Registrar of Companies of its intention to be regarded as an investment company.

Except for the fact that it may not distribute capital profits, an investment company may calculate its maximum dividend on the same basis as any other public company. However, it is afforded greater flexibility by Sec. 265 of the Companies Act 1985 which provides an alternative method of calculating the maximum dividend payable. An investment company can, subject to a number of conditions, pay a dividend equal to the amount of its accumulated realised revenue profits less its accumulated revenue losses (both realised and unrealised). Thus, it may ignore any capital losses subject to the restriction that, after the payment of the dividend, the company's assets must be equal to or greater than 1½ times its liabilities. Thus, if an investment company wishes to take advantage of the provision in Sec. 265 of not restricting its dividend by virtue of the existence of capital losses, it must apply this 'asset ratio test'.

It should be noted that the asset ratio test will be affected by the way in which it is proposed to fund the dividend in that the result will depend on whether the dividend will reduce assets (if paid out of a positive cash balance) or increase liabilities (if paid from an

---

21 Note that the excess of realised profits over unrealised losses is zero rather than the 'mathematical' excess of minus 15.

22 For a detailed list of conditions readers should refer to Companies Act 1985, Section 266.

overdraft). Suppose, for example, that an investment company has assets of £1200 and liabilities of £600. Then the maximum dividend on each basis will be:

(a) Dividend paid out of cash (i.e. liabilities held constant)

	Initial position £	After dividend £	Maximum dividend £
Assets	1200	900(3)	300
Liabilities	600	600(2)	

(b) Dividends paid out of an overdraft (assets held constant).

	Initial position £	After dividend £	Maximum dividend £
Assets	1200	1200(3)	
Liabilities	600	800(2)	200

The various provisions outlined above are summarised in Table 3.1 and illustrated in Example 3.2.

Table 3.1 Tests for maximum dividend

Type of company	Test
Private	The dividend must not exceed accumulated realised profits less accumulated realised losses.
Public (other than investment companies)	The dividend must not exceed accumulated realised profits less accumulated realised losses, less accumulated net unrealised losses.
Investment companies	The maximum dividend is the higher of: (a) the amount derived from the above rule applicable to all public companies with the modification that realised capital profits must be excluded; and (b) the amount of accumulated realised revenue profits less accumulated revenue losses, both realised and unrealised, provided that, after payment of the dividend, assets are equal to at least one and a half times the liabilities.

EXAMPLE 3.2

The balance sheet of Company A is summarised below:

	£	£
Total assets		4000
less Total liabilities		1000
		3000
Share capital		200
Share premium account		800
Unrealised profits		
Revenue	100	
Capital	200	300
Unrealised losses		
Revenue	(200)	
Capital	(800)	(1000)
Realised profits *less* realised losses		
Revenue	2300	
Capital	400	2700
		3000

We will now work out the maximum dividend on the assumption that Company A is (a) a private limited company, (b) a public limited company and (c) an investment company.

(a) *Private company*   For such a company, the maximum dividend is the accumulated net realised profits, that is £2700.

(b) *Public company*   The public company is subject to the capital maintenance rule that, after distribution, the net assets must equal the share capital plus undistributable reserves. In this case the undistributable reserves comprise only the share premium account, for the excess of unrealised profits over unrealised losses is zero. Hence, the maximum dividend is given by:

	£	£
Net assets		3000
less Share capital	200	
Share premium	800	1000
Maximum dividend		2000

In the case of the public company, the maximum dividend of the private company (£2700) has been reduced by the net unrealised losses of £700. (Unrealised losses £1000 less unrealised profits £300.)

(c) *Investment company*   By definition, an investment company must not distribute its capital profits. Hence our starting point must be realised revenue profits of £2300 subject, however, to the capital maintenance rule. Under this rule, the maximum dividend would be £2000 as for the public company in (b) above.

Using the alternative method allowed by Sec. 265 the maximum dividend is the excess of the realised revenue profits over net unrealised revenue losses, i.e. £2300 − (200−100) = £2200, subject to the application of the asset ratio test.

(i) If a dividend of £2200 was paid in cash, total assets would fall from £4000 to £1800 which is more than 1.5 times the liabilities of £1000.

(ii) If the dividend of £2200 was paid by overdraft, liabilities would increase to £3200 which would require asset cover of 1.5 x £3200 = £4800, i.e. more than the existing assets of £4000.

Hence the maximum dividend is £2200, but only if such a payment did not increase the liabilities. The lower limit of the maximum dividend is £2000 (as this can be justified on the alternative capital maintenance rule) while a dividend of between £2000 and £2200 would be possible if only a proportion of the dividend was paid out of an overdraft.

REALISED PROFITS [23]

It is clear from the above discussion that the most important task in determining a company's distributable profits is deciding what constitutes its realised profits less losses. Given the importance of the term, we might expect the Companies Acts to provide us with a comprehensive definition, but we would be extremely disappointed.

The Companies Act provides both specific and general guidance; while the specific guidance is helpful, the general guidance is much less helpful. Let us look at the more detailed guidance first.

Section 275 Companies Act 1985 states that provisions are realised losses except for a provision made in respect of a fall in value of a fixed asset appearing on a revaluation of *all* the fixed assets of the company, whether including or excluding goodwill. It also provides that where a fixed asset is revalued and depreciation is subsequently based on the revalued amount, the excess of depreciation based on the revalued amount over depreciation based on historical cost is to be treated as a realised profit. Thus the unrealised profit on revaluation is gradually converted into realised profit over the remaining useful life of the asset. Put another way, whatever is done in the profit and loss account, it is necessary only to charge depreciation based on historical cost in arriving at the realised profits of a company.

To give an example of such depreciation, let us suppose that a company purchased a fixed asset for £50 000 when its expected useful life was ten years and its expected residual value was zero. Using the straight line method of depreciation, the annual charge would be £5000 and, after four years, the net book value would be £30 000. If, after these four years, the asset were revalued to £42 000, there would be an unrealised revaluation surplus of £12 000, that is £42 000 less £30 000. The future annual depreciation charge in accordance with SSAP 12 (Revised) 'Accounting for depreciation' would normally be £42 000 ÷ 6 = £7000.

The excess of the revised depreciation charge of £7000 over historical cost depreciation of £5000 will then be treated as realised profits of the company year by year for the purpose of determining its distributable profits. Thus, by the end of the ensuing six years, the original unrealised revaluation surplus of £12 000 will have been regarded as realised and hence distributable.

23 This section on realised profits draws heavily on the ICAEW research paper *The Reporting of Profits and the Concept of Realization*, B. V. Carsberg and C. W. Noke, ICAEW, 1989.

Quite clearly the realised profits of a company may be a different figure from the balance on its profit and loss account!

Let us turn next to the more general guidance provided by the law. As a consequence of Companies Act 1989, the Companies Act 1985, Section 275, now contains the following definition:

> References ... to 'realized profits' and 'realized losses', in relation to a company's accounts, are to such profits or losses of the company as fall to be treated as realized in accordance with principles generally accepted, at the time when the accounts are prepared, with respect to the determination for accounting purposes of realized profits or losses ... .

This hardly provides an adequate definition of realised profits. Rather it leaves the definition of realised profits to accountants subject, of course, to the need for judicial interpretation in the Courts if the accountants' methods are challenged. For reasons which we discuss below, accounting standard setters have found it extremely difficult to provide a satisfactory definition of realised profits.

A basic problem is that the definition includes reference, not to generally accepted accounting principles, but to 'principles generally accepted with respect to the determination for accounting purposes of realised profits'. There is some considerable doubt over whether such principles actually exist. Accounting principles have been primarily concerned with a different objective, namely providing a true and fair view of a company's position and results. In attempting to achieve such an objective, accountants have been more concerned with the recognition of profit than with whether it is realised or distributable.

Paragraph 12 of Schedule 4 to Companies Act 1985 further complicates matters by stating that:

> The amount of any item shall be determined on a prudent basis, and in particular:
>
> (a) only profits realized at the balance sheet date shall be included in the profit and loss account ... .

Many accountants see this as providing an undesirable constraint on the development of more informative accounting.[24] Indeed the ASC invoked the true and fair override to avoid the requirement to comply with the above principle in cases where it was thought to be inappropriate. One example is the treatment of exchange gains on foreign currency loans outstanding on a balance sheet date which we discuss in Chapter 10.

Given the above position, it is perhaps not surprising to find little guidance on how to determine realised profits. One source of guidance was the ICAEW Technical Release 481, issued in 1982, which came to the conclusion that:

> A profit which is required by SSAPs to be recognized in the profit and loss account should normally be treated as a realized profit, unless the SSAP specifically indicates that it should be treated as unrealized.

Although this might have seemed an attractive way forward, it does seem to be a rather suspect interpretation of the law. Indeed, it appears to be somewhat close to a tautology: a profit and loss account must only include realised profits but, by definition, whatever an accountant puts in the profit and loss account is realised!

---

24 *See*, for example, 'The ASC in chains: whither self-regulation now?', Professor David P. Tweedie, *Accountancy*, March 1983, pp. 112–20.

Given the above difficulties, the ASC requested the Research Board of the ICAEW to commission a study and the resulting paper 'The Reporting of Profits and the Concept of Realization', by B. V. Carsberg and C. W. Noke, was published in 1989. If the ASC was expecting guidance on what was and what was not a realised profit, it must have been extremely disappointed. Carsberg and Noke identified six different meanings of realisation which have been used.

We shall focus on just two of these possible concepts of realisation. The narrower of the two is that embodied in the definition of prudence contained in SSAP 2:

> revenue and profits are not anticipated, but are recognized by inclusion in the profit and loss account only when realized in the form either of cash or of other assets the ultimate cash realization of which can be assessed with reasonable certainty; provision is made for all known liabilities (expenses and losses) whether the amount of these is known with certainty or is a best estimate in the light of the information available.

(Para. 14)

This concept concentrates on the reasonable certainty of the ultimate receipt of cash. Clearly realisation has occurred if cash has been received but realisation is also deemed to occur if certain types of assets, such as debtors, are held which are reasonably certain to be turned into cash.

The wider concept regards profit as realised if it can be assessed with reasonable certainty. Thus, it considers the main purpose of the concept as being to ensure reliability of measurement.

Readers may find the distinction between these two concepts difficult to grasp so it is perhaps helpful to look at some examples.

Where a company makes a cash sale, there is no doubt that the profit is realised under either concept. Similarly where a sale is made on credit, the profit is treated as realised subject to the possible need for a provision for doubtful debts. The creation of the debt payable in the short term provides evidence of the ultimate cash proceeds and also provides a reliable measure of the profits.

Let us think next of an investment in a listed security which increases in price during a period. Under the narrower concept of realisation, profit would not be considered realised because the ultimate cash proceeds at some unspecified time in the future cannot be assessed with reasonable certainty. However, under the wider concept, profit would be treated as realised because the listed price of the share on the balance sheet date provides reliable evidence that a profit has been made. Conventionally accountants would adopt the narrower concept and would treat the holding gain as unrealised.

When we turn to foreign exchange gains on unsettled short-term debtors and creditors, we find that SSAP 20 requires that such gains be taken to the profit and loss account as realised profits. Under the narrower concept of realisation, these would not be treated as realised profits in view of the fact that the exchange rate may reverse between the balance sheet date and the date of receipt or payment. However, under the wider concept, there is reliable evidence, in the form of a published exchange rate, for the fact that a profit has been made. It is true that this may be reversed in the subsequent period but that will be a matter for the subsequent period. Here the ASC appears to have adopted the wider concept of realisation, although, interestingly, the adoption of this wider concept is not applied to the treatment of exchange gains on unsettled long-term monetary items for here the gains are specifically described as unrealised.

We hope that these examples provide an indication of the lack of consistency in defining realised profits in practice. In order to provide some consistency, Carsberg and Noke recommended that the standard setters should prepare a statement defining realisation and, in their view, the definition should be framed in terms of the reliability of measurement. Some progress is being made insofar that in Chapter 4 of the draft Statement of Principles the ASB confirms that only realised gains should be included in the profit and loss account and proposes that a gain be regarded as realised when any one of the following occur:

(a) the gain is the result of a transaction whose value is measurable with sufficient reliability, or
(b) the gain results from a change in an asset or liability of a type not held for a continuing use in the business, and the resultant asset or liability is readily convertible to known amounts of cash or cash equivalents, or
(c) the gain results from the extinction of a liability.

Thus it appears that the ASB is moving to a position where either reliability of measurement or reasonable certainty of the conversion to cash would justify a gain being regarded as realised.

Do the provisions make sense?

The law has much to answer for in introducing references to realised profits without providing an adequate definition. By requiring that only such undefined profits be included in the profit and loss account, the law has placed a constraint on the development of accounting practice. In the past the ASC avoided the problem by invoking the true and fair override but this was a piecemeal solution. The ASB, in contrast, is now, through the development of its Statement of Principles, seeking both to define more precisely what is meant by recognition and realisation and to make financial statements more informative and understandable by ensuring that only realised gains are included in the profit and loss account with recognised gains and losses, being included in the statement of total recognised gains and losses (*see* Chapter 6).

It is possible to question the philosophy on which the law of distributable profits is based and to press for changes to that law. Why, after all, should dividends be restricted to distributable profits defined in terms of realisation?[25]

Let us approach the question in two stages. First, why should dividends be restricted to profits and, second, if such a restriction is to apply, why should it relate to realised profits?

If a company's directors are acting in the interests of its shareholders then whether or not a distribution is made should depend on the rates of return available to shareholders outside the company compared with the rates of return available within the company. If the company has inferior investment opportunities to those of the shareholders, then the restriction of a dividend to the distributable profits of the company would lead to an inefficient allocation of economic resources. The position of creditors needs to be considered and there is a case for protecting the 'buffer' available to creditors. In practice it is likely that the buffer will only be of relevance if the company goes into liquidation or

---

25 The ideas which follow may be explored in E. A. French, 'Evolution of the dividend law of England', in *Studies in Accounting*, W. T. Baxter and S. Davidson (eds), ICAEW, London, 1977 and D. A. Egginton, 'Distributable profit and the pursuit of prudence', in *Accounting and Business Research*, Number 41, Winter 1980.

substantially reduces its scale of operations. In such circumstances the real protection for creditors is the amount which will be realised from the sale of assets. In the case of some assets, especially current assets, realisable values may be well in excess of book values, but in the case of many fixed assets, particularly of a failed company, book value might exceed net realisable value. Hence, it might be argued that the test that should be applied is to specify that after distribution the realisable value of the company's assets exceed, possibly by a safety margin, the amounts due to creditors.

Even if we accept that dividends should be restricted to profits why should the distribution be limited to realised profits?

It is sometimes argued that if a gain is realised, then the money is available to pay the dividend without the need to consider asset valuation. However, as Professor Egginton has pointed out, the argument has two weaknesses, one damaging and the other fatal! The damaging weakness is that conventional accounting often treats profits as realised well before cash is received. The fatal weakness is that even when profits have been received in cash, this cash will usually have been converted into other assets long before any dividends are paid. Hence, whether profits have been received or not, there is no guarantee that cash is available.

This is an area of the law which includes a number of poorly thought out rules based on dubious reasoning, and accountants are forced to operate within an extremely unhelpful framework. It is of some consolation that in the vast majority of cases the limiting factor in determining a dividend is not the availability of distributable profits but the availability of cash and the alternative uses to which it may be put!

RECOMMENDED READING

R. H. Parker, G. C. Harcourt and G. Whittington (eds), *Readings in the Concept and Measurement of Income*, 2nd edn, Philip Allan, Oxford, 1986.

B. V. Carsberg and C. W. Noke, *The Reporting of Profits and the Concept of Realization*, ICAEW, London, 1989.

PART II
Financial reporting in practice

CHAPTER 4

Assets: tangible and intangible

INTRODUCTION

In this and the following chapters we will discuss a number of problems of accounting measurement and disclosure in the context of current financial accounting practice, which might be described as a 'modified historical cost accounting' system. While efforts to replace historical cost accounting by current cost accounting as the main basis of accounting have failed, the debate has had a considerable impact on financial accounting practice. Of course, in the UK at least, historical cost accounting has always been 'modified' to the extent that assets could be revalued for the purposes of the accounts and that company legislation required limited information to be provided regarding the market value of assets.

More recent developments which shift the balance from historical cost accounts include the 'alternative accounting rules' of the Companies Act 1985 which govern the use of current values in published accounts and the drafting of SSAPs and Financial Reporting Standards which, so far as possible, are now framed from the standpoints of both historical cost and current cost accounting. So, while we shall now concentrate on historical cost accounts, current cost accounts will not be far from our minds. The documents discussed in this chapter are:

ED 51   'Accounting for fixed assets and revaluations' and Discussion Paper
'The role of valuation in financial reporting'.

FRED 7   'Fair values in acquisition accounting'

SSAP 12 'Accounting for depreciation'

SSAP 19 'Accounting for investment properties'

SSAP 4   'Accounting for government grants'

SSAP 9   'Stocks and work in progress'

SSAP 13 'Accounting for research and development'

ED 52   'Accounting for intangible fixed assets'

ACCOUNTING FOR FIXED ASSETS AND REVALUATIONS

Fixed assets typically constitute a substantial proportion of an entity's assets so it is surprising that there is as yet no accounting standard on the subject.[1] The ASC attempted to remedy this by issuing Exposure Draft 51, 'Accounting for fixed assets and revaluations', in May 1990 and Exposure Draft 53, 'Fair value in the context of acquisition accounting', in July 1990. The ASB has attempted to move matters forward by issuing two discussion papers: 'The role of valuation in financial reporting', issued in March 1993, and 'Fair values in acquisition accounting', issued in April 1993. The latter has now resulted in an exposure draft with the same title, FRED 7, issued in December 1993. We shall discuss these documents in this section of the chapter.

ED 51

Exposure Draft 51 covers all fixed assets, including intangible assets, and in particular provides a general framework to which can be related existing and proposed standards relating to specific fixed assets. It includes a consideration of the definition of a fixed asset, the determination of the cost of the fixed asset and matters relating to the revaluation of fixed assets.

What is a fixed asset?

We need to start by deciding what is an asset. The ASC drawing on the IASC *Framework for the Preparation and Presentation of Financial Statements*[2] defines an asset as 'a resource controlled by the enterprise as a result of past events and from which future economic benefits are expected to flow to the enterprise'. (ED 51, Para. 6.)

For the asset to be recognised in the accounts not only should there be a probability that the future economic benefits will flow to or from the enterprise but the asset must have a cost. Note that the key elements are **control** (not ownership), **future economic benefits** and **cost**.

To qualify as a fixed asset, the item must be employed in the business with the intention that it should be used on a continuing basis. Thus the Exposure Draft defines a fixed asset as follows:

A fixed asset is an asset that:

(a) is held by an enterprise for use in the production or supply of goods and services, for rental to others, or for administrative purposes and may include items held for the maintenance or repair of such assets;

(b) has been acquired or constructed with the intention of being used on a continuing basis; and

(c) is not intended for sale in the ordinary course of business.[3]

---

1 The essential characteristics of an asset and the tests which should be applied to decide whether an asset should be included in the balance are discussed in some detail in FRED 4, 'Reporting the Substance of Transactions', see Chapter 6.

2 International Accounting Standards Committee, *Framework for the Preparation and Presentation of Financial Statements,* 1989.

3 ED 51, Para. 57.

The definition is clear enough but it does not answer all possible questions. To what extent should an item be regarded as a single asset or a collection of assets?[4] A factory is clearly a collection of assets while a motor car would almost always be treated as a single asset. But the question is not always capable of a simple answer. Take as an example, trailers which are towed by articulated trucks. The tyres of the trailers constitute a substantial portion of the total cost of the trailer but have a much shorter life than that of the bodies of the trailers. The owner of a large trailer fleet might well find it sensible to treat the tyres separately from the bodies and, for example, to apply a different depreciation pattern to the tyres as compared to the bodies.

Clear-cut rules cannot be provided to deal with such situations, in the words of the Exposure Draft: judgment is required.

The cost of a fixed asset

The principle under the historical cost convention is clear enough. The cost of a fixed asset is its purchase price or the expenditure incurred in its production together with, in each case, the expenditure incurred in bringing the fixed asset to working condition for its intended use at its intended location.

With this definition there can be no dispute about inclusion of expenditure on carriage and installation of the fixed asset in its cost. Production overheads can also be included in the case of self-constructed assets but the Exposure Draft would not permit the inclusion of administrative or general overheads unless they can be reasonably attributed to the purchase of the fixed asset or bringing it into use.

A distinction also needs to be drawn between essential commissioning costs and those which are due to what the Exposure Draft refers to as 'inefficiencies'. Essential commissioning costs which can include the cost of running plant at less than normal capacity for a limited period can be included in the cost of the fixed assets. Costs arising from inefficiencies such as industrial disputes should be charged to the profit and loss account.

In general the cost of fixed assets constructed by an enterprise for its own use (self-constructed assets) should be determined in the same way as the cost of finished goods, which is the subject of a later section of this chapter. As will be seen in that section, it is impossible, even if it is desirable, to lay down specific rules about the treatment of overheads, and thus the cost of self-constructed assets would be subject to considerable variation depending on the methods used. One difference between finished goods and self-constructed assets is that in the former any 'errors' will generally be reversed in the next accounting period, while in the case of the self-constructed assets the effect of any errors will be retained in the accounting system for a much longer period. Thus, if a 'self-constructed asset' is 'overvalued' the profit for the year of construction will be overstated. The consequence is that future depreciation charges will be overstated, but the 'excess profit' will not be totally eliminated until the asset is fully written off.

Capitalisation of borrowing costs

Considerable uncertainty surrounds the question of whether borrowing costs should be

---

4 We shall return to the question of whether assets should be valued on an individual basis or in aggregate as a 'business unit' in Chapter 18.

capitalised when the asset, say a building, is paid for in advance, often by a series of progress payments or in the case of an asset which takes a considerable time to bring into service. The debate about whether or not borrowing costs should be capitalised is often conducted with a fervour reminiscent of the more extreme medieval religious conflicts, but the basic point is, however, extremely simple.

The only point at issue is when the cost of borrowing should be charged to the profit and loss account. If the cost is not capitalised it will be charged over the life of the loan, while if it is capitalised the cost will be charged to the profit and loss account over the life of the asset as part of the depreciation expense. The rationale for the view that borrowing costs should be capitalised can best be demonstrated by the use of a simple example.

Assume that the client, A Limited, is offered the following choice by the builder, B Limited: 'The building will take two years to construct, you can either pay £1.0 million now or £1.2 million in two years' time.'

If A Limited decides to select the first option, it may well have to borrow the money on which it will have to pay interest. If A Limited selects the second option, it will still have to pay interest, but in this case the interest will be included in the price paid to B Limited.

The above example is extreme, but it does highlight the principles involved. If we assume that both companies have to pay the same interest rate, then A Limited will be in exactly the same position at the end of two years whatever option is selected, and it does not seem sensible to suggest that the cost of the building is different because in one case the interest is paid directly by the client while in the second case the interest is paid via the builder.

The Exposure Draft puts the two sides of the case. The arguments for capitalisation are that the borrowing costs are part of the total expenditure required to bring the fixed asset into use and the point about comparability demonstrated in the above illustration.

It also puts three arguments against capitalisation, two of which are weak. The weak arguments are:

(i)   It is illogical to treat the borrowing costs incurred during the period of construction of the fixed asset differently from those which are incurred when the asset is in use. But is it illogical, given the comparability argument advanced above?

(ii) That borrowing costs are usually incurred to support the whole of the activities of the enterprise and any attempt to associate borrowing costs with a particular fixed asset will often be arbitrary. But the amount of capital tied up in the asset while it is being constructed will be known and to this can be applied the enterprise's average cost of borrowing for the period.

The stronger counter argument focuses on comparability. An enterprise with a high proportion of equity capital might not need to borrow money but instead finance the purchase from retained earnings. There is still a cost, but it is an opportunity cost not an actual cost, and unless a notional charge is made to represent the opportunity cost, such an enterprise will carry its fixed assets at a lower amount than a highly geared enterprise which does capitalise borrowing costs. The making of a notional charge would be prohibited under the provisions of ED 51 (Para. 74(e)).

The Exposure Draft finds the arguments for and against the capitalisation of interest charges finely balanced and hence allows enterprises to choose whether or not to capitalise borrowing costs on fixed assets which take a substantial period of time to bring into service. It does, however, call for consistent treatment by enterprises. Thus, if an enterprise decides to capitalise borrowing costs, it must do so for all qualifying assets, but the overriding materiality convention would, of course, mitigate the effect of this proposal.

If the borrowing is directly associated with the acquisition of the asset, the actual cost should be capitalised. Otherwise a capitalisation rate should be determined by relating the borrowing costs incurred in financing expenditure on fixed assets during a period to the borrowings outstanding during that period.

The Exposure Draft also calls for the disclosure of the enterprise's policy concerning the capitalisation of borrowing costs and details of the total borrowing cost capitalised during the period analysed between the different types of fixed assets involved.

Enhancement costs

One of the more slippery areas of accounting is the distinction between repairs and enhancement with the temptations often pulling in opposite directions. The enterprise wishing to minimise its tax bill would tend to write off as much as possible to repairs, while an enterprise more concerned with showing a good profit would opt for capitalisation.

The Exposure Draft proposes that expenditure on improvements to a fixed asset should be capitalised. To qualify for this treatment the expenditure must result in an increase in the expected future benefits from the asset.

VALUATIONS

Historical cost accounting does suffer from a number of limitations, but at least it can be argued to be based on a simple and consistent rule. Record only those items which have a historical cost, and only record the historical cost of those items. So why ruin it by allowing enterprises to show some, but not all assets, at a valuation made at whatever date they choose? ED 51 rehearses the arguments for and against allowing enterprises to show assets at a valuation in an otherwise historical cost balance sheet. The positive argument is that it provides useful information to users of accounts in that the recognition of valuations 'enables performance ratios measuring the effectiveness with which capital has been employed to be calculated more satisfactorily' (ED 51, Para. 31).

True, but while the calculation may be 'more satisfactory', a curious term, it would only be meaningful if all the assets are shown at their current valuation.

The arguments against are that to allow selective revaluations undermines the integrity of the historical cost system and allows enterprises too much discretion over their reported results and financial position. Information about significant differences between current market values and balance sheet carrying values can be provided in notes to the accounts.

The phrasing of ED 51 suggested that the ASC would have preferred to prohibit the inclusion of asset valuations in historical cost accounts but recognised that it would have been impractical to do so. It is recognised that in the UK land and buildings are the assets most likely to have been revalued. If asset valuation was prohibited, it would mean either that the fixed assets concerned would have to be restated at their historical cost or that, for a considerable period, balance sheets would include some assets at cost and others at out-of-date valuations.

The Exposure Draft therefore attempted to overcome the problem in a different way. Its aims were to improve the consistency in the way enterprises undertake valuations and, through the provision of information, enable comparisons to be made between enterprises which revalue assets and those which do not. The main points are that an enterprise should be consistent in that it should treat all fixed assets in the same class in the same way, they should all be shown at valuation or all at historical cost, and that, if assets are shown at valuation, then they should be at current but not necessarily annual valuations, i.e. assets would have to be revalued at regular intervals, at least every five years.

The ASB Discussion Paper 'The role of valuation in financial reporting' recognised the problems of our present system and considered the possibilities of either reverting to an 'unmodified' or pure historical cost system or moving to a current value system. It rejected both alternatives and, instead, proposed an evolutionary approach within the present hybrid system of accounting. It earmarked certain assets for regular revaluation, namely those for which supplementary information is already required by law and which are traded in a ready market.[5]

The relevant assets are:
(i)   Properties (excluding fixed assets specific to the business)
(ii) Quoted investments
(iii) Stock of a commodity nature and long-term stock where a market of sufficient depth exists.

The Discussion Paper did not discuss the thorny problem of what should be done with the gain or loss on a revaluation. Under present law, such unrealised gains or losses cannot be taken to the profit and loss account unless the true and fair override is used.[6] Hence it would appear to be necessary to take them to the Statement of total recognised gains and losses.

Classification of fixed assets

For the purposes of the exposure draft *a class* is a category of fixed assets having a similar nature or function within the business; subdivision by reference to geographical location should be ignored.

Thus, if an enterprise owns a chain of shops, it should value all or none, wherever they are located. It is not clear whether the reference of 'similar nature' means that leasehold shops could be treated differently from those held on freehold. It is to be hoped that any standard resulting from ED 51 will be more precise in its definition.

Frequency of valuation and qualifications of valuers

Valuations should be kept up to date. At a minimum assets should be revalued every five years, but revaluations should be made more frequently if there is a material difference between the current value and the carrying value in the balance sheet. This means that an 'informal' revaluation will need to be made at each balance sheet date and, if it appears that there has been a material change, a qualified valuer would need to be instructed to carry out a full valuation. The Exposure Draft argues that to ensure the credibility of the financial statements the valuers should be experienced and possess appropriate qualifications.

5 'The role of valuation in financial reporting', ASB Discussion Paper, ASB, London, March 1993.
6 See the discussion of listed investments in Chapter 9, page 226.

The valuation of land and buildings should be made by an external valuer, except in the case of an enterprise which employs a substantial number of qualified valuers. In this case the actual valuations can be made by qualified employees, but the basis of the valuations should be reviewed by external valuers. The valuation of other assets can be made by qualified employees.

The basis of valuation – open market value and depreciated replacement cost

The ASC believed that in order to preserve the objectivity of historical cost accounts, any fixed assets included at their current valuation, should be valued by reference to their *open market value*. There were two exceptions – intangible assets and investment properties.[7]

The open market value is essentially the price that would be obtained in the market for the asset under 'normal conditions'. The full definition is:

> The *open market value* of a fixed asset is the best price at which the enterprise's interest in the asset might reasonably be expected to be sold at the date of valuation, assuming:
>
> (a) a willing seller;
> (b) a reasonable period in which to negotiate the sale, taking into account the nature of the market and the state of the market;
> (c) that values will remain static during this period;
> (d) that the asset will be freely exposed to the open market; and
> (e) that no account will be taken of any additional bid by a purchaser with a special interest.
>
> (ED 51, Para. 58.)

An asset's open market value is an exit value (*see* page 46) as it is based on the price for which it could be sold but differs from the net realisable value in that the value is based on the 'best price' and not the net proceeds from a hypothetical sale.

ED 51 does not discuss why this particular variant of current value was chosen. A possible justification for choosing open market value over net realisable value is that it reflects better the continuing use of the asset than a value more closely related to the disposal of the asset.

But why open market value rather than replacement cost? In many cases the differences between the selling and buying prices will be comparatively small but, in the case of fixed assets, the selling price is likely to be less than the buying price. Hence, the definition of open market value given in ED 51 is 'more prudent' than one based on the price (the owner of the asset) would have to pay to acquire the asset.

The value of land is heavily dependent on the uses to which the land can be put as specified through planning consents. The Exposure Draft therefore proposes that the open market value of an asset should reflect its value in its existing use, unless the enterprise is committed to changing the use of the asset and has obtained all the necessary consents.

In the explanatory note to the Exposure Draft, at paragraph 43, it is stated that

> An open market value will normally be obtainable in the case of land and buildings but the depreciated replacement cost basis may have to be used for specialized land and buildings such as oil refineries, power stations and dock installations or land and buildings located in particular

---

7 The valuation of intangible assets is discussed on pages 100 to 104, while investment properties are the subject of pages 87 to 88.

geographical areas for special reasons or of such a size, design or arrangement as would make it impossible for the valuer to arrive at an open market value.

This paragraph is apparently the basis of the relevant section (paragraph 82) of the proposed standard which states that assets should be valued at open market value except in circumstances in which it would not be practical.

But is the problem really one of a practicality or is it a concern about the outcome? Is the concern that the open market value will be close to zero? If so, should not the low value be reflected in the accounts? The lack of any substantial argument to justify the choice of one basis of valuation rather than another is a weakness of ED 51.

Permanent diminutions

The Exposure Draft distinguishes, but not clearly, between a downward revaluation of an asset and the recognition of a *permanent diminution* in its value. A permanent diminution is defined as 'a diminution in the amount recoverable from its future use and subsequent disposal which is not expected to reverse in the foreseeable future'. (ED 51, Para. 59.)

Once recognised, a permanent diminution should be charged to the profit and loss account and not debited to the revaluation reserve (*see below*).

A number of examples are given of the circumstances which might give rise to a permanent diminution – these include:

(a) significant technological developments;
(b) physical damage;
(c) structural changes in external economic conditions leading to reduced demand for the output produced by the fixed asset.

It seems that the essence of the distinction is that permanent diminutions means that the asset has become, either in physical or economic terms, damaged, in other words it is a 'lesser asset'. Consider, for example, a machine with an open market value of £10 000 which is capable of producing 100 units per hour, and suppose that as a result of technological change a new machine comes onto the market the operating costs and other characteristics of which are exactly the same, but which is capable of producing 200 units per hour. Then, so long as the cost of the new machine is less that £20 000 the open market value of the existing machine will fall. In economic terms, the existing machine has become a lesser asset and it is unlikely that the decline in value will be reversed.

The rationale for ED 51's approach is that revaluations can go up and down and it is not unreasonable to set the ups against the downs, but it would not be appropriate to set off a permanent diminution which represents a change in the nature of the asset (in the sense described above) against changes in the values of other assets.

The revaluation reserve

Revaluation surpluses and deficits should be carried to the revaluation reserve where they can be netted off. If the resulting balance is a debit, ED 51 proposes, on the grounds of prudence, that it be charged to the profit and loss account as additional depreciation.

The revaluation reserve should relate only to assets which are still owned by the enterprise.[8] Thus, when an asset shown at its valuation is sold, the amount of the revaluation reserve relating to that asset should be transferred to the profit and loss account.

Comparability

One of the aims of ED 51 is to facilitate comparability on an historical cost basis between enterprises which value assets and those which do not. Hence, in order to enable users of the accounts to see what the profit would have been had the enterprise carried all its fixed assets at historical cost, transfers made from the revaluation reserve to the profit and loss account should be clearly identified in financial statements.

In addition, the Exposure Draft, building on the requirement of the Companies Act, 1985 in respect of the adoption of the alternative accounting rules,[9] requires in respect of any class of asset shown at valuation, that the gross historical cost and the aggregate depreciation based on the historical cost should be disclosed in the notes to the financial statements. (ED 51, Para. 101(d).)

Valuation and depreciation

If in a period of fluctuating prices assets were revalued each year, with the difference between the current valuation and the figure shown in the preceding balance sheet taken direct to the revaluation reserve, then depreciation would not be recognised in the accounts in respect of the asset. Thus, in terms of conventional accounting the profit for the period would be overstated because an important expense, that relating to the consumption of fixed assets, would be absent from the profit and loss account.[10]

One way round the problem would be to charge or credit the profit and loss with revaluation deficits or surpluses, but this would result in a confused set of financial statements based on a mixture of historical and current value principles.

Unfortunately the Exposure Draft does not deal fully with the problem of depreciation. It does state that if valuation is to be used in place of historical cost for any class of fixed asset, then subsequent depreciation should be based on the valuation. (ED 51, Para. 36.) It also states that for each period there should be a transfer 'from the revaluation reserve to the profit and loss account reserve of an amount equal to the difference between depreciation for the period calculated on the basis of the historical cost carried at a valuation and the actual depreciation charge based on the revalued amounts in respect of those fixed assets' (ED 51, Para. 96), and that when a revalued asset is sold then 'any amount relating to it should be transferred to the profit and loss account reserve' (ED 51, Para. 97).

Thus, the fixed asset should be depreciated each year based on its opening balance sheet value and, if the asset is subsequently revalued, the surplus, or deficit, to be taken to the revaluation reserve should be the difference between the open market value and the book

---

8 Thus the reserve differs from reserves of an apparently similar nature which are a feature of current cost accounts. (*See* Chapter 16.) Current cost (revaluation) reserves represent additional amounts which need to be invested in an enterprise to maintain its operating capability and hence will not be adjusted when a particular asset is sold.

9 Companies Act, 1985 Schedule 4, Para. 33.

10 In Chapter 18 we introduce a system of accounting which does not attempt to measure depreciation but simply records changes in the values of fixed assets.

value at the date of revaluation. Subsequent depreciation should be based on the revalued amount. Hence, if an asset is revalued during the year, the depreciation charge in the profit and loss account will comprise two elements based on the different valuations.

The above points are best illustrated by an example.

EXAMPLE 4.1

Jaz Limited acquired a fixed asset for £10 000 at the beginning of year 1. Its estimated life is 10 years and its expected residual value is zero. The company uses straight line depreciation.

Thus, at the end of year 2 the fixed asset, if carried at historical cost, will be recorded as follows:

Cost	£10 000
less Accumulated depreciation	2 000
Net book value	£8 000

Let us assume that the company decides to show the fixed asset as at the end of year 2 at its open market value of £12 000. Then the relevant balance sheet figures will be:

Fixed asset at valuation	£12 000
Revaluation reserve	£4 000

Let us also assume that there is no change in the estimated life of the asset, i.e. as at the end of year 2, its expected life is eight years.

We will first consider the simple case, that after year 2 there is no significant difference between the current open market value and the carrying value in the balance sheet.

In year 3, the depreciation charge in the profit and loss account will be £1500 (£12 000 ÷ 8).

Then the relevant balance sheet figures as at the end of year 3 will be:

Fixed asset at revalued amount		12 000
less Depreciation, 1/8 of £12 000		1 500
		£10 500
Revaluation reserve		
Opening balance	4 000	
less Transfer to P&L		
Reserve (£1500−£1000)	500	£3 500

At the end of year 10, both the fixed asset and the revaluation reserve will be written off, which is consistent with the assumption of a zero residual value.

While the depreciation charge in the profit and loss account for year 3 will be £1500 the net effect on the profit and loss reserve will be a debit of £1000 (the historical cost depreciation) because of the transfer of £500 from the revaluation reserve.

Now let us assume that at the end of year 4 the open market value is £11 000.

The balance sheet figures before the adjustments consequent upon the valuation are:

Fixed asset at revalued amount		£12 000
less 2 years' depreciation		3 000
		£9 000
Revaluation reserve		
Opening balance	3 500	
less Transfer to P&L Reserve	500	£3 000

As a result of the revaluation the figures will be:

Fixed assets at revaluation		£11 000
Revaluation reserve		
Balance as above	3 000	
add Surpluses on revaluation		
£11 000 − £9000	2 000	£5 000

Disclosure requirements

We will not waste space in reproducing the disclosure requirements and transitional provisions of ED 51. The main points on disclosure are that the requirements are extensive and are designed to allow for comparisons to be made on an historical cost basis between enterprises which show some of their fixed assets at valuation and those which retain strict adherence to the historical cost basis of valuation.

Summary of ED 51

The main points of ED 51 are summarised in Table 4.1.

Table 4.1 Main points of ED 51

1 Definition of fixed assets	Future economic benefits, cost and intention to use on a continuing basis.
2 Cost of fixed assets	Expenditure to bring to intended use in intended location; should include production overheads, can include borrowing costs
3 Basis of valuation	Open market value or, if not possible, depreciated replacement cost. Valuations undertaken by qualified valuers.
4 Permanent diminution	To be distinguished from downward revaluations and charged to profit and loss account.
5 Revaluation reserve	Relates only to existing fixed assets.
6 Depreciation	Profit and loss charge based on carrying value but write back difference between depreciation based on valuation and historical cost to P&L account reserve.
7 Disclosure	Extensive and, in particular, allows for comparability on an historical cost basis.

ACQUISITION OF A COLLECTION OF ASSETS AND LIABILITIES

When an entity purchases a business or subsidiary undertaking, it obtains control of a collection of assets and liabilities which will usually include tangible and intangible assets. The determination of the 'cost' of these individual assets and liabilities for inclusion in the financial statements or consolidated financial statements of the acquiring entity requires the allocation of the total cost to the identified assets and liabilities. This topic was the subject of ED53 'Fair value in the context of acquisition accounting', which was issued by the ASC in 1988, and FRED 7 'Fair values in acquisition accounting', issued by the ASB in 1993.

FRED 7 is written in the context of acquisitions and hence we shall return to it when we discuss business combinations and acquisitions in Chapters 8 and 9. However it contains certain points of principle which are relevant when any collection of assets and liabilities is acquired for a global price. It also considers the position where a non-cash consideration, such as shares in the acquiring company, is given.

If we concentrate on a situation where a non-cash consideration is involved, we need to do two things:

(a) Put a fair value on the purchase consideration given.
(b) Determine the 'costs' of the individually identified assets and liabilities by assigning a fair value to each of these assets and liabilities.

Usually (a) and (b) will not be equal, giving rise to purchased goodwill, that is the excess of the purchase consideration over the sum of the fair values of the individual assets less the fair values of any liabilities taken over. Such goodwill may be positive or negative. While goodwill is almost always encountered in a situation involving a group of companies, an individual company may find that it has goodwill to deal with if, for example, it acquires an unincorporated business such as a sole trader or partnership.

Fair value of the consideration

The fair value of ordinary shares forming part of a purchase consideration should be based on the cash that would have been received from the issue of the shares had there been no knowledge of the transaction; for a listed security this will usually be based on the average price for a period prior to the announcement of the transaction. If there is not a market for the share, the price should be estimated by reference to a listed share with similar attributes. It will be appreciated that in practice such estimates will usually involve subjective judgment.

In some cases the purchase consideration may not be payable immediately; in which case, if material, the amount of the purchase consideration should be discounted to give its present value.

Part of the consideration might be contingent on the outcome of some future unknown event. A sporting example is when a footballer's transfer fee will be increased if at some stage in the future he becomes an international. In business, or more strictly in other forms of business, the total purchase consideration might depend on the future profitability of the business acquired. In such cases FRED 7 proposes that the fair value of the contingent element of the purchase consideration should be based on the probable, or most likely, outcome and when the actual amount is known an adjustment be made to goodwill (Para. 31).

Fair value of the identifiable assets

The basic principle is that identified assets and liabilities which are to be recognised in the financial statements should be recorded at their fair values at the date of acquisition. If we concentrate on assets, their fair value is based upon the 'Value to the Business' principle illustrated in Figure 4.1 and which is discussed in more detail in Chapter 16.

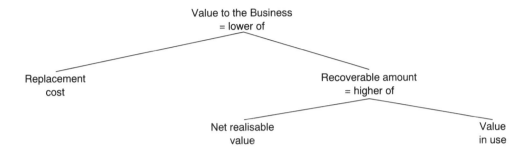

Fig. 4.1

For assets which the acquiring entity intends to keep, the fair value will be given by their replacement cost, that is the estimated amount which it would have cost the acquiring entity to purchase the individual asset directly. However this estimated amount depends upon perceptions and the time at which they are made.

FRED 7 proposes that the appraisal of fair values should be based on the evaluation of the state of the acquired business as it was at the date of acquisition and in particular that valuations should not reflect increases or decreases resulting from the acquirer's intentions for future actions, include provisions for future operating losses or the costs of reorganisation and integration (Para. 11).

Although the evaluation is to be made as at the date of acquisition the proposals of the exposure draft would allow the acquiring entity a period for investigation. Ideally the identification and valuation of assets and liabilities should be completed by the date on which the first post-acquisition financial statements of the acquirer are approved by its directors (Para. 27). If this does not prove possible then provisional valuation should be made which should then be amended, if necessary, in the next financial statements with a corresponding adjustment to goodwill (Para. 28). If any subsequent adjustment has to be made they should be recognised as gains or losses in the period in which they are identified other than those which may be regarded as the correction of fundamental errors which should be accounted for as prior period adjustments (Para. 29).

Now all this fine tuning about whose perception and when it may be applied does highlight the fact that historical cost accounting often has to rely on such arbitrary arrangements. A robust form of current cost accounting would have no difficulties in this area as it would encourage, if not require, all assets to be revalued in the light of current knowledge.

We will now move away from the question of fixed assets acquired in exchange for a non-cash consideration, although we will return to this theme in Chapters 8 and 9, to consider other matters which may need to be considered in determining a fixed asset's carrying value under the modified historical cost accounting system.

DEPRECIATION

Depreciation is the subject of SSAP 12. This was originally issued in December 1977; amended in November 1981 (which changed the treatment of investment properties, *see below*) and revised in January 1987.

The 1977 version of SSAP 12 was firmly rooted in historical cost accounting while the 1987 edition is relevant to both historical and current cost accounts. For it should be noted that the adoption of current cost accounting based on the deprival value or value to the business approach to asset valuation does not avoid the problems of depreciation.

Depreciation is defined in SSAP 12 as 'the measure of the wearing out, consumption or other reduction in the useful economic life of a fixed asset whether arising from use, effluxion of time or obsolescence through technological or market changes. (Para. 10.) Depreciation 'should be allocated so as to charge a fair proportion of cost or valuation of the asset to each accounting period expected to benefit from its use.' (Para. 3.)

There are of course a number of standard depreciation methods (with which we will assume readers are familiar) but the standard gives little guidance, and that mostly negative, on their relative merits and the circumstances in which they should be used. The standard simply states that:

> There is a range of acceptable depreciation methods. Management should select the method regarded as most appropriate to the type of asset and its use in the business so as to allocate depreciation as fairly as possible to the periods expected to benefit from the asset's use. Although the straight line method is the simplest to apply, it may not always be the most appropriate. (Para. 8.)

It is unfortunate that the ASC did not feel that it was able to provide more specific guidance about the criteria that should be employed in selecting the accounting policy for depreciation. The depreciation charge may be one of the largest expense items in the profit and loss account of a company, particularly one which operates in a capital intensive industry. If the profit figure is to have any meaning, the choice of depreciation policy must be justifiable as something more than a random selection from a number of standard depreciation methods.

Although it would have been helpful to have some guidance on the choice of depreciation method, the omission of such guidance is really not surprising. Professor Arthur Thomas has argued very persuasively that the choice of depreciation method, like many other accounting allocations, must be arbitrary.[11] The need for depreciation rests upon the accruals concept and this requires, *inter alia*, the matching of costs against revenues. The revenues of virtually every business arise from the joint use of a number of assets, both tangible and intangible, and it follows that it will usually be impossible to determine how much of the total revenue is produced by one particular fixed asset. If it is impossible to determine the revenues produced by a particular fixed asset, then it is impossible to select a depreciation policy which matches cost against those revenues.

One response to this difficulty would be to develop an accounting system which does not involve the use of arbitrary allocations,[12] but such an approach has not found favour with accountants. The alternative is to continue to make allocations, such as depreciation, but to recognise that there is no perfect answer.

11 Arthur L. Thomas, *The Allocation Problem in Financial Accounting Theory*, Studies in Accounting Research No. 3, AAA, 1969.
12 *See* Chapter 18.

The standard, SSAP 12

SSAP 12 is concerned both with the accounting treatment of depreciation and with its disclosure. We will first deal with the accounting aspects.

The key point of the standard is that all fixed assets covered by the standard and which have a finite useful economic life should be depreciated. The assets specified as being outside the scope of the standard are:

(a) Investment properties which are dealt with in SSAP 19 'Accounting for investment properties' (*see* pp. 87 to 88).
(b) Goodwill, which is dealt with in SSAP 22 'Accounting for goodwill' (*see* Chapter 8).
(c) Development costs, which are dealt with in SSAP 13 'Accounting for research and development' (*see* pp. 101 to 103) and
(d) Investments (*see* Chapter 9).

Depreciation should be based upon the historical cost of an asset except that where an asset has been revalued, subsequent depreciation should be based on the revalued amount.

Depreciation of buildings

Prior to the publication of the original version of SSAP 12 in 1977 many companies did not provide for the depreciation of freehold buildings, it being argued that buildings appreciated in value and that the appreciation, not reflected in the accounts, more than offset the omitted depreciation change. Clearly such an argument is fallacious on a number of grounds, notably that the netting off of two amounts, which may be of very different values, and is not consistent with the provision of a 'true and fair' view.

The position is now that, save with the exceptions listed above, all fixed assets should be depreciated, except freehold land which is not subject to depletion by the extraction of minerals etc.

The 1977 version of SSAP 12 did not exclude investment properties from its scope and required all buildings, including those held for investment to be depreciated. This was fiercely contested by property companies whose profits would, of course, be substantially reduced if they had to provide for depreciation on their buildings. It was argued that the profits of property companies would be distorted if depreciation were charged to the profit and loss account while the surpluses on revaluation had, under the provisions of SSAP 6 ('Extraordinary items and prior year adjustments'), to be credited to reserves.

The ASC's response (which may, according to taste, be described as reflecting the committee's weakness or flexibility) was to allow property companies exemption from this provision and this exemption was confirmed with the issue, in 1981 of SSAP 19, 'Accounting for investment properties', which specified the conditions under which depreciation need not be charged with respect to properties held as investments (*see* p. 87).

Changes in the estimates of asset lives

Prevailing practice for many years was that once an estimate was made of an asset's useful economic life, no adjustment was made even if the asset continued to be used even after it was fully depreciated; a practice justified by the prudence concept. If a revision of the estimated useful life was made there was, prior to the issue of SSAP 12, variation in the way that the change was reflected in the accounts. Some companies made an adjustment in the year in which the revision was made to make the net book value equal to that which it would have been had the asset been depreciated *ab initio* on the basis of the revised estimate. The alternative method, which was required by the original version of SSAP 12, was to write the existing net book value off over the asset's revised remaining life.

The 1987 version of SSAP 12 has approached the issue in a different way. Like the original SSAP 12, it specifies that the useful economic lives of assets should be reviewed regularly and, when necessary, revised. It suggested that the review should take place at least every five years, and more frequently when circumstances warrant. While it is not explicitly stated, the implication is that assets which continue to be used should not be fully written off in the accounts.

It suggested that if the regular reviews are made there will be no material distortion of future results if the net book value is written off over the revised remaining useful economic life. However, and in this aspect the 1987 version is more permissive than the original, where future results would otherwise be distorted an adjustment to accumulated depreciation should be recognised in the accounts in the year in which the change was made. Hence, the revised SSAP 12 permitted the replacement of many small distortions by one large distortion! In its defence, the one large distortion would normally be treated as an exceptional item and disclosed in accordance with the provisions of the then extant SSAP 6 'Extraordinary items and prior year adjustments'. SSAP 6 has now been withdrawn but the treatment of the adjustment to accumulated depreciation is covered by FRS 3 'Reporting Financial Performance' which requires that any such adjustment should be recognised as an exceptional item included under the same statutory format heading as the ongoing depreciation charge (FRS 3, Para. 33h). A consequential amendment has been made to paragraph 18 of SSAP 12.

Changes in the method of depreciation

The standard states that a change from one method to another is permissible only if the new method will give a fairer presentation of the results and financial position. If a change is made, the current net book value should be written off over the remaining useful economic life using that new method.

Changes in the book value of assets

An asset should be written down if its net book value exceeds its estimated 'recoverable amount' which is defined in the standard as the greater of the net realisable value of an asset and, where appropriate, the amount recoverable from its further use; a definition based on the value to the business concept of current cost accounting.

Disclosure requirements

Depreciation is a very subjective figure which is heavily influenced by the methods used and estimates made by the business. Thus, in order to help users interpret financial statements and compare the results of companies which use different methods, SSAP 12 calls for the disclosure of more detailed information than is required by the Companies Act. The standard requires that the following should be disclosed for each major class of depreciable asset:

(a) the depreciation methods used;
(b) the useful economic lives or the depreciation rates used;
(c) total depreciation for the period;
(d) the gross amount of depreciable assets and the related accumulated depreciation.

(SSAP 12, Para. 25).

When there has been a change in the method of depreciation, the effect, if material, should be disclosed in the year of change. The reason for the change should also be disclosed (SSAP 12, Para. 26).

If assets have been revalued, the effect on the depreciation charge should, if material, be disclosed in the year of revaluation (SSAP 12, Para. 27).

INVESTMENT PROPERTIES

In response to the criticisms of the initial requirement that all companies depreciate buildings, the ASC modified its position, as evidenced by the issue in November 1981 of SSAP 19 'Accounting for investment properties', in respect of properties which are not held for consumption as part of the business's operations but held as investments. It was argued that, for the proper appreciation of the position of the enterprise, it is of prime importance for users of the accounts to be aware of the current value of the investment properties and the changes in their values, For this purpose investment properties are defined as an interest in land and/or buildings:

(a) in respect of which construction work and development have been completed; and
(b) which is held for its investment potential, any rental income being negotiated at arm's length.

The following are specifically excluded from the definition:

(a) A property which is owned and occupied by a company for its own purposes is not an investment property.
(b) A property let to and occupied by another group company is not an investment property for the purposes of its own accounts or the group accounts.

The general issue of carrying fixed assets at valuation is covered in ED 51 'Accounting for Fixed Assets and Revaluation' and is the central theme of the discussion paper 'The Role of Valuation in Financial Reporting'. There is a fundamental difference between SSAP 19 and ED 51 in that the former requires the revaluation of the assets concerned while the latter permits, somewhat reluctantly, the practice of revaluation. The discussion paper indicates that the ASB are moving to remove that discrepancy in that it proposes the regular revaluation of certain assets, including properties.

In outline SSAP 19 specifies:

(i) Investment properties should not be subject to a depreciation charge as otherwise required by SSAP 12, except for properties held on a lease which should be depreciated on the basis set out in SSAP 12 at least over the period when the unexpired term is 20 years or less.' (SSAP 19, Para. 10.) In other words leaseholds with more than 20 years to run can be depreciated while other leases must be depreciated.

(ii) Investment properties should be included in the balance sheet at their 'open market value'. The phrase 'open market value' was not defined in the standard but has since been defined in ED 51 as the best price at which the asset might reasonably be expected to be sold. The bases of valuation should be disclosed in a note to the accounts (*see* (v) below).

(iii) Changes in the value of investment properties should be shown as a movement on an investment revaluation reserve, unless a deficit on revaluation exceeds the balance on the reserve in which case the deficit should be charged to the profit and loss account.[13]

(iv) The carrying value of the investment properties and of the investment revaluation reserve should be displayed prominently in the financial statements.

(v) The names of the persons making the valuation, or particulars of their qualifications, should be disclosed together with the bases of valuation used. If a person making a valuation is an employee or officer of the company or group which owns the property, this fact should be disclosed.

The ASC noted that adherence to the provisions of SSAP 19 would represent a departure from the specific requirement of the then extant Companies Act, 1981 that any fixed asset which has a limited useful economic life should be depreciated, a provision which also appears in the Companies Act, 1985.

In justifying this departure the ASC drew attention to Section 1 of the Companies Act 1981 (*see* Sec. 226 Companies Act 1985) which states that the need to give a true and fair view in the financial statement overrides any particular specific requirement of the Act. The ASC believed that the treatment of investment properties required by SSAP 19 represented an example of a situation where the use of a method other than that specified in the Companies Act will more closely adhere to the overriding requirement of the disclosure of a true and fair view. In such circumstances the accounts must include a statement giving particulars of the departure from the specific requirements of the Act with the reasons for and effect of the departure.[14]

Not everyone would agree with the stance taken by the ASC in so far that it can be argued that a far fuller picture would be disclosed if both the increase in value and the amount of the value that has been consumed by the passage of time are disclosed in the accounts.

THE ACCOUNTING TREATMENT OF GOVERNMENT GRANTS

It is convenient to discuss the accounting treatment of government grants at this stage because the topic is often closely related to the subject of fixed assets and depreciation. The topic is the subject matter of SSAP 4, 'The accounting treatment of government grants' which was originally issued in 1974. The standard proved to be inadequate not only because it was itself poorly conceived but also because of other developments. Grants themselves became more complex than was envisaged when SSAP 4 was published, while the provisions of the standard proved to be inconsistent with those of the Companies Act 1985 and of International Accounting Standard No 20 'Accounting for government grants and disclosure of government assistance' which was issued in 1982. Hence a revised

---

13 Under the provisions of FRS3 'Reporting Financial Performance' the changes would be included in the Statement of total recognised gains and losses.

14 Companies Act 1985, *see* Sec. 226(5) (as amended by Companies Act 1989, Sec. 4).

standard, SSAP 4 (revised) 'Accounting for government grants' was issued in July 1990.

The two accounting concepts on which SSAP 4 (revised) is based are accruals and prudence. The first implies that grants should be credited to the profit and loss account so as to match the expenditure towards which they are expected to contribute, the second that grants should not be recognised in the profit and loss account until the conditions for their receipt have been satisfied and that there is a reasonable assurance that the grants will be received.

Readers may feel that the reference to the accruals and prudence conventions is unnecessary because they are two of the four fundamental accounting concepts. However, by presenting the accruals concept in the way stated above, the ASC avoided a discussion of a fundamentally different alternative approach that all government grants should be regarded as a source of finance provided by government and hence retained in the balance sheet as a non-distributable reserve; including it as a reserve would imply that it is an element of owners' equity, but a part which has been provided by the government.

There are certain advantages of such an approach including clarity – it would describe clearly what has actually happened – and comparability in that it would assist comparisons between, for example, the two companies, one operating in an area where grants are available and the other not.

Revenue related grants

Revenue related grants, according to the original SSAP 4, did not produce any accounting problems 'as they clearly should be credited to revenue in the same period in which the revenue expenditure to which they relate is charged' (SSAP 4, Para. 2).

This may have been a reasonable description of the situation in 1974, but subsequently grants took many different forms and were derived from different sources than was the case in 1974. In the latter context it is noteworthy that in the original SSAP 4 the ASC did not see a need to define government; by implication government was the UK Central Government. In contrast the revised SSAP 4 defines government as including 'government and intergovernmental agencies and similar bodies whether local, national or international' (SSAP 4, Para. 21); it thus includes the European Community.

The matching of grants received to expenditure is straightforward when the grant is made towards specified items of expenditure. However, certain grants might not be related to specific items of expenditure; they might, for example, be paid to encourage job creation. In such circumstances the recognition of the grant in the profit and loss account should be matched with the identifiable *net* costs of achieving the objective. As is pointed out in the explanatory note to the revised standard, this may not be straightforward as account needs to be taken of the associated income generated by the activity in arriving at the net cost. If, for example, the grant is given on condition that jobs are created and sustained for a period of, say, three years, the grant should be matched to the net cost of providing the jobs. Thus, if the revenue generated by the activity is higher in the third year, a higher proportion of the grant should be recognised in the earlier years.

In some cases the grant may be paid to support one activity, training, for instance, but will only become payable when the company incurs expenditure in another, usually related, area – perhaps the purchase of capital equipment. In other words the grant will not be paid unless the company purchases the equipment but the size of the grant depends on the company's training expenditure. SSAP 4 provides that where such a link is established the grant should be matched to the expenditure to which it is intended to support, in this case training, but, as is the general rule under SSAP 4, nothing should be credited to the profit and loss account until the necessary conditions have been fulfilled – in this case until the equipment has been purchased.

The part of any revenue related grant received but not yet recognised in the profit and loss account should be included in the balance sheet as deferred income.

Capital related grants

Two methods of dealing with capital related grants are identified in SSAP 4 (revised).

(a) Show the grant as deferred income which is credited to the profit and loss account over the life of the asset on a basis consistent with the depreciation policy adopted for the asset.
(b) Reduce the cost of the asset and hence reduce the annual depreciation charges.

The other possible option of not crediting the grant at any stage to the profit and loss account but retaining it in the balance sheet as a source of funds is not considered for the reasons given earlier.

In choosing between the two alternatives the ASC came to the surprising – if not astonishing – conclusion that 'both treatments are acceptable and capable of giving a true and fair view' (SSAP 4 (revised), Para. 15). It is difficult to see how showing in the balance sheet the cost of an asset at 100 per cent of its purchase price or, say, depending on the size of the grant, 80 per cent of the price can both show a 'true and fair' view – it does seem the ASC had on this occasion, distorted that splendidly elastic phrase too far.

The ASC's position appears even stranger in that it records that it had received Counsel's opinion that the second alternative, the reduction in cost, is illegal in the light of Paragraphs 17 and 26 of Schedule 4 of the Companies Act, 1985. However, the ASC stuck to its guns. Both alternatives are available to enterprises under the provisions of SSAP 4 (revised), but only the first can be used by enterprises whose financial statements are governed by the Companies Acts.

Disclosure requirements

The disclosure requirements of SSAP 4 (revised) require the following information to be revealed:

(a) The accounting policy adopted in respect of government grants (this in any case is required by SSAP 2 'Disclosure of accounting policies').
(b) The effects of government grants on the results of the period and the financial position of the enterprise.
(c) Information regarding any material effect on the results of the period from government assistance other than grants (for example, free consultancy or subsidised loans) including, if possible, quantitative estimates of the effect of the assistance.
(d) Any potential liability to repay grants should, if necessary be disclosed in accordance with SSAP 18 'Accounting for contingencies'.

STOCKS AND LONG-TERM CONTRACTS

Introduction

It used to be said in jest that in drawing up the annual accounts of an enterprise the first figure to be set down was that of profit, then all the ascertainable figures, until finally the value of stock emerged as a balancing item. This sentiment is certainly echoed in the introductory remarks to the original version of SSAP 9, 'Stocks and work in progress', issued in May 1975:

> No area of accounting has produced wider differences in practice than the computation of the amount at which stocks and work in progress are stated in financial accounts. This statement of standard accounting practice seeks to define the practices, to narrow the differences and variation in those practices and to ensure adequate disclosure in the accounts.

Partly, but not wholly, due to changes in company law, the treatment of long-term contracts in the original version of the standard was found to be unsatisfactory and a revised version of the standard was issued in September 1988. From now on all references will be to the revised version.

SSAP 9 differs from most other statements in that a large proportion of the document is devoted to appendices which deal with practical problems. The ASC was of the view that the problems which arise in this area are of a practical rather than of a theoretical nature. Appendix 1 deals with the relevant practical considerations but, as is always the case with appendices, it did not form part of the statement of standard accounting practice. There are two other appendices; Appendix 2, which consists of a glossary of terms and Appendix 3, which is concerned with the presentation of information relating to long-term contracts.

We will assume that readers are familiar with the basic principles of stock valuation and the different methods employed in the historical cost system and, hence, we will concentrate on the few, but important, principles underlying SSAP 9.

Stocks other than long-term contracts

> The amount at which stocks are stated in periodic financial statements should be the total of the lower of cost and net realizable value of the separate item of stock or of groups of similar items.

> (SSAP 9, Para. 26.)

A simple enough statement. Stock should normally be shown at cost but might sometimes be written down. But to state that, stock should normally be stated at cost does not take us very far, for, as readers will be aware, the determination of the cost of stock and work in progress is by no means a simple task and much of the statement, including the appendices, is devoted to that subject. The basic principle is that the cost of stock and work in progress should comprise 'that expenditure which has been incurred in the normal course of business in bringing the product or service to its present location and condition. Such costs *will* [our emphasis] include all related production overheads, even though these may accrue on a time basis' (SSAP 9, Paras 17–19).

The cost of stock and work in progress is to include costs of production and conversion (as defined in the statement). The specification of the treatment of overheads reflects one way in which the standard fulfils its objective of narrowing variations in practice. There has been much debate on the extent to which production overheads should be included in the valuation of stock. At one extreme – the variable costing approach – is the view that overhead allocation is by its very nature arbitrary and that stock should be valued by reference to the costs (usually just direct material and labour), which can be directly related to the stock in question. A view which lies between this extreme and the ASC's position is that production overheads which relate to activity rather than time (e.g. cost of power) should be included in the cost of stock. These approaches are rejected by SSAP 9, which requires the inclusion of all production overheads, including those which accrue on a time basis. It appears that this alternative was adopted because the ASC felt that all production overheads, whether or not they arise on a time basis, are required to bring the stock to its 'present location and condition'.

Costs which include time-related production overheads will, all other things being equal, vary with the level of output; the lower the output the greater the cost of, say, rent per unit. Thus, the statement refers to the need to base the allocation of overheads on the company's normal level of activity,[15] so ensuring that the cost of unused capacity is written off in the current year. Appendix 1 of SSAP 9 provides some guidance on the question of how the normal level of activity should be determined, but it is clear that judgment will have to play a part in the resolution of this matter.

The ASC specifically rejected the argument that the omission of production overheads can be defended on the grounds of prudence. This emerges in Appendix 1, Para. 10, which states:

> The adoption of a conservative approach to the valuation of stocks and long-term contracts has sometimes been used as one of the reasons for omitting selected production overheads. In so far as the circumstances of the business require an element of prudence in determining the amount at which stocks and long-term contracts are stated, this needs to be taken into account in the determination of net realizable value and not by the exclusion from cost of selected overheads.

The conventional methods of stock valuation (FIFO, LIFO, etc.) are described in the glossary of terms. The actual standard does not give any guidance about the methods which should be used; but the ASC's view of the principle which should be followed is given in Appendix 1, where it is stated that 'management must exercise judgment to ensure that the methods chosen provide the fairest practicable approximation to cost'.[16] It can be seen that the ASC placed emphasis on the need to show as accurately as possible the cost of stock and rejected those methods such as LIFO which are used, especially in the United States, to produce a profit figure which approximates to a current cost operating profit.

We will now turn to the methods which must be adopted when stock is to be written down. We will not, however, at this stage refer to the problems of establishing the net realisable value, which has been dealt with in Chapter 3.

SSAP 9 requires that stock should be written down to its net realisable value. Prior to the publication of the standard, some companies stated stock at replacement cost where this was lower than net realisable value and cost. The use of replacement cost is rejected in SSAP 9 on the grounds that it may result in the recognition of 'a loss which is greater than that which is expected to be incurred'. (SSAP 9, Para. 6.)

Our final comment on the provisions of SSAP 9, Para. 26 quoted at the beginning of

---

15 *See* SSAP 9, Appendix 1, Para. 8.
16 SSAP 9, Appendix 1, Para. 12.

this section, relates to the requirement that the comparison of cost and net realisable value should be on an item by item basis or by reference to groups of similar items. The reason for this is that this provision is given in Para. 2, where it is stated that 'To compare the total realisable value of stocks with the total cost could result in an unacceptable setting off of foreseeable losses against unrealised profits'. In other words the practice contravenes the concept of prudence.

Long-term contracts

Long-term contracts merit separate consideration. Because of the time taken to complete such contracts, to defer recording turnover and the recognition of profit until completion might in the words of the standard 'result in the profit and loss account reflecting not so much a fair view of the activity of the company during the year but rather the results relating to contracts which have been completed by the year end (SSAP 9, Para. 7).

Thus, SSAP 9 states that it is appropriate (and by appropriate the ASC meant that companies should) to take credit for ascertainable turnover and profit while contracts are in progress, subject to various conditions specified in the standard.

This may well be an eminently practical and sensible view, but it does seem to be in conflict with the attitude adopted in SSAP 2, 'Disclosure of accounting policies', where it is stated that 'where the accruals concept is inconsistent with the prudence concept the latter prevails'. The provision of SSAP 9 relating to long-term contracts does appear to suggest that the accruals concept should prevail over prudence.

The provision that attributable profit should (not might) be recognised in the financial statements was perhaps the most controversial aspect of the original SSAP 9. A number of large companies had consistently eschewed the recognition of profit on uncompleted contracts and some continued this practice after the implementation of SSAP 9, accepting the consequential qualifications in their audit reports.

In addition, there would appear to be a conflict between this requirement of SSAP 9 and the legal requirement that only realised profits may be credited to the profit and loss account (*see* Chapter 3). Even if attributable profit on long-term contract work in progress is not realised, it may, nonetheless, be included in the profit and loss account if this is necessary to give a true and fair view. Our use of this true and fair view override on a number of occasions in the UK has aroused considerable criticism from our partners in the EC, who did not envisage that it would be used so often.

Definition of long-term contracts

A long-term contract can relate to the design or construction of a single substantial asset or the provision of a service (or a combination of assets or services which constitute a single project) where the activity falls into different accounting periods. If a contract is to fall within the definition, it will normally have to last for more than a year, but shorter contracts may also be included if they are sufficiently material so that the failure to record turnover and attributable profit would distort the financial statements.

Turnover, related costs and attributable profit

Long-term contracts should be assessed on a contract by contract basis and reflected in the profit and loss account by recording turnover and related costs as contract activity progresses.

(SSAP 9, Para. 28)

Also

> Where it is considered that the outcome of a long-term contract can be assessed with reasonable certainty before its conclusion, the prudently calculated attributable profit should be recognized in the profit and loss account as the difference between the reported turnover and related costs for that contract.

> (SSAP 9, Para. 29)

So the accounting seems pretty straightforward and obvious:

> Reported turnover − Related costs = Attributable profit.

But how are the various elements determined?
The actual standard does not help very much although some guidance is given:

> Turnover is ascertained in a manner appropriate to the stage of completion of the contract, the business and the industry in which it operates

> (SSAP 9, Para. 28)

Some assistance is also provided in Appendix 1 (Para. 23) where it is stated that turnover may be ascertained by reference to valuation of the work carried out to date. Alternatively there may be specific points where separately ascertainable sales values and costs can be identified because, for example, delivery or customer acceptance has taken place. The section goes on to state that the standard does not provide a definition of turnover because of the number of different possible approaches. It does, however, point out that the standard does require disclosure of the means by which turnover is ascertained.

Neither the standard nor any of the appendices refer to the calculation of the related cost, so we will now turn to this and the estimation of the attributable profit. We will start with two conceptually simple cases.

If the outcome of a long-term contract cannot be ascertained with reasonable certainty, no profit should be reflected in the profit and loss account. However, if despite the uncertainty the contract is not expected to make a loss, 'it may be appropriate to show as turnover a proportion of the total contract value using a zero estimate of profit.' (SSAP 9, Para. 10.)

In the latter situation in order to satisfy the relationship between turnover, cost and profit, the related costs would be made equal to the reported turnover. If on this basis, related costs appeared to be greater than the actual costs incurred to date, the turnover would be reduced and made equal to the actual costs.

The second 'simple' case is where the contract is expected to make a loss then, in accordance with the prudence concept, the whole of the loss should be recorded as soon as it is foreseen. Turnover would be determined in the normal way and the related cost would be equal to the actual cost to date plus the provision for foreseeable future losses.

Now let us consider a case where it would be necessary to recognise some profit. Attributable profit is defined as:

> that part of the the total profit currently estimated to arise over the duration of the contract, after allowing for estimated remedial and maintenance costs and increases in costs so far as not recoverable under the terms of the contract, that fairly reflect the profit attributable to that part of the work performed at the accounting date.

> (SSAP 9, Para. 23)

Thus, it is first necessary to estimate the total profit and then decide how it should be allocated. The principles involved are illustrated in Example 4.2.

EXAMPLE 4.2

Suppose that Engineer Limited started a three-year contract at the beginning of year 1 with a total contract value of £18 000 and costs of £12 000 which it is anticipated will be incurred as follows:

Year 1	Year 2	Year 3	Total
£3000	£6000	£3000	£12 000

The expected profit is thus £6000.

Case 1

We will assume that both turnover and profit are to be recognised in proportion to the costs incurred. Hence, assuming all goes to plan, the contract would be reported in the profit and loss accounts as follows:

	Year 1 (25%) £	Year 2 (50%) £	Year 3 (25%) £
Reported turnover	4500	9000	4500
Related costs	3000	6000	3000
Attributable profit	£1500	£3000	£1500

Case 2

Depending on the nature of the contract it might be deemed appropriate to record turnover on a different basis, perhaps on the values placed on the work completed to date by an independent consultant.

Assume that the value of the work certified is as follows:

	Value of work certified £	Value of work completed in year £	Fraction
End of Year 1	3000	3000	1/6
End of Year 2	9000	6000	1/3
End of Year 3	18000	9000	1/2

Profit might be based on cost (*Case 2a*) or turnover (*Case 2b*) which would result in the reporting of the following figures:

Case 2a

Profit related to cost

	Year 1 £	Year 2 £	Year 3 £
Reported turnover	3000	6000	9000
Related cost	1500	3000	7500
Attributable profit	£1500 (25%)	£3000 (50%)	£1500 (25%)

Case 2b

Profit related to turnover

	Year 1 £	Year 2 £	Year 3 £
Reported turnover	3000	6000	9000
Related cost	2000	4000	6000
Attributable profit	£1000 (1/6)	£2000 (1/3)	£3000 (1/2)

Thus, we can see that under the provisions of SSAP 9 even in this simple case, three different patterns of turnover, cost and profit might be reported, and in practice more variations are possible.

Now let us assume that all does not go to plan and the actual cost in Year 2 was £8000 rather than the expected £6000, but that no further difficulties are expected and that the original estimate for the cost of Year 3 of £3000 still holds.

Consider the position as at the end of Year 2; there are two possibilities which will be illustrated by reference to *Case 2a* above.

Either the additional unexpected expenditure can be written off in Year 2 reducing the profit for the year by £2000 to £1000, leaving the profit for Year 3 at £1500 or the revised profit less that already recognised in Year 1 could be spread over Years 2 and 3 on the basis of cost, i.e. in the ratio 8:3.

The revised profit is £4000 and the profit recognised in Year 1 was £1500, hence the profits for the remaining two years would be:

Year 1	£1818	(8/11)
Year 3	£682	(3/11)
	£2500	

Thus, we have the paradox that the profit for Year 3 is reduced because of difficulties experienced in Year 2. This does not appear to be sensible, but the approach would be permissible under the terms of SSAP 9.

Example 4.2 illustrates the point that the related cost is normally a balancing figure derived from the relationship between reported turnover and attributable profit. The statement does not deal with the situation where related costs exceed actual costs. Suppose that we have the following for the first year of a contract:

	£
Reported turnover	20000
Related cost	16000
Attributable profit	£4000
Actual cost to date	£13000

In practice it is likely that the turnover figure would be reduced to £17 000 to make the equation balance.

Long-term contracts and the balance sheet

Before moving to a discussion of the way in which long-term contract balances are shown in the balance sheet, we need to introduce another factor, payments on account, which is defined as 'all amounts received and receivable at the accounting date in respect of contracts in progress (SSAP 9, Para. 25).

The relevant section of the standard reproduced below is perhaps unnecessarily complex.

Long-term contracts should be disclosed in the balance sheet as follows:

(a) the amount by which recorded turnover is in excess of payments on account should be classified as 'amounts recoverable on contracts' and separately disclosed within debtors;
(b) the balance of payments on account (in excess of amounts (i) matched with turnover; and (ii) offset against long-term contract balances) should be classified as payments on account and separately disclosed within creditors;
(c) the amount of long-term contracts, at costs incurred, net of amounts transferred to cost of sales, after deducting foreseeable losses and payments on account not matched with turnover, should be classified as 'long-term contract balances' and separately disclosed within the balance sheet heading 'Stocks'. The balance sheet note should disclose separately the balances of:
(i) net cost less foreseeable losses; and
(ii) applicable payments on account;
(d) the amount by which the provision or accrual for foreseeable losses exceeds the costs incurred (after transfers to cost of sales) should be included within either provisions for liabilities and charges or creditors as appropriate.

(SSAP 9, Para. 30.)

To unravel the above it is best to start by concentrating on the situation where there are no losses, either incurred or contemplated.

Let us start by looking at the costs.

If the actual costs incurred to date exceed the cumulative related costs (the total charged to cost of sales), there is an asset *long-term contract balances* which is separately disclosed within stocks.

As stated earlier the standard does not consider a situation where related costs exceed actual costs; in practice this will not arise because, in all probability, turnover would be adjusted.

Let us now consider the receipt of cash from the customer.

If the cumulative reported turnover exceeds cumulative payments on account there is an asset *amounts recoverable on contracts* which is separately disclosed within debtors.

If the reverse holds (more cash received on account than reported as turnover), the credit balance is set off against long-term contract balances. If the credit (payments less turnover) is greater than the debit (long-term contract balances), the resulting credit is described as *payments on account* which is separately disclosed within creditors.

Thus in respect of each contract, which have to be considered separately, the possible combinations of assets and liabilities are:

(a) two assets: long-term contract balances and amounts recoverable on contract; or
(b) a liability: payments on account.

The above points are illustrated in Example 4.3.

EXAMPLE 4.3

No losses

Assume that the position on three contracts at a year-end is as follows:

	(1) £	(2) £	(3) £
Cumulative turnover	520	520	520
Cumulative actual cost	510	510	510
Cumulative related cost	450	450	450
Cumulative payments on account	440	555	630

The cumulative attributable profit for each of the contracts is £70, i.e. £520 − £450.

The relevant balance sheet items are shown below. Note that each contract will be considered on an individual basis, balances arising on one contract are not set off against balances on other contracts and hence the figures that will appear in the balance sheet are shown in the total column.

	Contract			Total
	(1) £	(2) £	(3) £	£
Stock – long-term contract balances	60 (a)	25 (b)	NIL	85
Debtors – amount recoverable on contracts	80	NIL	NIL	80
Creditors – payments on account	NIL	NIL	50 (c)	50

Notes (a) Actual costs *less* related costs; £510 − £450 = £60

(b) Long-term contract balance as (a),		£60
less Excess of payments on account		
over turnover, £555 − £520		£35
		£25
(c) Long-term contract balance, as (a)		£60
less Excess of payments on account		
over turnover, £630 − £520		£110
		(£50)

Foreseeable losses

All losses, as soon as they are foreseen, should be recognised in the financial statements. The estimate of future loss should be charged to the profit and loss as part of the related cost. The credit is first offset against the long-term contract balance (before any set-off for the excess of cumulative payments on account over cumulative reported turnover). If the long-term contract balance is insufficient to cover the expected loss, the balance is included within either provisions for liabilities and charges or creditors, as appropriate, i.e. depending on the degree of certainty with which the estimate is made.

EXAMPLE 4.4

Consider the following two contracts:

	(1)	(2)
	£	£
Cumulative turnover	200	110
Cumulative actual costs	250	200
Cumulative related costs	250	110
Cumulative payments on account	180	160
Losses to date (£250 − £200)	50	–
Expected future losses	40	70

If we assume that this is the first year of each contract, the profit and loss account will include the following:

	(1)	(2)	Total
	£	£	£
Turnover	200	110	310
Related costs (cost of sales)	290	180	470
Gross loss	£90	£70	£160

If the projects were other than in their first year, the amounts included would depend on what had been charged or credited in the previous years.

The various balance sheet figures are:

	(1) £	(2) £	Total £
Stock – long-term contract balances	NIL	NIL	NIL
Debtors – amounts recoverable on contracts	20[a]	NIL	20
Creditors – payments on account	NIL	30[b]	30
Provision/accrual for foreseeable losses	40	NIL	40

Notes

(a) Cumulative turnover less cumulative payments on account, £200 – £180 = £20.

(b) For contract 2, actual costs exceed related costs so we start with a long-term contract balance of £90 i.e. £200 – £110.

Expected future losses of £70 are set off against that balance, reducing it to £20.

But, there are excess payments on account, £50 since payments on account, £160, exceed turnover, £110. This credit balance, £50, is set off against the debit, £20, representing the long-term contract balance.

The net credit of £30 will appear in the balance sheet as a provision or accrual as appropriate.

INTANGIBLE FIXED ASSETS

Introduction

Certain assets are described as intangible and, although it is difficult to develop a precise definition of what accountants mean by this adjective, ED 52 'Accounting for intangible fixed assets' (May 1990) provided the following definition of intangible fixed assets.[17]

> An intangible fixed asset is a fixed asset that is non-monetary in nature and without physical substance.

The term should therefore include such assets as brands, development expenditure, goodwill, leases of tangible fixed assets, patents, trademarks and possibly investments although, as we shall see, ED 52 specifically excludes coverage of some of these.

Like tangible assets, intangible assets have value because they are expected to produce future benefits for the entity. Thus, in principle, the same accounting treatment should be applied to both tangible and intangible assets. If an entity purchases an intangible asset, it should be treated in the same way as a purchase of a tangible asset. Similarly, if a firm incurs expenditure to develop an intangible asset, such as research knowledge or a trained workforce, this should be treated in the same way as expenditure on the construction of a fixed asset. As we have seen, this was the basic approach proposed in ED 51 'Accounting for fixed assets and revaluations'. However, important features of intangible fixed assets are a high degree of uncertainty about the future benefits which they will generate and a poor link between the cost incurred and the value created.

The existence of this high level of uncertainty about the future benefits from a particular

17 ED 52 'Accounting for intangible fixed assets', Para. 37.

intangible asset gives rise to a conflict between two of the fundamental accounting concepts of SSAP 2. The accruals concept requires the matching of costs with appropriate revenues, while the prudence concept requires expenditure to be written off in the period in which it arises, unless its relationship to the revenue of a future period can be established with reasonable certainty. Thus, where an intangible asset is acquired or created, the accruals concept would require the capitalisation of its cost and subsequent amortisation or depreciation but, given that the future benefits are usually very uncertain, the prudence concept would require the expenditure to be written off. SSAP 2 is quite clear that where there is a conflict between the accruals concept and the prudence concept, the latter is to prevail.[18] With this conflict in mind we shall look first at the accounting treatment of research and development and then at the more general proposals of ED 52.

Accounting for research and development

Many enterprises spend large sums of money on research and development in the hope that, by incurring such expenditure, future profits will be higher than they otherwise would be. In other words they incur expenditure on research and development in the expectation of creating an intangible asset which will yield benefits in the future. By the very nature of the process, some research and development activities will be unsuccessful and hence no asset will be created. Any expenditure on such projects must certainly be written off against profits of the year in which it is incurred. Other research projects will be successful and will result in the creation of an asset. Under historical cost accounting expenditure on unsuccessful projects should be written off against the profits of the year in which it was incurred while expenditure on successful projects should be capitalised at an appropriate figure[19] and written off against profits of the periods in which benefits are expected to arise.

The accounting treatment proposed above seems quite clear, but two major problems arise as soon as an attempt is made to apply it. First, even where a project appears to have been successful, the size and timing of future benefits are often very uncertain; if such is the case the prudence convention would appear to require the expenditure to be written off. Second, the people who must make the decision on whether or not the research and development has been successful are not independent of the entity but are the directors who are interested in the outcome of the research and development. Because of their involvement, such directors may be susceptible to bias, either innocent or fraudulent, and, in view of the uncertainties involved, it may be extremely difficult for an auditor to challenge the views of the directors.

Accounting for research and development was the subject matter and title of SSAP 13 which was originally issued in 1977. A later version SSAP 13 (revised), which was issued in 1989, follows the same principles, although it increases the amount of disclosure required. We shall refer to SSAP 13 (revised) 'Accounting for research and development' (January 1989).

This SSAP, like its predecessor, follows the definitions of research and development expenditure adopted by the Organisation for Economic Co-operation and Development, which divides such expenditure into three categories:

18 SSAP 2, Para. 14(b).
19 The appropriate figure will be cost or lower recoverable amount.

(a) pure (or basic) research: experimental or theoretical work undertaken primarily to acquire new scientific or technical knowledge for its own sake rather than directed towards any specific aim or application;

(b) applied research: original or critical investigation undertaken in order to gain new scientific or technical knowledge and directed towards a specific practical aim or objective;

(c) development: use of scientific or technical knowledge in order to produce new or substantially improved materials, devices, products or services, to install new processes or systems prior to the commencement of commercial production or commercial applications, or to improve substantially those already produced or installed.

Given the uncertainties surrounding the benefits from research and development expenditure and the requirement of SSAP 2 that, in case of conflict, prudence should prevail over the accruals concept, one approach would be to write off all such expenditure to the profit and loss account as incurred.[20]

Although this approach may be simply applied and removes the need for judgment on the part of directors and auditors, many people would argue that it makes little economic sense. To take an example, we may think of two similar companies which have spent an identical amount on research and development. The efforts of one company have been successful while the efforts of the other company have not. If both companies are required to write off all research and development expenditure as it is incurred, then this essential difference between the two companies is not apparent from an examination of their accounts. An important element of business reality does not feature in the accounts.

SSAP 13 takes a less conservative approach. Although it requires companies to write off all expenditure on pure and applied research as it is incurred, it permits, but does not require, the capitalisation of certain development expenditure which must then be matched against the revenues to which it relates.

The adoption of this permissive approach introduces the possibility of bias on the part of directors, who must decide whether or not an asset exists on a balance sheet date. In order to reduce this bias to a minimum, the standard lists the following conditions which must be satisfied before development expenditure may be carried forward:[21]

(a) there is a clearly defined project; and

(b) the related expenditure is separately identifiable; and

(c) the outcome of such a project has been assessed with reasonable certainty as to:
   (i) its technical feasibility; and
   (ii) its ultimate commercial viability considered in the light of factors such as likely market conditions (including competing products), public opinion, consumer and environmental legislation; and

(d) the aggregate of the deferred development costs, any further development costs, and related production, selling and administration costs is reasonably expected to be exceeded by related future sales or other revenues; and

(e) adequate resources exist, or are reasonably expected to be available, to enable the project to be completed and to provide any consequential increases in working capital.

20 This was, in fact, the approach adopted in the first exposure draft on this subject ED 14 'Accounting for research and development' (January 1975), although it was modified in the subsequent exposure draft ED 17 'Accounting for research and development (revised)' (April 1976).

21 SSAP 13 (revised), Para. 25.

While the prudence convention does not win outright, it has the upper hand and development expenditure may only be carried forward if the above, rather stringent conditions, are met.[22]

In order to facilitate interpretation, the standard requires that the notes to the accounts contain a clear explanation of the accounting policy followed although this would, in any case, be required under the provisions of SSAP 2. It requires disclosure of the total amount of research and development expenditure charged in the profit and loss account, analysed between the current year's expenditure and the amortisation of deferred development expenditure.[23] Finally, it requires disclosure of movements on the deferred development expenditure account each year. The Companies Act specifically requires that the directors explain why expenditure has been capitalised and state the period over which the costs are being written off.[24]

ED 52 'Accounting for intangible fixed assets'

At the same time that it issued ED 51 'Accounting for fixed assets and revaluations' in May 1990, the ASC also issued ED 52 'Accounting for intangible fixed assets'. Although these two documents, together with SSAP 12 (revised) 'Accounting for depreciation', were intended to provide a framework of accounting for intangible fixed assets, the exclusions from the scope of ED 52 were considerable.[25]

They comprise accounting for research and development, leases of tangible fixed assets, goodwill and investments, all of which are covered by other pronouncements.[26]

With such extensive exclusions a reader might wonder what are the intangible fixed assets with which ED 52 is concerned? While they include such assets as copyrights, patents and trademarks, it was undoubtedly the accounting treatment of brands which prompted the issue of this Exposure Draft.

As we shall see in Chapter 8, one of the consequences of SSAP 22 'Accounting for goodwill' was that a number of large companies started to include brands on their balance sheets.[27] The propriety or impropriety of this generated heated discussions and it was to this subject that ED 52 was mainly addressed.

The Exposure Draft specifies the following conditions for recognising an intangible fixed asset in a balance sheet.[28]

(a) either the historical costs incurred in creating it are known or it can be clearly demonstrated that they are readily ascertainable; and
(b) its characteristics can be clearly distinguished from those of goodwill and other assets; and
(c) its cost can be measured independently of goodwill, of other assets and of the earnings of the relevant business or business segment. In order for this to be possible when the historical cost of acquired assets is deemed to be their fair value, there will normally need to be an active

22 The Companies Act 1985 requires that costs of research are charged to the profit and loss account (Schedule 4, Para. 3(2)(c)) but permits the carrying forward of development costs 'in special circumstances' (Schedule 4, Para. 20(1)). Satisfaction of the criteria for the carrying forward of development expenditure in SSAP 13 is now generally accepted as providing the 'special circumstances' referred to in the Act.
23 This was not required by the original SSAP 13 (1977) although it was required by IAS 9 'Accounting for research and development activities' (1978).
24 Companies Act 1985, Schedule 4, Para. 20(2).
25 ED 52, Para. 5.
26 The other pronouncements are SSAP 13 (revised), SSAP 21, SSAP 22/ED 47 and ED 55 respectively.
27 *See* Chapter 8 'Business combinations and goodwill', p. 220.
28 ED 52, Para. 38.

market in intangible assets of the same kind independently of the purchase and sale of businesses or business segments

The application of these criteria to brands is dealt with in the explanatory note.

When we turn to the explanatory note, we find that the ASC took the view that brands cannot be distinguished from goodwill and hence that, for accounting purposes, they should be subsumed under goodwill and accounted for in accordance with SSAP 22/ED 47 'Accounting for goodwill'.[29] This is also the line taken by the ASB in the Discussion Paper 'Goodwill and Intangible Assets' published in December 1993.

Although ED 52 encouraged companies to provide note disclosure of brands including brand names and the amount of any purchased goodwill which is attributable to them, it attempted to prohibit accounting for brands separately from goodwill.

Once brands have been dealt with, the proposed accounting treatment of remaining intangible fixed assets was straightforward. Provided they satisfy the above recognition criteria, such intangible assets should be included at historical cost and amortised over their useful economic life subject to a maximum period of 20 years.[30]

As with all fixed assets, any permanent fall in value should be recognised and charged to the profit and loss account.

An intangible asset may be revalued only if the criteria for recognition are satisfied, in particular the historical cost must be ascertainable. In such a case, the revalued amount should be the depreciated replacement cost or lower recoverable amount and, in accordance with the provisions of ED 51 and SSAP 12, subsequent amortization should be based on that amount.

Apart from keeping brands as a separate item out of balance sheets and the imposition of an arbitrary ceiling on the useful economic life of intangible assets, ED 52 required intangible fixed assets to be treated in the same way as tangible fixed assets.

RECOMMENDED READING

Excellent up-to-date and detailed reading on the subject matter of this chapter and on much of the contents of this book is provided by the most recent edition of:

UK GAAP, Principal authors and editors Mike Davies, Ron Paterson and Allister Wilson, Ernst and Young, Longman, London,

and by recent editions of the annual survey of published accounts:

Financial Reporting, ICAEW, London.

---

29 ED 52, Para. 23.
30 In exceptional circumstances, where it can be demonstrated that a figure in excess of 20 years is more appropriate, that period may be used but this may in no case exceed 40 years. (ED 52, Para. 41.) This is the same treatment as that proposed for purchased goodwill (ED 47, Para. 52).

CHAPTER 5

Accounting for liabilities

INTRODUCTION

We will deal in this chapter with the relatively neglected subject of liabilities. The relative, if not absolute, neglect of the topic is evidenced by the fact that there is at the time of writing no accounting standard on the general subject of liabilities. The closest we have is FRS 4 'Capital Instruments' which closely follows FRED 3 'Accounting for Capital Instruments' (December 1992) which was issued as recently as November 1993.

The topics covered in this chapter together with the relevant reporting standard and statements are:

FRS 4   'Capital Instruments'

SSAP 17   'Accounting for Post Balance Sheet Events'

SSAP 18   'Accounting for Contingencies'

SSAP 24   'Accounting for Pension Costs'

SORP   'Pension Scheme Accounts'

THE THREE SOURCES OF CAPITAL FUNDING

A company acquires capital funding through three sources.

- From owners – either through direct contribution of share capital or the retention of profits
- By borrowing
- Through gifts.

The last named might seem an unusual source but in fact governments and other agencies do make significant contributions to some companies.

We discussed the subject of accounting for government grants in Chapter 4 where we pointed out that a logical case could be made for retaining on the balance sheet a section, separate from owners' equity and liabilities, representing the volume of funds that have been provided by government and similar agencies; however, as we pointed out, SSAP 4 'Accounting for Government Grants' does not take this line. Instead the standard requires that the government grant should be credited to the profit and loss account either immediately or over time. Hence, a transfer is made between the 'gift' source of finance and shareholders' funds; the grant is hence treated as a gift to the owners rather than to the business itself. A more unusual form of gift is sometimes found in small family-owned businesses where a very long-term loan is granted, possibly interest free, where there is no intention that the loan should be repaid under foreseeable circumstances. In such, admittedly rare, cases the source of finance would be treated as a liability.

Apart from gifts, we have two sources of capital funding which are often referred to as debt and equity.[1] There are two key issues associated with the subject of accounting for these sources of funds. The first relates to separating the sources of funds between liabilities and shareholders funds (while the twofold categorisation holds for the accounts of single companies a third category, minority interest, will be found in consolidated financial statements). The second issue is how the interest on liabilities should be calculated and how it should be allocated over the life of the respective liability.

The distinction between liabilities and shareholders' funds

In the 1980s there emerged a bewildering array of new methods of raising finance. These methods involved many forms of financial instruments which are undoubtedly debt but also many which are of a hybrid nature having features of both debt and equity. Examples of the hybrid securities are convertible bonds where holders are given the right to convert into equity shares at a favourable price at some future time. Often the terms are such that the conversion is virtually certain to occur and existing shareholders' benefit from a relatively low rate of interest until conversion when their ownership interest in the company is diluted.[2]

Some accountants have argued that such hybrid securities should be included in a separate section of the balance sheet but, as we shall see below, FRS 4 requires that any securities which have any element of liability should be treated as such and reject the notion of separate presentation of hybrids.

The calculation and treatment of interest

Until the publication of FRS 4 there was little to guide the accountant on the general subject of liabilities. Company law, of course, does bear on the subject but as we shall show it hinders rather than helps because existing legislative requirements are based on woolly if not misguided economic principles.

Whilst the ingenuity of capital market is such that there are in practice many complex capital issues at issue, the main conceptual points can be illustrated by examining the simple case of a long-term loan or debenture.

Discounts and premiums on debentures

Debentures may be issued at a discount or a premium and may be redeemed at a discount or a premium. The difference between the issue and redemption price is as important in determining the cost of debenture finance, that is the return (before tax) to the lender, as is the coupon rate of interest.

To illustrate, let us consider three issues of debentures, each with a nominal value of

1 The use of the word equity to describe the source of funds provided by owners can sometimes lead to confusion because in the context of companies with share capital the distinction is made between equity shares and other forms of share capital, such as preference shares.

2 For an introduction to these and other novel financial instruments, readers are referred to D. J. Tonkin and L. C. L. Skerratt, eds, *Financial Reporting 1988–1989*, ICAEW, 1989: chapter entitled 'Complex Capital Issues', by B. L. Worth and R. A. Derwent, and L. C. L. Skerratt and D. J. Tonkin, eds, *Financial Reporting 1989–1990*, ICAEW, 1989: chapter entitled 'Complex Capital Issues', by S. Parkinson.

£100 and each for a five-year period.

(a) Debenture A carries a coupon rate of 20 per cent per annum: it is to be issued and redeemed at par.
(b) Debenture B carries a coupon rate of 16 per cent per annum: it is to be issued at a discount of £12, at a price of £88, and is to be redeemed at par.
(c) Debenture C carries a coupon rate of 18 per cent per annum: it is to be issued at par but redeemed at a premium of £15 at £115.

We shall assume that the interest on each debenture is payable annually at the end of each year and shall ignore taxation and transaction costs.

The effective interest rate on debenture A is 20 per cent and the terms of debentures B and C have been chosen to produce identical effective interest rates of 20 per cent. In other words, if we discount the cash flows from and to the debenture holders, all these debentures produce a net present value (NPV) of zero at a 20 per cent discount rate (Table 5.1).

Table 5.1

Debenture		NPV at 20%
A		$+100 - 20a_5 - 100v^5$
	=	$+100 - 20(2.9906) - 100(0.4019)$
	=	$+100 - 59.8 - 40.2$
	=	0
B		$+88 - 16a_5 - 100v^5$
	=	$+88 - 16(2.9906) - 100(0.4019)$
	=	$+88 - 47.8 - 40.2$
	=	0
C		$+100 - 18a_5 - 115v^5$
	=	$+100 - 18(2.9906) - 115(0.4019)$
	=	$+100 - 53.8 - 46.2$
	=	0

In all cases the effective rate of interest, that is the average cost of the finance, is 20 per cent, but whereas for Debenture A this is all paid in interest, for Debentures B and C the cost is partly paid as a difference between the redemption price and the issue price.

Accounting for Debenture A poses no problems. The annual interest expense of £20 (20% x £100) will be charged in the profit and loss account each year while the liability will appear at the nominal value of the debentures, that is £100. Accounting for Debentures B and C does pose some problems and we will deal with each in turn.

Discount on debentures

Debenture B is issued at a discount. While the interest of £16 (16% x £100) will undoubtedly be charged to the profit and loss account each year, it is also necessary to decide how to account for the discount on issue, the amount of £12.

The liability would be recorded at the nominal value of £100 and company law gives us permission to treat the discount on debentures as an asset.[3] Once we have recorded the

3 Companies Act 1985, Schedule 4, Para. 24(1).

discount as an asset, the next question is how this should be dealt with. As the discount is effectively part of the cost of the finance, we might expect this cost to be reflected in the profit and loss account. However, company law specifically permits the writing off of discounts on debentures to a share premium account.[4]

Thus, where a company has a share premium account, we may either write off the discount to share premium account or we may write off the discount to profit and loss account. In the latter case it is possible to write off the discount immediately or to write it off over the five-year period. Let us look at each possibility in turn.

Use of share premium account

Although company law clearly permits the writing off of this discount to share premium account, this results in part of the cost of borrowing bypassing the profit and loss account and hence in an overstatement of profits. This odd quirk of company law has been around for some time, as have its critics.

As long ago as 1962, the Jenkins Committee, which was set up to advise the government on changes in company legislation, reported that it thought that the law should be amended:[5]

> ... to prohibit the application of the (share premium) account in writing off the expenses and commission paid and discounts allowed on any issue of debentures or in providing for any premiums payable on redemption of debentures, since these are part of the ordinary expenses of borrowing.

Despite the numerous Companies Acts which have been enacted since 1962, this oddity remains and it is difficult to see how it can be justified. The charging of a discount to the share premium account means that the profit and loss account does not bear the full cost of the borrowing, but it also seems to be inconsistent with the rationale for creating a share premium account in the first place. The purpose of a share premium account is to ensure that, with certain exceptions, subscribed capital cannot be repaid to shareholders. If the profit and loss account is relieved of part of the cost of the business, then, effectively, part of the subscribed capital is available for distribution.

Charge to profit and loss account

In the view of the authors, the discount should be charged to the profit and loss account over the period of the debt, so our next question is 'How should this be done?' No specific guidance is provided by the law except that[6]

> it shall be written off by reasonable amounts each year and must be completely written off before repayment of the debt.

In practice, discounts appear to be written off on a straight line basis, but it is also possible to write them off using a method based on present value principles such as the effective rate method.[7]

Using the straight line method the charge to the profit and loss account in respect of

---

4 Companies Act 1985, Sec. 130(2).
5 Report of the Company Law Committee, Cmnd 1749, HMSO, London, 1962, Para. 163.
6 Companies Act 1985, Schedule 4, Para. 24(2)(a).
7 This is also called the 'actuarial method' (ASC in particular in SSAP 21), the 'compound yield method' (Inland Revenue) and the 'interest method' (FASB).

the discount would be £12 ÷ 5 = £2.4 so that, together with the annual interest payment, the annual expense would be:

Interest payment	£16.00
Amortisation of discount	2.40
	18.40

The more sophisticated approach would record the liability at the present value of the cash flows discounted at the market rate of interest, which we have assumed to be 20 per cent. The interest expense each year would be found by multiplying the present value of the cash flows at the start of the year by the effective interest rate. As can be seen from Table 5.2, this results in an increasing liability and an increasing interest expense throughout the term of the loan.

Table 5.2

(i) Year	(ii) Opening balance	(iii) Interest 20% of (ii)	(iv) Total (ii) + (iii)	(v) Payment at year end	(vi) Closing balance (iv) − (v)
	£	£	£	£	£
1	88.0	17.6	105.6	16.0	89.6
2	89.6	17.9	107.5	16.0	91.5
3	91.5	18.3	109.8	16.0	93.8
4	93.8	18.8	112.6	16.0	96.6
5	96.6	19.4*	116.0	116.0†	−

* Includes rounding adjustment.
† Interest 16.0 + Redemption price 100 00.

This is the approach which is required in the USA.[8] It is also the approach which is required by SSAP 21 'Accounting for leases and hire purchase contracts' when accounting for the obligation under a finance lease[9] and is now the only method which is permitted under the provisions of FRS 4.

Premium on redemption

Debenture C, which carries a coupon rate of interest of 18 per cent is issued at par but redeemed at a premium of £15. Under the existing legal framework it is not clear whether the liability should be recorded initially at the nominal value of £100 or at the amount payable, the redemption price of £115. If it is recorded initially at £100, then a premium must be provided by the end of the five-year period. If it is recorded initially at £115, then an asset 'premium on debentures' must also be established and we have a situation analogous to the issue of a debenture at a discount which has been discussed above. In either case it is necessary to decide how to deal with the premium.

8 Readers are referred to Richard Macve, 'Accounting for long-term loans', in *External Financial Reporting*, Bryan Carsberg and Susan Dev (eds), Prentice-Hall, 1984. This essay in honour of Professor Harold Edey discusses the treatment of long-term loans in both the UK and USA.
9 *See* Chapter 6.

Not surprisingly we find that the law permits the write-off of this premium to share premium account but, for the reasons explained above, the authors are of the view that it should be charged to the profit and loss account over the life of the debentures.

While the straight line method appears to be used most often in practice, the authors would favour the use of the effective interest method, producing the amounts for expense (column ii) and liabilities (column vi) shown in the following table:

Table 5.3

(i) Year	(ii) Opening balance	(iii) Interest 20% of (ii)	(iv) Total (ii) + (iii)	(v) Payment at year end	(vi) Closing balance (iv) − (v)
	£	£	£	£	£
1	100.0	20.0	120.0	18.0	102.0
2	102.0	20.4	122.4	18.0	104.4
3	104.4	20.9	125.3	18.0	107.3
4	107.3	21.5	128.8	18.0	110.8
5	110.8	22.2	133.0	133.0*	−

* Interest 18.0 + Redemption price 115.0

FRS 4 'CAPITAL INSTRUMENTS'

The objective of FRS 4 is:

> to ensure that financial statements provide a clear, coherent and consistent treatment of capital instruments, in particular as regards the classification of instruments as debt, non-equity shares or equity shares; that costs associated with capital instruments are dealt with in a manner consistent with their classification, and, for redeemable instruments, allocated to accounting periods on a fair basis over the period the instrument is in issue; and that financial statements provide relevant information concerning the nature and amount of the entity's sources of finance and the associated costs, commitments and potential commitments. (Para. 1.)

Some basic definitions

We should start by defining the term 'capital instruments':

> All instruments that are issued by reporting entities which are a means of raising finance, including shares, debentures, loans and debt instruments, options and warrants that give the holder the right to subscribe for or obtain capital instruments. In the case of consolidated financial statements the term includes capital instruments issued by subsidiaries except those which are held by another member of the group included in the consolidation. (FRS 4, Para. 2.)

Another important definition is that of 'finance costs'; these are:

> The difference between the net proceeds of an instrument and the total amount of the payments (or other transfers of economic benefit) that the issuer may be required to make in respect of the instrument. (FRS 4, Para. 8.)

FRS 4 – The main provisions

With these two definitions in mind the main points of FRS 4 can be briefly summarised.

Balance sheet presentation

Capital instruments must be categorised into four (single companies) or six (consolidated accounts) groups as shown in the following table.

Table 5.4

	Analysed between	
Shareholders' funds	Equity interests	Non-equity interests
Liabilities	Convertible liabilities	Non-convertible liabilities
Minority interests in subsidiaries	Equity interests in subsidiaries	Non-equity interests in subsidiaries

We have already referred to the various hybrid forms of capital instruments issued in recent years which seem to combine elements of debt and equity. Because of their complexity and the lack of a clear accounting standard there was inconsistency in treatment and opportunities, which were from time to time taken, to paint the balance sheet in a more favourable light than reality might allow. All other things being equal the higher the level of debt relative to shareholders' funds the higher the degree of risk because failure to pay interest could lead to the insolvency of the company whilst the failure to pay dividends would not have such a devastating effect. Similarly, from the point of view of equity shareholders a high level of non-equity shares mean that equity holders are subject to greater uncertainty in terms of their returns because of the prior claims of the non-equity holders. Hence the possibility of painting the balance sheet in a rosy hue if there are possibilities that instruments which are essentially debt can be presented as part of shareholders' funds or if non-equity interests can be classified as part of equity shares. As will be seen, the provisions of FRS 4 are such to ensure that if an instrument contains any element of debt it should be treated as such or, if the instrument is part of shareholders' funds, then if the instrument contains any trace of non-equity it should be recorded as such.

Allocation of finance costs

Finance costs associated with liabilities and shares, other than equity shares, should be allocated to accounting periods at a constant rate on the carrying amount. This is the actuarial method as described on page 109. Initially capital instruments should be recorded at the net amount of the issue proceeds and only the direct costs incurred in connection with the issue of the instruments should be deducted from the proceeds in arriving at this net amount. The finance cost for the period is added to the carrying amount and payments deducted from it. Thus, as shown in the earlier example, the carrying figure in the balance sheet may not be the same as the nominal value of the liability, but in the case of redeemable instruments this would result in the carrying amount at the time of redemption being equal to the amount payable at that time. A consequence of this is spelt out in more detail in the actual standard where it is stated:

> Gains and losses arising on the repurchase or early settlement of debt should be recognised in the profit and loss account in the period during which the repurchase or early settlement is made. (FRS 4, Para. 32.)

Scope

The standard covers all entities whose financial statements are intended to give a true and fair view irrespective of size or ownership. However, investment companies are exceptions in that they need only charge to the profit and loss account finance costs which relate to revenue; those which relate to capital should be charged in the statement of total recognised gains and losses (see page 146). The other main exclusions from the reporting standard are:

(a) Warrants issued to employees under employee share schemes
(b) Leases, which should be dealt with in accordance with SSAP 21, and
(c) Equity shares issued as part of a business combination which is treated as a merger.

The distinction between shareholders' funds and liabilities

The key test is that a capital instrument is a liability if it contains an obligation to transfer economic benefit, including contingent obligations. Such a distinction seems reasonably straightforward in that it is usually clear whether an instrument requires the company to make some sort of transfer to the owner of an instrument or whether any such transfer is made at the discretion of the company. There are two exceptions to the general rule. The first relates to an obligation which would only arise on the insolvency of the issuer. If there is no expectation of that event and the entity can be accounted for on a going concern basis that contingent liability can be ignored. Similarly, an obligation which would only crystallise if a covenant attached to a capital instrument is breached can also be disregarded unless, of course, there is evidence that such a breach will occur.

Warrants

Share warrants are instruments which state that the holder or bearer is entitled to be issued with a specified number of shares, possibly upon the payment of an additional fixed price. In the view of the ASB, the original amount paid for the warrant must be regarded as part of the subscription price of the shares which may, or may not, be issued at some time in the future and it is for this reason that FRS 4 specifies that warrants be reported within shareholders' funds (FRS 4 Para. 37).

The Board does, however, recognise that the topic of warrants raises a number of issues which are outside the scope of FRS 4. It refers (see the section on the development of the FRS, paragraphs 11–13) in particular to the view that if the price paid on the exercise on the warrant is less than the fair value of the shares issued that this should be reflected in the financial statements by, presumably, increasing shareholders' funds and recognising as an expense the 'cost' incurred in issuing shares in this way. Another controversial issue is what should be done if the warrant lapses without being exercised. Should the amount initially subscribed to the warrant continue to be treated as part of share capital or regarded as a gain by the company? The issue depends essentially on whether the warrant holders are regarded as sharing in the ownership of the company. If they are so regarded then the benefit from the lapse in the warrant is not a gain to the company but a transfer between owners and hence the initial subscription should be treated as part of share capital. If on the other hand the warrant holders are not regarded as owners, the view taken by the ASB, the amount released by the lapse of the warrants should be reported as a gain within the statement of recognised gains and losses.

In summary, the provisions of FRS 4 relating to the taking up and lapsing of warrants are:

(a) When a warrant is exercised, the amount previously recognised in respect of the warrant should be included in the net proceeds of the shares issued (Para. 46).

(b) When a warrant elapses unexercised, the amount previously recognised in respect of the warrant should be reported in the statement of total recognised gains and losses (Para. 47).

The distinction between equity and non-equity

FRS 4 reinforces the requirements of company legislation by requiring that the balance sheet should show the total amount of shareholders' funds with an analysis between the amount attributable to equity interests and the amount attributable to non-equity interests (Para. 40).

The need here is to distinguish between equity and non-equity interests. Company law provides a succinct definition of equity share capital which means

> in relation to a company, its issued share capital excluding any part of that capital which, neither as respects dividends nor as respects capital carries any weight to participate beyond a specified amount in a distribution.[10]

The ASB believe that that definition does not give sufficient guidance in the more complex cases and hence it provides a far more detailed statement of the distinction which starts with a definition of non-equity shares. These are shares possessing any of the following characteristics:

(a) Any of the rights of the shares to receive payments (whether in respect of dividends, in respect of redemption or otherwise) are for a limited amount that is not calculated by reference to the company's assets or profits or the dividends on any class of equity share.

(b) Any of their rights to participate in a surplus in a winding up are limited to a specific amount that is not calculated by reference to the company's assets or profits and such limitation had a commercial effect in practice at the time the shares were issued or, if later, at the time the limitation was introduced.

(c) The shares are redeemable according to their terms or the holder, or any party other than the issuer, can require their redemption (FRS 4, Para. 12).

Following all the above, equity shares are defined simply as 'shares other than non-equity shares' (FRS 4, Para. 7).

The general drift of the ASB thinking is clear. Its definition attempts to ensure that only 'true' equity is treated as such. In so far that the existence of non-equity capital represents

---

10 Companies Act 1985, section 744.

a risk which may be taken into account by equity shareholders when making investment decisions, this approach can be seen as being protective of the interest of potential equity shareholders.

The balance sheet treatment of liabilities

The distinction between convertible and non-convertible liabilities

A convertible debt is one which allows the holder of the security to exchange the debt for shares in the issuing company on the terms specified in the loan instrument.

Current practice is to report convertible debt as a liability, a practice which FRS 4 notes is uncontroversial where conversion is uncertain or unlikely. But there are those who would argue that if conversion is probable then convertible debt should be reported outside liabilities in order to give a fairer representation of the economic position of the company. In drafting FRS 4 the ASB, arguing that a balance sheet is a record of the financial position of a company at a point of time, not a forecast of future events, specified that all convertible debt should be included with liabilities. As we shall see in the section of this chapter dealing with the disclosure requirements of the standard, adequate information must be provided regarding the terms and conditions relating to the various capital instruments in issue.

There is a more sophisticated line of argument which suggests that merely reporting convertible debt as part of liabilities ignores the equity rights which are inherent in the issue of convertible debt. The International Accounting Standard Committee, for example, in its exposure draft E40 proposes that so-called 'split accounting' be required for convertible debt. Under this approach the proceeds of issue of convertible debt are allocated between the two components, the equity rights and the liabilities. The consequence of this is that the finance charge relating to the debt is increased over that which would be recorded if the whole of the proceeds of the issue were treated as a liability. The reason for this being that the total amount payable to the convertible debt holders, assuming no conversion, consists of a string of interest payments and the redemption price, remains the same irrespective of the method of accounting used. If the initial current value of the security is smaller, as it would be if the proceeds of the issue were split, then the finance cost would be increased to cover the amount of the proceeds which were allocated to the equity interest.

Happily for lovers of simplicity, the ASB rejected this more complex presentation and the relevant standard practice for the presentation of convertible debt is straightforward.

> Conversion of debt should not be anticipated. Convertible debt should be reported within liabilities and the finance cost should be calculated on the assumption that the debt will never be converted. The amount attributable to convertible debt should be stated separately from that of other liabilities.
>
> (FRS 4, Para. 25.)

> When convertible debt is converted, the amount recognised in shareholders' funds in respect of the shares issued should be the amount at which the liability for the debt is stated as at the date of conversion. No gain or loss should be recognised on conversion.
>
> (FRS 4, Para. 26.)

Debt maturity

As recognised in company legislation, users of accounts need to be given adequate information about the scheduling of the repayment of debt in order to help them assess the companies' short-term solvency and long-term liquidity position.

The requirements of FRS 4 are a little more extensive than those of the Companies Act in that they include an additional cut-off date of two years. The requirement is that:

> An analysis of the maturity of debt should be presented showing amounts falling due:
>
> (a) in one year or less, or on demand;
> (b) between one and two years;
> (c) between two and five years; and
> (d) in five years or more.

(FRS 4, Para. 33.)

> The maturity of the debt should be determined by reference to the earliest date on which the lender can require repayment.

(FRS 4, Para. 34.)

Life is of course not without its complications and the ASB had to consider the case of a borrower who had already made arrangements to re-finance the existing loan. The question here is whether the maturity of the loan should be measured by reference only to the capital instrument currently in issue or whether account should be taken of the re-financing arrangements that have been established. It would clearly be misleading to ignore the significant fact that facilities have been established in order to extend the period of the loan and therefore the ASB state:

> Where committed facilities are in existence at the balance sheet date that permit the re-financing of debt for a period beyond its maturity, the earliest date at which the lender can require repayment should be taken to be the maturity date of the longest refinancing permitted by a facility in respect of which all the following conditions are met:
> (a) The debt and the facility are under a single agreement or course of dealing with the same lender or group of lenders.
> (b) The finance costs for the new debt are on a basis that is not significantly higher than that of the existing debt.
> (c) The obligations of the lender (or group of lenders) are firm: the lender is not able legally to refrain from providing funds except in circumstances the possibility of which can be demonstrated to be remote.
> (d) The lender (or group of lenders) is expected to be able to fulfil its obligations under the facility.

(FRS 4, Para. 35.)

This is clearly a stringent set of conditions.

In order that the users of the accounts are made aware of the use of the above provision it is also required that:

> Where the maturity of debt is assessed by reference to that of refinancing permitted by facilities in accordance with paragraph 35, the amounts of the debt so treated, analysed by the earliest date on which the lender could demand repayment in the absence of the facilities, should be disclosed.

(FRS 4, Para. 36.)

The allocation of finance costs

Debts

The actuarial method, whereby the finance cost is allocated over the life of the debt at a constant rate on the carrying amount, is the only method allowed by the standard (paragraphs 27–29). When the debt is issued it is recorded at the net proceeds and the carrying amount is then increased by the finance costs and reduced by payments. All entities, other than investment companies, must charge the finance costs to the profit and loss account.

Accrued finance costs, to the extent that they will be paid in the next period, may be included with accruals but even if this option is exercised, the accrual must be included in the carrying value for the purpose of calculating the finance costs and any gains or losses on repurchase or early settlement (FRS 4, Para. 30).

In some cases the amount payable on the debt may be contingent on uncertain future events such as changes in a price index. Such events should not be anticipated and the finance costs and carrying amount should only be adjusted when the event occurs (FRS 4, Para. 31).

Because of the special features of investment companies they may include the element of finance costs, and any gains on losses on redemption or repurchase, which relate to capital, in the statement of total recognised gains and losses (FRS 4, Para. 52).

Non-equity shares

The treatment of finance costs relating to non-equity shares is based on the same principles as debt (FRS 4, Para. 42) with two additional specific rules. These are:

> Where the entitlement to dividends in respect of non-equity shares is calculated by reference to time, the dividends should be accounted for on an accruals basis except in those circumstances (for example where profits are insufficient to justify a dividend and dividend rights are non-cumulative) where ultimate payment is remote. All dividends should be reported as appropriations of profit.

> (FRS 4, Para. 43) and

> Where the finance costs for non-equity shares are not equal to the dividends the difference should be accounted for in the profit and loss account as an appropriation of profits.

> (FRS 4, Para. 44.)

An example of a situation where there may be a difference between the finance costs and the dividends are shares which may be redeemed at a premium.

We have already introduced the 'constant rate of return' method earlier in this chapter in the illustrative section on debentures (pages 106–10). There we showed that the method was logical and allocated the cost of borrowing fairly over the period of the loan, as well as ensuring that the whole of the finance costs are charged to the profit and loss account. The use of the method would also achieve consistency across the wide range of different capital instruments in issue. The problem with the method is not so much it is difficult to understand, especially when compared to the treatment of interest costs in SSAP 21 'Accounting for leases and hire purchase contracts', but that it represents a radical departure from existing practice. Whilst the method itself is reasonably straightforward there will be some confusion because of the difference between the constant rate of interest and the nominal or coupon rate, but that does not seem an unreasonable price to pay for the advantages of the method. The consequences of the adoption of these provisions of FRS 4 will be interesting. Will the fact that the real interest charge will have to be reported irrespective of the nominal rate affect the behaviour of the issuers of capital instruments? Will there, for example, be a move from complexity to simplicity if the real cost of interest has to be shown and all liabilities reported as such no matter how the loan is packaged?

Issue costs

The calculation of the constant rate of interest and the initial carrying value in the balance sheet depend upon the 'net proceeds' of the issue of the capital instruments. The net proceeds are defined as:

> The fair value of the consideration received on the issue of a capital instrument after deduction of issue costs.

(FRS 4, Para. 11.)

Issue costs are defined as

> The costs that are incurred directly in connection with the issue of a capital instrument, that is, those costs that would not have been incurred had the specific instrument in question not been issued.

(Para. 10.)

The use of the phrase 'fair value' reminds us that the carrying value of the capital instrument will not always be found without some degree of estimation. An example of such a case would be the joint issue of a debt and warrant. The amount received for the issue of the joint instrument will need to be allocated to provide the fair value of the debt and warrant, the most likely source of evidence is market values.

The standard is restrictive as to what should be included in issue costs (Para. 96). Such costs should not include any which would have been incurred had the instrument not been issued, such as management remuneration or indeed the costs of researching and negotiating alternative sources of finance. Those costs which do not qualify as issue costs should be written off to the profit and loss account as incurred. The standard requires that issue costs be accounted for by reducing the proceeds of the issue of the instrument and should not be regarded as assets because they do not provide access to any future economic benefits. The consequence of setting the issue costs against the net proceeds is to increase the interest charge in the profit and loss account, in other words it ensures that the issue costs are written off over the life of the capital instrument.

Back to the share premium account

It might be thought that the proposals would include the stipulation that entities subject to the Companies Act should no longer take advantage of the provision whereby they can charge issue costs and discounts against the share premium account. The proposals only go some way towards this desirable end. Issue costs, which would include discounts, have to be charged to the profit and loss account but the standard specifically draws attention to the fact that the issue costs may subsequently be charged to the share premium account by means of a transfer between reserves (Para. 97).

FRS 4 and consolidated financial statements

There are a number of special issues relating to consolidated financial statements.

There may be circumstances when shares issued by a subsidiary and held outside the group should be included in liabilities rather than minority interest (FRS 4, Para. 49). This treatment is required when the group, taken as a whole, has an obligation to transfer economic benefit, for example if another member of the group has guaranteed payments relating to the shares.

In addition:

(a) The amount of minority interests shown in the balance sheet should be analysed between the aggregate amount attributable to equity interests and amounts attributable to non-equity interests (FRS 4, Para. 50).

(b) The amounts attributed to non-equity minority interests and their associated finance costs should be calculated in the same manner as those for non-equity shares. The finance costs associated with such interests should be included in minority interests in the profit and loss account (FRS 4, Para. 51).

Some further explanation is required regarding the circumstances under which shares issued by subsidiaries would not be shown in minority interest. As already noted, one of the FRS 4 principles is that if any element of obligation to transfer economic resources attaches to a capital instrument then it should be treated as a liability. Thus, if guarantees have been given in respect of dividends payable on the shares or on their redemption there is a liability, albeit contingent, to transfer economic resources. In such circumstances the shares should be included under liabilities.

A particular case described in the explanatory note (Para. 90) is that of subordinated guarantees given by group companies in respect of shares issued by subsidiaries. It is noted that the intent of some guarantees of this type is that the rights of the holder of the shares in relation to the group should be the same as the holder of preference shares of the parent. If this is the case then the shares should be included as part of non-equity minority interests.

Disclosure requirements

FRS 4 is very much concerned with the provision of adequate, some might argue more than adequate, disclosure, and in the previous pages we have referred to a number of the proposals which bear on this matter. The remaining disclosure requirements may be briefly summarised as follows:

(a) *Disclosure relating to shares* (Paras 55–59)

    (i) An analysis should be given of the total amount of non-equity interests in shareholders' funds relating to each class of non-equity shares and series of warrants for non-equity shares.

    (ii) A brief summary of the rights of each class of shares should be given, other than for equity shares with standard characteristics. Details should also be provided of classes of shares which are not currently in issue but which may be issued as a result of the conversion of debt or the exercise of warrants.

    (iii) Details of dividends for each class of share and any other appropriation of profit in respect of non-equity shares should be disclosed.

(b) *Disclosure relating to minority interests* (Paras 60–61)
   (i)   The minority interests charge in the profit and loss account should be analysed between equity and non-equity interests.
   (ii) If there are non-equity minority interests the rights of the holders against other group companies should be described.

(c) *Disclosure relating to debt* (Paras 62–64)
   (i)   Details of convertible debt should be provided.
   (ii) Brief descriptions should be provided where the legal nature of the instrument differs from that associated with debt, for example, when the obligation to repay is conditional.
   (iii) Gains and losses on the repurchase or early settlement of debt should be disclosed in the profit and loss account as separate items within or adjacent to 'interest payable and similar changes'.

(d) *General disclosure requirements*
   (i)   When the disclosure requirements relating to the amounts of convertible debt, non-equity interests in shareholders' funds and non-equity interests in minority interests are given in the notes the relevant balance sheet caption should refer to the existence of the relevant capital instruments (Para. 54).
   (ii) Where the brief summaries required in respect of a(ii), b(i), c(i) and c(iii) above cannot adequately provide the information necessary to understand the commercial effect of the relevant instruments, that fact should be stated together with particulars of where the relevant information may be obtained. In any event the principal features of the instruments should be stated (Para. 65).

Application notes

FRS 4 includes a section on Application Notes which describe how the principles of the reporting standard should be applied to capital instruments with certain features. The instruments covered in this section are:

Auction market preferred shares (AMPS)	Index linked loans
Capital contributions	Limited recourse debt
Convertible capital bonds	Participating preference shares
Convertible debt with a premium put option	Perpetual debt
Convertible debt with enhanced interest	Repackaged perpetual debt
Debt issued with warrants	Stepped interest bonds
Deep discount bonds	Subordinated debt
Income bonds	

Space does not allow coverage of these notes and the interested reader should refer to the standard itself.

ACCOUNTING FOR THE POST BALANCE SHEET EVENTS

One of the desirable characteristics of accounting reports discussed in Chapter 1 was 'timeliness', i.e. the need to publish accounts as quickly as possible. However, there will inevitably be some delay between the end of the accounting period and the date of publication (which is not to say that the duration of the delay could not often be reduced), and this leads one to the question of how the accountant should treat significant events which occur during this period.

The main principle underlying SSAP 17, issued in 1980, is that users should be presented with information that is as up to date as possible and be informed of any significant events which have occurred since the end of the accounting period. The provisions are uncontroversial and straightforward and may therefore be briefly summarised.

A distinction is drawn between events which occur before and after the date on which the directors approved the financial statements, and the standard covers only those events which occurred prior to the date of approval. The point is made, however, that directors have a duty to ensure the publication of details of any events which occur after the date of approval if they have a material effect on the financial statements.

The date of approval is normally the date of the board meeting at which the financial statements are formally approved (or in the instance of an unincorporated association the corresponding date). In the case of group accounts the date is that on which the accounts are approved by the directors of the holding company.

Post balance sheet events are classified as either *adjusting* or *non-adjusting* events.

Adjusting events are those which provide additional evidence in respect of conditions existing at the balance sheet date and will therefore call for the revision of the amounts at which items are stated in the financial statements. A very obvious example of an adjusting event would be the receipt of cash from a debtor which could affect the provision against doubtful debts. Events such as the proposal of a dividend, a transfer to reserves and a change in the tax rate are also regarded as being adjusting events.

Non-adjusting events are those which do not relate to conditions existing at the balance sheet date and will not affect the figures included in the financial statements. Examples of non-adjusting events are the issue of shares; major changes in the composition of the company and the financial effect of the losses of fixed assets or stocks as a result of a disaster such as fire or flood. The last-mentioned instance is an example of a non-adjusting event because the fire or flood did not affect the condition of the asset concerned at the balance sheet date.

The standard also requires the disclosure, as a non-adjusting event, of the reversal after the balance sheet date of transactions undertaken before the year end with the prime intention of altering the appearance of the company's balance sheet. These alterations comprise those commonly referred to as 'window dressing', for example, the borrowing of cash from an associated company to disguise an acute short-term liquidity problem.

It may be that some event occurs after the balance sheet date which because of its effect on the company's operating results or financial position, puts into question the application of the going concern convention to the whole (or to a significant part) of the company's accounts. The standard is to some extent inconsistent in respect of the treatment of such events in that in Part 1 of the standard it states that 'Consequently these [the events] may fall to be treated as adjusting events' (SSAP 17, Para. 8). This suggests that a distinction should be drawn between events which represent the materialisation of a situation which existed at the balance sheet date (adjusting events) and those which are constituted by completely fresh disasters which did not exist at the balance sheet date (i.e. non-adjusting events). However, the standard itself (Para. 22) requires that the accounts should be amended as a consequence of any material post balance sheet event which casts doubt on the application of the going concern convention.

The actual standard may be summarised as follows:

1 Financial statements should be prepared on the basis of conditions existing at the balance sheet date.

2 A material post balance sheet event requires changes in the amounts to be included in financial statements where:
   (a) it is an adjusting event; or
   (b) it indicates that the application of the going concern concept to the whole or a material part of the company is not appropriate. (Note that for the reasons given above it might be argued that there is a conflict between requirements 1 and 2(b).)

3 A material post balance sheet event should be disclosed where:
   (a) its non-disclosure would hinder the users' ability to obtain a proper understanding of the financial position; or
   (b) it is the reversal or maturity after the year end of a transaction, the substance of which was primarily to alter the appearance of the company's balance sheet (window dressing).

4 In respect of any material post balance sheet event which has to be disclosed under the provisions of (3) above, the following should be stated in the notes to the accounts:
   (a) the nature of the event: and
   (b) an estimate of its financial effect or a statement that it is not practicable to make such an estimate. The financial effect should be shown without any adjustment for taxation but the taxation implications should be explained if such is necessary to enable a proper understanding of the financial position to be obtained.

5 The date on which the financial statements are approved by the Board of Directors should be disclosed.

It should be noted that the Companies Act 1985 requires that all liabilities and losses in respect of the financial year (or earlier years) shall be taken into account including those which only became apparent between the balance sheet date and the date of the approval of the accounts.

ACCOUNTING FOR CONTINGENCIES

Company law has for many years required the disclosure by way of a note to the accounts of information concerning contingent liabilities. Such a practice can be argued to be asymmetric in that no regard is paid to contingent assets. Accounting for contingencies is the subject, and title of, SSAP 18 issued in 1980, the purpose of which is twofold. It modified existing accounting practice by requiring disclosure of information relating to contingent assets as well as standardizing the methods used to define and disclose contingent liabilities and assets.

The term contingency is defined as follows:

> Contingency is a condition which exists at the balance sheet date, where the outcome will be confirmed only on the occurrence or non-occurrence of one or more uncertain future events. A contingent gain or loss is a gain or loss dependent on a contingency. (SSAP 18, Para. 14.)

There is obviously a close link between SSAP 18 and SSAP 17 ('Accounting for post balance sheet events') in that if what was an uncertain future event at the balance sheet date, crystallises before the accounts are approved by the directors it would be regarded as an adjusting event which would result in the modification of the balance sheet value of the related asset or liability. Similarly, a material contingency which arises between the balance sheet date and the date of approval would be treated as a non-adjusting event and hence disclosed under the provisions of SSAP 17.

One of the major problems that may be experienced in the implementation of SSAP 18 is that the statement does not attempt to define what is meant by 'a condition which exists at the balance sheet date' although it goes some way towards this by explicitly excluding uncertainties associated with accounting estimates such as the lives of fixed assets and the amount of bad debts. While some situations such as a pending legal action can clearly be identified as an existing condition there are many other situations which will require the application of judgment.

We will now summarise the provisions of SSAP 18 before providing further comment.

1 A material contingent loss should be accrued in financial statements where it is probable that a future event will confirm a loss which can be estimated with reasonable accuracy on the date on which the financial statements are approved by the board.
2 A material contingent loss not accrued under 1 above should be disclosed except where the possibility of loss is remote.
3 Contingent gains should not be accrued and should be disclosed only if it is probable that the gain will be realised.
4 The following information should be given in respect of contingent items which are disclosed: (a) the nature of the item, (b) the uncertainties which are expected to affect the outcome, and (c) a prudent estimate of the potential financial effect (made at the date of the approval of the accounts) or a statement that it is not practicable to make such an estimate. In the case of a contingent loss the amount can be reduced by any amount which is accrued and by the amount of any component where the possibility of loss is remote.
5 The financial effect should be stated before taking taxation into account but the taxation implication should be explained if such is necessary to give a proper understanding of the financial position.
6 Where there are a large number of items of the same nature which are subject to the same uncertainties the financial effect of each contingency need not be estimated as the amount can be based on a group of similar transactions.

Item 1 raises the question of what should be done if the loss is probable but the amount cannot be estimated with reasonable accuracy. Should they simply be disclosed or should a provision be made in the accounts? In view of the requirement of Para. 12(b) of the 1st Schedule of the 1981 Act, now paragraph 12(b) of the 4th Schedule to the Companies Act, 1985, which was enacted after the issue of SSAP 18, a provision should be made if a liability or loss is likely to occur.

SSAP 18 advocates an asymmetrical approach to contingent gains and losses as shown below:

	Contingent	
Outcome	Loss	Gain
Probable	Accrue	Note
Possible	Note	Ignore
Remote	Ignore	Ignore

(Possible has been used by the authors to describe a situation which falls between 'probable' and 'remote'.)

Given the weight of opinion in favour of rejecting the traditional interpretation of prudence (*see* Chapter 1) it is unfortunate that the ASC did not, at the very least, require the disclosure of possible contingent gains.

The standard requires that the financial effect should be shown on a prudent basis. Presumably this means the maximum amount of any possible loss or, more strictly, the upper bound of the range of reasonable expectations, i.e. larger values which have a low probability of occurrence may be ignored. Similarly, the lower bound of the range of reasonable expectation of possible gains should be disclosed. However, given the general movement towards more informative financial statements, it might be argued that it would be better to provide a more realistic estimate of the value of a contingent item. The point may be illustrated by the use of the following example:

Suppose that the company is facing litigation for damages and that the directors assess there is a probability of 0.4 of having to pay damages and costs. If the company wins the action it will be able to recover all its costs. If the company is penalised it must pay the total costs for both parties – say £40 000 – and damages which might with equal probability be £50 000, £100 000 or £150 000. The possible outcomes and their associated probabilities are as follows:

Outcome of action	Probability	Cost and damages
Win	0.6	Nil
Lose	0.4 x ⅓	£90 000
Lose	0.4 x ⅓	£140 000
Lose	0.4 x ⅓	£190 000

Thus the expected outcome is

$$£0.6 \times 0 + 0.4 \times £(⅓)(90\ 000 + 140\ 000 + 190\ 000) = £56\ 000$$

It can be seen that the 'estimate of the financial effect' could be presented in a number of different ways. The maximum loss should the company lose the action, £190 000, could be stated; alternatively, the range of possible outcomes, should the action be lost might be presented (£90 000 to £190 000). A third option is the 'expected value' of £56 000 which takes account of the probabilities as well as the magnitudes of the possible outcomes. Accounting is not yet at the point where the concept of expected values can be used especially in the case of isolated events of the type used as the example. However, item (5) in the above summary of requirements appears to allow this approach to be used where there are a number of contingent items of a similar type. In the case of a company which had discounted a large number of bills of exchange, information about the likely loss will be equally, if not more, valuable than a note stating the total amount of bills outstanding at the balance sheet date.

ACCOUNTING FOR PENSION COSTS

Introduction

The provision of occupational pension schemes for employees is now common practice in the UK. Some schemes are contributory, that is the cost is shared by both employees and employer, while others are non-contributory, that is the whole cost falls on the employer. In either case the cost to the employer may be both substantial and difficult to determine, but the legal disclosure requirements are minimal and, in the past, accounting practice was rudimentary. The publication of SSAP 24, 'Accounting for pension costs', in 1988 represented an important development in that it sought to fill a large hole in the accounts of many companies.

In order to understand accounting for pensions it is necessary to know something about pension schemes.

One distinction which may be made between pension schemes is whether they are funded or unfunded. In the case of the funded scheme, contributions are paid into a separate fund which is usually administered by trustees, who invest the contributions and meet the pension commitments. The contributions are invested in a portfolio of property and/or securities either directly or indirectly by the purchase of insurance policies. In unfunded schemes contributions are not placed in a separate fund but are reinvested in the employer's business and pensions are subsequently paid on a 'pay-as-you-go' basis. An unfunded pension scheme is obviously the more risky from the point of view of the employees and the vast majority of pension schemes in the UK are funded.

Another distinction which needs to be made is between 'defined contribution' schemes and 'defined benefit' schemes.

Under defined contribution schemes the contributions are determined and the employees receive pensions on the basis of whatever amounts are available from those contributions and the returns earned from their investment. Such a scheme poses few problems for the accountant. As the contributions are fixed the amount to be charged as the cost of providing pensions is clearly determinable as the amount payable by the employer in respect of a particular year.

Under a defined benefit scheme the retirement benefits are determined, sometimes on the basis of average salary over the employee's period of service but more often on the basis of salary in the final year or years before retirement. For such a scheme the cost of pensions in a particular year is much more difficult to determine. It depends not upon the contribution payable in respect of a year but upon the pensions which will be paid in the future. The pensions payable depend on such factors as the future rate of increase in wages and salaries, the number of staff leaving the scheme before retirement and the life expectancy of pensioners and, where relevant, their dependants. In addition the cost in the year of providing future pensions depends upon the rate of return to be earned on contributions and reinvested receipts. It is the need to take a very long-term view in the face of great uncertainties which makes accounting for defined benefit schemes such a difficult problem for the accountant.

Fortunately for employees, but unfortunately for accountants, most UK pension schemes, certainly those of major employers, are of the defined benefit variety. We will first examine how the costs of these schemes are estimated.

Defined benefit schemes – actuarial consideration

Given the long-term nature of pension schemes, it is necessary to involve actuaries in the calculation of the costs of defined benefit schemes. Most schemes are subject to a formal actuarial review every three years. The task of the actuary is to assess the level of contribution required to fund the estimated pension payments.

There are a number of different methods that are used by actuaries which, in general, share a common aim of finding a level contribution rate, as a proportion of pensionable pay, which, if the actuary's assumptions are correct, would ensure that the pension fund would be sufficient to pay the pensions as they fall due. Suppose for example, that we have a new pension scheme which has one employee, aged 41, due to retire in 24 years time at 65 and with a life expectancy thereafter of 15 years.

The actuarial calculations might proceed as follows:

> Present salary   £20 000
> Assume, that his or her salary will increase by 6% per year.
> Hence, salary on retirement = £20 000 $(1.06)^{24} \simeq$ £81 000

If on retirement a pension of half final salary is payable, the fund will require to be sufficient to pay £40 500 per annum for 15 years. Assuming, for simplicity that the pension contribution is paid at the end of each year and that the assets in the fund will earn 8 per cent per annum for that period, the capital value of the fund at retirement age will need to be £346 660.

Assume, that in the period until retirement, the annual return on investments is 7 per cent. Then 13 per cent of the staff members' salary will need to be paid into the fund.[11]

Two approaches are mentioned in SSAP 24[12] – *the accrued benefits* and *prospective benefits* methods. In broad terms, accrued benefits methods are based on the assumption that the flow of new entrants to the scheme will be such as to preserve the existing average age of the workforce. In contrast, prospective benefit methods normally only consider the existing workforce and seek to find a stable contribution rate for that group until the last member retires or leaves. The size of the fund will, hence, tend to be larger in the case of a scheme using a prospective benefit approach because it takes the ageing of the existing workforce into account.

---

11 On the date of retirement the required balance on the fund x is given by:

$$x = £40\ 500 \sum_{j=1}^{15} (1.08)^{-j} = £346\ 660$$

Let y be the required fraction of the annual salary which needs to be paid in the fund then

$$£346\ 660 = y\ £20\ 000 \sum_{j=1}^{24} (1.06)^{j}\ (1.07)^{24-j}$$

from which $y = 0.13$.

12 Other methods will be found in a paper published jointly by the ICAEW and the Faculty of Actuaries in May 1986, *Pension Fund Terminology: specimen descriptions of commonly used valuation methods.*

The accounting principles underlying SSAP 24

Prior to the adoption of SSAP 24 many companies simply showed their contribution to the pension scheme as the pension cost for the period. The contribution may have been affected by factors other than those relating solely to the needs of the fund. Employers might, for example, increase the contribution for a year, or for a limited period with a view to reducing contributions in the future. Conversely, employers have in periods of financial stringency reduced their contributions. Such actions may have been effective in achieving the desired ability to manipulate the levels of reported profit, but they did little to help users of accounts assess the total costs of employment for the period.

The accounting objective set by SSAP 24 is to require employing companies to recognise the cost of providing pensions on a systematic and rational basis over the period in which they benefit from the services of their employees. This cost may well not be equal to the contribution made to the pension scheme in any period.[13]

Thus, in a very simple world the actuary's task is to estimate what proportion of pensionable pay would be needed to be paid into the scheme each year to pay for the pensions and the whole of this (in the case of a non-contributory scheme) or a part of this (in a contributory scheme) would represent the cost to the employer. This cost can be regarded as the regular pension cost.

But we do not live in such a state of simplicity and both the world and employers change their minds. The world changes its mind through altered interest rates, changes in the level of earnings and by allowing people to die other than when predicted by the actuary. Employers can also change their minds (or have their minds changed for them) and vary the conditions under which pensions are paid.

Thus, there will be variations to the regular cost and a large part of SSAP 24 is devoted to discussing how to account for these variations. Variations from the regular cost may be due to the following:

(a) Experience surpluses or deficiencies – the results of the world not being as the actuary expected it to be when he or she last worked out the regular cost.
(b) Changes in actuarial assumptions and methods and retroactive changes in benefits or conditions of membership.
(c) Discretionary pensions increases.

Experience surpluses or deficiencies

Suppose that the regular cost had been estimated at 18 per cent of pensionable pay but, because the interest earned on the fund's investments had been lower than expected and the rate of wage increase higher, it might be found that the rate should have been 20 per cent. The actuary will no doubt take these changes into account when estimating the regular costs for the future but we have also to consider how to deal with the shortfall, i.e. the experience deficit.

Should it be charged to the past, by making a prior year adjustment, charged to the profit and loss account in the year it is discovered or charged to the future?

SSAP 24 specifies that with certain exceptions, to which we will refer later, material experience deficits, and surpluses, should be dealt with by adjusting current and future

---

13 Since tax relief is based on the contributions paid to the scheme the difference has deferred tax implications, *see* Chapter 7.

costs and not by immediately expensing (or crediting) the amount. In accordance with the main accounting objective of SSAP 24, the normal period over which the effect of the deficiency or surplus should be spread is the expected remaining service life of the current employees in the scheme after making suitable allowances for future withdrawals, or the average remaining service lives of the current membership. There are three exceptions to the general rule:

(a) Where there is a significant reduction in the number of employees covered by the scheme (*see below*).
(b) Where prudence requires a material deficiency to be made up over a shorter period. This exception is strictly limited to cases where a significant additional payment has to be paid into the scheme arising from a major transaction or event outside the actuarial assumptions and normal running of the scheme; a possible example is the consequence of a major mismanagement of the assets of the pension scheme. The standard does not specify the period over which the additional charge should be spread; it merely allows a shorter period than would otherwise be required.
(c) Where a refund is made to employers subject to deduction of tax within the provisions of the Finance Act 1986, or similar legislation. In such cases the employer may (not must) depart from the normal spreading rule and recognise the refund in the period in which it occurs.

The exception arising from a significant reduction of employees merits further comment. There have been many instances in recent years where reorganisation schemes have resulted in significant redundancies. These have often led to large surpluses on the pension funds with a result that future contributions are reduced, eliminated for a period (a 'contribution holiday') or contributions refunded.

In such instances the benefit should not be spread over the lives of the remaining workforce but instead recognised in the periods in which the benefits are received. They should, in general, not be anticipated in the sense of taking credit immediately the facts are known, but recognised on a year-by-year basis. But to this rule there is an exception, where the redundancies are related to a sale or termination of an operation, for in such a case FRS 3 'Reporting Financial Performance' must be followed. (SSAP 24, which of course predates FRS 3, refers to SSAP 6 in this context.) It may not be appropriate to defer recognition of a pension cost or credit because FRS 3 requires that provisions relating to the sale or termination of an operation be made after taking into account future profits of the operation or on the disposal of the assets.

The following example serves as a summary of the above and illustrates the variations between the contributions made to the scheme and the costs of pensions charged to the profit and loss account.

EXAMPLE 5.1

Slick Limited is a small company which established a non-contributory defined benefit funded scheme in 19X1. Its year end is 31 December.

For arithmetical simplicity we will assume that the annual pensionable salary bill was £1 000 000 before the reorganisation referred to in paragraph C below and £600 000 thereafter.

A   On the inception of the fund in 19X1 the actuary estimated that a contribution rate of 20 per cent on pensionable salaries would be required.

19X1–19X3
The charge to the profit and loss account will equal the contribution paid to the fund in each year, that is 20 per cent of £1 000 000 = £200 000.

B   At the first triennial actuarial valuation in 19X4 the regular cost was estimated to be 21 per cent. There was at that stage an experience deficit of £75 000 which was paid into the fund by the employer in 19X4. The average remaining service life of the employees at that date was 15 years.
   The position for each of the years 19X4–19X6 will be as follows:

19X4	£	£
Charge to profit and loss account		
Regular cost: 21% of 1 000 000		210 000
Experience deficit spread over 15 years		
£75 000 ÷ 15		5 000
Amount paid to fund		
21% of 1 000 000	210 000	
Experience deficit	75 000	
	285 000	215 000
Prepayment at 31 December 19X4		70 000
	285 000	285 000

19X5	£	£
Prepayment at 1 January 19X5	70 000	
Charge to profit and loss account –		
as above		215 000
Amount paid to fund – regular cost –		
21% = 1 000 000	210 000	
	280 000	215 000
Prepayment at 31 December 19X5		65 000
	280 000	280 000

19X6	£	£
Prepayment at 1 January 19X6	65 000	
Charge to profit and loss account –		
as above		215 000
Amount paid to fund – regular cost –		
as above	210 000	
	275 000	215 000
Prepayment at 31 December 19X6		60 000
	275 000	275 000

C   The next valuation took place in 19X7, a year in which the company undertook a major reorganisation involving a substantial number of redundancies.
   The surplus resulting from redundancies was estimated to be £200 000 which is to be recouped by a reduction of £50 000 in the contributions otherwise payable for each of the

four years 19X7–19Y0. We shall assume that this event constitutes a 'sale or termination' of an operation as defined in FRS 3.

In addition there was an experience surplus of £56 000 arising from events other than the reorganisation. The remaining average service life of the employees was 14 years.

The regular cost is estimated to be 18 per cent of £600 000 and the experience surplus of £56 000 is to be deducted in arriving at the 19X8 (not 19X7) payment.

For each of the years 19X7–19X9 the accounting treatment will be as follows:

19X7	£	£	£
Prepayment at 1 January 19X7		60 000	
Charge to profit and loss account in respect of regular cost and experience deficit/surplus.			
Regular cost – 18% x 600 000	108 000		
add 19X4 experience deficit			
75 000 ÷ 15	5 000		
	113 000		
less 19X7 experience surplus			
56 000 ÷ 14	4 000		109 000
Credit to profit and loss account in respect of surplus on termination		200 000	
Amount paid to fund			
18% x 600 000	108 000		
Reduction in respect of surplus on termination	50 000	58 000	
		318 000	109 000
Prepayment at 31 December 19X7			209 000
		318 000	318 000

19X8	£	£	£
Prepayment at 1 January 19X8		209 000	
Charge to profit and loss account			
– as above			109 000
Amount paid to fund – as above	58 000		
less Experience surplus	56 000	2 000	
		211 000	109 000
Prepayment at 31 December 19X8			102 000
		211 000	211 000

19X9		£	£
Prepayment at 1 January 19X9		102 000	
Charge to profit and loss account			
– as above			109 000
Amount paid to fund – as 19X7		58 000	
		160 000	109 000
Prepayment at 31 December 19X9			51 000
		160 000	160 000

The above may be summarised as follows:

	Profit & loss account expense	Cash payment	Balance sheet prepayment at year end
	£000	£000	£000
A 19X1–19X3			
19X1	200	200	–
19X2	200	200	–
19X3	200	200	–
B 19X4–19X6			
19X4	215	285	70
19X5	215	210	65
19X6	215	210	60
C 19X7–19X9			
19X7 Ordinary	109 ⎱	58	209
Extraordinary	(200) ⎰		
19X8	109	2	102
19X9	109	58	51

The prepayment at 31 December 19X9 may be analysed as follows:

	£
19X4 Experience deficit 9/15 x £75 000	45 000
19X7 Experience surplus 11/14 x £56 000	(44 000)
	1 000
19X7 Surplus on reorganisation £200 000 – £(3 x 50 000)	50 000
	51 000

Note
The deferred tax implications have been ignored.

Changes in actuarial assumptions and methods and retroactive changes to the scheme

The effect of changes in the assumptions and methods used by the actuary should be treated in the same way as experience deficits and surpluses – they should be spread over the period of the expected remaining service lives of the current employees.

The same rule should be applied if there are retroactive changes in benefits and membership. Such changes, often called past service costs, may give improved benefits, e.g. increasing the proportion of final salary which will be paid as pension, or give employees credit for periods of service before they joined the scheme.

In some cases a surplus on a pension fund may be used to improve benefits and if, as a result, a provision which the company had made in its own accounts is no longer necessary, that provision should be released over the estimated remaining service life of the current employees.

Discretionary pension increases

A pension scheme might allow for pension increases within its rules, in which case they will be taken into account in the actuarial calculations, as should any increases required by legislation.

Other increases are discretionary on the part of the employer, whether paid direct or through the pension scheme. If such increases are granted on a regular basis, SSAP 24 states that the preferred treatment is to allow for them in the actuarial calculations. If this is not done, the full capital value of the increase should be provided in the year in which it is granted, not in the years in which it is paid, to the extent to which the increase is not covered by the surplus on the fund.

The same procedure should be followed in the case of an *ex gratia* pension granted to an employee on retirement, such as a long-serving member of staff who for some reason has not been a member of the scheme. Thus, for example, if it is estimated that the amount which would need to be invested to produce the desired pension at the estimated rates of interest is £400 000 then that amount should be charged to the profit and loss account in the year of retirement.

A non-recurring increase which is granted for one period only with no expectation of repetition should be charged to the period in which it is paid to the extent that it is not covered by a surplus.

We have now completed our main discussion of the accounting principles underlying SSAP 24, but we will deal with a number of related issues before turning to disclosure.

Related issues

The effect of discounting

The statement points out that financial statements normally show items at their face value without discounting, but by their very nature actuarial assumptions do make allowances for interest so that future cash flows are discounted to their present values. The statement points out that the question of whether items should be discounted in financial statements is a general one and on this general issue SSAP 24 should not be regarded as establishing standard practice.

In the special case of unfunded schemes the question of discounting cannot be avoided. The annual charge for pensions in any unfunded scheme is made up of two elements: the charge for the year (which is equivalent to the contribution to a funded scheme) plus interest on the unfunded liability. In an unfunded scheme the assets to support the pension are retained within the business and the latter element represents the return on those investments.

Group schemes

It is common for a number of companies in a group to use a single group scheme in which it is accepted that a common contribution rate can be used, even if when calculated company by company different rates would emerge. The standard allows this practice to continue and for lesser disclosure in the case of subsidiary companies, although full details have to be provided in the accounts of the holding company.

Foreign schemes

In principle all pension costs should be accounted for in accordance with the standard and hence consolidation adjustments may be required in the case of overseas subsidiaries. However, where countries overseas have very different pension laws or where the cost of making the necessary actuarial calculations is excessive, the contributions to the relevant overseas scheme can be treated as the costs for the period.

Scope

The standard is not restricted to instances where employers have a legal or contractual commitment to pay pensions; it also covers cases where the employers implicitly, through their actions, provide or contribute to employees' pensions.

Disclosure requirements

The main accounting principle is fairly straightforward. Estimate the regular cost and, subject to certain exceptions, spread the cost or benefit from variations over the remaining service lives of the current employees.

Given the uncertain nature of the estimates that are involved and the length of the time period over which they have to be made, it is not surprising that the standard requires extensive disclosure of surpluses or deficiencies in respect of defined benefit schemes, just stopping short of asking for the colour of the actuary's eyes.

It would not be helpful to repeat the requirements here but they can be summarised as follows:

(a) Nature of the scheme.
(b) Accounting and funding policies.
(c) Date of last actuarial review and status of the actuary; i.e. whether or not an officer of the company.
(d) The pension cost for the period, together with an explanation of significant changes compared with the previous period, and any provisions or prepayments included in the balance sheet.
(e) The amount of any deficiency and action, if any, being taken in consequence.
(f) Details of the last formal valuation or review of the scheme including:
    (i) actuarial method used and main actuarial assumptions;
    (ii) market value of the assets;
    (iii) level of funding expressed in percentage terms of the benefits accrued by members and comments on any material surpluses or deficiency so revealed.
(g) Details of any commitments to make additional payments and the effect of any material changes in the company's pension arrangements.

An appendix to the standard provides some useful hypothetical examples of what might be disclosed by different types of companies but, a little surprisingly, does not provide an example of an unfunded scheme.

SSAP 24 – concluding comments

The cost of pensions is significant and in the past, because of the lack of legislative and professional rules, was open to manipulation by companies who wished to smooth their reported profits as, for example, larger contributions could be made in good years than in bad.

SSAP 24 has led to the reduction in the range of methods used in practice and has gone a considerable way in ensuring that users of accounts are provided with a 'systematic' and 'rational' view of the cost of providing for pensions.

PENSION SCHEME ACCOUNTS

In the previous sections, we have considered the measurement of pension costs and the disclosure of pension information in the accounts of an employer. A related, although somewhat different, problem is the form and content of the accounts of the pension scheme and the ASC issued a Statement of Recommended Practice on this topic.[14] This is too specialised a topic for a general textbook on advanced financial accounting but, for completeness, we have decided to include a very brief summary of the statement.

Reporting by pension schemes is largely governed by trust law and, at the time of writing, no statutory framework for such reporting exists. The result is that considerable variety is found in the reports issued by different pension schemes and the quality of some of these reports leaves much to be desired.

The statement recommends that the annual report of a pension scheme should comprise four elements:

(a) A trustees' report covering such matters as membership statistics, changes in benefits, financial growth of the scheme, the actuarial position and the investment policy and performance.
(b) Accounts designed to give a true and fair view of the financial transactions of the accounting period and a statement of the assets and liabilities at the accounting date.
(c) An actuarial report by a qualified actuary on the ability of the pension fund to meet accrued benefits.
(d) An investment report giving additional detail on investments, investment policy and performance.

Both the accounts under (b) and the actuarial report under (c) are prepared by experts and both are necessary for members and employers to appreciate the position of the pension scheme. Clearly, the ASC has no authority to regulate the contents of the actuary's report so the statement concentrates on the accounts.

It is recommended that the accounts comprise:

(a) a revenue account which records the financial inflows and outflows of the fund;
(b) a net assets statement which discloses the size and disposition of the net assets;
(c) a reconciliation of the movement in the net assets to the revenue account.

---

14 SORP: 'Pension scheme accounts' , ASC, London, May 1986.

Part 4 of the statement provides a detailed list of items which should be included in the accounts.

The statement recommends the use of the accruals basis of accounting but also recommends the inclusion of assets at their current values. Needless to say, it also recommends that the accounts include a statement of all significant accounting policies.

Readers who wish to study this topic in greater detail are referred to the SORP.

RECOMMENDED READING

Excellent up-to-date and detailed reading on the subject matter of this chapter is provided by the most recent edition of:

UK GAAP, Principal authors and editors Mike Davies, Ron Paterson and Allister Wilson, Ernst and Young, Longman, London.

More specialised reading includes the following:

A. T. Cabourne-Smith, 'Accounting for post balance sheet events', *Accountants Digest No. 101*, ICAEW, London, 1981.

A. T. Cabourne-Smith and R. L. Cohen, 'Accounting for Contingencies', *Accountants Digest No. 113*, ICAEW, London, 1981/2.

R. Macve, 'Accounting for Long-term Loans', in *External Financial Reporting*, Bryan Carsberg and Susan Dev (eds), Prentice-Hall, London, 1984.

C. J. Napier, *Accounting for the Cost of Pensions*, ICAEW, London, 1983.

J. M. Young and N. J. C. Buchanan, *Accounting for Pensions*, Woodhead-Faulkner, Cambridge, 1981.

P. G. C. Carne and P. P. E. Ogwuazor, 'Accounting for pension costs', *Accountants Digest No. 237*, ICAEW, London, Winter 1989/90.

CHAPTER 6

Financial statements – form and content

In this chapter we will deal with two comparatively recent developments in accounting practice which relate to the way in which financial statements are presented and the tests which should be applied in deciding what should be included in them. In the first section of the chapter we will concentrate on changes to financial position, the profit and loss account, statement of total recognised gains and losses and the reconciliation of movements of reserves and, in particular, the attempts of standard setters to make these statements more informative to users. In the second section we will shift our attention to the balance sheet and discuss issues relating to the recognition of assets and liabilities for inclusion in the balance sheet which, of course, will also have an impact on the statements reflecting changes in financial position.

REPORTING FINANCIAL PERFORMANCE

Introduction

Financial statements report on past performance but they are also used as an aid in the prediction of future performance (*see* Chapter 1). Prediction is usually heavily dependent on an extrapolation of the past. Suppose, to take a simplistic example, one wants to predict future profits in order to place a value on a business. The obvious starting point is the current level of profit and recent rates of growth (or decline). Suppose the current profit is £M3.0 and growth has been on average 3 per cent per year over the recent past, the predictor would start by thinking whether the growth rate is likely to continue into the future or whether a different rate should be used. But in performing this simple extrapolation the predictor will need to consider the extent to which the future will differ from the past. What proportion, for example, of the company's existing activities will be sustained in the future and what will be eliminated.

The desire to show separately what might be termed continuing and non-recurrent elements of the business resulted in the past in a loss of comparability in that different companies dealt with the issue in different ways. From time to time, abuse occurred because companies attempted to play down the effect of bad decisions by treating the resulting losses as a non-recurring item.

The ASC first dealt with this topic in April 1974 through the issue of SSAP 6 'Extraordinary items and prior adjustments, which was reissued in a revised form in August 1986. SSAP 6 was replaced in 1992 by the more wide ranging FRS 3 'Reporting Financial Performance'.

Extraordinary items and prior adjustments (SSAP 6)

Since FRS 3 is in many respects a development of SSAP 6 it will be useful to briefly summarise SSAP 6 before dealing in more detail with the provisions of the new FRS.

The problem which gave rise to the issue of SSAP 6 was the variety of practice concerning the treatment of income and expenditure which was regarded as being 'non-recurring'. Two extreme positions could be identified. At one extreme all items were passed through the profit and loss account, while at the other extreme any items which could be argued as not relating to the normal activities of the business (non-recurring items) were charged or credited direct to reserves or adjusted against the opening balance of retained profits. The latter method is known as 'reserve accounting'.[1] In practice, most companies adopted a position between the two extremes.

The argument in favour of reserve accounting was that a profit or loss based only on the 'normal activities' of the business gave a fairer indication of the business's maintainable profit. It was suggested that such a profit figure would provide the more useful basis for estimating future profits than the profit resulting from a profit and loss account which included all items irrespective of their nature.

The view of the ASC, as evidenced by the provisions of SSAP 6, was that all revenue items should pass through the profit and loss account. The reasons for this view were as follows:

(a) The inclusion and disclosure of the non-recurring items enables the profit and loss account for the year to give a better view of a company's profitability and progress.
(b) The exclusion of non-recurring items requires the exercise of subjective judgment and may lead to variation in the treatment of similar items and hence to a loss of comparability between the accounts of different companies.
(c) The exclusion of non-recurring items could result in them being overlooked in any review of results over a series of years. Thus, while the nature of the items will, by definition, change, many businesses, especially larger ones, will often have items which are 'non-recurrent' and continually to exclude them from the profit and loss account would result in a distorted view of profit being shown.

The wholly sensible view of the ASC was that the legitimate advantages of reserve accounting could be obtained, without the drawbacks listed above, if adequate disclosure is provided in accounts. In essence SSAP 6 required that all profits and losses recognised in the year should be shown in the profit and loss account. There were, however, two exceptions – prior year adjustments and certain items which, either by law or under the provisions of an accounting standard, were specifically permitted or required to be taken directly to reserves.

While the standard did in general reject the use of reserve accounting it did accept the notion that it is possible, and helpful to users, to distinguish between the results of *ordinary activities* of the business and *extraordinary (non-recurring)* profits and losses. Thus the standard prescribed if there were any extraordinary items, that the following elements should be included in the profit and loss account:

- post-tax profit before extraordinary items;
- extraordinary items (less taxation attributable thereto);
- post-tax profit after extraordinary items.

1 The two approaches are also often described, particularly in the USA, as 'all inclusive income' and 'current operating income', respectively.

In addition items of an abnormal size and incidence but which may be regarded as deriving from the ordinary activities of the business, *exceptional items*, should be disclosed but included in the derivation of the profit before extraordinary items.

The above provisions of SSAP 6 were incorporated into statute law by the Companies Act 1985 but the Act does not attempt to define the various terms, a task left to the standard setters.

FRS 3 'Reporting financial performance'

FRS 3 is based on the same principles as SSAP 6 but includes three important changes.

(a) It provides more precise and more useful definitions of the key terms and in particular limits drastically the circumstances under which an item can be classed as extraordinary.
(b) It puts greater emphasis on reporting the effects of discontinued operations. This has led to a change in the format of the profit and loss accounts of enterprises which have discontinued operations during an accounting period.
(c) It requires the inclusion of three additional elements in the financial statements:
  (i)   a statement of total recognised gains and losses, including the profit or loss for the period together with all other movements on reserves reflecting recognised gains and losses attributable to shareholders.
  (ii) a reconciliation of movements in shareholders' funds bringing together the performance of the period, as shown in the statement of recognised gains and losses, and all other changes in shareholders' funds in the period, including capital contributed by or repaid to shareholders.
  (iii) a note, which would be of relevance to companies which had revalued assets at some stage in their history, reconciling the profit or loss disclosed in the accounts with that figure which would have been disclosed had the company not revalued assets, i.e. the profit based on the strict application of the unmodified historical cost convention.

We will deal with each of these later in the chapter.

As FRS 3 superseded SSAP 6 there were consequential changes in other standards (FRS 3, Para. 33). In most cases the changes merely involved a change in the cross reference from SSAP 6 to FRS 3 but in some standards, notably SSAP 3 'Earnings Per Share' (*see* Chapter 14) and SSAP 12 'Accounting for Depreciation' (*see* Chapter 4), the changes were more fundamental, reflecting FRS 3's more restrictive definition of extraordinary items.

Exceptional and extraordinary items

The key definitions relating to exceptional and extraordinary items provided in FRS 3 are:

Ordinary activities

Any activities which are undertaken by a reporting entity as part of its business and such related activities in which the reporting entity engages in furtherance of, incidental to, or arising from, these activities. Ordinary activities include the effects on the reporting entity of any event in the various environments in which it operates, including the political, regulatory, economic and geographical environments, irrespective of the frequency or unusual nature of the events.

Exceptional items

Material items which derive from events or transactions that fall within the ordinary activities of the reporting entity and which individually or, if of a similar type, in aggregate, need to be disclosed by virtue of their size or incidence if the financial statements are to give a true and fair view.

Extraordinary items

Material items possessing a high degree of abnormality which arise from events or transactions that fall outside the ordinary activities of the reporting entity and which are not expected to recur. They do not include exceptional items nor do they include prior period items merely because they relate to a prior period.

The last sentence of the definition of 'Extraordinary Items', which has to be read a few times to be understood, simply means that an item does not become extraordinary simply because it is recognised in the profit and loss account in a period following the one in which it occurred.

The definition of exceptional activities contained in FRS 3 is much wider than the corresponding definition in SSAP 6. As a consequence the definition of extraordinary items provided in FRS 3 is very much more restricted than the SSAP 6 version with the result that, in the words of the ASB, extraordinary items are now likely to be 'extremely rare' (FRS 3, Para. 48). Because of this FRS 3, unlike SSAP 6, does not provide examples of extraordinary items. An illustration of the extent of the change is one of the examples provided in SSAP 6, the expropriation of assets, which is now regarded as part of the ordinary activities of the business because of the revised definition of that term. Another of the major examples of extraordinary items provided in SSAP 6 is the consequence of the discontinuity of a separate segment of the business which as we will explain below is now treated in an entirely different way.

The question of whether an item should be regarded as exceptional is essentially a matter of judgment related to whether knowledge of the item will provide the users of the financial statement with a clearer picture of the performance of the company. By definition exceptional items must be material but thereafter the recognition of such items depends on size or incidence. The meaning of 'incidence' in this context is not clear, nor is it explained in FRS 3, but it presumably relates to items which lie somewhere between material and large but which will nonetheless have some significance in assessing the maintainable profits of the enterprise. Thus, for example, the profit or loss on the sale or termination of operations of a type which do not satisfy the rather tight conditions for recognition as discontinued operations (*see* page 141) may not be large but may yet be significant in judging the future profitability of the business perhaps because had the operation not been terminated large losses would have been sustained in the future.

Prior period adjustments

These are defined as:

Material adjustments applicable to prior periods arising from changes in accounting policies or from the correction of fundamental errors. They do not include normal recurring adjustments or corrections of accounting estimates made in prior periods.

In some ways it is unfortunate that the ASB did not use a different name for this type of adjustment because as is pointed out in FRS 3 (Para. 60), the vast majority of items relating to prior periods arise from the corrections and adjustments which are the natural result of estimates inherent in periodic financial reporting and are therefore not covered by the definition of prior period adjustment; perhaps a title such as Fundamental Prior Period Adjustment would have been preferable.

The normal run of adjustments relating to prior periods are dealt with in the profit and loss account of the period in which they are identified. They are not exceptional or extraordinary merely because they relate to a prior period, but if their effect is material then they would be disclosed as an exceptional item or, in very rare cases, an extraordinary item.

The explanation to the statement emphasises consistency as a fundamental accounting concept and that a change in accounting policy should therefore be made only when it can be justified that the new policy gives a fairer presentation of the financial position of the reporting company. An adaptation or modification of an accounting basis caused by transactions or events that are clearly different in substance from those which occurred in the past does not give rise to a change of accounting policy and hence does not result in a prior period adjustment (FRS 3, Para. 62).

The second element in the definition of prior period adjustments is the correction of fundamental errors. To be treated as prior period adjustments such errors would need to be of such significance that the financial statements which contained them could not show a true and fair view.

Prior period adjustments – disclosure requirements

Prior period adjustments should be accounted for by adjusting the opening balance of reserves for the cumulative effect of the adjustments and by restating the comparative figures for the preceding period. In addition the cumulative effect of the adjustment should be noted at the foot of the statement of total recognised gains and losses of the current period whilst the effect of the prior period adjustments on the results for the preceding period should be disclosed where practicable (FRS 3, Para. 29).

Reflecting the results of discontinued operations

A company cannot maintain the profits of operations which it no longer carries out, and thus it seems reasonable to ensure that financial statements discriminate clearly between the results which have been achieved by that part of the enterprise which will continue, and the results achieved or losses sustained by those parts of the organisation which had been closed or sold during the course of the year.

In order to achieve this FRS 3 calls for what is, in effect, two profit and loss accounts; one covering those operations which will continue in the future, which includes acquisitions made during the year, and one dealing with any part of the enterprise that was sold or terminated during the course of the year.

The way in which the information is disclosed, whether by way of note or on the face of the profit and loss account, is to a large measure left to the accountant guided by two examples provided in the Appendix to FRS 3. The discretion is not unlimited, however, because as a minimum there should be shown on the face of the profit and loss account analyses of turnover and operating profit as between discontinued and continuing operations.

Adjustments are also required in the comparative figures because only the results of those operations which are regarded as continuing at the year end should be included in the proceeding year's figures for continuing operations. This is an important measure which helps the users of the financial statements to gain a clearer picture of the progress of the company.

One of the two illustrations provided in the standard is reproduced below:

	Continuing operations		Discontinued operations	Total	Total
	Acquisitions				
	1993	1993	1993	1993	1992 as restated
	£ million	£ million	£ million	£ million	£ million
Turnover	550	50	175	775	690
Cost of sales	(415)	(40)	(165)	(620)	(555)
Gross profit	135	10	10	155	135
Net operating expenses	(85)	(4)	(25)	(114)	(83)
Less 1992 provision			10	10	
Operating profit	50	6	(5)	51	52
Profit on sale of properties	9			9	6
Provision for loss on operations to be discontinued					(30)
Loss on disposal of discontinued operations			(17)	(17)	
Less 1992 provision			20	20	
Profit on ordinary activities before interest	59	6	(2)	63	28
Interest payable				(18)	(15)
Profit on ordinary activities before taxation				45	13
Tax on profit on ordinary activities				(14)	(4)
Profit on ordinary activities after taxation				31	9
Minority interests				(2)	(2)
[Profit before extraordinary items]				29	7
[Extraordinary items] (included only to show positioning)				–	–
Profit for the financial year				29	7
Dividends				(8)	(1)
Retained profit for the financial year				21	6

Earnings per share	39p	10p
Adjustments	xp	xp
[to be itemised and an adequate description to be given]		
Adjusted earnings per share	yp	yp

[Reason for calculating the adjusted earnings per share to be given]

Required Note:	1993			1992 (as restated)		
	Continuing	Dis-continued	Total	Continuing	Dis-continued	Total
	£ million	£ million	£ million	£ million	£ million	£ million
Turnover				500	190	690
Cost of sales				385	170	555
Net operating expenses						
Distribution costs	56	13	69	46	5	51
Administrative expenses	41	12	53	34	3	37
Other operating income	(8)	0	(8)	(5)	0	(5)
	89	25	114	75	8	83
Operating profit				40	12	52

The total figure of net operating expenses for continuing operations in 1993 includes £4 million in respect of acqusitions (namely distribution costs £3 million, administrative expenses £3 million and other operating income £2 million).

What constitutes discontinuity?

FRS 3 defines discontinued operations in the following way:

Discontinued operations
Operations of the reporting entity that are sold or terminated and that satisfy all of the following conditions.

(a) The sale or termination is completed either in the period or before the earlier of three months after the commencement of the subsequent period and the date on which the financial statements are approved.
(b) If a termination, the former activities have ceased permanently.
(c) The sale or termination has a material effect on the nature and focus of the reporting entity's operations and represents a material reduction in its operating facilities resulting either from its withdrawal from a particular market (whether class of business or geographical) or from a material reduction in turnover in the reporting entity's continuing markets.
(d) The assets, liabilities, results of operations and activities are clearly distinguishable, physically, operationally and for financial reporting purposes.

Operations not satisfying all these conditions are classified as continuing.

The objective of FRS 3 is clearly laudable in attempting to help users extrapolate past results into the future but the drawing of a distinction between continuing and discontinued operations is clearly open to abuse. Most businesses continually modify their range of operations; some product lines or activities will be dropped in the course of the year and these will usually be those which are less successful. Hence, if there were no limits on what could be designated as discontinued operations a business could make the 'continuing operations' part of the profit and loss account look very healthy by shunting the results of all abandoned product lines or activities into the discontinued operations section.

In order to prevent, or rather minimise, the opportunity for whitewashing the profit and loss account in this way the ASB has laid down a reasonably rigorous definition of what constitutes discontinuity. As can be seen above there are four tests all of which must be satisfied. The first two tests are fairly clear; the discontinuity must either be completed in the year or within three months of the balance sheet date, or even earlier if the date of approval of the financial statements is within that three-month period. Also, the termination must be permanent and not a temporary withdrawal from a particular market. Condition (d) is also reasonably straightforward. It requires that the 'operation' must have constituted a distinct chunk of the business in operation, physical and financial terms. Further elaboration of that point is provided in Paragraph 44 of the standard. To satisfy the condition, the operation must have been a revenue and cost centre to which all material items of revenue and costs were specifically assigned or, to put it another way, one where only a very small reliance had to be placed on the allocation of joint costs and revenues.

Paragraph (c) of the definition requires that the sale or termination must have had a material effect on the nature and focus of the enterprise but this does seem to beg the question of what is meant by the focus of the reporting entity's operations. The ASB goes some way to answering the question in so far that it states 'the nature and focus of the reporting entity's operations refers to the position of its products or services in their markets including the aspects of both quality and location' (FRS 3, Para. 42).

An example is given of a hotel company which sells its existing chains of hotels which operate at the cheaper end of the market and then buys a chain of luxury hotels. This, it is stated, can be regarded as 'changing its focus' and hence the sale could be treated as a discontinued operation even though the company stays in the hotel business. Similarly a sale of all its hotels in one country might also be regarded as a discontinuity even if, as a result, hotels are purchased in another country.

Two points need to be made about this example. The first relates to the use of the term 'chain' which implies that the hotels were operated as an identifiable group which was sold in its entirety. The sale of only the cheap hotels in a chain which were operated under the same name as the remaining luxury hotels and which shared common services would probably not satisfy the 'separateness' tests specified in paragraph (d).

The second point is that paragraph (c) requires that for the sale to be treated as a discontinuity it must represent 'a material reduction in its operating facilities resulting either from its withdrawal from a particular market (whether class of business or geographical) or from a material reduction in turnover in the reporting entity's continuing markets' (FRS 3, Para. 4c).

There is, perhaps, an ambiguity here. Can the sale be treated as a discontinuity if the material reduction in operating facilities in one market is replaced by an equivalent increase in another market? The example provided in paragraph 42 suggests that it can but this is not clear from the wording of paragraph (c) of the definition which places stress on the 'material reduction in operating facilities'. In reviewing the standard the ASB might consider revising its definition to make it clear that a change in the style of operation which does not materially affect the totality of operating facilities can still be treated as a discontinuity for the purposes of the standard.

Acquisitions

In estimating future results account needs to be taken of the effect of any acquisitions made during the year. Normally (the exception being the use of the merger method of consolidation) only post-acquisition results will be included in the profit and loss account but the user of the accounts will want to know the full year results of the company acquired. The Companies Act 1985 (Schedule 4A, Para. 13) requires that information relating to the profit or loss of any group or company acquired from the start of the financial year of the acquired undertaking to its date of acquisition should be shown in a note to the financial statement. The note must also state the date of the start of the financial year of the acquired undertaking and provide information relating to the previous accounting period.

The additional requirements of FRS 3 are, that there should be shown:

(a) on the face of the profit and loss account; analyses between continuing operations, acquisitions and discontinued operations of turnover and operating profit;
(b) on the face of the profit and loss account or in the notes; a similar threefold analysis of each of the statutory profit and loss format items between turnover and operating profit.

Acquisitions are shown as part of continuing operations except when an operation is both acquired and discontinued in the course of the year; then it should be treated as discontinued.

If it is not possible to determine the post-acquisition results of the new operation, then either an indication of the contribution of the acquired operation to turnover and operating profit should be disclosed or, if that is not possible, an explanation should be provided of the reasons for the company's inability to provide the information.

What should be included in the results of discontinued operations?

If an operation is sold or terminated in a year then two elements of profit or loss arise. One is the trading profit or loss to the date of termination, the other is the profit or loss on the disposal of the assets constituting the operation. FRS 3 provides that both should be included in the determination of the profit or loss on ordinary activities before taxation, albeit separately identified. This is in contrast to the provisions of SSAP 6 whereby profits or losses on the sale of a business segment were treated as extraordinary items and hence shown after the derivation of profit or loss on ordinary activities.

One of the members of the ASB, Robert Bradfield, did not vote for the adoption of the standard and one of his reasons for this explained in his dissenting view (published alongside the standard) was the inclusion of profits or losses on the disposal of operations in the figure for pre-tax profit. Bradfield believed that the Standard placed undue emphasis on the pre-tax profit figure which may be misleading if it includes the profits or losses on disposal especially as the tax effects, as allowed by FRS 3, are only shown in the notes (*see* page 145). The view of the majority of the members of the ASB, expressed in the section of the Standard entitled 'A development of the Standard' is that the FRS 3 approach does not place emphasis on a single number because the admittedly complex presentation is based on a 'information set' approach that highlights a range of important components of performance. However, if a single measure of performance is to be used, for example, in calculating earnings per share then it should be based on its 'all-inclusive' concept which avoids the inconsistencies which were experienced in the application of SSAP 6.

Provision for future losses

There is a great temptation to say that if the company has to take its medicine then it should drink deeply of it. Thus if the company decides that it should either eliminate entirely or reduce extensively its loss-making operations in, say, the United States, the announcement will have an adverse effect on share prices and there would be less confidence in the company's future; a confidence which the company will want to restore as quickly as possible. One way of helping to restore confidence quickly may be to lump as much of the loss into the 'bad news' year as possible and to relieve future years of the burdens of those losses.

To provide for everything in sight, and possibly just a wee bit more, may well be prudent but it is likely to be exceedingly misleading.

Consider the following two series of numbers.

Results (£M)

| | Year | | | | | |
	1	2	3	4	5	Total
A	L10	L2	–	P2	P4	L6
B	L16	P1	P2	P3	P4	L6

(L = Loss P = Profit)

To oversimplify, let us suppose that series A represents the 'truth' but B represents the results of the company if an excess provision of £6M is made in the 'bad news' year, year one. The 'prudent' approach under B suggests that the company is immediately restored to profit in the year two and then makes steady growth whilst in fact the 'true' position is that profit is not restored until year four but that the real rate of improvement is then higher than is shown by the prudent approach.

Now let us see how this matter is dealt with in FRS 3, remembering that in accordance with normal practice any permanent diminution in asset values should be recorded. The essential point of FRS 3 (Para. 18) is that provisions should be made for the direct cost of sale or termination and any operating losses of the operation up to the future date of sale or termination (after in each case taking account of related profits) *if and only if* there exists a binding sale agreement or the company is demonstrably committed to the sale or termination because, for example, the action is covered by detailed formal plans from which the company cannot realistically withdraw.

The provision would be included as part of discontinued operations only if the related event qualifies as a discontinuity. Note that the conditions for discontinuity and the condition precedent for making a provision are different and that provisions can be made for operations which are for the purposes of FRS 3 treated as continuing.

When in the subsequent period the operation is actually closed, its results for that period should not be lumped together but shown under the statutory format headings, but there also needs to be full disclosure on the face of the profit and loss account showing the way in which the provisions made in prior years have been utilised, indicating how much has been used to cover operating losses and how much to cover the loss on sale or termination of the discontinued operation.

Taxation

In deciding how taxation should be disclosed the ASB had before it two main options. One was to relate the tax charge on the face of the profit and loss account to its basic elements, for example continuing and discontinuing operations, and extraordinary and exceptional items, and to show the total tax charge by way of a note. The alternative was to show the total tax charge on the face of the accounts and provide the analysis in the notes. By and large, with the exception of extraordinary items, the ASB adopted the latter approach.

The disclosure provisions are of both a general and specific nature. The general elements of the Standard (Para. 23) are:

(a) Any special circumstances that affect the overall tax charge or credit for the period, or that may affect those of the future periods, should be disclosed by way of a note to the profit and loss account and their individual effects quantified.

(b) The effects of a fundamental change in the basis of taxation should be included in the tax charge or credit for the period and separately disclosed on the face of the profit and loss account.

In addition there are specific disclosure provisions relating to:

(a) Profits or losses on the sale or termination of an operation.
(b) Costs of fundamental reorganisation or restructuring:
(c) Profits or losses on the disposal of fixed assets.

In each case relevant information should be provided in the notes showing their effect on the tax charge.

Taxation and extraordinary items

FRS 3 provides (Para. 22) that the tax on extraordinary items should be shown separately as a part of the extraordinary profit or loss either on the face of the profit and loss account or in a note. Any subsequent adjustments to the tax on extraordinary profit or loss should also be shown as extraordinary items.

A dissenting view

We have already referred to the dissenting view of Robert Bradfield. One of the major elements of Bradfield's opposition to the provision of FRS 3 was his belief that users of accounts would not fully appreciate the taxation effect on the trading results attributable to shareholders (he made a similar point relating to minority interest). As an example Bradfield quotes the case of an international group of companies where the pre-tax trading profits in a low tax regime fell and those in a high tax regime increased by an identical amount. Such a change would leave the shareholder materially worse off but this would be masked in FRS 3.

The point is a good one and needs further consideration. This needs to be conducted in the light of a broader consideration relating to the reaction of shareholders and other users of accounts to the far more complex structure of financial statements that are appearing as a result of FRS 3. A particular issue is the balance between the information disclosed on the face of the accounts and in the notes to the accounts.

Minority interests

In the case of consolidated financial statements the information disclosure requirements for minority interests are very similar to those for taxation. The effect of three specific items referred to above (the termination of an operation, the fundamental reorganisation of operations and the profit or loss on disposal of fixed assets) on minority interests should be noted. If there are any extraordinary items which affect minority interests then the extent of the extraordinary profit and loss attributable to minority shareholders should be shown separately as a part of the extraordinary item either on the face of the profit and loss account or in a note.

The statement of total recognised gains and losses

One of the confusing aspects, especially so for the layman, of pre-FRS 3 traditional accounting was the ambiguity surrounding the treatment of gains and losses which were thought sufficiently significant to be allowed to have an impact on the balance sheet but yet were not reflected in the profit and loss account, and were instead dealt with by direct transfer to and from reserves. A good example of this type of transaction was the unrealised surplus on the revaluation of assets.

The traditional profit and loss account is based on a 'narrow concept' of realisation (*see* page 66) which treats as profits only those gains which have resulted in the receipt of cash or the acquisition of assets which are reasonably certain to be turned into cash. Unrealised gains are shunted into reserves (because of the prudence convention anticipated losses are generally taken to the profit and loss account) and are reported as part of the movement of reserves, a statement whose significance is not readily appreciated by many users of financial statements.

FRS 3 does not fundamentally challenge the narrow concept of realisation but in drafting the standard the ASB emphasises that gains and losses may be excluded from the profit and loss account only if they are specifically permitted or required to be taken to reserves by an accounting standard or, in the absence of a relevant accounting standard, by law (Para. 37). However, even with this stipulation the ASB believes that an incomplete impression of the company's financial performance would be obtained if attention was directed exclusively to the profit and loss account.

Accordingly FRS 3 requires that companies publish an additional primary statement, which should be presented with the same prominence as the other primary statements, the 'Statement of Total Recognised Gains and Losses', which should show the total of recognised gains and losses in so far as they are attributable to shareholders. (Note that the immediate write-off to reserves of purchased goodwill is not a recognised loss; see SSAP 22 'Accounting for Goodwill', Paras 6 and 7.)

The illustration in FRS 3 of this statement is shown below:

Statement of total recognised gains and losses	1993	1992 as restated
	£ million	£ million
Profit for the financial year	29	7
Unrealised surplus on revaluation of properties	4	6
Unrealised (loss)/gain on trade investment	(3)	7
	30	20
Currency translation differences on foreign currency net investments	(2)	5
Total recognised gains and losses relating to the year	28	25
Prior year adjustment	(10)	
Total gains and losses recognised since last annual report	18	

It is, perhaps, worth making the obvious point that gains and losses should not be double counted. Hence, a gain which was previously recorded as unrealised should not be recognised again in the period in which it is realised. For example, the realisation of a profit on the sale of a previously revalued fixed asset would be reflected in the statement of the movement of reserves, where it would appear as a transfer from the revaluation reserve to the profit and loss account.

The prominence given to the statement of total recognised gains and losses is an example of the 'information set' approach which the ASB hopes will divert the focus of attention from the single 'bottom line' figure of profit for the period.

Two additional notes

Reconciliation of movements in shareholders' funds (Para. 28)

The profit or loss for the period together with any recognised gains or losses not reflected in the profit and loss account measures the performance of the company during the period but there are other changes in shareholders' funds which affect the company's financial position, notably the declaration of dividends and the injection and withdrawal of capital. FRS 3 hence requires the publication of an additional note reconciling the opening and closing balance of shareholders' funds.

With the present state of the art associated with the treatment of goodwill as reflected in SSAP 22, the write off to reserves of purchased goodwill is not a recognised loss and hence cannot be included in the recognised gains and losses statement but it has to appear somewhere. The movement of shareholders' funds note provides a convenient home for the write off as shown in the following illustration taken from FRS 3:

Reconciliation of movements in shareholders' funds	*1993*	*1992 as restated*
	£ million	*£ million*
Profit for the financial year	29	7
Dividends	(8)	(1)
	21	6
Other recognised gains and losses relating to the year (net)	(1)	18
New share capital subscribed	20	1
Goodwill written-off	(25)	
Net addition to shareholders' funds	15	25
Opening shareholders' funds (originally £375 million before deducting prior year adjustment of £10 million)	365	340
Closing shareholders' funds	380	365

The note may be included as a primary statement but if it is, it should be shown separately from the statement of total recognised gains and losses (Para. 59).

It is important to see how the profit and loss account, statement of total recognised gains and losses and the reconciliation of movements in shareholders' funds fit together. This can best be seen by studying the comprehensive note showing the movement of reserves required by company legislation. The example shown below is consistent with the previous illustrations.

Reserves	*Share premium account*	*Revaluation reserve*	*Profit and loss account*	*Total*
	£ million	*£ million*	*£ million*	*£ million*
At beginning of year as previously stated	44	200	120	364
Prior year adjustment			(10)	(10)
At beginning of year as restated	44	200	110	354
Premium on issue of shares (nominal value £7 million)	13			13
Goodwill written-off			(25)	(25)
Transfer from profit and loss account of the year			21	21
Transfer of realised profits		(14)	14	0
Decrease in value of trade investment		(3)		(3)
Currency translation differences on foreign currency net investments			(2)	(2)
Surplus on property revaluation		4		4
At end of year	57	187	118	362

Note: Nominal share capital at end of year £18 million (1992 £11 million).

Note of historical cost profits and losses (Para. 26)

If there is a material difference between the results disclosed in the profit and loss account and that which would have been produced by an 'unmodified' (i.e. no asset revaluations) financial statement, a note of the historical cost profit or loss for the period should be presented. The note should include a reconciliation of the reported profit on ordinary activities before taxation to the equivalent historical cost figure and show the retained profit from the financial year as would have been reported on the historical cost basis.

The more common types of adjustments which will be found include:

(a) Gains recognised in prior periods in the statement of total recognised gains and losses but realised in the current period, as under the strict historical cost convention the whole of the gain would be reported in the current period.

(b) The difference between the depreciation charges based on historical cost and such charges based on the revalued amounts.

The standard allows two exceptions (Para. 55):

(a) adjustments made to cope with hyper-inflation in foreign operations; and

(b) the practice of market makers and other dealers in investments of marking to market value where this is an established industry practice.

Where full historical cost information is unavailable or cannot be obtained without unreasonable expense or delay, the earliest available values should be used.

The note should be presented immediately following the profit and loss account or the statement of total recognised gains and losses. The FRS 3 example of the note is presented below:

Note of historical cost profits and losses

	1993	1992 as restated
	£ million	£ million
Reported profit on ordinary activities before taxation	45	13
Realisation of property revaluation gains of previous years	9	10
Difference between a historical cost depreciation charge and the actual depreciation charge of the year calculated on the revalued amount	5	4
Historical cost profit on ordinary activities before taxation	59	27
Historical cost profit for the year retained after taxation, minority interests, extraordinary items and dividends	35	20

Two reasons are cited by the APB to support the publication of this additional note:

(a) Currently undertakings are allowed to decide whether to revalue assets and, if so, when. The results of undertakings which have revalued assets at different times are thus not comparable but the strict historical cost profit figure can be compared.

(b) Some users of financial statements wish to assess the profit or loss on the sale of assets on the basis of their historical cost rather than, as required by the standard, on their revalued carrying amount.

Summary

Accountants have struggled for a long time to find a way of separating out unusual items in order to help users make an informed judgement of the progress of the company and estimate its potential for the future. FRS 3 is an important milestone in that development.

Its provisions have resulted in the production of far more complex profit and loss accounts than had traditionally been produced, a development in tune with the view of the ASB that the desire for understandability should not mean that complex items should be excluded from financial statements if the information is relevant to decision making (ASB, Statement of Principles, Para. 38).

There is a danger, however, that the complexity may drive users to focus even more closely on the single figure elements such as operating profit after tax rather than seeking the intended understanding of how that figure has been derived. The jury is still out on the issue as it will take some time to assess the impact of FRS 3, which was after all only implemented for accounting periods ending on or after 22 June 1993.

OFF AND ON THE BALANCE SHEET

In order for the reader of accounts to judge properly the progress and standing of a company it is necessary for the accounts to show all the assets which are used to generate its profit and to describe fully its liabilities. With the present state of its art, accountancy is not capable of listing and valuing all assets. Those which relate to people – their skill, contacts and knowledge – are often the most important assets of a business which are as yet not shown separately in balance sheets. Other intangible assets are also important but, particularly where they have been generated internally and not acquired for an identifiable cost, these too are often absent from the balance sheet. But accepting all this, it would not be unreasonable to expect the accounts to reflect all the tangible assets employed in a business and to show all its liabilities. A reasonable expectation but one which is not always achieved.

A phenomenon, which has long been with us, but which has grown in importance in recent years is 'off balance sheet finance' schemes whereby what are, or have all the essential economic characteristics of, liabilities are excluded from the balance sheet. Since 'nothing is for nothing', the avoidance of recording the liability also means the exclusion of assets. While the phenomenon is as old as accounting, the term 'off balance sheet financing' is a relatively new one; many of the activities which are now so described would probably in the past have been described as 'window dressing', a much less respectable term.

There are a number of reasons for adopting off balance sheet financing. In some instances taxation is the spur, in other cases a desire not to show the true level of borrowing. Highly geared companies are regarded with some caution and it might be extremely advantageous to eliminate both assets and liabilities from the balance sheet, if, by so doing, the gearing ratio is reduced. It might also be that a company's articles or agreements with existing creditors set a limit on its level of borrowings; off balance sheet financing might be used to circumvent such a restriction.[2]

The ASC first addressed the subject in 1984 when it issued SSAP 21 'Accounting for leases and hire purchase contracts' which as the title suggests dealt with only one, albeit important, aspect of the general problem. Hence, in March 1988 the ASC published ED 42 'Accounting for special purpose transactions' which, following a period of consultation, was withdrawn and replaced in May 1990 by ED 49 'Reflecting the

---

2 A useful description of different forms of off balance sheet finance will be found in K. V. Peasnell and R. A. Yaansah, *Off Balance Sheet Financing*, Certified Accountant Publications, London, 1988.

substance of transactions in assets and liabilities'. This was itself replaced in 1993 when the ASB issued FRED 4 'Reporting the substance of transactions'. We will deal in this section of the chapter with SSAP 21 and FRED 4.

ACCOUNTING FOR LEASES AND HIRE PURCHASE CONTRACTS

Introduction

Under a hire purchase agreement the user has the option to acquire the legal title to the asset upon the fulfilment of the conditions laid down in the contract, usually that all the instalments are paid. By contrast, under a leasing agreement in the UK no legal title passes to the lessee at any time during the currency of the lease. The lessor rents the asset to the lessee for an agreed period and, although the lessee has the physical possession and use of the asset, the legal title remains with the lessor.

In some cases a lease will be for a relatively short period in the life of the particular asset and the lessor may lease the same asset for many short periods to different lessees and in such cases he will usually be responsible for the repairs and maintenance of the asset. This type of lease is described as an *operating lease*. In other instances the lease may be for virtually the whole life of the asset with the lessor taking the whole of his profit from one transaction, such a lease is known as a *finance lease*. Typically, the lessee of a finance lease will in practical terms treat the leased asset in very much the same way as it would an owned asset, the lessee for example, will often be responsible for the asset's repair and maintenance.

The distinction between finance and operating leases is, however, not clear cut and we will return to the way in which they can be differentiated in our discussion of SSAP 21 'Accounting for leases and hire purchase contracts' (*see* page 158).

For the accountant, operating leases pose few problems. Amounts are payable for the use of an asset. From the point of view of the lessee the amounts payable are the cost of using an asset for particular periods and hence are charged to the profit and loss account using the accruals concept. So far as the lessor is concerned the amounts receivable represents revenue from leasing the asset and are credited to the profit and loss account. The leased asset is treated as a fixed asset by the lessor and depreciated in accordance with normal policy.

It is the financing lease which poses problems for the accountant. Prior to the introduction of SSAP 21, financing leases were usually treated by both the lessee and lessor in the same way as operating leases. However, it was widely recognised that such treatment, while being justified on a strict legal interpretation of the agreement, failed to recognise the financial reality or substance of the transaction. The substance of the transaction was that the lessee acquired an asset for his exclusive use with finance provided by the lessor; which in economic terms has few (if any) differences from the case of an asset purchased on credit. If accounts are to be 'realistic' as described in Chapter 1 it is necessary to find a way of accounting for finance leases which accords with the reality of the transaction rather than its legal form. As we shall see the general issue is the subject of FRED 4 'Reporting the substance of transactions' but because of the growth of the leasing industry and the distorting effects of the then prevalent accounting treatment, the ASC issued SSAP 21 in advance of a comprehensive standard. Fortunately SSAP 21 is consistent with the provisions of FRED 4. The International Accounting Standards

Committee also specifically requires that the substance and financial reality of a transaction rather than its legal form, should determine the appropriate accounting treatment.[3]

The alternative treatment which accords with the substance of the transaction is, from the point of view of the lessee, to include in the lessee's balance sheet an asset representing the lease and a liability representing the obligation to make payments under the terms of the lease. At the inception of the lease the asset would be equal to the liability but this relationship does not hold thereafter. The asset would be written off over its life (or the length of the lease if shorter) while the liability would be eliminated by the payments. These payments are not, as in the case of an operating lease, charged entirely to the profit or loss account nor are they in general wholly set off against the liability. Instead the payments are split between that element which is regarded as representing the repayment of the liability and the remainder which is debited to the profit and loss account as the financing (or interest) charge. The alternative approach is referred to as the *capitalisation* of the lease.

The lack of reality consequent upon the failure of a lessee to capitalise financial leases is highlighted by the problems that would be experienced when comparing two companies, one of which leases most of its assets, with the other purchasing fixed assets using loans of one sort or another. The latter company's balance sheet would show the assets which it used to generate its revenue thus allowing users of accounts to estimate the rate of return earned on those assets, while the former company's balance sheet would if the leases were not capitalised understate its assets. Similarly, the latter company's balance sheet would indicate the liabilities which would have to be discharged if it is to continue in business with its existing bundle of assets while the former company's balance sheet would not.[4]

We have so far considered only how the lessee should treat a finance lease. Let us now consider the matter from the point of view of the lessor. The lessor's balance sheet would not include the physical asset but a debtor for the amounts receivable under the lease. Thenceforth the payments received under the terms of the lease should be split between that which goes to reducing the debt with the balance being credited to the profit and loss account. We shall see later in this section how the division can be made.

In order to understand part of the reason why leasing became popular, the reluctance on the part of most companies to capitalise leases, and the provisions of SSAP 21, it is necessary to understand the way in which leases are treated for the purposes of taxation. Unlike hire purchase contracts and credit sales agreements, where the user obtains grants and capital allowances, in the case of a lease it is the legal owner, the lessor, who receives grants and capital allowances on the asset. The lessee receives no allowances but obtains tax relief on the amounts payable under the lease. Capital allowances are only of value to a company which has sufficient taxable profit. Hence, to their mutual advantage, one company with large taxable profits is able to lease assets to another company which does not have sufficient taxable profits to take full advantage of capital allowances. Thus the company with insufficient taxable profits can acquire fixed assets at a lower effective cost than would have been the case with alternative methods of financing.

The effect of what might well be described as the distortion of the tax system described above was undoubtedly one of the major causes of the growth of leasing. Hence, there was a good deal of opposition to the proposal that lessees should capitalise finance leases

---

3 IAS 1, Paras 9b and 17.
4 It is for this reason that finance leases were described as providing an 'off balance sheet' source of finance.

as it was feared that a change in accounting practice might precipitate changes in taxation law whereby finance leases would be treated in the same way as hire purchase contracts.

Other factors which hindered the development of a standard requiring the capitalisation of finance leases included concerns about the possible extension of the principle to other types of non-cancellable contracts, for example those for the regular supply of raw materials or labour, and fears about the potential complexity of any standard. However, the ASC did issue SSAP 21, 'Accounting for leases and hire purchase contracts', in August 1984 and, amongst other things, this required lessees to capitalise finance leases and lessors to include in their balance sheets, not the fixed asset but the debtor for the net investment in the lease. It is perhaps somewhat ironic that, after studying the problem for some nine years, the ASC issued this standard just after the Finance Act 1984 had considerably reduced the tax advantages of leasing.

We will start by examining the treatment of finance leases in the books of the lessee. This will not only enable us to show the basic principles involved but also introduce some terms which will make it easier to understand SSAP 21.

Let us start with a simple example.

Lonbok Limited, a company whose year end is 31 December, leases a machine from Salat Limited on 1 January 19X1. Under the terms of the lease Lonbok is to make four annual payments[5] of £35 000 payable at the start of each year. Lonbok Limited is responsible for all the maintenance and insurance costs, so these are not covered by the payments under the lease.

The first step is to decide the amount at which the leased asset should be capitalised, i.e. shown as an asset and a liability in the first instance. SSAP 21 requires that:

> At the inception of the lease the sum to be recorded both as an asset and as a liability should be the present value of the minimum lease payments, derived by discounting them at the interest rate implicit in the lease.
>
> (SSAP 21, Para. 32)

To do that we need to know what is meant by the minimum lease payments and the interest rate implicit in the lease. These terms are a defined in SSAP 21.

Minimum lease payments

The minimum lease payments are the minimum payments over the remaining part of the lease term (excluding charges for services and taxes to be paid by the lessor) and:

> (a) in the case of the lessee, any residual amounts guaranteed by him or by a party related to him; or
>
> (b) in the case of the lessor, any residual amounts guaranteed by the lessee or by an independent third party.
>
> (SSAP 21, Para. 20)

---

5 In practice lease payments are usually made at monthly, quarterly or six-monthly intervals, but, in order to illustrate more clearly the principles involved, in our example we will assume that the payments are made at annual intervals. More realistic examples of the type of calculations that have to be made in practice, including leases which do not, conveniently, start on the first day of the year can be found in the guidance notes to SSAP 21.

In the Lonbok example we will assume that there are no residual amounts and thus the minimum lease payments at the inception of the lease are the four annual payments of £35 000.

Interest rate implicit in a lease

The interest rate implicit in a lease is the discount rate that at the inception of a lease when applied to the amounts which the lessor expects to receive and retain produces an amount (the present value) equal to the fair value of the leased asset. The amounts which the lessor expects to receive and retain comprise (a) the minimum lease payments to the lessor (as defined above) plus (b) any unguaranteed residual value, less (c) any part of (a) and (b) for which the lessor will be accountable to the lessee. If the interest rate implicit in the lease is not determinable, it should be estimated by reference to the rate which a lessee would be expected to pay on a similar lease.

(SSAP 21, Para. 24)

A key element in the above definition is fair value and hence we need to know how this is found:

Fair value

Fair value is the price at which an asset could be exchanged in an arm's length transaction less, where applicable, any grants receivable towards the purchase or use of the asset.

(SSAP 21, Para. 25)

Note that while knowledge of the implied interest rate is required to determine the appropriate accounting treatment in the books of the lessee it is found by reference to the cash flows of the lessor. In practice the lessee may not know or be able to estimate the various cash flows but we, at this stage, assume that the lessee can obtain all the necessary data.

If we let FV be the fair value, L_j the lease payment in year j (payable at the beginning of each year) and R_n the estimated residual values received at the end of year n, the last year of the lease, then using standard present value techniques the implied rate of interest r is found from the solution of the following equation:

$$FV = \sum_{j=0}^{n} \frac{L_j}{(1+r)^j} + \frac{R_n}{(1+r)^n}$$

If we assume that in the case of the Lonbok/Salat lease that the fair value is £108 720 and that there is no residual value (i.e. $R_n = 0$) then substituting in the above equation we get:

$$£108\ 720 = \sum_{j=0}^{3} \frac{£35\ 000}{(1+r)^j} \quad or \quad \sum_{j=0}^{3} \frac{1}{(1+r)^j} = 3.1064$$

Inspection of tables showing the present value of an annuity shows that 3.1064 represents an interest rate of 20 per cent.[6]

Thus the interest rate implicit in the lease is 20 per cent and hence the present value PV of the minimum lease payments can be found as follows:

$$PV = £35\,000(3.1064)$$
$$= £108\,720$$

This is of course equal to the fair value as in the simple case the only cash flows which the lessor will receive are the minimum lease payments. Later we will describe the circumstances where the two series of cash flows (i.e. the lessee's and the lessor's) might be different and the effect of these differences on the calculations.

We can now show how the lease will be treated in the books of Lonbok (the lessee). The original entry recording the lease is:

Dr Leased asset	£108 720	
Cr Liability under lease		£108 720

From this time onwards the two accounts are dealt with separately. The leased machine will be depreciated over the shorter of the length of the lease or the asset's expected life, using the company's normal depreciation policy for assets of its type, while the liability will be gradually extinguished as payments are made during the primary period of the lease. The only problem which remains is how to spread the total interest charge over the primary period of the lease. This same problem is, of course, encountered in accounting for hire purchase transactions.

The total interest charge may be calculated as follows:

Payments under lease, 4 x £35 000	£140 000
less 'Cost' as above	108 720
Interest	£31 280

Theoretically the best approach is to use the actuarial or annuity method which produces a constant annual rate of interest (in this case 20%) on the outstanding balance on the liability account. This is the method specified in SSAP 21 which does, however, allow the use of any alternative method which is a reasonable approximation to the annuity method.[7]

Assuming that all payments are made on the due dates, the liability account in the books of Lonbok for the term of the lease can be summarised as follows:

	19X1 £	*19X2* £	*19X3* £	*19X4* £
1 Jan opening balance (19X1 cost)	108 720	88 470	64 170	35 000
1 Jan Cash	35 000	35 000	35 000	35 000
	73 720	53 470	29 170	–
31 Dec Interest, 20% of above	14 750	10 700	5 830	–
31 Dec Closing balance	£88 470	£64 170	£35 000	–

6 This and other necessary present value calculations can be made by use of standard computer packages.
7 The method is the only one permitted under the provisions of FRS 4 'Capital investments'.

The account provides us with the interest charge to the profit and loss account for each year and the liability for inclusion in each balance sheet, although it is of course necessary to distinguish between the current portion of the liability (i.e. due within a year) and the rest for the purpose of balance sheet presentation. The amount of interest charged to the profit and loss account declines over the life of the lease because the outstanding balance is reduced by the annual payments.

One commonly used alternative to the annuity method is the 'sum of the year's digits' method or 'Rule of 78'.[8] If the sum of the digits method is used in the above illustration the results would be:

Total interest charge	£31 280
Sum of the year's digits, 1 + 2 + 3	6
Interest charged to profit and loss account	
19X1, ⅜ of £31 280	15 640
19X2, ⅔ of £31 280	10 430
19X3, ⅙ of £31 280	5 210
	£31 280

Although the use of the annuity method is conceptually superior, a comparison of the annual interest charges under the two methods reveals similar patterns of interest charge and thus the 'sum of the year's digits method is often used as a convenient approximation to the annuity method:

Year	Annuity method	Sum of the year's digits method
	(£)	*(£)*
19X1	14 750	15 640
19X2	10 700	10 430
19X3	5 830	5 210
	£31 280	£31 280

The impact of residual values

Let us now complicate matters by assuming that the asset which is the subject of the lease has a residual value. We will assume that the manufacturer who originally supplied the asset to Salat has agreed to reacquire the asset at the end of the lease. The sum is dependent on the condition of the machine and the market factors at the end of the lease, but the manufacturer has guaranteed to pay £10 000 whatever the circumstances. Let us assume that at the inception of the lease it is anticipated that the manufacturer will actually pay £20 000. Let us also assume that Lonbok and Salat agree that they will divide any sums realised on the disposal of the asset in the ratio 35 : 65. Thus, at the inception of the lease it is estimated that Lonbok will receive £7000 (of which £3500 is guaranteed) and Salat £13 000 (£6500 guaranteed).

---

8 It is called the Rule of 78 because if the method is based on the monthly intervals and if the digit 1 is assigned to January, 2 to February and so on the sum of the digits for the year is 78.

For the purposes of calculating the implicit interest rate the distinction between the guaranteed and unguaranteed elements of the residual value can be ignored as both have to be taken into the calculation, but the distinction may be important when deciding whether the lease is a finance or operating lease (*see* page 158).

If we return to the equation on page 154 and substitute the estimated value on realisation receivable by Salat the equation becomes:

$$108\ 720 = \sum_{j=0}^{3} \frac{35\ 000}{(1+r)^j} + \frac{13\ 000}{(1+r)^4}$$

Use of tables, or a programmable calculation on a computer shows that the above equation will be satisfied when r is approximately 25 per cent. This is a higher rate of interest than the 20 per cent which was previously calculated as Salat obviously earns a higher return due to the introduction of the residual value as an additional cash flow.

So far as Lonbok is concerned the minimum lease payments are unchanged but they will now be discounted at the higher rate of 25 per cent which will produce an initial value of the leased asset of:

$$£35\ 000(2.952) = £103\ 320$$

The annual payments of £35 000 are the same as in the original example except that the liability which is to be paid off is lower (£103 320 not £108 720). Hence the finance charge in the profit and loss account will be higher in the second example. This reflects the fact that in the first example the lease payments can be regarded as acquiring the whole of the productive use of the asset in that a zero residual value was assumed while in the second case the same annual lease payments only acquired a proportion of the asset's productive capacity.

It will be noted that the estimated realisable value which Lonbok expects to receive had no effect on the calculation of the amount by which the lease should be capitalised nor on the way in which the annual lease payments should be split. This is because these depend on the minimum lease payments. The recognition of the estimated realisable value does have an effect on the amount that has to be depreciated which is the present value of the minimum lease payments less the estimated realisable value. Thus, the depreciation charges which would emerge from our two sets of assumptions are as follows (assuming the straight-line method is used):

Assumption 1 $\dfrac{£108\ 720}{4}$ = £27 180

Assumption 2 $\dfrac{£(103\ 320 - 7\ 000)}{4}$ = £24 080

In the above examples we assumed that the lessee knows (or is able to find out from the lessor) the fair value of the asset and the estimated realisable value which the lessor expects to receive. In practice this may well not be the case and certain estimates will have to be made. Often the fair value will be known[9] and the interest rate estimated from a knowledge of other leases of a similar type.

SSAP 21, 'ACCOUNTING FOR LEASES AND HIRE PURCHASE CONTRACTS'

We are now in a position to discuss the specific requirements of SSAP 21. This is a detailed standard and we will not attempt to cover all its aspects but will instead concentrate on the important elements and those which might give rise to particular difficulties of understanding. The ASC have published guidance notes on SSAP 21 and readers should refer to this booklet for a more detailed explanation of the provisions of the standard.

We will first deal with a number of general issues before concentrating on the impact of the standard on the accounts of lessees and hirers. A discussion of the more specialised topic of accounting for lessors will be deferred to the concluding part of this chapter.

Scope

The standard covers leases and hire purchases contracts and is applicable to accounts based on both the historical cost and current cost conventions. The standard does not apply to leases of the rights to exploit natural resources such as oil or gas, nor does it apply to licensing agreement for items such as motion pictures, videos, etc. Stress is also laid on the point that the standard does not apply to immaterial items. Thus a company that leases some of its office equipment may not need to capitalise the lease but continue to treat a finance lease in the same way as an operating lease.

Distinction between finance and operating leases

The basic distinction between the two different types of leases has already been explained (*see* page 151). SSAP 21 states that:

> A finance lease is a lease that transfers substantially all the risks and rewards of ownership of an asset to the lessee.
>
> (Para. 15)

It is presumed that a lease is a finance lease if at the start of the lease the present value of the minimum lease payments amounts to substantially all (normally 90% or more) of the fair value of the leased asset. The present value should be calculated by using the interest rate implicit in the lease. However, the Standard recognises that in exceptional circumstances this initial presumption may be rebutted if the lease in question does not transfer substantially all the risks and rewards of ownership to the lessee. It may sometimes be the case that the lessor will receive part of his return by way of a guarantee from an independent third party, possibly the manufacturer of the asset, in which case the lease may be treated as a finance lease by the lessor but as an operating lease by the lessee.

---

9 Unless the asset concerned is highly specific the prudent lessee will obviously wish to know how much it would cost to purchase the asset before signing a lease.

Hire purchase contracts

With the vast majority of hire purchases contracts the 'risks and rewards' pass to the hirer and hence may be regarded as being akin to finance leases. In such cases the standard specifies that they should be treated in a similar way to finance leases. However, in exceptional circumstances a hire purchase contract may be accounted for on the same principles as an operating lease.

Accounting by lessees

Finance leases

A finance lease should be capitalised; hence the lease should be recorded as an asset and an obligation to pay rentals. At the inception of the lease the asset will equal the liability (although this equality will not hold over the life of the lease) and will be the present value of the minimum lease payments, derived by discounting them at the interest rate implied in the lease.

The Standard states:

> that the fair value of the asset will often be a sufficiently close approximation to the present value of the minimum lease payments and may in these circumstances be substituted for it.

> (Para. 33)

In most circumstances the fair value will be a sufficiently close approximation to be used, for, by definition, if the present value of the minimum lease payments does not equal 90 per cent or more of the fair value, then it is presumed that the lease is an operating and not a finance lease.

If the fair value cannot be determined, possibly because the asset concerned is unique, then the present value can be found by discounting the minimum lease payments by the interest rate implicit in the lease. If the latter cannot be determined the rate may be estimated from that which applied in similar leases.

Total payments less than fair value

In some circumstances the combined impact of any grants which may be available and taxation allowances received by the lessor may be such as to bring the total (i.e. not the present value) lease payments below the fair value. The standard specifies (Para. 34) that if this occurs the amount to be capitalised and depreciated should be reduced to the minimum lease payments. A negative finance charge should not be shown.

In other words if, say, the total of the payments to be made under the lease is £10 000 and the fair value of the asset is £12 000, the asset and liability on the inception of the lessee are both £10 000. The payments under the lease will all be applied to reducing the liability and no part of them will be charged to the profit and loss account as a finance charge. The only charge in the profit and loss account will be the annual depreciation charge.

Rentals

Rentals payable should be apportioned between the finance charge (if any) and a reduction of the outstanding obligation. The total finance charge should be allocated to accounting periods so as to produce a constant annual rate of charge (i.e. the annuity method), or a reasonable approximation thereto.

The guidance notes suggest that in most circumstances, especially where the lease is for 7 years or less and interest rates are not high that the Rule of 78 will be an acceptable approximation to the actuarial method. In the case of small (relative to the size of the companies) leases it is suggested that the straight-line method, whereby the total finance charge is recognised on a time basis, may be acceptable.

Note that FRS 4 'Capital instruments' does not give any latitude as to use of the method of allocating finance charges (or finance costs as they are called in FRS 4); only the actuarial (or annuity) method is allowed. However, the concept of materiality could be cited to justify the use of a simpler method such as the Rule of 78 if the figures produced by the two methods are fairly close or the totals are not material in the context of the entity's total operation.

Depreciation

A leased asset should be depreciated over the shorter of the length of the lease or the asset's useful life. However, in the case of hire purchase contracts, because of the presumption that the asset concerned will be acquired by the hirer, the asset should be depreciated over its useful life.

Operating leases

The accounting treatment by the lessee in respect of operating leases is fairly straightforward in that the whole of the payments are charged to the profit and loss account. The only slight complication is that the standard requires the rental to be charged on a straight-line basis over the lease term (unless another systematic and rational basis is more appropriate) even if the payments are not made on such a basis. Hence, if the term of the lease requires a heavy initial payment a proportion of the payment can be treated as a prepaid expense.

More commonly lessees are granted so-called 'rental holidays' in that they do not have to pay anything for an initial period. In such circumstances the standard requires a charge to be made to the profit and loss account for the period of the rental holiday which would be treated as an accrual in the balance sheet. Thereafter the charge to the profit and loss account would be less than the payments made in the year (as rental, like other holidays, have to be paid for) with the excess reducing the balance sheet accrual. Particularly significant examples of this type of arrangement are leases of buildings by government agencies to business in areas where the government wants to encourage the creation of jobs.

Disclosure requirements in the accounts of lessees and hirers

Finance leases

For disclosure purposes information relating to hire purchase contracts with characteristics similar to finance leases should be included with the equivalent information regarding leases.

1 *Fixed assets and depreciation* The lessee may either:

   (a) Show separately the gross amounts, accumulated depreciation and depreciation expense for each major class of leased asset, or

(b) Group the above information with the equivalent information for owned assets[10] but show by way of a note how much of the net amount (i.e. net book value) and the depreciation expense relates to assets held under finance leases.

2 *Obligations* The lessee must both:

(a) Disclose the obligations related to finance leases separately from other obligations and liabilities, and
(b) Analyse the net obligations under finance leases into three components (the figures may be combined with other obligations):
    amounts payable in next year;
    amounts payable in second to fifth years;
    amounts payable thereafter.

3 *Finance charges* The lessee must disclose the aggregate finance charge allocated to the period.

4 *Commitments* The lessee must show by way of a note the amount of any commitment existing at the balance sheet date in respect of finance leases which have been entered into but whose inception occurs after the year end.

5 *Accounting policies* Accounting policies adopted for finance leases must be stated.

Operating leases

1 *Current rentals* The lessee must disclose the total rentals charged as an expense, analysed between amounts payable in respect of the hire of plant and machinery and those charged in respect of other operating leases. (The Companies Act, of course, requires disclosure of the charge for the hire of plant and machinery.)

2 *Future rentals* The lessee must show the payments which he or she is committed to make during the next year, analysed between those in which the commitment expires:

(i) within that year;
(ii) in the second to fifth years inclusive; and
(iii) over 5 years from the balance sheet date.

Commitments in respect of leases of land and buildings and other operating leases must be shown separately.

3 *Accounting policies* The accounting policies adopted for operating leases must be stated.

Accounting for finance leases by lessors – general principles

The provisions of SSAP 21 regarding the accounting treatment of finance leases by lessors are relatively difficult for two main reasons. First, the basic method is not simple since – as will be shown – it depends on complex calculations of what constitutes the lessor's investment in a particular lease while, second, the standard permits the use of alternative methods and simplifying assumptions so that a host of different methods can be justified under the terms of the standard.

---

10 Since it is the right to use the asset rather than the asset itself which is capitalised there is some doubt as to whether it should be called a tangible asset and included with the owned tangible assets. The ASC ignored such niceties and for the purposes of balance sheet presentation the leases are regarded as tangible assets.

We will first describe the basic principles underlying the provisions of SSAP 21 relating to the treatment of finance leases by lessors.

Balance sheet presentation – the measurement of net investment

Lessors should not include in their balance sheets the assets subject to the leasing contracts but instead record as a debtor the *net investment* in the lease after making any necessary provisions for bad and doubtful debts. In order to explain this term and describe how profit is recognised, we will need to reproduce certain definitions included in SSAP 21.

Net investment

The net investment in a lease at a point in time comprises:

(a) the gross investment in a lease; *less*
(b) gross earnings allocated to future periods.

(SSAP 21, Para. 22)

Thus, we need to know what is meant by the gross investment and gross earnings.

Gross investment

The gross investment in a lease at a point in time is the total of the minimum lease payments [see page 153] and any unguaranteed residual value accruing to the lessor.

(SSAP 21, Para. 21)

Gross earnings

Gross earnings comprise the lessor's gross finance income over the lease term, representing the difference between his gross investment in the lease [see above] and the cost of the leased asset less any grants receivable towards the purchase or use of the asset.[11]

(SSAP 21, Para. 28)

In order to illustrate the effect of the above definitions assume that the details relating to a particular lease are as follows:

Cost of asset	£12 000
Grant receivable by lessor	£2 000
Lease term	5 years
Annual rental	£3 000
Estimated residual value accruing to the lessor	£500

Let us see how one measures the net investment at the inception of the lease and at the end of the first year.

---

11 The paragraph goes on to modify the definition to deal with the use of a possible option available in SSAP 21 relating to the treatment of tax-free grants.

At inception:	£
Minimum lease payments, 5 x £3000	15 000
Estimated residual value	500
Gross investment	15 500
less Gross earnings (£15 500 – £10 000)	5 500
Net investment	£10 000

Hence, at inception the net investment is equal to the cost of the asset less grants receivable by the lessor.

Assume that the gross earnings recognised in the profit and loss account in the first year are £2500 (we shall describe in the following section how this figure is calculated). Then the net investment at the end of the first year is:

	£
Minimum lease payments, 4 x £3 000	12 000
Estimated residual value	500
	12 500
less Gross earnings allocated to future periods	
£5500 – £2500	3 000
Net investment	£9 500

The recognition of gross earnings

The total gross earnings on any lease is reasonably easy to calculate since the minimum lease payments will be known and, generally, the residual value, if any, can be estimated. The difficulty lies in allocating the gross earnings to the different accounting periods. The standard followed existing practice in the leasing industry by specifying that (other than in the case of hire purchase contracts) the interest should be allocated on the basis of the lessor's *net cash* investment in the lease and not on the basis of the net investment. Specifically Para. 39 of SSAP 21 states:

> The total gross earnings under a finance lease should normally be allocated to accounting periods to give a constant periodic rate of return on the lessor's *net cash investment* in the lease in each period. In the case of a hire purchase contract which has characteristics similar to a finance lease, allocation of gross earnings so as to give a constant periodic rate of return on the finance company's *net investment* will in most cases be a suitable approximation to allocation based on the net cash investment. In arriving at the constant periodic rate of return, a reasonable approximation may be made.

To an extent the above is familiar in that it is the counterpart of the annuity method prescribed for use by lessees in that the annual finance charge should be such as to produce a constant rate based on the decreasing obligation. The difference is that while the reduction in the obligation is relatively easy to calculate the determination of the net cash investment is somewhat more difficult.

The meaning of net cash investment

The meaning of the net cash investment can be more easily understood if one assumes that a separate company is established by the lessor for each lease and then measuring or estimating the cash flows in and out of that company. The net cash investment is then the balance of cash, which might be positive or negative, in the company at any point in time. The various cash flows may be summarised as follows:

Table 6.1

Cash flows out	Cash flows in
1 Cost of the asset	(a) Grants received against purchase or use of asset
2 Cost of setting up the lease	(b) Rental income received
3 Tax payments on rental and interest received	(c) Tax reductions on capital allowances[12] and on interest paid
4 Interest payments on cash invested in the lease	(d) Interest earned when the net cash investment becomes a surplus
5 Profit withdrawn	(e) Residual value at the end of the lease

If one thinks in terms of a single lease company and the cash flows associated with it, it can be seen that the company will start with an 'overdraft' – the cost of the asset and of setting up the lease – but that this will be reduced if a grant is received and as capital allowances for the purchase of the asset are received. The overdraft will be reduced as lease payments are received but will be increased by virtue of the interest payments made on the overdraft. Profit may also be withdrawn (and for this purpose profit may be regarded as including the contribution made by the 'single lease' company to the operating expenses of the enterprise of which it actually forms part) which will also increase the overdraft. At some stage the overdraft may be eliminated and replaced by a cash surplus on which interest may be deemed to be earned. The interest 'payments' and 'receipts' will also have taxation consequences which will respectively increase the cash surplus (or reduce the overdraft) or decrease the cash surplus. Finally, if the lessor receives a residual value this will increase the surplus.

It is on the basis of the above considerations that SSAP 21 defines net cash investment as follows:

> The *net cash investment* in a lease at a point in time is the amount of funds invested in a lease by a lessor, and comprises the cost of the asset plus or minus the following related payments and receipts:
>
> (a) government or other grants receivable towards the purchase or use of the asset;
> (b) rentals received;
> (c) taxation payments and receipts, including the effect of capital allowances;
> (d) residual values, if any, at the end of the lease term;
> (e) interest payments (where applicable);
> (f) interest received on cash surplus;
> (g) profit taken out of the lease.
>
> (SSAP 21, Para. 23)

---

12 Since in actuality the 'single-lease' company is not separate and distinct the reductions in tax payments due to the receipt of capital allowances and the charging of expenses can be treated as cash receipts since they are covered by tax payment otherwise payable by the lessor (if this were not the case the lessor should not be in the leasing business in the first place!).

The actuarial method after tax

The guidance notes to SSAP 21 describe a number of ways of allocating the gross revenue to accounting periods based on the net cash investment. Of these the most accurate is the '*actuarial method after tax*'. This method produces a constant rate of return on the net cash investment over that period of the lease in which the lessor has a positive investment (i.e. before any cash surplus is generated). The phrase 'after tax' does not imply that it is after tax profit which is allocated but simply that the tax cash flows are included in the measurement of the net cash investment.

The actuarial method after tax is illustrated in Example 6.1.

EXAMPLE 6.1

Gasp plc, the lessor, acquired an asset for £7735 which it leased out on the following terms:

Period	5 years
Rental	£2 000 per year payable in advance on 1 January of each year
Residual value	Zero

Gasp's year end is 31 December and tax in respect of any year is payable on 1 January of the next year but one. The tax rate is 50 per cent and capital allowances of 100 per cent are receivable in the first year.

The annual rate of return earned over the period when there is a net cash investment is 12 per cent while it is estimated that surplus cash can be invested at 5 per cent (both rates are before tax).

The interest paid by Gasp on the funds invested in the lease will be ignored.

The cash flows and the profit recognised on the lease are set out in Table 6.2

Table 6.2 Hypothetical cash flows – figures in brackets represent cash flows out

Date	Cost £	Rent £	Tax £	Profit taken on lease £	Interest on cash surplus £	Net cash investment £
1 Jan X0	(7735)	2000				(5735)
31 Dec X0				(688)		(6423)
1 Jan X1		2000				(4423)
31 Dec X1				(531)		(4954)
1 Jan X2		2000	2868			(86)
31 Dec X2				(11)		(97)
1 Jan X3		2000	(1000)			903
31 Dec X3					45	948
1 Jan X4		2000	(1000)			1948
31 Dec X4					98	2046
1 Jan X5			(1023)			1023
31 Dec X5					52	1075
1 Jan X6			(1049)			26
1 Jan X7			(26)			–

Notes
(a) The profit taken on the lease has been calculated at 12 per cent of the net cash investment at the start of each year (e.g. £688 = 0.12 x £5735) while the interest on the cash surplus has been calculated at 5 per cent of the opening balance (e.g. £45 = 0.05 x £903). Interest on the cash surplus in 19X6 has been ignored (otherwise the calculation would never end)
(b) The tax computation for 19X0 (tax payable on 1 January 19X2) is as follows;

	£
Capital allowances (100%)	7735
less Rental income received	2000
Adjusted profit	£5735
Tax thereon, 50% of £5735 =	£2868

In subsequent years the tax payment is 50 per cent of the sum of the rental income and the interest earned on the cash surplus

Although the lease will generate an annual rental of £2000 for each of the five years after tax, profit recognised in respect of the lease is £688 in year 1, £531 in year 2 and £11 in year 3.[13] It may be thought that this is a very imprudent way of recognising profit in that most of the profit is taken in the first two years of the lease. However, it must be recognised that the profit reported is that which is generated by the lessor's financing activities and is calculated by reference to the amount that he has invested in the lease. As Table 6.2 shows the investment falls to zero, to be replaced by a cash surplus by 1 January 19X3.

Arithmetically all the figures in Table 6.2 can be found if you know the cash flows, which will be specified in the agreement, and either the profit on the lease (12%) or the re-investment rate (5%). Thus, if one of the two rates is known the other can be calculated, with the aid of a computer or a lot of patient trial and error. In practice, of course, the lessor will have made his calculations of these rates when agreeing the terms of the rental with the lessee. Thus he would start by deciding, on the basis of market conditions and competitive forces, the return he would require on the lease (taking into account the return on any surplus cash invested[14]) and hence work out the rent he would need to charge.

The next step is to calculate the proportion of the annual receipts of £2000 which is deemed to represent the reduction in the amount due from the lessee. The calculation is based on the figures in Table 6.3. This table also shows the necessary transfers to and from the deferred taxation account if it is judged necessary to establish such an account.

13 Observant readers will note that the sum of these is, at £1230, more than the 50 per cent of the difference between the minimum lease payments and the cost of the asset, i.e. 50 per cent of (£10 000 – £7735) = £1132. This is because the interest on the cash surplus is included in the total profit, i.e. £1230 = 50 per cent of £(10 000 – 7735 + 45 + 98 + 52).
14 The surplus cash will probably be invested in another lease, thus the rate of return on the surplus cash will be the return from the new lease. The return on the new lease will *inter alia* depend on the return on any surplus cash it may generate which it may be presumed will be invested in yet another lease and so on *ad infinitum*. In practice, to avoid having to estimate returns on leases (or other investments) which will arise in the future, a prudent estimate of the return on surplus cash is used in the calculations.

Table 6.3

	19X0 £	19X1 £	19X2 £	19X3 £	19X4 £	19X5 £	Total £
1 Rental	2000	2000	2000	2000	2000		10 000
2 Capital repayments	(624)	(938)	(1978)	(2045)	(2098)	(52)	(7 735)
3 Gross earnings	1376	1062	22	(45)	(98)	(52)	2 265
4 Interest				45	98	52	195
5 Profit before tax	1376	1062	22	–	–	–	2 460
6 Taxation	2868	(1000)	(1000)	(1023)	(1049)	(26)	(1 230)
7	4244	62	(978)	(1023)	(1049)	(26)	(1 230)
8 Deferred tax	(3556)	469	989	1023	1049	26	–
9 Net profit	£688	£531	£11	–	–	–	£1 230

Table 6.3 is constructed from the bottom up. The figures in line 9 are taken from Table 6.2. The net profit is then grossed up at the appropriate tax rate (50%) to give line 5. Line 6 which shows the actual tax payments is also taken from Table 6.2 which means that line 8 (deferred tax) can be derived. Line 4 is taken from Table 6.2 and hence the gross earnings (line 3) and capital repayments (line 2) can be deduced. If, taking into consideration the affairs of the company as a whole, it is decided that it is not necessary to account for deferred tax, one could start Table 6.3 at line 5 and work up from there.

It must be emphasised that Table 6.3 is used only to calculate the capital repayment and, if appropriate, the deferred taxation transfers. For the purposes of the balance sheet presentation SSAP 21 requires that the amount due from the lessee should be the net investment (not the net cash investment) in the lease. Thus in the instance of Gasp plc the asset would be recorded as follows:

Balance sheet date	Gross investment £	Gross earnings allocated to future periods £	Net investment £
31 Dec X0	8000	889	7111
31 Dec X1	6000	(173)	6173
31 Dec X2	4000	(195)	4195
31 Dec X3	2000	(150)	2150
31 Dec X4	–	(52)	52

The gross earnings allocated to future periods are found from row 3 of Table 6.3. Thus, for example, the figure at 31 December 19X0 is £(1062 + 22 – 45 – 98 – 52) = £889 and so on.

The method produces the apparently absurd result that the net investment at certain dates is greater than the remaining lease payments, the extreme case being that at 31 December 19X4 when a net investment of £52 is produced notwithstanding the fact that the lease has terminated. This odd result derives from the fact that a larger profit is taken in the early years of the lease in consequence of the anticipated return on the surplus cash invested; thus, for example, the net investment at 31 December 19X3 of £2150 can be regarded as representing the final lease payment of £2000 plus the anticipated interest receipts of £150 (£98 in 19X4 and £52 in 19X5).

The above example assumed the existence of 100 per cent first-year capital allowances and a high nominal rate of corporation tax as these assumptions make it easier to show the effect of tax on the net cash investment.

Alternative approaches to accounting for finance leases and hire purchase contracts

As stated on page 163, Para. 39 of SSAP 21 specifies that in the case of hire purchase contracts gross earnings can be allocated on the basis of the company's net investment. The reason for this is that in the case of hire purchase, capital allowances are granted to the hirer and hence the tax cash flows will not have the same significance to the hire purchase company as they have for a leasing company.

The same paragraph allows the use of alternative methods for both hire purchase and leasing companies which give 'reasonable approximations' to that which produces a constant rate of return of the net cash investment. A number of alternatives are described in the guidance notes to SSAP 21 which include the investment period method, which is similar to the actuarial method after tax. Other methods described are the 'Rule of 78' and the actuarial method before tax. These two methods are primarily intended for use with hire purchase contracts but they can be used for finance leases where the amounts concerned are not judged to be material.

A lessor may, if he or she chooses, write off the initial direct costs in arranging a lease over the period on a 'systematic and rational basis'.[15] This provision applies to both finance and operating leases.

Accounting for operating leases by lessors – general principles

The basic principles are contained in Paras 42–44 of SSAP 21. These are:

> An asset held for use in operating leases by a lessor should be recorded as a fixed asset and depreciated over its useful life.
>
> (Para. 42)

> Rental income from an operating lease, excluding charges for services such as insurance and maintenance, should be recognized on a straight-line basis over the period of the lease, even if the payments are not made on such a basis, unless another systematic and rational basis is more representative of the time pattern in which the benefit from the leased asset is receivable.
>
> (Para. 43)

> Initial direct costs incurred by a lessor in arranging a lease may be apportioned over the period of the lease on a systematic and rational basis.
>
> (Para. 44)

The accounting treatment of operating leases by the lessor is thus straightforward, subject only to the problems of dealing with cases where payment is not received on a straight-line basis and deciding on the circumstances where an alternative systematic and rational basis would be appropriate. These issues are similar to those faced by the lessee (*see* page 160).

15 SSAP 21, Para. 44.

Disclosure requirements for the lessor in respect of finance and operating leases and hire purchase contracts

The requirements, contained in Paras 58–60 of SSAP 21 are as follows:

1 The net investment in (i) finance leases and (ii) hire purchase contracts should be disclosed. Note that separate totals need to be given for leases and hire purchase contracts. In the case of the remaining disclosure requirements information regarding leases and hire purchase contracts can be combined.
2 The gross amount of assets held for use in operating leases and the related accumulated depreciation charge should be disclosed.
3 Disclosure should be made of:
   (a) the policy adopted for accounting for operating leases and finance leases and, in detail, the policy for accounting for finance lease income;
   (b) the aggregate rentals receivable in respect of an accounting period in relation to (i) finance leases and (ii) operating leases; and
   (c) the cost of assets acquired, whether by purchase or finance lease, for the purpose of letting under finance leases.

Sale and leaseback transactions

The standard makes specific reference to sale and leaseback transactions which arise when the vendor/lessee sells an asset but continues to have the use of it on the basis of a lease granted by the purchaser/lessor. No problems arise with regard to the treatment of a sale and leaseback transaction in the accounts of the lessor who will record the asset purchased at cost and then, depending on the nature of the lease, follow the provisions of SSAP 21 in the usual way. The position regarding the vendor/lessee is different in so far that there are circumstances where the sales and leaseback transactions will have to be accorded special treatment. The nature of the circumstances depends on the type of lease.

Finance leases

The key characteristic of a finance lease is that the 'risk and reward' associated with the asset rests with the lessee. Hence when a vendor engages in a sale and finance leaseback transaction, he retains the 'risk and reward'. It is therefore argued that in such circumstances it would be wrong to recognise a profit or loss on the sale of the asset concerned in the year in which the sale and leaseback is effected.

Thus SSAP 21 states:

> In a sale and leaseback transaction which results in a finance lease, any apparent profit or loss (that is, the difference between the sale price and the previous carrying value) should be deferred and amortized in the financial statements of the seller/lessee over the shorter of the lease term and the useful life of the asset.

> (Para. 46)

If the asset was sold for its fair value, the provisions of Para. 46 could be avoided by revaluing the asset prior to sale and hence removing any difference between the sale price and the carrying value. However, to the extent that the vendor retains the 'risk and reward' any profit on the sale should not be regarded as being realised, but it would be reasonable to recognise gradually the realisation of any profit over the shorter of the lease term and the useful life of the asset.

If the asset were not sold for its fair value it is likely that the consequence would be that the lease rental payments would be higher (if the asset were sold for more than its fair value) or lower than those which would be charged if the asset had been sold for its fair value. Hence it is reasonable to set the apparent profit or loss against the rental charges.

Operating leases

In the case of an operating lease the 'risks and rewards' are transferred along with the legal title to the asset. Hence any profit or loss on the sale of the asset should be recognised immediately as long as the asset was sold at its fair value.

If the asset is sold for an amount in excess of its fair value, the excess should be written back to the profit and loss account over the shorter of the remainder of the lease term or the period to the next rent review (if any).

Postscript to SSAP 21

Since accounting for lessors is a specialised subject we have concentrated on the main principles. Interested readers will need to study SSAP 21 and the associated guidance notes to gain a full understanding of the topic.

REFLECTING THE SUBSTANCE OF TRANSACTIONS

Introduction

The vast majority of transactions of the vast majority of companies are simple and straightforward. A fixed asset or an item of stock is purchased for cash or on credit and the impact on the company's assets and liabilities can be easily assessed. But occasionally a company will enter a complex set of transactions which involve a series of different events which if viewed in isolation might give a misleading picture.

Let us suppose X Limited 'sells' some land to Y Bank for £1 000 000 with an option to reacquire it for, say, £1 080 000 in six months' time.

Is it a genuine sale or is it a device to borrow money, 'off the balance sheet', for six months? And, if it is the latter, would the financial statements show a more realistic picture if the asset were not treated as a sale, but retained as an asset with the corresponding recognition of the obligation to 'repay' the bank?

The task is to determine the substance of the transaction. The doctrine of 'substance over form' is found in many attempts to construct a conceptual framework of accounting. Many interpretations have been made of the phrase but it is perhaps most readily understood as the belief that financial statements should, when there is conflict, be based on economic (or commercial) reality rather than legal form.[16]

---

16 For a comprehensive discussion on the subject see B. S. Rutherford, *The Doctrine of Substance over Form*, Certified Accountants Publications, London, 1988.

FRED 4 'Reporting the substance of transactions'

Introduction

FRED 4 does not refer specifically to the concept of substance over form but it is nevertheless one of the underpinnings of the proposed standard in that it is stated that the objective of FRED 4 'is to ensure that the substance of the entity's transaction is reported in the financial statements' (Summary, Para. a).

The key step in determining the substance of a transaction is the determination of whether or not it has given rise to new assets or liabilities or increased or decreased existing assets or liabilities. However, not all assets and liabilities so identified will, under the terms of FRED 4, qualify for recognition in the primary financial statements, so the draft proposes certain 'tests of recognition'.

In order to determine 'substance' FRED 4 emphasises the need to identify all aspects and implications of a complex transaction and points out that some aspects will be uncertain or contingent and that greater weight needs to be given to those aspects which are likely to have a commercial effect in practice. FRED 4 suggests that the accountant needs to consider the expectations and motivation of all parties to the transaction and points out that, whatever is the substance of the transaction, it will normally have a commercial logic for all the parties and hence, if a transaction appears not to make sense, this might indicate 'that not all related parts of the transaction have been identified or that the commercial effect of some element of the transaction has been incorrectly assessed' (Para. 43). In other words it suggests that if the accountant digs deep enough the reality of the transaction will emerge.

The proposed standard is relevant to those complex transactions whose substance is not readily apparent and whose commercial effect may not be fully reflected by their legal form. Common features of such transactions are:

(i) the severance of legal title to an item from the ability to enjoy the principal benefits and exposure to the principal risks associated with it;

(ii) the linking of a transaction with one or more others in such a way that its commercial effect cannot be understood without reference to the series as a whole; and

(iii) the inclusion in a transaction of one or more options whose terms make it highly likely that the option or options will be exercised.

The structure of FRED 4

FRED 4 deals with the following main issues:

(i) the identification of assets and liabilities and tests of recognition for inclusion in the financial statements

(ii) the treatment of options

(iii) the circumstances under which it is permissible to relate assets and associated liabilities – so called 'linked presentation'

(iv) the very limited circumstances under which it is permissible to offset assets and liabilities

(v) additional disclosure requirements

(vi) the treatment of 'quasi-subsidiaries', where the relationship between two entities is effectively, but not legally, one as between parent and subsidiary.

We will in the following pages examine the proposals of FRED 4 in the above order.

The identification of assets

An asset is defined as:

> 'Rights or other access to future economic benefits controlled by an entity as a result of past transactions or events'
>
> (FRED 4, Para. 2)

Whilst in the context of an asset, control is defined as:

> 'Control of rights or other access to future economic benefits means the ability to obtain those future economic benefits and to restrict the access of others.
>
> (Para. 3)

While the existence of future benefits is an essential criterion for the identification of an asset, it is not implied that the asset should be valued by reference to those benefits, although the present value of the asset's expected future benefits will provide an upper limit to its carrying value.

All assets carry some risk and the allocation of that risk between the various parties to a transaction will usually be a significant indication of whether the transaction has resulted in the acquisition or disposal of an asset. *Risk* is the potential variation between the actual and expected benefits associated with the asset and includes both the potential for gain as well as exposure to loss. Normally the party which has access to the benefits also has to face the risks and in practice the question of whether an asset should be identified is often dependent on an assessment of where the risk falls.

Control in this context is related to the means by which an entity ensures that the benefits accrue to itself and not to others and must be distinguished from the day-to-day management of the asset. Whilst control normally rests on the foundation of legal rights, the existence of such rights is not essential as commercial, or even moral, obligations may be significant factors.

The existence of an asset depends on a past and not a future event. Thus, in straightforward transactions it is easy to draw a distinction between a right to immediate control over future economic benefits and a right to acquire such control in the future. Both rights can be regarded as creating assets, but in the second case the asset is simply the option. The position in linked transactions may be different. An option may be simply a device to ensure that effective control of future benefits will be retained by the party who ceases, temporarily, to be the legal owner. Then the terms of the option may be such that the costs of exercising it are negligible compared to the benefits; in other words it would be commercial madness not to exercise the option. In such a case the accounting treatment (is there an asset and if so what is it?) will have to be decided by reference to the rights and obligations (including those taking effect in the future) which result from the transactions as a whole and which exist at the balance sheet date.

The identification of liabilities

A liability is defined as:

> As entity's obligations to transfer economic benefits as a result of past transactions or events.
>
> (FRED 4, Para. 4)

Little is said in FRED 4 on the nature of liabilities, the topic is treated in greater detail in the ASB's 'Statement of principles' and in FRS 4 'Capital instruments' (*see* Chapter 5). However, as with assets, the point is made that a liability is not only created by a legal relationship.

Tests for recognition of assets and liabilities

Assets and liabilities, although identified in terms of the above, should only be recognised in the primary financial statements if:

(a) there is sufficient evidence of the existence of the item (including, where appropriate, evidence that a future inflow or outflow of benefit will occur); and

(b) the item can be measured at a monetary amount with sufficient reliability.

(FRED 4, Para. 17)

An obvious example of an item which although identified would not be 'recognised' in the primary financial statements is a contingent liability.

The above general criteria for recognition are taken from Chapter 4 of the, ASB's draft 'Statement of principles' where it is pointed out that the effect of prudence is such that less evidence would be required for recognition of liabilities than assets.

In addition to the general tests reference may also have to be made to another FRS, a SSAP or statute. If a transaction is covered both by the standard emerging from FRED 4 and one or more of the other sources of authority, the standard or statute which contains the more specific provisions should be applied (FRED 4, Para. 18).

The proposed standard also covers situations where assets should cease to be recognised. An asset should cease to be recognised only if no significant rights or other access to material economic benefits relating to the asset are retained and any risk relating to the asset is immaterial (FRED 4, Para. 19). This formulation makes the point that an asset involves not only the potential of benefits but also the real possibility that access to those benefits will be effective in practice.

Options

One of the characteristics of complex transactions is the existence of options and in deciding how to treat them consideration needs to be given to all aspects of the series of transactions of which the option is part. If, after such consideration, it is decided that there is no genuine commercial possibility that the option will be exercised, the exercise of the option should be ignored whilst, if there is no genuine commercial possibility that the option will fail to be exercised, its future exercise should be assumed (FRED 4, Para. 16).

In assessing whether there is a genuine commercial possibility that an option will be exercised it should be assumed that the parties will act in accordance with their economic interests and that the parties will remain both liquid and solvent, unless it can reasonably be foreseen that either will not be the case. Thus, actions which the party will take only in the event of a severe deterioration in liquidity or creditworthiness that is not currently foreseen should not be taken into account.

There will be some circumstances which fall between the two certainties – the exercise or non-exercise of the option. In such a case the asset itself which would appear in the balance sheet of the entity with the right to acquire would be not the asset but the option to acquire the asset. To return to our simple example which involved X Limited 'selling' some land to a bank for £1m with an option to repurchase. If the price at which the option would be exercised is such that it is virtually certain to be less than the then market price

FRED 4 would require the transaction to be treated as a loan. If, conversely, the option price is virtually certain to be more than the prevailing market price then it would be presumed that the option would not be exercised and the transaction should be treated as a sale. But suppose there exists uncertainty, in that the option price lies within a range in which the market price of the land might reasonably be expected to fluctuate. In that case the asset that X Limited would show would be the option to reacquire the land and the cost of that asset would be the extra finance costs which the borrower would incur in a transaction which involved an option as against a straightforward borrowing which did not include an option.

Linked presentation

A borrower can finance an item on such terms that the provider of finance has access only to the item financed and not to the entity's other assets. A well-known example of this is the factoring of debts. In some such arrangements, whilst the provider of finance has only recourse against the specified item, the 'borrowing' entity retains rights to the benefits generated by the asset, and can repay the finance from its general resources if it wishes to preserve those rights. In such situations the entity has both an asset and a liability and linked presentation would not be appropriate.

Linked presentation, which as we shall see involves the setting off on the face of the balance sheet the liability against the asset, is only possible in situations where the finance *has* to be repaid from the benefits generated by the asset and the borrowing entity *has no right* to keep the item or to repay the finance from its general resources. The remaining conditions which have to be satisfied are set out in the draft standard (Para. 21); the essence of these conditions is that the borrower is under no legal, moral or commercial obligation to repay the loan other than from the benefits generated from the asset.

The question to be answered is what is the nature of the asset which is retained by the borrowing entity and in particular what rights and benefits are associated with that asset. The issue is best explained by introducing the example used in FRED 4.

Suppose that an entity transfers title to a portfolio of high quality debts of 100 in exchange for non-returnable proceeds of 90 plus rights to a further sum whose amount depends on whether and when the debts are paid. If we assume that the 90 is under no circumstances repayable then there are three ways of presenting the position in the balance sheet:

(a) Show the asset as 100 and a liability, distinct and separate, of 90. The problem with this form of presentation is that it would not reflect clearly the fact that the 90 liability has no relevance to the remaining assets of the entity and would, in particular, give a misleading view of the security of the entity.

(b) Set off the two amounts and show 10 as an asset. This may appear to be the most sensible procedure but it is argued that because the eventual return to the entity depends on the behaviour of the whole portfolio of debts which has been factored the risks remaining are the normal risks which could be related to that total portfolio of debt.

(c) Use what FRED 4 describes as the 'linked presentation' method, that is to show on the face of the balance sheet both the gross asset of 100 less possibly a small deduction for the normal provision against doubtful debts, and a deduction of 90. It is claimed that this presentation shows both that the entity retains significant benefits and risks relating to the whole portfolio of debts and that the claims of the provider of the finance are limited solely to the funds generated by the debts.

The proposed provision which would require the use of the linked presentation approach in certain specified conditions is one of the more significant ways in which FRED 4 differs from ED 49 and the proposal is one which the ASB has specifically asked for comment in the consultative period.

The art of financial statement preparation is not well served by over-elaboration and the drawing of fine distinctions based on immaterial differences. The 'linked presentation' proposal smacks of over-elaboration and its application would provide only marginal assistance to the users of accounts while adding the possibility of confusion. To take the ASB's own example, what is the asset, 100 or 10? Ignoring bad debts it is 10, the maximum that will be received in the future from the asset; 90 has been received but would in no circumstances have to be repaid so it is not a liability. Why suggest that it is? The obvious way of accounting for the transaction is to show the asset at 10 less an appropriate provision against doubtful debts. The fact that the provision is actually based on 100 rather than 10 can be explained in the notes if the fact is material.

The conditions which would have to be satisfied if linked presentation is to be used are stringent and it is likely that the proposal would apply only to a very limited range of transactions.

Offset

It is a general requirement of UK Company Law that assets and liability should not be netted off. The only exception is where a right of set-off exists between monetary assets and liabilities, such as for example, bank balances and overdrafts with the same party. Whilst in practice the proposals of FRED 4 would normally lead to the same result as the consequence of following the statutory requirements, FRED 4 is couched in rather more restricted terms. The proposed standard is

> Debit and credit balances should be aggregated into a single net item where, and only where, they do not constitute separate assets and liabilities: assets and liabilities should not be offset.

(Para. 24)

It is stated (Para. 68) that for an offset to occur all the following three conditions must be met.

(a) That the reporting entity has an unconditional right to insist on a net settlement.
(b) That the reporting entity's ability to insist on a net settlement is assured beyond doubt. It is essential that there is no chance that the entity could be required to transfer economic benefits to the other party whilst being unable to enforce its own access to economic benefits. For example, it is necessary that the legal arrangements should be secure enough to ensure that the ability to insist on a net settlement would survive at the insolvency of the other party.
(c) That the reporting entity does not bear significant risk associated with the gross amounts. The two items will need to be of the same kind so the changes in the amount of benefits relating to one would be mirrored by changes in the amounts of benefits flowing from the other. An example of the situation where this will not be the case is one where the items are denominated in different currencies.

Disclosure

In the world of complex transactions some assets may differ in some ways from most other assets and some liabilities, such as limited recourse finance, may differ from the generality of liabilities. A common example of a different form of asset is one which, while it is available for use in the trading activities of the enterprise, may not be available as security for a loan. In all such cases sufficient information should be provided to help the users of the financial statements appreciate the nature of the assets and liabilities involved (FRED 4, Para. 26).

Additional disclosure might also be required when, although the analysis of the transaction leads to the view that assets and liabilities need not be recognised in the balance sheet, it nonetheless appears that there are risks or benefits involved about which users need to be informed if they are to understand the commercial effect of a transaction. In some cases, the items might be specifically required to be disclosed by company law or accounting or reporting standards, for example, a contingent liability (FRED 4, Para. 25).

Quasi-subsidiaries

FRED 4 observes that there can be instances where, although the relationship between two companies may not constitute a parent/subsidiary relationship as defined by statute, the dominant company might have as much effective control over the assets of the other as would have been the case had the company been a subsidiary. A simple example is one where the dominant company holds less than 50 per cent of the equity of the other company but has an option to acquire additional shares which would take its holding over 50 per cent.

The draft standard refers to the controlled company as a quasi-subsidiary which it defines as follows:

> A quasi-subsidiary of a reporting entity is a company, trust, partnership or other vehicle which, though not fulfilling the definition of a subsidiary, is directly or indirectly controlled by the reporting entity and represents a source of benefit inflows or outflows for that entity that are in substance no different from those that would arise were the vehicle a subsidiary.

(FRED 4, Para. 6)

The concept of substance over form requires that a company which is in effect a subsidiary should be treated as such and this is supported by Section 227 (6), Companies Act, 1985 as amended by the Companies Act 1989, which specifies that, if in special circumstances, compliance with any provisions of the Act with respect to the matters to be included in a company's group accounts or in the notes thereto is inconsistent with the true and fair view requirement, the directors shall depart from that specific provision to the extent necessary to give a true and fair view. FRED 4 points out that the nature of quasi-subsidiaries is such that their existence will usually constitute such special circumstances. Thus, they should be included in the group accounts in the same way as legally defined subsidiary undertakings. If the dominant company does not have legally defined subsidiaries, then the notes to accounts should include the consolidated accounts of the dominant and quasi-subsidiary companies (FRED 4, Para. 30).

The conditions under which subsidiaries are permitted or required to be excluded are set out in FRS 2 'Accounting for subsidiary undertakings', but the grounds for exclusion are not generally applicable to quasi-subsidiaries which by definition need to be included in the consolidation if a true and fair view is to be obtained. FRED 4 concludes that the only circumstances under which quasi-subsidiaries should be excluded is when the quasi-subsidiary is held only with a view to subsequent sale and has not previously been included in the entity's consolidated accounts (FRED 4, Para. 31).

One set of circumstances is identified in the draft standard where the accounting treatment of a quasi-subsidiary would differ from that of a fully-fledged subsidiary. This occurs when the quasi-subsidiary holds either a single item or a single portfolio of similar items which are financed in such a way as to require the use of linked presentation. In the case of a quasi-subsidiary, linked presentation should be used in the consolidated balance sheet if the requirements which need to be met can be satisfied by the group (Para. 32). The difference in the case of a legal subsidiary is that linked presentation should only be used on the consolidated balance sheet if it is also applicable to the subsidiary's own balance sheet, in other words all the conditions need to be met by the subsidiary itself. This particular refinement is required in order to comply with the Companies Act under which the subsidiary is part of the group as legally defined and hence its assets and liabilities are assets and liabilities of the group and need to be treated in the consolidation in the normal way (FRED 4, Para. 80).

The section of FRED 4 on quasi-subsidiaries does not incorporate any major items of principle, unless the point about linked presentation discussed above is regarded as such, but mainly provides guidance and authority on the use of the override principle of the Companies Act.

Summary of FRED 4

The main elements of the draft standard have been dealt with in the text so there is little point in reproducing them here. We will, however, summarise the main points in the following list:

1 The substance of transactions should be recorded; greater weight should be given to aspects which are likely to have a commercial effect.
2 Complex transactions should be analysed to see whether the enterprise's assets or liabilities have been affected.
3 If assets and liabilities are identified then general tests need to be applied to see whether they should be recognised. Reference may also need to be made to other FRSs, SSAPs or statute.
4 Essentially there are four possible outcomes to the analysis:
   (a) Record the asset and liability separately
   (b Apply linked presentation
   (c) Offset (very rare)
   (d) Ignore the transaction.
5 Adequate disclosure is required, in particular (i) where the asset or liability recognised in the financial statements differs in some respects from the generality of assets and liabilities and (ii) where, although identified, assets or liabilities are not recognised, in the primary and financial statements.
6 Quasi-subsidiaries should be treated in much the same way as legal subsidiaries.

FRED 4 application notes

There are five application notes covering: consignment stock; sale and repurchase agreements; factoring of debts; securitised assets and loan transfers. Each application note has three sections: *features* which describe the nature of required transactions; *analysis* which analyses the transaction in terms of the framework of FRED 4 and *required accounting* which is the proposed standard covering recognition in the financial statement and disclosure in the notes. In addition each note contains tables and illustrations which are intended for general guidance and which do not form part of the proposed standard.

Postscript to FRED 4

The provisions of FRED 4, if implemented, would constitute a complex, if not over-complex, reporting standard which would only apply to a small minority of financial statements. However, in the cases where the standard would apply its effect would often be significant because complex transactions typically involve large amounts. The aims of the ASB in attempting to minimise off balance sheet financing is entirely laudable but it remains to be seen whether any reporting standard which emerges from FRED 4 would provide a set of principles sufficiently comprehensive and robust to cope with ingenuity of the capital markets.

RECOMMENDED READING

T. M. Clark, *Leasing*, McGraw-Hill, Maidenhead, 1978.

Coopers & Lybrand Deloitte, *Accounting for Lessees following SSAP 21*, London, 1984.

Coopers & Lybrand Deloitte, *Accounting by Lessors following SSAP 21*, London, 1984.

B. A. Rutherford, *The Doctrine of Substance over Form*, Certified Accountants Publications Limited, London, 1988.

Pauline Weetman, *Assets and Liabilities: Their Definition and Recognition*, Certified Accountants Publications Limited, London, 1989.

CHAPTER 7

Taxation

INTRODUCTION

The treatment of taxation in accounts is regulated not only by the Companies Acts, with which readers are assumed to be familiar, but also by three Statements of Standard Accounting Practice: SSAP 5, 'Accounting for valued added tax' (April 1974); SSAP 8, 'The treatment of taxation under the imputation system in the accounts of companies' (amended version December 1977); and SSAP 15, 'Accounting for deferred taxation' (October 1978, revised 1985).

Although the treatment of value added tax may require complex book-keeping arrangements, it poses few theoretical problems and is therefore not dealt with in this book. The treatment of taxation under the imputation tax system does pose certain difficulties, while the appropriate treatment of deferred taxation is an extremely controversial subject. Both topics are covered in this chapter.

THE TREATMENT OF TAXATION UNDER THE IMPUTATION TAX SYSTEM

The imputation tax system

Readers are assumed to be aware of the law relating to the taxation of companies and hence only a brief summary is provided. It is assumed throughout this section that the rate of corporation tax is 33 per cent and the rate of advance corporation tax (ACT) is one quarter.

When a company makes a distribution to shareholders in a particular period then, to the extent that the distribution has not been paid out of franked investment income (*see* page 180) of that same period, the company must pay over to the Inland Revenue ACT amounting to one-quarter of the distribution or, where appropriate, the excess of the distribution over franked investment income. For this purpose the year is divided into four quarters which run to 31 March, 30 June, 30 September and 31 December, although special rules are provided where a company's year does not end on one of these four dates. ACT must be paid within 14 days of the end of each quarter.

At the end of its accounting period the corporation tax payable on profits is computed. Profits include both income (apart from franked investment income) and chargeable gains. ACT in respect of distributions made during that accounting period is set against corporation tax on profits subject to an overriding maximum of 20 per cent of those profits. The balance, or mainstream corporation tax, is payable nine months after the end of the company's accounting period or within 30 days from the date of issue of the assessment if this is later.

Where a company resident in the UK carries on activities overseas, the profits made overseas will usually be subject to both overseas taxation and UK corporation tax, although, as we shall see, the UK tax payable may be reduced by all or part of the overseas tax payable.

SSAP 8

This Statement of Standard Accounting Practice requires that the following items should be included in the taxation charge in the profit and loss account and, where material, separately disclosed:[1]

(a) The amount of United Kingdom corporation tax specifying:
  (i)   the charge for corporation tax on the income of the year (where such corporation tax includes transfers between the deferred taxation account these should also be separately disclosed where material);
  (ii) tax attributable to franked investment income;
  (iii) irrecoverable ACT;
  (iv) the relief for overseas taxation.
(b) The total overseas taxation, relieved and unrelieved, specifying that part of the unrelieved overseas taxation which arises from the payment or proposed payment of dividends.

We shall examine each of these items in turn, discussing both the treatment in the profit and loss account and the associated treatment in the balance sheet. Deferred taxation will be dealt with later.

Corporation tax

At the end of each accounting period a company will compute the corporation tax payable on its profits, that is its income and chargeable gains, for the period.

The resulting liability will be deducted from the relevant ordinary or extraordinary profits in the profit and loss account and credited to a corporation tax payable account.

This corporation tax is payable nine months after the end of the company's accounting period and will therefore be included in the balance sheet as a creditor falling due within one year. Although the balance sheet formats provide headings for 'other creditors including taxation and social security', the Companies Act 1985 specifically requires the disclosure of the amount for creditors in respect of taxation and social security separately from other creditors.[2]

Tax on franked investment income

Frequently a company which is resident in the UK receives dividends, more generally distributions, from one or more other companies also resident in the UK. The amount of such dividends plus the associated tax credits is known as 'franked investment income'. Thus, if a company receives a dividend of £800 and the relevant rate of tax credit is one-quarter, the franked investment income is £1000. Such franked investment income is not subject to corporation tax.

1 SSAP 8, Para. 22.
2 Companies Act 1985, Schedule 4, Notes on the balance sheet formats (9).

Although it would be possible to ignore the tax credit altogether and merely to record as a source of income the amount of the dividend received, this would be inconsistent with the treatment of other sources of income. SSAP 8, Para. 13, therefore requires that the franked investment income, that is the 'gross' amount, should be shown as income while the tax credit should be shown as part of the taxation charge. Using the figures above, receipt of the dividend would be recorded as part of the profit and loss account entries as follows:

	£	£
Income from investments		1 000
less Taxation:		
Corporation tax, etc	X	
Taxation on franked investment income	200	X

As we have seen, it is possible for a company which receives franked investment income to reduce the amount of ACT payable in respect of a distribution by the amount of the tax credit on that franked investment income for the same period. It should be noted that this merely affects the amount of ACT payable and does not alter the accounting treatment discussed above.

ACT

When a company pays a dividend it will, assuming it has received insufficient franked investment income, also have to pay an amount of ACT within 14 days of the end of the relevant quarter or other shorter period. It follows that whenever a company provides for a dividend in its accounts it must also provide for the associated ACT payable. Such ACT payable is a current liability and, like the dividend payable, is extinguished when payment is made. The creation of this liability for ACT involves a credit entry in an account for 'ACT payable' but it is, of course, necessary to have a debit entry in an account which may be described as 'ACT recoverable'. As explained earlier, the law allows this amount to be set off against corporation tax payable for the accounting period in which the dividend is paid, i.e. not that for the period in which the dividend is proposed. The treatment may best be illustrated by means of an example:

Let us suppose that we are dealing with a company which prepares accounts annually to 31 December and pays mainstream corporation tax nine months after that date. In the year ended 31 December 19X1 it pays an interim dividend of £160 000 on 17 July and has a taxable profit of £2 000 000. It follows that ACT amounting to £40 000 (one-quarter of £160 000) becomes payable on 14 October 19X1, 14 days after the end of the quarter in which the dividend is paid. Mainstream corporation tax, payable on 30 September 19X2, is computed as follows:

	£000
Corporation tax for accounting year ended	
31 December 19X1 – 33% of £2 000 000	660
less ACT on dividend paid in year ended	
31 December 19X1	40
Mainstream corporation tax	620

The relevant book-keeping entries relating to taxation, assuming that all payments are made on the due dates, are:

ACT payable

19X1	£	19X1	£
14 Oct Cash	40 000	17 Jul ACT recoverable	40 000

ACT recoverable

19X1	£	19X1	£
17 Jul ACT payable		31 Dec Corporation	
	40 000	tax payable	40 000

Corporation tax payable

19X1	£	19X1	£
31 Dec ACT		31 Dec Profit and	
recoverable	40 000	loss account	660 000
Mainstream CT c/d	620 000		
	660 000		660 000
		19X2	
		1 Jan Balance b/d	620 000

The profit and loss account for 19X1 includes a corporation tax charge of £660 000 while the balance sheet on 31 December 19X1 contains a current liability for mainstream corporation tax of £620 000 payable on 30 September 19X2.

The example may now be expanded to include not only the interim dividend paid but also a proposed final dividend of £400 000 payable on 20 March 19X2. The payment of this dividend will give rise to a payment of ACT of £100 000 on 14 April 19X2, 14 days after the end of the relevant quarter. As the final dividend is recognised as a current liability on 31 December 19X1, it is also necessary to provide for the current liability for ACT by crediting the 'ACT payable' account. Correspondingly it is necessary to debit the 'ACT recoverable' account.

It is the date of payment of the dividend which determines the appropriate accounting year for set-off.[3] Thus, as the final dividend is not paid until 20 March 19X2, the ACT will be set off against the corporation tax payable on profits for the year ended 31 December 19X2. In this example, such corporation tax is not payable until 30 September 19X3. In other words at 31 December 19X1 the ACT of £100 000 is not recoverable for 21 months. It therefore represents a deferred asset to be shown as a debtor in the balance sheet or, more usually for reasons which will become apparent, set against any relevant credit balance on the deferred taxation account. The appropriate accounting entries in respect of taxation, repeating those dealt with above, are as follows:

3 Note that it is the date of payment of the dividend, *not* the date of payment of the ACT, which determines the appropriate year for set-off. Thus, ACT in respect of a dividend paid on 14 November 19X1 may be set off against the corporation tax liability for the year to 31 December 19X1, even though that ACT is not paid until 14 January 19X2.

ACT payable

19X1		£	19X1		£
14 Oct	Cash	40 000	17 Jul	ACT recoverable	40 000
			31 Dec	ACT recoverable (re proposed (dividend)	100 000

ACT recoverable

19X1		£	19X1		£
			31 Dec	Corporation tax payable	40 000
17 Jul	ACT payable	40 000			
31 Dec	ACT payable	100 000			

Corporation tax payable

19X1		£	19X1		£
31 Dec	ACT recoverable	40 000	31 Dec	Profit and loss account	660 000
	Mainstream CT c/d	620 000			
		660 000			660 000
			19X2		
			1 Jan	Mainstream CT payable 30 Sep 19X2 b/d	620 000

The profit and loss account for 19X1 will, as before, include the corporation tax charge of £660 000. The balance sheet on 31 December 19X1 will include two current liabilities in respect of taxation:

	£
ACT payable on 14 April 19X2 in respect of final dividend for 19X1	100 000
Mainstream corporation tax for 19X1 payable on 30 September 19X2	620 000
	720 000

It will also include the amount of £100 000 in respect of ACT recoverable either as a debtor due after more than one year or as a reduction in the credit balance on deferred taxation account.

So far, we have assumed that the company has had sufficient profits subject to corporation tax for the set off of ACT to be possible. In such a case, the payment of ACT does not increase the amount of corporation tax payable but simply advances the date on which some of it is paid. However, where a company pays a large dividend in relation to its taxable profits, the set off may be restricted and, in the extreme case, a company may have no corporation tax liability against which to set the ACT.[4] In such cases it is necessary

---

4 The problem of 'surplus' ACT has become particularly acute for UK companies which pay dividends out of foreign profits. Because double tax relief is set off against corporation tax on the foreign profits before ACT, some companies have permanent or 'structural' surplus ACT. The Inland Revenue published a consultative document 'Corporation Tax: surplus ACT: proposals for reform' in 1993.

to consider whether or not any debit balance on ACT recoverable account should be regarded as an asset or instead written off to the profit and loss account as 'irrecoverable advance corporation tax'.

In considering this question it is most important not to confuse the treatment of ACT recoverable for taxation purposes with its accounting treatment. For taxation purposes ACT unrelieved due to insufficient taxable profits for the accounting period may be carried back for six years or carried forward indefinitely. If it is carried back, then the ACT is, of course, recovered. If it is carried forward, then nothing that is done in the accounts will remove the right of ultimate set-off for taxation purposes. However, the ACT will only be recovered if there are sufficient taxable profits in future years and, if the company is not expected to generate such taxable profits, then it may be argued that prudence dictates that the ACT recoverable should no longer be regarded as an asset but should instead be written off to the profit and loss account. This need to write off ACT recoverable does not apply where it is set off against a credit balance on deferred taxation account but only where the ACT recoverable is treated as a separate deferred asset. In this case SSAP 8 states that it is prudent only to have regard to the immediate and foreseeable future and suggests that this should normally not extend beyond the next accounting period.[5]

Overseas taxation

A company resident in the UK is liable to corporation tax on all its profits whether they arise in the UK or overseas. As profits which have arisen overseas are usually subject to taxation in the relevant overseas country, they may therefore be subject to double taxation. Similarly, where a UK company receives dividends from the taxed profits of an overseas subsidiary, such dividends are neither franked investment income nor group income and hence are subject to UK corporation tax.

It is usually possible to obtain relief for such double taxation, although the precise nature of the relief depends upon the terms of any double taxation convention between the UK government and the relevant overseas government. Where there is no double tax convention, it is still possible to obtain unilateral relief for double taxation.

In some cases it is possible to obtain relief against UK corporation tax for the whole of the overseas taxation payable but, in other cases, some of the overseas taxation may be unrelieved. One example of the latter is where the rate of overseas taxation on overseas profits exceeds the rate of UK corporation tax on those same profits. To illustrate, let us suppose that a UK company has taxable profits of £300 000 overseas and an additional £2 000 000 in the UK. The rate of overseas corporation tax is 50 per cent while the rate of UK corporation tax is 33 per cent.

The corporation tax payable overseas is 50 per cent of £300 000, that is £150 000, while the corporation tax payable in the UK is 33 per cent of £(2 000 000 + 300 000), that is £759 000. As the UK corporation tax payable on overseas income is only £99 000 (33 per cent of £300 000) this is the maximum relief which may be given against the overseas taxation of £150 000.

Following the layout of Appendix 1 to SSAP 8, the taxation charge in the profit and loss account would therefore include the following:

---

5 SSAP 8, Para. 6.

	£000
Corporation tax on income – 33% of £2 300 000	759
less Relief for overseas taxation	99
	660
Overseas taxation	150
	810

We have now illustrated all of the items which SSAP 8 requires to be disclosed in the profit and loss account or notes to the accounts.

ACCOUNTING FOR DEFERRED TAXATION

Timing differences

Although accounting profits form the basis for the computation of taxable profits in the UK, for most companies there are substantial differences between the two. Such differences may be divided into two categories: (a) permanent differences; (b) timing differences.

In the case of permanent differences certain items of revenue or expense properly taken into account in arriving at accounting profit are not included when arriving at taxable profit. Examples are regional development grants received, amounts spent on entertainment and depreciation of non-industrial buildings.

In the case of timing differences, the same total amount is added or subtracted in arriving at both accounting profits and taxable profits over a period of years, but it is added or subtracted in different periods. Whatever is given is taken away! It is the existence of such timing differences which gives rise to the perceived need to account for deferred taxation.

There are a number of variations between accounting practice and taxation law which give rise to timing differences and, at the present time, the more important are:

(a) short-term differences from the use of the receipts and payments basis in taxation computations and the accruals basis in financial statements; these differences normally reverse in the subsequent accounting period although they may be replaced by new originating differences;

(b) availability of capital allowances in taxation computations which are different from the related depreciation charges in financial statements;

(c) capitalisation of finance leases where, so far as the lessee is concerned, tax relief is given in respect of the rentals payable for an accounting period while the profit and loss account is charged with depreciation of the leased asset and interest on the finance provided;

(d) pension contributions payable allowed for tax purposes which differ from the pension cost determined in accordance with the provisions of SSAP 24;

(e) unrealised revaluation surpluses on fixed assets, for which a taxation charge does not arise until the gain is realised on disposal of the asset;

(f) realised surpluses on the disposal of fixed assets which are subject to rollover relief for taxation purposes;

(g) tax losses carried forward to be used against taxable profits which arise in the future.

One of the four fundamental accounting concepts listed in SSAP 2 is the 'accruals' concept, under which expenses are matched against the revenues recognised in a particular accounting year. While some accountants might argue that taxation is an appropriation of profit, the vast majority would classify it as an expense. If it is so regarded, then it follows that taxation is subject to the accruals concept and that the taxation charge should be matched against the accounting profit to which it relates.

To illustrate, let us consider an example of a short-term timing difference.

Sabah Limited makes up its accounts annually to 31 December and has an operating profit of £1 800 000 in both 19X1 and 19X2. There are no permanent differences but there is a timing difference. On 1 July 19X1 Sabah invested £2 000 000 to earn interest at a fixed rate of 16 per cent per annum payable on 30 June 19X2. The interest of £320 000 is taxable in the year it is received at the rate of 33 per cent while the company accrues interest in its financial statements. If no provision is made for deferred taxation, the profit and loss accounts for the two years 19X1 and 19X2 would appear as follows:

Profit and loss accounts for the years ended 31 December 19X1 and 19X2

	19X1	19X2
	£000	£000
Operating profit	1800	1800
Interest receivable	160	160
Profit before taxation	1960	1960
less Corporation tax:		
33% x 1 800 000	594	
33% x (1 800 000 + 320 000)		700
Profit after taxation	1366	1260

The picture shown by these profit and loss accounts is, arguably, misleading and, in particular, any prediction of the 19X2 profit after tax using the accounts of 19X1 may tend to be too high. Tax of £105 600 (33% x £320 000) is payable in respect of the interest received in 19X2. If half of the interest received is recognised in the profit and loss account for 19X1 and half in the profit and loss account for 19X2, then, arguably, it makes sense to spread the tax bill over the same periods by the use of a deferred taxation account:

Profit and loss accounts for the years ended 31 December 19X1 and 19X2

	19X1	19X2
	£000	£000
Operating profit	1 800	1 800
Interest receivable	160	160
Profit before taxation	1 960	1 960
less Taxation:		
Corporation tax (as above):		
33% x 1 800 000	594	
33% x (1 800 000 + 320 000)		700
Deferred tax:		
On originating timing difference,		
33% x 160 000	53	
On reversing timing difference,		
33% x 160 000		(53)
	647	647
Profit after taxation	1 313	1 313

In 19X1 the accounting profit exceeds the taxable profit by £160 000, while in 19X2 the taxable profit exceeds the accounting profit by that same amount. As may be seen above, the use of a deferred taxation account in this simple situation results in a tax charge based on the accounting profit of each period. In 19X1 the profit and loss account is debited and a deferred taxation account is credited with tax on the originating timing difference of £160 000 while, in the following year, the deferred taxation account is debited and profit and loss account effectively credited with tax on the reversing timing difference of £160 000.

Few would quarrel with the use of a deferred taxation account in such simple circumstances. However, things are not always so simple so let us now explore the timing differences which arise where capital allowances exceed depreciation.

SSAP 12 'Accounting for depreciation' requires that fixed assets should be depreciated as 'fairly' as possible over the lives of those assets estimated on a 'realistic' basis. Subject to these parameters and, in particular, the opinions of its auditors, each company may select its own depreciation methods. A long-standing feature of the tax system is that the depreciation charge as shown in the financial statements is not an allowable charge in arriving at taxable profits. Instead relief for tax purposes is given through capital allowances. The major reason for this has been the wish of governments to prevent companies from delaying the payment of tax by the adoption of unreasonably accelerated methods of depreciation. Conversely, at some times, the government has used the capital allowance system to encourage investment by granting generous capital allowances for expenditure on certain types of fixed assets. For example, from 1972 to 1984, companies were allowed to claim a first year allowance of 100 per cent in respect of expenditure on plant and machinery, thus obtaining tax relief for the whole cost of such assets in the year of acquisition. The existence of such 100 per cent first year allowances led to substantial timing differences for many companies.[6]

---

6 To these were added timing differences relating to stock appreciation relief. This relief was given, in three different forms, between April 1973 and March 1984 to provide companies with some relief from taxation for the effect of price increases on their trading stocks.

The current system of capital allowances is less generous than the above and, in respect of plant and machinery, there is now no first year allowance, only a writing down allowance of 25 per cent, applied on a reducing balance basis. However, even with this less generous system, substantial timing differences still arise and it is instructive to examine the case of an asset with a five-year life.

Let us assume that Hongbo Limited makes up accounts annually to 31 December. On 1 January 19XI it purchases a machine for £500 000. The machine has an expected life of five years at the end of which its residual value is expected to be £120 000.[7]

The company uses the straight-line method so that the annual depreciation charge is £76 000 ((500 000 – 120 000) ÷ 5).

The depreciation charge and writing down allowance are therefore as given in columns (*ii*) and (*iii*) of Table 7.1.

Table 7.1

(i) Year	(ii) Depreciation	(iii) Capital allowances	(iv) Difference (iii) – (ii)	(v) Tax on difference at 33%	(vi) Balance at year end on deferred tax a/c
	£000	£000	£000	£000	£000
1	76	125	49	16	16
2	76	94	18	6	22
3	76	70	–6	–2	20
4	76	53	–23	–8	12
5	76	38	–38	–12	–
	380	380	0		

This table shows how the deferred tax account is built up. In years 1 and 2 there are originating timing differences: capital allowances exceed depreciation so that taxable profits are lower than accounting profits. The tax charge in the profit and loss account must be increased and there is a resulting credit balance on the deferred taxation account. In years 3 to 5 there are reversing timing differences: Capital allowances are less than depreciation so that taxable profits exceed accounting profits. The tax charge in the profit and loss account is reduced thus 'drawing down' and finally extinguishing the balance on the deferred taxation account.

If we assume that the company has a constant profit of £2 m before depreciation and taxation and that there are no permanent differences or other timing differences, the consequences of accounting for deferred taxation may be seen:

---

7 For illustrative purposes, the expected residual value has been assumed to approximate the tax written down value at the end of five years, namely $500\,000\,(1 - 0.25)^5 = 118\,652 \simeq 120\,000$.

Profit and loss account for the year to 31 December

	19X1	19X2	19X3	19X4	19X5
	£000	£000	£000	£000	£000
Profit before depreciation	2 000	2 000	2 000	2 000	2 000
Depreciation	76	76	76	76	76
	1 924	1 924	1 924	1 924	1 924
Taxation					
Corporation tax @ 33%[8]	619	629	637	643	647
Deferred tax – as per					
Table 7.1	16	6	(2)	(8)	(12)
	635	635	635	635	635
Profit after tax	1 289	1 289	1 289	1 289	1 289

The use of a deferred taxation account in this situation results in a tax charge which is 33 per cent of the accounting profit of each period. It is therefore possible to argue that the use of the deferred taxation account is necessary to comply with the accruals concept and that comprehensive tax allocation, that is the making of a full provision for deferred taxation, provides useful information. However, it is important to bear in mind the simplifications which have been made.

First, we have assumed that the rate of corporation tax is the same in each of the five years. Were the rate of tax to change, then it would be necessary to make a choice on whether to apply the 'deferral' method or the 'liability' method of accounting for deferred taxation.

Under the deferral method all reversing timing differences in respect of an asset are, in principle, reversed at the same rate of tax as that applied to the originating timing difference on that asset. To apply this method to a multi-asset firm strictly involves extensive record keeping and hence, when it is used in practice, it is usual to apply an approximate 'net change' method. Thus, where there is a net originating difference for a group of assets in a particular year, it is dealt with at the current rate of tax. If, however, there is a net reversing difference in respect of those assets, it is reversed using some rule of thumb, such as FIFO or the average rate of tax on accumulated timing differences.

Under the liability method, whenever there is a change in the rate of tax, the balance on the deferred taxation account is adjusted to that current rate of tax on accumulated timing differences. Subsequent reversing differences are made at the new rate of tax. It follows that, to operate the liability method, it is not necessary to keep such detailed records as those required for the deferral method as calculations may be made in total. To give one example: to calculate the balance on deferred taxation required because of the differences in capital allowances and depreciation on fixed assets, it is merely necessary to know the differences between the net book value and tax written down value of the relevant assets and the current rate of tax on the balance sheet date. The liability method is therefore much simpler to apply than the deferral method and has been the more popular of the two methods.

The second simplification which we have made is to assume that Hongbo Limited

8 Corporation tax payable for each year is calculated as follows (£000):
19X1 (2 000 – 125) = 1875 x 33% = 619
19X2 (2 000 – 94) = 1906 x 33% = 629
19X3 (2 000 – 70) = 1930 x 33% = 637
19X4 (2 000 – 53) = 1947 x 33% = 643
19X5 (2 000 – 38) = 1962 x 33% = 647

purchased one machine in 19X1 but made no further purchases in 19X2–19X5. We shall now explore the position where a company makes regular purchases by assuming that Hongbo Limited purchases one machine each year at a constant cost of £500 000. The depreciation charges and writing down allowances for tax purposes are then as shown in columns (*ii*) and (*iii*) of Table 7.2.

Table 7.2

(i) Year	(ii) Depreciation	(iii) Capital allowances	(iv) Difference (iii) − (ii)	(v) Tax on difference at 33%	(vi) Balance at year end on deferred tax a/c
	£000	£000	£000	£000	£000
19X1 (1 machine)	76	125	49	16	16
19X2 (2 machines)	152	219	67	22	38
19X3 (3 machines)	228	289	61	20	58
19X4 (4 machines)	304	342	38	13	71
19X5 (5 machines)	380	380	−	−	71
19X6 (5 machines)	380	380	−	−	71

From Table 7.2 it can be seen that the balance on the deferred tax account gradually builds up and that, eventually, a steady state is reached in 19X5. From 19X5 capital allowances and depreciation are equal and originating timing differences offset reversing timing differences. Thus, if Hongbo Limited continues to invest a constant amount each year, there will be no net reversal of timing differences and the balance on the deferred tax account will remain constant at £71 000.

We could develop this theme further by assuming that the cost of the machine increased year by year and, in such a case, we would find again that there would be no net reversing differences with the consequence that the balance on the deferred tax account would become larger and larger.

An examination of the accounts of companies which used comprehensive tax allocation in the 1970s shows how rarely there was a draw-down or reduction in the deferred tax balance from year to year and how large the balance on deferred taxation account could become.[9]

Such a deferred taxation balance, using comprehensive tax allocation, was normally disclosed as a separate item in the balance sheet of a company and certainly not as part of the shareholders' equity. If the balance was not part of the shareholders' equity, then a knowledge of elementary accounting would suggest that it was a liability. However, this may be questioned. As we have seen, for many companies it may well not have been payable in the foreseeable future and, in such cases, its inclusion in the balance sheet may therefore have been regarded as inconsistent with the going concern concept.

The inclusion of a full provision for deferred taxation in the balance sheet of a company undoubtedly posed problems of interpretation in many cases. If the amount was not part

---

9 For example, the accounts of Thorn Electrical Industries for 1978 showed that deferred taxation was approximately one-third of its long-term capital. This fell enormously when the company adopted partial tax allocation in 1979.

of the shareholders' equity, then it must presumably have been included as part of other long-term capital in measuring gearing, although in this case many UK companies which used comprehensive tax allocation appeared to be rather highly geared!

As we shall see, problems such as these caused the ASC to depart from comprehensive tax allocation in favour of partial tax allocation.

Attempts at standardisation: ED 11 to SSAP 15

The Accounting Standards Steering Committee made its first attempt at a standard method of accounting for deferred taxation when it issued ED 11, 'Accounting for deferred taxation', in May 1973. This proposed that companies should account for deferred taxation on all material timing differences using the deferral method; thus it favoured comprehensive tax allocation. The ensuing SSAP 11, which was published in August 1975, followed this approach, although it permitted companies to use either the deferral method or the liability method.

SSAP 11 came under such heavy criticism from industry that its starting date was postponed indefinitely and it was eventually withdrawn. The ASC was criticised for this withdrawal and many saw it as a manifestation of weakness, that is the ASC bending in the face of opposition rather than taking a strong line. Others saw it as an example of the ASC rightly responding to criticism, although even such supporters would argue that critics should make their views known during the exposure period rather than after a standard has been published.

ED 19, which was issued in May 1977, adopted a very different approach from SSAP 11. Instead of requiring comprehensive tax allocation, it permitted partial tax allocation in certain circumstances. Thus, instead of requiring companies to perform a mechanical calculation to provide for deferred taxation on all timing differences, it recognised that not all timing differences would reverse in the foreseeable future and consequently permitted a more subjective approach which took into account the circumstances of the particular company. Even where a company took advantage of this permissive approach, it was still required to provide a note to the balance sheet showing the potential deferred taxation on all timing differences and this potential deferred taxation was to be calculated using the liability method.

SSAP 15 was originally issued in 1978 and reissued in a revised form in 1985, following the publication of an Exposure Draft (ED 33). The basic principle of SSAP 15 is to permit companies to make a partial provision, using the liability method, so long as the amount of the potential deferred tax not provided for is stated by way of note.

The current version of SSAP 15 differs from the original on the matter of the balance of proof. In the original version SSAP 15 started with the presumption that full provision should be made unless it could be shown that the liability (or asset) would not crystallise. The current version is more even-handed: if it is probable that the liability (or asset) will crystallise, then provide; if it is probable that it will not crystallise, then do not provide.

The approach of SSAP 15 (1985)

Under the provisions of SSAP 15, companies are required to account for timing differences to the extent that it is probable that a liability or asset will crystallise but not to account for timing differences to the extent that it is probable that a liability or asset will not crystallise (Paras 25 and 26). The decision on whether deferred tax liabilities or assets will or will not crystallise involves looking into the future and should be based upon reasonable assumptions (Para. 27).

In calculating the amount of any provision, the liability method must be used (Para. 24) and the major components of the provision must be disclosed in the balance sheet or notes to the accounts (Para. 27). In addition the total amount of *unprovided* deferred taxation should be disclosed as a note, analysed into its major components (Para. 40). It follows that accountants now need to know not only how to calculate a partial provision but also how to calculate a full provision, so that the amount unprovided may be disclosed.

Whereas a full provision for deferred taxation may be made on the basis of the knowledge of what has happened in the past, in order to make a partial provision, it is necessary to look into the future. Thus, it is necessary to look at financial plans or projections covering a period of years sufficient to enable an assessment to be made of the likely pattern of future tax liabilities (Para. 28). The Appendix, which is for guidance only, states that this period may be relatively short – say, three to five years – where the pattern of timing differences is expected to be regular (Appendix, Para. 4). Where such regularity is not expected, it will be necessary to peer even further into the future.

Although the SSAP is silent on the matter, the Appendix also states that 'The combined effect of timing differences should be considered when attempting to assess whether a tax liability will crystallise, rather than looking at each timing difference separately' (Appendix, Para. 4). Given that the objective is to arrive at a meaningful provision in the circumstances faced by each particular company, such a global approach is undoubtedly sensible, although it does sometimes make it difficult to give the required analysis of the provision.

In spite of this requirement to look at the combined effect of timing differences, for explanatory purposes, we shall look first at each of the seven major categories of timing difference identified earlier in this chapter. We shall assume a company which makes up accounts to 31 December and that we are deciding what, if any, provision is necessary at 31 December 19X1.

(a) Receipts and payments versus accruals

In order to decide whether or not to provide for deferred taxation at 31 December 19X1, it is necessary to look into the future to see whether or not a reversing difference is likely to occur.

Let us return to the example of Sabah Limited which invested £2m on 1 July 19X1 to earn interest at a fixed rate of 16 per cent payable on 30 June 19X2. The interest is taxable in the year of receipt while, in its financial statements, the company accrued interest as it was earned, that is £160 000 in 19X1 and £160 000 in 19X2. Whether or not a provision for deferred taxation is required at 31 December 19X1 depends upon whether the difference is likely to reverse without being replaced by a similar difference. This depends upon whether this is a short-term loan or a loan for a much longer period.

If the loan is for one year only, then the timing difference will reverse in 19X2. Taxable profits in 19X2 will exceed accounting profits by £160 000 and a provision for deferred taxation amounting to £52 800 (33% £160 000) will be required at 31 December 19X1.

If we assume that the loan is to be repaid to Sabah Limited with final interest on 30 June 19X4, then the expected future timing differences will be as follows:

	19X2	19X3	19X4
	£000	£000	£000
Reversing timing difference	160	160	160
Originating timing difference	160	160	–
Net reversing difference	–	–	160

In the absence of any other timing difference, taxable profits in 19X4 will be greater than accounting profits for that year and it is therefore necessary to provide for deferred taxation of £52 800 (33% of £160 000) at 31 December 19X1.

(b) Capital allowances and depreciation

In the example of Hongbo Limited, we have seen that where a company regularly purchases fixed assets eligible for accelerated capital allowances, new originating differences may exceed reversing timing differences. Thus, there may be a hard core of timing differences which are not expected to reverse while the company continues to operate under existing tax legislation. In such a case full provision for deferred tax is not necessary.

Where the expenditure on eligible fixed assets is erratic, then reversing timing differences may exceed future originating differences so that a net reversing difference occurs and a tax liability crystallises. In such a case, a provision for deferred taxation will be necessary, although there may be differences of opinion about the precise amount of the provision.

To illustrate, let us assume that a company, Teluk plc, is calculating the necessary provision at 31 December 19X1 and that, taking into account expected expenditure, capital allowances and depreciation, it has produced the following forecast for the next four years:

Forecast for the years ended 31 December

	19X2	19X3	19X4	19X5
	£000	£000	£000	£000
Capital allowances	1 000	1 000	600	1 200
Depreciation	800	900	950	1 000
Net originating differences	(200)	(100)	–	(200)
Net reversing differences	–	–	350	–

In the year ended 31 December 19X4, the taxable profits are expected to exceed the accounting profits by £350 000 and, given that the rate of tax in the year to 31 December 19X4 is expected to be 33 per cent, the tax involved is 33 per cent of £350 000, which is £115 500. The most prudent partial provision on 31 December 19X1 would therefore be £115 500.

However, it may be argued that this is too prudent and that it is necessary to take a cumulative view of the position in future years. On this basis the net reversing difference in the year to 31 December 19X4 is preceded by net originating differences in the years 19X2 and 19X3. Thus, it will be possible to make additional provisions in those two years so that the minimum amount to be provided at 31 December 19X1 may be calculated as follows:

	£000	£000
Net reversing differences in 19X4		350
less Future net originating differences		
19X2	200	
19X3	100	
		300
		50
Minimum provision necessary at 31 December 19X1		£
£50 000 x 33%		16 500

If this approach is adopted, then the provision at 31 December 19X1 will be £16 500 and, providing the forecasts are met, provisions of £66 000 (£200 000 x 33%) and £33 000 (£100 000 x 33%) will be made in 19X2 and 19X3 respectively. By the beginning of the year in which the net reversing difference occurs, there will be an accumulated provision equal to taxation on the net reversing difference, in this case £115 500.

SSAP 15 provides no guidance on how such a partial provision should be calculated and this leaves considerable scope for variations in practice.

(c) Capitalisation of finance leases

As we have seen in Chapter 6, SSAP 21 requires a lessee to capitalise finance leases. A consequence of this is that the profit and loss account is charged with depreciation and finance charges (interest) rather than with the rentals payable. As taxation relief is granted on lease rentals payable, the capitalisation of leases gives rise to timing differences.

In order to determine the amount of provision required in accordance with the principles of SSAP 15, it is necessary to look into the future. Considering both finance leases already entered into and capitalised before the balance sheet date and the finance leases which the company expects to enter into in the foreseeable future, forecasts of the depreciation of leased assets, finance charges and rentals payable in each year must be made. The forecast charges in the profit and loss account must then be compared with the rentals payable to determine whether or not a net reversing difference is expected to occur in the foreseeable future.

Let us suppose that Uchanya plc is preparing its accounts to 31 December 19X1 and that the directors have prepared the following forecasts for the next four years:

Forecasts for the years ended 31 December

	19X2	19X3	19X4	19X5
	£000	£000	£000	£000
Depreciation of leased assets	400	440	350	400
Finance charges re leased assets	160	200	180	200
	560	640	530	600
Rentals payable under finance leases	540	610	600	550
Net originating differences	20	30	–	50
Net reversing differences	–	–	(70)	–

In 19X2, 19X3 and 19X5, there will be net originating differences as taxable profits will exceed accounting profits. Only in 19X4 is there a net reversing difference when taxable profits are below accounting profits. To account for deferred taxation in this situation would require the setting up of a deferred tax asset. While it would be possible to set up a deferred tax asset for £23 100 (33% x £70 000), it is also possible to argue that an asset for only £6600 (33% x £20 000) should be recognised at 31 December 19X1. This is the deferred tax on the cumulative timing differences in 19X2, 19X3 and 19X4, namely 33% x (70 000 – 20 000 – 30 000) = 33% x £20 000 = £6600. Note that the considerations in this situation are the same as those which applied in the case of capital allowances and depreciation.

(d) Pension contributions and pension costs

As we have explained in Chapter 5, the objective of SSAP 24 'Accounting for pension costs' is to require companies to recognise the cost of providing pensions on a systematic and rational basis over the period during which they benefit from the services of the employees. This necessarily involves companies taking a long-term view.

Because tax law allows the pension contributions payable by the company as a tax expense, rather than the cost determined in accordance with SSAP 24, there is frequently a timing difference and hence the need to account for deferred taxation. However if companies use the partial approach required by SSAP 15, they are providing deferred tax on differences which reverse in the foreseeable future, usually three to five years. It follows that the time horizon used to determine the deferred tax in respect of pension costs will usually be much shorter than that used in determining the pension cost.

The ASB addressed this inconsistency in 'Amendment to SSAP 15 Accounting for deferred tax' issued in December 1992. This amendment permits companies to use the same recognition criteria for the deferred tax applicable to pensions as it uses in determining the pension cost itself. Thus companies may use either the full provision basis or the partial provision basis in accounting for the deferred tax implication of pensions and other post-retirement benefits. The ASB clearly recognised that this amendment provided only an interim solution to the inconsistency pending comprehensive reviews of both SSAP 15 and SSAP 24.

(e) Unrealised revaluation surpluses on fixed assets for which a taxation charge does not arise until the gain is realised on disposal

Taxation on a revaluation surplus only becomes payable when that surplus is realised, and then only if no rollover relief is available. It follows that a provision for deferred tax will only be necessary if the directors intend to sell the revalued asset in the foreseeable future in circumstances where it is not possible to take advantage of rollover relief. If such a sale is not expected, then no provision for deferred taxation is necessary. If such a sale is expected, then deferred tax should be provided and deducted from the revaluation surplus which is taken to reserves.

(f) Surpluses on disposals of fixed assets which are subject to rollover relief

As under (e) above, tax will only become payable on such a surplus if the replacement asset is sold and no rollover relief is possible at that time. Where such a sale is not envisaged in the foreseeable future, no provision for deferred taxation is necessary. Where such a sale is envisaged, then deferred tax should be provided and charged against the realised surplus on disposal.

(g) Tax losses carried forward

Where a company is unable to obtain a more immediate benefit from a tax loss, that loss may be carried forward to set off against future profits. It follows that such a tax loss, incurred in the past, is an asset in that it will reduce tax payable in one or more future periods. SSAP 15 specifically draws attention to the fact that such a loss for tax purposes is a timing difference.[10]

Deferred tax relating to current trading losses may be treated as recoverable when[11]

(i)   the loss results from an identifiable and non-recurring cause; and

(ii) the enterprise, or predecessor enterprise, has been consistently profitable over a considerable period, with any past losses being more than offset by income in subsequent periods; and

(iii) it is assured beyond reasonable doubt that future taxable profits will be sufficient to offset the current loss during the carry-forward period prescribed by tax legislation.

The tax on such recoverable tax losses would reduce the tax charge in the current profit and loss account, perhaps making it negative, and would normally be deducted from any relevant provision for deferred taxation in respect of the other timing differences which have been discussed above.

A global approach

We have now looked at each of the major categories of timing differences individually but, as explained above, it is in fact necessary to look at the combined effect of all timing differences when determining the amount of the necessary provision for deferred tax on a particular date. Hence it would be necessary to prepare a table incorporating the forecast timing differences expected by a particular company and if, for example we bring together some of the income items discussed above, such a table might include the following:

Forecast timing differences

	19X2 £000	19X3 £000	19X4 £000	19X5 £000
Receipts and payments/accruals				
Reversing difference	160	–	–	–
Accelerated capital allowances				
Net originating differences	(200)	(100)	–	(200)
Net reversing difference	–	–	(350)	–
Capitalised finance leases				
Net originating differences	20	30	–	50
Net reversing difference	–	–	(70)	–
	(20)	(70)	280	(150)

---

10 SSAP 15, Para. 19.
11 Appendix to SSAP 15, Para. 14. Para. 15 contains similar rules in respect of deferred tax on capital losses.

In such a case, the minimum provision necessary on 31 December 19X1 would be calculated as follows:

	£	£
Net reversing difference in 19X4		280 000
less Net originating difference		
19X2	20 000	
19X3	70 000	
		90 000
		190 000

Minimum provision necessary at 31.12.19X1:
  £190 000 @ 33%   62 700

The charge/credit to the profit and loss account for 19X1 will be the difference between £62 700, the required provision at the year end, and the opening balance on the deferred tax account in respect of such income items.

Any attempt to provide the analysis of the amount provided over its major components immediately runs into difficulties because of the interaction between timing differences, especially in 19X2. However, it would probably be calculated as follows:

Amount provided in respect of:

	£
Accelerated capital allowances	
350 000 − (200 000 − 160 000) − 100 000	
= 350 000 − 40 000 − 100 000	
= 210 000; which at 33% =	69 300
Capitalised finance leases	
70 000 − 20 000 − 30 000	
= 20 000; which at 33% =	(6 600)
	62 700

We conclude this chapter with an hypothetical example of the note supporting the provision for deferred taxation in a balance sheet:[12]

Example of note to accounts
Deferred taxation

	Provided £000	*Unprovided* £000
Accruals and provisions	(40)	–
Accelerated capital allowances	160	480
Capitalised finance leases	(30)	(50)
	90	430
Revaluation of fixed assets and		
chargeable gains on disposal	40	90
	130	520
less ACT recoverable	20	–
	110	520

12 For clarity, we have excluded comparative figures.

RECOMMENDED READING

I. P. A. Stitt, *Deferred Tax Accounting*, ICAEW, London, 1985.

R. Munson, 'Deferred Tax', *Accountants Digest No. 174*, ICAEW, London, 1985.

P. Weetman (ed), 'SSAP 15 Accounting for Deferred Taxation', ICAS, Edinburgh, 1992.

CHAPTER 8

Business combinations and goodwill

BUSINESS COMBINATIONS

Introduction

Words such as merger, amalgamation, absorption, takeover and acquisition are all used to describe the coming together of two or more businesses. Such words do not have precise legal meanings and, as they are often used interchangeably, the American description 'business combinations' best describes the subject matter of this chapter.

A company may expand either by 'internal' or 'external' growth. In the former case it expands by undertaking investment projects, such as the purchase of new premises and plant, while in the latter case it expands by purchasing a collection of assets in the form of an established business. In this second case we have a business combination in which one company is very much the dominant party, acquiring control of that other business either with or without the consent of the directors of that business.

Where such 'external' growth is contemplated, it will be necessary to value the collection of assets it is proposed to purchase. It will usually be necessary to determine at least two values: (a) the value of the business to its present owners (this will determine the minimum price which will be acceptable); (b) the value of the business when combined with the existing assets of the acquiring company (this will determine the maximum price which may be offered). In some cases it may be possible to apply capital budgeting techniques to arrive at these values but often other methods of valuation, such as those discussed in Chapter 14, will be used.

In other circumstances two or more companies may both see benefits from coming together. Thus, two companies may consider that their combined businesses are worth more than the sum of the values of the individual businesses. For such a combination, the individual businesses must be valued to help in the determination of the proportionate shares in the combined business, although, of course, the ultimate shares will to a considerable extent depend upon the bargaining ability of the two parties.

Table 8.1 gives some indication of the importance of business combinations in the years 1983–1992. It shows acquisitions and mergers of industrial and commercial companies within the UK.[1]

---

1 This information has been taken from the CSO publication *Financial Statistics*.

Table 8.1

| Year | Number of companies acquired | Consideration (£ million) | | | |
		Total	Cash	Ordinary shares	Pref. shares/ loan stock
1983	447	2 343	1 026	1 261	56
1984	568	5 474	2 946	1 838	690
1985	474	7 090	2 857	3 708	525
1986	842	15 370	4 062	8 761	2 548
1987	1 528	16 539	5 711	9 974	853
1988	1 499	22 839	15 993	4 993	1 853
1989	1 337	27 250	22 356	3 520	1 374
1990	779	8 329	6 402	1 533	393
1991	506	10 434	7 278	3 034	121
1992	433	5 939	3 767	2 127	46

Some reasons for combining

Purchase of undervalued assets

As we shall see in the chapter on valuation of securities and businesses (Chapter 14), the same collection of assets may have different values to different people. As a result, it is often possible for one business to purchase another business, that is a collection of assets, at a price below the sum of the values of the underlying assets. If we take limited companies, for example, the shares of a company may be standing at a relatively low price because the current management is making poor use of the assets or has not communicated good future prospects to the shareholders. Even though the acquiring company purchases the shares at a price higher than the existing market price, it may be able to acquire underlying assets which have a much higher value than the price paid. Indeed, as many asset strippers have shown, even the sale of assets on a piecemeal basis may generate a sum considerably in excess of the price paid for those assets.

Economies of scale

The combination of two businesses may result in economies of scale, that is to say the cost of producing the combined output will be less than the sum of the costs of producing the separate outputs or, alternatively, the combined output will be greater for the same total cost. Such economies of scale may exist not only in production but also in administration, research and development and financing.

Concentrating first on production, economies of scale may arise for such reasons as the following: set-up costs and marketing costs may be spread over larger outputs; indivisible units of high cost machinery may become feasible at higher levels of output; where capacity is dependent on volume and cost is dependent on surface area, as in the case of storage tanks, such area–volume relationships may result in less than proportionate rises in costs.

When we turn to administration, a large organisation may attract and make better use of scarce managerial talent and enable the firm to employ specialists. Large organisations may also be able to attract suitable people to administer research and development programmes and to use the results of those programmes more effectively. In addition, the larger organisation is often in a position to raise and service capital more cheaply than a smaller organisation.

Economics textbooks devote considerable space to discussions of the theoretical bases for economies of scale and governments have often encouraged and supported combinations on the grounds that they would improve the efficiency of British industry, in particular its competitiveness in international markets. For reasons discussed below, there is now less confidence that benefits will be obtained from combinations and certainly in the 1980s, the Conservative government was much less committed to intervention than some previous governments.

Various techniques have been developed to examine whether and to what extent economies of scale exist in practice. Although there appears to be scope for economies of scale in many industries, these do not appear automatically after a business combination, but have to be planned. A number of studies[2] have found that the performances of many combined businesses have been rather disappointing. In particular there are diseconomies of large organisations, due mainly to the problems of administering large units, which may often outweigh the benefits afforded by economies of scale.

Elimination or reduction of competition

By eliminating or reducing competition, it may be possible for a company to make larger profits; combining with another business may be one means of achieving this end. Although integration may occur for many reasons, one reason may be that it is possible to reduce competition both by vertical integration, that is by combining with a firm at an earlier or later stage of the production cycle, or by horizontal integration, that is by combining with a firm at the same stage in the production cycle.

To illustrate, a firm at one stage of production may combine with a firm at an earlier stage of production, that is a supplier, thus ensuring a ready source of supply and perhaps putting it in a position to charge a lower price than competitors at the second stage, and hence squeeze them out of business. The extent to which this is possible would depend upon the structure of the market, that is the extent to which there are monopolistic or competitive elements present.

Combination with a firm at the same stage of production would reduce the number of competitors by one and again may give rise to higher profits as a result of the increased industrial concentration; although, much would depend upon the structure of the industry before and after the combination. The combination of two small firms in a very competitive industry might have little effect, whereas the combination of two giants might turn an oligopoly into a virtual monopoly.

There are obvious dangers to the public at large from mergers which reduce the level of competition and it is for this reason that we have legislation on monopolies and mergers.[3] Under such legislation the Secretary of State for Trade and Industry and the

---

2 *See*, for example, G. Meeks, *Disappointing Marriage: A Study of the Gains from Merger*, Cambridge University Press, Cambridge, 1977, or G. D. Newbould, *Management and Merger Activity*, Guthstead, London, 1970.

Director General of Fair Trading have discretionary powers to refer certain mergers[4] to the Monopolies and Mergers Commission, an independent body of economists, accountants, lawyers, businessmen and trade unionists supported by a full-time staff. This commission decides whether or not a merger is likely to have effects which are against the public interest. If it concludes that the merger is likely to have adverse effects, the Secretary of State may take various courses of action; thus, he may forbid a proposed merger, reverse one which has already taken place or impose restrictions on the future operations of the merged businesses.

Reduction of risk

By combining with a firm which makes different products, a business is often able to reduce risk. Thus one reason for a combination involving businesses in different industries may be a desire to generate an earnings stream which is less variable than the separate earnings streams of the two individual businesses. Such a reduction of risk is usually considered to be an advantage and will often lead to an increase in share values, although it may be argued that a shareholder may be better able to reduce risk by the selection of his or her own portfolio of shares.

Use of price/earnings ratios

In many business combinations, one company has been able to increase the wealth of its own shareholders by combining with a company which has a lower price/earnings ratio. To illustrate let us take a simple example of two companies:

	Company A	Company B
Earnings	£10 000	£10 000
Number of ordinary shares	100 000	100 000
Earnings per share	10p	10p
Current market price	£1.50	£1.20
P/E ratio	15	12

Let us suppose that company A issues 80 000 shares valued at £120 000 (80 000 at £1.50) in exchange for 100 000 shares in company B valued at £120 000 (100 000 at £1.20). If there is no change in earnings after the combination, the earnings of the combined companies as reflected in the group accounts will be £20 000 and the earnings per share 11p, that is £20 000 divided by 180 000 shares in A. If the market continues to use the P/E ratio of company A, that is 15, the price of a share in company A after the combination will be £1.65. This is greater than £1.50, the price of a share in company A before the combination and hence advantageous to the original shareholders in the company. It is also advantageous to the original shareholders in company B who now hold 80 000 shares in company A valued at £132 000 compared with their former holdings of 100 000 shares in company B which were valued at £120 000.

It may be argued that the market is unlikely to apply the same P/E ratio to the combined

---

4 These are mergers where the gross value of assets being transferred exceeds £30 million or where the merger would create or enhance a monopoly share (25% or more) of the relevant market in the UK or a substantial part of the UK.

earnings as it previously did to the earnings in company A as a separate company. An 'average' P/E ratio of 13.5, calculated as shown below, would perhaps be expected:

	Earnings	Values
Company A	£10 000	£150 000
Company B	£10 000	£120 000
Combined	£20 000	£270 000

The average P/E ratio is 270 000/20 000 = 13.5.

This does not appear to happen in practice, and the resulting P/E ratio is usually well above this 'average' P/E ratio because the market anticipates a better future.

Thus, even though benefits such as economies of scale and reduction of competition do not materialise, some companies have been able to increase the wealth of their shareholders by acquiring other companies with lower P/E ratios.

Managerial motives

Under traditional economic theory, the role of management is to respond in a rational, but more or less automatic way, to circumstances which present themselves. Thus if, for example, economies of scale are perceived to be likely if two businesses combine, such a combination will be pursued in order to maximise the wealth of shareholders.

Gerald Newbould,[5] examined all the major mergers which occurred during the UK merger boom of 1967 and 1968 and found that the role of management in these mergers was very different from that suggested by economic theory. Thus, *inter alia*, he found that often the period between preliminary discussions of a merger and the public announcement of intention to proceed was so short that little fundamental analysis of the benefits or disbenefits of such a combination was possible.

He also found that in many cases no attempts had been made to obtain the benefits of synergy after the merger and that often performance of the merged businesses was disappointing. Other studies have come to similar conclusions.[6]

The above factors suggested that the usual financial and economic reasons put forward for mergers were, in practice, not of prime importance. What seemed to be a more important determinant of mergers among large companies was the objectives of managers. In order to cope with increasing uncertainty, managers desired to increase their market power or to defend their market position. Although such activities could well further the interests of shareholders, they may have even greater benefits for the managers themselves. Thus, a less uncertain life, in particular less chance of the company itself being taken over, a larger empire and perhaps larger remuneration due to control of such an empire may be extremely important motivating forces.

Whatever the ultimate objective, managerial motives seemed to play a much larger role in merger activity than traditional economic theory allowed.

5 G. D. Newbould, *op. cit.*
6 *See* footnote 2 to this chapter.

Methods of combining

In order to be able to account for combinations, we must first explore some of the methods which may be used to effect them. Such methods may best be classified as to whether or not a group structure results from the combination.

Let us take as an example two companies, L and M, and assume that the respective boards of directors and owners have agreed to combine their businesses.

Combinations which result in a group structure

Two such combinations may be considered.

In the first case, company L may purchase the shares of company M and thereby acquire a subsidiary company; alternatively company M may purchase the shares of company L.

The choice of consideration given in exchange for the shares acquired will determine whether or not the shareholders in what becomes the subsidiary company have any interest in the combined businesses. Thus if company L issues shares in exchange for the shares of company M, the old shareholders in company M have an interest in the resulting holding company and thereby in the group whereas, if company L pays cash for the shares in company M, the old shareholders in M take their cash and cease to have any interest in the resulting group.

In the second case, a new company, LM, may be established to purchase the shares of both L and M. Thus, the shareholders in L and M may sell their shares to LM in exchange for shares in LM. The resulting group structure would then be as shown in Figure 8.1. The shareholders in LM would be the former shareholders in the two separate companies and their respective interests would depend, as in all the examples in this section, upon the valuations placed upon the two separate companies, which would in turn depend in part upon bargaining between the two boards of directors.

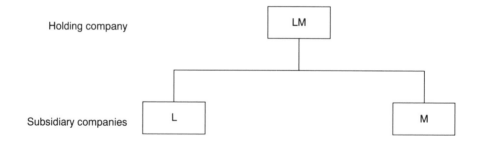

Fig. 8.1

It is possible for company LM to issue not only shares but also loan stock in order to purchase the shares in L and M. It would be difficult for payment to be made in cash as LM is a newly formed company, although it could, of course, issue other shares or raise loans to obtain cash.

Combinations not resulting in a group structure[7]

Again, two such combinations may be considered.

First, instead of purchasing the shares of company M, company L may obtain control of the net assets of M by making a direct purchase of those net assets. The net assets would thus be absorbed into company L and company M would itself receive the consideration. This would in due course be distributed to the shareholders of M by its liquidator.

As before, the choice of consideration determines whether or not the former shareholders in M have any interest in the enlarged company L.

Second, instead of one of the companies purchasing the net assets of the other, a new company may be formed to purchase the net assets of both existing companies. Thus, a new company, LM, may be formed to purchase the net assets of company L and company M. If payment is made by issuing shares in LM, these will be distributed by the respective liquidators so that the end result is one company, LM, which owns the net assets previously held by the separate companies and has as its shareholders the former shareholders in the two separate companies.

Preference for group structure

The above are methods of effecting a combination between two, or indeed more, companies. Virtually all large business combinations make use of a group structure, rather than a purchase of assets and net assets and FRED 6 'Acquisitions and mergers', paragraph 2, actually restricts the definition of a business combination to 'a transaction where one or more entities become subsidiary undertakings of another entity'. Such a structure is advantageous in that separate companies enjoying limited liability are already in existence. It follows that names, and associated goodwill, of the original companies are not lost and there is no necessity to renegotiate contractual arrangements. All sorts of other factors will be important in practice; some examples are the desire to retain staff, the impact of taxation and stamp duty and whether or not there is a remaining minority interest. A group structure also permits easy disinvestment by sale of one or more subsidiaries.

Choice of consideration

As discussed above, the choice of consideration will determine who is interested in the single business created by the combination and will therefore be affected by the intentions of the parties to the combination. It will also be affected by the size of the companies and by conditions in the market for securities and the taxation system in force.

The main possible types of consideration are cash, loan stock, ordinary shares, some form of convertible security or any combination of these.

Let us look at the effect of each of these before turning to some factors which influence the choice between them.

Cash

Where one company purchases the shares or assets of another for cash the shareholders of the latter company cease to have any interest in the combined businesses.

---

7 As will be seen below, such combinations would not fall within the definition of a business combination contained in the most recent official pronouncement FRED 6.

From the point of view of the selling shareholders, they take a certain cash sum and will be liable to capital gains tax on the disposal of their shares.

From the point of view of the purchasing company, its cash holdings will decrease. It has sometimes been suggested that the use of cash will give a better chance of success if opposition is anticipated and, providing the earnings of the company which is purchased are greater than the earnings which would be made by using cash in other ways, there will be an increase in the earnings per share.

Loan stock

In this case the selling shareholders, either directly or indirectly, exchange shares in one company for loan stock in another company. Hence an equity investment is exchanged for a fixed interest investment, which may or may not be an advantage, depending upon the relative values of the securities and the circumstances of the individual investor. Any liability to capital gains tax will be deferred until ultimate disposal of the loan stock.

From the point of view of the shareholders of the purchasing company, there may be an advantage in that the level of gearing will be increased. In addition, interest on the loan stock will be deductible for corporation tax purposes.

Ordinary shares

A share for share exchange is often the method used in combinations involving large companies. Here the shareholder simply exchanges shares in one company for shares in another company.

There are many potential benefits for the selling shareholders, although the extent to which they exist will depend upon the exact terms of the combination and the relative values of the shares. The selling shareholder continues to have an interest in the combined businesses with the benefits mentioned in the second section of this chapter and will not be subject to capital gains tax on the exchange. Against this the value of the security received is not certain but will depend upon market reaction to the combination.

From the point of view of the combined companies a share exchange does not affect their liquidity. The extent to which it is beneficial for the existing shareholders of the company must depend upon the relative values of the shares.

Although shares were popular in the mid-1980s, cash was by far the largest part of the total consideration in every year since 1987.[8]

Convertible loan stock

The issue of convertible loan stock has become more common and has sometimes been used in connection with business combinations. In such a case, the shareholders in one company exchange their shares for convertible loan stock in another company.

From the point of view of a selling shareholder, he exchanges an equity investment for a fixed interest security, but one which is convertible into an equity investment at some time in the future if he so wishes. Thus if in the future share prices move in his favour he will be able to take up his equity interest while, if they move against him, he will be able to retain his fixed interest investment. Again, any liability to capital gains tax is deferred until ultimate disposal of the convertible stock or equity shares issued in exchange.

From the point of view of the company issuing such securities, the interest on the loan

---

8 *See* the statistics on page 200 for an analysis of the total expenditure for each of the years 1983–1992 between cash, ordinary shares and fixed interest securities.

stock is deductible for taxation purposes and the debt is self-liquidating if loan holders convert loan stock into ordinary shares. If loan holders do convert, the tax deductibility is, of course, lost and in addition there is a reduction in gearing and possible dilution of the existing shareholders' interest.

The choice in practice

As has been seen above, the various forms of consideration which may be used have advantages and disadvantages. The choice in any business combination will depend upon a large number of factors, some of which are discussed in this section.

It is convenient to distinguish between an agreed combination where the two sets of shareholders in the individual companies are to be shareholders in the new or enlarged company and a situation where one party is dominant and is seeking to obtain control of the other company as cheaply as possible.

In the first of these cases the major part of the consideration must obviously be equity shares although, if a situation of surplus cash or low gearing is expected after the combination, an opportunity may be taken to pay part of the consideration in cash or some form of loan stock.

In the second case the choice of consideration will be affected considerably by the nature of the companies involved and the market situation. Where the biddee company is small or opposition is expected, a cash bid may be preferred. Loan stock may be attractive where rates of interest are low and especially if they are expected to rise. Where, however, it is felt that the shares of the dominant company are overpriced relative to those of the other company, then a share issue is likely to be most attractive.

Accounting for business combinations

Accounting for business combinations is a topic which has been the cause of considerable controversy in many countries. The traditional method of accounting for combinations in the UK was the 'acquisition' or 'purchase' method but, in the 1960s, a new method began to find favour. This was the 'merger' or 'pooling of interests' method which had been extensively used in the USA. ED 3 'Accounting for acquisitions and mergers', which was published in 1971, attempted to define situations in which each method should be used but, for reasons explained below, was never converted into a Statement of Standard Accounting Practice. Changes introduced by the Companies Act 1981 made it possible to make progress and SSAP 23 'Accounting for acquisitions and mergers' was issued in April 1985. This standard was the subject of considerable criticism and, in 1990, the ASC issued a revised version ED 48. The ASB then issued its own exposure draft, FRED 6 'Acquisitions and mergers', in May 1993. We shall explore these attempts at standardisation after we have distinguished between the 'acquisition' and 'merger' methods of accounting.

Acquisition and merger accounting

As stated above, the acquisition method has traditionally been used to account for business combinations and, where the consideration for shares or assets purchased is wholly cash or loan stock, this is agreed to be the correct method of accounting. However, where the consideration given is wholly or predominantly ordinary shares, many accountants would argue that the acquisition method is inappropriate. Here the shareholders in one company exchange their equity holding in that company for an equity interest in another company, a holding company if shares are purchased or an enlarged company if net assets are purchased. In such circumstances, use of the acquisition method frequently produces inconsistencies in the treatment of the two combining companies. These inconsistencies are avoided by the use of the merger method but, as we shall see, consistency is obtained only at a price.

Under acquisition accounting, an investment in a subsidiary would normally be recorded at the fair value of the consideration given. Where the fair value of any shares issued exceeds their par value, a share premium account or merger reserve would normally be created in the parent company's accounts.[9] In the consolidated accounts, the investment would be replaced by the underlying separable assets and liabilities of the subsidiary at their fair values, representing their 'cost' to the group. Any difference between the cost of the investment and the sum of the values of the separable assets and liabilities is recorded as goodwill. Preacquisition profits of the subsidiary are no longer available for distribution and the results of this new subsidiary are only brought into the consolidated profit and loss account from the date of acquisition.[10]

Under the merger method of accounting, the investment in the subsidiary company would normally be recorded in the parent company's accounts at the aggregate of the nominal value of any shares issued plus the fair value of any other consideration. Thus, the carrying value of the investment would not be the fair value of the consideration given and no share premium account or merger reserve would be created.

In the consolidated accounts, the investment would be replaced by the underlying separable assets and liabilities, not at fair value, but at their book values in the subsidiary's own accounts subject to adjustments necessary to achieve consistency of accounting policies for the group. The preacquisition profits of the new subsidiary are not frozen but are aggregated with those of the parent company, and the results of the new subsidiary are brought into the consolidated profit and loss account for the whole period as if the companies had always been merged. No goodwill is recorded, and any difference between the nominal value of shares issued plus the fair value of any other consideration given and the nominal value and share premium accounts in respect of shares purchased is treated as an adjustment to consolidated reserves.

The essential differences between the two methods can be illustrated in a simple example involving a share for share exchange.

EXAMPLE 8.1

Column 1 shows the summarised balance sheets of H Limited and S Limited before combination. H buys the shares in S in a share for share exchange. In order to concentrate on the essential differences between the two methods, we will assume that the current value of a share in both H Limited and S Limited is agreed to be £3. Hence H issues 800 shares in exchange for the 800 shares in S. We shall also assume that the sum of the fair values of separable net assets in H and S are £1800 and £1500 respectively.

---

9 The conditions for the creation of a merger reserve, rather than a share premium account, will be discussed below.

10 The acquisition method of accounting is considered in much greater depth in the next chapter

Columns 2 and 3 show the parent company's balance sheet using the principles of the acquisition method and merger method respectively.[11]

Summarised balance sheets

	1	2	3
	Before combination	After combination	
		Acquisition method	Merger method
	£	£	£
H Limited			
Net assets (Fair values £1800)	1 600	1 600	1 600
Shares in S Limited – at 'cost'		2 400	800
	1 600	4 000	2 400
£1 ordinary shares	1 000	1 800	1 800
Share premium/merger reserve		1 600	
Retained profits	600	600	600
	1 600	4 000	2 400
S Limited			
Net assets (Fair values £1500)	1 200	No change	
£1 ordinary shares	800	No change	
Retained profits	400		
	1 200		

If the acquisition method is used, the shares issued by H will be valued at their fair value at the date of issue, that is at £3 per share. The investment in subsidiary will be shown at a cost of £2400 while a share premium or merger reserve of £1600 will be recorded. Column 2 of the summarised balance sheets above reflects these entries.

If the merger method is used, the shares issued by H will be valued at their par value and the investment in subsidiary will be shown at a 'cost' of £800. This is shown in column 3 above.

We may now prepare the consolidated balance sheet of H Limited and its subsidiary S Limited using the acquisition and merger methods respectively.

11 This is not strictly correct in that the treatment of the investment in the parent company's accounts is legally independent of what method of accounting is used in the consolidated accounts. Thus, if merger relief is available, H does not have to create a share premium/merger reserve in its own accounts even though such a merger reserve will be required in its consolidated accounts. What we have done is logically consistent with the subsequent treatment of the combination in the consolidated accounts.

Consolidated balance sheet of H Limited and subsidiary S Limited

	1 Acquisition method £	2 Merger method £
Net assets: H 1600 + S 1500	3 100	
H 1600 + S 1200		2 800
Goodwill on consolidation		
2400 – 1500	900	
	4 000	2 800
£1 ordinary shares	1 800	1 800
Share premium/Merger reserve	1 600	
Retained profits: H only	600	
H + S		1 000
	4 000	2 800

Column 1 shows the consolidated balance sheet immediately after the combination using the acquisition method. In preparing the consolidated balance sheet the excess of the cost of investment in the subsidiary (£2400) over the sum of the fair values of the separable assets and liabilities (£1500) is shown as goodwill on consolidation. The effect of using this method may be summarised as follows:

(a) *Retained profits*: Before the combination H had retained profits of £600 and S had retained profits of £400. However, the consolidated balance sheet only includes the retained profits of H and those of S have been frozen. Thus, if H receives a dividend from the preacquisition profits of S, this must reduce the carrying value of the investment. The dividend received cannot be used as the basis for a dividend payment to the shareholders in H.

(b) *Net assets*: While the net assets of H are shown on the basis of their book values (£1600), those of S are included at their fair values (£1500).

(c) *Goodwill*: The goodwill in the consolidated balance sheet relates to S. None appears in relation to H.

Many would question whether this gives a true and fair view of the combination. After all, exactly the same people are interested in the net assets after the combination as before, although their proportionate interests will probably have changed as a result of the bargaining process. All that has happened is that the shareholders in S have exchanged their shares in S for shares in H, which now in turn owns S. Thus, two sets of shareholders have come together for their mutual benefit. Why then should the retained profits of one company be frozen while those of the other are not? Why should the net assets of one company be shown at fair values while those of the other are shown at their historical cost values? Why should we recognise goodwill for one company but not for the other?

  A further criticism could be made of the method in that the consolidated balance sheet would look very different if, instead of the acquisition of shares in S by H, S had acquired the shares of H. This is a perfectly feasible alternative means of combination. The results produced will therefore vary depending upon what may in fact be an arbitrary choice of the holding company.

Consideration of questions like this have led to the development of merger accounting.

Under the *merger method*, shares issued in exchange for other shares are valued not at their fair value, but at their par value. Thus, using our simple example, the 800 shares issued by H would be valued at £1 each, that is £800, rather than at £3 each. Correspondingly, the investment in S would be shown at a 'cost' of only £800. Column 3 of the summarised balance sheets (p. 209) reflects this entry.

Column 2 of the consolidated balance sheets provides the resulting consolidated balance sheet. From this it may be seen that the precombination retained profits of the two individual companies are still available for dividend while the net assets of both companies are shown at their historical-cost-based valuation. It is as if the companies had been combined since the cradle and it follows that, in preparing the consolidated profit and loss account, the results of both companies would be included for the whole year irrespective of the date on which the combination occurred.[12] In preparing the consolidated accounts, necessary adjustments must, of course, be made to reflect uniform accounting policies throughout the group.

While the use of the merger method results in a consistent treatment of the profits and net assets of the two companies, it does, of course, have the result that all the assets are valued on the basis of historical costs, which are arguably of little relevance to users of the accounts. Under the acquisition method, the assets of at least one company are shown at their fair values at the date of the combination, and to move from such a position to one where all assets are shown on the basis of their historical costs to the separate companies is regarded by some accountants as a step in the wrong direction.

One way to avoid this consequence of merger accounting would be for both companies to restate the carrying values of the separable assets and liabilities at their fair values at the date of combination so that the assets and liabilities of both companies would be shown on a consistent basis at fair value rather than at out of date values. Such a method, the 'New entity method', was proposed in International Exposure Draft E 22, issued in 1981, and mentioned in an appendix to ED 31 which regarded it as a variant of merger accounting using current values.[13] It has not appeared in later pronouncements.

In the above example the par value of the shares issued by H was the same as the par value of the shares purchased. In most combinations this will not be the case and, in addition, the consideration may include cash and loan stock. Any difference between the par value of the shares issued plus the fair value of any other consideration and the par value of the shares purchased and any share premium account in respect of these shares would be dealt with as a movement on the consolidated reserves.

We have now explored the differences between acquisition accounting and merger accounting. Providing shares are used to purchase shares or net assets in another company, so that two sets of shareholders have an interest in the resulting combined business, we have the theoretical possibility of applying the merger method of accounting. We shall now explore the way in which the use of such a method has been regulated by some of the official pronouncements.

---

12 This is to be contrasted with the position using the acquisition method of accounting where the consolidated profit and loss account will only include the results of a new subsidiary from the date of acquisition. This topic is considered in some detail in the following chapter.
13 ED 31 'Accounting for acquisitions and mergers', ASC, London, 1982.

Towards an accounting standard

The fate of ED 3

In January 1971 the ASC issued ED 3, 'Accounting for acquisitions and mergers', in which it attempted to distinguish between two types of business combination and specify the appropriate accounting treatment for each. If the combination was an acquisition, the acquisition method of accounting had to be used while, if the combination satisfied the definition of a merger, merger accounting had to be applied.

Even when this Exposure Draft was issued, there was some doubt as to the legality of the merger method under the existing law. As has been shown, use of the merger method requires that shares issued are recorded as being issued at their nominal value rather than their market or fair values. Although the Exposure Draft referred to legal opinion to the contrary, such a treatment seemed to many to be illegal under Sec. 56 of the Companies Act 1948 (now Sec. 130, Companies Act 1985) which stated quite clearly:

> Where a company issues shares at a premium, whether for cash or otherwise, a sum equal to the aggregate amount or value of the premiums on those shares shall be transferred to an account, to be called 'the share premium account'....

The recording of shares issued at their par values, when their fair value was in excess of par value, had already been held to be illegal in the case of *Henry Head & Co. Ltd* v. *Ropner Holdings*[14] and, in view of the questionable legality of the proposals in ED 3, the Exposure Draft was withdrawn.

The illegality of the merger method was subsequently confirmed in the case of *Shearer* v. *Bercain Ltd*[15] and little progress was possible until the Companies Act 1981 legalised the use of the merger method of accounting in certain circumstances.

The Companies Act 1981

The Companies Act 1981 relieved companies from the need to create a share premium account in certain circumstances and these provisions are now contained in Companies Act, 1985, Sections 131–134. This so-called merger relief is available when one company issues equity shares to purchase equity shares in another company and ends up with an equity holding of 90 per cent or more. In such circumstances, the company does not have to create a share premium account either in respect of the equity shares issued or any non-equity shares issued in exchange for non-equity shares.[16]

Thus, if one company issues equity shares to acquire 95 per cent of the equity shares of another company, it is not necessary to create any share premium account in respect of that transaction. If, however, one company already holds 20 per cent of the equity shares in another company and then purchases an additional 75 per cent of those shares, the relief from the need to create a share premium account applies only to the equity shares issued to obtain the 75 per cent holding, that is the purchase which takes the total holding to 90 per cent or above.

The main consequence of the above provisions was that they permitted, although they did not require, the subsequent use of merger accounting.

14 *Henry Head & Co. Ltd* v. *Ropner Holdings* (1951) All E.R. 994.
15 *Shearer* v. *Bercain Ltd* (1980) S.T.C. 359.
16 Relief from the requirement to create a share premium account is also provided in the case of certain group reconstructions which involve the transfer of ownership of a company within a group (Companies Act 1985, Sec. 132).

Once the merger method had been legalised, the ASC was able to turn its attention to the circumstances in which this method should be used. Before we look at the provisions of SSAP 23 (April 1985), ED 48 (February 1990) and FRED 6 (May 1993), we shall examine some of the matters which had to be considered and resolved.

Criteria for use of the merger method

Use of merger accounting would seem to offer certain advantages where there is a uniting of interests, that is where the equity shareholders in two separate companies pool their interests to become equity shareholders in a combined entity.

As described above, the Companies Act 1985 allowed (but did not require) the use of the merger method providing at least 90 per cent of the equity shares of the acquired company were part of the pool or, to put it another way, even when up to 10 per cent of the equity shares did not become part of the pool. Within this legal framework, the ASC had to decide what conditions were necessary for the use of the merger method of accounting and whether, if those conditions were satisfied, use of the merger method should be obligatory or optional. In this section some of the factors that had to be considered are discussed briefly.

First, although there must be a uniting of interests, to what extent is it necessary to obtain the approval of the two sets of shareholders? Do all the shareholders in the two companies have to agree to the merger or only some minimum proportion? The law requires the holding in the offeree company to exceed 90 per cent but it says nothing about obtaining the agreement of the shareholders in the offeror company. Clearly it would be possible to impose much more stringent conditions here.

Second, there is the question of relative size. If one company is much smaller than the other then, even though all shareholders in both companies agree to a uniting of interests, the end result may well be a situation in which one set of shareholders is dominant in the combined entity with the other set of shareholders having insignificant influence. Is this really a uniting of interests or merely an 'acquisition' using equity shares as the consideration?

Third, in order for there to be a uniting of interests, the consideration must be equity shares. If the consideration is wholly cash or loan stock, resources leave the combining businesses and one set of shareholders ceases to have any equity interest in the combination and there is definitely no uniting of interests. A difficulty arises where the consideration consists mainly of equity shares but also partly of cash or loan stock. Does this disqualify the combination for treatment as a merger? If it does not do so in principle, then what is the maximum percentage of the consideration which may be given in a form other than equity shares?

These were the main questions to be answered in specifying the circumstances in which merger accounting could be used although, as we shall see, the Companies Act 1989 has subsequently restricted the proportion of non-equity consideration which may be included in the total consideration. Given the nature of the questions, answers can only involve arbitrary choice and hence it is not surprising that the selection of a suitable set of criteria has posed problems for standard setting bodies here and overseas.

The approach of SSAP 23

SSAP 23 permitted the use of merger accounting if all of the following conditions were satisfied.[17]

---

17 SSAP 23, Para. 11.

(a) the business combination results from an offer to the holders of all equity shares and the holders of all voting shares which are not already held by the offeror: and

(b) the offeror has secured, as a result of the offer, a holding of (i) at least 90 per cent of all equity shares (taking each class of equity separately) and (ii) the shares carrying at least 90 per cent of the votes of the offeree: and

(c) immediately prior to the offer, the offeror does not hold (i) 20 per cent or more of all equity shares of the offeree (taking each class of equity separately), or (ii) shares carrying 20 per cent or more of the votes of the offeree: and

(d) not less than 90 per cent of the fair value of the total consideration given for the equity share capital (including that given for shares already held) is in the form of equity share capital: not less than 90 per cent of the fair value of the total consideration given for voting non-equity share capital (including that given for shares already held) is in the form of equity and/or voting non-equity share capital.

If we concentrate on a situation in which two companies are combining by forming a holding company/subsidiary company relationship and we assume that both companies have only voting equity shares in issue, the conditions may be summarised in the following way.

Any initial holding of one company in the other could not exceed 20 per cent, the offer had to be made to all remaining shareholders and had to result in a total holding of 90 per cent or more. Not less than 90 per cent of the fair value of the total consideration given for shares both in the present transaction and, in past transactions, had to be in the form of voting equity shares.[18]

Where the initial holding exceeds 20 per cent, there is a presumption, albeit rebuttable, of significant influence requiring the use of the equity method of accounting under SSAP 1. The equity method is based on the principles of acquisition accounting and is therefore incompatible with the use of merger accounting.

The requirement that the total holding is 90 per cent or more is necessary to comply with the Companies Act condition for the use of merger relief and the final condition that 90 per cent or more of the fair value of the total consideration was in the form of voting equity shares limited the non-share consideration to 10 per cent. Hence, there was a limit on the resources leaving the group.

The SSAP 23 conditions did not require the combination to be approved by the shareholders in the offeror company. Nor did it concern itself with the relative sizes of the two companies. Even when the conditions were satisfied, the use of merger accounting was not compulsory: acquisition accounting could still be used.

The use of these conditions in SSAP 23 have led to a number of difficulties and have been superseded by new conditions for the use of merger accounting, inserted in the Companies Act 1985 by the Companies Act 1989.[19] We shall explore these difficulties and provisions before turning to the later thinking of the standard setters as embodied in ED48 and FRED 6.

---

18 As we shall see below, this last criterion has been tightened considerably by Companies Act 1989 which requires that the fair value of any consideration other than equity shares must not exceed 10 per cent of the *nominal* value of equity shares issued.

19 Companies Act 1985, Schedule 4A, Para. 10.

Experience of SSAP 23

If we compare the consequences of using acquisition accounting and merger accounting in our simple example above, it is not hard to see why a company may prefer to use the merger method if it is available for a particular business combination. Under the merger method, the balance sheet figures for separable net assets are lower and no amount emerges for goodwill. Subsequent reported profits will be higher as depreciation will be based on lower asset values and there will be no goodwill to amortise. Thus, the merger method will result in higher returns on capital employed in the company's subsequent accounts than would be disclosed if the acquisition method were used.

Given the desire of companies to report their affairs in the best possible light, it is perhaps not surprising that numerous attempts have been made to exploit the conditions included in SSAP 23 in order to be able to apply merger accounting. Let us look at a few examples.

Under SSAP 23 it was not possible to use merger accounting if the purchasing company held 20 per cent or more of the equity shares in the other company immediately prior to the offer. Where one company held more than 20 per cent in the other, it was easily able to reduce the holding below 20 per cent by 'warehousing' shares with a banker or other third party. Thus, by temporarily selling enough shares to take the holding below 20 per cent and buying them back in the general offer, it was able to satisfy this particular condition.

Other rather blatant exploitations of the specific conditions were the so-called 'vendor placing' and 'vendor rights' schemes. These were used where one company wished to buy shares in another for cash, or some other non-equity share consideration, but also wished to use merger accounting. A payment in cash would mean resources leaving the group and would require the use of acquisition accounting. In order to avoid this some companies made a share for share exchange but gave the shareholders in the acquired company the power to convert the shares which they received into cash immediately, either by placing them with a third party or by selling them back to the shareholders in the acquiring company. The former was a vendor placing and the latter a vendor rights scheme.

The end result was that shares had been purchased for cash but in such a way that merger accounting could be used. While no resources left the group, there was certainly no pooling or uniting of shareholders' interests of the two companies!

It is quite clear that some companies have been applying the letter rather than the spirit of the standard and the above perceived abuses of the standard brought much criticism from commentators.

Towards a new standard

Following the Companies Act 1989, which implemented the EC Seventh Directive on consolidated accounts, conditions for the use of merger accounting have now been incorporated in the law, and these conditions differ somewhat from those included in SSAP 23. This change, together with the criticisms discussed above, have necessitated a revision of SSAP 23.

The legal conditions for the use of merger accounting are contained in Schedule 4A to Companies Act 1985.[20] They may be listed as follows:

20 Schedule 4A, Para. 10. Schedule 4A was inserted in Companies Act 1985 from Schedule 2 Companies Act 1989.

(a) that at least 90 per cent of the nominal value of the relevant shares in the undertaking acquired is held by or on behalf of the parent company and its subsidiary undertakings;

(b) that the proportion referred to in paragraph (a) was attained pursuant to an arrangement providing for the issue of equity shares by the parent company or one or more of its subsidiary undertakings;

(c) that the fair value of any consideration other than the issue of equity shares given pursuant to the arrangement by the parent company and its subsidiary undertakings did not exceed 10 per cent of the nominal value of the equity shares issued; and

(d) that adoption of the merger method of accounting accords with generally accepted accounting principles or practice.

Although these conditions do not fix a maximum shareholding immediately prior to the combination, condition (c) that the fair value of any non-equity consideration does not exceed 10 per cent of the *nominal* value of the shares issued is much stricter than the SSAP 23 condition that it did not exceed 10 per cent of the fair value of the total consideration given. Whereas the purpose of the SSAP 23 condition was clear, the new legal condition appears to lack any economic validity whatsoever.

Condition (d) leaves it to the standard setters to specify any further rules for the use of merger accounting and later thinking of the ASC and ASB can be found in ED 48 and FRED 6 respectively.

ED 48 'Accounting for acquisitions and mergers' was issued in February 1990 at the same time as Exposure Draft ED 47 'Accounting for goodwill'. As we shall see later in this chapter, ED 47 proposed that purchased goodwill be amortised through the profit and loss account. Given that such a charge would reduce reported profits subsequent to a combination, it might be expected that a large number of companies would attempt to use merger accounting which suppresses the emergence of any amount for goodwill. ED 48 was undoubtedly concerned to limit the use of merger accounting and to try to prevent some of the abuses which we have discussed above.

The approach taken in ED 48 and FRED 6 owes much to the Canadian standard setters[21]: Merger accounting may only be used for a merger, that is a business combination where no party can be identified as acquirer or acquiree. If a dominant partner can be identified then the combination will be an acquisition. Thus FRED 6, Para. 3, defines a merger as:

> A business combination which results in the creation of a new reporting entity formed from the combining parties, in which the shareholders of the combining entities come together in a substantially equal partnership for the mutual sharing of the risks and benefits of the combined entity, and in which no party to the combination in substance obtains control over any other, or is otherwise seen to be dominant, whether by virtue of the proportion of its shareholders' rights in the combined entity, the influence of its directors or otherwise.

This definition, which provides the general condition for the use of merger accounting is supplemented by five more detailed criteria, which we summarise below.[22]

(a) No party is portrayed as acquirer or acquiree.

---

21 *See* CICA Handbook, Sec. 1580, 'Business Combinations'.
22 FRED 6, Para. 10.

(b) All parties, as represented by directors or their appointees, participate in establishing the management structure and in selecting the management personnel of the combined entity.

(c) Relative sizes of the combining entities are not so disparate as to give one party dominance. (The explanatory note 52 suggests that one party should be presumed to dominate if it has a proportional equity interest which is more than 50 per cent larger than that of any other party.)

(d) No more than an immaterial proportion of the fair value received by any party is represented by non-equity. The explanatory notes provide no guidance on what percentage should be classed as immaterial.

(e) Equity shareholders of all of the combining entities have an interest in the whole combined entity and not just in a part of it.

FRED 6 envisages that where the criteria are satisfied, merger accounting must be used. There is to be no choice. However less combinations are likely to satisfy these criteria and the ASB envisages that, in future, the use of merger accounting will be even rarer than it has been in the past. Indeed FRED 6 even solicits views on an alternative approach which would prohibit the use of merger accounting except for internal group reconstructions, where no minority interests are involved.

Given the out-of-date balance sheet values produced by merger accounting, the abuses which have occurred and the infrequent use of merger accounting in recent years, this alternative approach would seem to have much to commend it!

GOODWILL

Introduction

Goodwill is the term used by accountants to describe the difference between the value placed on a firm and the sum of the fair values of the assets and liabilities of the firm which are identified and recorded separately in the accounting system. There are two reasons why these values will not be equal. First, most firms possess not only the predominantly tangible assets listed in a balance sheet but also such intangible assets as 'managerial ability', 'efficient staff' and 'regional monopoly' which contribute to the value of the firm and yet are not included in a balance sheet. Second, there is the simple economic fact that assets operating together frequently have a much higher value than the sum of the values of those same assets operating separately.

Goodwill is usually only recorded in an accounting system when a company purchases an unincorporated business or acquires a subsidiary or associated undertaking and prepares consolidated accounts. In the former case the goodwill arises in the accounts of the purchasing company itself while, in the latter case, the goodwill arises only in the consolidated accounts. In both cases the goodwill is described as 'purchased goodwill' to distinguish it from internally generated goodwill.

In the past goodwill has been calculated as the difference between the price paid and the sum of the book values of the individually identified assets less liabilities in the books of the acquired firm or company. Although this may simplify calculations, it makes little economic sense as the values in the books of the acquired firm or company are irrelevant in determining the historical cost of assets to the acquiring company or group. In accounting for an acquisition it is necessary for the acquiring company or group to value the individual assets and liabilities at their fair values, which determine their historical cost to the acquiring company or group.[23] Thus, the total cost of the collection of net assets, tangible and intangible, must be apportioned between those assets and liabilities which are to be identified separately in the accounting system and those which are not so identified. The latter group are recorded in the accounting system as a balancing figure which is described as goodwill. Such goodwill will normally be positive, but SSAP 22 takes the view that it may be negative.[24]

This may occur when the price paid for the collection of net assets is less than the sum of the fair values of the separable net assets. The standard warns us that, where negative goodwill emerges, the amounts allocated to the separable net assets should be reviewed to ensure that their fair values have not been overstated.

Internally created goodwill is not recorded, while goodwill which results from a market transaction is. It is therefore important to recognise that when a goodwill figure appears in a set of accounts, it does not relate to the whole reporting entity but merely to one segment which has been acquired by purchase.[25] Once the purchase has been made that segment will usually be merged with the other assets of the enlarged entity and may, indeed, no longer be separately identifiable.

With this background we may proceed to examine the problem of accounting for goodwill, assuming for the most part that the goodwill figure is positive.

Accounting for goodwill

Some possibilities

At the date of acquisition, goodwill represents the cost of acquiring certain intangible assets. As such is the case, the accruals concept would seem to dictate that the cost should be carried forward and matched against revenues of the periods expected to benefit from the use of such intangible assets. However, the future benefits may be extremely uncertain and there may be no way of determining which benefits arise from the particular collection of intangible assets. Hence, the prudence convention would appear to suggest that no asset should be recognised, rather that the amount paid for goodwill should be written off.

Given that there is a conflict between fundamental accounting conventions, it is not surprising to find that various methods of accounting for goodwill have been proposed. If we ignore the impractical suggestion that goodwill for the whole entity be revalued on each balance sheet date, the various proposals may be summarised as follows:

(a) Retain goodwill at cost, unless there is a permanent fall in the value.

---

23 *See* Companies Act 1985, Schedule 4A, Para. 9, which requires the use of fair values when a subsidiary is acquired, and SSAP 1, Para. 26 (a), which requires a similar treatment in the case of an associated company. Companies Act 1985, Schedule 4A, requires a tabular presentation of the book values and fair values for each class of assets and liabilities, including the amount of goodwill, together with an explanation of any significant adjustments made (Para. 13(5)).

24 SSAP 22, 'Accounting for goodwill', ASC, London, December 1984, Para. 8. Some accountants would not admit this possibility, arguing that the price paid must place a ceiling on the sum of the 'costs' of the separable net assets.

25 An exception to this general position occurs when the net assets of one firm are purchased by a newly formed entity. An example is the conversion of a sole tradership or partnership into a limited company. Provided the limited company acquires only the net assets of the firm and owns no other assets, the goodwill figure will relate to the whole business.

(b) Write off (amortise) the cost of goodwill over a period of years, which could be (i) its useful life, or (ii) a specific number of years, or (iii) its useful life subject to a maximum number of years.

(c) Write off goodwill immediately against reserves.

Some writers have argued that, in view of the unique nature of goodwill, the amount under (a) or (b) should appear, not as an asset, but as a 'dangling debit', that is as a deduction from share capital and reserves. This treatment can be regarded as a 'half-hearted' adoption of options (a) or (b) in that the information is provided but in such a way as to cast doubt upon its relevance.

Let us look at each of the proposals in turn.

The retention of goodwill at cost would seem to be justified only if the asset has an indefinite life. It is expected that this would rarely be true in the case of the particular intangible assets purchased, although the purchased benefits may, of course, be replaced by subsequent activities. If the intangible assets acquired do not have an indefinite life, it is necessary to recognise the possibility of a fall in the value of goodwill, but the determination of whether or not such a permanent fall has occurred will be an extremely difficult, if not impossible, task. It will certainly be difficult where the segment of the business which gave rise to the goodwill is no longer separately identifiable.

The amortisation of goodwill over a period of years is also subject to difficulties. In the first case, it is usually very difficult, if not impossible, to determine the useful life of goodwill, a residual category of assets measured by a balancing figure. In the second case, the selection of a specific number of years such as 5 or 40 is merely arbitrary, although the selection of a long period has the advantage that the results of no one period are significantly affected. The third case merely combines the difficulty of the first with the arbitrariness of the second.

The third proposal recognises that, after the year of acquisition, the retention of a goodwill figure relating to part of the business is unlikely to provide information useful to those interested in the affairs of the entity. It therefore requires its removal from the balance sheet by an immediate write-off against reserves.

In view of the different proposals which have been made and their associated problems, it is not surprising that the ASC experienced considerable difficulty in deciding upon an appropriate standard accounting practice.

The approach of SSAP 22

Unless it was prepared to use the true and fair override, the retention of goodwill at its cost was not an option available to the ASC. The Companies Act 1985 stated quite clearly that where goodwill is treated as an asset, it must be amortised systematically over a period not exceeding its useful economic life.[26] However, this still left the possibility of amortisation or of immediate write-off of goodwill against reserves for, in the latter case, goodwill is not treated as an asset and hence the legal requirement for amortisation does not apply.

While SSAP 22 preferred companies to write off goodwill immediately against reserves, it also permitted them to capitalise goodwill and to amortise it in arriving at the profit or

---

26 Companies Act 1985, Sec. 4, Para. 21.

loss on ordinary activities.[27] Both methods could be used simultaneously in respect of different acquisitions.

The preferred method had two major advantages. First, it avoided the difficult task of estimating the useful life of goodwill. Second, it resulted in a consistent treatment of purchased goodwill and internally generated goodwill. Given that the law does not permit companies to include internally generated goodwill in their balance sheets, the write-off of purchased goodwill results in the consistent position that no company shows goodwill in its balance sheet.

A major bias with the above requirements was that, if goodwill was capitalised and amortised, future profits and earnings per share would be reduced while, if goodwill was written off against reserves, there would be no impact on the profit and loss account at all! Not surprisingly the vast majority of companies adopted the preferred method of accounting under SSAP 22 often taking some pretty extreme steps to be able to do so.

Experience of SSAP 22

Before we explore the ways in which companies have responded to SSAP 22, it will, perhaps, be helpful if we illustrate how large goodwill may be in relation to the other net assets of a company at the date of acquisition. A good, but extreme example was provided in the annual accounts of Saatchi and Saatchi Company plc, a consulting firm, for the year to September 30 1986. The price paid for subsidiaries, the tangible net assets acquired and the resulting goodwill in respect of that year were as follows:

	£million
Cost of acquisitions	443.2
Net tangible assets	41.2
Goodwill	402.0

A more recent example is provided in the annual accounts of Thorn EMI plc for the year to March 31 1993, a year in which Thorn EMI plc acquired the Virgin Music Group Limited from Richard Branson:

	Total	Virgin Music Group Ltd	Other
	£m	£m	£m
Cost of acquisitions	653.7	593.0	60.7
Fair value of net assets acquired	17.3	14.1	3.2
Goodwill	636.4	578.9	57.5

In both of these cases, goodwill dwarfed the identifiable net assets, as might be expected in any successful company or group where people are the most important assets.

Given that large amounts have been paid to acquire valuable goodwill, there was a considerable reluctance among many companies to write off that goodwill in accordance with SSAP 22. One response has been to isolate an element of goodwill as 'brands' and

---

27 SSAP 22, Paras 32–35.

to retain this in the balance sheet.[28] Whether this is good accounting practice and whether the amount capitalised should be amortised or not has raised considerable controversy. The ASC issued an Exposure Draft ED 52 'Accounting for intangible fixed assets' (May 1990) in which it attempted to outlaw separate accounting for brands, but it remains to be seen what position will be taken in any subsequent ASB standard on this subject.

Once faced with the need to account for goodwill in accordance with SSAP 22, it is perhaps not surprising to find that the vast majority of companies chose immediate write-off rather than amortisation through the profit and loss account with its consequent impact on earnings per share. The way in which many large companies did so makes interesting reading.

If a company wished to adopt the policy of immediate write-off, the first question which had to be answered, on which SSAP 22 was silent, was which reserves could be used for the purpose of writing off goodwill. There was widespread agreement that the balance on the profit and loss account and any merger reserve could be used for this purpose, but there was much more dispute over whether the law permitted the use of a revaluation reserve. Although there was a large body of opinion to the effect that a revaluation reserve could not be used for this purpose, many companies chose to ignore this opinion.[29]

The next problem arose when the 'available' reserves were too small to absorb a write-off of goodwill and here we found two major responses.

Some companies effectively used share premium accounts to write off goodwill. They applied to the courts for a reduction of capital in order to be able to comply with the preferred method of accounting under SSAP 22. The share premium accounts were effectively relabelled, perhaps as a special reserve, thus becoming available to absorb the goodwill write-off.[30]

The second response was to create an appropriate reserve, a 'goodwill write-off' reserve, with a zero balance. The purchased goodwill could be written off against this goodwill write-off reserve resulting in a debit balance, a negative reserve, which was deducted from the share capital and reserves in the consolidated balance sheet.[31]

As well as provoking the above responses, the preference of SSAP 22 for immediate write-off appears to have had certain other consequences. By understating the fair values of the identifiable assets and liabilities, groups have been able to increase the amount labelled as goodwill. When this goodwill has been written off against reserves, future profit and loss accounts benefit from reduced depreciation charges on the tangible and intangible fixed assets.

A particular variant of the above has been the creation at acquisition of a provision for reorganisation costs. This reduced the identified net assets and hence increased the goodwill. The goodwill is written off and the provision is subsequently available to absorb costs which would otherwise have been charged to the profit and loss account. Any unused amount is then credited to the profit and loss account. While it is perfectly possible to

28 Some companies have gone further than this by including the values of internally generated brands as well as those which have been purchased. Good examples of companies which accounted for brands are Rank Hovis McDougall and Grand Metropolitan.

29 Since Companies Act 1989, the Revaluation Reserve is definitely *not* available for the write-off of goodwill, Companies Act 1985, Schedule 4. Para. 34.

30 Examples of companies which employed such an approach are Saatchi and Saatchi in 1985 and 1986 and Blue Arrow plc in 1987. A capital redemption reserve could presumably also be used in this way.

31 Examples of groups which have used this 'dangling debit disclosure' are Erskine House Group plc and TI Group plc.

justify the setting up of such a provision, it is thought that excessive provisions have been made by certain groups and the creation and use of such provisions had often been accompanied by inadequate disclosure.

It was developments such as the above which caused the ASC to issue a revised version of SSAP 22 in July 1989. The purpose of this standard was not to change the practice of accounting for goodwill, but to provide additional disclosure to help the users of accounts to understand what had been done.[32] Thus companies were required to show how goodwill had been dealt with, and to provide the table, subsequently required by law, showing the book values and fair values of each major category of assets and liabilities, together with an explanation of reasons for differences. In addition, it required disclosure of movements on provisions related to acquisitions and of information relating to the treatment of disposals of previously acquired businesses or business segments.

Even as the revised SSAP 22 was being issued, the accounting treatment of goodwill was under review and this led to the very different proposals in ED 47 'Accounting for goodwill', which was published in February 1990.

Towards a new standard

ED 47 took a very different view from SSAP 22. Whereas SSAP 22 favoured immediate write-off and permitted amortisation, ED 47 removed any choice and proposed that all goodwill should be amortised over its useful economic life. Whereas SSAP 22 attempted to achieve consistency between the treatment of purchased goodwill and non-purchased goodwill, ED 47 attempted to achieve consistency between the treatment of goodwill and other purchased intangible and tangible fixed assets. So, just as buildings, machinery and trademarks are depreciated over their useful economic lives, it argued that goodwill should be amortised.

ED 47 therefore proposed that positive goodwill should be amortised through the profit and loss account over its useful economic life using the straight-line basis or any other systematic basis which is more conservative and considered to give a more realistic allocation. However, it added the proviso that the useful economic life should not exceed 20 years, except in rare circumstances, and that the maximum life, even in those rare circumstances, should never exceed 40 years. These are provisions we do not find in standards dealing with tangible fixed assets! However, in common with the position with regard to tangible fixed assets, an annual review is required to ensure that the carrying value of the goodwill is not excessive.

The exposure draft admitted the possibility of negative goodwill, although where it arises it proposed a review of the fair values ascribed to the 'identifiable' assets and liabilities. The proposed treatment of any negative goodwill which remains after such a review is consistent with the treatment of positive goodwill, namely it is to be credited to the profit and loss account over a suitable period.

While the achievement of consistency with the treatment of other intangibles and tangible fixed assets would seem to be a worthwhile aim in the abstract, the authors have considerable doubts about the possibility of arriving at any meaningful figures by following a policy of amortisation.

Goodwill represents the residual category of net assets not identified separately in the accounting system and may include such assets as a high quality workforce and the

---

32 The additional disclosure requirements were contained in paragraphs 47–53 of the revised standard.

presence of barriers to entry. Such goodwill is measured as a balancing figure. To what extent is it possible to estimate the useful economic life of a residual class of net assets measured by a balancing figure? If this is not possible, then amortisation will result in highly dubious charges in the profit and loss account. Such an outcome seems to be recognised by the inclusion of references to 20 years and 40 years as the maximum useful economic life of goodwill.

As we have seen, the Exposure Draft proposed an annual review to ensure that the carrying value of the goodwill is not excessive. Here again, the authors have some difficulty in believing such a review to be possible. After all, what must be done is to assess the value at a particular date of goodwill acquired some years ago. The first problem is that no account must be taken of subsequently created goodwill. The second problem is that, in many cases, it is highly unlikely that the business segment, with which the goodwill was purchased, is still separately identifiable.

The accounting treatment of goodwill proposed in ED 47 was very different from that preferred by SSAP 22 and adopted by the vast majority of companies. Not surprisingly, there was considerable opposition to ED 47 and the proposals of the ASB have been anxiously awaited.

The ASB Discussion Paper

It was not until December 1993 that the ASB produced its first discussion paper on this subject entitled 'Goodwill and Intangible Assets'.

In its proposed treatment of intangible assets the discussion paper is clear: Purchased intangible assets, such as brands, should be subsumed within purchased goodwill and accounted for accordingly although purchased legal rights, such as patents, attaching to internally created intangible benefits should be capitalised at their historical cost and amortised appropriately (Paras 1.7 and 3.1.3).

However, when it turns to the subject of accounting for purchased goodwill there is much less certainty. The paper identifies the following six methods of accounting for goodwill, three based upon treating goodwill as an asset and three based upon the elimination of goodwill from assets:

A – Asset-based methods

1 *Capitalisation and amortisation over a predetermined life* subject to a maximum number of years, possibly 20, and subject to the usual test of recoverability at the end of each year.
2 *Capitalisation and annual review.* Under this approach, the value of goodwill is assessed at each balance sheet date using certain 'ceiling' tests described at length in appendix A to the Discussion Paper. These involve comparing the present value of the cash flows from the relevant segment of the business with the sum of the fair values of the separable assets and liabilities of that segment to determine the value of goodwill. Amortisation through the profit and loss account is only necessary if the value so determined is less than the existing carrying value of the goodwill.
3 *Combination of 1 and 2* with 1 being the norm and 2 being used when the goodwill has an indeterminate life expected to be more than 20 years.

B – Elimination methods

1 *Immediate write-off against reserves*, the preferred method of SSAP 22.
2 *Creation of a separate goodwill write-off reserve* with disclosure as a 'dangling debit', a deduction from share capital and reserves. Under this approach no further adjustment would be made to the goodwill write-off reserve unless the acquired segment of the group to which it relates is disposed of or closed.
3 *Variant of 2* involving creation of a separate goodwill write-off reserve but with an annual assessment of recoverability to ensure that the goodwill write-off reserve is reduced if the value of the goodwill has fallen permanently.

While the discussion paper provides extensive discussion of the merits and demerits of the various methods, it fails to identify any single proposed approach. Indeed it identifies two very different approaches which have support among Board members, namely methods A3 and B2 or B3.

Method A3 is itself a combination of A1 and A2 while methods B2 and B3 both involve the creation of a separate goodwill write-off reserve, either with (B3) or without (B2) a recoverability test. In other words the Board sees possible ways forward which might be described by a cynic as anything other than what is done at present (B1)!

It remains to be seen which method will be recommended by the ASB as standard accounting practice.

RECOMMENDED READING

J. A. Arnold, D. Egginton, L. Kirkham, R. H. Macve and K. Peasnell, 'Goodwill and other intangibles', ICAEW, London, October 1992.

T. E. Cooke, *Mergers and Acquisitions*, Blackwell, Oxford, 1986.

P. A. Holgate, 'Accounting for acquisitions and mergers', *Accountants Digest No. 189*, ICAEW, London, Summer 1986.

P. A. Holgate, 'Accounting for goodwill', *Accountants Digest No. 235*, ICAEW, London, Winter 1989/90.

M. C. Miller, 'Goodwill – an aggregation issue', *The Accounting Review*, April 1973.

M. A. Weinberg and M. V. Blank, *Takeovers and Mergers*, Vols 1 and 2, 5th edn, Sweet and Maxwell, 1989.

CHAPTER 9

Investments, groups and associated undertakings

INVESTMENTS

Introduction

The key to determine the treatment, in the investing company's accounts, of an investment in the shares of another company (the investee company) is intention. If the investment is to be for the long term, it will be treated as a fixed asset, while if it is intended to be for the short term, normally less than one year, it will be treated as a current asset.

In a traditional historical cost balance sheet, a fixed asset investment is shown at its historical cost unless its value has fallen permanently below historical cost when it is written down to that lower value. A current asset investment is shown at the lower of its cost and net realisable value.

For both types of investment it is usual to take credit in the profit and loss account of the investing company for dividends received and receivable, although dividends receivable are only recognised to the extent that they are in respect of accounting periods ended on or before the accounting year end of the investing company and have been declared prior to approval of the investing company's own accounts. Some companies are even more prudent and take credit only for dividends received in an accounting period.

The above accounting treatments provide limited information to users of the investing company's accounts and, in order to remedy this, some companies have taken advantage of the alternative accounting rules to show investments at their current value.[1] In such cases, any revaluation surplus must be taken to a revaluation reserve and any revaluation deficit must be taken to the revaluation reserve to the extent that that reserve contains a revaluation surplus in respect of the same investment but otherwise must be charged to the profit and loss account.

In its death throes in July 1990, the ASC issued Exposure Draft 55 'Accounting for investments' and this made proposals in respect of both fixed asset and current asset investments. It proposed that, where a company adopts the alternative accounting rules to show fixed asset investments at a valuation, that amount should be kept up to date by an annual revaluation.[2] However, its major proposal for change is in accounting for certain current asset investments, namely those which are 'readily marketable'. In the view

---

1 The rules on what is an acceptable current value differ for fixed assets and current assets respectively. (See Companies Act 1985, Schedule 4, Section C, Paras 31(3) and 31(4)). Thus, a current asset investment may be shown at its current cost, while a fixed asset investment may be shown at its market value or any other value which the directors consider to be appropriate. In the latter case, the method of valuation adopted and the reasons for adopting it must be stated.
2 ED 55 goes beyond ED 51 'Accounting for fixed assets and revaluations' which requires revaluations at least every five years.

of the ASC, such investments should be stated in a balance sheet at their quoted current value and any difference between that current value and the previous carrying value should be reflected in the profit and loss account. Hence the profit and loss account would reflect not only the dividends receivable but also any changes in the value of such an investment during an accounting year. In the view of the ASC any such change would be a realised profit or loss on the grounds that it has been reliably measured by reference to a quoted price.[3]

While many accountants would applaud the ASC for attempting to ensure that such changes in value are reflected in a profit and loss account, there are severe doubts about the legality of the proposed method of accounting for readily marketable current asset investments.[4] The proposed method does not comply with the historical cost accounting rules, which require current asset investments to be shown at the lower of cost and net realisable value, nor with the alternative accounting rules which require any revaluation surplus to be taken, not to the profit and loss account but to a revaluation reserve. When issuing the Exposure Draft, the ASC was aware that its proposals could only be introduced by relying on the true and fair override or if there were to be a change in the law.[5] As a consequence this proposal of ED 55 is unlikely to be introduced in its present form in the immediate future.

Investments carrying influence

While the present accounting treatments outlined above are still relevant in an investing company's own accounts, a fundamental change in the sort of information provided occurs when an investment carries influence over the affairs of an investee company.

Where the investment is sufficient to give the investing company control over the investee, the investee is a subsidiary undertaking and, subject to certain exceptions, the investing company must prepare group accounts. Since the enactment of Companies Act 1989, these group accounts must be consolidated accounts.[6] Relevant standard accounting practice is contained in FRS2 'Accounting for subsidiary undertakings' (July 1982).

Where an investment is such that it gives the investing company significant influence but not control over another entity, an associated undertaking or joint venture, the law requires the use of the equity method of accounting although, where the investee is a non-incorporated joint venture, it permits the use of proportional consolidation.[7] The source of standard accounting practice is SSAP 1 'Accounting for associated companies' (revised April 1982)[8] as amended by the ASB 'Interim Statement: Consolidated Accounts' (December 1990). At the time of writing, the ASB is still working on a proposed standard on associated undertakings and joint ventures.

In this chapter we look first at accounting for groups and then turn to the methods of

3 ED 55 'Accounting for investments', July 1990, Para. 43. As we have seen in Chapter 3, there are different ways of defining realisation. ED 55 takes the view that a profit or loss made due to a change in value of a readily marketable current asset investment is realised because the value of that investment can be reliably measured. In its view, the investment does not have to be converted into cash by sale before the profit can be treated as realised.
4 'Investments: conceptual clarity v legal muddle', R. Macve, *Accountancy*, March 1991, pp. 84–5.
5 ED 55, Preface, Paras 1.17 and 1.18.
6 Companies Act 1985, Sec. 227, Para. 2.
7 Companies Act 1985, Schedule 4A, Paras 19 and 20.
8 The original SSAP 1 'Accounting for associated companies' was issued in January 1971 and SSAP 1 (revised) was issued in April 1982.

accounting for associated undertakings and joint ventures. We assume that readers are familiar with the basic acquisition method of preparing consolidated accounts as used in the UK, including the cancellation of inter-company balances and the removal of unrealised inter-company profits.[9]

ACCOUNTING FOR GROUPS

What is a group?

Subject to certain exceptions which we discuss below, any UK company which is a parent company at its year end must prepare group accounts in addition to its individual accounts. Since the Companies Act 1989, these group accounts must be a set of consolidated accounts for the parent company and its subsidiary undertakings.[10]

Prior to the Companies Act 1989, a subsidiary had to be a company and a parent company/subsidiary relationship was defined as existing when the parent company was a shareholder and controlled the composition of the board of directors of the other company and/or when it held more than half of the equity share capital of that other company.[11]

This definition was thus based on both control and ownership and betrayed some confusion about why group accounts were required. While ownership and control usually go hand in hand, this is not always the case and, because the definition of 'equity share capital' was widely drawn, on some occasions one company was legally a subsidiary of two other companies at the same time!

In response to the EC Seventh Directive, which we discussed briefly in Chapter 2, the Companies Act 1989 has introduced a much clearer concept of a group for accounting purposes.

First, it required that consolidated accounts include the parent and all *subsidiary undertakings*. The latter is a new term which is not restricted to companies but includes partnerships and 'unincorporated associations carrying on trade or business with or without view to profit'.[12]

Second, it introduced a new definition of a parent/subsidiary relationship based not on ownership but upon control. Thus the relationship between a parent undertaking and a subsidiary undertaking is now defined as follows:[13]

> .
> .
> .

> (2) An undertaking is a parent undertaking in relation to another undertaking, a subsidiary undertaking, if –
> (a) it holds a majority of the voting rights in the undertaking, or
> (b) it is a member of the undertaking and has the right to appoint or remove a majority of its board of directors, or

---

9 FRS 2, Para. 39, standardises practice on the removal of such unrealised profits by requiring removal of the full amount to be set off against the group reserves and the minority interest respectively. The alternative of removing only the group share of the unrealised profit and leaving the minority interest unchanged is no longer permitted.

10 Companies Act 1985 (as amended by Companies Act 1989), Section 227. Before the Companies Act 1989, consolidated accounts were just one possible form which group accounts could take.

11 Companies Act 1985, Sec. 736.

12 Companies Act 1985 (as amended by Companies Act 1989), Sec. 259.

13 Companies Act 1985 (as amended by Companies Act 1989), Sec. 258.

  (c) it has the right to exercise a dominant influence over the undertaking –
    (i) by virtue of provisions contained in the undertaking's memorandum or articles, or
    (ii) by virtue of a control contract, or

  (d) it is a member of the undertaking and controls alone, pursuant to an agreement with other shareholders or members, a majority of the voting rights in the undertaking.

   .
   .
   .

(4) An undertaking is also a parent undertaking in relation to another undertaking, a subsidiary undertaking, if it has a participating interest in the undertaking and –
  (a) it actually exercises a dominant influence over it, or
  (b) it and the subsidiary undertaking are managed on a unified basis.

While paragraph (2) is concerned with the existence of legal power of control, the rather wider paragraph (4) reflects the very different definition of a group prevalent in Germany, namely a definition which rests on the existence of the *de facto* control rather than *de jure* control.

The more precise definition of a group introduced by the Companies Act 1989 helps us to keep clearly in our minds that the purpose of consolidated accounts is to show the assets and liabilities under common control and how these are being used. It will also help accountants to ensure that some of the many off balance sheet finance schemes which have exploited the previous definition of a subsidiary do now find their way on to the consolidated balance sheet. Indeed, as we have seen in Chapter 6, FRED 4 'Reporting the substance of transactions' has attempted to go even further than this in requiring the inclusion of quasi-subsidiaries in the consolidated accounts.[14]

The compass of group accounts

Since the Companies Act 1989 was passed, group accounts must take the form of a set of consolidated accounts, the only exception now being where such a set of consolidated accounts would not give true and fair view.[15] Thus a parent company must usually prepare a set of consolidated accounts showing the results and state of affairs of itself and all its subsidiary undertakings as a single economic entity.[16]

The law does, however, exempt the parent company from preparing group accounts in certain circumstances and permits the exclusion of subsidiary undertakings from the consolidated accounts in other circumstances. We shall deal with each in turn.

As a consequence of the government's programme for reducing the burdens on business, which we discussed in Chapter 2, the law has exempted a parent company from the need to prepare group accounts where the group qualifies as a small or medium-sized group, provided that it is not an ineligible group.[17]

As with the definitions of small and medium-sized companies, the definitions for small and medium-sized groups are framed by reference to turnover, balance sheet total (assets) and number of employees.[18]

---

14 *See* Chapter 6, pp. 176–7.
15 Companies Act 1985, Sec. 227.
16 Companies Act 1985, Sec. 228.
17 Companies Act 1985, Sec. 248. A group is ineligible if any of its members is a public company, a banking company, an insurance company or an authorised person under the Financial Services Act 1986.
18 Companies Act 1985, Sec. 249.

In addition to these exemptions based on size, a parent company does not have to prepare group accounts where it is itself an intermediate holding company with an immediate parent company in the European Community provided consolidated financial statements are prepared at a higher level in the group. There are a number of conditions which must be satisfied if this exemption is to apply, in particular, the higher level consolidated accounts must be prepared in accordance with law based on the EC 7th Directive and must be filed with the UK parent's individual accounts together with certified translations, where appropriate.[19]

Where a parent company is not able to take advantage of the above exemptions, it must prepare consolidated accounts for all the companies in the group which are under the control of the parent company. However, the law *permits* the exclusion of subsidiary undertakings from the consolidated accounts in the following circumstances:[20]

.
.
.

(3) ... a subsidiary undertaking may be excluded from consolidation where –
    (a) severe long-term restrictions substantially hinder the exercise of the rights of the parent company over the assets or management of that undertaking, or
    (b) the information necessary for the preparation of group accounts cannot be obtained without disproportionate expense or undue delay, or
    (c) the interest of the parent company is held exclusively with a view to subsequent resale and the undertaking has not previously been included in consolidated group accounts prepared by the parent company.

.
.
.

(4) Where the activities of one or more subsidiary undertakings are so different from those of other undertakings to be included in the consolidation that their inclusion would be incompatible with the obligation to give a true and fair view, those undertakings shall be excluded from consolidation.

This subsection does not apply merely because some of the undertakings are industrial, some commercial and some provide services, or because they carry on industrial or commercial activities involving different products or provide different services.

FRS 2 takes a more restricted view and specifically states that neither disproportionate expense nor undue delay can justify excluding material subsidiary undertakings from the consolidated accounts. However, whereas the law *permits* the exclusion of subsidiary undertakings from the consolidated accounts, FRS 2 *requires* their exclusion in certain circumstances and specifies the required accounting treatment for such excluded subsidiaries.[21] Thus, paragraph 25 of FRS 2 states that a subsidiary should be excluded from consolidation in three circumstances (see Table 9.1):

(a) Where severe long-term restrictions substantially hinder the exercise of the rights of the parent company over the assets or management of the subsidiary undertaking.
(b) Where the interest in the subsidiary undertaking is held exclusively with a view to subsequent resale and the subsidiary undertaking has not previously been consolidated in group accounts prepared by the parent company.

19 Companies Act 1985, Sec. 228.
20 Companies Act 1985 (as amended by Companies Act 1989), Sec. 229.
21 FRS 2 'Accounting for subsidiary undertakings', Paras 25–30.

(c) Where the subsidiary undertaking's activities are so different from those of other undertakings to be included in the consolidation that its inclusion would be incompatible with the obligation to give a true and fair view.

All three of these required exclusions follow from the legal provisions quoted above, except that FRS 2 emphasises that the circumstances envisaged under (c) are likely to be rare. In particular, the explanation to the standard emphasises that any differences between banking and insurance companies/groups and other companies/groups or between profit and not-for-profit undertakings is not sufficient of itself to justify non-consolidation.[22]

Table 9.1 Attitude to exclusion of subsidiary

	Companies Act 1985	FRS 2
Inability to exercise control	Permits	Requires
Disproportionate expense or undue delay	Permits	Forbids
Subsidiary acquired for resale	Permits	Requires
Different activities where inclusion would be incompatible with true and fair view	Permits	Requires*

*But expected to be rare

Having specified the circumstances under which subsidiary undertakings should be excluded, FRS 2 specifies the accounting treatment to be applied to such subsidiaries and the information to be disclosed. The required accounting treatment may be summarised as follows[23]:

(a) *Severe long-term restrictions.* If the parent company is denied control but retains significant influence over the excluded subsidiary, use the equity method of accounting. The equity method of accounting, which is the required method of accounting for associated undertakings, is described later in this chapter.

   If the parent does not even retain significant influence, treat the excluded subsidiary as a fixed asset investment showing it at the carrying value at which it would have appeared if the equity method had been in use when the restrictions came into force.[24] Subsequently take credit only for dividends actually received.

   In either case, it is essential to write down the investment if there has been a permanent fall in its value.
(b) *Subsidiary held exclusively with a view to resale.* This should be treated as a current asset and shown at the lower of cost and net realisable value.
(c) *Different activities.* In the rare circumstances where a subsidiary undertaking is excluded for this reason, the investment should be recorded in the consolidated financial statements using the equity method of accounting, and a separate set of financial statements for the subsidiary should be included with the consolidated financial statements.[25]

---

22 FRS 2, Para. 78e.
23 FRS 2, Paras 27–32.
24 This carrying value may be cost of the investment if the restriction existed at the date of acquisition (FRS 2 Para. 27).
25 Certain other disclosures are required in respect of subsidiaries, both included and excluded. Readers are referred to Companies Act 1985, Schedule 5 and to FRS 2, Paras 31–34.

Changes in the composition of a group

Consolidated accounts for a group are prepared to show the results of the group as a single economic entity. It follows that, subject to the removal of unrealised intercompany profit, the consolidated profit and loss account should include the profits or losses of all companies in the group for the relevant periods during which they were members of the group. The consolidated balance sheet should show the combined assets and liabilities of companies which are members of the group at the accounting year end. This simple requirement gives rise to many accounting problems where there is an acquisition or disposal of a subsidiary during the course of a year.

The first problem is to decide exactly when an acquisition or disposal occurs. The negotiations which lead to such an event are ofen long and drawn out, involving preliminary discussions, agreement in principle, a drawing up of terms, an offer, an unconditional acceptance and then payment of the consideration. In the 1970s various of these possible events were selected as fixing the date of acquisition or disposal and often the selection of the date appeared to have been influenced by a desire to show the largest possible profit in the consolidated accounts. Thus, when a new profit-making subsidiary is acquired, the earlier the selected date of acquisition, the greater the profits which will be included in the consolidated profit and loss account. Similarly, when the shares in a loss-making subsidiary are sold, the earlier the date of disposal the less the losses which serve to reduce the consolidated profits.

In order to remove discretion about the choice of possible date, FRS 2 defines the effective date of acquisition or disposal as the date on which control is obtained or relinquished.[26]

Control usually passes when an offer becomes unconditional and, in the case of a public offer of shares, this will be the date when the necessary number of acceptances has been obtained.

The consolidated profit and loss account must include the profits of any new subsidiary from the date of acquisition, as defined above, to the end of the accounting year and the profits or losses of any subsidiary sold from the beginning of the accounting year to the date of disposal.

FRS 3 'Reporting financial performance' specifically requires the disclosure of the aggregate results of continuing operations, acquisitions (as a component of continuing operations) and discontinued operations.[27]

Let us look first at the treatment of acquisitions and then consider some of the various types of disposal which may occur.

Treatment of an acquisition

Fair values and goodwill

When a company acquires a subsidiary undertaking, it pays a price to obtain control of the assets and liabilities of that subsidiary. In the balance sheet of the parent company it is necessary to record the investment at its cost while, in the consolidated balance sheet, it is necessary to recognise the individual assets and liabilities of that subsidiary.

---

26 FRS 2, Para. 45.
27 FRS 3 'Reporting financial performance', ASB, October 1992, Para. 14.

When a subsidiary is acquired for cash, the determination of the cost of the investment is easy but, when shares in a subsidiary are acquired in exchange for an issue of shares or other securities in the parent company or where part of the consideration is deferred or contingent on some future event, the determination of the cost may not be so clear cut.

Where the consideration is an issue of shares, it is necessary to determine the fair value of the shares and, if this exceeds the nominal value of the shares, to record a share premium or, where merger relief is available, a merger reserve.[28]

Similarly where other securities are issued, these should be valued at their fair value. Fair value is the market price of the securities when control is obtained or, if the securities are unquoted, the best approximation to the market price using the methods of valuation which we discuss in Chapter 14.

Where the consideration is deferred or contingent, a reasonable estimate of its fair value should be included.[29] This would be provided by the expected value of the amount payable, that is the present value of the amounts expected to be paid in future.

In preparing a consolidated balance sheet it is necessary to replace the investment in the subsidiary by the whole of the underlying assets and liabilities of the subsidiary showing any minority interest therein. Under the historical cost convention, these assets and liabilities must be included at their historical cost to the group and, for this purpose, the amounts at which they appear in the subsidiary's own balance sheet are, of course, irrelevant. Indeed the group may not recognise certain assets and liabilities which appear in the subsidiary's balance sheet and may recognise assets and liabilities which do not appear in the subsidiary's own balance sheet at all.

The difficulty which must be faced here is that the parent company has not bought the individual assets and liabilities of the subsidiary. It has paid a global price to obtain control over a collection of assets and liabilities and, in order to prepare a consolidated balance sheet, it is necessary to allocate the global price to the individual assets and liabilities using the concept of fair value.

The difference between the cost of the investment and the appropriate proportion of the sum of the fair values of the individual assets and liabilities will provide us with the goodwill. In FRED 7 'Fair values in acquisition accounting', the ASB explains the process thus[30]:

> Under the acquisition method of accounting the identifiable assets and liabilities acquired are included in the consolidated balance sheet at their fair values as at the date of acquisition, and the difference between those and the cost of the acquisition is recognised as goodwill or negative goodwill.

The ASB follows the law in using the adjective 'identifiable' and, although we shall continue to use this adjective, it does seem to be rather inappropriate. Many assets such as a good management team, a considerable research potential or a regional monopoly are identifiable but are not usually recognised in consolidated accounts except as a part of the goodwill figure.

FRED 7 provides some guidance on which assets and liabilities of the subsidiary should be recognised in the consolidated accounts. In particular it suggests that certain assets and liabilities not normally recognised in individual accounts should be recognised on

---

28 See Chapter 8, page 212.
29 Further guidance is provided by FRED 7 'Fair values in acquisition accounting', ASB, December, 1993.
30 FRED 7 'Fair values in acquisition accounting', ASB, December 1993, Para. 10.

consolidation and provides some examples, which include pension surpluses and deficiencies and contingent assets. It also proposes that the only liabilities to be included in the consolidated accounts are those which should have been recognised in the accounts of the acquired company prior to acquisition. By doing this, it attempts to outlaw the practice followed by some companies of making provisions for future reorganisation costs and losses of the subsidiary at the date of acquisition. The making of such a provision increases any positive goodwill figure and has the consequence that post-acquisition reorganisation costs are charged to the provision instead of to the consolidated profit and loss account. While the need to incur such reorganisation cost and losses, in integrating the new subsidiary into the group, will undoubtedly be relevant in fixing the purchase price, it has proved extremely difficult to police such provisions in practice and, in the case of certain companies, the provisions made appear to have been excessive.

Once the identifiable assets and liabilities have been listed it is then necessary to obtain their fair values; fair value is based on the concept of 'Value to the Business'.[31] The value to the business of fixed assets and stocks are given by the following formulae shown in Figure 9.1.

For a fixed asset:

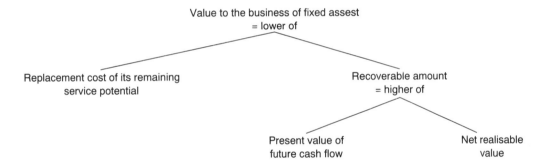

For stock and short term work in progress, the formula is simpler:

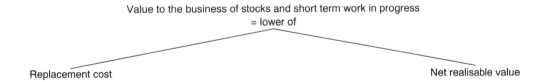

Fig. 9.1 Determination of fair value

Whereas the fair values of short-term and certain long-term debtors and creditors will be equal to their face values, it will be necessary to discount any long-term debtors and creditors which do not carry interest at the current market rate.

---

31 We discuss this concept in considerable detail in the context of current cost accounting in Chapter 16.

To help users of accounts to understand what has happened, Company Law requires companies to publish a table showing, for each class of assets and liabilities, the book values before an acquisition, the fair values at the date of acquisition, and an explanation for any significant adjustment made together with the goodwill on acquisition.[32]

FRED 7 proposes that the fair value adjustments are analysed between (a) revaluations, (b) adjustments to achieve consistency of accounting policies and (c) any other significant adjustments.[33]

An example of the table required by law is as follows:

Table 9.2

	Book value at acquisition	Fair value adjustments	Fair value to the group
	£000	£000	£000
Tangible fixed assets	420	140	560
Current assets	340	50	390
Creditors due within one year	(190)	–	(190)
Creditors due in more than one year	(200)	(30)	(230)
Provisions for liabilities and charges	(50)	(10)	(60)
	320	150	470
Goodwill			130
Consideration paid			600

In practice, the identification and valuation of assets and liabilities may take some considerable time. However FRED 7 proposes that all adjustments to fair values and purchased goodwill should be fixed by the date when the consolidated accounts for the first *full* financial year following the acquisition are approved by the directors.[34]

Before we look at a more complete example of an acquisition, let us examine the further complication caused when a subsidiary undertaking is acquired in stages. To take an example, one company may purchase 10 per cent of the equity shares in another company and then purchase a further 70 per cent of those shares at a later date. As control is only obtained at the time the latter purchase is made, the law requires that the combined cost of the 80 per cent (i.e. 10 per cent + 70 per cent) should be matched against that percentage of the sum of the fair values of the identifiable assets and liabilities to determine goodwill at the date on which control is obtained.[35]

This method will lead to a rather dubious figure for goodwill in that the price paid for the earlier purchase related to the fair value of the net assets and goodwill at the date of that purchase rather than their value at the much later date when control was obtained. However FRS 2 sees it as a practical means of applying acquisition accounting.[36]

The standard does recognise, however, that it will not always be appropriate and requires the use of the true and fair override to depart from the legal rule in certain circumstances. One example where this would be appropriate would be when the earlier purchase was sufficient to constitute the investee an associated undertaking for which

32 Companies Act 1985, Schedule 4A, Para. 12 (5).
33 FRED 7, Para. 33.
34 FRED 7, Para. 29.
35 Companies Act 1985, Sched. 4A, Para. 9.
36 FRS 2, Para. 89.

equity accounting was appropriate. The application of the equity method of accounting requires the use of fair values at the initial purchase date and use of the legally specified approach at a subsequent purchase which brings control would result in the post-acquisition profits and gains of the associated undertaking being reclassified as goodwill. In these circumstances, the standard requires that goodwill be calculated in stages, summing the differences between the cost of each purchase and the appropriate proportion of the fair value of the identifiable assets and liabilities at the date of each purchase. Such an approach would, of course, require the use of the true and fair override and the consequential disclosure that this had occurred.

The standard also deals with the situation where a company increases its stake in a subsidiary undertaking thus reducing or perhaps eliminating the minority interest.[37] In such a case it is essential to revalue the identifiable assets and liabilities in the subsidiary at the date of the increase in shareholding.

An example

We have seen that the consolidated profit and loss account must include the results of a new subsidiary from the date of acquisition to the end of the accounting year and that the consolidated balance sheet must include the assets and liabilities of the new subsidiary which is a member of the group at the year end. This general statement is best explored in the context of an example.

Let us take a company J Limited, which has many subsidiaries and makes up accounts to 31 December each year. J acquires a new wholly owned subsidiary, K Limited, during the year to 31 December 19X2. Control is obtained on 1 July 19X2. Summarised consolidated accounts of the J group (excluding K) and accounts for K Limited are given below:

Summarised profit and loss accounts for the year ended 31 December 19X2

	J Group £000	K Limited £000
Turnover	2 000	500
less Expenses	1 500	420
Profit from ordinary activities before tax	500	80
less Taxation	200	36
	300	44
less Minority interest	40	
	260	44
add Extraordinary profit (net of taxation and minority interest)	30	20
	290	64
less Dividends proposed	100	
	190	64
add Retained profits on 1 January 19X2	310	82
Retained profits	500	146

---

37 FRS 2, Para. 90.

Summarised balance sheets on 31 December 19X2

	J Group £000	K Limited £000
Fixed assets		
Goodwill	100	–
Tangible fixed assets	500	156
Investment in K Ltd – 40 000 shares at cost	200	–
Net current assets	300	100
	1100	256
less Long-term loans	170	50
	930	206
Share capital (£1 shares)	250	40
Revaluation reserve (created 1 July 19X2)	–	20
Retained profits	500	146
	750	206
Minority interests	180	–
	930	206

As K Limited was acquired on 1 July 19X2, the date on which control passed, it is necessary to value the identifiable assets and liabilities at their fair values on that date. In practice it is extremely helpful if their fair values are incorporated in the individual accounts of the subsidiary and this has been done in the balance sheet of K Limited to produce a Revaluation Reserve on 1 July 19X2 of £20 000.

The consolidated profit and loss account must include the results of K Limited from 1 July 19X2 to 31 December 19X2. If we assume that the sales and operating profit of K Limited accrued evenly over the year and that the extraordinary profit did not arise until October 19X2, the consolidated profit and loss account must include the following post-acquisition profits of K from 1 July 19X2 to 31 December 19X2:

		Post-acquisition
	£000	£000
Turnover	500 x ½	250
less Expenses	420 x ½	210
	80	40
less Taxation	36 x ½	18
	44	22
add Extraordinary profit	20	20
	64	42

The consolidated profit and loss account with relevant workings, will appear as follows [38]:

38 We have assumed that the extraordinary profit of K Limited remains extraordinary within the context of the group.

Consolidated profit and loss account for the year ended 31 December 19X2

	£000	£000
Turnover		
J group	2000	
K, ½ x £500 000	250	2250
Expenses		
J group	1500	
K, ½ x £420 000	210	1710
Profit from ordinary activities before tax		540
less Taxation		
J Group	200	
K, ½ x £36 000	18	218
		322
less Minority interest (no change as new subsidiary is wholly owned)		40
		282
add Extraordinary profit (net of taxation and minority interest)		
J group	30	
K (all post-acquisition)	20	50
		332
less Dividends proposed		100
		232
add Retained profits on 1 January 19X2		
J group only (K was not a member of the group at this date)		310
Retained profits on 31 December 19X2		542

Note that the retained profits brought forward do not include any profits in respect of K; after all, K did not become a member of the group until 1 July 19X2 so all retained profits before that date are pre-acquisition and represented by the net assets purchased on that date.

On the assumption that no major discontinuance is planned for K, the results of the new subsidiary will be included as part of the results of continuing operations and disclosed separately in accordance with the provisions of FRS 3.[39]

We next turn to the preparation of the consolidated balance sheet on 31 December 19X2. As K is a member of the group on that date, the balance sheet must include all of its assets and liabilities together with any goodwill on acquisition. In order to calculate the goodwill on acquisition we need to know the sum of the fair values of the identifiable assets and liabilities on 1 July 19X2. As these fair values have been incorporated in the accounts of K, they are equal to the sum of the share capital and reserves of K at the date of acquisition, which may be calculated as follows:

39 FRS 3, Para. 14.

K Limited

Net assets on 1 July 19X2	£000	£000
Share capital		40
Revaluation reserve		20
Retained profits		
On 1 January 19X2	82	
1 January to 30 June 19X2, 1/2×£44 000	22	104
		164

J Limited has paid £200 000 to acquire net assets which have an aggregate fair value of £164 000 on 1 July 19X2. Hence it has paid a premium of £36 000.

The consolidated balance sheet on 31 December 19X2, together with appropriate workings will appear as follows:

J Group
Summarised consolidated balance sheet on 31 December 19X2

		£000	£000
Fixed assets			
Intangible			
Goodwill	– Old J group	100	
	K	36	136
Tangible	– Old J group	500	
	K	156	656
Net current assets	– Old J group	300	
	K	100	400
			1192
less Long-term loans	– Old J Group	170	
	K	50	220
			972
Share capital, £1 shares			250
Retained profits, per consolidated profit and loss account			542
			792
Minority interest, as before			180
			972

Now that we have examined the basic principles for dealing with the acquisition of a new subsidiary, readers should be in a position to cope with various complications. Thus, the acquisition of a loss-making subsidiary or one in which profits do not arise evenly over the period should give few problems. Similarly, the acquisition of a partially owned subsidiary requires little modification to the approach we have adopted above.

Treatment of disposals

Just as companies acquire shares in subsidiaries, so too do they dispose of shares in subsidiaries. When we turn to disposals we may distinguish various categories of sales to outsiders[40] depending upon the shareholding, if any, which is retained:

(a) Sale of total shareholding
(b) Sale of part of shareholding such that the investee company remains or becomes
    (i) a subsidiary undertaking
    (ii) an associated undertaking
    (iii) a simple investment

In all cases it is necessary to recognise that different treatments are required in the individual accounts of the company making the sale and in the consolidated accounts.

We shall illustrate the principles involved in the context of a sale of the total shareholding and will then look briefly at partial disposals.

Sale of total shareholding

In the accounting records of the company which makes the sale, it is necessary to match the carrying value of the investment with the proceeds of sale to determine the profit or loss on disposal.

The disposal may, of course, have taxation consequences but, once the investing company has recognised the profit or loss and made any necessary provision for taxation, that is the end of the matter as far as that company is concerned.

When we turn to the consolidated accounts, matters are a little more complicated. In accordance with normal practice in the UK, post-acquisition profits of a subsidiary are credited to the consolidated profit and loss account year by year, whether or not they are distributed as dividend to the investing company. Hence, year by year, we recognise profits which are retained by the subsidiary company and so increase the net assets shown in the consolidated balance sheet by these amounts.

In the consolidated accounts, the profit or loss on disposal usually differs from that shown in the investing company's own profit and loss account. In the consolidated accounts the profit or loss on disposal will be the difference between the sale proceeds and the appropriate share of the underlying net assets of the subsidiary at the date of sale plus any goodwill on acquisition which has not been written off in the consolidated profit and loss account. Thus the difference between the profit on disposal shown in the investing company's records and in the consolidated accounts will depend on the change in the net assets of the subsidiary since acquisition. To the extent that the net assets of the subsidiary have grown, due to the profits made and retained between acquisition and disposal, these have been recognised in the consolidated profit and loss account as part of the group's results.

Let us start with a very simple example. L Limited has two wholly owned subsidiaries, M Limited and N Limited. The respective summarised balance sheets on 31 December 19X1 are given below.

---

40 Intra-group sales may also occur. In addition a parent company may lose control of a subsidiary even without a sale of shares where, for example, a rights offer by the investee is taken up by other shareholders but not by the existing parent. FRS 2 describes such a loss of control as a 'deemed disposal' and the principles involved in such a case are the same as those described in the text.

Summarised balance sheets on 31 December 19X1

	L	M	N
	£	£	£
Net assets	110 000	60 000	70 000
Investments in subsidiaries, at cost			
20 000 shares in M Limited	45 000		
30 000 shares in N Limited	70 000		
	225 000	60 000	70 000
Share capital, £1 shares	100 000	20 000	30 000
Retained profits	125 000		
at date of acquisition		10 000	20 000
post acquisition		30 000	20 000
	225 000	60 000	70 000

If we assume that there are no fair value adjustments and that goodwill has not been written off, the summarised consolidated balance sheet, with relevant workings, on 31 December 19X1 would appear as follows:

Summarised consolidated balance sheet on 31 December 19X1

	£	£
Goodwill		
M (£45 000 – £30 000)	15 000	
N (£70 000 – £50 000)	20 000	35 000
Other net assets		
(£110 000 + £60 000 + £70 000)		240 000
		275 000
Share capital, £1 shares		100 000
Retained profits		
L	125 000	
M post acquisition	30 000	
N post acquisition	20 000	175 000
		275 000

From this consolidated balance sheet we can see that the consolidated retained profits have been credited with £30 000 of post-acquisition profit retained by M and £20 000 post-acquisition profit retained by N. Thus, since acquisition, the net assets of these two companies have increased by £30 000 and £20 000 respectively due to the making and retention of profits.

Let us now suppose that L sells its shareholding in M for £100 000 on 1 January 19X2. In the books of L it is necessary to compute the profit or loss on disposal by matching the book value of the investment, here its cost, against the sale proceeds. Sale proceeds are £100 000 and the cost was £45 000 so that the profit on disposal is £55 000.

In order to concentrate on principles, we shall ignore taxation at this stage,[41] with the result that the profit and loss account of L for the year ended 31 December 19X2 will include a profit on disposal of shares in subsidiary amounting to £55 000.

---

41 The taxation implications are discussed later in the chapter.

As the investment in M was sold on the very first day of 19X2, we shall prepare the consolidated profit and loss account for the year ended 31 December 19X2 by aggregating the profit and loss account items of L and N, the two companies in the group for this year. Assuming that we have profit and loss accounts, and concentrating only on the essential figures, we may produce a draft consolidated profit and loss account as follows:

Profit and loss accounts – year to 31 December 19X2

	L	N	Total
	£	£	£
Operating profit	80 000	60 000	140 000
less Taxation	40 000	20 000	60 000
			80 000
add Profit on disposal of shares in M	55 000		55 000
			135 000
add Retained profits brought forward			
L	125 000		
N (post-acquisition)		20 000 }	145 000
Retained profits carried forward			280 000

Notice that the retained profits figure of £145 000 brought forward in this consolidated profit and loss account does not agree with the retained profits figure carried forward in the previous years' accounts and shown in the consolidated balance sheet on 31 December 19X1 as £175 000. The difference is, of course, the £30 000 post-acquisition retained profits of M Limited, which ceased to be a member of the group on 1 January 19X2. We cannot now say that this £30 000 never existed. What has happened is that we have previously taken credit for profits of £30 000 which are represented in the net assets of company M. Any proceeds received for the shares are in respect of the underlying net assets at the date of disposal. What we must do is to return our profits brought forward to £175 000 by adding £30 000 and correspondingly to reduce the profit on disposal:

Workings for consolidated profit and loss account – year to 31 December 19X2

	Total	Adjustment	Draft consolidated P and L account
	£	£	£
Operating profit	140 000		140 000
less Taxation	60 000		60 000
	80 000		80 000
add Profit on disposal of shares	55 000	–30 000	25 000
	135 000		105 000
add Retained profits brought forward	145 000	+30 000	175 000
Retained profits carried forward	280 000		280 000

Notice that we have not changed the retained profits carried forward. These relate to L and its subsidiary N, the only two companies in the group at the year end. All we have done is to rearrange the items in the consolidated profit and loss account in order to give a true and fair view of what has happened:

	£	£
Sale proceeds		100 000
less Net assets of M at date of disposal	60 000	
Goodwill on acquisition	15 000	75 000
Profit on disposal		25 000

The profit on disposal in the consolidated profit and loss account would be exactly the same if the goodwill had been written off directly to reserves in accordance with the preferred treatment of SSAP 22.[42] However, if goodwill had been amortised in the consolidated profit and loss account, only the unamortised amount applicable to M would be deducted. The amortised goodwill would have already reduced consolidated retained profits and hence the profit to be recognised on disposal would be larger.

The consolidated balance sheet on 31 December 19X2 poses no problems. At that date L has one subsidiary N and hence the consolidated balance sheet will be an aggregation for those two companies only.

Let us now complicate the example by assuming that the disposal occurs not on 1 January 19X2 but during the year to 31 December 19X2, for simplicity on 30 June 19X2. Let us assume that the proceeds on that date are £110 000 producing profit on disposal in the profit and loss account of L amounting to £65 000. Let us also assume that the profits of M arise evenly throughout the year.

M Limited
Summarised profit and loss account for the year to 31 December 19X2

	£
Operating profit	44 000
less Taxation	20 000
	24 000
add Retained profits brought forward	40 000
Retained profits carried forward	64 000

As explained above, we must make adjustments in the consolidated accounts to show the results as far as the group is concerned. First, we must restore the retained profits brought forward to £175 000 and reduce the profit on disposal by £30 000, as we did before. However, we must, in addition, make a second adjustment. The operating profit and taxation figures included in the total column above relate only to L and N. However, the group consisted of L, N and M for the first 6 months of the year. The profits made and retained by M during that first 6 months should therefore be included in the group profits. Such profits are, of course, represented by net assets at the date of disposal and hence we must also reduce our profit on disposal. The appropriate adjustment will be as follows:

42 This topic was addressed by the Urgent Issues Task Force in its Abstract 3 'Treatment of goodwill on disposal of a business', December 1991.

		£
Operating profits, ½ x £44 000	=	22 000
less Taxation, ½ x £20 000	=	10 000
		12 000

Our consolidated profit and loss account will therefore be arrived at as follows:

Draft consolidated profit and loss account of L Limited and its subsidiaries M Limited and N Limited for the year ended 31 December 19X2

	Total (L and N) as above	Adjustments	Draft consolidated P and L account
	£	£	£
Operating profit	140 000	+22 000	162 000
less Taxation	60 000	+10 000	70 000
	80 000	+12 000	92 000
add Profit on disposal of shares in subsidiary	65 000	−12 000 }	
		−30 000 }	23 000
	145 000		115 000
add Retained profits brought forward	145 000	+30 000	175 000
Retained profits carried forward	290 000		290 000

Notice again that the retained profit carried forward relates only to L and N, the companies in the group on 31 December 19X2. The profit on disposal amounts to £23 000 and may be explained as follows:

		£	£
Sales proceeds			110 000
less Net assets at date of disposal:			
On 31 December 19X1		60 000	
Increase in 6 months to 30 June 19X2		12 000	
		72 000	
Goodwill on acquisition		15 000	87 000
Profit on disposal			23 000

We have now examined the basic approach to the accounting treatment of disposals. Before we explore partial disposals, let us consider first the treatment of taxation and, second, the disclosure of the disposal in the consolidated profit and loss account.

Taxation

Under the UK taxation system, a chargeable gain or loss will occur when an investing company sells shares. Assuming that there is a gain, the profit in the accounts of the selling company will be reduced by taxation.

When we turn to the consolidated profit and loss account the treatment is again a little more complicated.

Let us take the last example in the previous section and assume that company L faces a liability to taxation at 25 per cent on the chargeable gain. Thus, on the gain of £65 000 in the accounts of L, the taxation would be £16 250 so that our profit on disposal in the profit and loss account of L would be as follows:

	£
Profit on disposal of shares in subsidiary	65 000
less Taxation	16 250
	48 750

When we turn to the consolidated profit and loss account an analysis of the component parts of the profit on disposal would be as follows:

	£
Sales proceeds	110 000
less Cost of investment	45 000
	65 000
Recognised in consolidated accounts:	
Post-acquisition profits retained:	
to 31 December 19X1	30 000
6 months to 30 June 19X2	12 000
	42 000
Profit on disposal	23 000
	65 000

What is happening is that although the post-acquisition profits have already borne Corporation Tax, they are being taxed again as a result of the disposal. It may therefore be argued that we should recognise this by apportioning the taxation charge to the three components:

	£		£
Post-acquisition profit			
to 31 December 19X1	30 000	x 25%	7 500
6 months to 30 June 19X2	12 000	x 25%	3 000
Profit on disposal	23 000	x 25%	5 750
	65 000		16 250

The second and third elements of this tax charge relate to the current year and should be included as part of the taxation expense in the consolidated profit and loss account. The first element relates to the retained profits brought forward and some accountants would argue that it should be treated as an adjustment to reserves. However such a treatment appears to be inconsistent with FRS 3 and, in the view of the authors, all three elements of the tax charge should be included in the consolidated profit and loss account. All three elements have arisen because of the disposal during the current year and should be reflected in the consolidated profit and loss account even though this may result in a relatively high tax expense in relation to the profits included. This could, if desired, be isolated as taxation related to discontinued operations although as we shall see below, this is not actually required by FRS 3.

Disclosure

In order to provide the results of the group, it is necessary to include as part of the consolidated profits those relating to the subsidiary M from the beginning of the year to the date of disposal. It is also necessary to include the profit on disposal of the subsidiary.

FRS 3 requires certain disclosures in the consolidated profit and loss account, namely that:

> The aggregate results of each of continuing operations, acquisitions (as a component of continuing operations) and discontinued operations should be disclosed separately.[43]

The relevant analysis of turnover and operating profit must be included on the face of the consolidated profit and loss account but an analysis of other statutory format headings between turnover and operating profit must be included either on the face of the consolidated profit and loss account or in the notes to the accounts.

If we assume that the sale of M falls within the FRS 3 definition of discontinued operations, an appropriate presentation for the relevant part of the consolidated profit and loss account for the L group would be as follows:

Consolidated profit and loss account – year to 31 December 19X2

	Continuing operations £	Discontinued operations £	Total £
Turnover			
Expenses – in accordance with statutory format		Analysed appropriately	
Operating profit	140 000	22 000	162 000
Profit on disposal of discontinued operations	–	23 000	23 000
Profit on ordinary activities	140 000	45 000	185 000
Taxation	60 000		
(10 000 + 16 250)		26 250 }	86 250
Profit on ordinary activities after tax	80 000	18 750	98 750

FRS 3 does not require an analysis of the taxation charge between continuing operations and discontinued operations. We have included it for completeness.

Partial disposals

Where one company sells part of a holding in a subsidiary undertaking, the principles applied are the same as those illustrated above. However the precise treatment depends upon the nature of the remaining investment. The investee may remain a subsidiary or the holding may be sufficient to make it an associated undertaking or a simple investment.

In all cases, it is essential to maintain a clear distinction between the entries in the accounting records of the selling company and those in the consolidation working papers.

43 FRS 3 'Reporting financial performance', ASB, October 1992, Para. 14.

In the records of the investing company it is necessary to match the appropriate proportion of the carrying value of the investment against the proceeds of disposal to produce a profit or loss on disposal. This may be subject to taxation but, now that we have explained the treatment of tax, we shall ignore it for the remainder of this chapter.

When we turn to the consolidated accounts, the position is somewhat different. We shall explore in detail the treatment where a subsidiary undertaking is retained and then look more briefly at the situation where an associated undertaking or simple investment is retained.

(1) *Retention of subsidiary* At the beginning of the year the consolidated retained profit will include the post-acquisition profits of all subsidiaries based on the respective holdings of those subsidiaries at that particular date. In order to give a true and fair view of the operations of the year, the consolidated profit and loss account must include the appropriate portion of profits or losses of all companies which were members of the group during the year. The consolidated balance sheet at the end of the year will be an aggregation of the balance sheets of all companies in the group as at that date.

This is best illustrated with an example. P Limited acquired an 80 per cent interest in Q Limited many years ago when the reserves of Q were £20 000. The summarised balance sheets of the two companies, together with a summarised consolidated balance sheet on 31 December 19X1, were as follows:

Summarised balance sheets on 31 December 19X1

	P £	Q £	Consolidated £
Goodwill on consolidation			32 000
Investment in Q Limited 32 000 shares at cost	80 000		
Other net assets	220 000	100 000	320 000
	300 000	100 000	352 000
Share capital, £1 shares	100 000	40 000	100 000
Retained profits	200 000		232 000
At date of acquisition		20 000	
Post acquisition		40 000	
Minority interest			20 000
	300 000	100 000	352 000

P sells 4000 shares in Q on 30 June 19X2 for £16 000. This produces a profit in the records of P amounting to £6000, as shown below, and leaves P with a 70 per cent shareholding in Q.

Sale of shares in subsidiaries

19X2		£	19X2		£
June 30	Investment account, cost of shares sold		June 30	Sale proceeds	16 000
	$\frac{1}{8}$ × £80 000	10 000			
	Profit on disposal	6 000			
		16 000			16 000

When we turn to the consolidated accounts our profit and loss account must include the result of Q as an 80 per cent owned subsidiary for the first 6 months of the year and as a 70 per cent owned subsidiary for the second 6 months. Our consolidated balance sheet on 31 December 19X2 will, of course, be based upon the 70 per cent holding at that date.

A simple approach is to prepare initially a consolidated profit and loss account on the basis of the holdings at the end of the year. Assuming that there are no unrealised profits on intercompany trading and that we have the individual profit and loss accounts as shown in the first two columns, we may proceed as follows.

Workings for consolidated profit and loss account for the year ended 31 December 19X2

	P	Q	Consolidated
	£	£	£
Operating profit	50 000	20 000	70 000
less Taxation	20 000	8 000	28 000
	30 000	12 000	42 000
less Minority interest, 30% x £12 000			3 600
			38 400
add Profit on disposal of shares in Q Limited	6 000		6 000
			44 400
add Retained profit brought forward	200 000		
Post-acquisition group share (70% x £40 000)		28 000 }	228 000
Retained profit carried forward			272 400

As in the previous section we may now make adjustments to show what has happened as far as the group is concerned. First, we must restore the retained profits brought forward to the figure shown in the consolidated balance sheet on 31 December 19X1 by adding £4000 and reduce the profit on disposal accordingly. Second, we must recognise that the minority interest was 20 per cent rather than 30 per cent for the first half of the year. Thus we must reduce the minority interest figure and also reduce the profit on disposal figure by 10 per cent of the profits of the first 6 months, which have of course increased the net assets underlying the shares sold. Assuming that the profits of Q arose evenly, we must therefore reduce the minority interest by £600 ($10\% \times \frac{1}{2} \times £12\,000$):

Workings for consolidated profit and loss account for the year ended 31 December 19X2

	Total based on 70% holding as above	Adjustment	Draft consolidated P and L account
	£	£	£
Operating profit	70 000		70 000
less Taxation	28 000		28 000
	42 000		42 000
less Minority interest	3 600	−600	3 000
	38 400		39 000
add Profit on disposal of shares in Q Limited	6 000	−600 ⎱ −4 000 ⎰	1 400
	44 400		40 400
add Retained profits brought forward	228 000	+4 000	232 000
Retained profits carried forward	272 400		272 400

Having made these adjustments, the operating profits of £39 000 after minority interest may be analysed as follows:

	£	£
Operating profit after taxation		
P(£50 000–£20 000)		30 000
Q		
6 months to 30 June 19X2, 80% x ($\frac{1}{2}$ x £12 000)	4 800	
6 months to 31 December 19X2, 70% x ($\frac{1}{2}$ x £12 000)	4 200	9 000
Per consolidated profit and loss account		39 000

With some rearrangement and additional information on turnover and expenses, readers should be in a position to prepare a consolidated profit and loss account for the group.

As before, the closing consolidated balance sheet poses no problems. At 31 December 19X2 P has one subsidiary, Q, in which it has a 70 per cent interest.

(2) *Retention of an associated undertaking* Where a parent company sells shares in a subsidiary undertaking but retains a holding sufficient to give significant influence over the investee, it retains an associated undertaking. In the individual accounts of the parent we match the relevant proportion of the cost of the investment against the proceeds of disposal to produce a profit or loss on disposal which may attract a taxation liability.

In the consolidated profit and loss account, we must recognise that the group has a subsidiary for part of the year but an associated undertaking for the remainder of the year. Thus for the first part of the year we must include all of the relevant profits of the subsidiary, subject to deducting any minority interests, together with the profit or loss on disposal. For the second part of the year we must include the appropriate proportion of the profits of the associated undertaking using the equity method of accounting.[44]

In the consolidated balance sheet at the year end, the investment in the associated

44 The equity method of accounting is discussed later in this chapter.

undertaking will appear at its cost, less any goodwill written off, plus the appropriate share of post-acquisition retained profits of that associated undertaking.

(3) *Retention of simple investment only* The treatment in the parent company's accounts is exactly the same as for other disposals. However the consolidated profit and loss account must include the whole of the profits of the subsidiary up to the date of disposal, subject to any minority interest, together with the relevant profit or loss on disposal. Subsequently there is only a simple investment so credit should be taken only for dividends received and receivable and the investment should be shown at the same value at which it appears in the parent company's own balance sheet.

While this sounds straightforward, it does give rise to the need to remove from the consolidated profit and loss account reserve the share of post acquisition retained profit included in relation to the simple investment retained.

To give an example, let us suppose that a parent company disposes of 90 per cent of the equity shares in a wholly owned subsidiary, thus retaining a 10 per cent holding.

The consolidated profit and loss account reserve will have included 100 per cent of the retained profits of the subsidiary from the date of acquisition to the date of disposal and these will be reflected in the net assets of the subsidiary at the date of disposal. Whereas the post-acquisition retained profits relating to the 90 per cent holding sold will be taken into account in calculating the profit on disposal, those relating to the remaining 10% holding must be removed if the investment is to be shown at its cost. Thus it would be necessary to have an adjustment to the consolidated profit and loss account reserve to remove the share of post-acquisition retained profits in respect of the remaining holding in a company which was previously a subsidiary.

In the consolidated balance sheet the investment would appear at its historical cost unless its value had fallen permanently below cost or the directors had decided to show the investment at a current value. As is the case with all disposals, preparation of the consolidated balance sheet poses no problems.

Having explored some of the major issues of accounting for groups we now turn our attention to accounting for associated undertakings and joint ventures.

ACCOUNTING FOR ASSOCIATED UNDERTAKINGS AND JOINT VENTURES

What is an associated undertaking?

Before SSAP 1, a long-term investment in another company was usually treated in one of two ways. Either it was a simple investment and was treated as a fixed asset as discussed above, or it was an investment in a subsidiary, in which case it was normal to prepare a separate set of consolidated accounts replacing the investment by the underlying assets and liabilities. The original SSAP 1, which was issued in January 1971, recognised an intermediate type of investment, an associated company, which it defined as follows.[45]

> A company (not being a subsidiary of the investing group or company) is an associated company of the investing group or company if:
> (a) the investing group or company's interest in the associated company is effectively that of a partner in a joint venture or consortium or

45 SSAP 1 'Accounting for the results of associated companies', ASC, London, January 1971, Para. 6.

(b) the investing group or company's interest in the associated company is for the long term and is substantial (i.e. not less than 20 per cent of the equity voting rights), and, having regard to the disposition of the other shareholdings, the investing group or company is in a position to exercise a significant influence over the associated company.

In both cases it is essential that the investing group or company participates (usually through representation on the board) in commercial and financial policy decisions of the associated company, including the distribution of profits.

Where an investing company is able to exert a significant influence over the investee company's distribution policy, it is able to influence the level of its own reported profit. It may, for example, compensate for its own poor results by ensuring that it receives a substantial dividend from the investee. The approach of taking credit only for dividends received and receivable would allow the investing company to smooth its profit. So far as the balance sheet is concerned, carrying the investment at its historical cost would mean that the assets under the influence of the investing company might be substantially understated. Thus, it was argued that where significant influence exists, the traditional method of accounting is inadequate.

Whether or not significant influence exists must depend upon the particular distribution of shareholdings. It could exist with a holding of 16 per cent of the equity shares of a company, if ownership of the remaining shares was highly dispersed, and may not exist with a holding of 40 per cent, if, for example, the remaining 60 per cent of the equity shares are held by one other person or entity.

As can be seen in para. (b) of the above definition, the original SSAP 1 specifically mentioned a holding of 20 per cent of the equity voting rights, and this led to a situation in which some accountants tended to apply a mechanical test, treating any investment of 20 per cent or more as an associated company and any investment of less than 20 per cent as a simple investment. Thus, some accountants preferred to use this objective cut-off point rather than to make a subjective judgment taking into account all of the relevant factors.

As part of its normal programme of reviewing standards the ASC reconsidered the principles of SSAP 1 and issued a revised SSAP 1, 'Accounting for associated companies' in April 1982. This provided a more satisfactory definition of an associated company:[46]

An associated company is a company not being a subsidiary of the investing group or company in which:

(a) the interest of the investing group or company is effectively that of a partner in a joint venture or consortium and the investing group or company is in a position to exercise a significant influence over the company in which the investment is made, or
(b) the interest of the investing group or company is for the long term and is substantial and, having regard to the disposition of the other shareholdings, the investing group or company is in a position to exercise a significant influence over the company in which the investment is made.

Significant influence over a company essentially involves participation in the financial and operating policy decisions of that company (including dividend policy) but not necessarily control of those policies. Representation on the board of directors is indicative of such

46 Revised SSAP 1, 'Accounting for associated companies', ASC, London, April 1982, Part 2, Para. 13. Paragraph (a) of this definition has subsequently been deleted by the ASB 'Interim Statement: Consolidated Accounts', Para. 38.

participation, but will neither necessarily give conclusive evidence of it nor be the only method by which the investing company may participate in policy decisions.

Although no figures appear in the above definition, a holding of 20 per cent of the equity voting rights still appears in the definitions section of the standard (Paras 14 and 15). Where the investing company or group holds 20 per cent or more of the equity voting rights, there is a presumption that the investee company is an associated company, but this presumption may be rebutted if the investing company or group can clearly demonstrate that it is not in a position to exercise significant influence. Conversely, where the investing company or group holds less than 20 per cent of the equity voting rights, there is a presumption that no significant influence, and hence no associated company, exists. To treat the investee company as an associated company in such circumstances requires the investing company both to demonstrate clearly that it is in a position to exercise significant influence and to obtain the concurrence of the associated company.[47] The revised statement thus provides an objective cut-off point at a holding of 20 per cent of the equity voting rights, but quite sensibly recognises that a classification based on one such figure will not always be appropriate.

Subsequent to the issue of the revised SSAP 1, the Companies Act 1989 has provided definitions of the newly introduced terms 'associated undertakings' and 'joint ventures'.[48]

> Where an undertaking ... manages another undertaking jointly ... that other undertaking ('the joint venture') may, if it is not –
>
> (a) a body corporate, or
> (b) a subsidiary undertaking of the parent company,
>
> be dealt with in the group accounts by the method of proportional consolidation (Para. 19(1)).
>
> An 'associated undertaking' means an undertaking in which an undertaking included in the consolidation has a participating interest and over whose operating and financial position it exercises a significant influence and which is not:
>
> (a) a subsidiary undertaking of the parent company, or
> (b) a joint venture dealt with in accordance with paragraph 19.
>
> Where an undertaking holds 20 per cent or more of the voting rights in another undertaking, it shall be presumed to exercise such an influence over it unless the contrary is shown (Paras 20(1) and 20(2))[49].

This is really rather bizarre drafting and, as we shall see, it has posed considerable problems in preparing a sensible standard. While the definition of associated undertakings always includes an incorporated joint venture, it includes an unincorporated joint venture only if the equity method of accounting is applied, not if proportional consolidation is used.

To define a joint venture by reference to the method used to account for it makes it extremely difficult to specify an appropriate accounting method for joint ventures!

---

47 Revised SSAP 1, Part 2, Paras 14 and 15.
48 Companies Act 1985, Schedule 4A, Paras 19 and 20.
49 An undertaking is defined as (a) a body corporate or partnership, or (b) an unincorporated association carrying on a trade or business, with or without a view to profit (Companies Act 1985, Sec. 259(1)). A participating interest means a long-term shareholding in another undertaking held for the purpose of securing a contribution to the activities by the exercise of control or influence (Companies Act 1985, Sec. 260(1)).

We shall return to this problem in due course but first we shall explore the similarities and differences between proportional consolidation and the equity method of accounting.

Possible methods of accounting

Where one company exercises significant influence over another company, it seems unreasonable to account for an investment in that company as a simple investment. To take credit in the profit and loss account merely for dividends received and receivable is not sufficient where the directors of the investing company are able to influence the level of those dividends. To show the investment in the balance sheet at its historical cost gives no guide to what is happening to the underlying net assets, the use of which is influenced by the investing company's directors. In order to evaluate the stewardship of their directors, shareholders in the investing company require further information.

If treatment as a simple investment is inadequate, there would appear to be two closely related possibilities. The first is *proportional consolidation*, and the second is the *equity method* of accounting. We shall look at each of these possibilities in turn before returning to the regulatory framework in more detail. In so doing we shall assume that the associated undertaking is a limited company rather than an unincorporated body.

Using the method of proportional consolidation we would remove the investment in the associated company from the investing company's balance sheet and replace it by the proportionate share of the assets and liabilities of the associated company on a line-by-line basis together with any goodwill on acquisition. In the profit and loss account of the investing company we would remove any dividends received or receivable already credited and take credit, instead, for the appropriate proportion of the revenues and expenses of the associated company on a line-by-line basis. The consolidated profits would then include the appropriate proportion of the post-acquisition profits retained by the associated company.

Using the equity method of accounting we would value the investment in the balance sheet at cost plus the share of post-acquisition profits retained by the associated company.[50] Thus, the carrying value of the investment in the balance sheet would be increased by the appropriate proportion of the increase in net assets of the associated company due to retained profits. The profit and loss account would be credited, not with dividends received and receivable, but with the appropriate proportion of the profits of the associated company. Conversely, it would be debited with the appropriate proportion of any losses.

The net effect on the profit and loss account under both proportional consolidation and the equity method is the same but the way in which information is disclosed is different. Under proportional consolidation, the share of revenue and expenses of the associated company are added to those of the investing entity on a line-by-line basis. Under the equity method of accounting it is usual to leave most of the revenues and expenses of the investing entity unchanged and to bring in the share of the profit from ordinary activities before tax, the tax on ordinary profits and the share of extraordinary profits and losses of the associated company as three separate entries.

Let us explore a balance sheet using each method of accounting.

---

50 Although the carrying value of the investment would be determined in this way, the revised SSAP 1 requires us to provide an analysis of the figure on a different basis which is explained below.

The summarised balance sheets of A Limited and B Limited on 31 December 19XI are as follows:

Summarised balance sheets on 31 December 19X1

	A Limited £	B Limited £
Fixed assets		
Tangible assets	90 000	40 000
Investment in B Limited		
5000 shares at cost	22 000	–
Net current assets	10 000	24 000
	122 000	64 000
Share capital, £1 shares	50 000	20 000
Retained profits	72 000	44 000
	122 000	64 000

A purchased its 25 per cent holding in B Limited some years ago when the retained profits of B were £28 000. Providing there have been no changes in share capital, this tells us that B's summarised balance sheet at the date of acquisition was:

	£
Net assets	48 000
Share capital	20 000
Retained profits	28 000
	48 000

A purchased a 25 per cent interest in these net assets for £22 000 and hence paid a premium on acquisition (goodwill) of £10 000, i.e. £22 000 less 25 per cent of £48 000.[51] Between the date of acquisition and 31 December 19X1 B has increased its retained profits by £16 000 (i.e. £44 000 less £28 000). A's share of this retained post-acquisition profit is 25 per cent or £4000. We may therefore replace the asset 'Investment in B Limited' shown in the balance sheet of A at £22 000, by the following items:

	£
Fixed assets	
Tangible assets, 25% of 40 000	10 000
Premium on acquisition (goodwill)	10 000
Net current assets 25% x 24 000	6 000
	26 000
less Retained profits (share of post-acquisition	
retained profits)	4 000
	22 000

---

51 In computing this premium, it is necessary to consider the fair values of the net assets at the date of acquisition rather than the values of those net assets in the accounts of B Limited but, for ease of exposition, we have assumed that fair values are equal to the book values.

Using proportional consolidation we would produce the following balance sheet grouping like items for the investing company and associated company together.

A Limited – Summarised balance sheet on 31 December 19X1 (using proportional consolidation)

	£	£
Fixed assets		
Intangible		
Premium on acquisition of investment in B Limited		
(Goodwill)		10 000
Tangible		
A Limited	90 000	
B Limited	10 000	
		100 000
		110 000
Net current assets		
A Limited	10 000	
B Limited	6 000	16 000
		126 000
Share capital (£1 shares)		50 000
Retained profits		
A Limited	72 000	
B Limited	4 000	
		76 000
		126 000

Using the equity method of accounting the investment is simply shown at cost plus the share of post-acquisition profits retained by the associated company, that is at £26 000 (£22 000 plus £4000):

A Limited – Summarised balance sheet on 31 December 19X1 (using equity method of accounting)

	£	£
Fixed assets		
Tangible assets		90 000
Investment in associated company (*see* below)		26 000
Net current assets		10 000
		126 000
Share capital, £1 shares		50 000
Retained profit		
A Limited	72 000	
B Limited	4 000	76 000
		126 000

The carrying value of the investment may be calculated as follows:

Cost of investment	22 000
add Share of post-acquisition profits retained by B Limited	4 000
	26 000

As discussed below, the revised SSAP 1 requires a more informative analysis of the carrying value:

	£
Share of net assets, 25% of £64 000	16 000
Premium on acquisition (Goodwill)	10 000
	26 000

Comparison of the way in which the investment is shown using the equity method of accounting with the balance sheet using proportional consolidation makes it clear why the equity method is often referred to as a 'one line consolidation'. The investment is shown at a value equal to the appropriate proportion of the net assets of the associated company at the balance sheet date plus any premium or less any discount on acquisition.

As we have seen in Chapter 8, SSAP 22 'Accounting for goodwill', requires that such a premium on acquisition should normally be written off immediately against reserves, although it also permits its amortisation through the profit and loss account on a systematic basis over its useful economic life.[52] For ease of exposition we have not done this but the reserves would, of course, be reduced by any amount written off and only the net tangible assets and any unamortised goodwill would be represented in the balance sheet using proportional consolidation and the equity method respectively. It may be observed that proportional consolidation provides greater information about the underlying assets and liabilities[53] and it is possible to argue that it is therefore more useful, particularly in the case of a joint venture.

The equity method of accounting and SSAP 1

As we have seen, the law requires the use of the equity method of accounting for associated undertakings, although it permits the use of proportional consolidation for non-incorporated joint ventures. The relevant standard practice is contained in SSAP 1 (Revised) as amended by the ASB 'Interim Statement: Consolidated Accounts', although this does not provide guidance on the accounting treatment of joint ventures.

Where the investing company prepares consolidated accounts, the equity method described in the previous section is applied. Where the investing company does not prepare consolidated accounts, it must prepare its own accounts following the traditional accounting principles for long-term investments. It must then either prepare a second set of accounts in which the full equity method of accounting is applied or provide supplementary information in the notes to its own accounts showing the relevant figures which would appear if the equity method had been used.

To illustrate the approach of SSAP 1 let us first take the situation where the investing company, C Limited, does have subsidiaries and does prepare consolidated accounts. The consolidated accounts for the group, together with the accounts of the associated company D Limited, in which C Limited holds 30 per cent of the equity shares, are given below for the year ended 31 December 19X1:

---

52 SSAP 22, 'Accounting for goodwill', ASC, London, 1984, Paras 32 and 34.

53 Revised SSAP 1, Para. 30, actually provides that more detailed information about the associated company's tangible and intangible assets should be given if the interests in the associated company is material and more detailed information would assist in giving a true and fair view.

Summarised profit and loss accounts for the year ended 31 December 19X1

	C Limited Consolidated P & L Account £	D Limited Associated Company £
Turnover	1 040 000	720 000
less Expenses	854 000	540 000
	186 000	180 000
add Dividend from D Limited	30 000	–
	216 000	180 000
less Taxation	106 000	60 000
(Consolidated tax charge includes £6000 in respect of dividend from D)		
	110 000	120 000
less Minority interest	10 000	–
	100 000	120 000
add Extraordinary profit (net of taxation and minority interest)	20 000	90 000
	120 000	210 000
less Dividends proposed	40 000	80 000
Retained profits for year	80 000	130 000
Movement on reserves for year		
Retained profits brought forward	400 000	240 000
Retained profits for year	80 000	130 000
Retained profits carried forward	480 000	370 000

The profit and loss account of C Limited and hence the consolidated profit and loss account includes a dividend of £24 000 receivable from D Limited. As was explained in Chapter 7 this is shown as gross income of £30 000, that is £24 000 × 100/80, and income tax of £6000. In the consolidated balance sheet, the long-term investment in D Limited is at present shown at its historical cost of £80 000.

Summarised balance sheets on 31 December 19X1

	C Limited Consolidated Accounts £	D Limited Associated Company £
Fixed assets		
Goodwill on consolidation	70 000	–
Tangible assets	510 000	420 000
Investment in associated company:		
45 000 shares (30%) at cost	80 000	–
Net current assets	280 000	360 000
	940 000	780 000
less Long-term loans	100 000	150 000
	840 000	630 000
less Deferred taxation	80 000	60 000
	760 000	570 000
Share capital £1 shares	200 000	150 000
Share premium	40 000	30 000
Retained profits	480 000	390 000
	720 000	570 000
Minority interests	40 000	–
	760 000	570 000

C Limited acquired its 30 per cent interest in D Limited some years ago when the retained profits of D were £60 000. It therefore paid a premium on acquisition of £8000.[54]

Let us concentrate first on the consolidated profit and loss account which, at present, includes £24 000 in respect of the dividend receivable from D Limited. This must be removed and replaced by the share of the profits or losses of the associated company whether or not distributed:

	D Limited £	30% share £
Operating profit	180 000	54 000
less Taxation	60 000	18 000
	120 000	36 000
add Extraordinary profit (net of tax)	90 000	27 000
	210 000	63 000

54 This premium is calculated as follows:

	£	£
Cost of investment		80 000
less Share of:		
Share capital	150 000	
Share premium	30 000	
Retained profits	60 000	
30% of	240 000	72 000
Premium on acquisition		8 000

We are implicitly assuming that the fair values of the assets and liabilities at the date of acquisition were equal to their book values and that there have been no changes to the share capital or share premium since that date.

Inclusion of these figures in the consolidated profit and loss account produces the following result:

Summarised consolidated profit and loss account for the year ended 31 December 19X1 (including results of associated company)

	£	£
Turnover (group only)		1 040 000
less Expenses (group only)		854 000
		186 000
add Share of profits of associated company		54 000
Profit from ordinary activities before tax		240 000
less Taxation		
Group (£106 000 – £6 000)	100 000	
Share of associated company	18 000	118 000
		122 000
less Minority interests		10 000
		112 000
add Extraordinary profit		
Group	20 000	
Share of associated company	27 000	47 000
		159 000
less Dividends proposed		40 000
Retained profit for year		119 000
Retained by group	80 000	
Retained by associated company	39 000	
	119 000	

We have brought in the share of profits amounting to £63 000[55] to replace the dividend receivable of £24 000. Thus we have brought in an extra £39 000 which is, of course, the share of profits retained by the associated company in respect of the year as noted at the foot of the consolidated profit and loss account.

When we turn to the movement on reserves we must include the share of all post-acquisition profits retained by the associated company. This statement includes the workings:

55 Share of ordinary profits   £54 000
    less Share of taxation   18 000
                              36 000
    add Share of extraordinary profit   27 000
                              £63 000

Movement on reserves for the year ended 31 December 19X1
(with workings)

	£	£
Retained profits on 1 January 19X1		
Group		400 000
Share of associated company post-acquisition profits		
30% x (£240 000 – £60 000)		54 000
		454 000
Retained profit for year, per consolidated profit and		
loss account		119 000
Retained profits on 31 December 19X1		
Group, per consolidated balance sheet	480 000	
Share of associated company		
30% x (£370 000 – £60 000)	93 000	
	573 000	573 000

At the end of the year we have therefore increased consolidated reserves by £93 000, the share of post-acquisition profits retained by the associated company, and we must therefore increase the carrying value of our investment by this figure in the consolidated balance sheet to keep it in balance. The carrying value of the investment is therefore £173 000, the cost of £80 000 plus £93 000.

C Limited
Summarised consolidated balance sheet on 31 December 19X1

	£
Fixed assets	
Goodwill on consolidation	70 000
Tangible assets	510 000
Investment in associated company	173 000
	753 000
Net current assets	280 000
	1 033 000
less Long-term loans	100 000
	933 000
less Deferred taxation	80 000
	853 000
Share capital, £1 shares	200 000
Share premium	40 000
Reserves	573 000
	813 000
Minority interests	40 000
	853 000

SSAP 1 requires that the investment in the associated company be analysed into three components:[56] (a) the investing group's share of the net assets other than goodwill of the associated company, (b) the investing group's share of the goodwill of the associated company and (c) the premium paid on the acquisition of the interest in the associated company after attributing fair values to the net assets acquired. In view of their intangible nature, (b) and (c) may be combined in one figure for disclosure purposes.

In our example there is no goodwill in the balance sheet of D Limited and, in the absence of details of the fair values of assets at the date of acquisition, an analysis would appear as follows:

	£
Investment in associated company	
Share of net assets other than goodwill	171 000
Premium on acquisition (goodwill)	8 000
	179 000

For ease of exposition we have, of course, ignored the requirement to write off goodwill. In order for the aggregation of net asset values of the associated companies with those of the investing group to be meaningful it is, of course, necessary for the accounting periods and policies of the associated company to coincide with those of the group. In practice this may pose problems requiring adjustment to the results of the associated company prior to aggregation. In addition further adjustments may be necessary to remove any unrealised profits due to intercompany trading.

When we turn to a company which does not prepare consolidated accounts, it is not possible to apply the equity method of accounting in the investing company's own accounts. In those accounts the profit and loss account will include dividends received and receivable, while, in the balance sheet, the investment will usually be shown at its historical cost.

In order to comply with the provisions of SSAP 1, the company must either prepare a second set of accounts in which the equity method of accounting is applied or provide similar information in notes to the accounts. In the former case, the treatment will be as illustrated above. In the latter case one or more supplementary notes will be necessary. Thus, there must be a note to the balance sheet showing the carrying value of the investment if the equity method were applied, together with an appropriate analysis of that figure, and a note to the profit and loss account showing the effect of applying the equity method of accounting.

We shall conclude this section by illustrating a possible note to the profit and loss account.

E Limited holds 25 per cent of the equity share capital of an associated company, F Limited, and has credited dividends received and receivable from F Limited in its own profit and loss account.[57] The summarised profit and loss accounts of the two companies are as follows:

56 SSAP 1, Para. 26. Although not relevant to this particular example, readers should be aware of the other disclosure requirements of SSAP 1. Thus, for example, Paras 27 and 28 require disclosure of loans between associated companies and the group while Para. 29 requires disclosure, where material, of balances representing normal trading transactions.

57 The dividends received and receivable from F Limited total 10 000 but, as was explained in Chapter 7, have been shown as gross income of £12 500, that is £10 000 × 100/80, and tax of £2500.

Summarised profit and loss accounts for the year ended 31 December 19X1

	E Limited	F Limited
	£	£
Operating profit	240 000	120 000
Dividends received and receivable from F Limited	12 500	–
	252 500	120 000
Taxation	80 000	40 000
Tax credit on dividends	2 500	–
	82 500	40 000
Profit on ordinary activities after taxation	170 000	80 000
Extraordinary items (net of tax)	45 000	20 000
	215 000	100 000
Dividends paid and payable	100 000	40 000
Retained profit for year	115 000	60 000

A possible note to the profit and loss account, in summarised form, would be as follows:

Note to the profit and loss account of E Limited
The effect of applying the equity method of accounting as required by SSAP 1, 'Accounting for associated companies', is as follows:

	£	£
Share of profits of associated company (25% of £120 000)		30 000
Share of taxation of associated company (25% of £40 000)		10 000
		20 000
add Profit of E Limited		
Per profit and loss account	170 000	
less Dividends from associated company	10 000	160 000
Profit from ordinary activities after taxation		180 000
add Extraordinary items (net of tax)		
E Limited	45 000	
Share of associated company (25% of £20 000)	5 000	50 000
		230 000
less Dividends paid and payable		100 000
Retained profit		130 000
Retained in investing company	115 000	
Retained in associated company (20 000 + 5 000 – 10 000)	15 000	
	130 000	

The Companies Act 1989 and subsequent pronouncements

Although it has not changed the basic approach to accounting for associated companies developed in SSAP 1 and discussed above, the Companies Act 1989 has introduced the term 'associated undertaking' and has distinguished between incorporated and unincorporated joint ventures.

The term associated undertaking is wider than 'associated company' in that it includes unincorporated undertakings; it is defined as follows:[58]

58 Companies Act 1985 (as amended by Companies Act 1989), Schedule 4A, Para. 20.

An associated undertaking means an undertaking in which an undertaking included in the consolidation has a participating interest and over whose operating and financial policy it exercises a significant influence, and which is not –

(a) a subsidiary undertaking of the parent company
(b) a joint venture dealt with in accordance with paragraph 19.

The law requires the use of the equity method of accounting for such associated undertakings but introduces a complication in (b). The paragraph referred to, paragraph 19 of Schedule 4A, permits but does not require the use of proportional consolidation for an *unincorporated* joint venture. Where proportional consolidation is used, that joint venture ceases to fall within the definition of an associated undertaking. Where proportional consolidation is not used, the unincorporated joint venture falls within the definition of an associated undertaking and, as for any incorporated joint venture or associated company, the equity method of accounting must be used.

The thinking behind the law appears to be that proportional consolidation should only be used for unincorporated joint ventures where there is a direct interest in the assets and liabilities of that venture. However, in the view of the authors, such an attempt to specify different accounting treatments for unincorporated and incorporated joint ventures ignores the fact that the purpose of any consolidation process is to present accounts which ignore the structure of the legal relationship between investor and investee and show the interest in the underlying profits, assets and liabilities. While it is possible to understand, although not necessarily to agree with, the reasons why the law would wish to limit proportional consolidation to unincorporated joint ventures, the drafting of the law can be criticised and has posed considerable difficulties for both the ASC and ASB in attempting to develop logical proposals on accounting for investments which give significant influence over the investee.

The way in which the ASC tackled the problem in ED 50 'Consolidated accounts' (June 1990) was to deal separately with joint ventures and, what it called 'associates'. The term associate was narrower than the term associated undertaking. ED 50 then *required* rather than permitted the use of proportional consolidation for unincorporated joint ventures except where such a joint venture retains profits and deals with its assets as if it were incorporated. In the latter case and for any incorporated joint ventures and associates, it proposed that the equity method should be used. The flow chart in Figure 9.2 summarises the position.

The Exposure Draft also proposed that the accounts of associates and joint ventures included in consolidated accounts should use the same accounting policies and be coterminous with those of the investing group or made up to a date not more than six months before, or shortly after, the date of the financial statements of the group.[59]

It also stressed the need to eliminate unrealised profits from intercompany trading and clarified the way in which this should be done:[60]

Where profits or losses have arisen on transactions between the group and its associate or joint venture which would require adjustment as unrealized if that associate or joint venture were a subsidiary, an adjustment should be made for the group's share of that profit or loss. Where the associate or joint venture involved in the transaction has been equity accounted, this adjustment should be taken in the consolidated profit and loss account against either the group

59 ED 50, Paras 116–118.
60 ED 50, Para. 115.

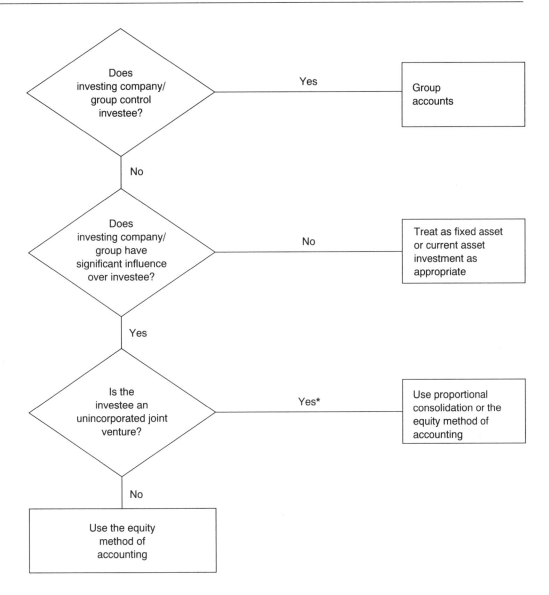

* The Companies Act 1985 permits a choice between proportional consolidation and the equity method of accounting. ED50 would have required the use of proportional consolidation.

Fig. 9.2 Treatment of investment

or the associate according to which recorded the profit on the transaction and against the asset which was the subject of the transaction if it is held by the group or else against the amount recorded for the associate. Where the joint venture has been proportionally consolidated, the adjustment should be made against the relevant item in the consolidated accounts.

While this Exposure Draft provided us with some guidance, it is clear that the ASB is unhappy with the ED 50 proposals regarding the accounting treatment of joint ventures:

... The Board reserves its opinion on how joint ventures should be treated until it has the time to consider this as part of its full review of consolidated accounts.[61]

While FRS 2 'Accounting for subsidiary undertakings' has been published in July 1992, we are still awaiting an ASB standard on associated undertakings and joint ventures.

RECOMMENDED READING

G. C. Baxter and J. C. Spinney, 'A closer look at consolidated financial statement theory', *CA Magazine*, January and February 1975.

S. J. Gray and A. G. Coenenberg (eds), *International Group Accounting,* Croom Helm, NJ, 1988.

S. M. McKinnon, *Consolidated Accounts: The Seventh EEC Directive*, A. D. H. Newham (ed), Arthur Young McClelland Moores, 1983.

C. Nobes, *Some Practical and Theoretical Problems of Group Accounting*, Deloitte Haskins & Sells, London, 1986.

A. Simmonds, A. Mackenzie and K. Wild, 'Accounting for subsidiary undertakings', *Accountants Digest No. 288*, ICAEW, London, Autumn 1992.

P. A. Taylor, *Consolidated Financial Statements: Concepts, Issues and Techniques*, Harper and Row, London, 1987.

---

61 Interim Statement: Consolidated Accounts, Para. A10, ASB, December 1990.

CHAPTER 10

Accounting for overseas involvement

THE PROBLEMS IDENTIFIED

Many firms based in the UK undertake transactions with firms in other countries and have branches and subsidiary and associated undertakings overseas.

In the first case, transactions undertaken between firms will often be expressed in foreign currencies and it will be necessary to translate these amounts into sterling in order to enter them in the accounting records of the UK firm. If the rate of exchange changes between the date of the transaction and the date of settlement it is necessary to decide how to deal with the resulting difference on exchange in the accounts of the UK company. If there is an intervening balance sheet date, then it is necessary to decide which rate of exchange should be used at the balance sheet date and how the resulting difference on exchange should be treated.

In the second case, that is where there is an overseas branch, subsidiary or associated undertaking, it is usual for the whole of the accounting records of the overseas unit to be kept in the local currency: indeed, the local law may require the preparation and publication of accounts in terms of the local currency. In order to combine the results of the overseas unit with the sterling results of the investing company and those of any similar UK units, the accounts expressed in foreign currency must be translated into sterling.[1] When exchange rates between currencies fluctuate over time, this need for translation poses two problems. First, it is necessary to decide what rates of exchange are appropriate for the individual assets, liabilities, revenues and expenses in the accounts of the overseas unit. No matter how this question is answered, the translation process invariably gives rise to differences on exchange. As a second problem, it is therefore necessary to decide how these differences are to be dealt with in the aggregated financial statements.

Until the ASC attempted to standardise the accounting treatment of exchange differences in ED 16,[2] professional accountancy bodies in the UK had provided little guidance on how the above questions should be answered. Official pronouncements[3] tended to describe various methods and to emphasise that selection between them is a matter of professional judgment, without providing any guidance as to the principles on which that professional judgment should be based. As a result many different methods have been used in practice.

In this chapter, we look first at accounting for transactions denominated in foreign currencies and then turn our attention to the more complex subject of translating the

---

1 Following the American terminology introduced by ED 21, the term 'conversion' is restricted to the exchange of one currency for another.
2 ED 16, 'Supplement to "Extraordinary items and prior year adjustments"', September 1975.
3 *See*, for example, recommendation N 25 of the ICAEW, issued in February 1968.

accounts of an overseas unit for the purposes of aggregation. The accounting treatment of both topics is now regulated by SSAP 20, 'Foreign currency translation', which was issued in April 1983.

ACCOUNTING FOR FOREIGN CURRENCY TRANSACTIONS

A UK company may purchase fixed assets, stocks or services from an overseas company and may, in addition, sell goods or services to an overseas company. It may also raise loans denominated in a foreign currency and make investments in the shares of an overseas company. Where the amounts involved are expressed in a foreign currency, it will be necessary to translate those amounts into sterling in order to incorporate them into the accounting records of the UK company. The approach which should be adopted is best illustrated by means of a number of examples.

EXAMPLE 10.1

Let us consider a UK company, Han Limited, which makes up its accounts to 31 December each year. On 12 September 19X1 it purchased a fixed asset, machinery, from a German company for 31 000 Deutschmarks when the rate of exchange was DM 3.1 to £1. It paid for this machinery on 15 November 19X1 when the rate of exchange was DM 2.95 to £1.[4]

At the date of purchase, 12 September 19X1, it is necessary to translate the foreign currency amount to record the cost of the fixed asset and the corresponding creditor in sterling. As there was no contractually agreed rate of exchange for settlement or forward exchange contract, the rate ruling on the date of purchase, that is DM 3.1 to £1, will be used.[5]

19X1			
Sept 12	*Dr* Machinery – at cost	£10 000	
	Cr Creditor – German company		£10 000

Purchase of machinery for DM 31 000 at exchange rate of DM 3.1 to £1.

The sterling cost of the machinery is £10 000 and it is this figure which will be depreciated over the expected useful life of the asset. No further adjustment to this cost is necessary whatever subsequently happens to the rate of exchange.

In order to pay for the machinery, Han Limited must arrange with its bankers to convert sterling into Deutschmarks. If bank charges are ignored, the payment of DM 31 000 on 15 November 19X1 would require sterling of £10 508 given that the rate of exchange is DM 2.95 to £1. Settlement would be recorded as follows:

---

4 Although the currencies used in this and the following examples are often real currencies, the rates of exchange used are fictitious and movements are exaggerated to illustrate the principles involved.

5 SSAP 20, Para. 48, states that, where appropriate, contractually agreed rates of exchange for settlement *should* be used. It also *permits* the use of rates of exchange fixed in related or matching forward contracts. The standard has been criticised for this permissive and rather *naïve* approach to forward contracts. After more than ten years in issue, it badly needs revising in this and other areas, in particular to incorporate some guidance on the appropriate treatment of foreign currency financial instruments, such as currency options and swaps.

19X1
Nov 15   *Dr* Creditor – German company   £10 508
          Cr Cash   £10 508

Being payment of DM 31 000 converted at DM 2.95 to £1.

The creditor is now settled but when we look at the account in the records of Han Limited, it shows a debit balance of £508.

Creditor – German company

19X1		£	19X1		£
Nov 15	Cash	10 508	Sept 12	Machinery	10 000

This is a difference on exchange which, in this case, is a loss due to the fact that sterling has weakened (that is become less valuable) against the Deutschmark between the date of purchase and the date of settlement. The loss is, of course, realised and SSAP 20 requires that it be charged to the profit and loss account in arriving at the profit or loss from ordinary activities for the accounting year ended 31 December 19X1.

EXAMPLE 10.2

The next complication which may arise is that the purchase and the payment occur in different accounting years. To illustrate this, let us assume that Han Limited purchased stock from a French company for 200 000 French francs on 20 November 19X1 when the rate of exchange was 10 francs to £1. It subsequently paid for the goods on 15 January 19X2 when the rate of exchange was 12 francs to £1. The rate of exchange on 31 December 19X1, the intervening balance sheet date, was 11.5 francs to £1.

Following the principles explained in Example 10.1, the purchase would be recorded as follows:

19X1
Nov 20   *Dr* Stock   £20 000
          Cr Creditor – French company   £20 000

Purchase of stock for 200 000 francs at 10 francs to £1.

The cost of stock is recorded at £20 000 and, as before, this figure is not affected by any subsequent changes in the exchange rate. If the stock is still held on 31 December 19X1 it is included in the balance sheet at the lower of cost and net realisable value. Cost will be determined in accordance with the company's normal accounting policy (e.g. FIFO, average cost, etc.).

When we turn to the creditor, a monetary amount, such an approach is not sensible and, in the absence of either contractually agreed exchange rates for settlement or forward exchange contracts, SSAP 20 requires that all monetary items are translated at the closing rate.[6] The closing rate is defined more precisely as follows:

---

6 But *see* preceding footnote.

The closing rate is the exchange rate for spot transactions ruling at the balance sheet date and is the mean of the buying and selling rates at the close of business on the day for which the rate is to be ascertained.[7]

On 31 December 19X1 the amount payable to extinguish the creditor is not £20 000 but a lower amount of £17 391, that is 200 000 francs, translated at the closing rate of exchange on that day – 11.5 francs to £1. When the liability is adjusted to this figure, the result is a gain on exchange:

Creditor – French company

19X1		£	19X1		£
Dec 31	Balance c/d	17 391	Nov 20	Stock	20 000
	Profit and loss account – gain on exchange	2 609			
		20 000			20 000
			19X2		
			Jan 1	Balance b/d	17 391

The gain on exchange has occurred because the sterling value of the liability has fallen between 20 November 19X1 and 31 December 19X1 which in turn is due to the strengthening of sterling against the French franc. SSAP 20 considers that, as there is objective evidence for the sterling value of the liability and, as such a gain on a short-term monetary item will shortly be reflected in cash flows, so the profit on exchange is a part of realised profit and hence should be included in the profit or loss from ordinary activities.

The gain recognised in 19X1 could, of course, be fully or partly offset by a loss in the subsequent year if sterling weakens against the franc between 31 December 19X1 and the date of settlement, 15 January 19X2. The treatment adopted is, of course, consistent with the accruals concept: the gain occurred in 19X1 and is reported in 19X1, while the loss would occur in 19X2 and be reported in 19X2.

In this particular example there is, of course, no loss in 19X2 but a further gain on exchange when settlement is made on 15 January 19X2. Ignoring bank charges, the amount payable in sterling is £16 667 (200 000 francs ÷ 12) so that the creditor's account appears as follows:

Creditor – French company

19X2		£	19X2		£
Jan. 15	Cash	16 667	Jan. 1	Balance b/d	17 391
	Profit and loss account – gain on exchange	724			
		17 391			17 391

---

7 SSAP 20, Para. 41.

As in 19X1, the gain on exchange is credited to the profit and loss account, this time for the year ended 31 December 19X2.

SSAP 20 requires similar adherence to the accruals principle in the case of long-term monetary liabilities although, as we shall see, the standard adopts a different stance on the realisation of gains on exchange on such long-term liabilities.

EXAMPLE 10.3

Let us suppose that Han Limited raised a long-term loan of 500 000 French francs on 1 October 19X1 when the rate of exchange was 10 francs to £1. The loan will be recorded in the accounting records of Han Limited at a figure of £50 000:

19X1			
Oct 1	*Dr* Cash	£50 000	
	Cr Long-term loan		£50 000

Being loan of 500 000 French francs translated at 10 francs to £1.

If, on 31 December 19X1, the rate of exchange is 11.5 francs to £1 then, under the provisions of SSAP 20, the liability must be translated into sterling at that rate to produce a figure of £43 478 (500 000 ÷ 11.5):

Long-term loan

19X1		£	19X1		£
Dec 31	Balance c/d	43 478	Oct 1	Cash	50 000
	Profit and loss account – gain on exchange	6 522			
		50 000			50 000
			19X2		
			Jan 1	Balance b/d	43 478

Restating the sterling liability at this figure produces a gain on exchange of £6522 and SSAP 20 requires that this be reported as part of the 'ordinary' profits of Han Limited.

Some accountants would argue that such a gain is realised on the grounds that there is objective evidence, in the form of an officially published exchange rate, that it actually occurred in 19X1. Others would argue that, because it relates to a long-term item which has not been repaid at the balance sheet date, the gain may be reversed by subsequent exchange rate movements before repayment and is therefore not realised at the balance sheet date. These two views reflect the lack of consensus on the precise meaning of realisation, which was discussed in Chapter 3.

Although SSAP 20 takes the view that exchange gains on unsettled short-term monetary items are realised, it takes the view that such gains on unsettled long-term monetary items are unrealised.[8] In the authors' view, this is an extremely uncomfortable position for it may result in a situation where a gain on a short-term item will be treated as realised even though we may know, at the time of preparing the accounts, that it has subsequently been reversed while a gain on a long-term item, where we have no such certain knowledge of reversal, will be treated as unrealised. The ASC appears to have adopted different definitions of realisation for short-term and long-term items. In the former case, the existence of an objective exchange rate seems crucial, no matter what happens to the exchange rate subsequently. In the latter case, the existence of the objective exchange rate seems unimportant and uncertainty about the ultimate cash payable appears to be dominant. Among such confusion, we should perhaps be thankful that, rightly or wrongly, there is little disagreement among accountants that exchange *losses* on unsettled monetary items, whether short-term or long-term, are realised.

Given the ASC's conclusion that exchange gains on unsettled long-term monetary items are unrealised, many accountants argue that the prudence concept dictates that such gains should not be included in the profit and loss account. Indeed, they may quote statutory support for their argument in that the Companies Act 1985 specifically states that: 'only profits realised at the balance sheet date shall be included in the profit and loss account'.[9] However, the law permits directors to depart from this principle if there are special reasons providing that the notes to the accounts give particulars of the departure, the reason for it and its effect.[10] SSAP 20 considers that such a departure from the realisation principle is essential if exchange gains and losses are to be treated symmetrically in accordance with the accruals principle. Thus, in contravention of SSAP 2, SSAP 20 requires that the accruals concept takes precedence over the prudence concept.[11] Hence, in the same way that exchange losses on long-term liabilities during the period are debited to the profit and loss account, so exchange gains for the period are credited to the profit and loss account.

As explained above, relevant disclosure must be made. In addition any such unrealised profits credited to the profit and loss account should be removed when calculating legally distributable profits.

EXAMPLE 10.4

It is possible for a UK company to raise a foreign currency loan which it then invests in the shares of an overseas company. The loan and investment may be in the same currency or, alternatively, the loan may be raised in one currency while the investment is made in a country with a different currency. For ease of exposition we shall assume that only one currency is involved.

Let us assume that Han Limited raised a long-term loan of US $300 000 on 1 October 19X1 when the rate of exchange was US $1.5 to £1. It immediately invested the proceeds in the shares of a US corporation so that, if we ignore the receipt and payment of cash, the summarised journal entry will appear as follows:

---

8 SSAP 20, Para. 65.
9 Companies Act 1985, Schedule 4, Para. 12(a)
10 Companies Act 1985, Schedule 4, Para. 15.
11 SSAP 2, Para. 14(b). '...provided that where the accruals concept is inconsistent with the "prudence" concept, the latter prevails.'

19X1

Oct 1 *Dr* Investment in US company   £200 000

  Cr Long-term loan (US)   £200 000

Being loan of US $300 000 raised to finance investment in US company translated at $1.5 to £1.

The investment may constitute the US company a subsidiary, an associated undertaking or merely a simple investment. Whichever is the case, the treatment in the accounting records of Han Limited will be exactly the same although the treatment in any consolidated accounts will differ.

Let us assume that the rate of exchange on 31 December 19X1 is $1.4 to £1. If Han Limited follows the rules explained in previous examples, certain difficulties will arise. Unless there had been a permanent fall in the value of the investment, the investment would be shown in the balance sheet at its cost of £200 000 while the loan, a monetary amount, would have to be translated at the closing rate of exchange and shown as a liability of £214 286 ($300 000 ÷ 1.4). Restating the loan at this amount produces a loss on exchange of £14 286 which would have to be charged to the profit and loss account.

Long-term loan – US dollars

19X1			19X1		
Dec 31	Balance c/d	£214 286	Oct 1	Cash	£200 000
			Dec 31	Profit and loss account – loss on exchange	14 286
		214 286			214 286

It may be argued that to make such a one-sided adjustment is misleading. Because of the adherence to historical cost accounting, the investment is retained at its historical cost in sterling while the liability is shown at its current sterling equivalent. SSAP 20 recognises the logic of this argument and *permits*, although it does not *require*, Han Limited to translate the investment at the closing rate of exchange rather than at the historical rate of exchange, thus:

Investment in US corporation

19X1			19X1		
Oct 1	Cost	£200 000	Dec 31	Balance c/d, 300 000 ÷ 1.4	£214 286
Dec 31	Gain on exchange	14 286			
		214 286			214 286

This produces a meaningless sterling figure for the investment, a figure which is neither the historical cost in sterling nor a current value in sterling, but it results in the creation of a gain on exchange which may be offset against the loss on exchange on the long-term loan. In this case the gain on the investment is exactly equal to the loss on the long-term loan and one may be offset against the other without any need to charge any gain or loss to the profit and loss account. If the loan and investment were for different currency amounts or in different foreign currencies, this equality of gain and loss is unlikely to exist. In such a case the provisions of SSAP 20 require that any exchange gain or loss on the investment should be taken direct to reserves. Any loss or gain on the loan should then be offset against the gain or loss on the investment. If the exchange loss/gain on the loan exceeds the gain/loss on the investment then it follows that the excess must be charged/credited to the profit and loss account.

The final problem addressed in this section is to what extent such an offset should be permitted. Should it be necessary to identify a particular loan with a particular investment? Should the offset be restricted to situations where the loan and investment are in the same currency? Where a large company has many loans denominated in various foreign currencies and many investments in various foreign currencies, should a global approach be permitted whereby any gains are set off against any losses? What criteria should be laid down to govern the use of this offset arrangement?

After receiving many different recommendations from those who commented on the offset arrangements included in ED 27, SSAP 20 specified the following conditions:[12]

(a) in any accounting period, exchange gains or losses arising on the borrowings may be offset only to the extent of exchange differences arising on the equity investments;
(b) the foreign currency borrowings, whose exchange gains or losses are used in the offset process, should not exceed, in the aggregate, the total amount of cash that the investments are expected to be able to generate, whether from profits or otherwise; and
(c) the accounting treatment adopted should be applied consistently from period to period.[13]

This must be recognised as a pragmatic solution to what is often a very difficult question to answer in practice: 'To what extent do foreign currency loans provide a hedge against foreign equity investments?'

Why the offset arrangement should apply to equity investments but not to other investments, such as a readily saleable property overseas, seems difficult to justify and displays the *ad hoc* nature of our approach to standard setting.

Summary

The accounting treatment of foreign currency transactions may be summarised as follows:

1 *Historical cost of non-monetary assets*
   The historical cost of assets purchased for foreign currency is not affected by subsequent changes in exchange rates except where a company exercises the option to use the closing rate to translate foreign equity investments financed by foreign currency borrowings.

---

12 SSAP 20, Para. 51. Although ED 27, 'Accounting for foreign currency translations', issued in October 1980, considered this topic within the context of consolidated accounts, it did not even mention such offset arrangements within the accounts of the individual company.
13 SSAP 20, Para. 51.

2 *Unsettled monetary items*

Unsettled monetary items should be translated at the closing rate, unless there is a contractually agreed exchange rate for settlement, in which case the latter *should* be used. If there are related or matching forward contracts in respect of trading transactions, the rates of exchange specified in those contracts *may* be used.

3 *Treatment of exchange gains and losses*

All exchange gains and losses on settled and unsettled transactions should be credited or charged to the profit and loss account as part of the profit from ordinary activities (unless they relate to transactions which are treated as extraordinary items) but note that:

Gains on unsettled long-term monetary items are not regarded as realised and hence an adjustment should be made when calculating the legally distributable profit.

ACCOUNTING FOR AN OVERSEAS SUBSIDIARY

Where a UK company has an overseas branch, subsidiary or associated undertaking which keeps its records in a foreign currency, it is necessary to translate the accounts in order to combine the figures with those of the UK company or group. In this chapter we assume that the overseas unit is a subsidiary although readers will appreciate that similar principles are appropriate for a foreign branch or associated undertaking.

As explained in the first section of this chapter, when exchange rates are changing the existence of an overseas subsidiary requires us to answer two questions. First, what rate of exchange should be used to translate the individual items in the accounts of the overseas subsidiary? Second, how should the resulting differences on exchange be treated in the accounts?

Turning first to the balance sheet of the overseas subsidiary, there are at least two rates of exchange which could be applied to each asset or liability. These are the historical rate or the closing rate. The historical rate is the rate of exchange ruling at the date the transaction occurred or, where appropriate, the rate of exchange ruling at the date of a subsequent revaluation. The closing rate is the rate of exchange ruling on the balance sheet date.

The major methods of translation which have been used make use of a combination of these rates and the following table illustrates how four methods deal with the major categories of asset and liability (Table 10.1).

Under the current/non-current method, current assets and liabilities are translated at the closing rate while fixed assets and long-term liabilities are translated at the appropriate historical rate.

Under the monetary/non-monetary method, monetary assets and liabilities are translated at the closing rate while non-monetary assets are translated at the historical rate.

Under the temporal method, which is discussed in more detail later in this chapter, the rate of exchange depends upon the basis of valuation used in the balance sheet of the overseas subsidiary. If items are shown at current value, which is automatically the case with monetary assets and liabilities, the closing rate is used.[14] Where items are shown at

---

14 This statement is only true within the confines of traditional accounts. Arguably the current value of a
  monetary item should take into account interest for the time period until maturity of the debt.

Table 10.1 Major methods of translation

	Current/ non-current		Monetary/ non-monetary		Temporal		Closing rate	
	H	C	H	C	H	C	H	C
Assets								
Fixed assets								
At cost less depreciation	•		•		•			•
At current value	•		•			•		•
Current assets								
Stock								
At cost		•	•		•			•
At current value		•	•			•		•
Debtors		•		•		•		•
Cash		•		•		•		•
Liabilities								
Long-term loans	•			•		•		•
Current liabilities		•		•		•		•

H = historical rate; C = closing rate.

a figure based upon historical cost an historical rate is appropriate and where items are shown at a figure based on a valuation, the rate of exchange at the date of the valuation is used.

From the preceding table, it can be seen that there is very little difference between the temporal method and the monetary/non-monetary method within the context of historical cost accounts. The most frequent instance of a difference occurs where stock is shown at net realisable value.

Under the closing rate method all assets and liabilities are translated at the closing rate of exchange.

When we turn to the profit and loss account, three possible translation rates may be distinguished: (a) historical rates, that is rates of exchange specific to each transaction; (b) average rate ruling during the year;[15] (c) closing rate on the balance sheet date. Under the first, the appropriate rate of exchange is that ruling on the date of the transaction. So, if depreciation is based upon an historical cost, the rate of exchange at the date of acquisition of the asset is appropriate. If depreciation is based upon a revalued amount, the rate of exchange at the date of revaluation is appropriate. Where revenues and other expenses arise on a particular day, the rate of exchange on that day is appropriate. In practice, for recurrent items such as wages, power, directors' remuneration etc., an average rate is used as an approximation to the historical or specific rate of exchange.

Under the second option, an average rate of exchange is used in its own right, whereas with the third approach the closing rate of exchange is used for all items in the profit and loss account.

When we consider rates of exchange applied to balance sheet items and profit and loss account items, the following combinations have been found:

15 This should, of course, be an appropriate weighted average and not merely a simple average of the opening and closing rates.

Balance sheet	Profit and loss account
Current/non-current	Historical or average
Monetary/non-monetary	Historical or average
Temporal	Historical or average
Closing rate	Average or closing rate

Thus there has been a wide choice in practice as to the appropriate combinations of rates of exchange.

Whichever combinations are used, there will inevitably be differences on exchange and there are various ways of dealing with them in the consolidated accounts:

(i)   Include as part of profit or loss from ordinary activities.
(ii) Treat as a movement on reserves.
(iii) Some combination of the above.

When the choice between relevant rates of exchange is coupled with the choice between the various ways of dealing with differences on exchange, there are a large number of possible combinations. Given such choice, it is not surprising that the ASC felt it necessary to reduce the diversity in practice by producing an accounting standard on this topic.

The solution proposed by the ASC

ED 21, wrongly entitled 'Accounting for foreign currency transactions',[16] was issued in September 1972 as the first comprehensive attempt towards standardising the accounting treatment of foreign currencies in the UK. It permitted companies to use either the temporal method or the closing rate method and laid down rules on the rates of exchange to be used for translation and the treatment of the differences on exchange.

If ED 21 had become a Statement of Standard Accounting Practice, it would certainly have reduced the choice of methods available to companies by outlawing the use of the current/non-current and the monetary/non-monetary methods. However, when applied to historical cost accounts, the temporal method and the closing rate method usually produce very different results and, hence, the degree of standardisation proposed by ED 21 was limited and the Exposure Draft was heavily criticised.

The subsequent ED 27, 'Accounting for foreign currency translations' issued in November 1980, and SSAP 20, 'Foreign currency translation', issued in April 1983, require the use of one method in most situations. The favoured method is now called the 'closing rate/net investment method' and this appears to be the method used by the majority of companies in the UK.[17]

The words 'net investment' were added to the title of the method to indicate the view which the method implicitly takes of the investment in the overseas subsidiary. The majority of overseas subsidiaries are thought to have a certain amount of autonomy and to operate primarily within the economic environment of an overseas country using the currency of that country. Using the terminology of the Financial Accounting Standards

---

16 Wrongly entitled because it dealt almost exclusively with foreign currency translation and gave little attention to foreign currency transactions.

17 'Financial reporting 1992–93: a survey of published accounts', ICAEW, shows that, of the companies surveyed in 1991–92 which had foreign operations, 98% used the closing rate/net investment method.

Board (FASB) Statement No. 52, the 'functional currency' of the overseas subsidiary is usually that of the country in which it operates.[18] The holding company is therefore regarded as having an investment in the net assets of the subsidiary rather than in its individual assets and liabilities. It follows that only the net investment is at risk from movements in the exchange rate and, as we shall see, use of the closing rate method is consistent with this position.

In some cases, however, the overseas subsidiary may not have significant autonomy. Thus the affairs of the overseas company may be closely linked with those of the parent company and its 'functional currency' may be sterling rather than the local currency. In such a case, SSAP 20 requires that the foreign accounts be translated using the temporal method so that the results are included as if the transactions had been undertaken by the parent company itself.

SSAP 20 provides little guidance on how to recognise situations where the temporal method is appropriate and, given the variety of situations found in practice, it has to be recognised that it will sometimes be extremely difficult to decide which method of translation to apply.

To summarise, under the provisions of SSAP 20, it is expected that the vast majority of companies should use the closing rate/net investment method while a small number of companies will be required to use the temporal method. It is therefore essential for us to look at both methods.

In the following two sections of this chapter we shall examine the principles of the closing rate/net investment and temporal methods using simple examples. We shall then compare and contrast the two methods before presenting, in the final section, a more complex example of the closing rate/net investment method.

Closing rate/net investment method

As we have seen, any method for translating the accounts of an overseas subsidiary must specify which rates of exchange are to be used for the various items in the accounts of that subsidiary and how the resulting differences on exchange are to be treated in the consolidated accounts.

The SSAP 20 version of the closing rate/net investment method lays down the following rules:

(a) All assets and liabilities in the balance sheet of the overseas subsidiary are to be translated at the closing rate. This, of course, determines the amount of the shareholders' interest although, as we shall see, it is sensible to translate the share capital and components of reserves at various rates of exchange.
(b) All profit and loss account items are to be translated at either the average rate or the closing rate.[19]
(c) All differences on exchange arising on translation are to be taken direct to reserves.

When the rate of exchange between sterling and the overseas currency is fluctuating, a difference on exchange will arise in respect of the opening net assets of the subsidiary,

---

18 *See* Appendix A to Statement of Financial Accounting Standard No. 52 for factors which should be taken into account in determining the functional currency of an overseas subsidiary.
19 ED 27 proposed the use of the average rate for profit and loss account items and, although this is standard practice in the USA and Canada, the comments on ED 27 showed that there was considerable opposition to the exclusive use of an average rate in the UK.

which are translated at a different rate at the year end from that used at the beginning of the year. A second difference will arise if the average rate of exchange is used to translate profit and loss account items for, in such a case, the increase in net assets as shown by the retained profit or loss is translated at the average rate while the resulting net assets are translated at the closing rate in the balance sheet. Both differences on translation are treated as movements on reserves.

Let us illustrate the method by means of a simple example.

EXAMPLE 10.5

Widening Horizons Limited, a UK company which owns and rents out properties, established a wholly owned overseas subsidiary, Foreign Venture Limited, on 31 December 19X1. Widening Horizons Limited subscribed £100 000 in cash for one million shares of 1 groucho each. On 31 December 19X1, the rate of exchange between currencies was 10 grouchos to £1.

Foreign Venture Limited immediately raised a long-term loan of 500 000 grouchos and purchased freehold land and buildings, suitable for renting, at a cost of 1 200 000 grouchos.

After these transactions, the opening balance sheet of the new subsidiary, in both foreign currency and sterling, is therefore as given below:

Foreign Venture Limited
Opening balance sheet on 1 January 19X2

	Grouchos	Rate of exchange (grouchos to £1)	£
Freehold land and buildings			
At cost	1 200 000	10	120 000
Short-term monetary assets			
Cash	300 000	10	30 000
	1 500 000		150 000
less Long-term loan	500 000	10	50 000
	1 000 000		100 000
Share capital			
1 000 000 share of 1 groucho	1 000 000	10	100 000

At this date only one rate of exchange is appropriate; it qualifies as both the historical rate and the closing rate. Once the balance sheet is translated into sterling, it is possible to match the cost of the investment shown in the records of Widening Horizons Limited at £100 000 against the share capital of Foreign Venture Limited to produce neither positive nor negative goodwill on consolidation.

During the following year to 31 December 19X2 Foreign Venture Limited collects rentals and incurs expenses with the result that its profit and loss account for the year and balance sheet on 31 December 19X2 are as follows:

Foreign Venture Limited
Profit and loss account for the year ended 31 December 19X2

	Grouchos	Grouchos
Rentals received		400 000
less Expenses		
Management expenses	115 000	
Depreciation of buildings	50 000	
Interest on long-term loan	75 000	240 000
Profit before taxation		160 000
less Taxation payable		60 000
Retained profit for year		100 000

Balance sheet on 31 December 19X2

	Grouchos
Freehold land and buildings	
At cost	1 200 000
less Depreciation	50 000
	1 150 000
Short-term net monetary assets	
(debtors plus cash less creditors)	450 000
	1 600 000
less Long-term loan	500 000
	1 100 000
Share capital	
1 000 000 shares of 1 groucho each	1 000 000
Retained profit	100 000
	1 100 000

Assuming that the relevant rates of exchange between grouchos and sterling are as given below, we may proceed to translate the accounts in accordance with the closing rate/net investment method:

	Grouchos to £1
1 January 19X2	10
Average for year to 31 December 19X2	8
31 December 19X2	6

The average rate, rather than the closing rate, has been applied in the profit and loss account.

Foreign Venture Limited
Profit and loss account for the year ended 31 December 19X2

	Grouchos	Rate of exchange	£
Rentals received	400 000	8	50 000
less Expenses			
Management expenses	115 000	8	14 375
Depreciation of buildings	50 000	8	6 250
Interest on long-term loan	75 000	8	9 375
	240 000		30 000
Profit before taxation	160 000		20 000
less Taxation payable	60 000	8	7 500
Retained profit for year	100 000		12 500

Balance sheet on 31 December 19X2

	Grouchos	Rate of exchange	£
Freehold land and buildings			
At cost	1 200 000	6	200 000
less Depreciation	50 000	6	8 333
	1 150 000		191 667
Short-term net monetary assets	450 000	6	75 000
	1 600 000		266 667
less Long-term loan	500 000	6	83 333
	1 100 000		183 334
Shareholders' interest:			
Share capital	1 000 000	10(HR)	100 000
Retained profits	100 000	Per P and L a/c	12 500
			112 500
Difference on exchange	–	Balance	70 834
	1 100 000		183 334

(*Note*: HR=historical rate)

The treatment of share capital merits special attention. It has been translated at the historical rate of exchange, that is the rate ruling at the date of acquisition.

If we assume for a moment that share capital had been translated at the closing rate of exchange of 6 grouchos to £1, this would have produced a sterling figure of £166 667 instead of the £100 000 shown. This would have reduced the difference on exchange, the balancing figure, by £66 667, but consideration must also be paid to the subsequent consolidation of the subsidiary's accounts with those of the parent company. In the consolidation workings the cost of the investment, £100 000, would be matched with the share capital of the subsidiary, £166 667 when translated at closing rate, to produce negative goodwill on consolidation of £66 667. This is clearly nonsensical since there was no goodwill on acquisition and the apparent negative goodwill would only have arisen because of the change in the exchange rate. In other words the £66 667 is a difference on exchange.

The wisdom of the method used in the example may now be seen. The application of the historical rate to share capital and, in a more general case, to preacquisition reserves as well, means first, that the total difference emerges in the translation of the subsidiary's balance sheet and, second, that there is no risk that an erroneous adjustment will be made to the goodwill on consolidation. This should be dealt with in accordance with the provisions of SSAP 22.

The total difference on exchange, a gain of £70 834, must be credited to consolidated reserves. It has arisen for two reasons. First, the opening net assets were translated at one rate on 1 January 19X2 and at a different rate on 31 December 19X2. Second, the increase in net assets, the retained profit, has been translated at one rate in the profit and loss account and at a different rate in the closing balance sheet. We may analyse the difference as follows:

Analysis of difference on exchange

	Grouchos	Opening balance sheet (10 grouchos to £1) £	Closing balance sheet (6 grouchos to £1) £	Difference £
Opening net assets				
Freehold land and buildings	1 200 000	120 000	200 000	80 000 (gain)
Cash	300 000	30 000	50 000	20 000 (gain)
	1 500 000	150 000	250 000	100 000
less Long-term loan	500 000	50 000	83 333	33 333 (loss)
	1 000 000	100 000	166 667	66 667

Increase in net assets during year				
Retained profit for year				
Per profit and loss account, 100 000 grouchos at 8 grouchos to £1			£12 500	
Per closing balance sheet (part of net monetary assets), 100 000 grouchos at 6 grouchos to £1			16 667	4 167 (gain)
Total gain on exchange				70 834

It is hoped that the above analysis helps to explain why the words 'net investment' have been added in the name 'closing rate/net investment' method. The loss on the opening long-term loan has effectively been offset against the gains on the opening assets so that it is only the gain on the opening *net* assets which is taken to reserves with the second part of the gain in respect of the retained profit for the year. If the closing rate had been used for profit and loss account items, this second part of the gain would not arise.

Let us assume that the accounts of the parent company are as given in the left-hand column below. Provided there are no unrealised intercompany profits or similar consolidation adjustments, we may proceed to consolidate by adding the figures for the parent company with the translated figures for the overseas subsidiary, treating the difference on exchange of £70 834 as a movement on reserves.

Widening Horizons Limited
Workings for consolidated profit and loss account for the year ended 31 December 19X2

	Widening Horizons Limited £	Foreign Venture Limited £	Consolidated £
Rentals received	500 000	50 000	550 000
less Expenses			
Management expenses	120 000	14 375	134 375
Depreciation	60 000	6 250	66 250
Loan interest	100 000	9 375	109 375
	280 000	30 000	310 000
Profit before taxation	220 000	20 000	240 000
less Taxation	100 000	7 500	107 500
	120 000	12 500	132 500
less Dividends proposed	60 000	–	60 000
Retained profit for year	60 000	12 500	72 500

Workings for movement on reserves for year to 31 December 19X2

	Widening Horizons Limited £	Foreign Venture Limited £	Consolidated £
Reserves on 1 January 19X2	420 000	–	420 000
add Retained profit for year	60 000	12 500	72 500
Gain on exchange	–	70 834	70 834
Reserves on 31 December 19X2	480 000	83 334	563 334

Workings for consolidated balance sheet on 31 December 19X2

	Widening Horizons Limited £	Foreign Venture Limited £	Consolidated £
Freehold land and buildings			
At cost	2 000 000	200 000	2 200 000
less Depreciation	350 000	8 333	358 333
	1 650 000	191 667	1 841 667
Investment in Foreign Venture Limited – at cost	100 000	–	–
Goodwill on consolidation – at cost	–	–	–
Short-term net monetary assets	330 000	75 000	405 000
	2 080 000	266 667	2 246 667
less Long-term loan	1 000 000	83 333	1 083 333
	1 080 000	183 334	1 163 334
Share capital	600 000	100 000	600 000
Reserves	480 000	83 334	563 334
	1 080 000	183 334	1 163 334

Once the translation has been undertaken, preparation of the consolidated accounts poses only the normal problems faced when consolidating a UK subsidiary and preparing the accounts using the formats required by company law.

Temporal method

This method was first proposed by an American, Leonard Lorensen, in a study published by the American Institute of Certified Public Accountants.[20] It was the only method permitted by the US FASB in their standard on the subject Financial Accounting Standard (FAS) 8, which was issued in October 1975. However, this standard attracted a great deal of criticism in the USA and has now been replaced by FAS 52, which was issued in December 1981 and, like SSAP 20, favours the closing rate method.

Under the temporal method, the rates of exchange to be used for translation are determined by the basis of measurement used for the various items in the accounts of the overseas subsidiary.

In the balance sheet, assets which are shown at a figure based on historical cost are translated at the relevant historical rate; assets which are shown on the basis of a revalued amount at some past date are translated at the rate of exchange ruling when the revalued amount was established; assets and liabilities which are shown at a current value, which includes all monetary assets and liabilities, are translated at the closing rate.

In the profit and loss account the rate of exchange used is similarly determined by the underlying basis of measurement: depreciation based on historical cost is translated at the relevant historical rate, revenues and expenses which have accrued over the year are

20 L. Lorensen, *Reporting Foreign Operations of US Companies in US Dollars*, Accounting Research Study No. 12, AICPA, New York, 1972.

translated at an average rate while revenues or expenses which relate to amounts established in previous years or to merely a part of the current year are translated at a specific rate or an appropriate average rate.

It follows that more extensive records are necessary than those required for use of the closing rate/net investment method.

Under the SSAP 20 version of the temporal method, all differences on exchange are to be credited or charged to the consolidated profit and loss account as a part of the ordinary profits for the year.[21]

Let us examine the temporal method by applying it to the same simple facts used in the previous example.

EXAMPLE 10.6

The opening balance sheet of Foreign Venture Limited, the new subsidiary established by Widening Horizons Limited, in both grouchos and sterling is repeated below:

Foreign Venture Limited
Balance sheet on 1 January 19X2

	Grouchos	Rate of exchange	£
Freehold land and buildings			
At cost	1 200 000	10	120 000
Short-term monetary assets			
Cash	300 000	10	30 000
	1 500 000		150 000
less Long-term loan	500 000	10	50 000
	1 000 000		100 000
Share capital	1 000 000	10	100 000

Widening Horizons Limited paid £100 000 for the investment and hence at the date of acquisition there is no goodwill on consolidation.

The accounts of Foreign Venture Limited for the year ended 31 December 19X2 are given below. The left-hand column gives the accounts in foreign currency while the right-hand column shows the results translated into sterling. For ease of reference, the relevant exchange rates are repeated:

	Grouchos to £1
1 January 19X2	10
Average for year to 31 December 19X2	8
31 December 19X2	6

In the profit and loss account the historical rate, that ruling when the buildings were purchased on 31 December 19X1, is applied to depreciation. For other items the average

---

21 Other variants of the temporal method exist. For example, the version of the temporal method required by the Canadian Institute of Chartered Accountants provides that unrealised gains and losses relating to long-term monetary assets and liabilities shall be amortised over the remaining life of the asset or liability.

rate is an appropriate approximation to the historical rate. A simple average of the opening and closing rates would only be appropriate if the revenue and expenses arose reasonably evenly over the year and the rate of exchange moved reasonably evenly. Otherwise an appropriate weighted average would have to be used.

Foreign Venture Limited
Profit and loss account for the year ended 31 December 19X2

	Grouchos	Rate of exchange (see note)	£
Rentals received	400 000	8(AR)	50 000
less Expenses			
Management expenses	115 000	8(AR)	14 375
Depreciation of buildings	50 000	10(HR)	5 000
Interest on long-term loan	75 000	8(AR)	9 375
	240 000		28 750
Profit before taxation	160 000		21 250
less Taxation payable	60 000	8(AR)	7 500
Retained profit for year	100 000		13 750

Note: AR=average rate, HR=historical rate.

In the balance sheet, the freehold land and buildings, shown at depreciated historical cost, is translated at the historical rate of exchange on 1 January 19X2 while all monetary assets and liabilities are translated at the closing rate.

As explained in the previous example, it is sensible to translate the share capital and, in a more general case, any pre-acquisition reserves at the historical rate in order to maintain the goodwill on acquisition at its 'historical cost' in the consolidated accounts. It is also necessary to translate the retained profit for the year at the same sterling figure as shown for retained profit in the profit and loss account. When this has been done the difference on exchange emerges as the balancing figure:

Balance sheet on 31 December 19X2

	Grouchos	Rate of exchange (see note)	£
Freehold land and buildings			
At cost	1 200 000	10(HR)	120 000
less Depreciation	50 000	10(HR)	5 000
	1 150 000		115 000
Short-term net monetary assets	450 000	6(CR)	75 000
	1 600 000		190 000
less Long-term loan	500 000	6(CR)	83 333
	1 100 000		106 667
Shareholders' interest:			
Share capital			
1 000 000 shares of 1 groucho			
each	1 000 000	10(HR)	100 000
Retained profit			
Per profit and loss account	100 000	Actual	13 750
			113 750
Difference on exchange	–	Balance	(7 083)
	1 100 000		106 667

Note: HR=historical rate, CR=closing rate.

As explained above, SSAP 20 requires any difference on exchange arising under the temporal method to be included in the ordinary profits and losses of the group.

If we assume that the accounts of the parent company are as given in the left-hand column below and that there are no consolidation adjustments for such matters as unrealised intercompany profits, we may proceed to consolidate. This requires adding the figures for the parent company with the sterling figures for the overseas subsidiary, treating the difference on exchange as part of the ordinary profits.

Widening Horizons Limited
Workings for consolidated profit and loss account for the year ended
31 December 19X2

	Widening Horizons Limited £	Foreign Venture Limited £	Consolidated £
Rentals received	500 000	50 000	550 000
less Expenses			
Management expenses	120 000	14 375	134 375
Depreciation	60 000	5 000	65 000
Loan interest	100 000	9 375	109 375
	280 000	28 750	308 750
Revenue less expenses	220 000	21 250	241 250
less Loss on exchange	–	7 083	7 083
Profit before taxation	220 000	14 167	234 167
less Taxation	100 000	7 500	107 500
	120 000	6 667	126 667
less Dividends proposed	60 000	–	60 000
Retained profit for the year	60 000	6 667	66 667

Workings for movement on reserves for year to 31 December 19X2

	Widening Horizons Limited £	Foreign Venture Limited £	Consolidated £
Retained profits on 1 January 19X2	420 000	–	420 000
add Retained profit for year	60 000	6 667	66 667
Retained profits on 31 December 19X2	480 000	6 667	486 667

Workings for consolidated balance sheet on 31 December 19X2

	Widening Horizons Limited £	Foreign Venture Limited £	Consolidated £
Freehold land and buildings			
At cost	2 000 000	120 000	2 120 000
less Depreciation	350 000	5 000	355 000
Carried forward	1 650 000	115 000	1 765 000

	Widening Horizons Limited £	Foreign Venture Limited £	Consolidated £
Brought forward	1 650 000	115 000	1 765 000
Investment in Foreign Venture Limited			
At cost	100 000	–	–
Short-term net monetary assets	330 000	75 000	405 000
	2 080 000	190 000	2 170 000
less Long-term loan	1 000 000	83 333	1 083 333
	1 080 000	106 667	1 086 667
Share capital	600 000	100 000	600 000
Retained profits	480 000	6 667	486 667
	1 080 000	106 667	1 086 667

From workings similar to the above, it is quite straightforward to produce the consolidated accounts for publication, although attention would have to be given to providing the more-detailed information in accordance with the formats prescribed by company law.

As would be expected in this case, there is no goodwill on consolidation. The loss on exchange is charged in the profit and loss account and would only be disclosed if it were an exceptional item.

There is no need to analyse the difference on exchange for the purposes of preparing the consolidated accounts. However, it is instructive to do so.

No difference on exchange relates to the freehold land and buildings. In the opening balance sheet of Foreign Venture Limited the freehold land and buildings were shown at cost and translated at 10 grouchos to £1. In the profit and loss account, depreciation of 50 000 grouchos was provided and this was translated at 10 grouchos to £1. In the closing balance sheet the asset is shown at cost less depreciation, again translated at 10 grouchos to £1.

The difference arises first because monetary assets and liabilities are translated at different rates in the opening and closing balance sheet and second because, for certain items, different rates are used in the profit and loss account and closing balance sheet. It may be analysed as follows:

Analysis of difference on exchange £

1 Opening balance of short-term net monetary assets   300 000 grouchos

    In opening balance sheet, 10 grouchos to £1   £30 000

    In closing balance sheet, 6 grouchos to £1   £50 000   Gain 20 000

2 Opening balance on long-term loan   500 000 grouchos

    In opening balance sheet, 10 grouchos to £1   £50 000

    In closing balance sheet, 6 grouchos to £1   £83 333   Loss 33 333

Carried forward   Loss 13 333

	£
Brought forward	Loss 13 333

3 Increase in short-term net
   monetary assets during year
   Per profit and loss account

Retained profit	100 000	grouchos
add Depreciation	50 000	grouchos
	150 000	grouchos

At 8 grouchos to £1	£18 750
Per closing balance sheet as part of short-term net monetary assets, at 6 grouchos to £1	£25 000
	Gain 6 250
Net loss	7 083

The differences on exchange may therefore be understood by thinking in terms of a flow of net monetary items:

Statement of source and application of net monetary assets/liabilities for the year ended 31 December 19X2

	Grouchos	Grouchos	Rate	£
Opening balance of net monetary liabilities:				
Long-term loan		500 000		
Short-term monetary assets		300 000		
		200 000	10	20 000
less Source of net monetary assets				
Retained profit plus depreciation		150 000	8	18 750
				1 250
Difference on exchange – balance (loss)				7 083
Closing balance of net monetary liabilities				
Long-term loan	500 000			
Short-term monetary assets	450 000			
	50 000			
		50 000	6	8 333

A critical look at the two methods

Some substantial differences

We have now illustrated the mechanics of the two methods of translation, using the same facts but rather large movements in the hypothetical exchange rates.

When exchange rates between currencies change over time the methods produce very different results from the same set of foreign currency accounts. Thus if we compare the translated amount of the fixed assets of Foreign Venture Limited, in the simple examples in the two preceding sections, we find the following results:

Fixed assets of Foreign Venture Limited on 31 December 19X2

	Net book value £
Closing rate/net investment method	191 667
Temporal method	115 000

It is true that the rate of exchange moved from 10 grouchos to £1 at the beginning of the year to 6 grouchos at the end of the year, but there are substantial changes in practice in the exchange rates between currencies. Table 10.2 contains movements in the rate of exchange between sterling and a number of major currencies over a 10-year period:

Table 10.2

	Rates to £1 at the end of		Change as a percentage
	December 1982	December 1992	
US dollars	1.6175	1.5330	− 5.2
Belgian francs	75.9000	50.3283	− 33.7
French francs	10.9100	8.3628	− 23.3
German Deutschmarks	3.8505	2.4408	− 36.6
Italian lire	2 216.8000	2 232.3525	+ 0.7
Japanese yen	380.9200	189.7900	− 50.2

Source: Bank of England.

To illustrate the effect of the differences between the two methods, let us suppose that a German subsidiary bought land in December 1982 and that this is shown in the balance sheet on 31 December 1992 as:

Land, at cost   1 000 000   Deutschmarks

Under the closing rate/net investment method, this cost would be translated at the closing-rate, while under the temporal method, it would be translated at the historical rate. Application of the two rates would produce very different sterling figures for the land:

Closing rate   1 000 000 ÷ 2.4408 = £409 702
Historical rate   1 000 000 ÷ 3.8505 = £259 707

When we turn to differences on exchange, we again find substantial differences between the methods. Under the closing rate/net investment method differences on exchange are treated as a movement on reserves, while under the temporal method they are considered to be part of the ordinary profit or loss for the year.

What then are the respective advantages and disadvantages of the two methods and why has SSAP 20 favoured the use of the closing rate/net investment method?

Advantages and disadvantages

In order to evaluate the two methods of translation, we must bear in mind how the translated figures are going to be used. If we were studying the accounts of an overseas company with a view to acquiring its shares, it might be useful to translate all items in the foreign currency accounts into sterling at the closing rate of exchange in order to produce figures which are meaningful in the home currency. Use of a constant rate of exchange for all items would maintain the same relationships in the sterling accounts as existed in the foreign currency accounts. Thus, for example, long-term liabilities would be the same proportion of fixed assets and the current ratio would be the same in sterling as in the foreign currency accounts.

However, when considering the translation of the accounts of a subsidiary company prior to consolidation, such a consideration would seem to be irrelevant. After all, we add the translated figures for the overseas subsidiary to those of the parent company and hence the relationship between items in the accounts of the overseas subsidiary will be completely lost. What would seem to be more important for meaningful aggregation in the consolidated accounts is that the bases of measurement used for the assets and liabilities are consistent.

If we accept the need to use consistent bases for consolidation then, in the context of historical cost accounting, it seems reasonable to aggregate the historical costs of the fixed assets and stocks of the subsidiary with the historical costs of the fixed assets and stocks of the parent company. Similarly, the amounts payable and receivable at the balance sheet date for both companies should be dealt with in a consistent manner.

Stated in this way, only the temporal method of translation is conceptually consistent with the historical cost basis of accounting and indeed any basis of accounting. The translation of an historical cost at an historical rate produces the historical cost in sterling, that is the amount which would have been incurred if a sum of money had been dispatched from the UK to purchase the asset. The translation of an historical cost at a closing rate would seem to produce a conceptual nonsense.

It was arguments such as these which led the US FASB to require the exclusive use of the temporal method in FAS 8 and probably also to the ASC permitting a choice between the closing rate method and the temporal method in ED 21. However, the temporal method is not without its problems.

First, there is the practical problem of keeping records. In order to translate fixed assets and stocks at historical rates of exchange, a detailed analysis of these items together with the respective rates of exchange has to be kept. Such a record is not required by those companies which use the closing rate/net investment method.

Second, the application of the method has caused large fluctuations in the reported profits of groups of companies from period to period, fluctuations which bear little relationship to the underlying operating performance of the overseas subsidiaries. Such volatility of reported earnings arises because of the requirement to include exchange gains and losses on long-term monetary items in the ordinary profits of the group and the problem could be solved by taking these particular exchange gains or losses direct to reserve or by spreading them over a period of years.

Third, the method produces misleading differences on exchange, which may in turn have adverse behavioural implications.

Let us take as an example a UK company which has an overseas subsidiary. In the balance sheet of the overseas subsidiary fixed assets and stocks are shown on the basis of historical cost and these are usually financed by net monetary liabilities and an equity interest. During a particular year sterling is weakening against the overseas currency, that is the other currency is becoming more valuable. In such a case the value of the overseas net assets to the UK company would be increasing and any potential dividends from the overseas subsidiary would be more valuable, as a given future dividend stream in the foreign currency would produce a greater amount of sterling. However, using the temporal method of translation, we would recognise no gains on the fixed assets but merely losses on the net monetary liabilities.

Thus, as a result of the movement in exchange rates, the overseas subsidiary is more valuable, but as a result of using the temporal method, the accounts show losses on exchange!

Under the provisions of both FAS 8 and SSAP 20, such losses on exchange reduced the profits from ordinary activities and hence the earnings per share. Given that no board of directors wishes to undertake activities which reduce profits or produce losses in the accounts, there is considerable evidence to indicate that 'profitable' overseas projects have been rejected because of the subsequent accounting losses which resulted from the use of the temporal method of translation.[22]

The closing rate/net investment method does not produce these misleading differences. Because the closing rate is applied to non-monetary assets as well as monetary assets and liabilities, it is possible to set off exchange losses on foreign currency borrowings against exchange gains on real assets and therefore eliminate the need to charge such losses in the profit and loss account. The use of such a cover method is felt by many to reflect the reality of the situation where fixed assets and stocks are financed by money raised overseas. Indeed, under the offset arrangements included in SSAP 20, this cover method is extended to loans raised by the parent company or other companies in the group so that where foreign currency borrowings have been used to finance, or provide a hedge against, group equity investments in foreign enterprises, exchange gains or losses on the borrowings may be set off against exchange differences arising on the retranslation of the net investment.[23]

To take into account exchange gains or losses on the monetary items without taking into account exchange losses or gains on real assets, as under the temporal method, is considered to be wrong by many accountants.

To summarise, the temporal method has the advantage of producing translated figures which are conceptually consistent with the underlying basis of measurement used while the closing rate/net investment method has the advantage of simplicity and manages to avoid the reporting of fluctuating profits and misleading differences on exchange by the use of one rate of exchange for both assets and liabilities.

The ASC had to balance the respective advantages and disadvantages of the two methods in producing SSAP 20. As we have seen, it favours the closing rate/net investment method for the majority of situations but requires the use of the temporal method where the trade of the foreign enterprise is more dependent on the economic environment of the investing company's currency than that of its own reporting currency. It does, however, recognise the limitations of the closing rate/net investment method where the foreign country suffers from hyper-inflation. In such a case it requires that the local currency financial statements be adjusted to reflect current price levels before the translation process is undertaken.[24]

---

22 *See*, for example, D. P. Walker, *An economic analysis of foreign exchange risk*, ICAEW Research Committee Occasional Paper No. 14, ICAEW, London, 1978.

23 SSAP 20, Para. 57 specifies the conditions under which this offset arrangement may be applied. As we shall see in the last section of this chapter, the exchange difference on the retranslation of the net assets in the consolidated accounts will usually differ from the exchange difference on the retranslation of the investment in the accounts of the parent company.

24 SSAP 20, Para. 26. This topic is addressed by IAS 29 'Financial reporting in hyper inflationary economies' and UITF Abstract 9 'Accounting for operations in hyper-inflationary economies', June 1993. These specifically require adjustments where the cumulative rate of inflation over a three year period is approaching or exceeds 100 per cent.

In the view of the authors, the use of the closing rate/net investment method is inconsistent with the subsequent consolidation of the resulting sterling figures. In our view, the logic of the method should lead us to include the results of an overseas subsidiary in the consolidated accounts by using the equity method of accounting. In this way the consolidated profit and loss account would include the appropriate proportion of the profit or loss of the subsidiary while the consolidated balance sheet would show a net investment in the overseas subsidiary. This is surely what the title of the closing rate/net investment method implies!

One aspect of a larger problem

We have seen that both of the major methods of translation have advantages and disadvantages and that it has been difficult to choose between them.

The difficulties which we face here may be seen as part of the much larger problem discussed in the early part of this book. In Chapter 3 we have seen, for example, that the addition of historical costs which have been incurred at different points in time results in an unhelpful total when the value of the pound has been changing over time. The movement of exchange rates between currencies presents us with similar problems and, given that we have not yet solved the problems of accounting where only one currency is involved, it is not surprising that there is considerable confusion when we introduce two or more currencies.

It might be suggested that the major stumbling-block is the traditional reliance on historical cost accounts, which are known to have so many defects. We cannot expect the choice of exchange rate to remedy these defects. If we were to depart from historical costs and instead to show assets and liabilities of the overseas company at their current values, only one rate of exchange would be appropriate. The closing rate is required by both the temporal method and the closing rate method and the resulting sterling figures may quite properly be aggregated with the current values of assets and liabilities of the parent company. It would still be necessary to determine the treatment of resulting differences on exchange but a major problem would have disappeared.

There would still, of course, be other problems in connection with foreign currencies. In all the examples we have assumed that our UK parent company prepares consolidated accounts so that sterling is the appropriate currency to use. Once we widen our horizons to look at a multinational company, which operates throughout the world and has shareholders in many countries, it is difficult to know even what the reporting currency should be, let alone what the resulting differences on exchange really mean.

To illustrate the sort of problem which we face, let us end this section with a very simple example:

Let us suppose that an individual habitually spends 6 months of every year in the UK and 6 months in the USA. On 1 January 19X2 he has wealth of $100 000 in the USA and £100 000 in the UK when the rate of exchange between the currencies is $2.5 to the £1. During the year he lives on income arising in the respective countries and ends the year with exactly the same money wealth in each country when the exchange rate has moved to $2 to £1.

Let us compare his wealth at the beginning and end of the year in dollars and sterling, respectively:

	$	£
Opening wealth – 1 January 19X2 (rate of exchange $2.5 to £1)		
UK, £100 000	250 000	100 000
USA, $100 000	100 000	40 000
	350 000	140 000
Closing wealth – 31 December 19X2 (rate of exchange $2 to £1)		
UK, £100 000	200 000	100 000
USA, $100 000	100 000	50 000
	300 000	150 000
Gain during year	–	£10 000
Loss during year	$50 000	–

As can be seen, if we ignore changes in the purchasing power of the respective currencies, the translation process produces a loss of $50 000 or a gain of £10 000 during the year, even though our individual has the same money wealth at the end as he did at the beginning.

Problems such as those discussed above obviously bedevil the multinational company. Although such companies prepare consolidated accounts in the currency of the country where the parent company is situated, it must be admitted that the figures produced are of dubious significance to many shareholders.

A more complex example

EXAMPLE 10.7: The closing rate/net investment method

A. Some years ago Home Country plc, a UK company, raised a long-term loan of $400 000 which it used to help purchase 80 per cent of the shares in Overseas Inc. at a total cost of $500 000.

B. Relevant rates of exchange were as follows:

	Dollars to £1
At date of acquisition	5
On 1 January 19X2	4
On 31 December 19X2	3

C. We shall first look at the treatment of the above transactions in the accounts of the parent company.

In accordance with the principles explained earlier in the chapter, the loan and investment would have originally been recorded at the following amounts:

Long-term loan ($400 000 ÷ 5)	£80 000
Investment in subsidiary ($500 000 ÷ 5)	£100 000

On 31 December 19X1 the loan would have been translated at the rate on that date and we shall assume that the company has also translated the investment at the closing rate at that date, as permitted by Para. 51 of SSAP 20. These items would have then appeared in the balance sheet as follows:

> **Home Country plc**
> **Extract from balance sheet on 31 December 19X1**
> Long-term loan denominated in dollars
> $400 000 ÷ 4   £100 000
>
> Investment in subsidiary
> $500 000 ÷ 4   £125 000

The difference on exchange between the date of acquisition and 31 December 19X1 would have been credited to reserves in past years, namely:

> Exchange gain on equity investment
> £125 000 – £100 000   £25 000
> *less* Exchange loss on dollar loan
> £100 000 – £80 000   20 000
> Net gain   5 000

When the balance sheet on 31 December 19X2 is prepared the foreign currency amounts will be translated at the closing rate of $3 to £1:

> **Home Country plc**
> **Extract from balance sheet on 31 December 19X2**
> Long-term loan denominated in dollars
> $400 000 ÷ 3   £133 333
>
> Investment in subsidiary
> $500 000 ÷ 3   £166 667

The difference on exchange to be treated as a movement on reserves in 19X2 in the accounts of the parent company is therefore as follows:

> **Home Country plc**
> **Part of movement on reserves for 19X2**
> Exchange gain on equity investment
> £166 667 – £125 000   £41 667
> *less* Exchange loss on dollar loan
> £133 333 – £100 000   33 333
> Net gain   8 334

D. The above figures for 19X2 are incorporated in the summarised accounts of Home Country plc for the year ended 31 December 19X2 which appear below:

Home Country plc
Profit and loss account for the year ended 31 December 19X2

	£
Profit before taxation	112 000
Dividend receivable from Overseas Inc. (net)	
(80% of £20 000)	16 000
	128 000
less Taxation	60 000
	68 000
add Extraordinary profit, net of tax	5 000
	73 000
less Dividends payable	30 000
Retained profit for year	43 000

Home Country plc
Movement on reserves for the year ended 31 December 19X2

	£
Balance on 1 January 19X2	133 666
Retained profit for year	43 000
Difference on exchange	8 334
Balance on 31 December 19X2	185 000

Home Country plc
Balance sheet on 31 December 19X2

	£	£
Fixed assets		
Tangible assets		400 000
Investment in subsidiary (80% holding)		166 667
Current assets		
Stocks	60 000	
Debtors	40 000	
Dividend receivable from Overseas Inc.	16 000	
Cash	5 666	
	121 666	
less Current liabilities	70 000	51 666
		618 333
less Long-term loans:		
Denominated in dollars	133 333	
Denominated in sterling	100 000	233 333
		385 000
Share capital		200 000
Reserves		185 000
		385 000

E. We may now turn our attention to the accounts of the overseas subsidiary.

The balance sheet of Overseas Inc. on 31 December 19X1 in dollars is given in the left-hand column while the relevant rates of exchange and resulting sterling amounts are given in the second and third columns respectively. It has been assumed that the assets of Overseas Inc. were revalued at their fair values at the date of acquisition to produce a revaluation reserve of $150 000. Other reserves at the date of acquisition are assumed to have been $100 000.

Overseas Inc.
Balance sheet on 31 December 19X1

	$	Rate of exchange	£
Fixed assets			
At revalued amounts at date of acquisition and subsequent cost less depreciation	1 000 000	4(CR)	250 000
Current assets			
Stocks	300 000	4(CR)	75 000
Debtors	200 000	4(CR)	50 000
Cash	100 000	4(CR)	25 000
	600 000		150 000
less Current liabilities	400 000	4(CR)	100 000
Net current assets	200 000		50 000
	1 200 000		300 000
less Long-term loan	600 000	4(CR)	150 000
	600 000		150 000
Share capital	100 000	5(HR)	20 000
Revaluation reserve – at date of acquisition by Home Country plc	150 000	5(HR)	30 000
Reserves			
Pre-acquisition	100 000	5(HR)	20 000
	350 000		70 000
Post-acquisition	250 000	Balance	80 000
	600 000		150 000

Notice that in translating the balance sheet, the share capital and preacquisition reserves have been translated at the historical rate at the date of acquisition with the intention of maintaining the goodwill on consolidation at its 'cost'. The balance of post-acquisition reserves, which is translated at £80 000, therefore includes all exchange differences which have arisen since the date of acquisition. The size of these exchange differences depends upon when the post-acquisition reserves were earned and the rates of exchange prevailing at those dates. The less the fluctuation in exchange rates since acquisition the lower will be the difference.

At first sight the use of historical rates for share capital and preacquisition reserves might be thought to be incorrect as far as the minority interest is concerned. However, the minority interest is 20 per cent of the net assets or total share capital and reserves and the way in which the individual components of the share capital and reserves are translated has no effect on the total figure.

F. The accounts of Overseas Inc. for the year ended 31 December 19X2 are given below. The left-hand column is in dollars, the centre column gives the relevant rate of exchange and the right-hand column gives the resulting sterling figures.

The profit and loss account has been translated at the closing rate rather than the average rate and, as we have seen earlier in the chapter, this avoids one difference on exchange.

Overseas Inc.
Profit and loss account for the year ended 31 December 19X2

	$	Rate of exchange (closing rate)	£
Operating profit	300 000	3	100 000
less Taxation	150 000	3	50 000
	150 000		50 000
add Extraordinary profit, net of tax	30 000	3	10 000
	180 000		60 000
less Dividends payable	60 000	3	20 000
Retained profit for year	120 000		40 000

Overseas Inc.
Balance sheet on 31 December 19X2

	$	Rate of exchange	£
Fixed assets			
At revalued amount or cost			
less depreciation	960 000	3	320 000
Current assets			
Stock	360 000	3	120 000
Debtors	240 000	3	80 000
Cash	160 000	3	53 333
	760 000		253 333
less Current liabilities			
(including dividend payable)	400 000	3	133 333
Net current assets	360 000		120 000
	1 320 000		440 000
less Long-term loan	600 000	3	200 000
	720 000		240 000
Share capital	100 000	5(HR)	20 000
Revaluation reserve			
(created at date of acquisition)	150 000	5(HR)	30 000
Reserves			
Pre-acquisition	100 000	5(HR)	20 000
Post-acquisition			
		Per balance	
at 1 January 19X2	250 000	sheet 31.12.19X1	80 000
(Net assets on 1.1.19X2)	600 000	4	150 000
Post-acquisition			
		Per P and L	
Current year – 19X2	120 000	account	40 000
	720 000		190 000
Difference on exchange	–	Balance	50 000
	720 000		240 000

Note that the balance sheet contains a suitable analysis of reserves and, in particular, that it is necessary to translate the post-acquisition reserves so that they agree with the previous year's accounts and with the profit and loss account balance for the year ended 31 December 19X2, respectively. An exchange gain of £50 000 emerges as the balancing figure. As the profit and loss account has been translated at the closing rate rather than the average rate, the whole of the difference on exchange relates to the opening net assets:

Difference on exchange

Opening net assets	$600 000	
Translation at beginning of year $600 000 ÷ 4		£150 000
Translation at end of year $600 000 ÷ 3		200 000
Gain on exchange		50 000

G. In order to prepare consolidated accounts, it is necessary to provide the usual analysis of the shareholders' interest in Overseas Inc. and to decide how to deal with the difference on exchange. In practice there will usually be many other adjustments in respect of such matters as unrealised inter-company profits but these are problems faced on any consolidation and are therefore not dealt with here.

The shareholders' interest in Overseas Inc. may be analysed as follows:

Overseas Inc.
Analysis of shareholders' equity on 31 December 19X2

	Total	Pre-acquisition	Post-acquisition	Minority interest
	£	£	£	£
Share capital	20 000	16 000		4 000
Revaluation reserve	30 000	24 000		6 000
Other reserves				
Pre-acquisition	20 000	16 000		4 000
Post-acquisition				
At 1 January 19X2	80 000		64 000	16 000
Retained profit 19X2	40 000		32 000	8 000
Difference on exchange 19X2	50 000		40 000	10 000
	240 000	56 000	136 000	48 000
Cost of investment				
(original cost)		100 000		
Goodwill on consolidation		44 000		

Group 80% spans the Pre-acquisition and Post-acquisition columns.

H. As shown in section C, the accounts of Home Country plc for 19X2 include an exchange gain on the equity investment of £41 667 and an exchange loss on the dollar loan of £33 333, together producing a net gain of £8334 which has been credited to reserves.

When we turn to the consolidated accounts it is still possible to set the loss on the dollar loan, which appears in the parent company's accounts, against the gain on the investment as permitted by SSAP 20, Para. 57. However, the appropriate exchange gain in the consolidated accounts is the parent company's share of the exchange gain resulting from the translation of the subsidiary's accounts, in this case 80 per cent of £50 000 = £40 000.

This treatment is in line with the general principle of consolidation whereby the cost of the investment in the parent company's balance sheet is replaced by the underlying net assets of the subsidiary.

As a consequence of this the net difference on exchange which is to be treated as a movement on reserves in the consolidated accounts will be:

	£
Gain on exchange in 19X2 in respect of Home Country's share of net assets in Overseas Inc., 80% of £50 000	40 000
less Loss on exchange in 19X2 in respect of dollar loan – per accounts of Home Country plc (*see* C above)	33 333
Net gain	6 667

I. An adjustment similar to that discussed in H above is necessary to calculate the balance of consolidated reserves brought forward at 1 January 19X2.

It is insufficient just to add together the reserves of Home Country plc and 80 per cent of the post-acquisition reserves of Overseas Inc. As shown in Section C, the reserves of Home Country plc on 31 December 19X1 include the following net exchange gain made since acquisition:

	£
Exchange gain on equity investment	25 000
less Exchange loss on dollar loan	20 000
Net gain	5 000

While the exchange loss on the dollar loan may be properly charged against consolidated reserves, the relevant exchange gain in the consolidated accounts is not that on the investment but the parent company's share of the gain on translating the subsidiary's accounts. We do not know the amount of this exchange gain but we do know that it is included in the figure of £80 000 for post-acquisition reserves shown in E above.

The balance of consolidated reserves on 31 December 19X1, that is brought forward on 1.1.19X2, may therefore be calculated as follows:

	£
Home Country plc	
Per company's own balance sheet (*see* D)	133 666
less Exchange gain on equity investment included in above figure	
(*see* this section above)	25 000
	108 666
Overseas Inc.	
Share of post-acquisition reserves at 1.1.19X2 including exchange	
differences on net assets since acquisition, 80% of £80 000 (*see* E)	64 000
	172 666

J. We are now in a position to consolidate:

Home Country plc
Workings for consolidated profit and loss account for the year to 31 December 19X2

Profit before taxation		
Home Country plc	112 000	
Overseas Inc.	100 000	212 000
less Taxation		
Home Country plc	60 000	
Overseas Inc.	50 000	110 000
		102 000
less Minority interest, 20% of (£100 000 – £50 000)		10 000
		92 000
add Extraordinary profit after tax		
Home Country plc	5 000	
Overseas Inc. net of minority interest, 80% of £10 000	8 000	13 000
		105 000
less Dividends payable by parent company		30 000
Retained profit for the year		75 000

Workings for movement on reserves for year to 31 December 19X2

	£	£
Balance on 1 January 19X2 (per I above)		172 666
Retained profit for year – per consolidated profit and loss account above		75 000
Exchange gain (per H above)		
Gain on net assets	40 000	
less Loss on foreign currency borrowings	33 333	6 667
Balance on 31 December 19X2		254 333

Workings for consolidated balance sheet on 31 December 19X2

	£	£
Fixed assets		
Tangible assets – at net book value		
Home Country plc	400 000	
Overseas Inc. (*see* note (a))	320 000	720 000
Intangible assets		
Goodwill on consolidation – at cost per analysis of equity interest (*see* G)		44 000
Net current assets (*see* note (b))		
Home Country plc	51 666	
Overseas Inc.	120 000	171 666
		935 666
less Long-term loans		
Home Country plc	233 333	
Overseas Inc.	200 000	433 333
		502 333

	£
Share capital	200 000
Reserves – as above	254 333
	454 333
Minority interest, per analysis of equity interest	48 000
	502 333

Notes
(a) Note that the revalued amount of the fixed assets of Overseas Inc. at the date of acquisition represents 'cost' to the group.
(b) An adjustment is necessary to cancel out the dividend receivable by Home Country plc. The amount is £16 000 but the effect on the total net current assets is, of course, nil.

It is now relatively straightforward to prepare the consolidated accounts for publication in the normal manner, although a greater amount of detail would be necessary to satisfy the disclosure requirements of company law and accounting standards. In order to simplify the example, goodwill on consolidation has not been written off.

RECOMMENDED READING

I. J. Martin, *Accounting and Control in the Foreign Exchange Market*, 2nd edition, Butterworths, London, 1993.

C. Nobes, 'A review of the translation debate', *Accounting and Business Research Number 40*, ICAEW, London, Autumn 1980.

J. Percy, *How to Account for Foreign Currencies*, Macmillan, Basingstoke, 1984.

L. Revsine, 'The rationale underlying the functional currency choice', in *Accounting Theory and Policy*, R. Bloom and P. T. Elgers (eds), Harcourt Brace Jovanovich, Orlando USA, 1987.

P. Wallace and B. D. G. Ogle, 'Foreign currency translation', *Accountants Digest Number 150*, ICAEW, London, 1983/84.

C. A. Westwick, *Accounting for Overseas Operations*, Gower, Aldershot, 1986.

CHAPTER 11

Expansion of the annual report

INTRODUCTION

The published annual reports of companies frequently include reports and statements other than those required by law. While some of these may be required by accounting standard, others are supplied voluntarily. The best example of a statement required by accounting standard is the cash flow statement, while some examples of statements which are frequently supplied voluntarily by large and listed companies, are the chairman's statement, the highlights statement and the historical summary. The first of these voluntary statements provides users with a review of the year's performance and sometimes includes an indication of future prospects, the second usually presents a comparison of certain key figures for the current and previous year and the Historical Summary provides a table of comparative figures for some five or more years. Less frequently included examples are the value added statement[1] and the employment report. In addition, many companies produce a separate simplified report which may be intended for either shareholders or employees but may be a general purpose statement not aimed at any group of users in particular. Since 1989, company law actually permits listed companies to prepare and distribute a Summary Financial Statement to shareholders who do not wish to receive the full accounts of the company.

In broad terms the objectives of most additional statements are the same – to assist users of accounts to obtain a more comprehensive view of the progress and future prospects of the company. This broad objective can be served in a number of ways and it is helpful to have a framework within which the statements can be analysed. Essentially the statements can be seen as constituting two groups depending on whether a statement:

(a) provides more data than is required by company law, or
(b) does not provide additional data but makes it easier to assimilate the data either by rearrangement of the figures or through the provision of simplified statements.

We might usefully refer to the first group as 'extended' statements and the second as 'rearranged and simplified' statements.

Extended statements include such documents as the Cash Flow Statement and Employment Report as well as any Operating and Financial Review.[2]

Rearranged and simplified statements can be derived from the published accounts of the company, except in the case of smaller companies, and include such documents as the Value Added Statement, the simplified report to employees and the Summary Financial Statement which may be sent to the shareholders of listed companies.

1 This Value Added Statement, which is discussed later in the chapter, should not be confused with Value Added Tax.
2 See the Statement 'Operating and Financial Review', ASB, London, July 1993.

It is interesting to question why companies should be required or choose to publish such rearranged and simplified statements. In part the reason may be behavioural in the sense that the publication of the document is intended to create better relations with employees and the community in general. Such an objective is clearly present in the case of simplified accounts prepared especially for employees. Another possible reason is the wish to remove the 'competitive advantage' possessed by investors and potential investors who have technical knowledge themselves or have ready access to professional advice.[3]

On the professional front, the first major developments in the drive towards the expansion of the annual report came in 1975 when the Accounting Standards Steering Committee issued both SSAP 10, 'Statements of source and application of funds' and *The Corporate Report*.[4] SSAP 10 required all but very small enterprises to prepare a statement of source and application of funds as part of their audited financial accounts. As discussed below, it has now been superseded by FRS 1, 'Cash Flow Statements'. *The Corporate Report*, which was issued as a discussion paper, argued that the then current reporting practices did not fully meet the needs of the various users of accounts and recommended that all significant economic entities should publish the following additional statements:

(a) A statement of value added
(b) An employment report
(c) A statement of money exchanges with government
(d) A statement of transactions in foreign currency
(e) A statement of future prospects
(f) A statement of corporate objectives.

The adoption of these recommendations would have resulted in the provision of substantially more information than that provided by the statutory financial accounts. While *The Corporate Report* remains an important document worthy of study, none of these recommendations have in fact been adopted by the ASC or ASB.

These professional initiatives were followed by two Green Papers.[5] The first, issued by a Labour administration in 1977 proposed that, for larger companies, substantial additional disclosure be provided. Thus it envisaged that the law should be changed to require more comprehensive financial statements including an added value statement, an employment statement, an international trade statement and more disaggregated information.

The second Green Paper, which was produced by a Conservative administration in 1979, proposed a three-tier classification of companies based on size and recommended that disclosure requirements should differ between tiers. It proposed that there should be a significant reduction in the amount of information to be disclosed by the smaller bottom-tier companies but an increase in the amount of information to be disclosed by the top tier, that is by large and listed companies. Although it supported experimentation with new statements by the accountancy profession, it did not envisage that the law should be changed to require these statements.

---

3 Supporters of the 'efficient market hypothesis' which, in its semistrong form, states that all available data relevant to the price of a share is immediately reflected in the market price, would presumably take the view that there is nothing to be gained from any requirement for companies to publish otherwise available data in a different form.

4 *The Corporate Report*, Accounting Standards Steering Committee, London, 1975.

5 'The future of company reports', Cmnd 6888, HMSO, London, 1977 and 'Company accounting and disclosure', Cmnd 7654, HMSO, London, 1979.

It was perhaps not surprising to find that the 1979 Green Paper was so opposed to the introduction of legal requirements for new accounting statements. Any such legal requirements would have sat uneasily with the philosophy of a government committed to deregulation and reducing the regulatory and administrative burdens on business.[6]

As we have seen in Chapter 2, as a result of implementing the EC Fourth Directive, UK company law now includes a three-tier classification of companies and disclosure requirements do differ between the tiers. The law also requires the provision of certain disaggregated information and, for larger companies, this requirement has been increased by SSAP 25 'Segmental reporting'.[7]

Even without legislative requirements, it is clear that the accountant must develop competence in producing and interpreting statements other than the traditional balance sheet and profit and loss account. This chapter concentrates on two of these, the Cash Flow Statement and the Value Added Statement. It then examines more briefly the historical summary, the subject of reporting about and to employees and finally the summary financial statement which listed companies may send to their shareholders.

CASH FLOW STATEMENTS

Background

It has long been recognised that the information provided by a balance sheet and profit and loss account gives users limited help in understanding how the liquidity of a company or group has been affected by its activities during a particular year. To remedy this, accounting standard setters in many countries have required companies to prepare 'funds statements', that is statements showing the sources and applications of funds. In the UK, SSAP 10 'Statement of source and application of funds' was first issued in July 1975 and required all companies with a turnover or gross income of £25 000 or greater to prepare such a statement.

One of the first difficulties which companies encountered in complying with SSAP 10 was that, although the statement defined net liquid funds as one component of funds, it did not actually define the term funds. As with profit, there are many possible definitions of funds including cash, working capital and all financial resources. The choice of definition determines what the statement seeks to explain and hence what is shown as a source or application. To take a simple example, the receipt of cash from debtors is a source of funds if the cash concept is adopted but merely a change in the constituent parts of funds if the working capital concept is used. As a second example, the issue of shares in exchange for the purchase of fixed assets, is neither a source nor an application if either the cash or working capital concepts are used, but it certainly changes the financial resources of a company.

In the USA, the funds statement had long been the subject of criticism[8] and, in November 1987, the FASB replaced the requirement for US companies to produce a funds statement with a requirement for them to produce a statement of cash flows.

---

6 *See*, for example, the White Papers 'Lifting the burden', Cmnd 9571 (1985) and 'Building business … not barriers', Cmnd 9794 (1986).
7 *See* Chapter 13.
8 *See*, for example, Loyd C. Heath 'Let's scrap the funds statement', *Journal of Accountancy*, October 1978.

Statement of Financial Accounting Standards number 95, 'Statement of cash flows', now requires relevant US companies to prepare a statement explaining the change in cash and cash equivalents by showing cash receipts and payments.

The ASC drew heavily on the US standard in preparing ED 54 'Cash flow statements' in 1990 and the ASB refined ED 54 to produce its first standard, FRS 1 'Cash flow statements' in September 1991. As a consequence relevant UK entities must now prepare a cash flow statement rather than a statement of source and application of funds.

The standard applies to all financial statements intended to give a true and fair view of the financial position and profit or loss except those of the following entities[9]:

(a) companies entitled to the small companies exemptions when filing accounts with the Registrar of Companies
(b) entities which would be so entitled if they had been incorporated under companies legislation
(c) wholly owned subsidiary undertakings of an EU parent undertaking provided the parent publishes appropriate consolidated financial statements in English which include a consolidated cash flow statement enabling a user to derive the totals of the amounts to be shown under each of the standard headings of FRS 1
(d) building societies which prepare a statement of source and application of funds in a prescribed format
(e) mutual life assurance companies.

We now turn to the preparation of a cash flow statement for a single company.

FRS 1 and the single company

The purpose of the cash flow statement is clear – to show the sources and uses of cash and cash equivalents during an accounting period. Cash and cash equivalents are defined as follows:

Cash

Cash in hand and deposits repayable on demand with any bank or other financial institution. Cash includes cash in hand and deposits denominated in foreign currencies (Para. 2).

Cash equivalents

Short-term, highly liquid investments which are readily convertible into known amounts of cash without notice and which were within three months of maturity when acquired; less advances from banks repayable within three months from the date of the advance. Cash equivalents include investments and advances denominated in foreign currencies provided that they fulfil the above criteria (Para. 3).

The inclusion of cash equivalents recognises that many companies invest surplus cash for short periods. The limitations of these to investments purchased within three months of

9 FRS 1, Para. 8.

maturity is an attempt to ensure that the amounts receivable are not subject to fluctuations in value due to interest rate changes.[10]

The cash flow statement is a statement of cash receipts and payments but, in order to achieve a consistent format to permit inter-company comparisons, FRS 1 requires that cash flows are classified under five standard headings:

Net cash flow from operating activities	X
Returns on investments and servicing of finance	X
Taxation	X
Investing activities	X
Net cash inflow (outflow) before financing	X
Financing activities	X
Change in cash and cash equivalents	X

Although it does not require a sub-total before investing activities, the standard specifically requires a sub-total before financing activities, as shown above.

We shall now look at the cash flows to be included under each of the five standard headings.

Net cash flow from operating activities

The net cash flow from operating activities is the cash flow relating to all those activities which are included in arriving at the operating profit of the entity. It may be calculated by the direct method (the gross method) or the indirect method (the net method) although only the resulting figure should be disclosed in the cash flow statement.

Direct method	
Cash receipts from customers	X
Cash payments to suppliers	(x)
Cash payments to and on behalf of employees	(x)
Net cash flow from operating activities	X

Indirect method	
Operating profit	X
Adjustments for items not involving a flow of cash:	
Depreciation	X
Profit on disposal of fixed asset	(x)
Increase in stocks	(x)
Increase in debtors relating to operating activities	(x)
Increase in creditors relating to operating activities	X
Net cash flow from operating activities	X

---

10 Some companies have criticised this definition of cash equivalents as being too narrow. They argue that treasury maturity horizons are frequently longer than three months. They also argue that companies borrow for the short term by issuing commercial paper, which does not qualify for inclusion as it is not an advance from a bank.

The direct method is undoubtedly easier for a non-accountant to understand but requires information which has traditionally not been provided by many companies' accounting systems. The indirect method effectively reverses all the accruals adjustments which have been made in arriving at operating profit and follows more closely the approach which has been taken previously in preparing statements of source and application of funds.

FRS 1 actually requires companies to prepare a note to the statement showing the calculations using the indirect method, thus providing a reconciliation of operating profit and net cash flow from operating activities. Sensibly this reconciliation, which can be extremely confusing for non-accountants, is not included in the main body of the statement.

The standard encourages companies to provide the information using the direct method where the benefits to users of the information outweigh the costs of providing it (Para. 70) but, on the basis of experience in the USA, we are unlikely to see many notes showing the cash flows using this direct method.[11]

Returns on investments and servicing of finance

FRS 1 requires us to separate returns on investments and payments to service financing from the capital flows to which they relate. The cash flows under this heading should therefore include the following items:

- Interest received, including any related tax recovered.
- Interest paid, including any tax deducted therefrom and paid to the relevant tax authority. The standard specifically requires the inclusion of interest paid even if it is capitalised and, of course, requires the inclusion of the interest element of finance lease payments.
- Dividends received, net of tax credits.
- Dividends paid, excluding any advance corporation tax.

Under this approach, consistent treatment of receipts and payments is achieved.

Taxation

The only amounts to be included under this heading are payments and receipts relating to tax on the company's revenue and capital profits. Thus this heading typically comprises payments of corporation tax and advance corporation tax.

Taxes for which the company acts as a collecting agent for the government, such as VAT, would normally be dealt with as part of the operating activities of the company. Cash flows would then be shown net of any VAT and an adjustment would be made to reflect the change in the amount payable to or recoverable from the government.

Investing activities

This heading comprises payments to acquire fixed assets or investments in other entities as well as receipts from the sale of fixed assets and investments.[12] Given that interest paid

---

11 SFAS 95 permits the presentation of the net cash flow from operating activities using either the direct method or the indirect method. However, according to recent AICPA surveys of accounting practices in the USA, only some 3 per cent of US companies surveyed actually used the direct method.

12 We shall look at the treatment of subsidiary and associated undertakings in the next section of this chapter.

which has been capitalised is included under 'Returns on investments and servicing of financing' above, it will not be included as part of the payment for the related fixed asset.

Financing activities

This heading embraces receipts from providers of finance and repayments of such finance:

- Receipts from issue of shares.
- Receipts from long-term and short-term borrowings, excluding those classified as cash equivalents.
- Payments to purchase or redeem share capital.
- Repayments of loans, except those classified as cash equivalents.
- Capital element of finance lease rental payments.

With this summary of the cash flows to be included under each heading, we are in a position to look at an example. Before we do so, we should recognise that the standard requires that the cash flow statement is supplemented by at least three notes, reconciling amounts shown in the cash flow statement with the company's profit and loss account and balance sheets:

(a) The first note should reconcile the operating profit to net cash flow from operating activities. In other words it is the net cash inflow from operating activities calculated using the indirect or net approach which we have discussed above.
(b) A second note should reconcile the change in cash and cash equivalents with the relevant opening and closing balance sheets. This may sometimes become complicated where several balance sheet items, or parts thereof, have been combined to arrive at cash and cash equivalents.
(c) The third note requires a reconciliation of the receipts and payments in the financing section of the cash flow statement with the related opening and closing balance sheet amounts.

We shall illustrate each of these notes in the following example.

EXAMPLE 11.1

Summarised accounts of a manufacturing company, Kamina plc, for the year ended 31 December 19X2, together with an opening balance sheet, are given below. The two right-hand columns by the balance sheet merely list differences between the opening and closing balances. The + column contains increases in assets and reductions in liabilities, while the − column contains reductions in assets and increases in both liabilities and the shareholders' interest.

Balance sheets on 31 December 19X1 and 19X2

	19X1	19X2	Change	
			+	−
	£000s	£000s	£000s	£000s
Fixed assets at net book value: (note (i))				
Freehold properties	800	1 140	340	
Plant and machinery	1 100	1 400	300	
Carried forward	1 900	2 540	640	

	19X1	19X2	Change +	Change −
	£000s	£000s	£000s	£000s
Brought forward	1 900	2 540	640	−
Current assets				
Stock	1 100	1 680	580	
Debtors (note (ii))	640	980	340	
Cash at bank	200	−		200
	1 940	2 660		
less Short-term creditors				
Bank overdraft	−	85		85
Creditors (note (iii))	685	890		205
Taxation payable (note (iv))	225	285		60
Proposed dividend	120	160		40
	1 030	1 420		
Net current assets	910	1 240		
	2 810	3 780		
less Long-term loans (note (v))	600	1 000		400
	2 210	2 780		
less Deferred taxation (note (vi))	380	479		99
	1 830	2 301		
Share capital and reserves				
£1 ordinary shares (note (vii))	1 000	1 100		100
Share premium (note (vii))	200	300		100
Retained profits	630	901		271
	1 830	2 301	1 560	1 560

Profit and loss account for the year ended 31 December 19X2

	£000s	£000s
Turnover		6 250
Cost of sales		3 750
Gross profit		2 500
Distribution costs	615	
Administrative expenses	1 047	1 662
Operating profit		838
Profit on sale of freehold property		40
		878
Interest payable (note (viii))		98
Profit on ordinary activities before tax		780
Taxation		
Corporation tax	180	
Deferred tax	109	289
Profit on ordinary activities after tax		491
less Dividends		
Paid	60	
Proposed	160	220
Retained profit for the year		271

The following information is relevant:
(i)   Fixed asset movements

	Freehold properties £000s	Plant and machinery £000s
Cost		
On 1 January 19X2	1 000	2 000
Additions	440	720
Disposal	(60)	–
On 31 December 19X2	1 380	2 720
Depreciation		
On 1 January 19X2	200	900
Disposal	(10)	–
Profit & loss account charge	50	420
On 31 December 19X2	240	1 320
Net book value	1 140	1 400

(ii)   A freehold property was sold for £90 000 and, at 31 December 19X2, £75 000 of this amount is included in debtors.
(iii)   Short-term creditors have been analysed as follows:

	31.12.X1 £000s	31.12.X2 £000s
Interest payable – £600 000 11% loan	33	33
£400 000 10% loan	–	10
Creditor for purchase of machinery	40	60
Trade and expense creditors	612	787
	685	890

(iv)   Taxation payable has been analysed as follows:

	31.12.X1 £000s	31.12.X2 £000s
Corporation tax payable		
30 September 19X2	120	–
30 September 19X3	–	135
Advance corporation tax payable on		
proposed dividend*	30	40
	150	175
Value added tax	75	110
	225	285

* The ACT rate is 25 per cent of the distribution.

(v) Long-term loans

	31.12.X1 £000s	31.12.X2 £000s
11% loan	600	600
10% loan raised 1 April 19X2	–	400
	600	1 000

Interest on the 11 per cent loan is payable annually on 30 June while interest on the new 10 per cent loan is payable half yearly on 30 September and 31 March.

(vi) Deferred taxation

	31.12.X1 £000s	31.12.X2 £000s
Deferred taxation on timing differences other than chargeable gain	410	533
less ACT recoverable	30	40
	380	493
Deferred taxation on chargeable gain on sale of property	–	14
	380	479

(vii) Share issues

40 000 £1 ordinary shares were issued for cash of £80 000 on 5 December 19X2 while a further 60 000 £1 ordinary shares were issued on 12 December 19X2 to acquire a freehold property valued at £120 000.

(viii) Interest payable is made up as follows:

	£000s
Interest on long-term loans	
11% loan	66
10% loan (from 1 April X2 to 31 December X2)	30
	96
Interest paid on bank overdraft	2
	98

We shall now examine the workings for this example in detail.

(A) Change in cash and cash equivalents

	£000s
Cash at bank on 1 January 19X2	200
Bank overdraft on 31 December 19X2	85
Decrease in cash and cash equivalents	285

(B) Net cash inflow from operating activities using indirect method:

	£000s	£000s
Operating profit		838
Adjustments:		
Depreciation – freehold buildings (note (i))	50	
– plant & machinery (note (i))	420	470
Increase in stocks		(580)
Increase in debtors from operating activities:		
per balance sheet on 31 December 19X2	980	
less debtor for sale of property (note (ii))	75	
	905	
per balance sheet on 31 December 19X1	640	(265)
Increase in creditors from operating activities:		
Trade and expense creditors per note (iii) (787 – 612)	175	
VAT per note (iv) (110 – 75)	35	210
Net cash inflow		673

Note: It is not necessary to deduct the profit on sale of the freehold property as this has not been included in arriving at the operating profit shown in the profit and loss account.

(C) Returns on investments and servicing of financing

	£000s	£000s
Interest paid (see notes (v) and (viii))		
On £600,000 11% loan		
Amount paid 30 June 19X2	66	
(Check 33 000+66 000–33 000)		
On £400 000 10% loan		
Amount paid 30 September 19X2		
$\frac{1}{2}$ x 10% x 400 000	20	
(Check 0+30 000–10 000)		
On bank overdraft	2	
		88
Dividends paid		
Final for 19X1	120	
Interim for 19X2	60	180
Payments		268

(D) Taxation – corporation tax and ACT

	£000s	£000s
Corporation tax paid 30 September 19X2		120
Advance corporation tax paid re:		
Final dividend for 19X1	30	
Interim dividend for 19X2	15	45
		165

Check:	£000s
Opening creditor per note (iv)	150
less ACT recoverable	30
	120
Profit and loss account charge	180
	300
less closing creditor net of ACT recoverable	
(175 000 – 40 000)	135
	165

(E)   Investing activities

	£000s	£000s
Purchases of fixed assets using cash		
Freehold properties – additions per note (i)	440	
less Purchased by means of share issue per note (vii)	120	
Cash purchases		(320)
Plant and machinery – additions per note (i)	720	
less Increase in creditors for plant and machinery		
purchases per note (iii) (60 000 – 40 000)	20	
Cash purchases		(700)
		(1020)
Sale of fixed assets – freehold property		
Net book value per note (i)		
(60 000 – 10 000)	50	
add Profit on disposal – per profit		
& loss account	40	
Proceeds as given in note (ii)	90	
less Debtor at 31 December 19X2	75	15
		(1005)

(F)   Financing activities

	£000s
Issue of ordinary shares for cash per note (vii)	80
New long-term loan – per note (v)	400
	480

We are now in a position to prepare the cash flow statement and accompanying notes.

Kamina plc
Cash flow statement for the year ended 31 December 19X2

	£000s	£000s
Net cash inflow from operating activities		673
Returns on investments and servicing of finance		
Interest paid	(88)	
Dividends paid	(180)	(268)
Taxation		
Corporation tax paid (including ACT)		(165)
Investing activities		
Payments to acquire fixed assets	(1020)	
Receipts from sale of fixed assets	15	(1005)
Net cash outflow before financing		(765)
Financing activities		
Issue of ordinary shares	80	
New long-term loan	400	480
Decrease in cash and cash equivalents		(285)

Notes to the cash flow statement

1 Reconciliation of operating profit to net cash inflow from operating activities

	£000s
Operating profit	838
Depreciation	470
Increase in stocks	(580)
Increase in debtors	(265)
Increase in creditors	210
Net cash inflow from operating activities	673

2 Reconciliation of changes in cash and cash equivalents with balance sheet

	£000s
Cash at bank on 31 December 19X1	200
Net cash outflow per cash flow statement	(285)
Bank overdraft on 31 December 19X2	(85)

3 Analysis of changes in financing during year

	Share capital including premium	Long-term loans
	£000s	£000s
Financing at 31 December 19X1	1 200	600
Cash inflows from financing	80	400
Proceeds of issue of shares to acquire freehold property	120	–
Financing at 31 December 19X2	1 400	1 000

The cash flow statement which we have prepared shows that, although the company has a positive net cash inflow from operating activities, there has been a net cash outflow before financing of £765 000. Of this, £480 000 has been covered by new finance raised but the remainder, £285 000, resulted in a fall in the cash balances of the company.

While FRS 1 specifically requires the disclosure of a sub-total before financing activities, the authors consider that it would be helpful for companies to disclose a sub-total after taxation, thus showing the net cash flow before both investing and financing activities. In the case of the above total the relevant sub-total would be a net cash inflow of £240 000 calculated as follows:

	£000s
Net cash inflow from operating activities	673
Returns on investments and servicing of finance	(268)
Taxation	(165)
Net cash inflow before investing and financing activities	240

Now that we have explored the preparation of a cash flow statement for a single company, we turn to the additional complications posed by the existence of subsidiary and associated undertakings and foreign currencies.

GROUPS, ASSOCIATED UNDERTAKINGS AND JOINT VENTURES

Groups

Where a company has subsidiary undertakings and prepares consolidated financial statements, it must prepare a cash flow statement which reflects the cash flows of the group.[13]

Following the normal consolidation techniques of acquisition accounting, which we have discussed in Chapters 8 and 9, a consolidated balance sheet includes the whole of the assets and liabilities of the parent undertaking and subsidiary undertakings even when those subsidiary undertakings are only partly owned. The cash flow statement will therefore explain changes in the cash and cash equivalents of all the undertakings in the group as shown in the consolidated balance sheets. Intercompany cash flows, resulting from sales, management charges or dividend payments between group companies, are irrelevant although dividends paid to any minority interests will, of course, be shown as a payment under the heading 'Returns on investments and servicing of finance'.

Where the parent company uses the direct or gross method to determine the cash flows from operating activities of the group, it will be necessary to introduce a system to collect the relevant information from subsidiaries and to ensure that intergroup cash flows are eliminated. Where the indirect or net method is used, it will be possible to rely largely on the adjustments made during the consolidation process although, even in this case, certain additional information will be necessary. Examples of such additional information are analyses of group debtors and creditors so that those relating to operating transactions can be identified and included while those relating to non-operating transactions can be

---

13 A parent company which is itself a wholly owned subsidiary of an EU parent undertaking does not have to provide such a cash flow statement if the parent prepares consolidated financial statements, which include a cash flow statement, in English.

dealt with in computing receipts and payments included under the other headings in the cash flow statement.

When a company acquires a new subsidiary undertaking and acquisition accounting is used, the consolidated profit and loss account will include the profits or losses of that new subsidiary from the date of acquisition to the end of the period and the consolidated balance sheet will include the whole of the assets and liabilities of the subsidiary, whether it is wholly or partly owned.[14] It follows that when we try to determine the reasons for differences between items in the opening and closing balance sheets, we find that part of the change will be due to the assets, liabilities and any minority interest of the subsidiary undertaking at the date of acquisition as well as to the payment made to acquire the subsidiary. So, for example, if we focus on the change in cash and cash equivalents between the beginning and end of the year, we find that part of the change is due to any cash payment made by the parent company to acquire the new subsidiary while a further part is due to the balance of cash and cash equivalents held by the subsidiary at the date of acquisition. The cash payment which must be shown in respect of the purchase of subsidiary undertakings under the heading 'Investing activities' is therefore calculated as follows:

	£000s
Cash consideration paid	X
less Cash and cash equivalents of subsidiary undertakings at date of acquisition	X
Cash payment	X

Where a subsidiary is acquired for a consideration other than cash, all that will appear in the cash flow statement will be the cash and cash equivalents of the subsidiary at the date of acquisition.

To enable users to understand what has happened, it is necessary to provide a note to the cash flow statement showing a breakdown of the assets and liabilities acquired together with the consideration paid. Such a note would take the following form:

Purchase of subsidiary undertakings

	£000
Net assets acquired:	
Tangible fixed assets	16 000
Investments	40
Stocks	13 000
Debtors	5 000
Cash at bank and in hand	2 500
Bank overdrafts	(1 000)
Other creditors	(5 500)
Loans	(3 000)
Minority interests	(40)
	27 000
Goodwill	3 000
	30 000

---

14 *See* Chapter 9.

Satisfied by:

Shares allotted	25 000
Cash	5 000
	30 000

Analysis of net outflow of cash and cash equivalents in respect of the purchase of subsidiary undertakings

	£000	£000
Cash consideration		5 000
Cash and cash equivalents[15] acquired		
Cash at bank and in hand	2 500	
Bank overdraft	1 000	1 500
Net payment		3 500

When a group disposes of a subsidiary undertaking the converse is the case. Any cash proceeds from the sale of shares in the subsidiary less any positive balance of cash and cash equivalents of the subsidiary at the date of disposal will be recorded as a cash receipt under the heading 'Investing Activities'. A note to the statement should then provide a list of the assets and liabilities of the subsidiary at the date of disposal together with the proceeds received and any profit or loss on disposal:

	£000
Net assets disposed of:	
Tangible fixed assets	5 000
Stocks	2 000
Debtors	3 000
Cash and cash equivalents	1 000
Creditors	(4 000)
	7 000
Profit on disposal	1 000
	8 000
Satisfied by:	
Loan stock	4 000
Cash	4 000
	8 000

The net cash receipt from disposal of subsidiary would be:

Cash received	4 000
less Cash and cash equivalents of subsidiary sold	1 000
	3 000

15 It is assumed that there are no cash or cash equivalents other than cash at bank and in hand and the bank overdraft.

Associated undertakings and joint ventures

When an investing company purchases or sells its interest in an associated undertaking or joint venture, any payment or receipt of cash will be included under the heading 'Investing activities'.

As we have seen in Chapter 9, standard accounting practice requires the use of the equity method of accounting for associated undertakings and incorporated joint ventures although it permits the use of proportional consolidation for unincorporated joint ventures.

Under the equity method of accounting, an investing company takes credit in its consolidated profit and loss account for its full share of the profits or losses of the associated undertaking or joint venture. The consolidated balance sheet includes the investment but the individual assets and liabilities do not include relevant amounts in respect of the associated undertaking. Hence cash and cash equivalents in the opening and closing consolidated balance sheets do not include the respective amounts for the associated undertaking.

Apart from the purchase and sale of an investment and, perhaps the making and repayment of a loan, the only recurrent receipt from an associated undertaking or incorporated joint venture, will be the dividend received. This should be shown as a receipt under the heading 'Returns on investments and servicing of finance' and should be separately disclosed in accordance with paragraph 19(b) of the standard.

Where an investing company uses proportional consolidation to account for an unincorporated joint venture, the position is a little different. Assets and liabilities shown in the opening and closing consolidated balance sheets will include the shares of the cash and cash equivalents of the joint venture. Hence the share of the cash flows of that joint venture must be included as receipts and payments in order to explain fully the change disclosed by comparing opening and closing balance sheet amounts. The net cash flow from operating activities must therefore include the share of cash flows of the joint venture as must the other headings of the cash flow statement.

As explained in Chapter 9, at present a company may use either the equity method or proportional consolidation for an unincorporated joint venture. Although the choice between methods has no impact on the ultimate profit or loss included, the impact of the choice on the cash flow statement could be important.

Foreign currency differences

As we have seen in Chapter 10, exchange differences frequently arise both when a company engages in foreign transactions and when the accounts of an overseas entity are translated prior to the preparation of consolidated financial statements. We shall examine the treatment of such differences in the preparation of a cash flow statement. Where a company enters into a foreign currency transaction then, unless there is an agreed rate for settlement or a forward exchange contract, the foreign currency amount will be translated into sterling at the rate on the transaction date. Any difference arising on monetary items between the date of the transaction and the date of settlement will be taken to the profit and loss account as part of the operating profit. Where a debtor or creditor is outstanding at a balance sheet date, the foreign currency amount will be retranslated at the closing rate and again any resulting difference on exchange will be taken to the profit and loss account as part of operating profit.

As far as the cash flow statement is concerned, the cash flows to creditors or from debtors are the amounts actually paid and received in sterling and, if a company wishes to use the direct method to calculate the cash flow from operations, it must ensure that it has an adequate accounting system in place to collect this information. However, it is possible to use the indirect method although it will then be necessary to analyse the difference on exchange which has been included in arriving at operating profit. To the extent that the differences on exchange relate to operating activities, no adjustment is necessary. However, to the extent that differences relate to other activities, such as the purchase of fixed assets on credit or the retranslation of a foreign currency loan, this must be removed from the operating profit to arrive at the net cash flow from operating activities.

To illustrate, let us take examples of a settled transaction and an unsettled transaction respectively. A company makes a purchase from an overseas supplier which is recorded in the accounting records at a sterling amount of £15 000. During the same accounting period settlement is made of £16 500 resulting in a loss on exchange of £1500, which is deducted in arriving at the operating profit shown in the profit and loss account. The cash payment is, of course, £16 500 and this is the amount which has been deducted in arriving at operating profit, albeit in two parts:

	£
Purchase	15 000
Loss on exchange	1 500
	16 500

Turning to an example of an unsettled transaction, let us assume that a company makes a sale, denominated in foreign currency, to an overseas customer and that the foreign currency amount invoiced is translated at £24 000. If the amount is still due at the ensuing balance sheet date, it will be translated at the closing rate of exchange to produce a different amount of, say, £26 000. The gain on exchange of £2000 will be credited to the profit and loss account in arriving at the operating profit.

As far as the cash flow statement is concerned, there has been no receipt. If we take the operating profit and make the usual adjustment for the change in debtors, this is exactly what will be included in the net cash flow from operating activities:

	£
Operating profit (including gain on exchange)	
Sale	24 000
Gain on exchange	2 000
	26 000
less Increase in debtors	26 000
Cash flow from this transaction	–

Whereas no adjustment is necessary in respect of exchange differences relating to operating activities such as purchases and sales, adjustments to the operating profit will be necessary in respect of other exchange differences. So, for example, an exchange difference relating to the purchase of a fixed asset on credit or the retranslation of a long-term loan must feature as an adjustment in moving from operating profit to net cash flow from operating activities. In the latter case the exchange difference will also have to be included in the note reconciling the opening balance sheet value of the loan with its closing balance sheet value.

Let us now turn to the translation of the accounts of a foreign subsidiary or associated undertaking. Here FRS 1 makes it clear what should be done.[16]

> Where a portion of a reporting entity's business is undertaken by a foreign entity, the cash flows of that entity are to be included in the cash flow statement on the basis used for translating the results of those activities in the profit and loss account of the reporting entity.

The vast majority of companies in the UK use the closing rate/net investment method under which profit and loss account items are translated at average or closing rate and assets and liabilities in the balance sheet are translated at the closing rate. Differences on exchange are taken to reserves and these will relate to opening assets and liabilities and, where an average rate is used in the profit and loss account, to the increase in net assets which has occurred during the year. Such differences thus explain changes in the balance sheet amounts including the change in cash and cash equivalents. The relevant parts of these differences on exchange must be included in the note reconciling opening and closing amounts for cash and cash equivalents. Similarly the relevant parts of the difference on exchange must be included in the note reconciling opening and closing share capital and loans. The parts of the difference relating to such items as opening fixed assets, stocks, debtors, and creditors will, of course, appear in relevant notes to the accounts but do not represent any receipt or payment of cash.

Where a company uses the temporal method of translation, exchange differences are taken to the consolidated profit and loss account and their treatment in preparing the cash flow statement will be exactly the same as that explained above for foreign currency transactions entered into by the company itself. After all, the purpose of the temporal method is to translate the foreign currency financial statements in such a way that the result is the same as if the investing company had itself entered into the transactions undertaken by the foreign entity.

Usefulness and deficiencies of the cash flow statement

Now that we have explored the preparation of the cash flow statement, it is time to explore briefly the usefulness and deficiencies of that statement.

As we have seen in Chapter 1, most users are concerned with the future performance of an entity and turn to the financial statements, as well as to other sources, for help in making a judgement about likely future performance. In assessing the cash flow statement, it is therefore necessary to ask how it helps users in this task.

The statement supplements the traditional accounts by focusing on changes in cash and cash equivalents in a way which provides answers to many pertinent questions which a user might wish to ask. Examples of such questions are as follows: Has there been an increase or decrease in cash balances? To what extent has cash been generated by operations of the company? Are payments of interest, dividends and taxation covered by the net cash generated by operating activities? Has cash been used to finance the purchase of fixed assets?

Answers to such questions as these undoubtedly help users to assess what has happened and what is likely to happen to the entity in future. However, like all the figures shown in a set of accounts, they cannot be used in isolation but must be interpreted as part of the whole collection of information. This may be illustrated by just one example.

16 FRS 1, Para. 36.

When a user looks at the relationship between receipts from long-term loans and the purchase of fixed assets, it is essential to bear in mind the position shown in the opening and closing balance sheets. Thus a failure of long-term loans to cover purchase of fixed assets in a particular year may merely reflect the fact that there were large cash balances at the opening balance sheet date, cash balances which have now been reduced to more appropriate levels.

While cash flow statements are still in their infancy, it is possible to make certain criticisms of FRS 1. Whereas a statement of cash receipts and payments would be easily understandable, the requirement to include both receipts and payments under the same heading frequently results in a statement which is riddled with brackets and therefore difficult to understand. The failure to require a sub-total before the heading 'Investing activities' means that it is not apparent, without additional work being done by the user, whether the net cash outflows on the servicing of finance and taxation are covered by the net cash flow from operating activities.

It is possible to make more technical criticisms about, for example, the definition of cash equivalents or the lack of guidance on the treatment of cash flows of an operating nature which are not charged in arriving at the operating profit for a period. An example of the latter is capitalised development expenditure. However, there is no doubt in the minds of the authors that the cash flow statement is an enormous improvement over its predecessor, the statement of source and application of funds.

THE VALUE ADDED STATEMENT

Background

As we have seen in the introduction to this chapter, *The Corporate Report* recommended that all significant economic entities should publish a value added statement as part of their annual accounts. Contrary to the traditional legal position, but in keeping with many current organisational theories, such a statement regards the entity as being operated by and for the benefit of a team of interests. Such a team is usually taken to include employees, suppliers of long-term capital and the government but to exclude other firms which supply goods and services. Thus, whereas the profit and loss account has traditionally shown the profit or loss of a period from the point of view of the equity shareholders, the value added statement shows the income of the larger entity and how this has been divided between the wider team of contributors.

The concept of value added

Once the team has been specified, the value added may be calculated as the difference between the value of the goods or services produced by the team, i.e. sales revenue, less the value of the goods and services purchased from outsiders, i.e. the cost of bought-in materials and services.

The value added statement is normally in two parts, the first of which shows the value added by the team while the second shows how that value added has been divided between the team members. The illustrative layout proposed in *The Corporate Report* was as follows:

A manufacturing company. Statement of value added for the year to 31 December 19X9

	£	£
Turnover		X
Bought-in materials and services		X
Value added		X
Applied the following way		
To pay employees'		
wages, pensions and fringe benefits		X
To pay providers of capital		
Interest on loans	X	
Dividends to shareholders	X	X
To pay government		
Corporation tax payable		X
To provide for maintenance and expansion of assets		
Depreciation	X	
Retained profits	X	X
Value added		X

As may be seen from the above illustration, so far as large companies are concerned, the value added statement is largely a rearrangement of information disclosed elsewhere in the company's published accounts. For this reason many people consider it to be a mere cosmetic device to place less emphasis on the profit figure. Others would stress that presentation has an important role to play and that the arrangement of information in the value added statement provides a better means of understanding the contribution of a company to society. In particular, the inclusion of relevant percentages of value added by the side of items in the second part of the statement would make people aware of the respective shares of the various team members.

Simple company

Content of statement

For a manufacturing or trading company the first figure in the value added statement will usually be the turnover figure which appears in its profit and loss account. From this is deducted the cost of bought-in materials and services, which comprise the cost of materials and services consumed. Examples of such bought-in materials and services are raw materials, fuel costs, hire of computing facilities, printing and stationery and audit fees: these are all goods or services bought from non-team members. In practice the cost of bought-in materials and services will usually be calculated as a balancing figure.

   Although the illustration in *The Corporate Report* does not deduct depreciation in arriving at value added, there is a very strong argument for doing so. The purchase of a fixed asset from another firm, a non-team member, is a bought-in item and it is only the fact that the asset has a long life which necessitates the charging of depreciation. Thus in arriving at value added, a preferred format would be:

	£	£
Turnover		X
less Bought-in materials and services		X
Depreciation	X	X
		X

In order to avoid confusion it is perhaps sensible to talk of the illustration in *The Corporate Report* as a statement of gross value added and the illustration above as a statement of net value added. A similar distinction between gross national product and net national product is found in national income statistics.

In the lower part of the statement we need to show how the value added during the period has been shared between members of the team. Following the order in the illustrative layout of *The Corporate Report* we would start with amounts payable to all employees, that is gross pay, employers' National Insurance contributions, employers pension contributions and pension payments and, to the extent that it is possible to arrive at them, fringe benefits. Theoretically we should disclose wages payable in respect of the sales of the year. However, most published statements have shown wages payable for the year and have ignored the changes in the labour content of work in progress or finished goods stock, thus losing the difference in the balancing figure for 'bought-in materials and services'.

Some companies have shown as payable to employees merely the net pay of employees, grouping PAYE and both employers' and employees' National Insurance contributions under the heading 'To pay government'. Although one can understand companies wishing to emphasise how much is paid over to the government there seems a lot to be said for showing only corporation tax payable under the government heading for reasons which will be discussed below.

The second group of members of the team in the illustrative layout are providers of financial capital. Under this heading will be shown interest payable on loans and dividends payable to shareholders for the period. Where tax is deductible from interest payable, interest should be shown gross of tax for the company is merely accounting for the recipient's income tax liability at the basic rate of taxation.

It is when we turn to the heading 'To pay government' that we find the most variety in practice. Some companies have merely shown corporation tax payable in respect of the period, that is both advance corporation tax and mainstream corporation tax. Others have shown all taxes paid to the government whether paid over on behalf of others or not. In this case the heading 'To pay government' might include such taxes as the following: corporation tax, employees' PAYE, National Insurance contributions, taxation deducted from interest payable, VAT, local rates, motor vehicle license fees, Customs and Excise duties.

There seem to be arguments in favour of both treatments. To include just the figure for corporation tax payable avoids the need for arbitrary distinctions and time-consuming analysis of the accounts to ascertain the totals of the various taxes listed above. It also has the advantage of agreement with the profit and loss account figure. On the other hand, it may be argued that the inclusion of all taxes payable to the government would facilitate international comparison. The inclusion of only one direct tax, corporation tax, would make such international comparisons difficult in that countries have different mixes of direct and indirect taxes.

The final heading in the illustrative layout is 'To provide for maintenance and expansion of assets'. For the reasons stated above, depreciation is usually better classified as a bought-in cost. This leaves only retained profit, and some description such as 'available for investment' would then be more appropriate. Some people would argue that it is wrong to include such an abstraction as a member of the team, for, after all, retained profits belong to the equity shareholders.

Non-trading items

In the previous section we have examined the value added statement of a simple trading or manufacturing company. Most companies also have what may be loosely described as non-trading items, examples of which are investment income and extraordinary profits and losses. Although it may be argued that investment income is a share of the value added distributable by another company rather than a part of the value added by the company with which we are concerned, that investment income is certainly a part of the value added available to share between team members. Indeed it is impossible to eliminate the investment income from the individual items in the second part of the statement and it must therefore either be deducted in total in the second part of the statement or, preferably, included separately in the first part of the statement. A similar treatment is appropriate for extraordinary items and, if this treatment is adopted, the first part of the value added statement would appear as follows:

	£	£
Sales		X
less Bought-in materials and services	X	
Depreciation	X	X
Value added by the company		X
add Investment income	X	
Extraordinary profits	X	X
Value added available		X

Group of companies – minority interests

Where a company prepares consolidated accounts the value added statement should be based upon the consolidated profit and loss account rather than the profit and loss account of the parent company. It will therefore show value added by the group. The minority interests in subsidiaries must therefore be treated as members of the team and their share of the value added included in the lower part of the statement. Two methods have been used in practice.

Some companies show, under the heading 'To pay providers of capital', the full share of minority interests in the current profits, whether or not these are distributable as dividends. Other companies split the share of profits applicable to minority interests, showing dividends paid and payable under the heading 'To pay providers of capital' and the retained profits applicable to the minority interest as a separate item under the heading 'Retained profits available for investment'. The latter would seem to be the better alternative as the treatment is consistent with that applied to the shareholders in the holding company.

Associated undertakings

Under SSAP 1 companies are required to include in their consolidated profit and loss accounts their full share of profits and losses of associated undertakings. Such an item should therefore be included as a separate component of value added in the top part of the statement.

In the second part of the statement there must be shown the share of the corporation tax payable by the associated undertaking and the share of retained profits which will either be held by the investing company, to the extent that a dividend is payable by the associate undertaking, or in the associate undertaking itself. Tax payable should be shown under the heading 'To pay government' whereas the retained profits should be shown under the heading 'Retained to provide for investment'. Notice that no item appears under the heading 'To pay employees' because the figure we have included as value added is the share of profits in associated undertakings, after payment to employees.

The current position

As discussed above, some people consider the value added statement to be a mere cosmetic device to divert attention from the profit figure while others consider it to be an instrument for improving industrial relations in the UK by emphasising the team nature of the entity.[17] Whatever the merits of the statement it is clear that, although many large listed companies have, at some time, produced a value added statement as part of their annual reports, the proportion of such companies producing the statement has never exceeded 40 per cent and that this proportion has declined considerably in recent years.

THE HISTORICAL SUMMARY

As we explain in Chapter 13, it is usually difficult to draw conclusions about the performance and position of a company from a profit and loss account and balance sheet without some yardstick of comparison. Company law clearly recognises this in requiring the disclosure of corresponding amounts for the preceding financial year.[18] Thus the law ensures that, at a minimum, users are able to compare the performance and position in the current year with that of the previous year. While such information is undoubtedly useful, comparative information for a longer period would be even more helpful in enabling users of the accounts to appreciate trends.

It was for this reason that, in the 1960s, the then Chairman of the Stock Exchange recommended that all listed companies should publish tables of relevant comparative figures for a ten-year period. Although this recommendation has never been incorporated into the Stock Exchange Regulations, nor into company law or accounting standards, it has become accepted practice for listed companies to provide a historical summary covering a five-year period. Five years has perhaps been chosen because this is the period specified for accountants' reports in prospectuses.

Given the lack of regulation, it is not surprising to find that the information included in a historical summary differs considerably from one company to another. While some companies only provide figures for turnover and profit for each of the five years, others provide summarised profit and loss accounts and balance sheets for the period. These are

---

17 *See* M. F. Morley, *The Value Added Statement*, Gee, London, 1978, Chapter 3.
18 Companies Act 1985, Schedule 4, Para. 4(1).

often supplemented by financial ratios, particularly earnings per share and dividend per share, and sometimes by a segmental analysis and/or non-financial information for the five-year period. Examples of the latter include the number of employees and the area of retail floor space available in each year. Readers familiar with the non-financial performance indicators published by nationalised industries will appreciate just how much detailed information of this type may be provided.

Given the lack of regulation and the fact that the historical summary is not subject to audit it is, of course, possible for directors to choose to disclose those elements of a company's performance which show their company in the most favourable light. Thus, they may choose to disclose increasing amounts for turnover and operating profit while suppressing the fact that the profit before taxation and earnings per share may have been declining. It is for this reason that some accountants have called for regulation of the content of the historical summary.[19]

In our view, the historical summary should include as a minimum the main headings and totals in the profit and loss account and balance sheet. The former would include turnover, operating profit, exceptional items, profit before taxation, profit after taxation, extraordinary items and dividends. The latter would include fixed assets, net current assets, borrowings and shareholders' interest. These should be supplemented by ratios for earnings per share, dividends per share and net assets per share.

In order to ensure comparability, in so far as this is possible, previously published figures should be adjusted to reflect changes in accounting policies and to correct any fundamental errors which have come to light. In addition, amounts shown for earnings per share, dividends per share and net assets per share should be adjusted to reflect any subsequent changes in the share capital such as bonus issues and rights issues. In order not to obscure trends, it is essential that both exceptional items and any extraordinary items should be disclosed separately. A brief description of these and of any major changes in the composition of the group should also be provided.

The main criticism which we would make of published historical summaries is that the vast majority are not adjusted for inflation. Although many users are able to make approximate adjustments for changes in the value of money by use of the published Retail Price Index, the trend shown by uncorrected information may be misleading for less sophisticated users.

To illustrate, let us assume that a company has reported its turnover for a five-year period as shown in the first line of Table 11.1 below. On the basis of the reported figures, turnover has been growing during the five-year period at a rate of approximately 3 per cent per annum.

However the second line of the table provides values for the average Retail Price Index each year and the third line provides the turnover for each year measured in average pounds for 1993.[20]

---

19 *See*, for example, R. M. Wilkins and A. C. Lennard 'Historical summaries', in *Financial Reporting 1987–88*, L. C. L. Skerratt and D. J. Tonkin (eds), ICAEW, London, 1988. Wilkins and Lennard suggested that the Stock Exchange should consider introducing a requirement for historical summaries and that this should be supplemented by a SORP, giving practical guidance on the detailed information to be included and how problem areas should be handled.

20 To measure the turnover for each year in average pounds for 1993 – £(1993)s – it is merely necessary to multiply the turnover for each year by the average RPI for 1993 and to divide by the average RPI for the year to which the turnover relates. Hence the turnover for 1989 measured in £(1993)s, rounded to the nearest £1000 is calculated as £600 × 140.7/115.2 = £733.

Table 11.1

Year to 31 December	1989	1990	1991	1992	1993
Turnover (£000s)	600	618	635	652	670
Average RPI for year	115.2	126.1	133.5	138.5	140.7
Turnover measured in £(1993)s (£000s)	733	690	669	662	670

Whereas the unadjusted figures show an increasing turnover, once we adjust for the fact that the value of the pound is falling, the 'real' turnover was, in fact, declining for four out of the five years.

The ASC recommended that such simple adjustments be made.[21] In our view it is quite indefensible for companies to publish five-year historical summaries without incorporating changes in the value of the pound. The need for such adjustments is, of course, greater the higher the rate of inflation.

REPORTING ABOUT AND TO EMPLOYEES

As we have seen in the introduction to this chapter, both *The Corporate Report* and the subsequent Green Papers favoured the expansion of the annual report to include an employment report.

Companies and other entities employ a large number of people who look to those entities for employment security and prospects while society at large expects employers to maintain certain standards of conduct in relation to its employees. *The Corporate Report* therefore took the view that significant economic entities should report employment information and recommended that the annual report should be expanded to include an employment report which should provide the following information.[22]

(a) Numbers employed, average for the financial year and actual on the first and last day.
(b) Broad reasons for changes in the numbers employed.
(c) The age distribution and sex of employees.
(d) The functions of employees.
(e) The geographical location of major employment centres.
(f) Major plant and site closures, disposals and acquisitions during the past year.
(g) The hours scheduled and worked by employees giving as much detail as possible concerning differences between groups of employees.
(h) Employment costs including fringe benefits.
(i) The costs and benefits associated with pension schemes and the ability of such schemes to meet future commitments.
(j) The cost and time spent on training.
(k) The names of unions recognised by the entity for the purpose of collective bargaining and membership figures where available or the fact that this information has not been made available by the unions concerned.

---

21 See the Discussion Paper 'Corresponding amounts and ten-year summaries in current cost accounting', ASC, 1982, and the Handbook 'Accounting for the effects of changing prices', ASC, 1986, Chapter 7.
22 *The Corporate Report*, Para. 6.19. Appendix 3 to that document provides an example of the sort of employment report envisaged.

(l) Information concerning safety and health including the frequency and severity of accidents and occupational diseases.

(m) Selected ratios relating to employment.

In the introduction to this chapter, we distinguished two types of statement. The employment report envisaged by *The Corporate Report* is an example of what we called an 'extended' statement. It is a general purpose statement to be included in the annual report of a company, which would provide much more information on employment than that required by company law. It should not be confused with another document, the employee report, which is an example of a 'rearranged and simplified' report, in this case a document separate from the annual report, intended for the use of employees.

Employee reports usually contain a simplified set of accounts together with a narrative review of those accounts. The emphasis is on making the information as easy to understand as possible and such reports try to avoid technical language and frequently include charts and diagrams which might show, for example, the changes in sales or profits over a number of years or the distribution of value added between the team members.

In large companies the employees are primarily interested in a part, rather than the whole, of the entity and frequently employee reports are used to give more detailed segmental information about geographical areas, divisions or plants. They can thus be tailor-made for the particular company and can be improved in response to suggestions from the users, that is the employees, themselves.

Perhaps not surprisingly, companies have been reluctant to publish employment reports, especially given the fact that there has been little published work explaining which users find the particular pieces of information useful and for what purposes they may be useful. On the other hand employee reports seem to be more widely used and these are often also issued to shareholders as a matter of course.

SUMMARY FINANCIAL STATEMENT

As we have seen in Chapter 2, company law has long required limited companies to send copies of their annual accounts, directors' reports and auditors' reports to every member and debenture holder of the company. However the Companies Act 1989 introduced new provisions whereby a *listed* company may instead send members a Summary Financial Statement.[23] Such a statement must explain that it is a summary of the full accounts, inform members that they are entitled to the full accounts and carry a warning that the summary financial statement does not contain sufficient information to permit a full understanding of the results or position of the company or group. It must contain a report by the auditor that the statement is consistent with the full accounts and that it complies with the law. It must also include any qualified auditor's report together with details of certain types of qualification.

While the Companies Act 1989 introduced these general principles, the detailed regulations have been introduced by statutory instrument.[24] This specified the minimum content of the Summary Financial Statement which comprises certain information from

23 Companies Act 1985, Sec. 251.
24 The Companies (Summary Financial Statement) Regulations 1990, SI 1990/515.

the directors' report and the main headings and associated amounts from the profit and loss account and balance sheet.

With regard to the information in the directors' report, it is necessary to disclose the names of all directors who served during the financial year and either the whole or a summary of the fair review of results and position, of post balance sheet events and of likely future developments. With respect to the results and position it is necessary to give the minimum headings shown in Table 11.2. Given that almost all listed companies prepare group accounts, we have provided a list for a consolidated profit and loss account and balance sheet.

Table 11.2 Minimum content of summary profit and loss account and balance sheet

Summary consolidated profit and loss account

	£
Turnover	x
Income from shares in associated undertakings	x
Other interest receivable and similar income less interest payable and similar charges	x
Profit (or loss) on ordinary activities before taxation	x
Tax on profit (or loss) on ordinary activities	x
Profit (or loss) on ordinary activities after tax	x
Minority interests	x
	x
Extraordinary items	x
Profit (or loss) for the financial year	x
Dividends paid and proposed	x
	x
Directors' emoluments (total only)	x

Summary consolidated balance sheet

	£	£
Fixed assets		x
Current assets	x	
Creditors: amounts falling due within one year	x	
Net current assets		x
Total assets less current liabilities		x
Creditors: amounts falling due after more than one year		x
		x
Provisions for liabilities and charges		x
		x
Capital and reserves		x
Minority interests		x
		x

As will be seen from Table 11.2 the summary financial statement is indeed a highly simplified statement and as the required warning states, it is unlikely to contain sufficient information to allow for a full understanding of the group's performance and position. In no way are such statements an attempt to improve financial reporting. Rather they represent a means of reducing the cost of sending full accounts to the vastly increased numbers of small shareholders as a consequence of the large privatisation issues of the 1980s!

RECOMMENDED READING

D. Davis and M. Blackwood, 'FRS 1 Cash flow statements', *Accountants Digest No. 287*, ICAEW, London, Summer 1992.

M. Renshall, R. Allan and K. Nicholson, *Added Value in External Financial Reporting*, ICAEW, London 1979.

Much useful information on current practice is included in the volume *Financial Reporting – A Survey of UK Published Accounts*, published annually by the ICAEW.

CHAPTER 12

Capital reorganisation, reduction and reconstruction

INTRODUCTION

There are many reasons for making changes to a company's capital structure and these range from those which are virtually cosmetic to those where the company's capital base has almost disappeared.

At the cosmetic end of the spectrum is the bonus (or scrip) issue designed to tidy up a balance sheet which might otherwise show a large number of different reserves. At the other end of the spectrum is the capital reconstruction scheme entered into as the only possible alternative to liquidation of the company. In such a case, the value of the company's assets may be less than the value of its liabilities with the probable result that the company will be unable to meet its debts as they fall due. The company must then reach some agreement with its debenture-holders and other creditors about how their liabilities are to be treated. To achieve economic viability, it will often be necessary to raise new capital from existing shareholders and if, as is likely, the company has accumulated losses, the new shares would probably be unattractive to investors. The writing down, or reduction, of share capital removes such losses from the balance sheet and brings a greater likelihood of earlier future dividends, thus making the shares more attractive.

Within this spectrum of reasons for a reorganisation of capital, there are numerous possibilities. A company may wish to raise new share capital and use a rights issue as a cheaper alternative to a general offer to the public; conversely it may wish to reduce its share capital in line with a smaller level of operations or perhaps to permit a shareholder director in a family company to retire. A capital reorganisation scheme may be used to effect a change in the relative rights of different classes of shareholders, perhaps when a company is involved in a business combination. Taxation considerations are important in leading a company to reorganise its capital so that its earnings may be distributed to members in a tax-efficient way.

In some cases the reason for the reorganisation is unique, that is it is only applicable in the circumstances of the particular company. A good example is the scheme of arrangement undertaken by European Ferries plc in 1984. Under this scheme, ordinary shareholders were permitted to convert their ordinary shares into preference shares and only those preference shares now carry the right to discounts on P & O ferries. The purpose of the scheme was to limit any future growth in the number of shareholders entitled to such discounts.

Changes in share capital such as bonus issues and rights issues are dealt with in more elementary textbooks on accounting. Here we concentrate on certain reorganisations of capital permitted under the provisions of the Companies Act 1985.

First, we look at the redemption or purchase of its own shares by a company under the provisions of the Companies Act 1985. We deal with both the purchase of shares other than out of capital, which may be made by any limited company with a share capital, and a purchase out of capital, which may only be made by a private limited company. In the following section we examine the more wide-ranging powers to reduce capital contained in the Companies Act 1985. Next we provide the background to other capital reorganisations including those which involve the alteration of creditors' rights. In the final section, we consider the design and evaluation of a capital reconstruction scheme to be undertaken as an alternative to liquidation.

REDEMPTION AND PURCHASE OF SHARES

Purchase not out of capital[1]

Until the Companies Act 1981, the only class of share that a company was able to redeem was redeemable preference shares. The Companies Act 1985 now permits limited companies both to issue redeemable shares of any class, and to purchase its own shares, whether or not they were issued as redeemable shares. The difference between a redemption and a purchase is that in the former case the shares will be reacquired on terms specified when the security was issued while in the case of a purchase the amount payable will depend on conditions prevailing at the date of purchase. Apart from this, the rules governing redemption and purchase are the same and, in order to avoid repetition, we shall merely use the term purchase throughout this section. In both cases the purchased shares are cancelled and cannot be reissued.

The Act distinguishes two categories of purchase, a market purchase and an off-market purchase. The market purchase is a purchase of shares listed on a recognised stock exchange or dealt in on the Unlisted Securities Market. It follows that such a purchase may only be made by a public company which has shares quoted on the relevant market. The off-market purchase is any other purchase of shares under a contract and may be made by both public and private companies. In view of the possibility that one particular shareholder may be beneficially treated, the Act lays down more onerous conditions for an off-market purchase than for a market purchase. Thus, whereas the market purchase may be made in accordance with a general authority passed by an ordinary resolution in general meeting, the off-market purchase requires approval of a specific contract by a special resolution in general meeting.

Private companies are in certain circumstances allowed to reduce their permanent capital by the purchase of their own shares and we shall deal with these provisions later in the chapter. With this exception the 1985 Act lays down very detailed rules to ensure that the permanent capital is maintained intact following the purchase. The general principle, which has applied for many years on the redemption of redeemable preference shares, is that the purchase must be made either out of distributable profits or out of the proceeds of a new issue of shares made for the purpose or by a combination of the two methods.

In many instances the purchase will be made at a premium, i.e. the purchase price will exceed the share's nominal value. Any premium payable on purchase must be paid out of

1 The relevant legal provisions are contained in the Companies Act 1985, Sections 159–170.

distributable profits unless the shares being purchased were originally issued at a premium,[2] in which case some or all of the premium may come from the proceeds of any new issue.

Where the purchase is made out of distributable profits an amount must be transferred to a capital redemption reserve, which is treated as paid-up share capital of the company. It would appear that the intention of the Act is that the amount of the transfer should be such as to ensure that the permanent capital following the purchase is maintained at the original level. However, probably unintentionally, due to the particular wording used in the Act, circumstances can arise which could result in either an increase or a reduction in permanent capital. The circumstances might occur where shares are purchased at a premium out of the proceeds of a fresh issue of shares itself made at a premium[3] and these will be illustrated in the examples which follow.

First let us assume that a company purchases shares without making a new issue of shares. In such a case the amount payable, including any premium, must come from distributable profits and, in order to maintain the permanent capital of the company, it is necessary to transfer an amount equal to the nominal value of the shares purchased from distributable profits to a capital redemption reserve, which is treated as paid-up share capital of the company. This is illustrated in Example 12.1.

EXAMPLE 12.1

Bratsk plc has the following summarised balance sheet:

	£
Net assets	1 500
Share capital – £1 shares	1 000
Share premium	200
(Permanent capital)	1 200
Distributable profits	300
	1 500

It purchases 100 £1 shares for £160 out of distributable profits.
Summarised journal entries together with the resulting balance sheet are as follows:

	£	£
Dr Share capital	100	
Premium on purchase	60	
Cr Cash		160
	160	160
Dr Distributable profits	160	
Cr Premium on purchase		60
Capital redemption reserve		100
	160	160

2 This means that where some of the shares in issue were issued at par with others having been issued at a premium it will be necessary to identify which particular shares are being purchased.
3 *See*, for example, Donald Jamieson, 'Companies Act 1981 and the maintenance of capital'. *Accountancy*, July 1983, pp. 103–5.

Summarised balance sheet after purchase of shares:

		£
Net assets	(1 500 – 160)	1 340
Share capital	(1 000 – 100)	900
Share premium		200
Capital redemption reserve		100
(Permanent capital)		1 200
Distributable profits	(300 – 160)	140
		1340

Notice that the permanent capital of the company remains unchanged at £1200.

Next let us assume that a company purchases shares out of the proceeds of a new issue. In the absence of any premium payable on purchase, discussed below, the nominal value of the shares purchased is replaced by the nominal value of and any share premium received on the new issue.

EXAMPLE 12.2

Chita Limited has the following summarised balance sheet:

	£
Net assets	1 500
Share capital – £1 shares	1 000
Share premium	200
(Permanent capital)	1 200
Distributable profits	300
	1 500

Chita purchases 100 £1 shares at their nominal value out of the proceeds of an issue of 80 £1 shares at a premium of 25p per share.

Summarised journal entries and the resulting balance sheet are as follows:

	£	£
Dr Cash	100	
Cr Share capital		80
Share premium		20
	100	100
Dr Share capital	100	
Cr Cash		100

Summarised balance sheet after purchase of shares:

Net assets	1 500
Share capital (1000 + 80 – 100)	980
Share premium (200 + 20)	220
(Permanent capital)	1 200
Distributable profits	300
	1 500

Once again, the permanent capital has been maintained at £1200.

Frequently, as in the case of Bratsk (Example 12.1) above, a premium is payable on the shares purchased. Such a premium must be paid out of distributable profits except that where the shares which are being purchased were originally issued at a premium, all or part of the premium now payable may be paid out of the proceeds of the new issue and charged against the share premium account. The amount which may be charged against the share premium account is the lower of:

(i) the amount of the premium which the company originally received on the shares now being purchased, and

(ii) the current balance on the share premium account, including any premium on the new issue of shares.

EXAMPLE 12.3

Dudinka Limited has the following summarised balance sheet:

Net assets	1 500
Share capital – £1 shares	1 000
Share premium	200
(Permanent capital)	1 200
Distributable profits	300
	1 500

Dudinka Limited purchases 100 £1 shares which were originally issued at a premium of 20p per share. The price paid is £180 and this is financed by the issue of 90 £1 shares at a premium of £1 per share.

Part of the premium payable may be financed from the proceeds of the new issue; the amount is the lower of the original share premium on the shares now being purchased and the balance of the share premium account, including the premium on the new share issue. In this case the amount is the lower of £20 (100 at 20p) and £290 (£200 + £90) and hence £20 may be debited to the share premium account. The balance must come from distributable profits.

Summarised journal entries and the resulting balance sheet are as follows:

	£	£
Dr Cash	180	
Cr Share capital		90
Share premium		90
	180	180
Dr Share capital	100	
Premium on purchase	80	
Cr Cash		180
	180	180
Dr Share premium	20	
Distributable profits	60	
Cr Premium on purchase		80
	80	80

Summarised balance sheet after purchase of shares:

Net assets (1 500 + 180 – 180)	1 500
Share capital (1 000 + 90 – 100)	990
Share premium (200 + 90 – 20)	270
(Permanent capital)	1 260
Distributable profits (300 – 60)	240
	1 500

So, even where the proceeds of the new issue are exactly equal to the amount payable on purchase, the restriction on the amount of any premium payable which may be charged against the share premium account will often result in part of the premium payable being charged against distributable profits and a consequent increase in the permanent capital of the company.

In the final example in this section, we look at a company which purchases shares but raises only part of the finance by making a new issue of shares. We shall assume that the shares are purchased at a premium and that the new shares are issued at a premium. As we shall see, it is in this situation that a reduction in the permanent capital of the company may occur.

EXAMPLE 12.4

Ivdel plc has the following summarised balance sheet:

	£
Net assets	1 500
Share capital – £1 shares	1 000
Share premium	200
(Permanent capital)	1 200
Distributable profits	300
	1 500

It purchases 100 shares which were originally issued at a premium of 50p per share. The agreed price is £180 and the company issues 40 shares at a premium of £1 per share to help finance the purchase.

The premium payable on purchase is £80 and part of this may come from the proceeds of the new issue and be charged to the share premium account. As explained above, this amount is the lower of the original premium (£50) and the balance on the share premium account after the new issue (£240). Hence £50 may be debited to the share premium account and the balance must be debited to distributable profits.

As part of the purchase price is being met from distributable profits, it is necessary to make a transfer to capital redemption reserve. Section 170(2) of the 1985 Companies Act requires the amount to be calculated by deducting the aggregate amount of the proceeds of the new issue from the nominal value of the shares purchased. In this case the amount of the transfer is therefore:

	£
Nominal value of shares purchased	100
less Proceeds of new issue	
(40 x £2)	80
Necessary transfer	20

Necessary journal entries and the resulting balance sheet are given below:

	£	£
Dr Cash	80	
Cr Share capital		40
Share premium		40
	80	80
Dr Share capital	100	
Premium on purchase	80	
Cr Cash		180
	180	180
Dr Share premium	50	
Distributable profits	30	
Cr Premium on purchase		80
	80	80
Dr Distributable profits	20	
Cr Capital redemption reserve		20

Summarised balance sheet after purchase of shares:

	£
Net assets (1500 + 80 – 180)	1 400
Share capital (1000 + 40 – 100)	940
Share premium (200 + 40 – 50)	190
Capital redemption reserve	20
(Permanent capital)	1 150
Distributable profits (300 – 30 – 20)	250
	1 400

In this case, the permanent capital has been reduced from £1200 to £1150 which does not appear to accord with the intended aim of maintaining permanent capital. The reason the reduction occurs is because the proceeds of the new issue are used to finance part of both nominal value and premium payable and yet this is not recognised in making the transfer to capital redemption reserve.

Let us illustrate: the proceeds of the new issue are £80 and, of this, £50 is used to finance the premium on purchase. This leaves only £30 to replace the nominal value of the shares issued. To maintain permanent capital of the company, the transfer to capital redemption reserve should be calculated as follows:

	£	£
Nominal value of shares purchased		100
less Net proceeds of new issue:		
Total proceeds	80	
less Utilised to finance part of premium payable	50	
		30
Transfer to capital redemption reserve		70

Such a transfer would maintain permanent capital at £1200 but it is not the transfer required by law. Section 170(2) makes no reference to 'net' proceeds and hence the law seems to permit such a reduction in capital for both public and private companies.

Purchase out of capital[4]

The permissible capital payment

Whereas failure to maintain capital in the circumstances discussed above may be an unintended effect of the legislation, the 1985 Act specifically permits a private, but not a public, company to purchase its shares out of capital. This provides such a company with a means for reducing its permanent capital without the formality and expense of undertaking a capital reduction scheme, which we discuss in the next section. Such an ability to purchase shares out of capital is of considerable benefit to, for example, a family-owned company where a member of the family wishes to realise his or her investment but no other member of the family wishes, or is able, to purchase it.

A purchase of shares out of capital results in a fall in the resources available to creditors and the 1985 Act therefore provides a number of safeguards to protect their interests. Before summarising these safeguards, we will explain the calculation of the permitted reduction in capital, what the Act describes as the 'permissible capital payment'.

The private company is not free to specify the amount of the payment out of capital. Rather the payment is restricted to the amount actually paid for shares less both the distributable profits and the proceeds of any fresh issue of shares made for the purpose of the purchase. Thus, a payment from capital may only be made when all distributable reserves have been utilised. Rules are laid down to ensure that the permanent capital of the company is not reduced by more than the permissible capital payment although these rules may still not succeed due to the problem discussed in connection with Example 12.4 above.

4 The relevant legal provisions are contained in the Companies Act 1985, Sections 171–177.

If the total of the permissible capital payment and the proceeds of a fresh issue of shares is less than the nominal value of the shares purchased, there would be a reduction in permanent capital in excess of the permissible capital payment. To prevent this, the law requires that the difference be transferred to a capital redemption reserve. If the permissible capital payment together with the proceeds of any fresh issue of shares exceeds the nominal value of the shares purchased, the excess may be eliminated by writing it off against any one of a number of accounts, including accounts for capital redemption reserve, share premium, share capital or unrealised profits. This ability to write off the excess to any one of these named accounts or, indeed, to deal with it in some other way, provides a private company with considerable flexibility to design its own capital reduction scheme.

We shall illustrate the above rules with two examples.

In Example 12.5 the purchase of shares is made partly out of capital and partly out of distributable profits while in Example 12.6 the purchase is, in addition, made partly out of the proceeds of a new issue of shares.

EXAMPLE 12.5

Kotlas Limited has the following summarised balance sheet:

	£
Net assets	1 250
Share capital – £1 shares	1 000
Distributable profits	250
	1 250

It purchases 200 £1 shares at a cost of £300. In the absence of a share premium account or a new issue of shares at a premium, the amount of the premium payable must be provided from distributable profits.

The permissible capital payment is:

	£
Amount payable	300
less Distributable profits	250
Permissible capital payment	50

As the permissible capital payment (£50) is less than the nominal value of the shares purchased (£200) it is necessary to make a transfer from distributable profits to a capital redemption reserve.

	£
Nominal value of shares purchased	200
less Permissible capital payment	50
Necessary transfer	150

Necessary journal entries and the resulting summarised balance sheet are given below:

	£	£
Dr Share capital	200	
Premium on purchase	100	
Cr Cash		300
	300	300

	£	£
Dr Distributable profits	250	
Cr Premium on purchase		100
Capital redemption reserve		150
	250	250

Summarised balance sheet after purchase of shares:

	£
Net assets (1250 – 300)	950
Share capital (1000 – 200)	800
Capital redemption reserve	150
(Permanent capital)	950

The permanent capital of the company has been reduced from £1000 share capital to £950. It has fallen by the amount of the permissible capital payment.

EXAMPLE 12.6

Nordvik Limited has the following summarised balance sheet:

	£
Net assets	1 250
Share capital – £1 shares	1 000
Share premium	200
(Permanent capital)	1 200
Distributable profits	50
	1 250

Of the £1 shares, 500 were issued at par when the company was formed and 500 were issued at a premium of 40p per share some years later.

Nordvik purchases 200 of the shares which were originally issued at par for an agreed price of £300 and finances the purchase in part by an issue of 50 shares at a premium of 60p per share.

As the shares purchased were not originally issued at a premium, no part of the premium payable may come from the proceeds of the new issue. The whole of the premium payable, that is the whole of the increase in value of these particular shares since their issue, must be charged against distributable profits.

In this case the permissible capital payment is:

	£	£
Amount payable		300
less Distributable profits	50	
Proceeds of new issue (50 x £1.60)	80	130
Permissible capital payment		170

In order to determine whether or not a transfer to capital redemption reserve is necessary, we must compare the proceeds of the new issue and the permissible capital payment with the nominal value of the shares purchased.

	£	£
Nominal value of shares purchased		200
less Permissible capital payment	170	
Proceeds of new issue	80	250
		(50)

In this case no transfer to capital redemption reserve is required. Rather the excess £50 may be charged to one of the accounts discussed above and we have chosen to debit it to the share premium account.

Necessary journal entries and the resulting summarised balance sheet are given below:

	£	£
Dr Cash	80	
Cr Share capital		50
Share premium		30
	80	80
Dr Share capital	200	
Premium on purchase	100	
Cr Cash		300
	300	300

	£	£
Dr Distributable profits	50	
Share premium	50	
Cr Premium on purchase		100
	100	100

Summarised balance sheet after purchase of shares:

	£
Net assets (1 250 + 80 – 300)	1 030
Share capital (1 000 + 50 – 200	850
Share premium (200 + 30 – 50)	180
(Permanent capital)	1 030
Distributable profits	–
	1 030

The permanent capital of the company has been reduced from £1200 to £1030 by the amount of the permissible capital payment of £170.

The safeguards

In view of the fact that there is a reduction in the permanent capital, that is a reduction in the net assets available to creditors and the remaining shareholders, the law provides a number of safeguards where a company wishes to make such a purchase of shares involving a payment out of capital. Thus, not only must the payment out of capital be permitted by the company's articles of association and authorised by a special resolution of the company, but the directors must also provide a statutory declaration of solvency to the effect that, having made a full enquiry into the affairs and prospects of the company, they have formed the opinion that the company will be able to pay its debts both immediately after the payment and during the following year. As the protection of creditors and shareholders rests on this continuing solvency of the company, the law requires that a report by the company's auditors on the reasonableness of the directors' opinion is attached to the statutory declaration.

After the payment out of capital has been authorised, the company must publicise it in an official gazette and either a national newspaper or by individual notice to each creditor. Any creditor, or any shareholder who did not vote for the special resolution, may then apply to the court for the cancellation of the resolution and the court may then cancel or confirm the resolution and may make an order to facilitate an arrangement whereby the interests of dissenting creditors or members are purchased.

If the directors' optimism subsequently proves not to have been well founded and the company commences to wind up within a year of the payment out of capital and is unable to pay all its liabilities and the costs of winding up, then directors and past shareholders may be liable to contribute. The directors who have signed the statutory declaration and/or past shareholders, whose shares were purchased, may have to pay an amount not exceeding in total the permitted capital payment.

Thus the Companies Act 1985 provides safeguards to protect creditors. The use of its provisions to make a purchase of shares partly out of capital is undoubtedly much cheaper and less burdensome than a reduction of capital under the provisions to which we turn next.

CAPITAL REDUCTION

The Companies Act 1985 gives companies a much wider power to reduce capital from that discussed above but it also imposes the more onerous condition that any such reduction must be confirmed by the court.

Providing it is authorised to do so by its articles of association, a limited company may reduce its share capital by passing a special resolution, which must be confirmed by the court. The Act gives a general power to reduce share capital but specifically lists three possible ways to reduce capital:[5]

(a) extinguish or reduce the liability on any of its shares in respect of share capital not paid up; or

(b) either with or without extinguishing or reducing liability on any of its shares, cancel any paid-up share capital which is lost or unrepresented by available assets; or

---

5 Companies Act 1985, Section 135.

(c) either with or without extinguishing or reducing liability on any of its shares, pay off any paid-up share capital which is in excess of the company's wants.

A capital reduction for the first and third of the possible reasons listed is extremely rare. With regard to the first, few companies now have partly paid shares in existence and hence there is invariably no liability in respect of partly paid capital which could be reduced. With regard to the third, although it might make good economic sense for directors to return 'permanent' capital to shareholders where better investment opportunities exist outside of the company than within it, most directors have been loath to relinquish their control over such resources and have usually found some way to employ them within the company.

Both of these capital reductions ((a) and (c)) do, of course, result in a reduction in the potential net assets or actual net assets available to creditors. Thus, in the first case, there is a reduction in the liability of members and hence in the potential pool of net assets available to creditors on a liquidation. In the third case, resources actually leave the company so directly reducing the pool of net assets to which the creditors have recourse. For these reasons the court must give any creditor an opportunity to object to the capital reduction and will usually only confirm the scheme if the debt of such a dissenting creditor is paid or secured.

The second of the three possible capital reduction schemes is the one most commonly found in practice. Thus, where a company has made losses in excess of previous profits, its net assets will be lower than its permanent capital. Given that such a position has been reached, it will often be sensible to recognise the fact by reducing the capital and writing off the losses so that a more realistic position is shown by the balance sheet and the company is allowed to make a fresh start. In particular, after such a scheme the company will be able to distribute realised profits without the need to first make good the accumulated realised losses and, in the case of a public company, net unrealised losses.[6]

The simplest way of carrying out such a capital reduction scheme is to reduce proportionately the nominal value of the ordinary shares outstanding. This has no effect whatsoever on the real value of the ordinary shareholders' interest since the same number of shares in the same company are held in the same proportions by the same people! Each shareholder has the same proportional interest in the net assets of the company after the scheme as before. This demonstrates the irrelevance of the par value and supports the argument that companies should be permitted to issue shares of no par value.[7]

To illustrate such a scheme, let us look at an example.

---

6 *See* Chapter 3.

7 A government committee under the chairmanship of Mr Montague Gedge reported in favour of the issue of shares of no par value as long ago as 1954, Cmnd 9112/5, HMSO, London, 1954.

EXAMPLE 12.7

Perm plc has the following summarised balance sheet:

	£
Net assets	1 200
Share capital	
1000 £1 ordinary shares, fully paid	1 000
500 £1 10% preference shares, fully paid	500
	1 500
Share premium	200
	1 700
less Accumulated losses	500
	1 200

The preference shares rank for dividend and repayment of capital in priority to ordinary shares. The company wishes to reduce its capital by an amount sufficient to remove the accumulated losses and to write down the net assets to a more realistic book value of £900. Thus it wishes to reduce permanent capital by £800, that is £(500 + (1 200 − 900)).

For illustrative purposes we shall consider two possible capital reduction schemes, the first involving a reduction of ordinary share capital only and the second involving the reduction of both ordinary share capital and preference share capital.

Scheme 1

As explained above, the total amount of the capital reduction is £800. However, for the purpose of a reduction of capital, a share premium account is to be treated as paid-up share capital of the company[8] so that £200 may be written off against the share premium leaving £600 to reduce the ordinary share capital from £1000 to £400, that is from £1 to 40p per share.

The balance sheet after the capital reduction would therefore appear as follows:

Summarised balance sheet after capital reduction

	£
Net assets	900
Share capital	
1000 40p ordinary shares	400
500 £1 10% preference shares	500
	900

The interest of preference shareholders and ordinary shareholders in the liquidation value of the company has not altered. Preference shareholders would receive the first £500 while ordinary shareholders would receive the remainder. If the company continues to trade, both sets of shareholders gain in the sense that the company will be able to pay dividends as soon as profits are made without any need to make good the past losses.

Scheme 2

Given the fact that preference shareholders as well as ordinary shareholders benefit from the capital reduction scheme, ordinary shareholders might argue that preference share

8 Companies Act 1985, Section 130(3).

capital as well as ordinary share capital should be reduced. However, as we shall see, a reduction in the par value of a preference share has a much more serious effect than the reduction in the par value of ordinary shares. Indeed a reduction in the par value of both preference shares and ordinary shares with no other changes, will lead to a fall in the real value of the preference shares, but a rise in the real value of the ordinary shares. This may be illustrated as follows.

As before, let us assume that the amount of the capital reduction is £800 and that, of this, £200 may be written off against the share premium account leaving £600 to be written off against share capital. Given that the ordinary share capital is £1000 and that the preference share capital is £500, it might be thought that the amount of £600 should be written off in the ratio 2:1 which would produce a balance sheet as follows:

Summarised balance sheet after capital reduction

	£
Net assets	900
Share capital	
1000 60p ordinary shares	600
500 60p 10% preference shares	300
	900

While this may initially appear fair, a little thought will make it clear that the preference shareholders have been unfairly treated.

Given that the par value of a preference share determines the amount of the preference dividend and the amount which the preference shareholders receive on a liquidation, preference shareholders will have suffered a real loss. They are worse off after the scheme than before. Conversely the ordinary shareholders are better off. Not only would they receive more on an immediate liquidation, as less would be paid to the preference shareholders, but they are also likely to receive higher future dividends, as a lesser dividend would be paid to the preference shareholders.

Careful attention must be paid to the likely effect of reducing the par values of different types of share capital. A capital reduction such as Scheme 2 is unlikely to be acceptable to the preference shareholders unless they are given some other benefit such as a holding of ordinary shares which will give them an opportunity to share in any future prosperity.

THE LEGAL BACKGROUND TO OTHER REORGANISATIONS

We have looked in some detail at the ways in which a company may reduce its share capital under the provisions of the Companies Act 1985. As we saw in the introduction to this chapter, there are many other ways in which a company may wish to reorganise its capital. For example, it may wish to alter the respective rights of different classes of shareholders, while, if it is in financial difficulties, it may need to reduce not only share capital but also the claims of creditors. In this section we look briefly at the legal background to such reorganisations.

First, it is necessary to make it clear that although the term 'capital reduction' has a clear legal meaning, as discussed above, the terms 'capital reorganisation', 'capital reconstruction' and, indeed, 'scheme of arrangement' do not. These terms tend to be used interchangeably although there is, perhaps a tendency to use the term 'capital reconstruction' for the more serious changes in capital structure; so in the final section of this chapter we look at a capital reconstruction scheme undertaken as an alternative to liquidation of the company. In the remainder of this section we will use the term reorganisation.

Any reorganisation which involves creditors will invariably be carried out in accordance with the procedures laid down in Secs 425–426 of the Companies Act 1985. These procedures are designed to protect the various parties involved by requiring court approval for the reorganisation. This sounds fine in theory but the Courts have been reluctant to pass judgement on the economic merits and fairness of schemes and have tended to concern themselves with deciding whether the scheme satisfies the required legal formalities.[9]

Under Secs 425–426, the company will apply to the court which will then direct meetings of the various parties affected to be held. The company must then send out details of the proposed scheme and, providing a majority in number representing three-quarters in value of those attending the various meetings agree and the scheme is sanctioned by the court, it will become binding on all parties once an office copy is delivered to the Registrar of Companies.

Sometimes a reorganisation entered into in accordance with the above provisions will involve the transfer of the whole or part of an undertaking from one company to another. In such a case, Sec. 427 gives the court wide powers to make provision for the transfer of ownership of assets, liabilities, rights and duties to the transferee company.

The above provisions may be used to effect a reorganisation even where there is no change in creditors' rights. However, alternative procedures are available in such cases which do not involve the formality and expense of going to court. Thus, it may be possible to vary the rights of two or more classes of shareholders by merely holding separate class meetings and obtaining the necessary majority votes, although a dissenting minority is given a right to object to the variation in an application to the court.

Another possible means of reorganisation is provided by Section 110 of the Insolvency Act 1986. Under this section, once a voluntary liquidation of the company is proposed, the liquidator may be given authority to sell the whole or a part of the undertaking to another company in exchange for shares or other securities in that other company. Thus, where it is desired to change the rights of two or more classes of its shareholders, the company may be put into voluntary liquidation and a new company may be formed with the desired mix of various classes of shares. The business of the transferor company may then be sold to the new company in exchange for the new shares, which may then be distributed to the shareholders in the transferor company to achieve the desired change. This procedure is much simpler than the use of a scheme under Sections 425–427 of the Act.

Invariably taxation considerations will be extremely important in most capital reorganisations and, in view of the complexity of the tax legislation, specialist advice is almost always necessary.

9 *See* L. C. B. Gower, *Gower's Principles of Modern Company Law*, 5th edition, Sweet & Maxwell, London, 1992, pp. 691–92 and 696–97.

CAPITAL RECONSTRUCTION

In this section we shall concentrate on the design and evaluation of a capital reconstruction scheme for a company which is in severe financial difficulties. It will be assumed that, in the absence of a capital reconstruction scheme, the liquidation of the company would be inevitable. This assumption will affect both the design of the scheme and the way in which it will be evaluated by the interested parties.

As the alternative source of benefits to interested parties is the amount receivable on liquidation, it is essential for us to recall the order in which the proceeds from the sale of assets must be distributed by a liquidator.

Distribution on liquidation

It is the duty of a liquidator to sell the assets of a company as advantageously as possible and to pay costs, creditors and shareholders in the following order:

1 Debts secured by a fixed charge. These must be paid out of the proceeds of sale of the particular assets. In practice a receiver will usually be appointed to sell the assets, which are the subject of the charge, and to pay the secured creditors the amounts due to them.

It will rarely be the case that the proceeds of sale are exactly equal to the costs of the receiver and the amount of the debt. Any excess will be paid over to the liquidator of the company while, to the extent of any deficiency, the creditors are treated in the same way as other unsecured creditors.

2 Costs of the liquidation, in the order specified by law.
3 Preferential creditors. These are listed in Schedule 6 to the Insolvency Act 1986 and include income tax deducted from employees' emoluments under PAYE, value added tax, car tax, social security contributions, contributions to pension schemes and remuneration of employees. There are limits to each of these categories so, for example, PAYE is preferential to the extent of one year's deductions, value added tax to six months, social security contributions up to one year and remuneration of employees for up to four months. To the extent that only a part of a debt is preferential, the remainder will be treated as an unsecured creditor.
4 Creditors secured by a floating charge.
5 Unsecured creditors, including the amounts mentioned in 1 and 3 above.
6 Shareholders of the company in accordance with their rights as laid down in the company's articles of association. Preference shares will normally be paid before any amounts are paid to ordinary shareholders.

Where the amounts available are insufficient to pay any of the above groups in full, each member of the particular group receives the same proportion of the amount of his debt. This proportion is determined as the amount available for a particular group divided by the total amounts due to that group.

Design of a capital reconstruction scheme

Given that a company is in financial difficulties, the objective in the design of a capital reconstruction scheme will be to produce an entity which is a profitable going concern. In some cases the financial difficulties may be so severe that this is impossible for, no matter how skilfully a capital reconstruction scheme is designed, it is not possible to turn the sow's ear into a silk purse. Where the financial difficulties are less severe and the company is capable of operating profitably, a capital reconstruction scheme may have a high probability of success. In order to achieve that success, it will usually be necessary to relieve the company of its burden of immediate debts and will often be necessary to raise new finance, probably by a new issue of shares.

Any capital reconstruction scheme which affects the rights of creditors and shareholders will require the necessary majorities of votes in favour of the scheme as required by Section 425 of the Companies Act 1985, together with the sanction of the court. Hence, to stand any chance of success the scheme must give each interested party the same or more than he would receive on liquidation of the company. In addition the scheme must be accepted as equitable by the various interested parties. It must ensure that no one class of creditor or shareholder is favoured at the expense of any other so that each creditor and shareholder is treated – and feels that he is treated – fairly.

The design of a capital reconstruction scheme is illustrated in the following example while the resulting scheme is evaluated in the final section of this chapter.

EXAMPLE 12.8

The balance sheet of Sakhalin plc on 31 December 19X5 is as follows:

Sakhalin plc
Balance sheet on 31 December 19X5

	£000s	£000s
Fixed assets at cost less depreciation		
Land and buildings	2 500	
Plant and machinery	1 000	3 500
Current assets		
Stock and work in progress	1 000	
Sundry debtors	1 500	2 500
		6 000
less Current liabilities		
Arrears of debenture interest	250	
Trade creditors	1 000	
Bank overdraft	3 000	4 250
		1 750
Financed by		
10% secured debentures (note (a))		1 250
1 million authorised and issued £1		
5% preference shares	1 000	
2 million authorised and issued £1		
ordinary shares	2 000	
	3 000	
less Accumulated losses	2 500	500
		1 750

The following information is available:

(a) The debentures are secured on the office premises, the net realisable value of which is estimated to be £900 000.

(b) The other land and buildings are estimated to have a net realisable value of £1 900 000.

(c) The net realisable value of the plant and machinery is estimated to be £500 000, of the stock and work in progress £750 000, and the recoverable debts are now estimated to be £1 425 000.

(d) The preference dividend has not been paid for 4 years.

(e) The debenture interest is 2 years in arrears.

(f) The articles provide that, on liquidation, the preference shareholders rank for repayment at par prior to any distribution to the ordinary shareholders.

From preliminary meetings of the directors and soundings of the interested parties the following information has also been obtained:

(g) The debenture holders are prepared to agree to a reconstruction scheme providing the rate of interest is increased from 10 to 15 per cent p.a., and they are given a fixed security on the total land and buildings, rather than just the office premises, of the company. They are also willing to accept ordinary shares in lieu of £125 000, that is one of the 2 years' interest in arrears.

(h) The bank is prepared to agree to a reconstruction scheme provided its debt is secured by a floating charge over the assets of the company, thus improving its position *vis-à-vis* any other creditors of the reconstructed company. They would be willing to provide the same amount of finance for the medium term.

(i) The trade creditors are unlikely to agree to any reduction in their claims but are thought to be willing to supply the reconstructed company and to continue to grant credit on normal terms.

(j) The preference shareholders would be willing to forego their arrears of dividend and to accept ordinary shares instead of preference shares.

(k) The directors consider that, if the company is able to raise an additional £1 million in cash by a rights issue, it will be able to commence trading successfully. Expected annual earnings before debenture interest and dividends will then be at least £300 000 and due to accumulated tax losses, no corporation tax will be payable in the foreseeable future.

(l) Debenture holders, preference shareholders and ordinary shareholders are willing to subscribe for new ordinary share capital in the company.

(m) Costs of the reconstruction scheme are expected to be £60 000.

(n) In the absence of a satisfactory scheme the company will have to be liquidated involving costs of £295 000.

From the above information it is possible to calculate the amount of the capital reduction required, namely:[10]

		£000s
(a)	To correct the value of plant and machinery	500
(b)	To correct the value of stock and work in progress	250
(c)	To correct the value of debtors	75
(d)	To eliminate the adverse balance on the profit and loss account	2 500
(e)	To provide for the costs of the scheme	60
		3 385
(f)	Less surplus on revaluation of land and buildings	300
		3 085

In order to begin to decide who must bear this loss in the reconstruction scheme, we must first examine what each class of creditor and shareholder would receive if the company were to be liquidated.

The realisable value of the assets and the way in which they would be distributed are as follows:

	£000s	£000s
Office premises	900	
less Payable to debenture holders		
secured on office premises	900	–
Other premises		1 900
Plant and machinery		500
Stock and work in progress		750
Sundry debtors		1 425
		4 575
less Costs of liquidation		295
Available for unsecured creditors		4 280
Unsecured creditors:[11]		
Bank overdraft		3 000
Debenture holders		
Capital	1 250	
Interest	250	
	1 500	
less Paid out of security as above	900	600
Trade creditors		1 000
		4 600

---

10 In a balance sheet assets should be shown at their 'going concern value' rather than their net realisable value. In order to avoid complicating the example by the introduction of another set of values, the realistic going concern values, assets have been written down to their net realisable values.

11 For simplicity it is assumed that there are no preferential creditors.

There would be £4280 available to meet unsecured creditors of £4600 with the result that each of these creditors, including the debenture holders to the extent that they are unsecured, would receive 93p in the £1. The various parties would therefore receive the following amounts on liquidation of the company:

	£000s
Bank (0.93 x £3 000 000)	2 790
Debenture holders (900 000 + 0.93 x 600 000)	1 460
Trade creditors (0.93 x 1 000 000)	930
Preference shareholders	0
Ordinary shareholders	0
	5 180

Thus all parties would lose on a liquidation and there is an incentive for them to agree to a suitable reconstruction scheme. It is clear that any losses under the scheme must fall most heavily on the shareholders.

One possible scheme of reconstruction would be as follows:

	Reduction *£000s*
(a) 2 million £1 ordinary shares to each be reduced to 1p ordinary shares	1980
(b) 1 million £1 preference shares to be cancelled in exchange for 1 million 1p ordinary shares	990
(c) The granting of an increased rate of interest of 15 per cent p.a. and a fixed charge on all premises to the debenture holders and the waiving of £125 000 of interest in arrears in exchange for 1 million 1p ordinary shares	115
(d) The granting of a floating charge on the debt due to the bank	–
(e) Consolidation of the 4 million 1p ordinary shares into 40 000 £1 ordinary shares	–
(f) The making of a rights issue of 25 £1 ordinary shares for each £1 ordinary share held thus raising cash of £1 000 000. Thus finance would come from old ordinary shareholders (£500 000), old preference shareholders (£250 000) and old debenture holders (£250 000)	–
Total reduction achieved as required	3085

After such a reconstruction scheme is carried into effect, the balance sheet would appear as shown below:

Sakhalin plc		
Balance sheet after scheme	£000s	£000s
Tangible fixed assets – at valuation		
Land and buildings		2 800
Plant and machinery		500
		3 300
Current assets		
Stock and work in progress	750	
Debtors	1 425	
Cash	1 000	
	3 175	
less Current liabilities		
Bank overdraft (secured)	3 000	
Debenture interest (1 year)	125	
Trade creditors	1 000	
Cost of reconstruction	60	
	4 185	(1 010)
		2 290
less 15% Debentures (secured on land and buildings)		1 250
		1 040
Share capital		
1 040 000 £1 ordinary shares, fully paid		1 040

Note The apparently poor current ratio is due to the fact that the bank overdraft is included in current liabilities, in accordance with normal practice, whereas it is in fact medium-term capital.

Evaluation of a capital reconstruction scheme

In evaluating a capital reconstruction scheme, as in designing it, the aim must be to establish the equity of the changes in rights as a result of the scheme. In most cases professional advisers are called upon by each class of member and creditor to evaluate the scheme from their point of view and, in order to do this, it is necessary to evaluate the scheme as a whole since the changes of relative rights will be extremely important.

The rights of participants fall into two classes, the capital repayment rights and the income participation rights. In order to make an appropriate comparison of these, it is helpful to set out the interest of the various parties in the company both before and after the proposed reconstruction.

In Example 12.9 we shall do this in respect of the scheme which has been proposed for Sakhalin plc in Example 12.8.

EXAMPLE 12.9

Table 12.1 **Evaluation of proposed scheme – comparison of interests**

Original class	Interest prior to scheme	Interest after scheme
Bank	£3 000 000 unsecured overdraft	£3 000 000 secured overdraft
Debenture holders	£1 250 000 partly secured 10% debentures plus £250 000 arrears of interest	£1 250 000 fully secured 15% debentures plus £125 000 arrears of interest plus one-quarter of the ordinary shares
Trade creditors	£1 000 000 unsecured debt	£1 000 000 unsecured debt
Preference shareholders	£1 000 000 £1 5% preference shares	One-quarter of the ordinary shares
Ordinary shareholders	All ordinary shares	One-half of the ordinary shares

We have already considered the amounts each class would receive should the scheme be rejected and the company forced into an immediate liquidation. These amounts need to be compared with the position following the reconstruction and we shall do so by evaluating three alternative possible outcomes. First, we shall assume that despite the scheme, the company goes into liquidation immediately following the end of the capital reconstruction. Second, we will assume that the earnings are as expected, about £300 000 per annum. Finally, we will assume that the earnings are more than anticipated; we will for this purpose, assume a figure of £500 000 per annum.

If we assume that the costs of the reconstruction scheme are paid, the position on the subsequent liquidation would be as follows:

Position on liquidation after scheme

	£000s	£000s
Amount receivable from sale of premises		2 800
less Debentures		
Capital	1 250	
Interest	125	1 375
		1 425
Amount realised from other assets:		
Plant and machinery	500	
Stock and work in progress	750	
Debtors	1 425	2 675
Cash (1 000 000 − 60 000)		940
Carried forward		5 040

	£000s
Brought forward	5 040
less Cost of liquidation	295
	4 745
less Bank secured by floating charge	3 000
	1 745
less Trade creditors	1 000
Available for ordinary shareholders	745
Divisible:	
Old debenture holders (¼)	186
Old preference shareholders (¼)	186
Old ordinary shareholders (½)	373
	745

So, on a liquidation subsequent to the scheme the original parties would receive the following amounts:

	£000s
Bank	3 000
Debenture holders (1 375 000 + 186 000)	1 561
Trade creditors	1 000
Preference shareholders	186
Ordinary shareholders	373
	6 120

Debenture holders and preference shareholders have, of course, subscribed £250 000 each for new ordinary share capital while ordinary shareholders have subscribed £500 000.

Let us next examine the interests of the various parties in the expected earnings of the reconstructed company.

As we have seen in note (k) on page 350, the annual earnings before debenture interest and dividends are expected to be at least £300 000 and no corporation tax is likely to be paid in the foreseeable future. It follows that these earnings may be divided:[12]

	£	£
Old debenture holders		
Interest 15% x £1 250 000	187 500	
Share of balance ¼ (300 000 − 187 500)	28 125	215 625
Old preference shareholders		
¼ (300 000 − 187 500)		28 125
Old ordinary shareholders		
½ (300 000 − 187 500)		56 250
		300 000

It is helpful to examine the position if earnings turn out to be higher or lower than expected and, for illustrative purposes, we look at the position if earnings are £500 000:

---

12 For simplicity we have ignored Advanced Corporation Tax.

	£	£
Old debenture holders		
Interest – as above	187 500	
Share of balance ¼ (500 000 – 187 500)	78 125	265 625
Old preference shareholders		
¼ (500 000 – 187 500)		78 125
Old ordinary shareholders		
½ (500 000 – 187 500)		156 250
		500 000

We are now able to set out the position of each party before and after the proposed scheme in order to draw conclusions about its acceptability:

Table 12.2

	Amount receivable on liquidation before scheme £000s	New capital introduced £000s	Position after scheme		
Original class			Amount receivable on liquidation after scheme £000s	Share of earnings £300 000 £000s	Share of earnings £500 000 £000s
Bank	2 790	–	3 000	n/a	n/a
Debenture					
holders	1 460	250	1 561	215.625	265.625
Trade creditors	930	–	1 000	n/a	n/a
Preference					
shareholders	–	250	186	28.125	78.125
Ordinary					
shareholders	–	500	373	56.250	156.250

The scheme would appear to offer advantages to all parties:

The bank converts unsecured debt into secured debt and stands to receive more in a liquidation after the scheme than in one before it.

On an immediate liquidation the debenture holders would receive £1 460 000 whereas if they invest a further £250 000 they will obtain a higher rate of interest on their debentures, a higher level of security and one-quarter of the ordinary shares in the reconstructed company. Although they would only receive £1 561 000 on a liquidation after the scheme, their share in future earnings is attractive. If the level of future earnings is £300 000 their rate of return is approximately 12.6 per cent, that is £215 625 divided by the amount of £1 710 000 (1 460 000 + 250 000) effectively invested. If future earnings are £500 000, the rate of return rises to approximately 18.2 per cent.

Trade creditors would receive more in a liquidation after the scheme than in one before it.

Both preference shareholders and ordinary shareholders would appear to benefit considerably from the scheme. Although they would not receive back their new investment if a liquidation occurred immediately after the scheme, their potential earnings yield is high.

If future earnings are £300 000, the yield is 11.25 per cent (28.125/250) while, if earnings are £500 000, the yield rises to 31.25 per cent (78.125/250).

If all the parties are happy with the scheme, they will vote in favour of it at their respective meetings. Provided it is then confirmed by the court, the scheme will become operative as soon as a copy of the court order is lodged with the Registrar. If any of the parties are unhappy with the scheme, it will be necessary to amend it. If, at the end of the day, agreement on a satisfactory scheme cannot be reached, the company will be liquidated.

RECOMMENDED READING

J. H. Farrar, N. E. Furey, B. M. Hannigan and O. P. Wylie, *Farrar's Company Law*, 3rd edition, Butterworths, London, 1991.

L. C. B. Gower, *Gower's Principles of Modern Company Law*, 5th edition, Sweet & Maxwell, London, 1992.

M. Wyatt, 'Purchase of own shares', *Accountants Digest No. 284*, ICAEW, London, 1992.

PART III

Interpretation and valuation

CHAPTER 13

Interpretation of accounts

INTRODUCTION

As we saw in Chapter 1, there are many different groups of people who are interested in the affairs of a business entity and who are therefore likely to use its accounts. Although the government as tax collector is interested mainly in the past, most users, including the government in other roles, are more interested in what is likely to happen in the future. Such people will therefore use the accounts for a past period to help them make a judgment on the likely future success or otherwise of the entity.

As we explained in Chapter 1, relatively little is known about the way in which accounts are used in the process of decision making but, at a general level, it is clear that different groups will place greater or lesser emphasis on particular aspects of a company's performance. To give an example, a potential long-term equity shareholder in a company will be interested in the potential returns and the riskiness of those returns in comparison with other investment opportunities, while a potential supplier of goods, that is a trade creditor, will be interested in whether or not he is likely to receive payment for goods supplied. Both users are interested in the future performance of the company but the emphasis of their interpretation will differ. When called upon to interpret a set of accounts, it is essential for the accountant to keep clearly in mind the purpose of the exercise.

Traditionally, textbooks on financial accounting have tended to concentrate on univariate analysis. Thus they examine and discuss one ratio at a time and show how it is possible to draw tentative conclusions by comparing the result for that ratio with some yardstick of comparison. By studying a number of ratios in this way, it is possible to piece together a picture of the company's performance and position. This is the predominant approach used in practice and occupies the second section of this chapter. In that section we shall assume that readers are familiar with the basic principles of ratio analysis.[1]

In the 1970s there was a move towards the use of multivariate analysis, that is a consideration of the impact of several ratios at the same time by using such statistical techniques as multiple regression analysis and discriminant analysis. The third section of the chapter examines this approach.

Many companies and groups of companies are now highly diversified and it is often difficult to draw conclusions from one set of accounts covering all such diverse activities. The final section of this chapter therefore examines the case for segmental reports and discusses some of the problems which must be faced in the provision of such information.

---

1 Readers who wish to revise this topic are referred to R. Lewis and M. Firth, *Foundation in Accounting*, Vol. 2, 2nd edn, Prentice-Hall, London, 1985.

UNIVARIATE ANALYSIS

Accounting systems

In this section we shall concentrate on the interpretation of historical cost accounts, although we shall refer to some differences in approach which may be necessary for the interpretation of current cost accounts.

In the case of historical cost accounts interpretation has become more difficult in a period when prices change. Many of the conclusions reached on the basis of the information contained in these accounts must be heavily qualified and many of the so called 'norms' for ratios, specified in traditional textbooks, are no longer relevant in a period where gains may be made from owing money and losses may be incurred by holding monetary assets.

Yardsticks of comparison

As readers will be aware, one figure in a set of accounts, or a ratio based on two figures in that set of accounts, are of little use unless the user has some yardstick of comparison. Although an internal user of accounts will have access to budgets as a suitable yardstick, the external user, with whom this book is concerned, must have recourse to other yardsticks. These are usually the results of previous periods, the results of other similar companies or industry averages for the same accounting period. Comparison with the results of previous periods is known as trend or time series analysis while comparison with the results of other firms, either individually or in terms of industry averages, is known as cross-sectional analysis. Both give rise to problems.

When trend analysis is employed, the results of each year will usually have been arrived at using consistent accounting policies.[2] Even so, the fixed asset values shown in historical cost accounts and the depreciation charges based on these tend to become more and more out of date as time passes. In addition, comparisons are difficult when the value of the measuring rod, the pound, is changing over time. In current cost accounts the former of these problems is largely removed because fixed assets are shown at their value to the business; however, unless such a current cost system incorporates adjustments for changes in the value of a pound, it is still difficult to compare results over time.

In addition to these difficulties caused by the accounting principles used, there is the more fundamental problem that the company's environment will change over time, with the result that performance which was considered satisfactory in the past may no longer be so. Thus, for example, a current ratio which might be considered to be acceptable in a period when additional short-term credit can be obtained cheaply and easily might be regarded as being dangerously low when short-term loans are very difficult to obtain.

When cross-sectional analysis is employed, even greater problems must be faced. First, there is the problem of finding a comparable business. This may be difficult as businesses may be diversified to a greater or lesser extent. Indeed, there can be substantial differences between businesses even when they operate within the same industry. Two examples will illustrate this point: (a) although two companies manufacture the same product, one company may own its own property while another company may rent its property; (b)

---

2 When this is not so, as in the case of a change in accounting policies, suitable adjustments must be made to render the figures comparable.

two companies may manufacture a similar finished product but whereas one company uses bought-in components, the other may manufacture all its components from raw materials.

In addition to these underlying differences, the fixed asset values which appear in a set of historical cost accounts tend, as was pointed out above, to become more and more out of date as time passes. This, together with the ability of directors to revalue assets on a piecemeal basis, introduces biases which depend on the dates of purchase or revaluation of the assets. Such biases are, of course, removed in current cost accounts.

To the above difficulties is added the wide choice of accounting policies available to reflect underlying business reality, with the result that one company may choose one set of policies while a second may choose a very different set.[3]

As readers may imagine, it is usually very difficult for an external user to make any adjustments for these differences, although he must bear them in mind when interpreting a set of accounts. Probably the best warning that may be given is that one must not be too dogmatic when interpreting accounts.

Aspects of performance

It is convenient to examine separately two aspects of performance of a company, profitability and liquidity. The continuance of a business depends both upon profitable operations and upon having enough cash to meet its commitments as they fall due. Although in the long run satisfactory profitability and liquidity are likely to accompany one another, in the short run it is quite possible for a company to be, on the one hand, profitable but illiquid or, on the other hand, liquid but unprofitable. In both cases there will be some doubt about the continuance of the business. Let us look at each of these aspects of performance in turn.

Profitability

Whether or not a company pursues profit maximisation as its objective, the majority of users of accounts will be interested in its profitability, that is how well the directors are using the resources at their disposal. Return on capital employed is frequently used as a measure of profitability, although it is necessary to exercise care in interpreting such a ratio. In particular, it is essential to be wary of undue reliance on a single ratio which attempts to summarise what may be an extremely complex business reality. The ASB took considerable pains to emphasise this point in FRS 3 'Reporting financial performance'.

If a profit and loss account shows that a company has made a profit of, say, £100 000, it is impossible to draw any conclusion from this one figure on whether the company has performed well or badly. The conclusion would differ if, on the one hand, assets worth £500 000 had been used and, on the other hand, assets worth £10 000 000 had been used to generate the profit. In the former case the return on assets or capital employed is 20 per cent while in the latter case it is only 1 per cent.

---

3 The Centre for Interfirm Comparison Limited, which conducts interfirm comparison schemes for firms in a number of industries, goes to considerable lengths to adjust the accounting data of participants to a common set of accounting policies. Although the Centre conducts schemes for the benefit of management rather than external users, its requirements for extensive adjustments indicate the difficulties of making comparisons if these adjustments have not been made.

A ratio of a measure of profit to a measure of capital employed is a first step towards assessing the profitability of most, although not all businesses.[4] Once such a return on capital employed has been calculated at, say, 20 per cent, it is still impossible to draw any conclusion about profitability without reference to one of the yardsticks of comparison mentioned in the preceding section.

Bearing in mind this need for comparison, let us try to be a little more precise in what we mean by return on assets or capital employed. Should we take operating profit, profit before interest and tax, profit available for shareholders, profit available for equity shareholders? Should we take gross assets or net assets, total capital employed whether short-term or long-term, long-term capital employed or just equity capital employed? Whichever of these capital figures we select should we use opening balance sheet figures, closing balance sheet figures or some average for the year?

Many combinations are possible and each may be useful for a specific purpose and also in helping us to build up a picture of the business. It is essential, however, that the numerator and denominator of each ratio are logically consistent.

We shall examine three ratios which measure different aspects of the return on capital employed:

$$\text{(a)} \quad \frac{\text{Profit available to equity shareholders}}{\text{Equity shareholders' interest}}$$

Equity shareholders and potential equity shareholders will be interested in the return which is being earned on equity capital employed in the business. This ratio provides an indication of the overall efficiency of the management not only in the operations of the business but also in arranging the financing position and taxation affairs of the company for the benefit of the equity shareholders.

When the ratio is calculated on the figures disclosed in historical cost accounts the profit to be taken is that after deducting interest, taxation and any preference dividends. The equity shareholders' interest is not just the equity share capital but the sum of equity share capital and all reserves. As the profits are earned over a period of time, it is preferable to use an appropriate average figure for the denominator.

Such a ratio based upon historical cost accounts suffers from the fact that the figure for equity interest shown in the balance sheet is based on out of date historical costs rather than current costs. Similarly, the profit figure is arrived at after charging out of date costs rather than current costs. These deficiencies are remedied to some extent where figures shown in current cost accounts are used to calculate the ratio.

When current cost accounts are used the numerator is the 'current cost profit attributable to equity shareholders'. The denominator is an appropriate average of the equity share capital plus all reserves, including any current cost reserve.

It is important to bear in mind that, although the equity shareholders' interest which appears in a current cost balance sheet will be based upon the current values of the assets which appear in that balance sheet, it will still exclude the value of many intangible assets, such as good management, which do not usually appear in balance sheets. It follows that, all other things being equal, a firm with a relatively high proportion of intangible assets

---

4 As neither historical cost accounts nor current cost accounts include a value for human capital employed, such a ratio based on the accounting data would be unhelpful for assessing the profitability of, for example, a professional accountancy practice.

will show a higher return on capital calculated on balance sheet figures than one with a low proportion of such assets. This point is also relevant to the following ratios.

$$\text{(b)} \quad \frac{\text{Profit before interest on long-term loans and taxation}}{\text{Long-term capital employed}}$$

This ratio indicates the return on all long-term capital employed. Long-term capital comprises the equity shareholders' interest, preference share capital and any long-term loans. As profit is earned during a period an appropriate average figure should be employed for the denominator.

Where current cost accounts are available the numerator will usually be the 'current cost operating profit' of the company and the denominator will reflect the current values of the assets identified in the current cost balance sheet.

Difficulties may often occur with bank overdrafts which, although legally repayable on demand, are often in practice part of the long-term capital of a company. Here it is necessary to make a judgment upon whether overdrafts are or are not long-term capital and then to frame the ratio accordingly. If bank overdrafts are considered to be part of long-term capital, the denominator will include the average overdraft and the numerator must therefore be the profit before charging interest on overdrafts. If they are not considered to be part of long-term capital, they will be excluded from the denominator and the numerator will be the profit after bank interest but before interest on long-term loans and taxation.

$$\text{(c)} \quad \frac{\text{Operating profit}}{\text{Operating assets employed}}$$

This ratio does not measure the overall success of the firm but abstracts from the financing and taxation position in order to measure what may be called operating efficiency. Thus it shows the rate of return which has been earned on the operating assets at the disposal of the directors, irrespective of how those assets have been financed.

The denominator should be an average of the operating assets employed by the firm, before the deduction of any current or long-term liabilities. The numerator should be the operating profit before interest on any sources of finance.

When a set of detailed financial accounts is available, it is possible to carry out a systematic analysis using a pyramid of ratios like the one illustrated below.[5] We have designed a pyramid for a manufacturing company but it is, of course, possible to design all manner of pyramids depending upon the circumstances of the particular company and the information required. The simple pyramid for a manufacturing company might take the form shown in Figure 13.1.

Ratio (1) provides the return on total assets expressed as a percentage. This may be analysed by examining ratios (2) and (3). Ratio (2) is the net profit margin on sales

---

5 Such an analysis is only possible if companies adopt profit and loss account formats 1 or 3 specifed in the Companies Act 1985, Schedule 4, Part 1.

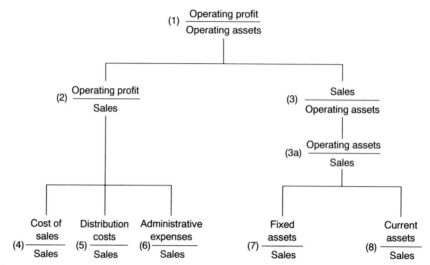

Fig. 13.1

expressed as a percentage while ratio (3) is the asset turnover in times per year. The relationship between the three ratios is expressed as follows:

$$\frac{\text{Profit}}{\text{Assets}} = \frac{\text{Profit}}{\text{Sales}} \times \frac{\text{Sales}}{\text{Assets}}$$

i.e. Ratio (1) = Ratio (2) x Ratio (3)

To give an example, if the result for ratio (2) is 10 per cent and the result for ratio (3) is two times per year, the result for ratio (1) is 20 per cent.

If the net profit margin on sales (ratio (2)) has deteriorated compared with previous years or is poor in comparison with the corresponding ratio of other companies, it is possible to move down the left-hand side of the pyramid to determine why this is so. By examining the results for ratios (4), (5) and (6), it is possible to see which ratios are increasing and hence causing ratio (2) to fall. If we assume that all ratios are expressed as percentages, the relationship between ratios (2), (4), (5) and (6) is expressed as follows:

Ratio (2) + Ratio (4) + Ratio (5) + Ratio (6) = 100%[6]

The higher the result for ratios (4), (5) and (6), the lower will be the result for ratios (1)

[6] This may be easily demonstrated. Let S be sales and let C_4, C_5, C_6 be cost of sales, distribution costs and administrative expenses respectively, assuming that all operating costs of the company are included under one of these headings. Then

$$\text{Ratio (2)} = \frac{S - (C_4 + C_5 + C_6)}{S}$$

while

$$\text{Ratio (4)} = \frac{C_4}{S} \quad \text{Ratio (5)} = \frac{C_5}{S} \quad \text{Ratio (6)} = \frac{C_6}{S}$$

It follows that

$$\frac{S - (C_4 + C_5 + C_6)}{S} + \frac{C_4}{S} + \frac{C_5}{S} + \frac{C_6}{S} = \frac{S}{S} = 1.$$

But $S/S = 1$ expressed as a percentage is 100%.

and (2). Hence at this stage we may say that high results for ratios (4), (5) and (6) are undesirable, although as we shall see later in this section, even this statement will have to be modified when we consider the interrelationships between the two sides of the pyramid.

Turning now to the right-hand side of the pyramid, we may explore how well the firm is utilising its assets to achieve sales. Ratio (3) shows the asset turnover and, provided that ratio (2) is positive, the higher the result for this ratio the better. Many people find it conceptually difficult to think in terms of asset turnover, and it is therefore useful to express the same measures in a somewhat different way. Whereas ratio (3) shows sales divided by assets, ratio (3a), its reciprocal, shows the value of assets per pound of sales. A result of two times per year for ratio (3) would therefore be equivalent to a result of £0.5 for ratio (3a). If similar measures are used for ratios (7) and (8), we have the advantage, for analytical purposes, that:

$$\text{Ratio (7)} + \text{Ratio (8)} = \text{Ratio (3a)}$$

Again we may tentatively say that the lower the results for ratios (7) and (8) the better.

It is possible to extend the pyramid downwards. Thus the utilisation of the various categories of fixed assets and current assets may be explored. To take an example let us examine the utilisation of current assets (Figure 13.2).

Current assets may be analysed into stocks, debtors and any other current assets and an examination made to determine to what extent a high value for ratio (8) is due to high results for ratios (9), (10) and (11). This may be the best that can be done with the information available in published accounts. The figures for stocks and debtors will, at best, be averages of the opening and closing balance sheet figures, and such simple averages may not be good approximations to the average, in the sense of typical, values for the period. Similarly, ratios (9) and (10) are both logically inconsistent for the reasons given below and could be improved with better information.

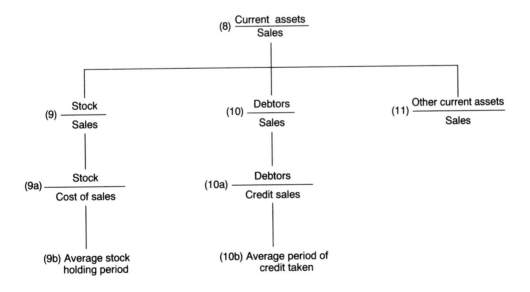

Fig. 13.2

Concentrating first on ratio (9), stocks are usually shown at cost while sales are at selling price. A consistent ratio would relate stocks to the cost of sales, as shown in ratio (9a), and from this we may arrive at the average stock holding period in days (ratio (9b)):

$$\text{Average stock holding period (Ratio (9b))} = 365 \times \frac{\text{Stock}}{\text{Cost of sales}}$$

A consistent ratio for (10) would relate debtors, not to total sales, but to credit sales. This is done in ratio (10a). Again we are able to arrive at an average period of credit taken by debtors, shown by ratio (10b):

$$\text{Average period of credit (Ratio (10b))} = 365 \times \frac{\text{Debtors}}{\text{Credit sales}}$$

We have now seen how, given sufficient data, it is possible to analyse performance in a systematic way. In addition we have seen that, looked at individually, high results for the cost ratios and for the asset utilisation ratios (3a), (7) and (8) are unfavourable. It is, however, most important not to be too dogmatic here and to bear in mind that there are links *across* the pyramid. To give an example, a high result for ratio (5), selling and distribution costs to sales, is by itself unfavourable. However, high expenditure on selling may increase sales with the result that it is possible to use assets more effectively and hence achieve favourable results for the asset utilisation ratios.

This emphasises that interpretation of accounts is an art by which we look for clues to performance. It is an art in which one should never be rigid in one's thinking.

Liquidity

Even a very profitable company may be forced into liquidation if it is unable to meet its debts. In view of this, most users of accounts are concerned with the liquidity of a company, which may conveniently be divided into short-term liquidity and long-term solvency.

The short-term liquidity position of a company has traditionally been assessed by looking at the relationship between current assets and current liabilities, or some components of current assets and current liabilities, on a balance sheet. These are essentially static measures, whereas debts are paid out of cash flows. A more recent tendency has been to look at ratios of a dynamic nature relating cash or funds flow to current liabilities. We shall look at these in turn, commencing with the static measures.

The current, or working capital, ratio relates current assets to current liabilities:

$$\text{Current ratio} = \frac{\text{Current liabilities}}{\text{Current assets}}$$

A result greater than 1 suggests that a company is able to pay its current liabilities out of current assets. However, the composition of the current assets is important; two companies may have the same result for the current ratio although, in one case the major part of current assets is stock while, in the other case, the major part of current assets is debtors. Because of this it is usual to supplement the current ratio with a 'liquid' or 'quick' asset ratio, relating the more liquid current assets, such as debtors, cash and short-term marketable securities, to current liabilities:

$$\text{Liquid ratio} = \frac{\text{Debtors + Cash + Short-term marketable securities}}{\text{Current liabilities}}$$

A ratio in excess of 1 is a much clearer indication, although still not conclusive evidence, that a company is able to meet its short-term debts.

Once the above ratios have been calculated it is usually still very difficult to say whether the results are good or bad. Although high results for the current ratio and the liquid ratio suggest a sound liquidity position, they may also suggest that an excessive amount of money is tied up unprofitably in stocks, debtors and cash. In addition, in an inflationary era, a large amount tied up in monetary assets will lead to monetary losses, that is losses of purchasing power, which most companies will be keen to avoid.

The above ratios are essentially static in nature and hence only give us indications of the short-term liquidity position to the extent that they are typical and that no window dressing has taken place. Window dressing occurs when action is taken to manipulate certain figures which appear in a set of accounts to produce more satisfactory results. The current ratio and liquid ratio are both particularly susceptible to such manipulation. This is best understood by recognising that if a ratio is greater than 1, the subtraction of the same amount from both numerator and denominator will make it larger whereas, if it is less than 1, the subtraction of the same amount from both numerator and denominator will make it smaller.[7]

Let us look at an example. A company forecasts that it will have a liquid ratio of 0.7 on its balance sheet date calculated as follows:

$$\frac{\text{Liquid assets}}{\text{Current liabilities}} = \frac{700\ 000}{1\ 000\ 000} = 0.70$$

The firm realises that this ratio is lower than that of previous years and considers that it is likely to have an adverse effect on the company's share price. It therefore delays the payment of creditors amounting to £300 000 so that the liquid ratio based on the reported results becomes:

$$\frac{700\ 000 + 300\ 000}{1\ 000\ 000 + 300\ 000} = 0.77$$

The possibility of such window dressing emphasises the dangers of assessing liquidity by taking the position at just one point in time. As current liabilities are paid out of cash flow, rather than out of a stock of current assets, analysts have developed ratios of a more dynamic nature. Two such ratios using cash flows are:

$$\text{(a)} \quad \frac{\text{Net cash inflow from operating activities}}{\text{Current liabilities}}$$

$$\text{(b)} \quad \frac{\text{Quick assets}}{\text{Daily outflow of cash on operations}}$$

---

7 If $A/B > 1$, then $(A - x)/(B - x) > A/B$. Conversely, if $A/B < 1$, then $(A - x)/(B - x) < A/B$. $(B > x > 0.)$

The former relates the source of cash from operations, as shown in the cash flow statement to the current liabilities at the close of a period. It therefore gives an indication of how long it takes to generate sufficient cash to pay off the stock of current liabilities. By dividing 365 days by the result for ratio (a), this information may be expressed in days. The second of the two ratios relates the quick assets, that is cash, debtors and marketable securities, to the average daily outlay of cash on operations. The former figure would be taken from the closing balance sheet while the latter would be approximated by taking the total operating expenses from the profit and loss account and deducting depreciation. It indicates how many days the firm would be able to continue operations if there were no further inflow of cash and is usually referred to as a 'defensive interval measure' or sometimes a 'no credit interval'. Neither of these ratios is without fault, but they do attempt to focus on the flows out of which debts are paid rather than on what may be an atypical position at one point in time. Of course they still suffer from the possibility that the current liabilities or quick assets included in the ratios may themselves be atypical.

We have so far focused on the short-term liquidity of a company. It is also important to consider the longer-term solvency, in other words the ability of the company to meet debts in the future.

Two ratios are of particular help here: the first is the gearing or leverage ratio, that is the relationship between debt and equity capital.

$$\text{(a)} \quad \frac{\text{Long-term debt and preference share capital}}{\text{Long-term debt, preference share capital and equity interest}}$$

This ratio is often calculated on the basis of balance sheet values, although to have any economic meaning it should properly be based upon current values. The higher the result for this ratio, the greater the proportion of the assets which is financed by non-equity capital and hence the greater the risk of debt holders suffering a loss on a liquidation. In addition the higher the result for this ratio, the greater the potential volatility of the earnings stream attributable to the equity shareholders.

Of course, this is a simple initial conclusion because, on the one hand, different forms of debt have different rights and security and, on the other hand, the realisable values of the assets on a liquidation may bear little relationship to their balance sheet values in either historical cost accounts or current cost accounts. Nevertheless it is frequently used to compare the financial position of one company with that of another.

The second ratio is commonly called 'times interest covered', that is the relationship between operating income and interest and preference dividends payable.

$$\text{(b)} \quad \frac{\text{Operating income before interest and taxation}}{\text{Interest payments (before taxation) and preference dividends payable}}$$

This ratio tries to capture the same feature as ratio (a) above by looking at the proportion of the total operating income which goes to suppliers of long-term capital other than equity shareholders. The lower the ratio the less certain are debt holders to receive their interest and preference shareholders their dividends; in other words, the greater the risk to lenders and preference shareholders.

In interpreting these ratios, it is, of course, essential to bear in mind the variability of the operating earnings. A company with stable earnings over time will be able to support a much higher level of debt than a company with variable earnings over time.

We must stress the undesirability of attempting to draw definite conclusions from the liquidity and solvency ratios. Instead the ratios should be used to help build up a picture of the company's overall position. Thus, one should ask such questions as: Are the current and liquid ratios becoming larger or smaller over time? Is the gearing increasing or falling? How do the ratios of this company compare with those of other companies in the industry? If the ratios are out of line with those of other companies, what are the possible reasons?

MULTIVARIATE ANALYSIS

Introduction

In the preceding section we concentrated on the univariate approach to interpretation. Under this approach one particular ratio is examined, comparisons are made with the results of previous years or of similar companies and tentative conclusions are drawn. This process is repeated in respect of another ratio and, gradually, by examining many ratios, a picture is built up of the position and likely future prospects of the company. The ratios are not combined together in any formal manner, but professional judgment is used to determine how much weight should be given to each of them.

A different approach involves considering several ratios simultaneously by means of multivariate analysis. Under this approach several ratios are combined by means of a formula to produce an index number and conclusions may be drawn by comparing that index number with the similar number for previous periods or for similar companies. One of the best documented areas in which such an approach has been applied is in the prediction of corporate failure and we shall concentrate on that particular application here.

The prediction of corporate failure

The failure[8] of a company will usually have serious repercussions for the individuals involved, such as shareholders, employees and creditors, and often for society at large. If it were possible to predict that a company was likely to fail, then it may well be possible for management to take steps to avoid failure and for other interested parties to take remedial action to mitigate the effects of failure in their own interests. A method which successfully predicts failure would therefore be very valuable, and considerable effort has been devoted to this problem by researchers.[9] Both univariate and multivariate approaches have been used, although we shall concentrate on the latter approach here.[10] As will be seen it is not possible to predict whether a particular company is going to fail. Rather it

---

8 Failure may be defined (and has been defined) in many ways in different studies. This may include insolvency, entry into receivership, creditors' voluntary liquidation or compulsory liquidation, the need for a reconstruction or receipt of government aid as alternatives to liquidation.

9 In this section we concentrate on methods of predicting failure based on information contained in a set of accounts. These methods may be said to concentrate on the symptoms rather than on the more fundamental defects of the company and the mistakes of its management. John Argenti has developed an 'A' score, based on both accounting data and on qualitative judgments of management. Interested readers are referred to 'Company failure – long range prediction not enough', *Accountancy*, August 1977, and to the extremely readable book, J. Argenti, *Corporate Collapse*, McGraw-Hill, New York. 1976.

10 For an example of the univariate approach, *see* W. H. Beaver, 'Financial ratios as predictors of failure', in *Empirical Research in Accounting*, Supplement to *Journal of Accounting Research*, 1966.

appears possible to say whether or not a particular company exhibits characteristics similar to other companies which have failed in the past.

Although the multivariate approach had been used in this context before, the most influential work on the prediction of failure was that of the American Professor E. I. Altman.[11] In a study published in 1968, he took a sample of 33 failed and 33 non-failed American manufacturing companies. He then examined many ratios to see which ratios taken together best discriminated between companies in the two groups. In the absence of any well-developed theoretical models which would explain why companies fail, he used a statistical technique known as 'multiple discriminant analysis'. By this means he found five ratios which could be combined to produce what is called a Z score, the level of which best captured differences between the failed and non-failed firms.

The discriminant function took the form:

$$Z = 0.012X_1 + 0.014X_2 + 0.033X_3 + 0.006X_4 + 0.010X_5$$

The five ratios were

$$X_1 = \frac{\text{Working capital}}{\text{Total gross assets}}$$

$$X_2 = \frac{\text{Retained earnings}}{\text{Total gross assets}}$$

$$X_3 = \frac{\text{Earnings before interest and tax}}{\text{Total gross assets}}$$

$$X_4 = \frac{\text{Market value of equity}}{\text{Book value of debt}}$$

$$X_5 = \frac{\text{Sales}}{\text{Total gross assets}}$$

Thus the Altman Z score combined ratios covering aspects of liquidity, re-invested earnings, profitability, gearing and asset turnover. There is no obvious economic reason why these emerged; it was simply that, statistically, they gave the best results.

Having arrived at the above equation, Altman then found that all companies with a Z score greater than 2.99 were non-failed companies while all companies with a Z score below 1.81 were failed companies.[12] It was impossible to be so categoric with companies which had a score between 1.81 and 2.99. Altman tested his statistical model on different samples of companies and found that one year before failure his model correctly classified companies to the failed or non-failed group accurately in 96 per cent of the cases. However, more generally he found that the percentage of correct classification declined considerably with data more than one year prior to failure.

11 *See*, for example, E. I. Altman, 'Financial ratios, discriminant analysis and the prediction of corporate bankruptcy', *The Journal of Finance*, 1968, or, E. I. Altman, *Corporate Financial Distress*, John Wiley, New York, 1983.

12 Strictly 'non-bankrupt' and 'bankrupt', respectively, using Altman's terminology.

It is important to bear in mind that Altman's researches and model relate to the manufacturing sector of the US economy in the period 1946–65. It therefore does not follow that his results would be applicable to other sectors or at other times; nor does it follow that his results would be relevant in the different conditions of the UK economy. What he did was to provide us with an approach to the prediction of failure which may be applied in other circumstances.

R. J. Taffler and H. Tisshaw applied the approach to UK data and developed two 'Z scales', one for quoted manufacturing enterprises and one for non-quoted manufacturing enterprises with turnover above £½ million.[13] For the sample of quoted manufacturing enterprises, statistical analysis resulted in the following formula:

$$Z = C_0 + C_1 R_1 + C_2 R_2 + C_3 R_3 + C_4 R_4$$

C_0 to C_4 are coefficients and R_1 to R_4 are the following ratios:

$$R_1 = \frac{\text{Profit before taxation}}{\text{Current liabilities}}$$

$$R_2 = \frac{\text{Current assets}}{\text{Total liabilities}}$$

$$R_3 = \frac{\text{Current liabilities}}{\text{Total assets}}$$

$$R_4 = \text{No credit interval}$$

$$= \frac{\text{Immediate assets} - \text{Current liabilities}}{\text{Operating costs excluding depreciation}}$$

Thus, the four ratios combine together various aspects of profitability and solvency to produce a Z score. When they turn to the unquoted manufacturing enterprises the formula comprises not four but five ratios.

Taffler and Tisshaw claim very good results for their formula but, because of their proprietary interest, have not been willing to publish the coefficients for their equations. It has not therefore been possible for others working in the same area to test and comment on the particular models put forward.

In a general textbook on financial accounting we have only been able to provide a brief introduction to multivariate analysis. Such techniques are being used by various investment institutions and large accounting practices to determine whether or not the going concern concept is or is not appropriate.

Segmental reporting and its problems

The financial statements of a company and the consolidated financial statements of a group summarise the results and financial position for the reporting entity as a whole.

---

13 A brief account of this work appears in R. J. Taffler, 'Z-scores: An approach to the recession', *Accountancy*, July 1991, pp. 95–7.

Thus, subject to the possible exclusion of one or more subsidiaries from consolidation in accordance with the provisions of FRS 2, the financial statements summarise all of the activities of the reporting entity, no matter how diverse these activities may be. Many companies and groups of companies operate in a number of different industries and in a number of different geographical areas, perhaps manufacturing in certain countries and supplying customers in other countries. The industrial and geographical segments of the entity may enjoy different levels of profitability and may be subject to very different risks and may have very different growth potentials. If users are to be able to assess past performance and to predict likely future performance of the entity as a whole, it may be argued that it is necessary for them to be provided with a detailed analysis in respect of the individual segments. The provision of such an analysis is known as segmental, analysed or disaggregated reporting.

Company law and the Stock Exchange have accepted the need for such segmental reporting for many years although, as we shall see, their requirements are limited. Many listed companies provide considerably more detailed information than has been required and there is some evidence that the provision of such information enables users to make more accurate predictions. Although an international accounting standard, IAS 14 'Reporting financial information by segment' was issued in 1981, SSAP 25 'Segmental reporting' was only issued in 1990. We shall look first at the requirements of company law and the Stock Exchange before turning to the provisions of SSAP 25.

So long as the disclosure of the information is not seriously prejudicial to the interests of the company, the Companies Act 1985 requires two analyses, the first where a company or group has carried on business of two or more classes that (in the opinion of the directors) differ substantially from one another and the second where a company or group has supplied geographical markets that (in the opinion of the directors) differ substantially from each other.[14]

In the former case, the law requires a description of each class of business together with the turnover and the profit or loss before taxation attributable to each class while, for the geographical segments, the law requires only an analysis of turnover. For listed companies, the Stock Exchange increases the amount of disclosure by requiring 'a geographical analysis of both net turnover and contribution to trading results of those trading operations carried on ... outside the United Kingdom and the Republic of Ireland', although the analysis of contribution is only required if the profit or loss from a specific area is out of line with the normal profit margin.[15]

The above requirements ensure the provision of a minimum amount of segmental information but leave a great many questions unanswered.

While some would question the wisdom of leaving the selection of reportable segments to directors, this would seem to be inevitable given the variety and complexity of modern businesses.[16] However, any segmental analysis provided may be highly misleading if there is substantial trading between segments, especially if this trading occurs at artificially determined prices, and yet the law and Stock Exchange do not require the disclosure of any intersegment turnover nor the basis of intersegment pricing. Where an analysis of profit or contribution is required, there is the problem of how to deal with common or

---

14 Companies Act 1985 Schedule 4 Para. 55(1) to 55(5).
15 *Admission of Securities to Listing*, Sec. 5, Chapter 2, Para. 21(c).
16 SSAP 25, Para. 9 defines a reportable segment by reference to the relative size of the segment, namely 10 per cent or more of external turnover, results or net assets.

joint costs which are not directly attributable to any one segment; examples would be interest cost and the cost of a head office. In addition, the segmental information would appear to be of limited use without some indication of the net assets employed in each segment but, immediately an attempt is made to provide such an indication of net assets, the accountant confronts the problem of how to deal with common or joint assets, that is assets used by more than one segment. We would expect to turn to the Accounting Standard for guidance on the above matters.

While the standard contains some provisions relating to the statutory segmental disclosure, which therefore apply to all companies, it also extends these requirements for any entity that:[17]

(a) is a public limited company or that has a public limited company as a subsidiary; or
(b) is a banking or insurance company or group ...; or
(c) exceeds the criteria, multiplied in each case by 10, for defining a medium-sized company under section 247 of the Companies Act 1985, as amended from time to time by statutory instrument.

Thus, segmental disclosure required by statute is increased for public companies and certain specialised companies as well as for large private companies, although such a large private company does not have to provide the additional information if its parent provides the required information.

The extent of the increase in disclosure may be seen in paragraph 34 of the standard:

> If an entity has two or more classes of business, or operates in two or more geographical segments which differ substantially from each other, it should define its classes of business and geographical segments in its financial statements, and it should report with respect to each class of business and geographical segment the following financial information:
>
> (a) turnover, distinguishing between (i) turnover derived from external customers and (ii) turnover derived from other segments;
> (b) result, before accounting for taxation, minority interests and extraordinary items; and
> (c) net assets.

The geographical segmentation should be given by *turnover of origin*, that is the area from which products or services are supplied and for which results and net assets will be determined. However, it should also be given by *turnover of destination* where it is materially different.[18]

The division of turnover between external sales and intersegment sales undoubtedly helps users to appreciate the interdependence of segments although the effect of such interdependence on results will be impossible to ascertain without some knowledge of the way in which intersegment prices are determined. While IAS 14 and ED 45, the predecessor of SSAP 25, require disclosure of the basis of intersegment pricing, SSAP 25 stepped back from actually requiring this.

The standard provides guidance on determining segmental results and increases the legal provisions by requiring the disclosure of net assets for each segment. As a consequence it should be possible to compute returns on capital employed for the different activities of the business.

---

17 SSAP 25, Para. 41.
18 SSAP 25, Para. 34.

Results are to be taken before taxation, minority interests and extraordinary items and normally before taking account of any interest receivable or payable. Net assets will normally be the non-interest earning operating assets less the non-interest bearing operating liabilities. Only if the interest income or expense is central to the business of the segment should it be included in arriving at the segmental result when, for consistency, the assets or liabilities to which it relates should be included in the segmental net assets. Interest excluded and other common revenues and costs should be excluded from the segmental analysis but included in the total results. Similarly, common assets and liabilities should be excluded from the segment net assets but included separately as part of the total net assets. This is essential if the segmental analysis is to agree with the related totals in the financial statements of the company or group and, where such agreement is not apparent, a reconciliation must be provided.[19]

The Appendix to SSAP 25 contains an illustrative segmental report covering both classes of business and geographical segment. The following table illustrates the sort of segmental report envisaged for classes of business only although, for simplicity, we have excluded comparative figures.[20]

From Table 13.1 it is possible to compare the profit margin on sales and the return on net assets for each segment:

Table 13.1   Illustrative segmental report

Classes of business (excluding comparative figures)	Industry A £000s	Industry B £000s	Group £000s
Turnover			
External sales	700	250	950
Intersegment sales	50	–	50
Total sales	750	250	1000
Profit before taxation			
Segment profit	150	100	250
less Common costs			60
			190
Share of profit before taxation of associated undertakings	40	–	40
Net assets			
Segment net assets	1500	400	1900
Unallocated assets			100
			2000
Share of net assets of associated undertaking	300	–	300
			2300

19 SSAP 25, Para. 37.

20 Note that the illustration includes the aggregate share of the results and net assets of associated undertakings. This is required if such associated undertakings account for at least 20 per cent of its total results or 20 per cent of its total net assets. (SSAP 25, Para. 36.)

Profit margin
Segment A $150 \div 750 = 20\%$
Segment B $100 \div 250 = 40\%$

Return on net assets
Segment A $150 \div 1500 = 10\%$
Segment B $100 \div \ \ 400 = 25\%$

Thus, it can be seen that the smaller segment, that is industry B, has the higher profit margin and the higher return on capital employed.

In practice such results could be compared with those for previous years to build up a picture of past trends and hence likely future progress. For example, given the results disclosed above, an investor would be much happier if the involvement of the company or group in industry B were growing as a proportion of its total activity than if the involvement in industry A were growing.

By requiring the disclosure of intersegment sales and of segmental net assets, the standard has certainly improved the usefulness of the legally required segmental disclosure. However, it will be more difficult to draw conclusions from a segmental report the higher the level of intersegment sales and the greater the proportion of common costs/revenues and common net assets.

Although potentially, the segmental information should be of considerable benefit to users, the inevitable discretion permitted to directors reduces that benefit substantially in practice.

RECOMMENDED READING

G. Foster, *Financial Statement Analysis*, 2nd edition, Prentice-Hall, Englewood Cliffs, N.J., 1986.

M. Pendlebury and R. Groves, *Company Accounts – analysis, interpretation and understanding*, Unwin Hyman, 1990.

E. Hodgson, 'Segmental reporting', *Accountants Digest No. 248*, ICAEW, London, Summer 1990.

CHAPTER 14

The valuation of securities and businesses

INTRODUCTION

More than a passing reference has been made elsewhere in this book to the fact that conventional accounting based on the historical cost convention does not reflect the current economic value of either individual assets or the business as a whole. It might then appear to be somewhat paradoxical that the results disclosed by a business's financial statement loom so large in the way in which businesses and shares in businesses are valued.

We shall in this chapter discuss the basic principles associated with the valuation of financial securities and businesses and consider the part played therein by accounting information.

The standard valuation model for any asset is based on the cash flows that will accrue to the owner as a result of his or her possession of that asset – the 'present value model' i.e.

$$V_0 = \sum_{j=1}^{\infty} \frac{C_j}{(1+k)^j}$$

Where V_0 is the value of the asset at time t_0, C_j is the cash flow to the owner which will be generated in year j and k is the discount rate.

We shall assume that the readers are familiar with the basic principles underlying present value calculations but we, nonetheless, emphasise two important assumptions that underlie the simple model presented above; one is that the discount rate k is constant, the other is that cash flows occur only at the end of each year.

It can be seen from the model that, in order to value an asset, estimates of C_j and k are required.

THE VALUATION OF SECURITIES

We shall in this section consider the valuation of holdings of securities which do not constitute a controlling interest in the enterprise. If the holding is sufficient to give a controlling interest, the focus of interest changes to the value of the business as a whole – a topic which will be covered in the second part of the chapter.

Ex post and *ex ante* valuations

It is convenient to distinguish between the *ex post* (after) and the *ex ante* (before) need to value securities, although as we shall show similar principles apply in each case. In an *ex post* valuation the purpose of the exercise is the determination of the value of the securities at a current or past date, while in an *ex ante* valuation the requirement is to estimate the value of the security at some future date.

Perhaps the most common reason for requiring an *ex post* valuation is taxation, particularly for inheritance and capital gains tax. The inclusion of investments in the balance sheet of the owner at current cost also gives rise to the need for an *ex post* valuation.

Ex ante valuations are also of considerable importance. The management of a company should consider the effect on the value of the company's securities of alternative courses of action when deciding upon such matters as the company's investment policy or capital structure. It is possible, for example, that diversification into a new area may influence the stock market's perception of the risk associated with the company's earnings. Thus, it seems reasonable that when management is contemplating such diversification it should consider the likely impact on security prices and not confine itself to an assessment of the change in the company's cash flow.

Valuation of fixed interest securities

Loans and preference shares are usually described as fixed interest securities even though the preference shareholders are entitled to a fixed rate of dividend rather than a fixed rate of interest.[1] Both may be irredeemable or redeemable at some specified date in the future.

In the case of fixed interest securities the future cash flows are known and so the only problem is the selection of an appropriate discount rate. As discussed below, this is likely to be different for loans and preference shares in view of the different risks involved. For the moment, we shall assume that the discount rate is known.

Where a security is irredeemable, it will yield the same sum of cash each year for the indefinite future. If we assume that the interest or dividend is payable annually and that the first receipt will occur in one year's time, then the value of the security will be given by the following formula:

$$V_0 = \frac{s}{k}$$

where V_0 is the value at t_0, s is the annual cash receipt and k is the discount rate. So, for example, if we wish to value 10 per cent irredeemable debenture stock which pays interest annually, when the discount rate is 16 per cent, we would proceed as follows:

Let us value £100 of debenture stock. This produces a cash flow of £10 (10% × £100) per annum so the value of this perpetual flow of £10 per annum would be:

$$V_0 = \frac{£10}{0.16} = £62.5$$

---

1 Some preference shares may, of course, be participating preference shares and both loans and preference shares may be convertible into ordinary shares. The valuation of these participating and convertible securities is not dealt with in this book.

Thus the value of £100 of this debenture stock would be £62.50.

Where the interest is payable half yearly or quarterly, it is still possible to use the above formula but s would then represent the half-yearly or quarterly cash receipt as appropriate while k would be the appropriate half-yearly or quarterly discount rate.

Redeemable fixed interest securities will yield the same sum of money each period until their redemption date when a return of capital will take place on some prescribed basis.

Consider a security which will pay an annual sum of £s for n years at which time a return of capital of £C will be made. The first receipt will occur in one year's time.

Using a present value model the value of this security would be given by:

$$V_0 = \sum_{j=1}^{n} \frac{s}{(1+k)^j} + \frac{C}{(1+k)^n}$$

Once the annual cash flow, the redemption date and value and a cost of capital are known, the actual calculations can be made painlessly given the possession of a suitably programmed calculator or a set of compound interest tables.

In choosing an appropriate discount rate for fixed interest securities, it is important to distinguish between loans and preference shares. The payment of loan interest is a contractual liability of the company and must be paid whether or not profits are made, whereas preference dividends may only be paid if there are distributable profits available and the directors decide to pay such dividends. On a liquidation, loan holders will be repaid before preference shareholders. Thus, it is clear that loan holders can be more certain of their income and capital than preference shareholders. Hence, loan holders are likely to apply a lower discount rate in arriving at the valuation of their securities than are the preference shareholders.

In general the appropriate discount rates will be derived from market comparisons. In the case of securities which are not listed on a stock exchange, a higher discount rate would be expected to compensate for the lack of marketability.

The valuation of ordinary shares

We shall first consider the usually simple task of valuing quoted shares. We shall then introduce a theoretical model and show how it may be applied to unquoted shares.

Quoted shares

In most circumstances the *ex post* valuation of quoted shares will present few difficulties as the valuation can be made by reference to the prices at which the shares were traded on the required valuation date. Typically, there will be a number of different prices quoted for any one day since prices will fluctuate during the day and the normal practice, for valuation purposes, is to take the average of the highest and lowest prices marked.

There are circumstances when the Stock Exchange price will not give a reliable guide to the value of a holding of shares. This will occur when the block of shares to be valued is large compared with the number of shares which are actively traded on the Stock Exchange. Clearly, if the normal level of activity in a company share runs at about 10 000 shares per day it is extremely likely that the hypothetical sale of 100 000 shares would only have been achieved at a lower price than that which actually prevailed on the appropriate date. Similarly, a purchase of a large block of shares would probably have to have been made at a higher price. Thus, in such circumstances, the realisable value of a large block of shares will be less than the product of the number of shares and the Stock Exchange price per share while the replacement cost of the shares would be greater than that figure. Valuation of such large blocks of shares therefore requires a considerable element of subjective judgment about the circumstances leading to the need for evaluation and about the likely effect on the market of a transaction of unusual size.

True and market value

We shall now consider whether it can be said that a share has a true or intrinsic value which may be different from its market value. There are different opinions on this matter. Some argue that there cannot be a difference between the two because (ignoring the problem of large blocks of shares) the value of a quoted share must be the same as the price at which it was traded and that it is not meaningful to talk of a 'true' value which differs from its market value. Advocates of this view believe that the price of a share is determined by the interaction of buyers and sellers, who are influenced by many factors including speculative motives, and that there is little point in attempting to analyse the results of any particular company in any great detail. The investment strategy of this school is to attempt to determine when share prices will change and to buy or sell depending upon whether they think that the share price will rise or fall. An extreme, and well-known, example of this approach is provided by the chartists, who claim that it is possible to identify patterns of past share price movements which may be used to determine whether the share price will rise or fall. It must be said that not everyone agrees that this is a valid approach.

An alternative view is that the share does have a true value based on the economic value of the company which, if the company is a going concern, will be based on the company's prospective dividends since they must ultimately be available to the shareholders. It is argued that due to differences in expectations and other market imperfections it is likely that the market price will not be the same as the true value but that over time the difference will be eroded as the participants in the markets come to share the same expectations. This view suggests that it would be profitable to attempt to identify and purchase those shares which are currently 'undervalued'.

We will concentrate on the second approach not only because of its importance in its own right but also because it provides a theoretical underpinning to the whole subject of the valuation of shares, whether quoted or unquoted.

Dividend valuation models

The first assumption we must make is that investors are only interested in the cash flows that will accrue to them as a result of their ownership of shares, i.e. we will assume that investors will ignore any non-pecuniary benefits (such as prestige from holding shares in the company or other perquisites available to shareholders).

We will consider initially a potential purchaser of a share who intends to hold that share for only a year and then to resell it. His outlay is the current purchase price; he will receive a dividend in one year's time and will then sell the share. We will assume at this stage that the purchaser could alternatively put his money in a risk-free bank account and leave it there to earn interest. There is, therefore, a cost to the individual that is the lost interest. We can consider this lost interest at his cost of capital.

Let us suppose that the price he pays to purchase the share is $£P_0$, the price for which he sells the share is $£P_1$, the dividend he receives at the year end is $£D_1$ and the cost of capital (expressed as a decimal) is k.

Now if the potential investor had deposited the purchase price in a risk-free interest-earning bank account at the beginning of the year (time t_0) he would at the end of the year (time t_1) have $£P_0(1 + k)$. Alternatively, if he purchases the share he would at time t_1 receive $£(P_1 + D_1)$. He will only purchase the share if he expects the purchase to make him at least as well off as his deposit in the interest earning account, i.e. if $P_0(1 + k) < P_1 + D_1$ or $P_0 < (P_1 + D_1)/(1 + k)$.

Let us assume that the participants in the market all make the same estimates of P_1, D_1, and k. Then a share which is cheaply priced, i.e. where $P_0 < (P_1 + D_1)/(1 + k)$, will be purchased and the price will be bid up until equilibrium is achieved when, $P_0 = (P_1 + D_1)/(1 + k)$.

We have thus derived a simple present value model of the value of a share based on its expected dividend for the year and its expected price in one year's time.

If we consider the subsequent purchaser (who will hold the share for one year only), then the same considerations will apply at time t_1 so that we can say that P_1 will be given by $P_1 = (P_2 + D_2)/(1 + k)$, where P_2 is the selling price of the share at time t_2, and D_2 is the dividend to be paid at time t_2. Thus we could state that

$$P_0 = \frac{D_1}{1+k} + \frac{D_2}{(1+k)^2} + \frac{P_2}{(1+k)^2}$$

and so, by extending the analysis for the whole life of the company,

$$P_0 = \frac{D_1}{1+k} + \frac{D_2}{(1+k)^2} + \frac{D_3}{(1+k)^3} + \ldots + \frac{D_n}{(1+k)^n}$$
$$= \sum_{j=1}^{n} \frac{D_j}{(1+k)^j}$$

If, therefore, we can estimate the dividends to be paid out for the rest of the life of the company, including the final or liquidating dividend and also the cost of capital, we can make an estimate of the equilibrium value of the share.

This represents a laborious calculation, quite apart from the fact that it is a difficult forecasting problem. To simplify this, it is sometimes possible to assume that the dividend can be expected to grow at a constant rate (less than the cost of capital) each year.

Let the rate of growth of the dividend be g and the cost of capital be k, which is greater than g; also let the dividend at time t_0 be D_0. Then we can state that the value of the share at time t_0 will be given by the expression[2]

$$P_0 = \frac{D_0(1+g)}{(k-g)}$$

---

2 This expression may be derived from the formula for the sum of a geometric progression.

Thus, if we use the assumption that the company will have a reasonably long life with dividends increasing at $100g$ per cent per year and has a constant cost of capital of $100k$ per cent, we can use the last declared dividend to estimate the value of a share.

If, however, the rate of growth of the dividend is greater than the cost of capital, we must discount the forecast dividends for the desired time horizon in order to arrive at a value for the share.

Estimation of the variables

There remains the problem of estimating the growth rate (g) and the cost of capital (k). Of these g is the simpler to estimate as it is usually possible to examine past data for the company and so estimate its past dividend growth rate. This, of course, assumes that the past rate will provide a good estimate of future growth. If other information about the expected future dividend pattern is available, extrapolation from past data may not be necessary.

Care should be taken to ensure that the dividends per share are adjusted to take account of any rights issue or other capital changes that may have taken place in the period under review.

EXAMPLE 14.1

Consider a company which has paid the following dividends:

Year	Dividend (pence per share)
1985	6.0
1986	6.2
1987	6.4
1988	6.8
1989	6.8
1990	7.2
1991	7.3
1992	7.5
1993	7.8

Graphically the above can be represented as shown in Figure 14.1.

Mathematical techniques are available which can be used to estimate the average percentage growth in dividends for the period, but we will describe a simple and quick method which will often give a reasonable first approximation.

We can see that dividends have increased from 6.0p per share in 1985 to 7.8p per share in 1993. A visual inspection of the graph indicates that these observations are reasonably close to the trend and it therefore seems safe to use them. The average increase in dividends is $1.8/8 = 0.22$p per year, but we are seeking the average percentage growth g, which can be calculated as follows:

$$D_0 (1 + g)^8 = D_8$$

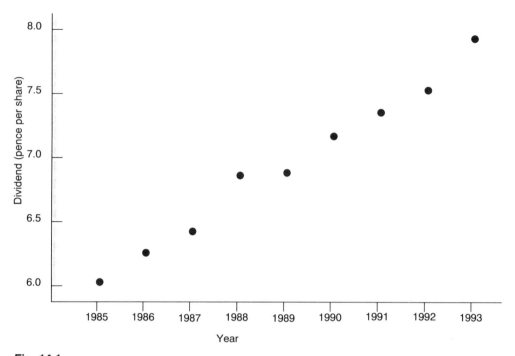

Fig. 14.1

where D_0 is the 1985 dividend and D_8 is the 1993 dividend, i.e.

$$6.0(1+g)^8 = 7.8$$
$$\frac{1}{(1+g)^8} = \frac{6.0}{7.8} = 0.77$$

$(1 + g)^8$ and hence g can be calculated by the use of logarithms, but an easier way is to make use of present value tables which give the value of $1/(1 + g)^n$ for different values of g and n. If we use the tables where $n = 8$ we find the following:

g	Present value
0.02	0.853
0.03	0.789
0.04	0.731

We can see that g lies between 0.03 and 0.04 and we could probably accept an estimate of say 0.035 (3½%). Given the other problems of estimation there seems little point in interpolating between 0.03 and 0.04 to find a more exact figure.

Where, however, the growth rate of the annual dividend is not constant in the period under consideration, some approximation must be made, such as taking a geometric mean[3] of the growth rates in the period under consideration.

Alternatively it may be possible to identify a cyclical trend in the dividend pattern and this could be used to forecast the dividends for the next 5 years, using a mean growth rate thereafter. In this way it is often possible to obtain a reasonable estimate of value from the dividend valuation model, i.e.

$$P_0 = \frac{D_1}{(1+k)} + \frac{D_2}{(1+k)^2} + \frac{D_3}{(1+k)^3} + \frac{D_4}{(1+k)^4} + \frac{D_5 + D_5\dfrac{(1+g)}{(k-g)}}{(1+k)^5}$$

(Since $P_5 = D_5[(1 + g)/(k - g)]$ this is simply the discounting of expected cash flows over a 5-year time horizon.)

Throughout the analysis which has been carried out so far it has been assumed that the cost of capital can be determined, and the proposition that it is the return which could be achieved by investment in a bank deposit account has not been retracted. It will, however, be clear that in the absence of unexpected inflation an investment in a deposit account with a sound bank can be regarded as a risk-free investment while it is evident that investment in the shares of a limited company is not risk free.

The risk associated with investment in the shares of a limited company can be explained in two main ways. First, the interest element, or dividend for ordinary shares, is not guaranteed but may fluctuate with the fortunes of the company and the whim of the directors. Second, the ability to recover one's capital at the end of the 'investment period' is dependent upon the sale of those shares. Since the sale of shares requires a market transaction the recovery of capital is dependent upon the state of the market and is by no means guaranteed.

It therefore seems reasonable that an investor will require a higher return from a risky investment compared with a risk-free investment. Strictly this depends on the assumption that the investor is risk averse, i.e. that he would prefer the certainty of receiving £X rather than enter an arrangement whereby he has a 50 per cent chance of receiving £(X + Y) and a 50 per cent chance of receiving £(X − Y). A risk preferrer might favour the risky prospect and therefore expect a lower rate on a risky investment because he enjoys the uncertainty and is attracted by the possibility of higher returns. Most investors may be assumed to be risk averse, an assumption that is evidenced by the taking out of insurance policies to reduce the level of risk experienced in life.

The introduction of risk into this analysis makes the estimation of the cost of capital more difficult. In practice the problem is often tackled by inflating the cost of capital based on a risk-free investment by a premium determined on some subjective basis depending on the investor's view of the riskiness of the investment. There are theoretical objections to this approach which are based upon the subjectivity of the risk assessment, and theoretical models have been formulated relating the premium to some objective measure of the risk of the proposed investment.

3 The geometric mean of n items is the nth root of the product of those items, e.g. the geometric mean, g, of the growth rates for periods 1 and 2, g_1 and g_2 is given by $g = \sqrt{g_1 \times g_2}$. This mean is appropriate for our analysis since the mean g for which we are searching is such that

$$D_0(1+g)^n = D_0(1+g_1)(1+g_2)\dots(1+g_n)$$

$$= D_0 \prod_{j=1}^{n}(1+g_j)$$

The best known model is the Capital Asset Pricing Model which relates the expected return on a share to its risk in the following way[4];

$$Ex_j = r + (Ex_m - r)\beta_j$$

This states that the expected return on share j (Ex_j), that is the appropriate cost of capital or discount rate, is a function of the risk-free rate of interest (r) and a risk premium. The risk premium depends upon the excess of the expected return on the market as a whole over the risk-free rate of interest ($Ex_m - r$) and the beta value of the particular share (β_j). This beta is a measure of what is called the systematic or non-diversifiable risk of the share. It is a measure of the riskiness of the share in relation to the market as a whole. The beta value for the market as a whole is defined as 1 so that, if a particular share has a beta value of 2, it is twice as risky as the market and hence demands twice the risk premium. Conversely, if the beta value for another share is 0.5, that share is half as risky as the market and requires half of the risk premium of the market. Beta values for UK companies and industry sectors are published by various sources.[5]

The Capital Asset Pricing Model rests on a large number of simplifying assumptions but, in spite of its elegance, the model enjoys only limited support from empirical studies. Use of the model to obtain a discount rate in practice requires the identification of the particular industry sector in which a company operates, so that an appropriate beta value may be obtained. This process becomes difficult where a particular company has diversified into different industry sectors for which different beta values are appropriate. Here again a large element of subjective judgment will be involved.

A further complicating factor in determining the cost of capital is that of a changing price level. If the price level of goods and services which would otherwise be bought with the capital that is invested is subject to change, then the value of the capital invested by the individual will change as its purchasing power will change. There are basically two ways of dealing with inflation in the valuation model.

The first is to adjust all items to real terms by expressing all cash flows in terms of purchasing power of a common, usually the current, date. However, if this is done then the cost of capital should also be measured in real terms to ensure that inflation is not counted twice.

The real cost of capital (for an investment of given level of risk), r, can be estimated as follows.

Let k be the 'nominal' cost of capital (i.e. the actual rate of return which is required on an investment of the given level of risk) and let m be the annual rate of inflation. Assume that £1.00 is invested at the start of the year; this is equivalent to an investment of £1(1 + m) in year-end pounds. However, at the year end the investor will receive £1(1 + k). Therefore the real rate of interest, r, is given by the equation

$$£1(1 + m)(1 + r) = £1(1 + k)$$

or

$$1 + m + r + mr = 1 + k.$$

If we assume that mr is very small, since it is the product of two small numbers, both much less than 1, then we can state that $r = k - m$.

4 This model (CAPM) is described in finance texts such as Richard A. Brealey and Stuart C. Myers, *Principles of Corporate Finance*, 4th edition, McGraw-Hill, 1991 and J. F. Weston and T. E. Copeland, *Managerial Finance*, second UK edition, adapted by A. F. Fox and R. J. Limmack, Cassell, 1988.
5 One such listing is published by the London Business School.

The estimate, therefore, of the real cost of capital is the nominal cost less the expected change in the price index.

The second alternative for valuing the investment in ordinary shares is to express all the cash flows which have been predicted in money terms at their expected price levels and to discount these cash flows at the money ('nominal') cost of capital. This method is probably simpler to understand since money figures will be used throughout the analysis, reducing the conceptual problems of identifying 'real' monetary units.

The determination of the cost of capital does, in the final analysis, depend upon the opportunity cost approach. The opportunity cost of an investment is the best alternative return which has been foregone by selecting this specific investment. This approach to determining the cost of capital is one of the most useful approaches available to those involved in the valuation of securities since it enables an estimate of the cost of capital to be made by comparison with other available investments. When such a comparison is being made it is important that the risk characteristics of the alternative investments are sufficiently alike to make the comparison meaningful.

This opportunity cost method of comparison is then the dominant approach used by market participants in their valuation calculations, especially in the case of shares in unquoted companies or in the search for underpriced shares in quoted companies. The typical procedure that would be followed would be to identify a comparable quoted company and to obtain its dividend yield (*see below*) which represents the first approximation to the opportunity cost of capital. This dividend yield will then be adjusted upwards by about a quarter to a third to reflect the lack of marketability of the unquoted shares. Additional adjustments will usually be made to reflect other differences between shares in the quoted company and those in the unquoted company. These might include differences in dividend cover, asset backing or growth prospects. The adjusted dividend yield will then be used as the cost of capital in order to capitalise the dividends of the unquoted share.

The opportunity cost method is therefore theoretically justifiable and applicable in practice: there are, however, two main practical problems inherent in this approach. There is the problem that no two companies are exactly alike, and great care must be taken when selecting a company with which comparisons are to be made. Ideally companies being compared should be in the same industry, be of approximately the same size and operate in the same market as a company whose shares are being valued. It is unlikely that the ideal company will be found. The other problem is that comparison can be made in respect of more than one aspect of a company's performance. It is rather like the problem faced by a judge in a music competition. Most people would not rank the participants in terms of only one of their attributes; they are likely to consider technique, expression, presence, etc., and balance these factors in their own minds before coming to a ranking decision. Similarly, when comparing the results of two companies, one would have to consider a number of factors in addition to the level of dividends upon which we have concentrated so far. These factors would be the assets and earnings of the companies because these will influence the expectation of future dividends. Only if the companies have sufficient earnings will they be able to maintain their dividend pay out.

The valuation of unquoted shares

In this section of the chapter we will first consider the main stock exchange indicators which provide a basis for comparison of companies. We will then present an example dealing with the valuation of the shares of an unquoted company.

In order to discuss the main stock exchange indicators we will make use of a hypothetical quoted company whose summarised accounts for the year t_0 to t_1 are given below:

Profit and loss account for the period t_0 to t_1

	£000s
Turnover	2000
Earnings	200
less Corporation tax (at 33% of taxable profit)	80
	120
Dividends paid	60
Unappropriated earnings for the period	60
Retained earnings at t_0	400
Retained earnings at t_1	460

Balance sheets

	t_0 £000s	t_1 £000s
Assets *less* current liabilities	1000	1060
less 9% debentures 2010	100	100
	900	960
Capital and reserves:		
1 million 50p ordinary shares	500	500
Reserves	400	460
	900	960

At time t_1, the company's shares are quoted at £1.50. For the period t_0 to t_1, the basic rate of income tax is 25 per cent and the rate for advance corporation tax (ACT) is one quarter.

In this section we will examine five ratios – the dividend yield, the dividend cover, the earnings per share, the price/earnings ratio and the earnings yield. Four of these ratios include the price of the company's shares and thus can be used to make a direct comparison between one share and another; the dividend cover ratio is different in that it serves as an indicator of risk associated with the dividend as well as giving some indication of the management's distribution policy.

Dividend yield

The dividend yield provides a measure of the return that the investor will receive on an investment. It is calculated on a pre-tax basis (for the recipient) and hence the dividend figure included in the calculation will be the gross dividend, i.e. the net cash payment received by the shareholder plus the tax credit.

In our example, the net dividend per share is given by £60 000/1 000 000 = 6p and, as the rate of ACT is ¼, the gross dividend is 6 + 6 x ¼ = 7.5. The dividend yield is then given by

$$\text{Dividend yield} = \frac{\text{Gross dividend per share}}{\text{Market price per share}} \times 100\%$$

$$= \frac{7.5}{150} \times 100 = 5.0\%.$$

Dividend cover

The purpose of this ratio is to help assess the likelihood that management will not have to reduce the dividend from its current level. The dividend cover is the ratio between the profit, excluding extraordinary items, attributable to the ordinary shareholders (i.e. profit after tax and any preference dividends) and the current dividend.

In the case of our example, profit attributable to shareholders is £120 000 and the dividend declared is 60 000. Therefore dividend cover = 120 000/60 000 = 2.[6]

In the USA the reciprocal of the dividend cover, the payment ratio, is a more commonly used statistic.

Earnings per share

The earnings per share ratio is one that is very simple in concept, but which is often difficult to calculate in practice. The basic concept is that the earnings of the company for the year should be apportioned to the ordinary shares in issue to give an indication of the amount of earnings which would be available to the holder of one ordinary share. This simple concept thus enables the earnings associated with holding an ordinary share in one company to be compared with those associated with holding an ordinary share in another company.

It is, however, on this matter of comparability that complications can and do arise. If the ratio is to be used meaningfully, then it must be calculated on a similar basis for every company, and the earnings must be representative of the company's earnings potential. It is clear that the earnings stated in companies' reports are not necessarily comparable with one another because different accounting policies may have been applied and there may have been differing levels of earnings from non-trading transactions which will not be representative of the companies' earnings potentials. The levels of taxation incurred may not have been consistent; one of the main reasons for the inconsistency of tax charges is because a company may have incurred irrecoverable ACT, thus increasing its tax charge because of its dividend policy.

In order to increase comparability, the earnings per share figure should be calculated on the consolidated profit of the period (after tax and after deducting minority interests and preference dividends but including any extraordinary items) divided by the number of equity shares in issue and ranking for dividend in respect of the period.[7]

This still leaves the problem of irrecoverable ACT. It can be argued that if such tax reduces the earnings available then this is a management decision and the reduced level of earnings should be shown in the calculation. This calculation using the higher tax charge in arriving at earnings is known as the *net* basis of calculating earnings per share.

The alternative argument is that the reported earnings per share should not be affected by the level of dividends actually payable when the figure is desired for the comparison of the performances of companies. In this case the lower tax charge that would have occurred had no dividend been declared is used in calculating the ratio and is known as the *nil* distribution earnings per share.

---

6 The position is more complicated where distribution of the full earnings would involve irrecoverable ACT and hence increase the taxation charge in the profit and loss account. In such cases a better method of calculating dividend cover would be:

$$\text{Dividend cover} = \frac{\text{Maximum dividend payable out of profits for the year}}{\text{Actual dividend for year}}$$

7 *See* SSAP 3, Para. 10 as amended by FRS 3, Para. 25.

For companies that do not suffer irrecoverable ACT there will be no difference between the net basis and the nil distribution basis of calculating earnings per share. We will ensure that this is the situation which we face in our example (*see below*), where there are also no extraordinary items.

Hence, if the earnings for the year attributable to the ordinary shareholders is £120 000 and the number of shares in issue is 1 000 000, then the earnings per share is 12p.

Some of the other problems which may occur in the calculation of the earnings per share, and a discussion of SSAP 3, will be found in the appendix to this chapter.

Price/earnings ratio

While the security valuation model developed so far rightly concentrates upon the dividend to be expected, consideration is given in practice to the company's earnings. This has been found to be useful because earnings represent an upper limit for dividend distribution.

The most common valuation tool based on earnings is the price/earnings (P/E) ratio, which is calculated as follows:

$$\text{P/E ratio} = \frac{\text{Price per share}}{\text{Earnings per share}}$$

In the case under examination, the earnings per share is 12p, as we showed above, and the share price is £1.50. Hence:

$$\text{P/E} = \frac{150}{12} = 12.5$$

The P/E ratio shows the investor the numbers of years' earnings that he will purchase with his investment and enables him to compare this investment with alternatives. The flaw in the argument is, of course, that the P/E ratio is based on the last known earnings figure while the investor is 'buying' future earnings. Thus, the shares of a company whose earnings are expected to grow will, all other things being equal, have a higher P/E ratio than the shares of a company whose earnings are not expected to increase. Similarly, a company whose earnings are considered by the market to be risky will have shares with a lower P/E ratio than a company with a more certain earnings stream.

Earnings yield

The earnings yield is an alternative way of relating the company's earnings to its share price and is given by

$$\text{Earnings yield} = \frac{\text{Earnings per share}}{\text{Share price}} \times 100\%$$

Unfortunately, the value of earnings per share most commonly used in such calculations is based on different assumptions from the value of earnings per share used to calculate the P/E ratio. For the purposes of calculating the earnings yield the earnings per share figure is the maximum dividend that could have been declared from the profits for the year, i.e. the grossed up earnings to allow for the tax credit; the so-called 'full distribution' basis (*see* page 389, fn 6). It is therefore necessary to determine whether the figure being used for valuation purposes is gross or net of tax so that consistent comparisons may be made.

EXAMPLE 14.2: VALUATION OF THE SHARES OF AN UNQUOTED COMPANY

The basic principle is that the value is the price that the shares would fetch if sold on the open market on the date in respect of which the shares are being valued. As was stated earlier this is done by looking at the price of shares of quoted, but otherwise similar, companies.

X Limited is an unquoted company whose accounts for the last 4 years disclosed the following:

Balance sheets

End of year	1	2	3	4
	£000s	£000s	£000s	£000s
Net assets	850	1000	990	1110
Share capital				
£1 ordinary shares	500	500	500	500
Retained earnings	200	300	390	510
Loans	150	200	100	100
	850	1000	990	1110

Results	Year 1	Year 2	Year 3	Year 4
	£000s	£000s	£000s	£000s
Earnings after tax	150	160	180	220
Dividend	50	60	90	100

We will attempt to place a value on the shares of X Limited as at the end of year 4 on the assumption that the shares being valued represent only a small proportion of the total issue.

There are two quoted companies, A plc and B plc, which appear to be similar to X Limited. The *Financial Times* listing at the end of year 4 shows the following:

High	Low	Stock	Price	+ or –	Div. net	Cover	Div. yield gross	P/E
135	100	A plc 50p ord.	130	+ 2	4.9	1.857	4.7	10
90	60	B plc 25p ord.	80	– 1	2.5	3.689	3.9	6

The 'price' is, of course, the price per share quoted in pence at the end of the day's business while 'high' and 'low' are the highest and lowest prices achieved during the preceding 12 months '+ or –' shows the change from the closing price on the preceding day. 'Div net' is the net dividend, i.e. before the addition of the tax credit while 'Cover' is the dividend cover. The yield is the dividend yield, which is calculated on the value of the dividend and associated tax credit, while the P/E ratio is calculated on the 'net' distribution basis (i.e. the earnings per share figure is computed after deducting the whole of the tax charge including irrecoverable ACT and irrecoverable overseas tax arising from a dividend distribution).

We will assume that none of the companies involved in the analysis has suffered irrecoverable ACT or overseas tax during the period under review.

We will now calculate the earnings per share, dividend per share and dividend cover for X Limited for the last four years:

	Year			
	1	*2*	*3*	*4*
Earnings per share	30p	32p	36p	44p
Dividends per share, net	10p	12p	18p	20p
Dividends per share, gross	12.5p	15.0p	22.5p	25.0p
Dividend cover	3.0	2.7	2.0	2.2

Note that the dividend cover calculation is based on the net dividend and that it has been assumed that the rate of ACT has been ¼ throughout the period.

We can see that both the earnings and dividends per share have grown steadily over the period. These are expressed in monetary terms and in a full analysis we should attempt to eliminate the effect of inflation. However, we will assume that the figures for year 4 which will be used in the comparison are not unrepresentative of the period.

The dividend cover has declined over the period from 3.0 to 2.2. The most recent figure is still acceptable and the decline should not, all other things being equal, affect the valuation, since it would appear that the dividend can be maintained given that it is more than twice covered.

Now it is clear from comparisons of dividend cover that X Limited lies between A plc and B plc. We will carry out calculations in order to estimate the price of X Limited in comparison to A plc and B plc, and it is worth noting that it will be necessary for the comparison company to have similarly assessed growth prospects for the valuations derived to be useful.

First we shall make an estimate of the share value using a dividend yield approach.

The gross dividend per share for X Limited is 25.0p. The gross dividend yield for A plc is 4.7 per cent. In order to adjust the figure for X Limited being an unquoted company we might increase it by about a third, giving a level of comparison of about 6.25 per cent. Thus we could produce a value for the shares of X Limited of £(0.25/0.0625) = £4.00. Alternatively, if we compare X Limited with B plc we would expect a gross dividend yield of about 5.2 per cent (3.9% x 1.33). Thus we would produce a value for the shares of X Limited of £(0.25/0.052) = £4.81.

The dividend valuation approach therefore gives values of £4.00 and £4.81.

We may similarly attempt to carry out a valuation using an earnings approach. Again we must adjust the P/E ratios of the quoted companies by about one-third to allow for the fact that X Limited is unquoted. In using P/E ratios, such an adjustment involves a reduction to reflect the fact that the shares in the unquoted company are less valuable than those in the quoted company. Thus we would apply P/E ratios of about 7 and 4 in comparison with the ratios of 10 for A plc and 6 for B plc.

The earnings per share of X Limited is 44p, thus the application of an earnings-based approach gives valuations for X Limited's shares of £3.08 and £1.76.

We would also look at the asset backing of X Limited's shares. This can be done using the net book value of the assets as disclosed by the historical cost accounts:

Net book value of assets at the end of year 4	=	£1 110 000
Loans outstanding	=	£100 000
Net book value of assets less loans	=	£1 010 000
Number of shares	=	500 000
Net book value per share	=	£2.05

If the shares are being valued on the assumption that the business is a going concern then the above figure may be of dubious value, but it might give some indication of the lowest possible share valuation. An examination of the current value of the assets may also be of interest, but this is likely to be of much greater relevance to a potential purchaser of a controlling interest in the business, which will be discussed later in the chapter.

Thus, we have five possible valuations of a share in X Limited:

(a) book value per share	£2.05
(b) comparison with A plc	
(i) on dividend yield	£4.00
(ii) on P/E ratio	£3.08
(c) comparison with B plc	
(i) on dividend yield	£4.81
(ii) on P/E ratio	£1.76

These figures represent a very large range, and it is obvious that if the company being considered is not comparable on a dividend cover basis with the quoted company a large discrepancy of prices between the earnings-based figure and the dividend-based figure will result, even though the growth prospects might be similarly assessed.

The wide range produced in the above analysis probably stems from the different dividend cover between X Limited and B plc although it will be necessary to consider whether there are other significant differences between the three companies. It seems unlikely that X Limited will increase its dividend cover to approximate with that of B plc, and therefore in the absence of evidence of comparability of other factors we will ignore the comparison with that company. It is also unlikely that X Limited will be broken up, and therefore a reasonable range for the valuation of the shares of X Limited would seem to be between £3.08 and £4.00.

While it is often necessary to value unquoted shares by reference to the market value of otherwise comparable quoted shares, it must be noted that the method does suffer from many severe limitations in that (a) the dividend policies of unquoted companies tend to be different from and less stable than those of their quoted counterparts: (b) the asset base and its financing of unquoted companies is likely to be different from the quoted companies with which they will be compared, the quoted companies being on the whole less volatile; (c) the value of quoted companies' shares is dependent upon the market and therefore will be volatile and not necessarily equal to their intrinsic worth.

The valuation of shares cannot be made simply by application of formulae. The valuer must balance the information derived from an analysis such as that described above with other information and, ultimately, apply his or her intuition and judgement before arriving at a conclusion.

Some, but by no means all, of the other factors which might be considered are as follows: (a) whether there are any restrictions upon the transfer of shares and the nature of any such restrictions; (b) the history and prospects of the company and the industries in which it operates; (c) the nature and quality of the company's management; (d) the prospects of a takeover or a merger; (e) the impact of inflation; (f) the results of a more detailed analysis of the company's accounts as discussed in Chapter 13.

The valuation of shares for statutory purposes

In valuing shares for statutory purposes such as the calculation of the liability of an individual to capital gains tax or inheritance tax, an agreement of valuation must be reached with the Shares Valuation Division of the Inland Revenue. This body has shown that it tends to calculate the value of an unquoted shareholding by comparison with the value of shares in similar quoted companies, making allowance for the differing circumstances of the companies and also discounting the share price so derived by between 10 per cent and 35 per cent on the basis of the restrictions of the articles of association of the company and the size of the shareholding in question.

In negotiations for the statutory valuation of shares it is necessary to consider the possibility of capital appreciation in addition to the points made in the previous section. Potential capital appreciation will be taken into account in the statutory valuation when it can be shown that it is likely to occur; such would be the case if, for example, the directors were already considering a new issue of shares at a higher price than the current valuation.

It must be remembered that the requirement for the valuation of shares for capital gains tax, as laid down in Schedule 10 of the Finance Act 1975, is that the value is the assumed price of an arm's length transaction given all the information a prudent purchaser might reasonably acquire. This is open to many interpretations and serves to illustrate the large range of values which could be maintained in the negotiations for the statutory valuations of shares in unquoted companies.

Readers who are faced with the problem of statutory valuation are urged to make reference to recent appeals dealt with by the Special Commissioners and the High Court to acquaint themselves with current precedent. These are frequently reported in the weekly and monthly accounting journals.

THE VALUATION OF A BUSINESS

Introduction

A business is an asset, and the same theoretical underpinnings can be applied to the valuation of a business as are applied to the valuation of individual assets. There is, however, one very important difference between a single asset and a business: this is that a single asset usually represents only a small proportion of the owner's wealth. It is unlikely that this will be so in the case of a business and hence its valuation will depend in part on the other assets owned by the person or group on whose behalf the valuation is being made. In other words the value of a business could be said to be given by: the value of the owner's total stock of assets on the assumption that the business is owned *less* the value of the owner's total stock of assets without the business.

The significance of the effect of the potential or existing owner's other assets can be seen by considering the example of valuation of a pharmaceutical business. Let us suppose that there are two potential purchasers – a photographic company and an engineering company. It is likely, all other things being equal, that the photographic company would place a higher value on the business than the engineers if, as is probable, the pharmaceutical and photographic businesses have common outlets which would enable the photographic company to use the same representatives to sell both types of product. This is an example of what is called positive *synergy*, i.e. the interaction of assets so that the combined earnings of two or more assets will exceed the sum of their potential separate earnings.

The bases of valuation of a business will be dependent on the circumstances in which the valuation is being made, and we should therefore consider the reasons why a valuation of a business is required.

Taxation

Tax legislation dictates that a business will have to be valued for the purposes of inheritance tax and capital gains tax when the proprietor of a business dies or transfers part or all of his or her interest in the business during his or her life.

Insurance

A prudent management will wish to insure its business. This is often done by reference to the tangible assets of the business only, and the problem then reduces to deciding on the value to be attached to the business's tangible assets, a subject which is dealt with in some detail elsewhere in the book.

There are, however, many businesses where such an approach would result in a significant undervaluation of the business because tangible assets constitute only a small proportion of its assets. Examples of such enterprises include management consultancies, advertising agencies and firms of accountants. In these and similar cases the major asset of the business is the skill and enterprise of its owners and employees and in many, especially smaller, concerns the greater proportion of these assets is provided by the owner himself. If this is the case, the owner should carefully consider the amount of life and disability insurance required to ensure that the value of the assets of the owner, or of his estate, will not decline should the owner be unable, by death or otherwise, to continue to work. In theory the amount of the insurance, the insurable risk, should, if we ignore the contribution of employees and other elements of 'goodwill', be equal to the value of the business less the value of the tangible assets.

Transfer of ownership

Both the potential vendor and the potential purchaser of a business will require valuation from their own particular standpoint and would, for the purposes of negotiation, wish to estimate the value which is in the minds of the other party to the transaction. We will discuss this topic in detail later in the chapter, but at this stage we will point out the particular problems faced by the potential purchaser.

A potential purchaser cannot be sure of retaining the trained labour force and management which are currently part of the business. Also, the potential purchaser may not be interested in the business as a whole but only in a part of it which she/he intends to keep as a going concern, selling off the other assets. In contrast, she/he may not wish to persist with any part of the business and may only be interested in one or a number of the assets of the business which she/he would find more expensive to acquire in any other way.

There is also the question of synergy to be considered; thus the degree of interaction between the business being acquired and the purchaser's present business may be such that the value of the business to the purchaser bears little relation to the value of the business on its own. The potential purchaser also faces the practical problem that she/he may not be able to obtain all the necessary information.

In addition to the above circumstances, which apply to most forms of business enterprise, a number of special factors apply in the cases of partnerships and companies.

Partnerships

If the business is a partnership the problems of valuation may be acute and frequent. Whenever there is a change in the partnership arrangements a valuation of both the 'old' and 'new' partnerships is required, for the ongoing partners will give up a share in the old partnership in return for a share in the new partnership. In practice the difficult problems involved are often dealt with, in so far as the valuation of the old partnership is concerned, by the addition to the tangible assets of a figure for goodwill based on such arbitrary formulae as x years purchase of the average profits of a past period. Such an approach is theoretically unsound because it is based on past results rather than future expectations, but the method is usually easy to apply and will reduce the possibility of disagreement arising between the partners.

The contribution of the partners to the new partnership is dealt with in the first instance by the selection of a profit-sharing agreement based on the capital and labour inputs of the partners, but this will, of course, only encompass the profits recognised by the accounting system and will ignore changes in the valuation of assets, especially goodwill. Thus, when there is next a change in the partnership arrangements the problem of the valuation of the business will again have to be faced.

Companies

When a company requires new capital and proposes to raise this by the issue of new shares it will be necessary to value the company in order that an appropriate and equitable price will be derived for the new issue. Often, when a company is faced with a takeover bid, it will be advantageous to obtain a valuation in order that the bid may either be defended or a fair price agreed for the company's shares.

In addition, there is also a need for the shareholders of the company to have some indication of the current value of the company in order that they may judge the stewardship of the directors by reference to the rate of return which they obtain on their investment. Indeed, it is argued that this knowledge should be in the possession of all investors on the grounds that the most efficient use of the nation's resources will be achieved if investment is steered towards those companies which offer the greatest return.

A valuation model based on earnings

The present value model which discounts future cash flows to their net present value which has already been introduced provides what most people would regard as the correct theoretical approach to the valuation of a business. However, in practice it is often difficult to make or obtain all the necessary data required and hence other approaches of varying degrees of crudity are often used.

We will start this section by discussing an earnings-based model, and, in particular, investigate the circumstances under which the differences between models based on cash flows and reported earnings may not be all that significant.

The standard valuation model may be presented thus:

$$V_0 = \sum_{j=0}^{\infty} \frac{Y_j - X_j}{(1+k)^j}$$

where V_0 is the value of the asset at time t_0, k is the discount rate, Y_j are the cash receipts generated by the asset in year j, X_j are the cash expenses associated with the asset in year j.

Now if C is the expenses of the business in year j on an accruals basis and R is the revenue of the business in year j on an accruals basis, then the profit of the business in year j is given by

$$P_j = R_j - C_j$$

Over the life of the business the cash receipts from sales must be the same as the revenue accrued (if bad debts and discounts are ignored), i.e.

$$\sum_{j=0}^{\infty} Y_j = \sum_{j=0}^{\infty} R_j$$

and the cash payments must be the same as the expenses calculated on an accruals basis (again ignoring bad debts and discounts), i.e.

$$\sum_{j=0}^{\infty} X_j = \sum_{j=0}^{\infty} C_j$$

If the net expenditure on fixed assets per year is approximately the same as the annual depreciation charge, and if the business investment in net current assets is approximately constant, then it follows that

$$Y_j \simeq R_j \quad \text{and} \quad X_j \simeq C_j$$

The valuation model can then be restated as follows:

$$V_0 = \sum_{j=0}^{\infty} \frac{Y_j - X_j}{(1+k)^j}$$

and thus

$$V_0 \simeq \sum_{j=0}^{\infty} \frac{R_j - C_j}{(1+k)^j} = \sum_{j=0}^{\infty} \frac{P_j}{(1+k)^j}$$

Therefore the value of the firm can be stated in terms of the discounted value of the expected profits to be earned over the firm's lifetime.

The nature of the discounting process is such that the later terms in the series have less impact on the overall valuation V_0 than the earlier terms. In other words, for a given P_j and k, $P_j/(1 + k)^j$ becomes smaller as j becomes larger. Thus, the importance of the assumptions referred to above relating to the purchase of fixed assets and investment in working capital is reduced as the years pass.

It might be argued that this formulation overstates the value of the business because not all the profit is paid to the proprietor, but some is reinvested in the business. Thus, the cash flow to the proprietor is less than the profit flow to the business. This is generally true, but the recognition of this point leads us to modify but not abandon our approach. A rational proprietor with a discount rate k would only reinvest the profits of the business where the expected rate of return on that investment was greater than k. Consider, for example, the reinvestment of I from the profits in year 1. Then the profit paid to the proprietor falls from P_1 to $P_1 - I$. However, this investment must earn at least rate k, so the profits in year 2 must be increased from P_2 to at least $P_2 + I(1 + k)$ if this was a 1-year investment.

Thus, in place of the valuation

$$V_0 = P_0 + \frac{P_1}{1+k} + \frac{P_2}{(1+k)^2} + \ldots + \frac{P_n}{(1+k)^n} + \ldots$$

we have, if it is assumed that the amount invested earns a return of k (i.e. that profits of year 2 are $P_2 + I(1 + k)$), a value, V_0', which is given by

$$V_0' = P_0 + \frac{P_1 - I}{(1+k)} + \frac{P_2 + I(1+k)}{(1+k)^2} + \ldots + \frac{P_n}{(1+k)^n} + \ldots$$

$$= P_0 + \frac{P_1}{(1+k)} + \frac{P_2}{(1+k)^2} + \ldots + \frac{P_n}{(1+k)^n} + \ldots$$

$$= V_0$$

The same analysis can be applied to investments made in later years.

If it is assumed that the amounts invested will earn a greater return than k then the value V_0 can be regarded as providing a lower limit of the range of values of the business.

We have thus established a theoretical model for the valuation of a business as a going concern, based upon the discounted value of the future earnings of the business.

Valuation of a business as a going concern

Initially, we will confine the discussion to the case of a business which is being valued as a going concern and whose management and assets will be unchanged as a result of the circumstances leading to the requirement for a valuation.

The direct application of our theoretical model poses several problems. The first and most obvious problem is that the model requires us to forecast earnings for the business for the remainder of its life. This, it will readily be recognised, is an impossible task. The second problem arises in the estimation of the discount rate, k, which should be used to carry out this calculation. Thus, in practice, the theoretical model is rarely applied as we have derived it, but rather various rule of thumb approximations are used to establish a range of values for the business which experience has shown might be indicated by the theoretical model were we able to use it.

The asset valuation approach

Our first approach to the problem of valuation will be an asset valuation approach. It can be argued that if a business is acquiring or retaining an asset, then the value of that asset to the business must, in the case of acquisition of the asset, be greater than the cost of that asset and, in the case of retention of the asset, be greater than the net realisable value of the asset. If, therefore, all the assets of the business are valued at their net realisable values, then the sum of those values will clearly be less than their value to the business and can be regarded as providing the lower bound to the range of values based on the asset valuation approach. This point is not as simple as it appears because of the difficulty in determining the net realisable value of assets and, as described in Chapter 3, the net realisable value of an asset depends on the circumstances under which it is assumed that the asset will be sold.

The upper bound of the range of assets will be the sum of the replacement costs of the company's assets so long as it is recognised that the assets include intangibles such as goodwill. The determination of the replacement cost of both tangible and in particular intangible assets does produce substantial practical difficulties.

Discounted earnings approaches

These approaches are related to the present value method, but contain a number of simplifying assumptions which facilitate their use. There is, however, a danger that the crudity of the assumptions may in certain circumstances mean that the links between the methods described and the present value method become tenuous.

A common theme of the simplified approaches is that one figure is selected as representing what is termed the *maintainable profit* of the business. This figure is sometimes based on the average profit for the recent past; in which case adjustments need to be made for changes in capital employed, inflation, etc. Alternatively, the profits of the most recent year or the forecast profit of the current year may be used to provide a first estimate of the maintainable profit. The first estimate, however derived, may then be adjusted on a more or less subjective basis by the valuer. He might feel that the current year, or recent past, does not provide a reasonable indication of the future and may, therefore, inflate or deflate the first estimate depending on his view of the likely future trend in profits.

The valuer will, especially in the case of smaller businesses, have to consider the extent to which profit is being distributed by way of remuneration. For example, the directors of a family-owned limited company may be paid a great deal more than the economic value of their services and part of their remuneration should be regarded as profit. In such an instance the reported accounting profit is understated in the sense that – all other things being equal – a higher profit could have been obtained if the family directors were replaced by professional managers paid at the market rate.

Sometimes an adjustment will have to be made in the opposite direction for it is not uncommon, especially at the start of a company's life, for directors to pay themselves less than the market rate of remuneration. We are now in a position to consider a simple discounted earnings approach.

Let us assume that an estimate of the maintainable profit has been obtained. The next step is to determine the capitalisation rate which will be necessary to fix the current value of an anticipated stream of future earnings. This is usually done by comparing the business concerned with a similar business of which the current value is known and whose maintainable profit can be estimated. The capitalisation rate derived from the relationship between current value and earnings in this case can be applied, after making any necessary adjustments, to the business which is to be valued.

One very convenient basis of comparison is the share price and earnings of a publicly quoted company undertaking a similar type of business since this will give a readily available price to earnings (P/E) ratio which can be applied to the earnings of the business. It is usual to apply a lower P/E ratio to the earnings of the business being valued than is currently applied to the earnings of a publicly listed company and the discount to cover the lack of marketability would usually be in the region of 25 to 33 per cent. In addition it will be necessary to make suitable adjustments to this P/E ratio to take into account differences, in such matters as asset backing and earnings growth, between the quoted company and the unquoted business.

One disadvantage of this approach is that the P/E ratio derived from the market is based on marginal transactions, i.e. the price which is associated with the transfer of a relatively small proportion of the shares in issue. This price is not obviously applicable for the valuation of the business as a whole because, on the one hand, the purchase of the business would mean that a larger parcel of shares was acquired (which would suggest that a lower P/E ratio should be used), while on the other hand the purchaser would be gaining control of the whole business (which might justify the use of a higher P/E ratio).

The above approach, together with the asset valuation method, is illustrated in Example 14.3. The data of this example will be used as the basis of a running example which will appear later in the chapter.

EXAMPLE 14.3

ABC Limited is an unquoted company which has been trading for 10 years in an inflation-free environment and has been earning profits consistently. It is required, for some reason whose tax effects and influence upon the path of the business will be negligible, to arrive at a valuation for the business. The following information is known about the business as at 31 December 19X9:

Profits for ABC Limited

19X0	£1 000	19X5	£15 000
19X1	£2 000	19X6	£14 000
19X2	£5 000	19X7	£16 000
19X3	£8 000	19X8	£14 000
19X4	£12 000	19X9	£17 000

The book values of the assets of the business in 19X0 were £10 000 and are now £70 000.

The book values of the assets of the business are believed to be reasonable approximations to their net realisable values, apart from the business premises, which have a book value of £20 000 but an estimated net realisable value of £60 000.

The net realisable value of ABC's assets is thus £70 000 + £(60 000 − 20 000) = £110 000 which, as argued above, might be regarded as the lower band of the range of values based on an asset valuation approach.

The maintainable profit of the business could be based on the average of the last 5 years' profits, which appear to be reasonably stable; hence the maintainable profit is £15 200.

Let us assume that the quoted shares of a similar business sell at a P/E ratio of 10 and that it is appropriate to discount this figure by 25% to take account of the reduced marketability of the shares of ABC Limited, i.e. the P/E ratio would be 0.75 of 10 = 7.5.

The simple discounted earnings method valuation of the business is then 7.5 x £15 200 = £114 000.

Super-profits method

It is sometimes suggested that the earnings stream of a business can be divided into two elements – the first is the expected return on the value of the tangible assets employed in the business while the second is an additional amount known as the *super-profit*. The super-profit is therefore the difference between the maintainable profit and the expected return on the tangible assets employed. The essence of the super-profit method is that the additional profits are regarded as riskier than the expected return and that the super-profit should therefore be capitalised at a lower multiple (or higher capitalisation rate) than the expected return.

A number of arguments can be advanced to support the view. One is based on the standard economic theory that in a perfectly competitive market, profits that are higher than the norm for the type of assets employed in the business will be eroded away because the existence of excess profits will encourage new entrants into the market. The new firms will drive down the price until the excess profits are eliminated. The strength of this argument does depend on the structure of the market involved and it has to be recognised that there may be barriers to entry whereby a monopolist can continue to reap excess profits in the long term.

The super-profits method has also been justified by reference to the transient nature of goodwill. It can be argued that the super-profits represent the profits generated by the existence of goodwill. Consider a new business which has tangible assets of £800 000 and that the normal return on assets of the type employed by the business is 12 per cent. Then the expected profit is £96 000. An existing business with identical tangible assets may be earning a profit of £120 000. The difference between the two profits, which may be regarded as the super-profit, is due to the fact that the existing business has created 'goodwill', e.g. has established good relationships with customers, a skilled workforce, etc. Now by its very nature goodwill will disappear if no steps are taken to ensure its survival. Thus, new employees will have to be trained, customers will have to be provided with satisfactory service and so on. When an existing business is acquired its goodwill will gradually disappear and it will, in effect, have to be replaced by the activities of the new owners. This view, if accepted, can be used as an argument for applying a lower multiple to the super-profits.

The theoretical weakness of the super-profits method is that the separation of maintainable profits into the two elements is artificial. The associated practical difficulty is the determination of the expected rate of return on assets of the type employed in the business. All businesses have some goodwill (although in very badly run firms goodwill may be negative) and thus it is unlikely that reference to similar businesses will yield the required return. It is sometimes suggested that the expected return might be related to the return on government securities, but an investment in a business will carry a greater risk and it will therefore be necessary to adjust for this difference.

The super-profits method is perhaps superficially attractive, but on more detailed consideration it is clear that it suffers from severe theoretical and practical shortcomings. Given its difficulties a valuer might well be advised to use the present value approach described earlier in the chapter, which would mean that he or she would not be confined to one figure of maintainable profit. He or she could estimate the future trend of profits, which would enable the consideration of the possibility of growth. The required discount rate could be obtained from an examination of similar businesses and would avoid the need to make the artificial distinction between normal and super-profits.

The mechanics of the super-profits method are illustrated in Example 14.4.

EXAMPLE 14.4

Data are the same as in Example 14.3.

Let us suppose that the 'normal' rate of return on assets of the type used by ABC Limited is 10 per cent. The 'super-profits' can then be calculated as follows:

	£
Expected maintainable profits (from Example 14.3)	15 200
less Normal return, 10% of £110 000	11 000
Super-profits	4 200

Let us assume that it is believed that the super-profits should be valued at 4 years' earnings, i.e. a multiple of four or a capitalisation rate of 25 per cent should be applied to the figure of £4200. It should be noted that one of the major defects of the super-profits method is that it is by no means clear how the required multiple should be determined.

The value of ABC Limited would then be determined as follows:

	£
Value of tangible assets	110 000[8]
Value of super-profits 4 x £4 200	16 800
	126 800

Valuation of a business for amalgamation with another

The valuation of a business which is to be amalgamated with another business is a more complex process because it cannot be made in isolation. From the point of view of the potential purchaser the maximum price that he would be prepared to pay is the difference between the value of the combined businesses and the value of his existing business.

If the amalgamation gives rise to positive synergy, the value of the amalgamated business will be greater than the sum of the values of the individual businesses taken in isolation. The basic principle can be simply stated, but the practical problems are immense in that the purchaser has to place a value on a business which has yet to be established. The purchaser will usually not only have to consider the tangible assets, which can be valued with relative ease, but also the intangible assets which may be particularly influenced by the synergical effect of the amalgamation.

In many amalgamations some of the assets of the acquired business will not be retained in the new business. The first step therefore in valuing a business for acquisition will be to determine the asset structure of the business and identify the assets which will not be required in the future. These assets must be valued at their net realisable value at the time at which they are expected to be sold and these figures discounted to the present time to ascertain the present value of the superfluous assets. In many cases, the sale of the superfluous assets will take place immediately and therefore no discounting will be necessary. The value of these assets may be considered to be a deduction from the purchase price of the business.

In practice the valuation figure must be the net realisable value of the surplus assets which are to be sold plus the present value of the additional earnings which will accrue to the acquiring business as a result of the acquisition. It is of course apparent that a major problem arises in determining the rate of interest at which the earnings of the business must be discounted, and this has already been discussed.

We will consider an example in order to assist with the explanation of this analysis.

---

8 This is of course equivalent to capitalising the expected return of £11 000 at 10 per cent.

EXAMPLE 14.5

ADG is a business which produces and sells to retailers a certain range of fashion clothes. It has made the following estimates of potential earnings for the next 10 years:

Year no	1	2	3	4	5	6	7	8	9	10
Earnings (£000)	120	140	170	200	210	220	240	260	280	300

XYZ is a business which owns a number of boutiques in a certain locality. The boutiques buy clothes from various suppliers and retail them. Each boutique has a manager and an assistant but all purchasing and policy decisions are taken centrally by the owner and her staff.

XYZ independently estimates its earnings for the next 10 years to be

Year no.	1	2	3	4	5	6	7	8	9	10
Earnings (£000)	10	15	20	25	28	31	33	34	35	35

The net assets of XYZ have a book value of £100 000, which includes 10-year leases on retail shops valued at about £60 000, a freehold shop and office valued at £20 000, stock worth £20 000 at retail prices, on which £12 000 is owing to suppliers.

ADG is interested in acquiring XYZ in order to provide some additional retail outlets. If it were to do this, it would retain most of the shops with their staff, but would not retain the owner, nor her staff nor the freehold shop and offices. It would use the shops to sell only its own clothes, and so improve its turnover and profit margin.

ADG have made the following estimates of costs and earnings if it were to acquire XYZ. Initially, it would sell the freehold shop and office for £20 000 and the leases on two of the shops for a further £10 000. This would entail the dismissal of 10 staff who would need to be compensated for loss of employment, which would cost ADG about £25 000. The entire stock of the shops would be sold as quickly as possible and replaced with clothing supplied by ADG. The estimated trading earnings of ADG with XYZ for the next 10 years are as follows:

Year no.	1	2	3	4	5	6	7	8	9	10
Earnings (£000)	125	150	200	230	255	270	280	300	320	350

Thus, ADG can assess the differences between its performance without XYZ and with XYZ. These differences are:

Year no.	1	2	3	4	5	6	7	8	9	10
Difference in earnings (£000)	+5	+10	+30	+30	+45	+50	+40	+40	+40	+50

Additional gains to ADG would be the sale of the freehold and the leasehold shops (£30 000) and of the stock (£20 000) less the liabilities due to suppliers (£12 000) and the cost of laying off the excess employees (£25 000): an immediate net gain of £13 000.

It is assumed that all other assets of the business would be retained. Thus, the figures to be discounted to give a present value for the acquisition are as follows:

Year no.	0	1	2	3	4	5	6	7	8	9	10
Earnings (£000)	13	5	10	30	30	45	50	40	40	40	50

In practice it may be difficult to decide upon the appropriate discount rate. The problem may be overcome by considering a range of discount rates within which it is likely that the appropriate rate will fall. We will assume that the selected range is 15–20 per cent.

The present values of the earnings stream are £157 620 when discounted at 15 per cent and £127 063 when discounted at 20 per cent, while the present values of the earnings of XYZ for the next 10 years should it continue as an independent business are £116 926 when discounted at 15 per cent and £93 598 when discounted at 20 per cent. The value of the business of XYZ on its own can therefore be seen to be less than its value to ADG at any given discount rate between 15 and 20 per cent, therefore agreement should readily be reached as to a purchase price since it will be advantageous for the owner of XYZ to sell at £117 000 or above and for ADG to buy at £127 000 or below, given that 15 per cent and 20 per cent represent the extremes of the possible discount rates applicable to this type of business.

As can be seen in the example, if the business can be put to a more profitable use by the new management and, if there is not a substantial difference between the discount rates used by the parties, it is likely that a price for the business will be agreed. If we retain the assumption about the comparability of the discount rates, it is clear that the converse holds in that if the business would be employed less profitably by the potential purchaser it is not likely that agreement could be reached as the business would be worth more to the potential seller than it is to the potential buyer. If the parties employ widely different discount rates the above conclusions may not apply.

Suppose for example that the owner of XYZ was content with a return of 10 per cent on capital. Then, discounting the earnings stream of XYZ at 10 per cent, would produce a present value of £149 606. If ADG expected a 20 per cent return on their investment then the value they would put upon the acquisition of the business would be £127 064. In such a case it would be impossible to fix a price which would not lead to a worsening of the perceived positions of one or both parties.

The value of control of a business

For a sole proprietor there is no question of ownership of a business without control, but for a partnership or a company it is possible to share in the ownership of a business without having control of the business. In using the word 'control' in this context we mean that the individual in question is able to determine the business policy or any particular action of the business without resort to persuading other owners of the business that this course of action is desirable.

When a business is jointly owned the value of the business to the controlling owner is in most cases greater, proportionately to the holding, than to the other owners. This has been clearly established in law in valuing shares for capital transfer tax purposes where a controlling interest in a company was recognised as carrying a higher proportionate value than a minority interest. The law, however, merely follows upon observed fact, since the valuation is based upon what a potential purchaser would be likely to pay for the holding being valued, given that there was access to all the information that would be available to a prudent potential purchaser. Thus, we must examine the underlying reasons for which a controlling interest in a business is proportionately more valuable than a minority interest.

The most obvious reason for this higher valuation is that the controlling interest enables the owner of that interest to arrange the affairs of the business in a way that best suits his own circumstances. This may appear to offend the profit maximisation principle which is assumed to apply to businesses, but it does in fact take us one step further in the analysis. The assumption of profit maximisation for a business is an extension of the principle of the maximising of utility for the individual. These two criteria do not necessarily coincide, but provided there are many owners with many preferences, it is a practicable solution to suggest that if maximum profit is available then the individuals will be able to get the most utility from spending it. However, the crux of the problem can be illustrated by supposing there is only one owner and examining the maximizing of his utility and the profit of the firm separately.

Assume that there are two possible paths for the business to follow producing the following dividend flows given differing reinvestment patterns:

Year no.	1	2	3	4	5
Path 1 dividends (£000s)	5	7	12	17	20
Path 2 dividends (£000s)	11	11	11	11	11

If the cost of capital to the business is 10 per cent then the present value of these dividends will be £43 376 if path 1 is followed and £41 700 if path 2 is followed. The profit maximisation assumption would indicate that path 1 should be followed.

Suppose, however, that the owner of the business requires more money in the early years and, if he is not able to take this money from the business, he must borrow it at 25 per cent interest and is prepared to do so. This means that the owner's discount rate is 25 per cent and therefore the present value of the dividends streams to him are £28 140 if path 1 is followed and £29 580 if path 2 is followed. He will choose to follow path 2.

Thus, the value to this individual from controlling the business, and thereby directing the business to follow path 2 rather than path 1 is £29 580 – £28 140 = £1440.

Now it is clear that if this business was owned by many shareholders and run by a professional manager it should follow path 1 because the manager could show that by reinvesting profits at a high rate in the early period the firm would be better off by £43 376 – £41 700, i.e. by £1676 in present value terms, whilst the individual we have considered would be worse off by £1140 if he were the sole recipient of these dividends.

Thus, we have shown that the net present value of the dividends stream from the business is dependent upon the rate at which the stream is discounted. Therefore the value which will be placed by an individual upon a business will depend upon her expected income stream and her own time preference rate. The control of a firm enables an individual to co-ordinate the discount rate used by the firm with that which optimises her own welfare.

There are, of course, other advantages to having control of a business which are concerned with status and the ability to use the business to help to achieve personal goals, but the difference in value between a minority and controlling interest stems from the difference between the individual's utility maximising position and profit maximisation. The difference will in nearly all cases make a controlling interest in a business proportionately more valuable than a minority interest.

The valuation of a business represents therefore much the same type of problem as does the valuation of other assets, but because the business is a complex asset and its ownership is often diverse the estimation involved is even more difficult.

APPENDIX: SSAP 3 'EARNINGS PER SHARE'

The importance of the earnings per share (EPS) measure and the uses to which it is put have been discussed in the main body of this chapter. It is therefore not surprising to find that there is an accounting standard, SSAP 3, which requires all companies having a listing on a recognised stock exchange for any class of equity to display *on the face* of its audited profit and loss account its EPS on the net basis (see below) for both the current year and the previous year. The basis of calculating these figures must be shown either in the profit and loss account or in the notes to the accounts. This will normally involve disclosing the earnings and the number of equity shares used in the calculation.

Since the primary use of the EPS measure is in decisions regarding the valuation of equity shares, SSAP 3 originally required that EPS be calculated on the basis of earnings from ordinary activities, that is before adding extraordinary profits or deducting extraordinary losses. Such extraordinary items were, by definition, expected not to recur frequently or regularly and hence would not contribute to the future 'maintainable' or 'normal' profits of the company. They were therefore excluded from the numerator in making the EPS calculation.

As we have seen in Chapter 6, it has proved extremely difficult to provide a robust definition which enables companies to distinguish between ordinary and extraordinary items consistently. Different companies appear to have treated similar items differently and frequently large listed companies have substantial extraordinary items in their profit and loss accounts year after year. As a consequence of this, FRS 3 'Reporting financial performance' has defined ordinary activities so widely that extraordinary items are likely to be extremely rare. It has also replaced the definition of earnings per share included in SSAP 3, by the following[9]:

> The profit in pence attributable to each equity share, based on the profit (or in the case of a group the consolidated profit) of the period after tax, minority interests *and extraordinary items* and after deducting preference dividends and other appropriations in respect of preference shares, divided by the number of equity shares in issue and ranking for dividend in respect of the period.

Hence the EPS measure now includes any extraordinary items. The ASB does envisage that some companies may wish to publish additional earnings per share figures and permits this provided that the additional figures are reconciled to the standard EPS and are not given more prominence than the EPS required by the standard.

For many companies, the EPS figures may be calculated with ease but there are a number of complicating factors including situations where the tax charge is affected by

---

9 SSAP 3, Para. 10 as replaced by FRS 3, Para. 25.

the level of distribution, when losses are incurred and where there either have been or might be, changes in a company's capital structure. Each of these will be discussed below.

Taxation and the level of dividends

While in most cases a company's liability to taxation is unaffected by the size of its dividends, there are instances where this will not be the case. The exceptions occur when the level of dividends is such as to make it impossible to recover, in the immediate future, ACT paid. In such a case the question arises as to what should be included as the tax deduction in arriving at the earnings figure – the actual tax charge or that which would have been charged if no distribution had been made.

If the actual tax charge is used we have what is termed the *net* basis of calculating EPS while if the alternative is adopted the result is called the *nil distribution* basis. The latter term is self-explanatory but it should be noted that even if the nil distribution basis is adopted, any tax resulting from the payment of a preference dividend should be deducted in calculating the earnings figure.

The main argument in favour of the use of the nil distribution basis is that it aids comparability between companies in that the EPS is not dependent on the level of distribution. Use of the net basis is justified by the view that it takes into account all relevant factors including the additional tax liabilities inherent in the dividend policy adopted by the directors for which they should be accountable to shareholders.

SSAP 3 specifies that the net basis should be used. However, the desirability, but not obligation, of also showing the EPS using the nil basis where the two methods would yield significantly different results is stressed.

Losses and unpaid preference dividends

If the earnings attributable to equity shareholders is negative the EPS should be calculated in the normal way with the result shown as a loss per share.

A related issue is the treatment of unpaid preference dividends. If the shares are cumulative the dividend for the period should be taken into account in arriving at the EPS whether or not it has been declared. In the case of non-cumulative preference shares only the dividend paid or proposed should be included.

Actual changes in equity share capital

EXAMPLE 14.6

It will be helpful to use a simple example. Let us assume that MM plc's earnings attributable to equity shareholders for 19X5 is £2.0 million and that at 1 January, the start of its financial year, it had in issue 20 million ordinary shares at 25p each and that on 1 October it issued a further 4 million 25p ordinary shares. What is the EPS for 19X5? The answer depends on the source of the issue, specifically whether it was a scrip (or bonus) issue or whether the issue was for cash (or other consideration) and, if for cash, etc., whether the issue was at, or below, the market price.

A scrip issue does not raise extra cash and merely represents a rearrangement of the equity interest in a company in that a transfer is made from reserves to equity share capital.

There are simply more shares in issue at the end of the year than there were at the beginning and, hence, to show the EPS appropriate to the new capital structure all that is required is to apportion the earnings over the shares in issue at the year end, 24 million, and thus the EPS is (£2 000 000 ÷ 24 000 000) x 100 = 8.0p.

To assist comparability, the EPS for the corresponding period should be adjusted accordingly. Similar considerations apply if shares are split into shares of a smaller nominal value.

Let us now assume that the issue of shares was made at the full market price, while recognising that in practice such an issue is nowadays a rare event, as most issues for cash take the form of rights issues to existing shareholders at a price below that which prevails on the market. To calculate the EPS where there has been an issue at the full market price all that is necessary is to calculate the *weighted* average number of shares in issue in the course of the year and divide the result into the total earnings of the year. The average is weighted to take account of the timing of the share issue.

In this case the company had 20 million shares in issue for 9 months and 24 million for 3 months. The appropriate weightings to be applied are hence ¾ and ¼ and the weighted average is ¾ x 20 000 000 + ¼ x 24 000 000 = 21 000 000 with the new EPS (£2 000 000/21 000 000) x 100 = 9.5p.

It will be noted that this figure exceeds the 8.0p per share in the scrip issue example and it will be instructive to consider why this is so. A company which makes a scrip issue raises no extra resources and hence, all other things being equal, will not increase its earnings. Thus, the only effect of the scrip issue is to divide the earnings over a greater number of shares. In contrast if shares are issued for cash, extra resources are obtained which, it is hoped, will increase earnings in the future. If the new investment generates the same rate of return as the existing assets of the business, then, all other things being equal, the EPS after an issue at the full market price will be the same as that which prevailed before the issue. However, in practice it will take some time to deploy the additional resources and in the first instance the additional cash will earn a small or even a negative return, hence the issue of shares for cash will normally reduce the EPS (from that which applied before the issue) until the new investment comes on stream.

A rights issue lies somewhere between the two extremes of a scrip issue and an issue at the full market price in that it combines elements of both since while additional cash is raised the original shares lose some of their value.

In order to distinguish between the two elements of a rights issue it is necessary to find what is called the *theoretical ex-rights price*. This is the price per share following the issue which would make the stock market value of the company immediately after the rights issue equal to the sum of the market value before the announcement of the issue and the proceeds of the rights issue.[10] Once the theoretical ex-rights price is determined the EPS calculation can be made on the assumption that there were two transactions, a scrip issue followed by an issue at the new market price.[11]

---

10 The actual price per share following the issue is not likely to be equal to the theoretical ex-rights price as the actual price is likely to be affected by the market's expectations of future results and dividend policy. It might, for example, be thought that the total dividend per share would at least be held constant following the issue and hence the total dividend payable increased and this expectation might, of itself, increase the market price.

11 The same result would be achieved if it was assumed that the transactions were made in the reverse order, i.e. an issue at the market price followed by a scrip issue. The above method, however, accords with the description given in SSAP 3 and we will hence concentrate on that alternative.

Let us assume that a company has in issue 12 000 shares which had a market price of £2 and 8 months after the start of the year makes a rights issue of 1 for every 3 shares held (a 1 for 3 issue) at a discount of 25 per cent, i.e. 4000 shares were issued at a price of £1.50 each raising £6000. The theoretical ex-rights price, x, is given by:

$$16\,000x = 12\,000 \times £2 + 4000 \times £1.5$$
$$16\,000x = £24\,000 + £6000$$
$$x = £1.875$$

We need to find the size of a hypothetical scrip issue which would, all other things being equal, have reduced the market price per share from £2 to £1.875.

Let X be the number of shares in issue following the scrip issue

$$\text{then } X \times £1.875 = 12\,000 \times £2$$

$$\text{or } X = 12\,000 \times \frac{£2}{£1.875} = 12\,800$$

Thus the scrip issue would be such as to increase the number of shares in issue from 12 000 to (12 000 x 2/1.875). We should note that the factor 2/1.875 is the:

$$\frac{\text{Actual market price before the issue}}{\text{Theoretical ex-rights price}}$$

We can now divide the rights issue into its two elements (a) the scrip issue and (b) the issue at the market price (or, in this case, at the theoretical ex-rights price).
Thus:

(i)	The company started with	12 000 shares
(ii)	The hypothetical scrip issue increased the shares to 12 000 x 2/1.875 or an additional	800 shares
(iii)	The hypothetical issue of 3200 shares at £1.875 raised £6000	3200 shares
	Thus the company finished with	16 000 shares

To calculate the EPS it is necessary to remember that, in the case of a scrip issue, the earnings were simply divided by the number of shares ranking for dividend at the end of the year (irrespective of the date of the scrip issue) while in the case of an issue at market price the average number of shares was used (weighted on the basis of the time of the issue). To combine these two methods we draw a line after the hypothetical scrip issue and say that at the end of 8 months there were 12 800 (12 000 x 2/1.875) shares in issue but, as the increase was due to a scrip issue, we will calculate the EPS on the assumption that the company had 12 800 shares for the whole of the 8-month period. Thus, the weighted average number of shares will be calculated on the basis that the company had 12 000 x 2/1.875 shares for 8 months and 16 000 shares for 4 months. The weighted average number of shares is then:

$$12\,000 \times \frac{2}{1.875} \times \tfrac{2}{3} + 16\,000 \times \tfrac{1}{3} = 13\,867$$

and, if the earnings for the year were £1664, the EPS would be 12p.

The method described above is that recommended in Para. 18 of SSAP 3 which states that the factor which should be used to inflate the number of shares prior to the issue to adjust for the bonus element should be:

$$\frac{\text{Actual cum rights price on last day of quotation cum rights}}{\text{Theoretical ex-rights price}}$$

In order to aid comparability the EPS figure for the prior year needs to be adjusted to take account of the hypothetical scrip issue. If 12 000 shares were in issue for the whole of the preceding year then for the purposes of restating the EPS this figure will be increased to 12 800, i.e. to 12 000 x (cum rights price)/(theoretical ex-rights price). Actually, a short cut can be taken as the same result can be obtained by multiplying the original EPS by the reciprocal of the above ratio, i.e. by (theoretical ex-rights price)/(cum rights price).[12]

Possible future changes in capital structure

If at the balance sheet date the company has contracted to issue shares at some time in the future the effect may be to dilute (reduce) the EPS in future. The same might happen if at the balance sheet date the company has already issued shares which have not yet ranked for dividend (and hence which have been excluded from the EPS calculation) but which may do so in the future. In such cases SSAP 3 requires that the fully diluted EPS be shown on the face of the profit and loss account together with the basic EPS so long as the dilution is material (5 per cent is stated to be material for this purpose). Where there is a material dilution the standard requires that:

(a) equal prominence should be given to both the basic and fully diluted EPS,
(b) the basis of calculation of the diluted EPS figure should be disclosed and
(c) the fully diluted EPS for the corresponding period should only be shown if the assumptions on which it was based still apply.

The contract to issue further shares may be in the form of warrants or options to subscribe for equity shares in the company or may be in the form of convertible debentures, loan stock or preference shares.

The basic principle is to show the maximum effect of the possible dilution and hence if the terms of the issue of the options or convertible securities are such that the conversion ratio varies, e.g. if the number of equity shares which will be issued in respect of the conversion of each £1000 of convertible loan stock reduces over time, the greatest possible number of potential additional shares should be used in the calculation. Further it should be assumed that the conversion had been effected on the first day of the accounting period or, if later, the date of issue of the security.

It would clearly be misleading to treat, say, convertible loan stock as both loan stock and equity capital and hence when calculating the fully diluted EPS it is necessary to add to the basic earnings the interest (less taxation thereon) payable in respect of the

---

12 Let P be the original EPS, P' the restated EPS, E the earnings, S the original number of shares in issue and F the ratio of the cum rights price to the theoretical ex-rights price. Then:

$$P = \frac{E}{S} \quad \text{and} \quad P' = \frac{E}{SF} = P \times \frac{1}{F}$$

convertible stock. Similarly, it would be misleading to assume that the cash received from the exercise of an option to purchase equity shares would not increase earnings and hence in such circumstances SSAP 3 states that the earnings for the period should, for the purposes of the calculation, be increased by an amount equivalent to that which would have been earned had the proceeds of the exercise of the option been invested in 2½ per cent Consolidated Stock on the first day of the period at the closing price of the previous day. Note that if convertible loan stock is actually converted during the year it is still necessary to show the fully diluted EPS for the year, that is the EPS which would have been generated if the conversion had taken place on the first day of the year.

When calculating the fully diluted EPS the denominator will always be greater than that used in the basic EPS calculation while in some circumstances the numerator will also be increased. Hence in some circumstances, such as a company with a low basic EPS and a large volume of convertible loan stock, the diluted EPS may actually be greater than the basic figure. In such cases SSAP 3 states that the conversion right would not be exercised and hence a fully diluted (or actually inflated) EPS figure should not be shown. If there is more than one type of security which falls to be treated as part of the calculation of the diluted EPS and if the inclusion of a security would be to increase the basic EPS, then that security should be totally excluded from the calculation.

In summary, SSAP 3 requires, in appropriate circumstances, the presentation of two figures for EPS on the face of the profit and loss account (with corresponding figures for the preceeding period) – the basic and fully diluted figures – and recommends the inclusion of a further figure in the notes to the accounts – the basic EPS calculated on the nil distribution basis.

Some of the points covered in the Appendix are illustrated in Example 14.7.

EXAMPLE 14.7

(A) PB plc's capital structure for the whole of the year ended 31 December 19X2 was as follows:

	£
200 000 £1 deferred ordinary shares	200 000
2 000 000 ordinary shares, 50p each	1 000 000
	1 200 000
Convertible loan stock (10%)	600 000
	1 800 000

Notes
(a) The deferred ordinary shares will not rank for dividend until 1 January 19X9 at which date they will each be divided into two 50p ordinary shares which will rank *pari passu* with the ordinary shares then in issue.
(b) The loan stock is convertible into 50p ordinary shares on the following terms. Each £100 of loan stock is convertible into 60 shares if the option is exercised on 1 January 19X6 or 50 shares if exercised on 1 January 19X7.
(c) Under the terms of a share incentive scheme certain executives have the option to purchase a total of 100 000 ordinary shares for £1.2 each.
(d) PB plc's earnings per share for 19X2 was £320 000/2 000 000 = 16.0p.

(B) On 30 September 19X3 the company made a 1 for 4 rights issue at £1.4 per share. The actual cum rights price on the last day of quotation cum rights was £2.0. No shares were issued under the terms of the share incentive scheme in 19X3 nor was there any increase in the company's obligations under the scheme.

(C) A summary of PB plc's profit and loss account for the year ended 31 December 19X3 is given below:

	£
Profit before interest and tax	660 000
less Interest	60 000
	600 000
less Corporation tax at, say, 25%	150 000
	450 000
Extraordinary loss, net of tax	50 000
Profit attributable to ordinary shareholders	400 000

(D) *Basic EPS*   In order to calculate the basic EPS it is necessary to work out the theoretical ex-rights price, x.

$$2\,500\,000 \times £x = 2\,000\,000 \times £2 + 500\,000 \times £1.4$$
$$2\,500\,000 \times £x = £4\,000\,000 + £700\,000$$
$$x = £1.88.$$

The weighted average number of shares in issue for 19X3 is given by:

$2\,000\,000 \times 2/1.88 \times 9/12$	=	1 595 744
$2\,500\,000 \times 3/12$	=	625 000
Weighted average		2 220 744

The basic EPS for 19X3 is

$$\frac{£400\,000}{2\,220\,744} \qquad = \qquad 18.0p$$

and the restated EPS for 19X2 is

$$16 \times \frac{1.88}{2} \qquad = \qquad 15.0p$$

(E) *Fully diluted EPS*

	19X3	19X2
	£	£
Earnings attributable to ordinary shareholders	400 000	320 000
Add: Interest on convertible loan stock (60 000 less tax at 25%)	45 000	45 000
Earnings from proceeds of share option scheme (£120 000) at 9% in 19X3, 8% in 19X2 less tax (*see below*)	5 400	4 800
	450 400	369 800

(It has been assumed that the yield on 2½% consolidated stock was 9% on 1.1.19X3 and 8% on 1.1.19X2.)

	19X3	19X2
Average number of ordinary shares	2 220 744	2 127 659[13]
Maximum increase due to:		
(i) Conversion of deferred shares	400 000	400 000
(ii) Conversion of loan stock	360 000	360 000
(iii) Options under incentive scheme	100 000	100 000
	3 080 744	2 987 659
Fully diluted EPS	14.6p	12.4p

RECOMMENDED READING

C. G. Glover, *Valuation of Unquoted Securities*, Gee & Co., London, 1986.

C. G. Glover, 'Valuation of Unquoted Shares', *Accountants' Digest No. 299*, Accountancy Books, London, 1993.

N. Eastaway and H. Booth, *Practical Share Valuation*, 2nd edn, Butterworths, London, 1990.

---

13 2 000 000 x 2/1.88 = 2 127 659.

PART IV
Accounting and price changes

CHAPTER 15

Accounting for inflation

INTRODUCTION

In Chapter 3 we suggested that the historical cost asset valuation/money financial capital maintenance system (conventional accounting) suffers from numerous shortcomings when tested against the purposes which financial accounting might sensibly be regarded as serving. This observation is not a new one[1] but the case for accounting reform was not widely accepted in the United Kingdom, especially by accountants, until the 1970s.

Why the change in attitude?

The obvious answer is the high rate of inflation which was a feature of the UK economy of that period; the annual rate of inflation was, for example, over 25 per cent in 1974. The apparent permanent increase in inflation highlighted the limitations of the conventional accounting model which we discussed in Chapter 3.

A striking example of the consequences of inflation on historical cost accounts was provided by the ASC in its 1986 publication *Accounting for the Effects of Changing Prices: a Handbook*, which will henceforth be referred to as the ASC Handbook. The example compared dividend distributions expressed as a percentage of (a) historical cost profit and (b) a measure of profit based on current cost principles. The results were derived from large samples of companies and covered the period 1980 to 1984, a period in which the UK had significantly lower inflation than in the 1970s. The results are shown in Table 15.1.

Table 15.1 Dividend distribution expressed as percentages of profit derived on (i) historical cost and (ii) current cost principles

	Historical cost (%)	Current cost (%)
1980	37	97
1981	40	111
1982	48	130
1983	50	94
1984	52	64

---

1 *See* Sir R. Edwards 'The nature and measurement of income', originally published as a series of articles in *The Accountant*, July–October 1938; reprinted *in Studies in Accounting* W. T. Baxter and S. Davidson (eds), ICAEW, London, 1977, pp. 96–140. This is only one, and by no means the earliest, of many references that could have been selected. In this classic paper Sir Ronald Edwards, an accountant who was both a university professor and successful businessman, clearly outlined many of the problems inherent in conventional accounting and discussed many important matters which are still controversial issues.

Note that using an historical cost perception it appeared that company directors had on average pursued prudent distribution policies, but the results based on current costs indicate that in some years the average dividend exceeded the amount required to be retained in the business to sustain its existing scale of operations.

So it seems that in periods of high inflation business financial results based on historical cost asset valuations and money financial capital maintenance paint a misleading and distorted picture of the financial progress of companies. But does the case for accounting reform disappear in periods when inflation is low? It is certainly true that support for reform on the part of most businessmen and professional accountants does depend on the rate of inflation. When inflation is high there is a strong pressure for change and exposure drafts and standards are issued, while when inflation falls the advocates of the status quo gain supremacy and the exposure drafts and standards are withdrawn. But the case for reform does not disappear.[2]

In its 1986 Handbook the ASC stated 'The limitations of historical cost accounts exist not only in periods of relatively rapid price changes but also when prices are changing more slowly.[3] Three reasons were advanced to support this view:

(a) Even with low annual rates of inflation, the cumulative effect of inflation over time is significant, for example, with 5 per cent inflation, prices double every 14 years.
(b) The accounting effects of previous high rates of inflation persist over a number of years.
(c) Rates of change of specific prices may be substantial even when the rate of inflation is relatively low.

THE PROGRESS OF ACCOUNTING REFORM

The path towards accounting reform has been long and tortuous and, as far as Britain is concerned, is outlined in Figure 15.1 which can be used as a guide to this and subsequent chapters.

There are two lines shown in Figure 15.1. One represents the current purchasing power (CPP) method, which takes account of general price changes but which ignores specific price changes; in terms of the analysis presented in Chapter 3 it is a system of accounting based on the combination of the adjusted historical cost asset valuation basis and the maintenance of real financial capital. A detailed exposition of CPP accounting is provided later in this chapter. The other line represents an approach generally known as current cost accounting (CCA) which in the United Kingdom combines a variant of the replacement cost approach to valuation with either the operating or the real financial capital maintenance concepts. This approach will be discussed in more detail in Chapter 16.

CPP accounting retains most of the significant features of historical cost accounting, and the only real change is the replacement of the money unit of measurement by the purchasing power unit. It will be seen that when compared to a system which attempts to measure current values the CPP model involves a far less radical departure from the

---

2 Michael Mumford 'The end of a familiar inflation accounting cycle', *Accounting and Business Research*, Vol. 9, No. 34, Spring 1978, pp. 98–104.
3 *Accounting for the Effects of Changing Prices: a Handbook*, ASC, London, 1986, p. 11.

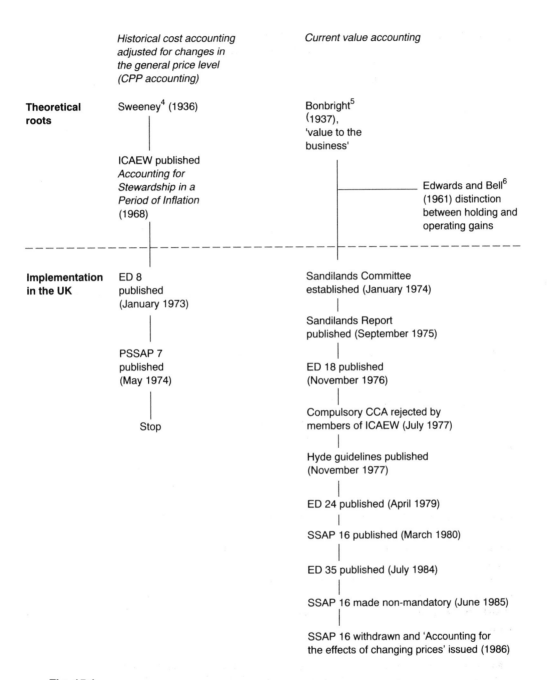

Fig. 15.1

4 F. N. Sweeney, *Stabilized Accounts*, Harper, New York, 1936 (reprinted by Arno Press, New York, 1977).
5 J. C. Bonbright, *The Valuation of Property*, Michie, Charlottesville, Va., 1937 (reprinted 1965).
6 E. O. Edwards and P. W. Bell, *The Theory and Measurement of Business Income*, University of California Press, Stanford, Calif., 1961.

conventional method, and it is perhaps not surprising that the first tentative steps on the path to accounting reform taken by the British accountancy profession were on the CPP route; much the same occurred in the United States and Australia.[7]

In 1968 the Research Foundation of the ICAEW published *Accounting for Stewardship in a Period of Inflation*. The title is instructive in that it suggests a far more restrictive view of the objectives of financial accounts than is accepted nowadays and does illustrate the extent of the changes that have since taken place. The methods outlined in that document were not original. They had been described in English by Sweeney in 1936[8] and his book was itself based on work done in Germany during the period of hyperinflation which followed the First World War. The significance of the publication was that it was produced by a body associated with a leading professional accounting institute and indicated that that body was apparently prepared to initiate reform. The seeds took a long time to germinate, and we had to wait until 1973 for the publication of ED 8 by the ASC. ED 8 proposed that companies should be required to publish, along with their conventional accounts, supplementary statements which would, in effect, be their profit and loss accounts and balance sheets based on CPP principles. ED 8 was followed by the issue of Provisional Statement of Standard Accounting Practice (PSSAP) 7, in May 1974. The inclusion of the word 'provisional' in the title of this standard (the only occasion on which this was done by the ASC) reflected the uncertainties in the mind of the accountancy profession on this matter, since it meant that companies were requested rather than required to comply with the standard.

Many users of accounting reports, including the government, were dissatisfied with this approach. Consequently, the government established its own committee of enquiry into inflation accounting in January 1974, i.e. after the issue of ED 8. The committee was chaired by Mr, now Sir, Francis Sandilands and its report (usually referred to as the Sandilands Report) was issued in September, 1975.[9] The committee recommended the adoption of a system of accounting known as 'current cost accounting' which is, as will be shown later, a very different creature from CPP accounting. As a result of the publication of the Sandilands Report, the ASC abandoned its own proposals and set up a working party, the Inflation Accounting Steering Group (IASG) to prepare an initial Statement of Standard Accounting Practice based on the Sandilands' proposals. The outcome of this group's labours was ED 18, 'Current cost accounting', which was published in November 1976. This publication came under a good deal of attack from many quarters, including those who supported the main principles of current cost accounting (CCA). The Exposure Draft was considered by many to be unnecessarily complicated and to deal with too many subsidiary issues. The draft was also attacked by many rank and file – some would say backwoods – members of the ICAEW, and their efforts resulted in the passing of a resolution in July 1977 by members of the Institute which rejected any compulsory introduction of CCA.

---

7 For example, in the United States the FASB (the US equivalent of the British ASC) produced an Exposure Draft in December 1974 which was similar in content to ED 8, but the Securities Exchange Commission (a US Government Agency) in 1976 called for the disclosure by larger companies of additional information concerning the replacement costs of fixed assets and stock. The subsequent US standard, FAS No. 33 'Financial reporting and changing prices', September 1979, required supplementary disclosure of both types of information, but this statement was superseded by FAS No. 89, with the same title, in December 1986. This encouraged, rather than required, such disclosure.

8 F. N. Sweeney, *op. cit.*

9 *Report of the Inflation Accounting Committee*, Cmnd 6225, HMSO, London, 1975.

This did not halt the advance of CCA. The government, in a discussion document issued in July 1977 (*The future of company reports*), reiterated its support for the adoption of CCA, while in November 1977 the accountancy profession issued a set of interim recommendations to cover the period until a revised set of detailed proposals could be formulated. These recommendations were called the Hyde guidelines after the name of the chairman of the committee responsible for the recommendations. A second Exposure Draft, ED 24, was published in April 1979 and was followed by the issue of SSAP 16 in March 1980. SSAP 16 was allowed to prevail for 3 years while the effect of the introduction of CCA was evaluated.

With certain exceptions, SSAP 16 applied to all companies listed on the Stock Exchange and to large unlisted companies. Such companies were required to publish current cost accounts together with historical cost accounts or historical cost information. The intention was that primacy should be given to the current cost accounts although, as we shall see, things did not turn out in the way intended by the ASC.

Current cost accounts did not replace the historical cost accounts and they were often presented and perhaps even more often regarded as being supplementary to the main, or as many no doubt believed the 'real' accounts. Many companies simply failed to comply with the provisions of SSAP 16, and while auditors were obliged to refer to the absence of current cost accounts in the audit report, such references were not regarded as important qualifications and the companies concerned did not seem to suffer as a consequence of their non-compliance.

Following the evaluation of the impact of SSAP16, ED 35 was published in July 1984. The basic principles of CCA were maintained, albeit with some modifications, but ED 35 proposed that companies should only be required to produce one set of accounts, based on historical costs with notes showing the effect of changing prices. The proposals of ED 35 were not implemented but instead SSAP 16 was made non-mandatory in June 1985. This was, however, not the end of the matter for in 1986 SSAP 16 was withdrawn and the ASC published its Handbook, *Accounting for the Effects of Changing Prices*. At that time the Presidents of the five leading accountancy bodies in the UK issued a joint statement endorsing the view of the ASC that companies should appraise and, where material, report the effect of changing prices. In addition the Presidents supported the view that accounting for the effect of changing prices is of great importance and agreed that a suitable accounting standard should be developed. Numerous reasons can be advanced to explain why it has not proved possible to introduce a generally acceptable system of current cost accounting. Prominent among them is the lack of agreement on the part of those advocating change as to how to account for changing prices and the associated problem that very many businessmen and accountants do not understand the basic principles underlying current cost accounting.

We shall continue this chapter with a discussion of the CPP method and will return to current cost accounting in Chapter 16.

CURRENT PURCHASING POWER (CPP) ACCOUNTING

Introduction

The elements of CPP accounting were introduced in Chapter 3 – that is the adjusted historical cost basis of valuation coupled with profit measurement based on the maintenance of real financial capital. Before describing how these can be combined to produce a coherent accounting model it is necessary to consider how, and from whose point of view, the purchasing power of money should be measured.

The prices of different goods and services change by different amounts, and the problem faced by those responsible for measuring changes in the purchasing power of money is to find a suitable average value to reflect the different individual price changes which have taken place during the period under review. This could be done by considering all the different goods and services which are traded in the country during the period and to compare their prices with those prevailing in the comparison or base period. This is a massive task, but it is possible to arrive at the required answer by indirect methods as is done in the United States in the calculation of the gross domestic product implicit price deflator.

An alternative approach is to select a sample of goods and services, measure the changes in their prices, and then average them. This method is used to construct the Index of Retail Prices (RPI), which is based on the price changes which affect 'middle income' households. In order to construct the index it is necessary to assign weights to the various price changes to take account of their relative importance. These weights are based on the spending patterns of a sample of householders which is drawn so as to exclude households with incomes which are significantly higher and significantly lower than the average.

One of the major provisions of PSSAP 7 was the stipulation that changes in the purchasing power of money should be measured by reference to the RPI. The consequence of this proposal was that changes in purchasing power were not to be measured from the point of view of the individual firm or even all firms but from the point of view of individual consumers. Thus it was the intention that CPP accounts should not be regarded as providing proxies to current value accounts, but rather as restatements of the conventional historical cost accounts in terms which attempted to adjust for the effect of inflation on shareholders and other individuals.

The basic principle underlying CPP accounts is that all monetary amounts should be converted to pounds of CPP in a manner which is analogous to the way in which sums expressed in different foreign currencies are translated to a common base. Assume that we are attempting to measure the CPP profit for a transaction which involved the purchase of goods for £200 in January 1993 and their sale for £300 in December 1993. The RPI was 137.9 at the date of purchase and 141.9 at the date of sale. If we wish to measure the profit in terms of purchasing power at December 1993 we would need to convert the £200, which represented January 1993 purchasing power, in terms of December 1993 purchasing power. In order to carry out such calculations it will be helpful if we use symbols which indicate the purchasing power associated with the monetary amount; we will do this by specifying that £(Jan.93) means January 1993 pounds and so on.

The calculation of CPP profit for the above transaction could then be shown as follows:

	£(Dec 93)
Sales	300.00
Purchases, £(Jan 93) 200 x $\dfrac{141.9}{137.9}$	205.80
£(Dec 93)	94.20

The equation:

$$£(Jan\ 93)\ 200 \times \frac{141.9}{137.9} = £(Dec\ 93)\ 205.80$$

means that a consumer would require £205.80 in December 1993 in order to be able to command the same purchasing power as was available from the possession of £200 in January 1993.

The consequence of the extension of the basic CPP principle to the profit and loss account is that all items will be expressed in terms of current (i.e. year-end) purchasing power, while the same will be true in the balance sheet. Thus, all items in the balance sheet will have to be converted in terms of year-end purchasing power except the so-called monetary assets and liabilities which are automatically expressed in such terms. Example 15.1 illustrates the preparation of CPP accounts in the absence of monetary assets and liabilities.

EXAMPLE 15.1

Bell Limited's historical cost and CPP balance sheets at 31 December 19X6 (on which date a hypothetical RPI was 120) are given below:

Bell Limited
Balance sheet as at 31 December 19X6

	Historical cost £	Note		CPP £(31 Dec. X6)
Fixed assets				
Cost	10 000	(a)		12 000
Accumulated				
depreciation	4 000	(b)		4 800
	6 000			7 200
Stock	3 300	(c)		3 600
	£9 300		£(31 Dec. 19X6)	10 800
Share capital	4 000	(d)		4 800
Retained earnings	5 300	(e)		6 000
	£9 300		£(31 Dec. 19X6)	10 800

Notes

(a) The fixed assets were purchased for £10 000 on 1 January 19X3 when the RPI = 100:

$$£(1 \text{ Jan X3}) \ 10 \ 000 \times \frac{120}{100} = £(31 \text{ Dec. X6}) \ 12 \ 000$$

(b) Bell Limited depreciates its fixed assets on a straight-line basis over 10 years (assuming a zero scrap value). Thus, at the end of 19X6 four-tenths of the asset has been written off and the accumulated depreciation figure is thus:

$$4/10 \text{ of } £(31 \text{ Dec. X6}) \ 12 \ 000 = £(31 \text{ Dec. X6}) \ 4 \ 800$$

(c) The company's stock was purchased for £3 300 on 30 September 19X6 when the RPI was 110:

$$£(30 \text{ Sep. X6}) \ 3 \ 300 \times \frac{120}{110} = £(31 \text{ Dec. X6}) \ 3 \ 600$$

(d) The share capital consists of 4 000 £1 ordinary shares which were issued on 1 January 19X3 when the RPI was 100:

$$£(1 \text{ Jan. X3}) \ 4 \ 000 \times \frac{120}{100} = £(31 \text{ Dec. X6}) \ 4 \ 800$$

(e) Had CPP accounts been prepared in the past the CPP retained earnings would have emerged in the same way that retained earnings emerge in the historical cost accounts. In this case the CPP retained earnings is found by treating it as the balancing figure in the CPP balance sheet. It is not possible to find the CPP retained earnings from its historical cost equivalent as the relationship between them depends on the aggregate of the differences between the CPP and historical cost figures of all the balance sheet items.

During 19X7 Bell Limited engaged in the following transactions:

(a) On 31 March 19X7 it sold half its stock for cash of £(31 Mar. X7) 5500. £(31 Mar. X7) 4400 of the proceeds were used to purchase additional stock while the balance was paid out as a dividend.

(b) On 1 July 19X7 one-quarter of the 1 January 19X7 stock was sold for £(1 July X7) 2750; the proceeds were used to pay for overhead expenses which may be assumed to accrue evenly over the year.

The RPI moved as follows:

Date	Index
1 January 19X7	120
31 March 19X7	121
1 July 19X7 (which may be assumed to be the average value for the year)	132
31 December 19X7	143

The CPP profit and loss account for the year ended 31 December 19X7 is given below:

Bell Limited
Profit and loss account

	£(31 Dec X7)	£(31 Dec X7)
Sales, £(31 Mar X7) 5 500 x $\frac{143}{121}$	6 500	
Sales, £(1 Jul X7) 2 750 x $\frac{143}{132}$	2 979	9 479
less Opening stock,		
£(30 Sep X6) 3 300 x $\frac{143}{110}$	4 290	
Purchases,		
£(31 Mar X7) 4 400 x $\frac{143}{121}$	5 200	
	9 490	
less Closing stock,		
£(30 Sep X6) 825 x $\frac{143}{110}$		
+ £(31 Mar X7) 4 400 x $\frac{143}{121}$		
	6 272	3 218
Gross profit		6 261
less Overheads,		
£(1 Jul X7) 2 750 x $\frac{143}{132}$	2 979	
Depreciation,		
£1(1 Jan X3) 10 000 x $\frac{1}{10}$ x $\frac{143}{100}$	1 430	4 409
Net profit		1 852
less Dividends,		
£(31 Mar X7) 1 100 x $\frac{143}{121}$		1 300
		552
Retained earnings, 1 Jan X7,		
£(1 Jan X7) 6 000 x $\frac{143}{120}$		7 150
Retained earnings, 31 Dec X7 £(31 Dec X7)		7 702

Bell Limited
CPP balance sheet as at 31 December 19X7

	£(31 Dec X7)	£(31 Dec X7)
Fixed assets:		
Cost, £(1 Jan X3) 10 000 × $\frac{143}{100}$	14 300	
Accumulated depreciation,		
£(1 Jan X3) 5 000 × $\frac{143}{100}$	7 150	7 150
Stock:		
£(30 Sep X6) 825 × $\frac{143}{110}$	1 072	
£(31 Mar X7) 4 400 × $\frac{143}{121}$	5 200	6 272
	£(31 Dec X7)	13 422
Share capital,		
£(1 Jan X3) 4 000 × $\frac{143}{100}$		5 720
Retained earnings		
(from the profit and loss account		7 702
	£(31 Dec X7)	13 422

Example 15.1 illustrates the necessity of identifying the dates on which the different transactions took place in order to determine the denominator of the conversion factor (i.e. the RPI at the date of the transaction): the numerator is always the same – the RPI at the balance sheet date. In the example it was practicable to deal with each sale separately, but in practice it would usually be found necessary to make some simplifying assumption, e.g. that the sales accrued evenly over the year, which would mean that the average value of the RPI would be taken as the denominator in the conversion factor. A similar approach would probably have to be taken in respect of purchases and overhead expenses.

The treatment of depreciation merits special attention. Note that in Example 15.1 the conversion factor used in the calculation of the depreciation expense in the profit and loss account and the fixed asset items in the balance sheet is 143/100. The denominator, 100, is the RPI at the date on which the fixed asset was acquired. It is sometimes suggested that when calculating the depreciation expense the denominator should be the average value of the RPI for the year on the grounds that 'depreciation is written off over the year'. This is indeed so, but the vital point which is missing in this argument is that the pound of depreciation which is being written off in 19X7 is a pound of 1 January 19X3 as it was pounds with a 1 January 19X3 purchasing power which were given up in exchange for the asset.

Monetary assets and liabilities

A common feature of inflation is that debtors gain in purchasing power while creditors lose.[10] And, because free lunches are not a common feature of our economy, it is – to use

10 It is possible for the contracts between lenders and borrowers to be drawn up in terms of purchasing power instead of monetary units. These are often called index-linked agreements.

the terminology of game theory – a zero-sum game; the debtors' gains equal the creditors' losses. In other words, all other things being equal, one effect of inflation is to transfer purchasing power from creditors to debtors.

The reason for this is that if a person borrows money in a period of inflation he will repay it in pounds of lower purchasing power (value) than those which he obtained when he was granted the loan. The longer the loan then, so long as the inflation continues, the greater will be the difference between the values of the pounds borrowed and of the pounds repaid. Thus, a houseowner with a mortgage whose income has kept step with inflation may well be among those hard-faced people who 'have done well out of inflation' in that their mortgage payments constitute a continually declining percentage of their income.

It is, of course, possible for creditors to protect themselves in some cases by increasing the interest rate to take into account the expected rate of inflation. If this is done, the market rate of interest will be based upon the market's view of the likely future rates of inflation. Thus, a quoted rate of interest may be broken down into two parts, one, which we may term the 'real' interest rate, is that which would have been charged in the absence of inflationary expectations; the balance represents the inflation premium. This point has a good deal of relevance to some important questions about the treatment of gains and losses on monetary items. We will return to this point later.[11]

If the above analysis is extended to a company, it can be said that a company will lose purchasing power in a period of inflation if, taking the year as a whole, it holds net monetary assets (in simple terms if its cash plus debtors exceeds its creditors). Conversely, it will gain in purchasing power if, on average, it is in a net monetary liability position. The calculation depends on the meaning of monetary assets and liabilities.

In PSSAP 7 monetary items were defined as 'Assets, liabilities, or capital, the amounts of which were fixed by contract or statute in terms of numbers of pounds regardless of changes in the purchasing power of the pound.[12]

Let us first consider the distinction between monetary and non-monetary liabilities. A non-monetary liability would be one in which the payment of interest, or the return on capital, or both, are not subject to a limit expressed in terms of a given number of pound notes. Such liabilities are rare in the private sector of the economy, but the British Government has issued a number of securities in which the returns are dependent on movements of the RPI. In contrast, the obligations on the part of the borrower of a monetary liability are fixed and are not affected by changes in purchasing power.

We will now turn to the distinction between monetary and non-monetary capital. Preference shares which do not entitle their owners to a share of any surplus on liquidation of the company are clearly monetary items in that the rights associated with them – the annual dividend and the repayment of principal – are subjected to upper limits which are expressed in monetary terms. Conversely, equity capital is a non-monetary item because no limits are placed on the amounts that can be paid to the owners of this type of capital. The effect of inflation on the relationship between equity and preference shareholders is similar to that on the relationship between debtors and creditors, i.e. equity shareholders will gain in purchasing power at the expense of preference shareholders because the latters' interests are fixed in money terms and will decline with a fall in the value of money. This point will be illustrated in Example 15.3.

11 *See* page 439.
12 PSSAP 7, 'Accounting for changes in the purchasing power of money', Para. 28.

Monetary assets are those assets the values of which are fixed in monetary terms, e.g. cash and debtors. Non-monetary assets, such as stock and fixed assets, are those assets whose values may be expected to vary according to changes in the rate of inflation. Consider as examples debtors and stock and suppose that a company has £100 invested in each of these assets. Assume that as a result of some catastrophe the RPI increases by 100 per cent (or the purchasing power of money falls by 50 per cent) overnight. The violent change in the RPI will not affect the debtors figure in that the asset will still only realise 100 £1 coins, but it is highly probable that it will have an effect on the stock figure as the cost of the stock will be likely to rise. In other words it would take $(100 + x)$ £1 coins to buy the stock using the less valuable pounds.

The classification of investments into monetary and non-monetary categories often appears to be difficult, but this is not really so because we can employ the same analysis as was used in our discussion of capital. If the investment is in a fixed interest security where the dividend or interest and the repayment of principal is fixed in monetary terms, then it is a monetary item. An investment in equity shares where there is no limit on the amount that can be received is a non-monetary item.

The computation of gains and losses on a company's net monetary position

We showed earlier that one effect of inflation is to transfer purchasing power from creditors to debtors; we will now show how the amount of the creditors' loss and debtors' gains can be calculated. We will at this stage concentrate on interest-free credit and hence ignore the possibility of creditors reducing or eliminating their loss by incorporating an inflation premium in the rate of interest charged.

Suppose that A Limited borrowed £(1 Jan. X4)300 from B Limited on 1 January 19X4 which is repaid on 30 September 19X4. The year end for both companies is 31 December 19X4. Assume that the RPI moved as follows:

Date:	1 January X4	30 September X4	31 December X4
Index no:	120	150	160

We will first consider the position from A Limited's point of view. The company borrowed 300 £1 notes when the index was 120 and repaid the same number of £1 notes when the index was 150. In order to calculate the gain on purchasing power involved we need to convert one or other of the pounds borrowed or repaid so that the comparison can be made in terms of common purchasing power. We will convert the pounds borrowed in terms of 30 September 19X4 purchasing power. The calculation could then be made as follows:

	£(30 Sep X4)
Purchasing power acquired, $£(1 \text{ Jan X4}) \, 300 \times \dfrac{150}{120}$	375
Purchasing power given up on repayment of the loan	300
Gain £(30 Sep X4)	75

The gain in purchasing power, expressed in 30 September 19X4 purchasing power, is thus £(30 Sep. X4) 75. If the company's year end is 31 December then for the purpose of the annual accounts the gain will have to be converted to 31 December 19X4 purchasing power:

$$\text{Gain} = \text{£(30 Sep X4) 75} \times \frac{160}{150}$$

$$= \text{£(31 Dec X4)80}$$

Note that the analysis has been confined to the borrowing made by A Limited. If A Limited has used all or part of the borrowing to invest in monetary assets (which would include keeping the cash in a bank) it would experience a loss in purchasing power due to the holding of a monetary asset in a period of inflation.

If we consider the creditor, B Limited, a similar analysis will show that its loss of purchasing power resulting from the loan is £(31 Dec X4) 80. In making the loan B Limited gave up purchasing power amounting to £(1 Jan X4) 300 or £(31 Dec X4) 400. The repayment of the loan increased B Limited's purchasing power by £(31 Sep X4) 300 or £(31 Dec X4) 320. Thus its loss of purchasing power is £(31 Dec X4) 80.

The above analysis can be generalised as follows:

Suppose that a monetary asset of £(1) A was acquired at time 1 when the RPI was I_1, was sold at time 2 when the RPI was I_2 and that the year end is considered to be time 3 when the RPI was I_3. Then the purchasing power given up by virtue of the investment in the monetary asset is given by:

$$\text{£(1)}A = \text{£(2)}A\, \frac{I_2}{I_1}$$

The purchasing power regained from the disposal of the asset is given by £(2)A. The loss of purchasing power in time 2 purchasing power is:

$$\text{£(2)}A\, \frac{I_2}{I_1} - \text{£(2)}A = \text{£(2)}A \left(\frac{I_1}{I_2} - 1 \right)$$

and the loss of purchasing power in time 3 (year end) purchasing power is:

$$\text{£(3)}A \left(\frac{I_2}{I_1} - 1 \right) \frac{I_3}{I_2} = \text{£(3)}AI_3 \left(\frac{1}{I_1} - \frac{1}{I_2} \right)$$

In the special case where the asset is still in existence at the year end, $I_2 = I_3$ and the loss can be stated as follows:

$$\text{Loss} = \text{£(3)}AI_3 \left(\frac{1}{I_1} - \frac{1}{I_3} \right) = \text{£(3)}A \left(\frac{I_3}{I_1} - 1 \right)$$

If £A is replaced by −£A the above approach can be used to calculate the gain in purchasing power resulting from holding a monetary liability in a period of rising prices.

In the above analysis we concentrated on a single monetary item, but in practice a company's net monetary position will fluctuate on a daily basis. The foregoing method can be adapted to deal with this problem in the following way.

Suppose that a company starts the year on 1 January with net monetary assets of £200, reduces its net monetary assets by £280 on 1 April and finally increases its net monetary assets by £100 on 1 October. If this were the case, the company would have held net monetary assets of £200 for 3 months (January–March), net monetary liabilities of £80 for the next 6 months (April–September) and been a net monetary creditor of £20 for the last 3 months of the year. An alternative way of viewing the position, which we will use to calculate the total loss or gain on the company's monetary position, is to say that it: (a) held a monetary asset of £200 for the whole of the year; (b) held a monetary liability of £280 for the 9-month period from April to December; (c) held a monetary asset of £100 for the 3-month period from October to December.

Assume that the appropriate index numbers are:

Date:	1 January	1 April	1 October	31 December
Index no.:	100	140	150	180

The loss or gain on each of the three hypothetical items can then be calculated by substituting the appropriate values in equation (15.1) as follows:

$$\text{(a) Loss} = £(31 \text{ Dec}) \ 200 \times \left(\frac{180}{100} - 1 \right)$$

$$\text{(b) Loss} = - £(31 \text{ Dec}) \ 280 \times \left(\frac{180}{140} - 1 \right)$$

$$\text{(c) Loss} = £(31 \text{ Dec}) \ 100 \times \left(\frac{180}{150} - 1 \right)$$

The total loss is given by:

$$£(31 \text{ Dec}) \left\{ 200 \left(\frac{180}{100} - 1 \right) - 280 \left(\frac{180}{140} - 1 \right) + 100 \left(\frac{180}{150} - 1 \right) \right\}$$

$$= £(31 \text{ Dec}) \left\{ - 200 + 280 - 100 + 200 \times \frac{180}{100} - 280 \times \frac{180}{140} + 100 \times \frac{180}{150} \right\}$$

$$= £(31 \text{ Dec}) \left(200 \times \frac{180}{100} - 280 \times \frac{180}{140} + 100 \times \frac{180}{150} \right) - £(31 \text{ Dec}) \ 20$$

Note that the second term in the right-hand side of the above expression, £(31 Dec) 20, is the balance of the company's net monetary assets at the year end. We can now see that it is possible to calculate a company's total gain or loss by first converting all changes to the company's net monetary assets to year-end purchasing power (this gives us the first term on the right-hand side of the expression) and then subtracting the actual balance of net monetary assets.

The loss in this case will be:

$$£(31 \text{ Dec}) \ 120 - £(31 \text{ Dec}) \ 20 = £(31 \text{ Dec}) \ 100$$

The above result may be interpreted as follows. If the company had been in a position to arrange its affairs so that cash, debtors and creditors had been in the form of non-monetary items whose values had changed exactly in step with inflation, it would have had 'net monetary assets' of £120 at the year end. It could have achieved this result had it been able to get its debtors to agree that they would repay the company with pounds which represented the same purchasing power as was represented by the amount of the debt at the date at which it was established, and had made a similar arrangement with its creditors. The company's bank balance is a special case of a creditor or debtor depending on whether or not the account is overdrawn.

The hypothetical £120 is then compared with the actual closing balance of £20 and it can be seen that the company's policy of holding net monetary assets over the year has resulted in a loss of purchasing power of £(31 Dec) 100.

The above argument can be generalised in the following fashion:

Let a_1, be the opening balance of net monetary assets plus the increases in net monetary assets for the first day of the year and let a_j, $j = 2, \ldots, 365$, be the increases in net monetary assets for day j. Then the loss of the holding of net monetary assets expressed in terms of year-end purchasing power, £(day 365), using equation (15.1), is given by:

$$\text{Loss} = \pounds(\text{day } 365) \left[a_1 \left(\frac{I_{365}}{I_1} - 1 \right) + a_2 \left(\frac{I_{365}}{I_2} - 1 \right) + a_3 \left(\frac{I_{365}}{I_3} - 1 \right) + \ldots + a_{365} \left(\frac{I_{365}}{I_{365}} - 1 \right) \right]$$

$$= \pounds(\text{day } 365) \left(I_{365} \sum_{j=1}^{365} \frac{a_j}{I_j} - \sum_{j=1}^{365} a_j \right)$$

Note that $\sum_{j=1}^{365} a_j$ represents the actual closing balance of net monetary assets which we can call A. Therefore:

$$\text{Loss} = \pounds(\text{day } 365) \left(I_{365} \sum_{j=1}^{365} \frac{a_j}{I_j} - A \right)$$

The use of computing facilities would make the above approach feasible in practice, but in preparing CPP accounts it is customary to take averages and assume that, depending on the circumstances, the increases in net monetary assets due to sales took place evenly either over the year as a whole or over each month or quarter, etc. If the annual assumption were made, the increase in net monetary assets would be assumed to have taken place at a date on which the general price index was at the average value for the year. If the calculation were done on a quarterly basis, the average values of the general price index for the quarters would be used.

Example 15.2 shows how one can calculate the loss or gain on a company's net monetary position.

EXAMPLE 15.2

On 1 January 19X2 Match Limited's monetary items were as follows:

	£
Balance at bank	8 000
Trade debtors	2 000
Trade creditors	6 000
Proposed dividend	1 000

A summary of the company's cash book for 19X2 revealed the following:

		£			£
1 Jan	Opening balance	8 000	1 Jan	Purchases of	50 000
Jan–Jun	Cash sales	5 000		fixed assets	
	Trade debtors	18 000	Jan–Jun	Trade creditors	16 000
1 Jul	Issue of ordinary		1 Jul	Payment of 19X1	
	shares	30 000		dividend	1 000
Jul–Dec	Cash sales	8 000	Jul–Dec	Trade creditors	20 000
	Trade debtors	24 000	31 Dec	Closing balance	6 000
		£93 000			£93 000

Credit sales for the year were

January–June	£21 000
July–December	£28 000

Credit purchases for the year were

January–June	£14 000
July–December	£21 000

The values of a suitable general price index at appropriate dates were

Date:	1 January	Average Jan–Jun	1 July	Average Jul–Dec	31 December
Index:	140	148	160	162	165

We must identify the changes in the company's net monetary balances. Note that the sale of goods results in an immediate increase in the company's net monetary assets regardless of whether the sale was made for cash or credit. If the sale was made on credit, the increase in debtors will increase the company's net monetary assets, but the consequence of this is that the payment of cash by debtors will not affect the total net monetary position of the company. Similarly, the payment of the proposed dividend does not affect the net monetary position of the company. It merely reduces cash and the liability of proposed dividends, both of which are monetary items.

The changes in the company's net monetary assets may be summarised as follows:

		Increase (£)	Decrease (£)	Net (£)	Balance (£)
1 Jan	Opening balance				
	Bank	8 000			
	Debtors	2 000			
	Creditors		6 000		
	Proposed dividend		1 000		
		£10 000	£7 000	£3 000	3 000
1 Jan	Reduction in cash				
	(purchase of fixed assets)		£50 000	£(50 000)	(47 000)
Jan–Jun	Increase in cash				
	(cash sales)	5 000			
	Increase in debtors				
	(credit sales)	21 000			
	Increase in creditors				
	(credit purchases)		14 000		
		£26 000	£14 000	£12 000	(35 000)
1 Jul	Increase in cash				
	(issue of shares)	£30 000		£30 000	(5 000)
Jul–Dec	Increase in cash				
	(cash sales)	8 000			
	Increase in debtors				
	(credit sales)	28 000			
	Increase in creditors				
	(credit purchases)		21 000		
		£36 000	£21 000	£15 000	£10 000[13]

The company's loss or gain on its monetary position can now be found by converting all changes in net monetary items to year-end purchasing power.

13 The closing balance of the net monetary assets is made up as follows:

	£
Bank	6 000
Debtors	9 000
	15 000
less Creditors	5 000
	£10 000

		Conversion factor	*Increase*	*Decrease*
1 Jan	Opening balance.	$\frac{165}{140}$		
	£(1 Jan X2) 3 000		3 536	
1 Jan	Decrease	$\frac{165}{140}$		
	£(1 Jan X2) 50 000			58 929
Jan–Jun	Increase	$\frac{165}{148}$		
	£(Jan–Jun) 12 000		13 378	
1 Jul	Increase	$\frac{165}{160}$		
	£(1 Jul X2) 30 000		30 938	
Jul–Dec	Increase	$\frac{165}{162}$		
	£(Jul–Dec) 15 000		15 278	
31 Dec	Balance			4 201
			£63 130	63 130

	£(31 Dec X2)
Actual balance of net monetary assets	10 000
Balance from above	4 201
Gain £(31 Dec X2)	5 799

Note that the company gained in purchasing power even though it disclosed positive net monetary assets in both the opening and closing balance sheets because it was, over the year as a whole, a net monetary debtor.

Example 15.3 combines the features of Examples 15.1 and 15.2 in that it demonstrates how a set of CPP accounts can be produced in a case where a company holds net monetary items. It also shows how a set of historical cost accounts can be 'converted' into CPP accounts.

EXAMPLE 15.3

(A) Parker Limited's historical cost and CPP balance sheets as at 1 January 19X5 (when the RPI was 150) are given below:

Parker Limited
Balance sheets as at 1 January 19X5

	Historical cost £	£	Notes, conversion factors	CPP £(1 Jan X5)	£(1 Jan X5)
Fixed assets					
Net book value		8 000	(a) $\dfrac{150}{100}$		12 000
Current assets					
Stock	1 200		(b) $\dfrac{150}{140}$	1 286	
Debtors plus cash	600	1 800	(c)	600	1 886
		9 800		£(1 Jan X5)	13 886
Share capital					
£1 10% preference shares	2 000		(c)	2 000	
£1 ordinary shares	4 000	6 000	(d) $\dfrac{150}{80}$	7 500	9 500
Reserve		2 400	(e)		2 986
Owner's equity		8 400			12 486
15% debentures		1 000	(c)		1 000
Current liabilities		400	(c)		400
		£9 800		£(1 Jan X5)	13 886

Notes
(a) The fixed assets were acquired when the RPI was 100.
(b) The stock was purchased over a period for which the average value of the RPI was 140.
(c) Monetary items.
(d) The ordinary shares were issued on a date at which the RPI was 80.
(e) The 'CPP reserve' is the balancing figure in the CPP balance sheet.

(B) During 19X5, Parker Limited issued 2000 £1 ordinary shares at a premium of 25 pence per share on 1 April when the RPI was 160 and purchased fixed assets of £(1 Sept X5) 3000; the RPI on 1 September 19X5 was 175.

Parker Limited's historical cost profit and loss account for 19X5 is given below:

Parker Limited
Profit and loss account

	£	£
Sales		12 000
less Opening stock	1 200	
Purchases	7 000	
	8 200	
less Closing stock	1 600	6 600
Gross profit		5 400
less Sundry expenses	1 450	
Debenture interest	150	
Depreciation (20% reducing balance)	2 200	3 800
		£1 600

No dividends were declared during the year.

A full year's depreciation has been provided on the fixed assets purchased on 1 September 19X5.

(C) In order to prepare the CPP accounts it is necessary to make certain assumptions about the dates on which the various transactions took place. It will be assumed that sales, purchases, expenses and debenture interest all accrued evenly over the year and that the average RPI for the year was 170. It will further be assumed that the average age of the closing stock was 2 months and that the RPI on 31 October 19X5 was 178. The RPI at the year end will be taken to be 180.

For convenience the RPI at appropriate dates are summarised below:

Date	Index
Issue of original ordinary shares	80
Purchase of original fixed assets	100
Purchase of opening stock	140
1 January 19X5	150
1 April 19X5 (issue of 2000 ordinary shares)	160
Average for 19X5	170
1 September 19X5 (purchase of fixed assets)	175
31 October 19X5 (purchase of closing stock)	178
31 December 19X5	180

(D) We will now calculate the losses or gains resulting from the company's monetary position. The loss or gain on short- and long-term items will be calculated separately. The calculations are usually done separately because of the different factors which give rise to a company's holding of short-term and long-term monetary items. The short-term items depend on the company's policy regarding its investment in working capital; in most cases the short-term items are equivalent to a company's net current assets excluding stock. The longer-term position is a consequence of the company's overall financing strategy and depends on the level of gearing at which the company operates.

The short-term position may be calculated as follows:

		Actual		Conversion factor	Year-end pounds	
		+	−		+	−
1 Jan	Opening balance	200		$\dfrac{180}{150}$	240	
1 Apr	Issue of shares	2 500		$\dfrac{180}{160}$	2 812	
Average for year	Sales *less* purchases, expenses + interest	3 400		$\dfrac{180}{170}$	3 600	
1 Sept	Purchase of fixed assets		3 000	$\dfrac{180}{175}$		3 086
31 Dec	Closing balance		3 100			3 566
					(31 Dec X5)	(31 Dec X5)
		£6 100	£6 100		£6 652	£6 652

The company's actual balance of short-term monetary items is £3100, but had the company been able to maintain the purchasing power of these items it would have had £3566. Hence, the loss on holding short-term monetary items for the year is £(31 Dec. X5) [3 566–3 100] = £(31 Dec. X5) 466.

The company's long-term monetary liabilities consist of the preference shares and the debentures. The opening balances for these items are:

	£(1 Jan X5)
Preference shares	2 000
Debentures	1 000
£(1 Jan X5)	3 000

The above balance is equivalent in year-end pounds to:

$$£(31\ \text{Dec X5}) \left[3\ 000 \times \frac{180}{150}\right] = (31\ \text{Dec X5})\ 3\ 600$$

However, since we are dealing with monetary items these values are not affected by the changes in the price level and the value at the year end is £(31 Dec. X5) 3000.

The company has therefore gained in purchasing power from holding monetary liabilities and the gain is given by:

$$£(31\ \text{Dec X5}) \left[3\ 000 \times \frac{180}{150} - 3\ 000\right] = £(31\ \text{Dec X5})\ 3\ 000 \left[\frac{180}{150} - 1\right]$$

$$= £(31\ \text{Dec X5})\ 600$$

(E) We are now in a position to prepare the CPP profit and loss account and balance sheet.

Parker Limited
CPP profit and loss account for the year ended 31 December 19X5

	£(31 Dec X5)	£(31 Dec X5)
Sales, $12\,000 \times \dfrac{180}{170}$		12 706
less Opening stock, $1\,200 \times \dfrac{180}{140}$	1 543	
Purchases, $7\,000 \times \dfrac{180}{170}$	7 412	
	8 955	
less Closing stock, $1\,600 \times \dfrac{180}{178}$	1 618	7 337
Gross profit		5 369
less Sundry expenses, $1\,450 \times \dfrac{180}{170}$	1 535	
Debenture interest, $150 \times \dfrac{180}{170}$	159	
Depreciation,		
$0.20 \times 8\,000 \times \dfrac{180}{100}$	2 880	
$0.20 \times 3\,000 \times \dfrac{180}{175}$	617	5 191
Net trading profit		178
Gain on long-term monetary items	600	
less Loss on short-term monetary items	466	134
Profit for the year	£(31 Dec X5)	312

CPP balance sheet as at 31 December 19X5

	£(*31 Dec X5*)	£(*31 Dec X5*)
Fixed assets		
Net book value:		
$(8\,000 - 1\,600) \times \dfrac{180}{100}$	11 520	
$(3\,000 - 600) \times \dfrac{180}{175}$	2 469	13 989
Current assets		
Stock, $1\,600 \times \dfrac{180}{178}$	1 618	
Cash *plus* debtors *less* creditors	3 100	4 718
	£(*31 Dec X5*)	18 707
Share capital		
£1 10% preference shares		2 000
£1 ordinary shares:		
$4\,000 \times \dfrac{180}{80}$	9 000	
$2\,000 \times \dfrac{180}{160}$	2 250	11 250
		13 250
Reserves		
Share premium account,		
$500 \times \dfrac{180}{160}$	562	
Reserves, 1 January 19X5,		
$2\,986 \times \dfrac{180}{150}$	3 583	
Profit for 19X5	312	4 457
Owners' equity		17 707
15% Debentures		1 000
	£(*31 Dec X5*)	18 707

The nature of the loss or gain on a company's net monetary position

One of the more important features of a set of CPP accounts is its disclosure of the loss or gain arising from the company's net monetary position. It attempts to show the results, from the point of view of the equity shareholders, of the financing policy adopted by the company in a period of changing prices.

The figures disclosed by CPP accounts have, however, been criticised on a number of grounds. One cause for criticism stems from the observation that the nominal interest normally includes some compensation for the fact that in a period of rising prices the debtor will discharge his or her debt in pounds of a lesser value than the pounds which or she borrowed. If, at the time the debt was issued, the market correctly assessed the future course of inflation, the 'gain' which apparently accrues to the borrower will be equal to the compensation for inflation which is included in the nominal rate of interest. If this were the case, it would seem sensible to set off the gain against the interest payable in the accounts of the borrower and to set off the corresponding loss against the interest receivable in the accounts of the lender. If this were done, the accounts would disclose the 'real' interest payable and receivable.

In practice the market will not be correct in its assessment of the future course of inflation and there will be a real loss or gain arising from the company's net monetary position. The loss or gain will depend on the difference between the anticipated and actual rates of inflation and thus, so far as interest-bearing loans are concerned, the debtor will not automatically gain nor the creditor automatically lose. The debtor will only gain if inflation turns out to be greater than that which was anticipated when the borrowing was made.

Suppose that £10 000 debentures were issued at a nominal rate of interest at 12 per cent and let us suppose that it is known that the market believed that prices would rise by 9 per cent each year for the period of the loan. It could thus be argued that the real rate of interest is 3 per cent.

Assume that the actual rate of inflation in 19X7 was 15 per cent. The items relating to the loan which would appear in the CPP profit and loss account for 19X7 would be:

Interest payable, 12% of £10 000	£1 200[14]
Gain on long-term borrowing, $£10\,000 \left(\dfrac{115}{100}-1\right)$	£1 500

It could, however, be argued that the following would provide a more realistic description of what in fact took place:

Interest payable, 3% of £10 000	£300
Gain on long-term borrowing,	
$£10\,000 \left(\dfrac{115}{100}-1\right) - 9\% \text{ of } £10\,000$	£600

In practice it is not possible to break down the nominal interest rate into the two elements – the real interest rate and the compensation for anticipated inflation – and hence it is not possible to present the CPP accounts in the above manner. However, it is clear that in the case of interest-bearing loans the loss and gains on the company's net monetary position will be overstated in the CPP accounts of the borrower and lender. There is thus a strong case for the suggestion that the loss or gain should be shown in the same section of the CPP profit and loss account as interest payable or receivable, and that the criticism referred to above is more concerned with the format of the CPP profit and loss account as proposed in PSSAP 7 than with the principles involved.

It must be emphasised that the above discussion refers only to interest-bearing items. The CPP profit and loss account will not overstate the loss or gain on such items as cash at bank on current account or trade creditors.

It has also been argued that it is misleading to measure the loss or gain by reference to changes in the RPI as this assumes that the alternative of putting, say, £10 000 into a bank

14 For simplicity it has been assumed than interest is paid at the year-end and the question of whether the interest should be deemed to have accrued evenly throughout the year, which would require the interest payment to be converted to pounds of year-end purchasing power, has been ignored.

account is the payment of a dividend of that amount. In reality only a very small proportion of the cash generated by a company is used to pay dividends; the greater proportion is recirculated in the business and is used to purchase stock and fixed assets and to pay wages and other overheads. It has been suggested that the loss in purchasing power experienced if a company deposited £10 000 in a bank account for 1 month should be measured by reference to the increase in prices of those items which will be purchased by the company.

The above argument can be countered by the assertion that the purpose of business activity is to increase future consumption and that physical assets are not acquired for their own sake. The objective of CPP accounts is to show the effect of changing prices on the consumption opportunities of the equity shareholders and not on the potential asset purchases of the firm.

Suppose that a slothful company starts the year with £100 000 in the bank and does nothing until the end of the year when it purchases assets the cost of which have increased by 10 per cent over the year. Let us also assume that the RPI has increased by 15 per cent over the same period. Is the loss on holding money £10 000 or £15 000? From the point of view of the equity shareholders it is £15 000. Had the £100 000 been distributed at the beginning of the year the shareholders could have consumed goods and services amounting to £100 000. As prices had on average gone up by 15 per cent over the year they would have required £115 000 at the year end to purchase an equivalent bundle of goods and services.

At the year end the directors of the company must decide how best to maximise the total potential consumption over time of their shareholders. If the directors decide to invest the whole of the £100 000 in assets it must be on the basis of the belief that such action will be more beneficial to the shareholders than would the distribution of the cash. The shareholders would sacrifice immediate consumption in return for what is hoped will be greater consumption opportunities in the future.

It can be seen that there are two steps in the argument. First, the potential consumption opportunities of the shareholders have fallen by £15 000 (measured in year-end pounds) over the year. Second, a sacrifice of the consumption opportunity of £100 000 at the year end is required if the investment is to be made.

To show the loss on holding money as £10 000 would not reflect the fact that the potential consumption opportunity of the equity shareholders had fallen by £15 000 over the year.

Strengths and weaknesses of the CPP model

As we pointed out in Chapter 3, an accounting model can be appraised in terms of the selected capital maintenance test and asset valuation basis. We will now evaluate the CPP model in this way.

The real financial (money) capital maintenance test appears to be a sensible choice. Money is not of itself a valuable commodity – its utility depends on what can be done with it or, in other words, what it can buy either now or in the future. Thus, given that the purchasing power of money does vary over time, it seems reasonable to suggest that it is more helpful for many purposes to use a bench mark based on the maintenance of real money capital rather than money capital. In particular, the use, in CPP accounting, of a price index based on changes in consumer prices does seem to be the appropriate basis for the preparation of financial statements which serve to show the impact of an entity's operations on the economic welfare of its owner. The case for the use of the real financial capital test in such circumstances can be highlighted by the presentation of a simple example.

Suppose that a sole trader conducts all his or her business on a cash basis such that his or her only business asset is cash and that the business has no liabilities. Assume that he or she starts the year with £10 000 and has £12 000 at the end of the year, during which time he or she has neither introduced nor withdrawn any cash.

The profit which would be disclosed by the conventional accounting method which uses the money capital test is £2000, but does this represent the owner's increase in 'well-offness' over the year? The question cannot be answered in the absence of any knowledge of the change in the purchasing power of money over the year. If the rate of inflation was less than 20 per cent, then it seems reasonable to suggest that the owner was better off at the end of the year than he was at the beginning of the year in the sense that he could purchase more goods and services. Similarly, if the rate of inflation was more than 20 per cent the owner would be worse off.

Let us now turn to the CPP basis of asset valuation. It is here that the CPP model is weak. As has already been stated, the CPP model does not purport to show the current economic value of assets since the basis of valuation is historical cost. With CPP accounting it is money and not the asset which is 'revalued'. Thus, the CPP model suffers from much the same limitations as historical cost accounting which were outlined in Chapter 3, and most authorities appear to agree that the CPP approach is not an adequate response to the criticisms of the conventional method.

Given the obvious usefulness of the real money capital test and the weakness of the CPP asset valuation basis, many people, including the authors, believe that it would be sensible to combine the profit measure based on real financial capital maintenance with a basis of asset valuation which does reflect current values. We shall introduce such an approach in Chapter 17 but in Chapter 16 we shall first introduce CCA.

RECOMMENDED READING

See end of Chapter 18.

Current cost accounting introduced

THEORETICAL ROOTS

In this chapter we will examine current cost accounting (CCA). We will start by discussing the two theoretical roots identified in Figure 15.1 (page 419), the contributions made by Edwards and Bell, and Bonbright. We will first discuss the ideas of Edwards and Bell.

Their seminal work, *The Theory and Measurement of Business Income*,[1] was published in 1961. The book represented a major advance in the development of current value accounting, and its particular contribution to the CCA model was the recognition of the distinction between holding and operating gains; we will concentrate on this aspect of their work.

The distinction between holding and operating gains

For the purposes of determining business profit[2] Edwards and Bell divided the activities of a company into holding intervals and sales moments – the latter being assumed to be instantaneous (*see* Figure 16.1). A sales moment is the instant in time when the company sells goods while a holding interval is the interval between successive sales moments.

Suppose that a company starts an accounting period with assets with a replacement cost of £40, and that at the end of the first holding period its assets have a replacement cost of £60. These are not necessarily the same assets, as the company might well have exchanged assets during the period. Thus a manufacturing company might have reduced its cash and increased its holding of raw materials, work in progress and finished goods. Since, by definition, the company has made no sales during the holding interval, the change in replacement cost must be due to an increase in the replacement cost of assets owned by the company.

Immediately after the first sales moment the replacement cost of the company's assets equals £90. These assets will consist of the receipts from sales plus those of the company's assets which were not sold. The total business profit so far (assuming that no capital has been introduced or withdrawn) is £50: the difference between the replacement cost of the assets immediately after the first sales moment and the equivalent value at the start of the accounting period.

---

1 E. O. Edwards and P. W. Bell, *The Theory and Measurement of Business Income*, University of California Press, Stanford, Calif., 1961.
2 Edwards and Bell, *op. cit.*, used the phrase 'business profit' to refer to the profit measurement related to assets valued at current cost. As defined by Edwards and Bell an asset's current cost is usually (but not always) the same as its replacement cost. For simplicity, we will assume that there is no difference between current cost and replacement cost.

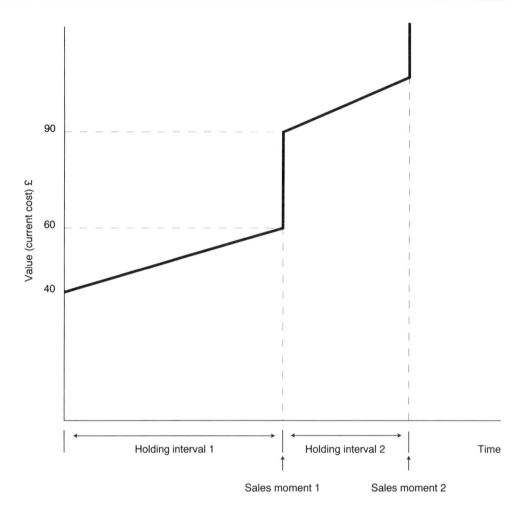

Fig. 16.1

The total business profit of £50 can be divided into two elements. Part of the profit, £20, is due to the increase in the replacement cost of the assets during the holding period. This, Edwards and Bell called the realisable cost saving although other terms used to describe it are holding gain and revaluation surplus. We will use the term holding gain. The replacement cost of assets at the moment of the first sale was £60, but as they were acquired with assets which had a current cost of £40, the company has gained, or saved, £20 by virtue of acquiring or manufacturing the goods sold in advance of the date of sale.

The remainder of the business profit, £30, is termed the *current operating profit*. This is the difference between the replacement cost of the assets before and after the sales moment. Now many of the company's assets will remain unchanged during the sales moment (i.e. will not be sold) and the current operating profit can be stated in terms of the assets that do change. Thus, the current operating profit can be said to be equal to the receipts from sales less the replacement cost of assets used up (or exchanged) in the sales moment.

The same approach can be used for each sales moment and, if we consider the accounting period as a whole, then, if it is assumed that no capital is introduced or withdrawn,

Business profit for period = Replacement cost of assets at end of period – replacement cost of assets at beginning of period

= Sum of current operating profits for all sales moments + Sum of holding gains for all holding intervals.

The approach described above is illustrated in Example 16.1.

EXAMPLE 16.1

Bow Limited started the year with the following assets:

	£
Stock, at replacement cost	600
Cash	400
	£1000

and finished the year with

	£
Stock, at replacement cost	900
Cash	500
	£1400

It will be assumed that the company has no operating expenses and that no capital was introduced or withdrawn. The total business profit is thus: £1400 – £1000 = £400.

The company's activities for the year were as follows:

				Stock	Cash
First	1 Jan	Opening balances		600	400
holding	17 Feb	Purchased stock for £200		200	(200)
interval		Stock had a RC of £900			
	31 Mar	at 31 March	HG	100	
				900	200
First	31 Mar	Stock with a RC of £300			
sales		sold for £450 (COP = £150)		(300)	450
moment				600	650
Second	1 Apr	Stock had a RC of £680			
holding		on 30 June	HG	80	
interval	30 Jun			680	650
Second	30 Jun	Stock with a RC of £280			
sales		sold for £300 (COP £20)		(280)	300
moment				400	950
Third	1 Jul				
holding	30 Sep	Purchased Stock for £450		450	(450)
interval		Stock had a RC of £900			
		at 31 Dec (the year end)	HG	50	
	31 Dec	Closing balances		£900	£500

where RC is the replacement cost, HG is the holding gain and COP is the current operating profit.

The total business profit of £400 can be analysed as follows:

Current operating profits		
First sales moment £(450 – 300)	150	
Second sales moment £(300 – 280)	20	170
Holding gains		
First holding interval £(900 – 800)	100	
Second holding interval £(680 – 600)	80	
Third holding interval £(900 – 850)	50	230
Business profit		£400

We will discuss the problems involved in distinguishing between holding and operating gains later when we introduce the CCA model. However, it might be useful if we commented that a company's holding gains might be argued to give some indication of its success in the acquisition or manufacture of inputs, e.g. the extent to which it benefited by purchasing stock before a price increase. In contrast, the current operating profit might be said to provide information about the company's success as a seller of goods – the extent to which, because of its efficiency or position in the market, it can sell goods for a price which is greater than the current cost of replacing them.

The distinction between realised and unrealised holding gains

The total holding gain for a period may be split into two elements – the realised holding gain (RHG) and the unrealised holding gain (UHG). The RHG is that part of the total which is associated with the assets which have been used up or consumed in the period; that is, the RHG is the difference between the current value of the asset at the date at which it is consumed (e.g. the date of sale in the case of stock) and the historical cost of the asset. Conversely, the UHG arises from the increase in value of the assets which remain on hand at the end of the period and is equal to the difference between the current value of the assets at the end of the period and their historical cost or, in the case of assets owned at the beginning of the period, their value at that date.

The position is complicated slightly when we consider the consumption of assets which were owned at the beginning of the period because part of the RHG is effectively the realisation of part or the whole of the UHG of earlier periods.

Example 16.2 illustrates these points.

EXAMPLE 16.2

Clive purchased 100 units of stock for £10 each on 1 December 19X7. No sales were made in December 19X7 and the RC of the units at 31 December 19X7 (Clive's year end) were £11 each.

Clive sold 60 units for £18 each on 30 June 19X8, at which date the RC of each unit was £13. No more sales were made in 19X8 but Clive purchased 20 units for £5 each on 10 October. The RC of stock on 31 December 19X8 was £16 per unit.

In 19X7 the only element of business profit is the UHG of £1 per unit or £100.

Now let us consider the year 19X8. Clive's assets at the start of the year, measured at RC, amounted to 100 units at £11 each or £1100. His assets at the end of the year were:

	£
Cash (60 x 18) − (20 x 15)	780
Stock 60 units at £16	960
	£1 740

Clive's business profit for 19X8 was therefore £1740 − £1100 = £640. Clive's COP for the year is given by:

	£
Sales 60 x £18	1 080
less RC of stock at the date of sale, 60 x £13	780
COP	£300

His RHG is given by:

RC of stock at the date of sale	780
less Historical cost of stock, 60 x £10	600
RHG	£180

But of the above RHG of £180 a part represents the realisation of a portion of the 19X7 UHG, the amount involved being 60 x £1 = 60.

Clive's UHG in 19X8 is given by:

	£	£
RC at year end of closing stock of 60 units		960
less RC at 1 January of unsold closing stock held on 1 January, 40 x £11	440	
Historical cost of stock purchased in the year, 20 x £15	300	740
UHG		£220

The total business profit (BP) for the year is given by:

BP = COP + RHG + UHG − (that part of the RHG which was
                                      included in the UHG or previous years).

Substituting the monetary values, we have:

BP = £(300 + 180 + 220 − 60) = £640

The relationship between historical cost profit and business profit

The relationship can be easily seen if we resort to some simple algebra.

Let R be the revenue from sales, C be the current value of assets used up in generating sales, and H be the historical cost of those assets. Then the COP is given by $R - C$ while the RHG is equal to $C - H$.

The historical cost profit (HCP) is of course the difference between revenue and the historical cost of the assets consumed or, to use the above symbols,

$$HCP = R - H$$
$$= (R - C) + (C - H)$$
$$= COP + RHG.$$

In other words the historical cost profit is the sum of the current operating profit and the realised holding gains.

Let us now consider the implications of the above statement. The following discussion will serve as an introduction to the CCA model which will be developed later, as well as providing further evidence of the weaknesses of the historical cost accounting model.

It can be seen that historical cost profit has, when compared with business profit, two possible defects. First, historical cost profit combines two arguably distinct elements, COP and RHG, and the conventional accounting model makes no attempt to separate them. Second, the historical cost approach ignores UHG, i.e. it takes no account of the current value of the assets held at the end of the period.

The significance of these two observations depends on the view that is taken of the most suitable concept of capital for the purposes of profit determination. If the view is taken that the enterprise should be able to replace its assets as they are used up if it is to maintain its wealth or capital, i.e. the operating capital maintenance approach, then it might be argued that RHG should not be regarded as being part of the profit for the period.

Of course if one takes a different view of what constitutes 'well-offness' then it might be that RHG could be regarded as being part of profit. Such a view is implicit in the historical cost approach. However, it might still be argued that one of the defects of historical cost accounting is its failure to disentangle COP and RHG. This argument is based on the view that a company's COP and RHG are the result of different circumstances, and knowledge of the two elements might help the user of accounts to understand how the company obtained its historical cost profit. In particular, it might assist users to estimate future profits. For example, it might be that in a given year a company makes a very much greater profit than it had achieved in previous years because of the existence of RHGs. Those wishing to predict future profits would then no doubt consider the extent to which they believe that the opportunities to achieve RHGs will continue in the future.

To the extent that accounting practice in the UK and other countries allows companies to revalue assets for balance sheet purposes, UHGs are to be found in what are otherwise historical cost accounts. It will, however, be noted that UHGs are not shown in the historical cost profit and loss account, but are carried to reserves.

The recognition of UHGs in historical cost accounting is partial, irregular (in the chronological and not moral sense) and is generally dependent on the whims of the directors.[3] Most adherents of current value accounting would not wish to include UHG as part of a company's profit. Even so, there is still a strong case for valuing assets at the current value, or in other words, systematically recognising UHGs. In CCA *all* UHGs on stocks and fixed assets are systematically recorded and reflected in the accounts.

The purpose of this section is to discuss the contribution of Edwards and Bell to the developments of CCA. This can perhaps best be understood by noting that CCA makes a sharp distinction between current cost operating profit and holding gains.

It must, however, be noted that not all authorities agree that it is possible to make a clear and sharp distinction between operating profit and holding gains or that, even if it were possible, question whether it would be desirable to do so. The distinction between operating and holding gains is clear in those cases when stock is replaced by more or less identical items. However, many traders do not act in this way but instead are prepared to switch from one line to another if they sense the opportunity of making greater profits. A trader might, for example, start the period with a warehouse full of carpets but use the cash flow generated from their sale to purchase refrigerators. In such a case it might be argued that it would not be realistic to include in the calculation of the trader's operating profit the replacement cost of carpets which the trader does not intend to replace. The designers of current cost accounting systems have been forced to include special provisions to deal with such cases.

Some would go further and argue that even if stock is to be replaced the distinction between holding and operating gains is artificial. Such advocates would say that the decision to carry on a business of necessity involves holding stock and hence most price changes in the stock holding period are just as much a part of the operations of the firm as the differences between current revenue and the current cost of goods sold.[4]

---

3 The Companies Act 1985 (Schedule 7, Para. 1(2)) does, however, require directors to make a suitable statement in the directors' report when, in their opinion, the difference between the book and market value of land, when it is held as a fixed asset, is significant.

4 *See* D. F. Drake and N. Dopuch, 'On the case for dictomising income', *Journal of Accounting Research*, Autumn 1965 and P. Prakash and S. Saunder, 'The case against separation of current operation profit and holding gain', *The Accounting Review*, January 1979.

Which 'current value'?

In Chapter 3 we pointed out that there are several ways of valuing an asset, each of which is of relevance in the determination of periodic accounting profit. In other words there is not one unique measure of profit but a whole set depending on the basis of asset valuation employed and the selected capital maintenance concept.

Let us for a moment ignore the problems associated with the choice of the capital maintenance concept and accept the argument that the present value approach to asset valuation should be rejected for the theoretical and practical reasons outlined in Chapter 3. We are then – if we are to use current values – left with the choice between the replacement cost and net realisable value approaches.

Clearly both are of relevance and a strong case can be made for requiring companies, or at least larger companies – to publish multi-columnar accounts which would show both the replacement costs and the net realisable values of their assets and, possibly, their historical costs. Thus, companies would be required to report profit on more than one basis. Against this the view has been expressed that the approach would be too costly for the producers of accounts and too complicated for the users of accounts.

The cost argument is not wholly convincing since if assets are to be employed properly businessmen will need to be aware of both the replacement cost and net realisable values of their assets. In addition, as will be seen, knowledge of both is required for the variant of current cost accounting which was favoured by the ASC. The second line of argument can – at least in the authors' view – be dealt with almost as easily. If it can be shown that there are a number of ways of measuring profit, then it surely is confusing and misleading to imply that there is only one. Considerations of practicability must limit the number of different profit figures which are reported, but it does seem reasonable to suppose that users of accounts should be able to cope with and benefit from the publication of two or three views of a company's results.

The foregoing argument has, it must be admitted, not been accepted by those charged with the task of reviewing accounting practice except in so far as it has been advocated that the current value accounts should be published along with historical cost accounts. Conventional wisdom has it that one set of current value accounts is enough. Thus, the question of which asset valuation method should be adopted is central to the current value accounting debate.

The net realisable value (NRV) approach possesses a number of virtues. The total of the net realisable values of a company's assets does provide some measure of the risks involved in lending to or investing in the company in that the total indicates the amount that would be available for distribution to creditors and shareholders should the business be wound up. This point is of course dependent on the problems associated with the determination of net realisable values which were discussed in Chapter 3, and in particular the assumptions that are made about the circumstances surrounding the disposal of the assets. It has also been argued, notably by Professor R. J. Chambers, that the profit derived from a variant of the net realisable value asset valuation basis,[5] shows, after adjusting for changes in the general price level, the extent to which the potential purchasing power of the owners of an enterprise has increased over the period. However, the potential would only be realised if all the assets were sold and it must be noted that in reality companies do not sell off all their assets at frequent intervals.

---

5 A method known as continuously contemporary accounting (CoCoA).

Advocates of net realisable value were in the past mostly to be found in academia but support for this view has emerged from a professional accountancy body in the form of a discussion document issued by the Research Committee of the Institute of Chartered Accountants of Scotland.[6] The model advocated by the committee and their arguments in favour of the net realisable value approach will be discussed in a little more detail in Chapter 18.

The general view of the supporters of current cost accounting is that in practice companies continue in the same line or lines of business for a considerable time, making only marginal changes to the mix of their activities. It is therefore argued that if only one current value profit is to be published then it should be based on the replacement cost approach. For if it is assumed that a company is going to continue in the same line of business then it should only be regarded as maintaining its 'well-offness' if it has generated sufficient revenue to replace the assets used up. Thus, replacement cost is the preferred choice of those groups in the UK and most overseas countries which have recommended the introduction of current value accounting. A strict adherence to the use of replacement cost, however, would not allow accounts to reflect the fact that companies do change their activities or the manner in which they conduct their present activities and that all the assets owned at any one time would not necessarily be replaced. Thus, some modification of the replacement cost approach is required.

Deprival value (value to the business)

A suitable basis of asset valuation which would lead to the use of replacement cost in those circumstances where the owner would – if deprived of the asset – replace it and the use of a lower figure if the asset was not worth replacement was suggested by Professor J. C. Bonbright in 1937. Professor Bonbright wrote, 'The value of a property to its owner is identical in amount with the adverse value of the entire loss, direct and indirect, that the owner might expect to suffer if he were deprived of the property.'[7]

Professor Bonbright's main concern was with the question of the legal damages which should be awarded for the loss of assets. He was not concerned with the impact of asset valuation on the determination of accounting profit. Others, notably Professor W. T. Baxter in the UK, recognised the relevance of this approach to accounting and developed the concept in the context of profit measurement. Professor Baxter coined the term 'deprival value', which neatly encapsulates the main point that the value of an asset is the sum of money which the owner would need to receive in order to compensate him exactly if he were deprived of the asset. It must be emphasised that the exercise is of a hypothetical nature; the owner need not be physically dispossessed of his asset in order for its deprival value to be determined. This approach was adopted by the Sandilands Committee and has, more or less, survived the various modifications to the original proposals and remains as the asset valuation basis underlying current cost accounting. Thus, in a current cost balance sheet, assets would be shown at their deprival value while a current cost profit and loss account would show the current operating profit, which is the difference between the revenue for the period and the deprival value of the assets consumed in the generation of revenue.

6 *Making Corporate Reports Valuable*, Kogan Page, London, 1988.
7 J. C. Bonbright, *The Valuation of Property*, Michie, Charlottesville, Va., 1965.

Before turning to a discussion of CCA, it might be helpful if we explored the meaning of deprival value in a little more detail. Ignoring non-pecuniary factors, the deprival value of an asset cannot exceed its replacement cost, for if the owner were deprived of an asset he or she could restore his original position through the asset's replacement. The owner might of course incur additional costs (e.g. a loss of potential profit) if there was any delay in replacement – the indirect costs referred to in Professor Bonbright's original definition. There may be circumstances where these additional costs may be so substantial that they will need to be included in the determination of the replacement cost, but generally these additional factors are ignored.

The owner might not feel that the asset was worth replacing, in which case the use of the asset's replacement cost would overstate its deprival value. Suppose that a trader owns 60 widgets whose current replacement cost is £3 per unit. Let us also assume that the trader's position in the market has changed since he acquired the widgets, that he will only be able to sell them for £2 each, and that this estimate can be made with certainty. The trader's other assets consist of cash of £100.

The trader's wealth before the hypothetical loss of the widgets is £220 (actual cash of £100 plus the certain receipt of £120). Let us now assume that the trader is deprived of his widgets. It is clear that he would only need to receive £120 in compensation, i.e. the net realisable value of the widgets, to restore his original position. If the trader were paid £180 (the replacement cost) he would end up better off.

In order for an asset's deprival value to be given by its net realisable value the net realisable value must be less than its replacement cost. Otherwise a rational owner (and in this analysis it is assumed that owners are rational) would consider it worth while replacing the asset.

We must now consider a different set of circumstances under which the owner would not replace the asset but has no intention of selling it. The asset may be a fixed asset which is obsolete in the sense that it would not be worth acquiring in the present circumstances of the business. The asset is still of some benefit to the business and it is thought that this benefit exceeds the amount that would be obtained from its immediate sale – i.e. its net realisable value. This benefit will, at this stage, be referred to as the asset's 'value in use'.

An example of this type of asset might be a machine which is used as a standby for when other machines break down. The probability of breakdowns may be such that it would not be worth purchasing a machine to provide cover because the replacement cost is greater than the benefit of owning a spare machine. It must be emphasised that the relevant replacement cost in this analysis is the cost of replacing the machine in its present condition and not the cost of a new machine. The machine may have a low net realisable value (which may be negative if there are costs associated with the removal of the machine) which is less than its value in use. In such circumstances an asset's deprival value will be given by its value in use, which would be less than its replacement cost but greater than its net realisable value.

As will be seen, the determination of an asset's value in use often proves to be a difficult task. In certain circumstances it may be possible to identify the cash flows that will accrue to the owner by virtue of his ownership of the asset and thus, given that an appropriate discount rate can be selected, its present value can be found. In other instances the amount recoverable from further use may have to be estimated on a more subjective basis. However, this estimate will approximate to the asset's present value and hence we will at this stage, use the term present value (PV) for simplicity.

The above discussion is summarised in Figure 16.2.

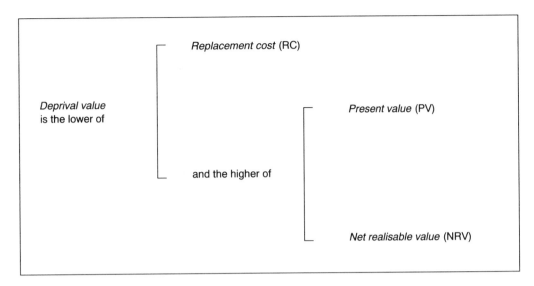

Fig. 16.2 A definition of deprival value

In the case of a fixed asset the replacement cost is the lowest cost of replacing the services rendered by that asset rather than the cost of the asset itself. The replacement cost of stock will depend on the normal pattern of purchases by the business and thus it will be assumed that the usual discount for bulk purchases will be available.

The net realisable value of work in progress which would, in the normal course of business, require further processing before it is sold needs careful interpretation. The conventional definition of net realisable value in relation to stock is the 'actual or estimated selling price (net of trade but before settlement discounts) less (a) all further costs to completion and (b) all costs to be incurred in marketing, selling and distributing'.[8] There is an alternative definition which is the amount that would be realised if the asset were sold in its *existing* condition less the cost of disposal. For the purposes of determining the asset's deprival value the higher of the two possible net realisable values will be taken.

Assume that a business holds an item of work in progress which could be sold for £200 in its existing condition, but which could, after further processing costing £30, be sold for £250. Also assume that its replacement cost is £350 and thus its replacement cost does not yield its deprival value.

In this case the asset's deprival value is £220 so long as the period required to complete and market the stock is brief enough for us to be able to ignore the effect of discounting. It is clear that before the hypothetical deprival of the asset the business would expect to receive £220 from its sale after taking account of the additional processing costs. If, on the other hand, the increase in the sales proceeds that would be expected if the asset were processed was less than the additional manufacturing costs, a rational owner would sell the asset in its existing condition and the net sales proceeds under these circumstances would give its deprival value.

In the context of Figure 16.2 six different situations can be envisaged:

8 SSAP 9, 'Stocks and long-term contracts'. Revised September 1988.

1 RC < NRV < PV; then the deprival value is given by the RC. In this case the asset's RC is less than both its NRV and PV. It is worth replacing and because its PV is greater than its NRV it is likely that the asset involved is a fixed asset which will be retained for use within the company.

2 RC < PV < NRV; then the deprival value is given by the RC. As (1) except that as the asset's NRV exceeds its PV the asset will be sold and is probably part of the trading stock of the business.

3 PV < RC < NRV; then the deprival value is given by the RC. The asset would be replaced and then sold. It is almost certain to be part of the trading stock.

4 NRV < RC < PV; then the deprival value is given by the RC. This is likely to be a fixed asset. It is worth replacing since its PV is greater than its RC.

5 NRV < PV < RC; then the deprival value is given by the PV. This asset is not worth replacing, but given that it is owned it will be retained since its PV is greater than its NRV. This is likely to be a fixed asset which would not now be worth purchasing but is worth retaining because of its comparatively low NRV.

6 PV < NRV < RC; then the deprival value is given by the NRV. This is the second case where the asset's value to the business is not its RC. The asset is not worth replacing nor is there any point in keeping it. It is obviously an asset which should be sold immediately. It might be an obsolete fixed asset whose scrap value is now greater than the benefit that would be obtained from its retention. Alternatively, the asset might be an item of trading stock in respect of which there has been a change in the business's place in the market, i.e. it can no longer acquire or manufacture the stock for an amount which is less than its selling price net of expenses.

It is clear that the deprival value of a fixed asset can only be given by its replacement cost or present value. The deprival value of an asset is based on its net realisable value only when it would be in the interest of the business to dispose of the asset. Thus, following the conventional definition of a current asset – an asset which will be used up within a year of the balance sheet date or within the operating cycle of the business, whichever is the longer – an asset whose deprival value is given by the net realisable value should be classified as a current asset.

The trading stock of a business is, by definition, an asset which is held for sale and hence its deprival value will either be its replacement cost or its net realisable value but not its present value (although in the case of stock which will not be sold for a considerable time its net realisable value may itself be based on the present value of future cash flows).

The deprival value of other current assets may be any of the three possible figures. Consider, as an example, the case of an unexpired insurance premium. Its deprival value is the loss which would be suffered if the insurance company could no longer honour its obligations. If the business felt that it was worth replacing the asset and would take out a new policy to cover the risk, the asset's deprival value would be given by its replacement cost. But suppose that it was believed that the cost of the new policy would outweigh the benefits that would be afforded by the policy. If the perceived benefits from the policy exceed the amount that could be obtained if the business surrendered the policy the asset's deprival value would be its 'present value' (or value in use), which would be an amount which is less than the replacement cost but greater than its net realisable value (or surrender value of the policy). It may be that the net realisable value exceeds the perceived benefit that would flow from the retention of the policy. In this instance the deprival value of the asset is its net realisable value but, if this was indeed the case, the business should in any event surrender the policy.

THE BASIC ELEMENTS OF CURRENT COST ACCOUNTING

We are now in a position to introduce the basic elements of current cost accounting. In order to be able to concentrate on the principles involved we shall first use very simple examples. A more detailed example will be provided in Chapter 17 together with a discussion of the thinking of the ASC as reflected in its Handbook.

The current cost balance sheet

In a current cost balance sheet both assets and liabilities should in principle be shown at current cost, that is at deprival value or value to the business.

The current cost of short-term monetary assets will be the same as the amounts at which they appear in historical cost accounts. Hence, the assets which will appear at a different amount in a current cost balance sheet will be non-monetary assets, usually tangible fixed assets, investments and stocks.

In theory, liabilities should also be stated in terms of their 'current costs'. To do this we need to turn the definition of current cost round and ask how much the debtor would gain if he or she were released from the obligation to repay the debt. Clearly, all other things being equal, the longer the period before the debt is due the less the gain from the extinction of the debt.

The 'current cost' or 'relief value' of a liability could be calculated by reference to its present value. Thus, if we ignore interest costs, the balance sheet figure for a debt of £100 000 repayable next month would be higher than a debt of the same nominal value repayable in ten years' time, the difference between the two figures depending on the discount rate.

While a strong case can be made for revaluing substantial longer-term liabilities, in practice it is rarely done and liabilities are usually shown at their nominal values.

The total owners' equity in a current cost balance sheet is, as in a historical cost balance sheet, the difference between the assets and liabilities, but part of it will be treated as a reserve reflecting the amounts needed to be retained within the business to deal with the effect of changing prices. The size of the reserve, and its appropriate description, will depend on the selected capital maintenance concept (*see* Chapters 3 and 17).

The current cost profit and loss account

A current cost profit and loss account includes a number of items not found in one based on the historical cost convention. The actual number will depend on the chosen capital maintenance concept which may be 'operating capital maintenance' or 'financial capital maintenance'. We shall look at each in turn.

Operating capital maintenance

We will first examine a current cost profit and loss account based on the maintenance of operating capital. Operating capital may be defined in a number of ways, but it is usual to think of it as the productive capacity of the company's assets in terms of the volume of goods and services capable of being produced. Thus, from this standpoint a company will only be deemed to have made a profit if its productive capacity at the end of a period is greater than it was at the start of the period after adjusting for dividends and capital introduced and withdrawn.

The most convenient way of measuring a company's output is by using as a proxy its *net operating assets*. So, a company will only be deemed to have made a profit if it has maintained the level of its net operating assets. As we shall see later there is as yet no agreement as to what constitutes net operating assets. At this stage we will regard net operating assets as a company's fixed assets, stock and all monetary assets less all liabilities.

As explained on pages 50 and 51 of Chapter 3, if the company is partly financed by creditors, the profit attributable to the equity holders is different from, and in periods of rising prices greater than, the entity profit (current cost operating profit) on the assumption that part of the additional funds needed to maintain the operating capital is provided by creditors.

There are four 'current cost adjustments' which might appear in a current cost profit and loss account and which may be regarded as 'converting' a historical cost profit into a current cost profit. The first three are the 'current cost operating adjustments' while the fourth is the gearing adjustment:

(a) Cost of sales adjustment (COSA). This is the difference between the current cost of goods sold and the historical cost.
(b) Depreciation adjustment. This is the difference between the depreciation charge for the year based on the current cost of the fixed asset and the charge based on its historical cost.
(c) Monetary working capital adjustment (MWCA). Monetary working capital may be defined as cash plus debtors less current liabilities. In order to operate most companies need to invest in monetary working capital as well as in fixed assets, thus they might need to hold a certain level of cash and sell on credit but will also be able to buy on credit. All other things being equal, an increase in prices will mean that a company will have to increase its investment in monetary working capital and the purpose of the MWCA is to show the additional investment required to cope with price increases. Of course some companies can operate with negative working capital, for example a supermarket chain which buys on credit but sells for cash. In such instances an increase in prices will result in a reduction in monetary working capital and the MWCA would then be a negative figure reflecting that reduction.
(d) The gearing adjustment. The gearing adjustment is the link between the current cost operating profit and the current cost profit attributable to the equity shareholders. It depends on the assumption that part of the additional funds required to be invested in the business as a result of increased prices will be provided by long-term creditors.

These adjustments are illustrated below.

Since X Limited started trading all prices have remained constant; hence the balance sheet as at 1 January 19X2, shown below, satisfies both the historical cost and current cost conventions.

Balance Sheet as at 1 January 19X2

	£		£
Share capital and		Fixed assets	
reserves	4 500	purchased 31 Dec XI	3 600
Loan (interest free)	4 500	Stock (200 units)	2 000
		Debtors	2 400
		Cash	1 000
	£9 000		£9 000

X Limited buys for cash and sells on one month's credit.

The company incurs no overhead expenses.

The fixed asset is to be written off over three years on a straight line basis.

The mark up is constant at 20 per cent on historical cost determined using the first-in first-out method of stock valuation.

Stock is held constant at 200 units: the monthly sales are 200 units. The cost of stock at the end of the previous month was £10 per unit, the cost of purchases increased by 10 per cent at the beginning of the month. The replacement cost of the fixed asset increased by 50 per cent on that date. Thereafter all prices held constant.

All profits are paid out by way of dividend at the end of each month.

We will first present the historical cost accounts for January 19X2:

Historical cost profit and loss account for the month of January 19X2

	£	£
Sales, 200 x £10 x 1.2		2 400
less Opening stock	2 000	
Purchases, 200 x £10 x 1.1	2 200	
	4 200	
Less Closing stock	2 200	2 000
		400
Less Depreciation 1/36 of £3 600		100
Profit for month		300
less Dividend		£300

Historical cost balance sheet as at 31 January 19X2

	£
Fixed assets	3 500
Stock	2 200
Debtors	2 400
Cash £(1000 + 2 400 − 2 200 − 300)*	900
	£9 000
Share capital and reserves	4 500
Loan (interest free)	4 500
	£9 000

* Opening balance plus debtors less purchases less dividends.

We will now look at the four adjustments on the assumption that the current cost of the assets is given by their replacement cost.

Cost of sales adjustment (COSA)

	£
Replacement cost of the 200 units sold	
200 x £10 x 1.1	2 200
Historical cost of goods sold	2 000
COSA	£200

Depreciation adjustment

	£
Depreciation charge for month based on the current cost of the fixed assets	
1/36 x £3600 x 1.5	150
Depreciation charge based on historical costs	100
Depreciation adjustment	£50

Note that in this simple introductory example we have assumed away the problem of the valuation of part used assets, i.e. there is no prior or backlog depreciation. We shall discuss the question of depreciation in more detail in Chapter 17.

Monetary working capital adjustment (MWCA)

The company's opening monetary working capital consists of a cash balance of £1000, which represents half its monthly purchases (at the old prices) and debtors of £2400 (one month's sales). Hence, if it is assumed that for operational reasons the company will need to maintain the same relative position, an increase in the cost of purchases of 10 per cent will mean that the company's investment in working capital will also need to increase by 10 per cent.

Its opening monetary working capital was £3400;[9] hence the MWCA is 10 per cent of £3400 = £340.

The current cost operating profit and operating capability

Before turning to the gearing adjustment it is instructive to see what has happened so far. We started with a profit on the historical cost basis of £300 and have made three adjustments, the cumulative effect of which is:

---

9 Debtors include the profit on the sales. Strictly the profit element should be eliminated from the calculation of the MWCA as follows:

	£
Cost of stock with debtors	
$\frac{10}{12} \times £2400$	2 000
Cash balance	1 000
MWC	£3 000
MWCA 10% of £3000	£300

We shall, however, ignore this complication at this stage.

	£	£
Historical cost profit		300
less COSA	200	
Depreciation adjustment	50	
MWCA	340	590
Current cost operating loss		£290

This example is based on the maintenance of operating capital and the current cost operating loss of £290 can be related to the company's operating capacity as measured by its holding of net operating assets in the following way.

In order to be in the same position at the end of the month as it was at the beginning the company would need:

(a) To be able to replace that part of the fixed asset that has been consumed during the period (we will assume for the sake of the argument that the asset can be replaced in bits). At current prices it will need to set aside £150 to replace one thirty-sixth of the asset. (1/36 × £5400 = £150)
(b) Hold stocks of £2200.
(c) Carry debtors equal to one month's sales at the new price, £2640. (£2400 + 10% of £2400)
(d) Hold a cash balance of £1100 (half the cost of one month's purchases).

We can now compare the required holding of assets with that which actually exists.

Required holding of assets

	£	£
Fixed assets		
remaining		3 500
required for replacement		150
Stock		2 200
Debtors		2 640
Cash		1 100
		9 590
Assets available at the end of the month		
Fixed assets	3 500	
Stock	2 200	
Debtors	2 400	
Cash	900	9 000
Shortfall		£590

The shortfall can be explained by two factors

	£
Dividend paid	300
Current cost operating loss	290
	£590

Thus, it appears that, if it is the company's intention to maintain its operating capital, it should not have paid the dividend, but even if the dividend had not been paid, the company's operating capital would have been reduced by £290.

Many advocates of CCA would say that the above line of argument is unduly prudent because it ignores the fact that part of the company is financed by long-term creditors. They would include a gearing adjustment of some kind.

The gearing adjustment

The purpose of the gearing adjustment is to show how much of the additional investment required to counter the effects of increased prices would be provided by longer-term creditors[10] on the assumption that the existing debt to equity ratio, in this example 1:1 will be maintained.

Unfortunately, the gearing adjustment is another example of a failure to agree on the most appropriate method and there are at least two ways of calculating the gearing adjustment. The most commonly used, the so-called restricted or partial gearing adjustment, was based on the assumption that the current cost profit attributable to shareholders should bear the burden of only that part of the cost of sales, depreciation and monetary working capital adjustments financed by the shareholders, in this case 50 per cent. Thus, the restricted gearing adjustment is a credit to current cost operating profit of 50 per cent of the total of the three adjustments i.e.:

	£
COSA	200
Depreciation adjustment	50
MWCA	340
	£590

Gearing Adjustment, 50% of £590 = £295

Putting all this together the current cost profit attributable to shareholders can be determined as follows:

	£	£
Historical cost profit		300
less COSA	200	
Depreciation adjustment	50	
MWCA	340	590
Current cost operating loss		290
Add Gearing adjustment		295
Current cost profit attributable to shareholders		£5

Thus, the company could pay a dividend of £5 and still maintain its operating capital so

---

10 Short-term creditors, such as trade creditors, have been ignored in this example. In practice, short-term creditors are included in monetary working capital.

long as the long-term creditors provide (or will provide if asked at some stage in the future) £295.

Some argue that this gearing adjustment is unduly restrictive because it fails to take into account unrealised holding gains (UHG) which will be reflected in a current cost balance sheet and which will reduce the debt : equity ratio thus affording the opportunity for further borrowings. In this case the unrealised holding gain on the fixed asset is 50 per cent of 35/36ths of £3600 = £1750.

The alternative, the natural or full[11] gearing adjustment is based on the sum of the UHG and the current cost adjustments – in this case 50 per cent of (£590 + £1750) = £1170 and thus the current cost profit attributable to shareholders becomes £880.

The use of the full gearing adjustment is based on the assumption that creditors would be prepared to lend the company an additional £1170 which would maintain the existing debt : equity ratio.

The current cost accounts

The current cost profit and loss account for January, using the restricted gearing adjustment, can be presented as follows:

Current cost profit and loss account for the month of January 19X2

	£	£
Sales		2400
Cost of goods sold:		
Historical cost	2000	
COSA	200	2200
		200
Depreciation:		
Historical cost	100	
Depreciation adjustment	50	150
		50
MWCA		340
Current cost operating loss		290
Gearing adjustment (restricted)		295
Current cost profit attributable to shareholders		5
Dividend, assumed equal to Profit		£5

A distinction can be made between the three current cost operating adjustments. One, the depreciation adjustment, represents the restated value of the cost of an asset consumed during the period and will thus be credited to the provision for depreciation. The other adjustments relate to the additional investments required to maintain operating capability and will be credited to a *current cost reserve account*.

Another adjustment is required in the balance sheet in respect of the fixed asset. At the beginning of the month the fixed asset's current cost (equal in this instance to its historical

---

11 In its Handbook the ASC refers to the restricted (partial) gearing adjustment as a Type 1 adjustment and the full (natural) version as a Type 2 adjustment.

cost) was £3600. This increased by 50 per cent to £5400 on the first day of the month. However, the decision to depreciate the asset on a straight line basis assumes that one thirty-sixth of the asset is used up in the month and hence 1/36 of the total gain of £1800, £50, is realised and the balance unrealised.

The total gain of £1800 is debited to the fixed asset account and credited to the current cost reserve account.

The gearing adjustment is debited to the current cost reserve account.

The current cost balance sheet as at 31 January 19X2 is therefore:

	£	£
Fixed assets at current cost	5400	
less Provision for depreciation	150	5 250
Stock		2 200
Debtors		2 400
Cash (assuming a dividend of £5*)		1 194
		£11 045
Share capital and reserves		4 500
Current cost reserve account (*see* below)		2 045
		6 545
Loan (interest free)		4 500
		£11 045

*1000+2400−2200−5

Current cost reserve

Gain on fixed assets	1 800
COSA	200
MWCA	340
	2 340
less Gearing adjustment	295
	£2 045

If we had used the full gearing adjustment, £1170, the current cost profit attributable to shareholders, and in this case the dividend, would be £880 thus reducing the assets to £10 170 and the current cost reserve to £1170. These figures illustrate the argument in favour of the full gearing adjustment because if the creditors did increase their loan by the amount of this gearing adjustment, £1170, the original debt : equity ratio of 1:1 would be maintained. The introduction of funds equal to the restricted gearing adjustment would not have the same effect because of the failure to recognise the unrealised holding gain.

The consequences of using the different approaches are illustrated in the following summary balance sheets which assume that additional borrowings, equal to the appropriate gearing adjustment, are obtained.

	Restricted gearing adjustment		*Full gearing adjustment*	
	£	£	£	£
Sundry assets		9 850		9 850
Cash		1 195		320
Carried forward		11 045		10 170

	Restricted gearing adjustment		Full gearing adjustment	
	£	£	£	£
Brought forward		11 045		10 170
Additional cash generated by fresh borrowings		295		1 170
		£ 11 340		£11 340
Share capital and reserves		4 500		4 500
Current cost reserve account		2 045		1 170
		6 545		5 670
Original loan	4 500		4 500	
Additional loan	295	4 795	1 170	5 670
		£ 11 340		£11 340
Debt : equity ratio		1:1.36		1:1

Financial capital maintenance

We will now consider current cost accounts based on the maintenance of financial capital. The focus here is on the shareholder and whether his or her interest in the company has increased in 'real' terms, that is after taking account of inflation. This approach deals with both changes in specific prices and inflation and may be described as a 'real terms current cost system'.

If it is assumed that no capital is introduced or withdrawn during the period, the 'real terms' profit can be found as follows:

(a) Measure the shareholders' funds at the beginning of the period based on the current cost of assets.
(b) Restate that amount in terms of pounds of purchasing power at the balance sheet date by use of a relevant index of general prices (such as the Retail Price Index (RPI)).
(c) Compare the restated amount from (b) with the shareholders' funds at the end of the year based on the current cost of assets. If shareholders' funds at the end of the period exceed the restated figure for the beginning of the period a 'profit' has been made; which in the ASC Handbook is described as 'Total Real Gains'.

Using our earlier illustration and assuming that on average prices increased by 20 per cent over one month and that no dividends were paid, we can calculate the total real gain as follows:

(a) Shareholders' funds based on current costs as at 1 January 19X2, £4500
(b) If prices increased on average by 20 per cent over the month, shareholders' funds would need to amount to £5400 (£4500 × 1.20) if real financial capital is to be maintained.

(c) **Calculation of total real gain**

	£
Shareholders' funds at 31 January 19X2 at current cost	
Fixed assets	5 250
Stock	2 200
Debtors	2 400
Cash (before dividend)	1 200
	11 050
less Loan	4 500
Funds at 31 January 19X2	6 550
Funds at 1 January 19X2, restated in terms of 31 January 19X2 purchasing power	5 400
Total real gains for January	£1 150

The above calculation gives no indication of how the gain was achieved. There are many ways of presenting a profit and loss account based on the maintenance of financial capital. One simple version based on our illustration is given below.

It starts in a similar fashion to the profit and loss account based on the maintenance of operating capital, in that it shows a current cost operating profit but without the inclusion of the monetary working capital adjustment which, along with the gearing adjustment, is inconsistent with the approach taken to monetary items in a system which does not seek to indicate the additional finance required to sustain a given level of net operating assets.

To the modified current cost operating profit are added the holding gains, distinguished between realised and unrealised. The cost of sales and depreciation adjustments are realised holding gains which means that they are debited in the first part of the statement but are added back, or credited, in the second section.

The sum of the modified current cost operating profit and the total holding gains is described as the 'Total Gains'.

Finally, the 'inflation adjustment' is deducted from the total gains to give the total real gains.

Profit and loss account for January 19X2
'Real terms' (based on the maintenance of financial capital)

	£	£
Sales		2 400
Cost of goods sold: historical cost	2 000	
: COSA	200	
Depreciation: historical cost	100	
: depreciation adjustment	50	2 350
Current cost operating profit		50
add Realised holding gains:		
Cost of sales adjustment	200	
Depreciation adjustment	50	
Carried forward	250	50

	£	£
Brought forward	250	50
Unrealised holding gains: fixed asset	1 750	2 000
Total gains		2 050
less Inflation adjustment		900
Total real gains		£1 150

RECOMMENDED READING

See end of Chapter 18.

CHAPTER 17

Current cost accounting: The ASC Handbook

INTRODUCTION

The ASC's 1986 publication *Accounting for the Effects of Changing Prices: a Handbook*, henceforth referred to as the Handbook, has already been introduced and placed in context, *see* page 421.

The *Handbook* differed from statements of standard accounting practice in that it was neither mandatory nor prescriptive. The ASC's objective in publishing it was: 'to explain and discuss the methods (for accounting for the effects of changing prices) which may be adopted and to identify those which the ASC considers most appropriate' (*Handbook*, Introduction). The *Handbook* was offered as a contribution to the debate about accounting for changing prices.

Although we shall see in Chapter 18 that the ASB envisages a much less adventurous approach to accounting for changing prices, the view of the ASC was that companies should be encouraged to appraise and, where material, report the effects of changing prices. In summary the message was: 'Please do something and, if you do something, this is probably the best way of doing it'.

The preferred method

The ASC view was that of the various methods available, the most appropriate way of accounting for changing prices is an approach based on:

> current cost asset valuation, with *either* the operating or financial capital maintenance concept using the nominal pound as the unit of measurement.

We have already discussed the current cost basis of asset valuation and the two capital maintenance concepts, and will return to that subject later, but at this stage we need to consider the selection of the nominal pound as the unit of measurement. This can be put negatively by saying that the ASC rejected the CPP approach.

The rejection of CPP

Although, as shown in Figure 15.1, the first serious attempts at accounting for changing prices in the UK was CPP accounting, the approach lost favour following the report of the Sandilands committee.[1]

---

1 *Report of the Inflation Accounting Committee*, Cmnd 6225, HMSO, London.

This committee rejected the CPP unit of measurement on a number of grounds including the view that it is not possible to measure inflation except on an individual basis because inflation is a personal matter depending on an individual's particular pattern of consumption. They wrote:

> Inflation does not exist as a quantifiable phenomenon independent of the price movement in any specific group of goods and services or of the spending pattern of any specific group of individuals or entities and is not a phenomenon capable of independent and objective measurement, affecting all individuals and entities in the same way. The rate of inflation will vary for different individuals and entities in the country according to the selection of goods and services which they buy.[2]

The Sandilands' proposals therefore eschewed the use of any broadly based price index.

To this one might respond that the estimate of the effect of inflation provided by the RPI is probably a better estimate of the experience of all shareholders, and everybody else, than the estimate of zero which is implied by the complete rejection of any attempt to take account of changes in general purchasing power.

Another reason why the Committee rejected CPP accounting in its pure form was that it does not disclose the current value of assets. This is a good reason but, as we have already seen in Chapter 16, it is possible to show the effects of changes in the general price levels in a system which reports the current cost of assets.

The partial return of CPP

Although the ASC prefers the nominal pound as the unit of measurement, it has not completely rejected CPP principles in so far as one of the two selected capital maintenance concepts – financial capital maintenance – is based on the measurement of the effects of changes in the general price level on shareholders' funds. The opening shareholders' interest is restated, using a general price index, in terms of year-end purchasing power and then compared with closing shareholders' interest which is automatically measured in terms of year-end purchasing power. The final profit figure derived from the maintenance of financial capital is thus in some respects a CPP profit.

While there may be a weak case for ignoring the effect of one year's inflation where it is not excessive, the same is certainly not true over a longer time period. Hence the ASC's proposals concerning the publication of corresponding amounts (the previous years' figures) and historical summaries include the suggestion that items be restated in terms of year-end purchasing power (*see* page 484).

The choice between the two capital maintenance concepts

The choice can be considered from two aspects: (a) the nature of the business and (b) the different interests of the various users of the accounts.

It is suggested that if it is possible to apply both concepts to a particular business then it would be helpful to produce information based on both concepts but there are certain types of business, *value-based companies*, where it may not be possible or, if possible, sensible to apply the maintenance of operating capital test.

2 *Ibid.*, p. 13.

Value-based companies

The phrase value-based companies is used to describe those companies where all or most of the profit is, by intention, derived from holding assets which increase in value, i.e. holding gains, rather than from trading. Examples of value-based companies include commodity traders, insurers, banks and investment trusts.

The problem of applying the operating capital maintenance test to value-based companies can be seen by examining the cost of sales adjustment. It will be found that either there is no meaningful cost of sales adjustment which can be calculated because the assets used up will not be replaced, or, if one can be calculated, it will eliminate the whole of the profit because the company's prime objective is the making of holding gains.

To judge the success of a value-based company, the best test is to see whether it has earned 'real' profits over and above inflation and this can only be determined by applying the financial capital maintenance test.

Different aspects of a business

Let us now consider businesses, other than value-based companies, where it is possible to think in terms of the maintenance of operating capacity. If one has to select between the two concepts, the decision should rest on what particular aspect of the company's performance it is most useful to report or, to put it in a slightly different way, from whose standpoint profit should be measured. We will consider two extreme cases.

A shareholder might be interested only in the return on his or her investment and would expect management to maximise the return by switching resources from one type of business to another whenever profitable opportunities arise. Such a shareholder would be much more interested in knowing whether his or her investment has been maintained in real terms than in knowing about whether the company has maintained its operating capacity, and is therefore likely to be more interested in a profit measure based on financial capital maintenance than one based on operating capital maintenance.

The other extreme is an employee who is interested in the continuity of his or her employment or a shareholder/owner of a company whose desire is to sustain it in its existing business. They will be particularly interested in a profit measure based on the maintenance of operating capital.

While we have presented extremes it is likely that all the parties would also be interested in the 'other' capital maintenance test and hence the ASC suggested that some companies may wish to provide information based on both concepts.

THE HANDBOOK: DETAILED TREATMENT OF VARIOUS ITEMS

We have already discussed the principles underlying the preparation of current cost accounts and will now discuss their application based on the methods of accounting for the effect of changes in prices as advocated in the Handbook.

Fixed assets

Plant and machinery

The current cost of a fixed asset is normally its *net current replacement cost*. The exception is where there has been a permanent diminution in its value when the asset will be written down to its recoverable amount.

The net current replacement cost of an asset is normally based on its gross current replacement cost (i.e. the replacement cost of a new asset) and the proportion of the asset that has been deemed to be used up. Thus, assume that an asset has a *gross current replacement cost* of £20 000 and, as at 31 December 19X1, that 40 per cent of it has been used up (say, for example, it has been depreciated at 10 per cent per annum on a straight line basis for four years assuming a zero scrap value).

Its net current replacement cost will be £12 000 and it will be included in a current cost balance sheet at 31 December 19X1 as follows:

	£
Gross current replacement cost	20 000
less Accumulated depreciation	8 000
Net current replacement cost	£12 000

Generally the most convenient way of finding the gross current replacement cost is by applying a relevant specific index adjustment to the cost; the index used need not be highly specific and the same index could be applied to the blocks of similar assets. The indices could be those prepared by government agencies[3] or be generally recognised privately produced indices or even indices compiled by a company on the basis of its own purchasing experience.

There may be circumstances where the use of an index of asset prices may not be appropriate; in such cases the gross current replacement cost should be based on expert opinion or other evidence of the current cost of assets. A particular example is where the speed of technological change is such that it would be unwise to rely on the use of any index of changes in specific prices. The problem is that we may not be comparing like with like. An index will disclose, say, that the average cost of machinery used in a particular industry has increased by, say, 60 per cent over the same period but will not show that its operating costs of the machinery was cut by, say 40 per cent over the same period.

The unthinking use of an index could lead to misleading results. Its use without correction would mean that the value of an asset would be overstated and the current cost operating profit for the period would be understated because it would be charged with both a high depreciation charge (which would be based on a machine with low operating costs) and the higher operating costs associated with the old machine.

It may be possible to overcome the problem by using a more broadly based index but, in material cases, it may be necessary to address the issue directly by an analysis such as the following:

---

3 The government regularly issues two volumes of index numbers. *Price Index Numbers for Current Cost Accounting* and *Current Cost Accounting: Guide to Price Indices for Overseas Countries*. Both volumes are published by HMSO.

Original cost of asset	£100 000
Price index	
(a) at date of acquisition of asset	100
(b) at the date of valuation	225
Gross current replacement cost of asset based on the movement	
of the price index, £100 000 x 225/100	£225 000
Estimated total life of machine	5 years

However, let us suppose that the current cost of a modern asset which may be deemed to be a modern equivalent of the asset being valued is £250 000 and also suppose that the annual operating costs of the new machine is £16 000 a year less than the old machine and that the life of the new machine is 5 years.

On a comparable basis the value of the asset is clearly less than £250 000. The difference is the capital value which is attributable to the saving of £16 000 per year in operating costs. If conventional discounting theory is used, the capital value is the present value of £16 000 per year discounted at the appropriate rate of discount. Let us suppose that the rate of discount is 15 per cent, then using annuity tables the capital value is £16 000 × 3.3522 = £53 635. Thus the gross current replacement cost of the asset under review is £196 365 (£250 000 − £53 635).

The net current replacement cost will depend on the proportion of the asset which has been considered to have been used up; this will depend on the asset's estimated life and the enterprise's accounting policy for depreciation.

Depreciation (including backlog depreciation)

Under CCA the depreciation charge is based on the value to the business of that part of the asset used up in the period. In principle the value to the business should be measured by reference to the value at the date of consumption, i.e. on average current costs, but it is normally acceptable to use year-end values.

CCA does present one complication – *backlog depreciation*. This arises from the need to revalue accumulated depreciation, i.e. that part of the asset which has already been written off. This may appear to be a strange and unnecessary procedure, but it is required because the value of the asset is based in the first instance on the restatement of the gross current replacement cost of the asset. In so far as part of the asset has been used up, the increase in gross current replacement cost of the asset will overstate the holding gain made in the year. A deduction must therefore be made in respect of that part of the asset which has already been used up. Thus, the accumulated depreciation at the start of the period must also be 'revalued' and the increase in this value (backlog depreciation) must be deducted from the increase in the gross current replacement cost to give the net holding gain for the period.

To illustrate the point, suppose that an asset was purchased for £10 000 on 1 January 19X2 when the appropriate price index was 100. Let us also suppose that: (a) the index remained constant until 31 December 19X4 when it rose to 120; (b) the asset is depreciated on a straight-line basis over 5 years with a zero scrap value, i.e. 20% of the asset is assumed to be used up each year; (c) the company's year end is 31 December. The book value of the asset on 31 December 19X3 is as follows:

Gross current replacement cost (which is also the historical cost	£10 000
Less Accumulated depreciation (2 years)	£4 000
Net current replacement cost	£6 000

The gross current replacement cost of the asset at 31 December 19X4 is £10 000 × 120/100 = £12 000. Given that sales revenue has accrued throughout the year, the current cost depreciation should be calculated using average values of the fixed assets. However, the Handbook permits the use of closing values as an approximation to this and in this illustration we shall use the closing value.

The CCA depreciation charge for 19X4, if based on the end of year value, is 20 per cent of £12 000, i.e. £2400. The value to the business, or net current replacement cost, of the asset at 31 December 19X4 is two-fifths of £12 000, i.e. £4800, as two-fifths of the asset remains to be used at that date.

Consider that portion of the asset which was deemed to be in existence at the beginning of the year (three-fifths of the original asset). Its value at the start of the year was £6000 and since the index increased by 20 per cent its year-end value was £7200. Thus the company experienced a holding gain or revaluation surplus of £1200 and this is the amount which is to be credited to the current cost reserve account.

The gross current replacement cost of the asset increased by £2000 (£10 000 to £12 000) and to take this amount, without adjustment, to the current cost reserve would be to overstate the gain.

The difference of £800 between £2000 and £1200 is the increase in value of that part of the asset which had been used up at the start of the year, i.e. two-fifths of £2000 = £800.

The argument can be illustrated graphically if it is assumed that the asset was made up of five equal blocks one of which is used up each year. The position at 1 January 19X4 was:

Gross replacement cost, £10 000

2 000	2 000	2 000	2 000	2 000

Accumulated depreciation, £4 000   Net replacement cost, £6 000

The position at 31 December 19X4 *before* recording the depreciation charge for 19X4 was:

Gross replacement cost, £12 000

2 400	2 400	2 400	2 400	2 400

Accumulated depreciation, £4 800   Net replacement cost, £7 200

	£
Increase in gross replacement cost, £12 000 − £10 000	£2 000
less Backlog depreciation, £4 800 − £4 000	800
Net surplus on revaluation	£1 200

The position at 31 December 19X4 *after* recognising the depreciation charge for the year was:

Gross replacement cost, £12 000

2 400	2 400	2 400	2 400	2 400

Accumulated
depreciation, £7 200

Net replacement
cost, £4 800

In practice a convenient way of calculating backlog depreciation is to follow the steps set out below:

1 Estimate the asset's gross current replacement cost at the year end.
2 Calculate the depreciation charge for the year.
3 Calculate the required balance on the accumulated depreciation account at the year end – $x\%$ of (1) where $x\%$ is the proportion of the asset which has been assumed to have been used up.
4 Backlog depreciation is then the difference between (3) and the sum of the opening accumulated depreciation and the depreciation charge for the year.

Land and buildings

The current cost of land and buildings will in principle be their open market value. A distinction is drawn between specialised and non-specialised buildings. Specialised buildings are those which by their nature are rarely sold except as part of the sale of the business in which they are used. Non-specialised buildings are, by contrast, generally sold as units in their own right. While it is easy to classify certain types of building – oil refineries are clearly specialised buildings, while office blocks are usually non-specialised – there are many instances where it will be difficult to make the distinction between the two types of building.

It is suggested that specialised buildings should be valued in the same way as plant and machinery[4] but that the underlying land should be valued on the same basis as non-specialised buildings.

Non-specialised buildings, such as the majority of offices, shops and general industrial units, are those which are commonly bought and sold, as one unit, together with the underlying land. Since the normal method of acquiring such assets is purchase in the open market, it is suggested that their net current replacement cost should be valued by reference to the estimated cost of purchasing the property on the open market and not by reference to the updated value of the cost of the building plus the current cost of the land. The use of indices is considered to be inappropriate because the market value of properties will often move in an individual way depending on their location, and the use of the individual valuations is therefore called for. In the case of land and buildings which will continue to be used by the business, their value can be increased by the cost of acquisition and

---

4 An exception to this rule is suggested in the case of buildings such as hotels, petrol filling stations and public houses which are conventionally recorded in the historical cost accounts at figures which include 'inherent trading potential' (or goodwill element). It is suggested that these buildings should be treated as non-specialised buildings because the method of valuation suggested for such buildings is a better basis of valuation of the goodwill element.

adaptation, although adaptation costs should be valued on the same principles as plant and machinery. In contrast, land and non-specialised buildings which are surplus to the present and future needs of the business should be valued at their open market value less costs of disposal, i.e. at their net realisable value.

Valuation need not be made annually, but it is expected that not more than five years should elapse between valuations, and should be made by professionally qualified and experienced valuers who could be in the employ of the company owning the asset.

It should be noted that because the values of non-specialised buildings and land are found by reference to their existing condition, only the net current replacement cost is shown in the current cost balance sheet, i.e. the gross current cost and accumulated depreciation are not recorded.

Depreciation of non-specialised buildings

In accordance with the provisions of SSAP 12, depreciation must be provided on buildings.

The Handbook does not provide an example showing how to depreciate non-specialised buildings but the following example is based on the guidance manual to ED 18.[5]

Suppose that XYZ Limited owned buildings which had a net current replacement cost of £550 000 on 1 January 19X3 and an estimated life of 21 years from 1 January 19X3. Let us assume that the buildings were revalued on 31 December 19X3, at which date a value of £600 000 was placed on the building but no change was made in the estimated life of the asset.

The depreciation charge is calculated by dividing the depreciable amount (estimated value of the buildings) by the life of the asset from the year end. The life is measured from the year end rather than the beginning of the year because the building was valued on the basis of its condition at the end of the year (i.e., after depreciation for the period).

The depreciation charge is thus £600 000/20 = £30 000. If the net current replacement cost of the building at 31 December 19X3 is £600 000 then the figure before charging depreciation for the year is £630 000. As the net current replacement cost at 1 January 19X3 was £550 000, the transfer to the current cost reserve is £80 000.

These adjustments can be conveniently summarised as follows:

	£
Debit land and buildings	50 000
Debit profit and loss account (depreciation expense)	30 000
Credit current cost reserve	80 000

Let us assume that the buildings are not revalued in 19X4. The depreciation charge for 19X4 will thus be the same as in 19X3, £30 000. The figure can be obtained by dividing the asset's net current replacement cost at the beginning of the year by the building's life measured at that date. This method can be used for all periods in which there is not a revaluation of the asset. Thus, if there is no revaluation in 19X5, the depreciation charge for the year is given by:

---

5 *Guidance Manual on Current Cost Accounting*, Inflation Accounting Steering Group, Tolley/ICAEW, London, 1976.

$$\frac{\text{Net current replacement cost at 1 January 19X5}}{\text{Estimated life as at 1 January 19X5}} = \frac{£570\,000}{19} = £30\,000$$

Investments

A company which is a parent company of a group should present information on the effects of changing prices in respect of the whole group (*see* Handbook, Appendix 7). There will normally be no need for it to provide current cost information for itself as a single company.

Investments included as fixed assets should be included in the balance sheet at the directors' estimate of current cost. Investments carried as current assets should be shown at the lower of their current replacement cost and net realisable value.

Stocks

A distinction is made between stock which is, or is not, subject to the cost of sales adjustment (COSA). The distinction, however, is not clearly made, and the classification will in many instances depend heavily on judgment. A more detailed discussion of stock not subject to COSA will be provided later, but in general such stock may be said to consist of items for which replacement costs cannot be determined and those where such a valuation would be inappropriate because there is no intention to replace them by the purchase of substantially similar items.

Stock subject to a COSA

The value to the business of an item of stock is the lower of its current replacement cost and the recoverable amount (in the case of stock, its net realisable value).

The Handbook suggests that when stock is valued on a 'first in first out' basis and the average age is short, less than three months, it would generally not be misleading if stock is shown in the balance sheet at historical cost.

The current replacement cost may be obtained from any of a number of sources, including suppliers' price lists and the use of indices. In appropriate cases use can be made of standard costs updated where necessary by the allocation of price variances. The current replacement cost of work in progress and finished goods is obtained by calculating the current replacement costs of the inputs (raw materials, labour and overheads) which have been required to bring the asset to its condition at the date of valuation. The existence of a suitable standard costing system would obviously help this process.

The problem of deciding whether stock should be written down to its net realisable value is little different from that which is experienced under historical cost accounting when the decision as to whether stock should be written down from cost to net realisable value has to be made. Strictly, each item of stock should be considered individually, but in practice the assessment might have to be made on the basis of the different categories of stock. If stock is written down to its recoverable value, the difference should be charged to the current cost profit and loss account and not debited to the current cost reserve account.

COSA

The COSA is the difference between the value to the business of the stock sold and its historical cost (i.e. the realised holding gain).

In principle the current cost profit and loss account should be charged with the value to the business of each item of stock sold measured at the date of sale. The informational needs if this were to be done for any but the smallest entities would be enormous, so in practice proxy measures are normally used. In most instances the assumption is made that the objective of charging the profit and loss account with the current cost of replacement will be adequately served by charging the profit and loss account with the average cost for the year.

If the volume of stock has remained reasonably constant over the year, or has changed at a more or less constant rate, the average cost for the period can be used. If these conditions do not hold, perhaps because stock is purchased or manufactured at a fairly constant rate while sales are made in large parcels at infrequent intervals, the calculations should be based on shorter periods, e.g. monthly.

The averaging method

The averaging method is commonly employed to calculate the COSA because it is simple to calculate and requires the minimum of additional data over and above that which is part of the historical cost system. In essence, with the averaging method the opening and closing stocks (based on the first in, first out (FIFO) convention) are expressed in terms of the average price for the period. No adjustment is made to the purchases figure on the grounds that this is automatically expressed in terms of the average price for the period. Thus, the three elements in the cost of goods sold expense (opening stock, closing stock and purchases) are all expressed in terms of the average cost for the period.

In order for the averaging method to be used the stock volume must either have been constant or increased (or decreased) at a constant rate over the period for which the calculation is made. The average purchase price may be calculated by using a simple average of the period's prices selected at regular intervals. The use of the averaging method is illustrated below.

Suppose that the following historical cost of stock information is available (based on the FIFO convention): opening stock, £30 000; purchases, £140 000; closing stock, £40 000. Let us also assume that the appropriate price indices for the stock in question were as follows: opening stock 100; average for the year, 130;[6] closing stock, 150. The cost of goods sold expense based on both historical cost and current cost principles is shown below:

	Historical cost (£)		Current cost (£)
Opening stock	30 000	(£30 000 x 130/100)	39 000
Purchases	140 000		140 000
	170 000		179 000
less Closing stock	40 000	(£40 000 x 130/150)	34 667
	£130 000		£144 333

6 The average for the year will be the average value of a series of index numbers for a number of dates spaced at regular intervals over the year. It is not necessarily the simple average of the indices applicable at the beginning and end of the year.

The COSA is then £144 333 − £130 000 = £14 333.

Note that the COSA does not depend on knowledge of the purchases figure and that it can be found by simply adjusting the opening and closing stocks as long as the three price index numbers are available.

The opening stock element of the COSA is

$$\pounds 30\ 000 \times \frac{130}{100} - \pounds 30\ 000 = \pounds 9\ 000$$

i.e. the difference between the opening stock valued at average price and its historical cost. Similarly, the closing stock element is

$$\pounds 40\ 000 - \pounds 40\ 000 \times \frac{130}{150} = \pounds 5\ 333$$

i.e. the difference between the historical cost of closing stock and its value based on the average price for the period.

In times of rising prices the historical cost of closing stock will be greater than the closing stock figure based on average prices because, using FIFO, the units comprising the closing stock will have been deemed to have been purchased at more recent prices, which will be higher than the average. However, since closing stock is deducted in order to arrive at the cost of goods sold the reduction in the value placed on closing stock will add to the COSA.

The formula for calculating the COSA can be expressed as follows. Let S_1 and S_3 be the historical cost (based on the FIFO convention) of opening and closing stock, respectively. Let P_1, P_2 and P_3 be the price indices applicable to opening stock, the average cost for the period and closing stock, respectively. The COSA is then given by:

$$\text{COSA} = S_1 \left(\frac{P_2}{P_1} \right) - S_1 + S_3 - S_3 \left(\frac{P_2}{P_3} \right)$$

$$= \frac{S_1}{P_1} (P_2 - P_1) + \frac{S_3}{P_3} (P_3 - P_2)$$

The above formula is also applicable in periods when prices are falling. In this case the COSA will represent a realised holding loss which will be credited to the current cost profit and loss account and debited to the current cost reserve account.

In principle the indices applied to both opening and closing stocks should relate to the date on which the stock was acquired (or more precisely to the date on which stock would have to have been ordered for delivery on the date of acquisition). However, the Handbook suggests that the year-end indices can be used if the results so derived are not significantly different from those which would be obtained from the use of the indices applicable to the dates of acquisition.

In the above example the COSA was calculated for the year as a whole. This is acceptable if the volume of stock remains approximately constant or increases or decreases gradually. If the volume of stock is subject to severe fluctuations, the calculations should be made at more frequent intervals, possibly monthly.

It must be emphasised that the averaging method is only one method which can be used to arrive at the COSA. In the case of large units it may be possible to identify the value to the business of specific items when they are sold. In other cases the LIFO method may be used to arrive at the charge to the profit and loss account, but this method should not of course be used to find the balance sheet value of stock.

Stock not subject to a COSA

The discussion of stock has so far been based on the assumptions of a simplistic world in which stock when sold is replaced by more or less identical items. In such instances it is possible to make a clear distinction between a realised revaluation surplus (which is represented by the COSA) and an operating gain.[7] However, there are many situations where it would either be impossible or misleading to make such a distinction. An obvious example of a case where the use of a COSA would not be appropriate is provided by a trader who does not deal with a limited range of goods but instead is prepared to switch from one line to another whenever he senses the opportunity of making greater profits.

As discussed earlier (page 468), a company which is primarily concerned with stock which will not be replaced – value-based companies – will probably decide to use the financial capital maintenance approach which does not *require* the calculation of a COSA. The purpose of including a COSA in a financial capital maintenance current cost profit and loss account is to give some indication of how the total gains for the year were derived; the COSA will not affect the total gain reported as the debit in arriving at the current cost operating profit is exactly offset by the credit of the realised holding gain.

If the operating capital maintenance concept is used, then stock not subject to a COSA could be included with monetary working capital and hence any related price changes might be accounted for through the monetary working capital adjustment.

Whatever capital maintenance concept is selected, all stock should be shown on the balance sheet at its current cost, which may be derived from the use of price indices or by reference to market prices.

OPERATING CAPITAL MAINTENANCE – TWO, THREE OR FOUR CURRENT COST ADJUSTMENTS?

The ASC recognised that there was, and still is, no consensus about the best way of applying the operating capital maintenance test. There is general agreement about the need for a depreciation adjustment and a cost of sales adjustment, but different views are taken on the need for the monetary working capital and gearing adjustments. Hence, in respect of the latter adjustments the Handbook is not dogmatic but simply describes how they might be calculated should the company decide that they should be included in the current cost accounts.

---

7 It may be argued that this approach does not really arrive at the operating gain. After all, the decision to operate of necessity involves holding stock and hence price changes in the period of stock holding are just as much a part of the operations of the firm as the differences between sales and revenue and the current cost of goods sold. For a consideration of this point readers are referred to D. F. Drake and N. Dopuch, 'On the case for dichotomising income', *Journal of Accounting Research,* Autumn 1965 and P. Prakash and S. Sunder, 'The case against separation of current operating profit and holding gain', *The Accounting Review*, January 1979.

Monetary working capital adjustment

The decision whether to include an MWCA depends on the view taken as to the composition of net operating assets, the proxy measure of operating capital. A list of the most commonly used definitions is provided in paragraph 3.6 of the Handbook, which is reproduced below in Table 17.1.

Table 17.1 Net operating assets – commonly used definitions

(a) Fixed assets and stock
(b) Fixed assets, stock and monetary assets (excluding fixed or long-term monetary assets)
(c) Fixed assets, stock and all monetary assets
(d) Fixed assets, stock and all monetary assets less all liabilities
(e) Fixed assets, stock and all monetary assets less liabilities (excluding long-term borrowings)
(f) Fixed assets, stock and monetary assets (generally excluding cash) less short-term liabilities (generally excluding bank overdrafts)

The authors believe that in so far as it is necessary for a company to maintain a positive balance in net monetary assets, or is in a position to be financed in part by 'negative net monetary assets', then if the company uses the operating capital maintenance concept and financial statements are to reflect the effect of changing prices it is necessary to include an MWCA. This should be based on those net monetary assets which are required for the day-to-day operations of the business, hence excess cash holdings which may be used for dividend or for major capital investment should be excluded.

Probably the most useful definition of monetary working capital was that provided in SSAP 16, which defined monetary working capital as the aggregate of:

(a) trade debtors, prepayments and trade bills receivable, plus
(b) stock not subject to a cost of sales adjustment, less
(c) trade creditors, accruals and trade bills payable,

in so far as they arise from the day-to-day operating activities of the business as distinct from transactions of capital nature.[8]

The standard went on to point out that bank balances and overdrafts may fluctuate with the volume of stock or the items in (a), (b) and (c) above. It was argued that the part of bank balances or overdrafts arising from those fluctuations should be included in monetary working capital together with any cash floats required to support day-to-day operations.

One obvious example of a situation where bank balances or overdrafts should be included in monetary working capital is provided by a business which, because of the seasonal nature of activities, exhibits considerable fluctuations in its holding of stock and its investment in debtors. The most likely consequence of the business's net reduction in its investment in stock plus debtors less creditors is an increase in its bank balance (or a reduction in its overdraft). If prices rise in the period during which the business's bank balance is high, the business will only be able to purchase a lesser quantity of stock, etc., unless additional working capital is obtained. In such an example the temporary increase in the bank balance should be included as part of the monetary working capital and a MWCA should be calculated by reference to the total amount of working capital required in the circumstances of the business, irrespective of its composition.

8 SSAP 16, Para. 44.

Calculation of the MWCA

The MWCA is calculated in the same way as the COSA and the averaging method described on pages 475–77 is usually found to be the most convenient approach. If the averaging method is used, the calculation will be based on the opening and closing balances of items included in monetary working capital, appropriate price indices relating to the beginning and end of the period and the average price index for the period.

The calculations can be done for the year as a whole or separate calculations may be made for lesser periods. It is important to ensure that the MWCA is calculated by reference to the same periods as the COSA. The reason for this is the relationship between stock and the remaining elements of working capital. In general, if stock is decreased the other elements of working capital are increased and vice versa.

In principle separate index numbers should be used to calculate the various elements of the MWCA. The index for debtors should be based on the movements of the costs of the goods and services sold which gave rise to the debtors.

In many cases the index used for the stock of finished goods will be suitable for debtors, but adjustments may be required if, for example, certain products are sold primarily for cash while others are sold on credit, since it is the costs of the inputs used in the manufacture of the goods sold on credit which are relevant to the debtors adjustment. Strictly, the calculation should be based on the debtors figure less the profit element, but the total debtors could be used where this gives a fair approximation.

The index for creditors should be based on movements of the items which are financed by creditors. Thus, changes in wage rates which should in general be included in the debtors index will often be immaterial so far as the index for creditors is concerned. Despite the fact that these two indices will normally reflect different price movements, where the percentage changes in debtors and creditors indices over the period are similar, a single index can be used.

As is the case with the COSA, regard must be paid to the average age of the debtors and creditors when applying the index if to do so would yield a materially different adjustment than would be obtained by the index numbers relating to the ends of the periods over which the calculation is made. Thus, if, for example, the average age of debtors is one month, the value of the appropriate index number at 30 November should be applied to the closing balance of debtors if the business has a 31 December year end.

If stock not subject to a COSA is included in monetary working capital, the appropriate index should be based on price changes most appropriate to the stock in question and the general nature of the business. In the absence of a more suitable index a general index should be applied.

If cash or overdrafts are included in monetary working capital, the index should be based on the price movements of the items which will be purchased by the cash.

If a business's monetary working capital is a net liability and if the net liability exceeds the value of stock subject to a COSA, the excess is not regarded as financing working capital and should be excluded from the MWCA calculation. The excess is included in the net borrowing figure and will therefore affect the gearing adjustment (*see below*).

We will now present an example to illustrate the calculation of both the COSA and MWCA.

EXAMPLE 17.1

Suppose that Fowl Limited's current assets and current liabilities at 1 January and 31 December 19X5 are as follows:

	1 January		31 December	
	£	£	£	£
Current assets				
Stock at historical cost		60 000		90 000
Trade debtors		20 000		65 000
Prepayments		1 200		1 400
Cash in hand		2 000		2 200
		83 200		158 600
less Current liabilities				
Trade creditors	30 000		80 000	
Accrued expenses	5 000		7 000	
Dividends payable	16 000		20 000	
Corporation tax	20 000		44 000	
Bank overdraft	22 000	93 000	15 000	166 000
Net current assets		£(9 800)		£(7 400)

Assume:
(a) that the price movements relevant to stock, debtors and creditors follow the same path, thus enabling us to use the same index for all these items;
(b) that in view of the rapid turnover of stocks, debtors and creditors the index numbers at the beginning and end of the period can be used;
(c) that the business is not subject to any seasonality and that the COSA and MWCA can be calculated for the year as a whole;
(d) that the company's bank overdraft does not fluctuate with the level of stock, trade debtors and creditors and that it does not require cash floats to support its day-to-day operations. Thus, cash and overdrafts are excluded from the MWCA calculation;
(e) that the appropriate index numbers referred to in paragraph (a) are: 1 January, 120; average for the year, 125; 31 December, 140.

Under these assumptions, the cost of sales adjustment using the formula for the averaging method given on page 476 is:

$$\text{COSA} = \frac{£60\ 000}{120}\ (125 - 120) + \frac{£90\ 000}{140}\ (140 - 125) = £12\ 143$$

On the basis of the definition of monetary working capital given on page 478 and the above assumptions, monetary working capital at 1 January and 31 December is:

	1 January		31 December	
	£	£	£	£
Trade debtors		20 000		65 000
Prepayments		1 200		1 400
		21 200		66 400
less Trade creditors	30 000		80 000	
Accrued expenses	5 000	35 000	7 000	87 000
		£(13 800)		£(20 600)

Note that the cash, dividends payable, corporation tax and the bank overdraft have not been included.

At both 1 January and 31 December the monetary working capital is a net liability, but, as the net liabilities are less than the stock subject to the COSA at both dates, nothing has to be added to net borrowings (*see below*).

Using the averaging method the MWCA is given by:

$$\text{MWCA} = \frac{-£13\,800}{120}(125 - 120) + \frac{-£20\,600}{140}(140 - 125) = -£2782$$

As the MWCA is negative, £2782 will be credited to the current cost profit and loss account and debited to the current cost reserve account.

In a case such as this, when the same index numbers are used in the COSA and MWCA calculations, the combined figure of £9361 (£12 143 – £2782) could be shown in the current cost profit and loss account.

The gearing adjustment

We have already described the rationale for a gearing adjustment and the fact that the *Handbook* describes two types; the restricted and full adjustments described in the *Handbook* as Type 1 and Type 2 adjustments respectively (*see* pages 460 to 461). The *Handbook* does not state any preference between the two, or indeed whether there should be a gearing adjustment at all. The authors believe that in the context of current cost accounts based on the maintenance of operating capital, the gearing adjustment does provide useful information and, of the two versions presented in the Handbook, the full adjustment is the more logical in that it attempts to measure the effect of all relevant price changes.

In this section we shall concentrate on the technical aspects of the topic and will first consider the measurement of *average net borrowing* and the *gearing ratio* which are required to calculate either type of gearing adjustment.

Average net borrowing

Net borrowings can be defined as:

(a) the aggregate of all liabilities and provisions fixed in monetary terms (including preference share capital, convertible debentures and deferred tax but excluding proposed equity dividends), other than those included as part of monetary working capital and those which are, in substance, equity capital; less

(b) the aggregate of all current assets other than those subject to a cost of sales adjustment and those included as part of monetary working capital.

(*Handbook*, Para. A5.10).

The average net borrowing may be calculated by using a simple average of the opening and closing balance sheets, unless there have been substantial changes during the year in which case a weighted average would be more appropriate.

If, unusually, net borrowing is negative, then no gearing adjustment is made.

In summary, net borrowing will, in most cases, be made up of all those monetary items which are not part of the equity shareholders' interest (preference shares are part of net borrowing) or monetary working capital.

The gearing ratio

The gearing ratio (R) is the ratio of the average net borrowing during the period (L) to the sum of average net borrowing and average equity shareholders' interest (including proposed dividends) (S) i.e.

$$R = \frac{L}{L + S}$$

Some readers, having noted that one needs the shareholders' interest from the current cost balance sheet in order to calculate the gearing adjustment, may be puzzled about how to proceed given that one needs the gearing adjustment in order to complete the current cost balance sheet. The answer to this apparent paradox is that the gearing adjustment simply represents a transfer between the current cost reserve account and the profit and loss account, which are both part of the shareholders' interest. It is therefore necessary initially to prepare draft current cost accounts without the gearing adjustment in order to find the shareholders' interest and net borrowing; the inclusion of the gearing adjustment will then be a final adjustment which will change the composition but not the total of shareholders' interest.

EXAMPLE 17.2

Suppose that the current cost balance sheets (before the calculation of the gearing adjustment in the case of 19X7) at 31 December 19X6 and 19X7 are as follows:

	19X6		19X7	
	£000	£000	£000	£000
Fixed assets		11 200		12 300
Net current assets				
Stock	3 000		4 300	
Monetary working capital	500		2 200	
	3 500		6 500	
Proposed dividends	(200)		(300)	
Other current liabilities (incl. tax)	(600)	2 700	(400)	5 800
		13 900		18 100
Debentures	(4 000)		(4 000)	
Deferred tax	(600)	(4 600)	(700)	(4 700)
		£9 300		£13 400
Share capital and reserves				
Ordinary shares		5 000		6 000
Share premium		–		500
Current cost reserve		3 200		4 100
Other reserves		1 100		2 800
		£9 300		£13 400

Movement on current cost reserve

	£000
Balance 1.1 19X7	3 200
add COSA and MWCA	600
Increase in current cost of fixed assets	300
Balance 31.12.19X7	£4 100

In order to calculate the gearing adjustments it will be helpful to recast the balance sheets to show net borrowing and equity shareholders' interest.

Equity shareholders' interest:		
Share capital and reserves	9 300	13 400
Proposed dividends	200	300
Total equity shareholders' interest	£9 500	£13 700
Net borrowing:		
Other current liabilities	600	400
Debentures	4 000	4 000
Deferred tax	600	700
Total net borrowing	£5 200	£5 100

The average net borrowing is given by:

$$L = \frac{£5\,200 + £5\,100}{2} = £5\,150$$

and the average equity shareholders' interest by:

$$S = \frac{£9\,500 + £13\,700}{2} = £11\,600$$

The gearing ratio is then given by:

$$\frac{L}{L + S} = \frac{£5\,150}{£5\,150 + £11\,600} = 0.31$$

The two gearing adjustments are then:

Restricted – Type 1

Gearing ratio x current cost operating adjustments
0.31 x £600 = £186

Full – Type 2

Gearing ratios x all holding gains in 19X7
0.31 x £(600 + 300) = £279

CORRESPONDING AMOUNTS AND TREND INFORMATION

'For yet another year, sales have reached a new high' is the sort of statement which used to appear far too frequently in chairmen's reports. Inflation made it easy for companies to present their results with a rosy glow when in reality the failure of the company to keep in step with the fall in the value of money should have been the cause for great concern.

The ASC recognised this and suggest that to avoid distortion, adjustments should be made both to the corresponding amounts, figures for the previous period, which are required by the Companies Act and to any historical summaries, typically for a five- or ten-year period, which although not required by law, are a common feature of financial statements.

If the corresponding amounts are restated into units of constant purchasing power, it is still necessary to show the figures before adjustment in order to comply with the Companies Act.

EXAMPLE 17.3

We will conclude this chapter by providing a comprehensive example based firstly on the maintenance of operating capital and secondly on the maintenance of financial capital.

The historical cost and current cost balance sheets of Ant Limited as at 31 December 19X4 are given below:

	Historical cost £	Current cost £	Difference £
Fixed assets			
Cost	180 000	212 400	
less Accumulated depreciation	18 000	21 240	
	162 000	191 160	29 160
Current assets			
Stock	50 000	52 174	2 174
Debtors	60 000	60 000	
Current liabilities			
Creditors and accrued expenses	(30 000)	(30 000)	
Dividends payable	(5 000)	(5 000)	
Overdraft	(50 000)	(50 000)	
	187 000	218 334	31 334
Long-term liabilities			
10% debentures	(60 000)	(60 000)	
	£127 000	£158 334	£31 334
Share capital			
£1 ordinary shares	100 000	100 000	
Current cost reserve	–	36 466	36 466
Profit and loss account	27 000	21 868	–5 132
	£127 000	£158 334	£31 334

Ant Limited started trading on 1 January 19X4. As a current cost balance sheet has been prepared at the end of its first year of trading, the balance on the current cost reserve account at 31 December 19X4 can be analysed as follows:

	£	£
Unrealised surpluses		
Fixed assets	29 160	
Stock	2 174	31 334
Realised surpluses – the cumulative total of the current cost adjustments that have been passed through the profit and loss account including the gearing adjustment		5 132
		£36 466

Normally when current cost accounts are prepared for the first time the current cost reserve will include only unrealised surpluses at the date of introduction of the system and it would not be possible to identify past realised surpluses.

Ant Limited's historical cost trading and profit and loss account for the year ended 31 December 19X5 and balance sheet as at that date are given below:

Ant Limited
Trading and profit and loss account for the year ended 31 December 19X5

	£	£
Sales		500 000
less Opening stock	50 000	
Purchases	390 000	
	440 000	
less Closing stock	90 000	350 000
Gross profit		150 000
less Sundry expenses	56 000	
Debenture interest	6 000	
Depreciation	28 000	90 000
Profit before taxation		60 000
less Corporation tax		16 000
		44 000
less Dividends		
Paid	8 000	
Proposed	15 000	23 000
		21 000
Retained profits 1 January 19X5		27 000
Retained profits 31 December 19X5		£48 000

Balance sheet as at 31 December 19X5

	£	£	£
Fixed assets			
Cost		380 000	
Accumulated depreciation		46 000	334 000
Current assets			
Stock		90 000	
Debtors		100 000	
Balance at bank		9 000	
less Current liabilities		199 000	
Creditors	50 000		
Accrued expenses	4 000		
Dividends payable	15 000		
Corporation tax	16 000	85 000	114 000
			448 000
10% debentures			60 000
			£388 000
Share capital			
£1 ordinary shares			300 000
Share premium account			40 000
Profit and loss account			48 000
			£388 000

Notes
(a) On 1 July 19X5 the company issued 200 000 £1 ordinary shares at a premium of 20 pence per share.
(b) On 1 July 19X5 the company purchased fixed assets costing £200 000. There were no sales of fixed assets in the year. The company depreciated its fixed assets at 10 per cent per annum on a straight-line basis assuming a zero scrap value.

The workings required in order to prepare the current accounts will be organised in the following sections:

A Fixed assets and depreciation
B COSA and stock
C MWCA
D Gearing adjustment
E Movement on the current cost reserve account

A *Fixed assets and depreciation*
A1 The appropriate price index for fixed assets moved as follows:

Date:	1 January 19X5	1 July 19X5	31 December 19X5
Index:	118	132	144

A2 An analysis of the fixed assets held on 1 January 19X5 revealed that they had all been purchased on 1 January 19X4 at a cost of £180 000.

A3 The gross replacement cost of fixed assets at 31 December 19X5 is:

	£
Opening balance per current cost balance sheet, £212 400 x 144/118	259 200
Assets purchased on 1 July 19X5, £200 000 x 144/132	218 182
	£477 382

A4 The current cost depreciation charge for 19X5 based on the average gross current replacement cost is:

	£
On fixed assets held on 1 January 19X5, 10% of $\frac{1}{2}$ (£212 400 + £259 200)	23 580
On fixed assets purchased on 1 July 19X5, 5% of $\frac{1}{2}$ (£200 000 + £218 182)	10 455
	£34 035

A5 The depreciation adjustment is then

	£
Current cost depreciation	34 035
less Historical cost depreciation	28 000
Depreciation adjustment	£6 035

A6 Required balance on accumulated depreciation at December 19X5:

	£
Fixed assets held on 1 January 19X5 (and purchased on 1 January 19X4), 20% of £259 200	51 840
Fixed assets purchased on 1 July 19X5, 5% of £218 182	10 909
	£62 749

A7 Backlog depreciation:

	£	£
Accumulated depreciation at 31 December 19X5		62 749
less Accumulated depreciation		
(per current cost accounts)		
at 1 January 19X5	21 240	
CCA depreciation charge for 19X5	34 034	55 275
Backlog depreciation		£7 474

A8 The CCA balance sheet figures are then

	£
Gross replacement cost (A3)	477 382
less Accumulated depreciation (A6)	62 749
Net replacement cost	£414 633

A9 The net credit to the current cost reserve is

	£
Increase in gross replacement cost	
Assets held on 1 January 19X5, £259 200 – £212 400	46 800
Assets purchased on 1 July 19X5, £218 182 – £200 000	18 182
	64 982
less Backlog depreciation	7 474
Net credit	£57 508

B COSA and stock

B1 Assume (i) that all the stock is subject to a COSA; (ii) that the averaging method can be used and that the adjustment can be made for the year as a whole (note that this can only be done if similar assumptions can be made about the MWCA); (iii) that the average age of stock is 3 months; (iv) that the appropriate price index for stock moved as follows:

Date:	1 October 19X4	Average for 19X5	1 October 19X5	31 December 19X5
Index:	115	128	140	150

B2 The COSA for 19X5 is given by:

$$\text{COSA} = \frac{£50\ 000}{115}(128-115) + \frac{£90\ 000}{140}(140-128) = £13\ 366$$

B3 The unrealised revaluation surplus on the stock held on 31 December 19X5 is given by:

	£
Current replacement cost at 31 December 19X5,	
£90 000 × $\frac{150}{140}$	96 429
less Cost of stock	90 000
Unrealised surplus	£6 429

B4 The credit to the current cost reserve account is:

	£	£
Realised surplus, i.e. COSA		13 366
Increase in unrealised surplus		
Unrealised surplus at 31 December 19X5	6 429	
Unrealised surplus at 1 January 19X5	2 174	4 255
		£17 621

C *MWCA*

C1 Assume (i) that the overdraft and balance at bank do not fluctuate with the level of stock, debtors or creditors, and hence should not be included in monetary working capital; (ii) that the ages of debtors and creditors can be ignored and the year-end index numbers can be used in the calculation; (iii) that the appropriate price indices are as follows:

	1 January 19X5	Average for 19X5	31 December 19X5
Date			
Debtors index	120	133	146
Creditors and accrued expenses index	115	125	135

C2 The MWCA is then given by

$$\text{Debtors,} \ \frac{£60\,000}{120}(133 - 120) + \frac{£100\,000}{146}(146 - 133) = \quad 15\,404$$

$$\text{Creditors and accrued expenses,}$$

$$\frac{-£30\,000}{115}(125 - 115) - \frac{£54\,000}{135}(135 - 125) \quad = \quad \frac{-6\,609}{£8\,795}$$

D *Gearing adjustment*

D1 In order to calculate the gearing ratio it is necessary to construct a draft CCA balance sheet as at 31 December 19X5. It will be helpful if we first summarise the adjustments that have been made to the current cost reserve and the profit and loss account:

	£
Balance current cost reserve 1 January 19X5	36 466
add Increases for 19X5	
Fixed assets (A9)	57 508
Stock (B4)	17 621
MWCA (C2)	8 795
Balance before gearing adjustment at 31 December 19X5	£120 390

The balance on the CCA profit and loss account as at 31 December 19X5 (before making the gearing adjustment) is:

	£	£	£
Balance on CCA profit and loss account at 1 January 19X5			21 868
Increase in retained earnings in 19X5, historical cost profit and loss account		21 000	
less Current cost adjustments			
Depreciation adjustment (A5)	6 035		
COSA (B2)	13 366		
MWCA (C2)	8 795	28 196	(7 196)
Balance of CCA profit and loss account at 31 December 19X5 before the gearing adjustment			£14 672

D2 A draft CCA balance sheet (before the gearing adjustment) can now be prepared. For convenience the balance sheet will be arranged so as to disclose the totals of net operating assets, shareholders' interest and net borrowing.

CCA balance sheet as at 31 December 19X5 (before making the gearing adjustment for 19X5)

	£	Workings
Net operating assets		
Fixed assets	414 633	A8
Stock	96 429	B3
Debtors	100 000	
Creditors	(50 000)	
Accrued expenses	(4 000)	
	£557 062	
Shareholders' interest		
Share capital	300 000	
Share premium	40 000	
Profit and loss account	14 672	D1
Current cost reserve	120 390	D1
Proposed dividends	15 000	
	£490 062	
Net borrowing		
Balance at bank	(9 000)	
Corporation tax	16 000	
Debentures	60 000	
	£67 000	

Only the shareholders' interest and net borrowing are required to calculate the gearing proportion. In practice it will often be simplest to calculate the net operating assets and net borrowing, thus deriving shareholders' interest as the balancing figure.

D3 As the gearing ratio is based on average values it is necessary to analyse the opening balance sheet to derive the required totals:

Analysis of CCA balance sheet as at 1 January 19X5

	£
Net operating assets	
Fixed assets	191 160
Stock	52 174
Debtors	60 000
Creditors	(30 000)
	£273 334
Shareholders' interest	
Share capital	100 000
Current cost reserve	36 466
Profit and loss account	21 868
Proposed dividends	5 000
	£163 334
Net borrowing	
Overdraft	50 000
Debentures	60 000
	£110 000

D4 The required averages are then calculated as follows:
Shareholders' interest (S) = 0.5 (163 334 + 490 062) = £326 698;
Net borrowing (L) = £0.5 (110 000 + 67 000) = £88 500.
The gearing ratio is then given by:

$$\frac{L}{L + S} = \frac{88\,500}{88\,500 + 326\,698} = 0.21$$

D5 The total of the current cost adjustments (*see* D1) is £28 196 and the Type 1, restricted, gearing adjustment is therefore 0.21 x £28 196 = £5921.

E *Movements on the current cost reserve*

E1 The Handbook suggests that a full set of financial statements based on the current cost convention should include a statement showing the movement in current cost reserve distinguishing between the realised and unrealised elements.

E2 The balance on the current cost reserve account at 31 December 19X5 is

	£
Balance (excluding gearing adjustment) from D1	120 390
less Gearing adjustment (D5)	5 921
Balance at 31 December 19X5	£114 469

E3 The above balance can be analysed in the manner described below, which will enable the realised and unrealised elements to be identified. Special reference needs to be made to the treatment of the depreciation adjustment for the year, i.e. the difference between the current cost and the historical cost depreciation charges. The excess depreciation is credited to the accumulated depreciation account and not the current cost reserve. It does, however, have an impact on the current cost reserve as it represents a transfer from the unrealised to the realised section of the account. This is because depreciation is a measure of the consumption of an asset and hence is a measure of the surplus on the fixed assets which has been realised during the year.

	Unrealised (£)	Realised (£)	Total (£)
Fixed assets			
Line 1: Balance at 1 January 19X5	29 160		
Line 2: Increase for year (A9)	57 508		
Line 3: Depreciation adjustment (A5)	(6 035)	6 035	
Stock			
Line 4: Balance at 1 January 19X5	2 174		
Line 5: Increase in unrealised surplus (B4)	4 255		
Line 6: COSA (B2)		13 366	
Line 7: Realised surpluses at 1 January 19X5		5 132	
Line 8: MWCA (C2)		8 795	
Line 9: Gearing adjustment (D5)		(5 921)	
	£87 062	£27 407	£114 469

E4 Using the above table a suitable statement can be prepared:

Current cost reserve	£	£	£
Balance at 1 January 19X5 (Lines 1, 4 and 7)			36 466
Revaluation surpluses reflecting price changes			
Fixed assets (Line 2)	57 508		
Stocks and work in progress (Lines 4, 5 and 6)	17 621	75 129	
MWCA (Line 8)		8 795	
Gearing adjustment (Line 9)		(5 921)	78 003
			£114 469
Of which:			27 407
Realised			87 062
Unrealised			£114 469

We can now present the current cost accounts, to save space we will not reproduce all the notes which are suggested in the Handbook.

Ant Limited
Current cost profit and loss account for the year ended 31 December 19X5, based on the operating capital maintenance concept

	£	£	Workings
Turnover		500 000	
Cost of sales		(350 000)	
Gross profit		150 000	
Distribution costs and administrative expense		(84 000)	
Historical cost operating profit		66 000	
Current cost operating adjustments (Note 1)		(28 196)	D1
Current cost operating profit		37 804	
Interest payable	(6 000)		
Gearing adjustment	5 921	(79)	D5
Current cost profit on ordinary activities before taxation		37 725	
Tax on profit on ordinary activities		(16 000)	
Current cost profit for the year		21 725	
Dividends paid and proposed		23 000	
Current cost loss retained		£(1 275)	

Note 1 Current cost operating adjustments

	£
Cost of sales	13 366
Money working capital	8 795
Working capital	22 161
Fixed assets (depreciation)	6 035
Current cost operating adjustments	£28 196

Current cost balance sheet as at December 19X5, based on the operating capital maintenance concept

	£	£	Workings
Fixed assets			
Tangible assets		414 633	A8
Current assets			
Stocks	96 429		B3
Debtors	100 000		
Cash at bank and in hand	9 000		
	205 429		
Creditors: Amounts falling due within one year:			
Trade creditors	(50 000)		
Other creditors			
sundry	(4 000)		
taxation	(16 000)		
proposed dividend	(15 000)		
	(85 000)		

	£	*Workings*
Net current assets	120 429	
	535 062	
Creditors: Amounts falling due after more than one year		
10% Debentures	(60 000)	
	£475 062	
Capital and reserves		
Called-up share capital	300 000	
Share premium account	40 000	
Other reserves (Note 2)	135 062	
	£475 062	

Note 2 Other reserves

	£	
Current cost reserve	114 469	E4
Profit and loss account (£21 868–£1 275)	20 593	
	£135 062	

We will now present accounts based on the maintenance of financial capital.

EXAMPLE 17.4

Facts are as in Example 17.3 with the following additional information.
Assume that the index of retail prices moved as follows:

Date:	1 January 19X5	30 June 19X5	31 December 19X5
Index:	150	172	188

Note that the assets and liabilities will be shown at the same figures irrespective of whether the balance sheet is based on the maintenance of operating capital or financial capital. The only difference is the composition, but not the total, of owners' equity. In an 'operating capital' balance sheet, owners' equity includes a current cost reserve while in a 'financial capital' balance sheet it will include a financial capital maintenance reserve.

We will assume that as at 31 December 19X4 the relevant figures in the 'financial capital' balance sheet were:

	£
Financial capital maintenance reserve	30 000
Profit and loss account	28 334
	£58 334

£58 334 is the sum of the current cost reserve (£36 466) and the profit and loss account balance (£21 868) shown on the 'operating capital' balance sheet appearing on page 485.

Most of the workings required for this example have already been presented in Example 17.3 and references will be made to that example. The only new working is that required to calculate the inflation adjustment.

F *Inflation adjustment to shareholders' funds*

There was a share issue on 1 July 19X5 and hence there needs to be separate adjustments for the opening balance and the proceeds of the share issue.

F1 *Inflation adjustment*

	£
Opening capital £158 334 (188/150 − 1)	40 111
Share capital issued on 1 July 19X5	
£240 000 (188/172 − 1)	22 326
	£62 437

There are a number of ways of presenting the current cost profit and loss account based on the maintenance of financial capital. The virtue of the format used in this example is that it provides a detailed analysis of the holding gains.

Ant Limited
Current cost profit and loss account for the year ended 31 December 19X5 based on the maintenance of financial capital

	£	£	Workings
Historical cost profit for year before interest and taxation		66 000	
Interest		(6 000)	
Tax on profit		(16 000)	
Historical cost profit for year		44 000	
Cost of sales adjustment	(13 366)		
Depreciation adjustment	(6 035)	(19 401)	
Current cost retained profit		24 599	
Unrealised holding gains arising during the year (Note (a))	63 937		
Realised holding gains	19 401		
	83 338		
Realised holding gains previously recognised as unrealised (Note (b))	(8 209)		
Total holding gains	75 129		
Inflation adjustment to shareholders' funds	(62 437)		F1
Real holding gains		12 692	
Total real gains		37 291	
Dividends, paid and proposed		23 000	
Amount retained		£14 291	

Note (a) Unrealised holding gains arising during the year:

	£	Workings
Fixed assets	57 508	A9
Stock	6 429	B4
	£63 937	

Note (b) Realised holding gains previously recognised as unrealised:

	£	*Workings*
Depreciation adjustment	6 035	A5
Stock, unrealised holding gain at		
1 January 19X4	2 174	B4
	£8 209	

Current cost balance sheet as at 31 December 19X5 based on the maintenance of financial capital

The assets and liabilities of the company will be shown at the same amounts as those shown in the current cost balance sheet on page 494 totalling £475 062. However, the shareholders' interest, in particular the reserves, will be different:

	£
Net assets as before	475 062
Capital and reserves	
Called-up share capital	300 000
Share premium account	40 000
Financial capital maintenance reserve (Note (c))	92 437
Profit and loss account reserve (Note (c))	42 625
	£475 062

Note (c) Movement on reserves during the year

	Financial capital maintenance reserve	*Profit and loss reserve*
	£	£
Balance at 1 January 19X5	30 000	28 334
Increase during year	62 437	14 291
Balance at 31 December 19X5	£92 437	£42 625

RECOMMENDED READING

See end of Chapter 18.

CHAPTER 18

Beyond current cost accounting

INTRODUCTION

In this concluding chapter we shall assess the virtues of current cost accounts against the prime purposes served by the publication of periodic financial statements which we identified in Chapter 3 as control, taxation, consumption and valuation.

We shall then see whether current cost accounting can be further developed as a fully stabilised set of accounts based on a CPP unit of measurement or whether the answer is to adopt a totally different approach. Accordingly, we will introduce the proposals outlined in *Making Corporate Reports Valuable*[1] which advocate further study towards the implementation of a system of accounting based on the net realisable value basis of asset and liability measurement.

We will conclude by looking briefly at the approach envisaged by the ASB as outlined in its Discussion Paper 'The Role of Valuation in Financial Reporting', issued in March 1993.

THE UTILITY OF CURRENT COST ACCOUNTS

Control

Current cost accounts are likely to be more helpful than historical cost accounts or current purchasing power accounts in helping shareholders and others to assess how well or badly the directors have employed the resources which have been entrusted to them, especially through the use of such measures as return on capital employed. The current cost accounts attempt to show the current values of the assets of the company and whether or not the net assets have increased during a period after allowing for specific price changes. Thus, it may be argued that the current cost accounts would provide a better vehicle for the exercise of control by shareholders and others.

There are obvious weaknesses with the ASC Handbook's current cost model, notably the complete absence of regard to changes in the general price level found in the operating capital maintenance variant, and the partial treatment provided by the financial capital maintenance approach.

---

1 P. N. McMonnies (ed), *Making Corporate Reports Valuable*, Institute of Chartered Accountants of Scotland and Kogan Page, London, 1988.

Taxation

If one makes the not unreasonable assumption that a government would only wish to levy taxation on any surplus that is generated after the substance of the business has been maintained, then it can be seen that CCA is likely to provide a better basis for taxation than the historical cost or CPP methods.

It must be recognised that the amount of taxation payable by a company depends not only upon the way in which its taxable profit is calculated, but also upon the nominal tax rate applied to that taxable profit. Even if the government were to adopt current cost profits, rather than historical cost profits, as the basis for the computation of taxable profits, it might still wish to raise the same amount from the taxation of business profits. If such were the case, there would be a redistribution of the tax burden within the business sector, with no change in the total burden on that sector.

Current cost accounting does *prima facie* seem to provide a suitable basis for taxation, but since equity and clarity are desirable characteristics of any system of taxation much more will have to be done if taxes are to be based on current cost accounting. In particular, the degree of choice allowed to companies, especially with regard to the capital maintenance concept, would need to be reduced.

It is unlikely that the Inland Revenue would accept the degree of subjectivity involved in any system of current cost accounting which has yet been developed.

The treatment of the gearing adjustment is also likely to require careful consideration. It is reasonable to include the gearing adjustment in arriving at the profit subject to taxation, as it does offset the cost of interest which is charged to the accounts, so only the real cost of interest as opposed to the nominal charge would be allowed against tax. However, if this were done, there would be a strong case for not taxing the whole of the interest payments received by lenders, thus allowing them some relief from inflation. Such a change would have significant consequences for the whole of the tax system – both personal and corporate – and is unlikely to be made without a good deal of discussion.

Consumption

As is the case with taxation, the extent to which financial accounts will assist in the making and monitoring, by shareholders and others, of the consumption or dividend decision depends on the concept of capital which is to be 'maintained'. While at its present state of development there is no general agreement as to the most suitable capital maintenance concept for CCA, it does not seem unreasonable to suggest that both the operating and financial capital bases provide more useful information than that provided by the historical cost model which, as we have argued at various places in this book, can be extremely dangerous in so far that dividends may be paid unwittingly out of capital.

In developing the CCA model its advocates have placed considerable emphasis on the dividend decision, but in some respects this aim has resulted in a degree of complexity which has hindered the acceptance of current cost accounting. The gearing adjustment is perhaps the most striking example. Such complexity may be inevitable in a system of accounting which does attempt to reflect reality – for reality is rarely simple. To take the dividend decision as an example, the desires of a short-term shareholder and a director/shareholder interested in security of employment will, as we argued at page 468 be very different. If CCA is complex because it tries to present information which will be of value to both groups, should such complexity be condemned?

In developing CCA the emphasis has been placed, for quite understandable reasons, on the needs of larger companies. But it is usually in the humbler parts of the business world that we would find disasters caused by a level of consumption (through drawings or dividends) unsupported by profits. If those responsible for the conduct of small and medium-sized enterprises are presented, as they are, with historical cost accounts which indicate they have generated a healthy profit, can one be surprised if some of them 'blow the lot', rather than intuitively estimating the cost of sales and other adjustments in order to see how much of that apparent profit needs to be retained to keep the business operating at its existing level?

If it is not yet possible to devise a suitable method for applying CCA principles in a way which would be appropriate to the circumstances of smaller enterprises, then, at the very least, the traditional historical cost accounts should carry a health warning.

Valuation

The sum of the values of the assets less liabilities of a business as shown in a current cost balance sheet will not, other than in the simplest of cases, be the same as the value of the businesses as a whole, but it is likely that the current cost total will give a better approximation to this value than the figures that are disclosed by the historical cost accounts.

It is not necessary at this stage to spell out the reasons why there is a difference between the total of the values of the individual assets less liabilities and the value of the business as a whole, as the subject of the valuation of a business was discussed earlier. The main reason for the difference is that which is covered by the concept of goodwill, which recognises that an existing business will usually possess substantial intangible assets such as reputation, established relationships with suppliers and customers, and managerial skills, which are not recorded in a balance sheet.

The liabilities section of the balance sheet provides another possible reason for the difference. It must be remembered that, under present proposals, liabilities are included at their nominal amounts and not at their current values.

The above discussion of goodwill was based on the assumption that the value of the business was greater than the total of the values of the assets less liabilities. The reverse can also be true, and a potential weakness of the CCA model is that it can overstate the value of the assets in particular because of the existence of interdependent assets. This problem arises from the fact that assets will be valued at their replacement cost unless a permanent diminution in value has been recognised. If each asset is considered individually and the values aggregated, it may be seen that they are collectively not worth replacing and thus that a value less than the sum of their replacement values should be placed on them. An often quoted hypothetical example of this situation is that of a railway line which runs through two tunnels. Assume that the present value of the railway line is £400 000 and the replacement cost of each tunnel is £250 000. If each tunnel is considered in isolation, it is clear that if either were destroyed it would be worth replacing, and thus would be valued for CCA purposes at £250 000. However, it is clear that if both tunnels were simultaneously destroyed they would not be replaced because the total replacement cost would exceed the benefit that would be derived from the action.

The above example is highly artificial, but the principles can obviously be extended to more complex and practical examples. The sum of the replacement costs of machines and other assets situated in a factory may easily be greater than the price that would be paid for the factory as a whole. Indeed, this position may be only too common in the case of declining industries, such as shipbuilding.

It is true that the position described above can and does exist under historical cost accounting. Accountants are reasonably good at ensuring that there is a write-down in the book value of individual assets, where their recoverable value falls below their net book value, but often fail to make the corresponding adjustment when there is a severe decline in the fortunes of the business as a whole. The questioning of the applicability of the going concern concept is relevant in those instances where the ability of the company to continue in business is an issue, but such questioning does not cover the intermediate position where the business can still survive but where its value has fallen below the total book value of the assets less liabilities. Clearly, given the fact that the total of the assets is likely to be higher in current cost accounts, this particular problem is likely to occur more frequently than is the case with historical cost accounting.

Thus, while it will generally be true that the current cost balance sheet totals will provide a closer approximation to the value of the business than historical cost information, there will still be substantial differences between the two values. This is not to be taken as a criticism of CCA in that the designers of the system did not set this as one of the objectives of CCA. However, it is likely that many laymen will not fully appreciate this point, and there may well be some confusion on the part of the general public, who may believe that a system of current cost accounts should tell them how much a business is worth.

INTERIM SUMMARY

CCA is certainly not the perfect system of accounting in that there is more than one way of reflecting the activities of a business. Neither is it a perfect system of accounting in that, even within its own parameters, it is capable of improvement. The important practical test of whether the work that has gone into the development of CCA and the effort that is required in preparing the accounts are worth while is whether the provision of such accounts will enable better decisions to be made.

Attempts have been made to answer this question including the studies commissioned by ASC on the implementation of SSAP 16. The conclusion was that there were some advantages to be gained from the publication of current cost information in that its availability provided a better basis for decision making than a complete reliance on historical cost information. However, the CCA model as presently developed does not represent the final stage in the reform of accounting practice and further changes can be expected to occur.

CPP AND CCA COMBINED

The relationship between accounting for changes in specific prices and accounting for changes in general prices has always been uneasy. As described in Chapter 15, the early moves to reform in the UK tended to polarise the position – the reformed models were either based on CPP or CCA ignoring inflation. More recently, the financial capital maintenance variant of the ASC Handbook's CCA model does include an 'inflation adjustment' applied to opening shareholders' funds. But in a sense this is not accounting for inflation but an expedient to deal with the particular problem of value-based companies which cannot be easily accommodated by the operating capital maintenance concept.

So why not combine the best features of CCA and CPP? Such an approach has been advocated by a number of accountants, mostly of the academic variety.[2] The change in shareholders' equity derived from a set of fully stabilised[3] financial statements based on 'value to the business' asset valuation is the same as that derived from the ASC Handbook's approach, but there is an important difference because of the treatment of price changes during the year and because of the treatment of monetary items. A fully stabilised set of financial statements will, for example, show the loss or gain on holding monetary assets.

The basic principles can be illustrated in the following example.

EXAMPLE 18.1

Guy started a business on 1 January 19X3 with £1000 which he used to purchase 100 units of stock for £10 each. Trading was not overactive during the year and the only sales were 60 units for £18 each on 31 December 19X3.

For simplicity we will assume that he incurred no overheads during the year. Let us suppose that the general price level increased by 10 per cent over the year while the replacement cost of stock increased by 15 per cent. Then Guy's only sales transaction can be analysed as follows:

	£
Cost of sales	600
Inflation increase	60
Cost of sales restated in current pounds (at 31.12.19X3)	660
Price increase in excess of inflation	30
Replacement cost at date of sale	690
Sales	1 080
Profit	£390

Now if we had prepared a standard CCA profit and loss account we would also have shown a profit of £390 as this is the difference between the sales proceeds and the current cost of the stock consumed. The major difference between the CCA approach and the above is that in the latter the CCA cost of sales adjustment of £90 has been broken down into two elements, (a) £60, which represents the amount by which the cost of the stock held needed to increase in order to keep step with inflation, and (b) £30, the amount by which the increase in the current cost of the stock exceeded inflation. The justification for disaggregating the CCA cost of sales adjustment in this way is that, if account is taken of the fall in the value of money, then the whole of £90 cannot be regarded as a realised holding gain as £60 merely represents that which is required to keep step with inflation and is not a 'real gain'. In consequence that element of the nominal gain which is required to keep step with inflation

---

2 *See*, for example, W. T. Baxter *Accounting Values and Inflation*, McGraw-Hill, London, 1975.
3 Fully stabilised means that all items are expressed in forms of a constant purchasing power, usually the unit of purchasing power on the balance sheet date.

(£60 in this case) is sometimes known as the *fictitious holding gain* while the *real realised holding gain* (or loss) is the difference between the current cost of the asset at the date at which it is consumed and the restated historical cost (i.e. the historical cost adjusted for the change in the general price level).

If we now turn our attention to the closing stock the same approach can be used, i.e.:

	£	£
Current cost of closing stock £400 x 1.15		460
Historical cost of closing stock	400	
Inflation adjustment (fictitious unrealised holding gain) 10%	40	440
Real unrealised holding gain		£20

Opening financial capital was £1000 and if real financial capital is to be maintained this amount must be enhanced by 10 per cent to take account of the fall in the value of money.

On the basis of the above considerations Guy's accounts for 19X3 would appear as follows:

Profit and loss account 19X3

	£
Sales	1 080
Current cost of goods sold	690
Operating profit	£390

Statement of gains/losses 19X3

	£
Operating profit	390
Realised real holding gain	30
Unrealised real holding gain	20
	£440

Balance sheet as at 31 December 19X3

	£	£
Capital 1.1.X3	1 000	
Inflation adjustment 10%	100	1 100
Reserves		
Realised gains		
Operating	390	
Holding	30	420
Unrealised gains		20
		£1 540
Stock at current cost (40 items @ £11.50)		460
Cash (60 @ £18)		1 080
		£1 540

The capital and reserves section of the balance sheet well illustrates the different views that may be taken with regard to distribution. If it is accepted that capital is maintained if assets less liabilities at the balance sheet date equal opening capital after adjusting for inflation, then the maximum that could be distributed without diminishing capital is £440. If it is argued that only realised profits should be distributed then the dividend should be restricted to £420. If it is argued that the business must retain sufficient funds to maintain the same level of activity (i.e. be able to replace the 60 units sold) the maximum dividend is equal to the realised operating gain of £390.

This last line of argument brings us to the current cost account approach that it is the operating capability of the business that must be kept intact if capital is to be maintained. Thus, it can be seen that within the combined CCA/CPP approach it is possible to focus on a profit calculated on the basis of physical capital maintenance. The authors, along with most other writers on the subject, would not, however, advocate this be done as they believe that the concept of 'operating capability' is unclear and ambiguous. However, even if the maintenance of real financial capital is taken to be the bench mark used to measure profit it may still be of value to show what proportion of the operating profit has been paid out by way of dividend so that users can see the extent to which the reserves of the business have increased or decreased after setting aside a sum to allow for increases in specific prices over the rate of inflation. The formulation used in the above simple example would allow this assessment to be made as well as showing the extent to which the total gains are realised.

Before turning to a slightly more complex example, we will discuss those issues which we were able to sidestep in our very simple example – the monetary working capital and gearing adjustments.

The monetary working capital and gearing adjustments arise from the attempts to measure changes in operating capability. The first because it attempts to show the increased investment required in monetary working capital while the second strives to show the extent to which the increased investment in stocks, fixed assets and monetary working capital would be provided by creditors. These adjustments are not required in a stabilised accounting system based on the maintenance of real financial capital. In such a system the impact of inflation on monetary items is the loss or gain on both the business' short- and long-term monetary positions as described in Chapter 15.

Example 18.2 illustrates one way of combining current cost asset valuation with the maintenance of real financial capital.

EXAMPLE 18.2

Suppose that Park Limited started business on 1 January 19X2. On that date the company issued 12 000 £1 shares and £4000 of debentures and purchased fixed assets for £12 000 and stock of £6000. The purchases were partly financed by an overdraft of £2000.

Park's balance sheet at 1 January 19X2 is then

	£		£
Share capital	£12 000	Fixed assets	£12 000
Debentures	4 000	Stock (100 units)	6 000
		Overdraft	(2 000)
	£16 000		£16 000

We will assume that all transactions took place on 1 July 19X2. On that date Park Limited purchased another 400 units for £75 (total £30 000) and sold 380 units for £36 000. Closing stock at FIFO cost is thus £9000.

Overhead expenses, including debenture interest, all paid for cash on 1 July 19X2, amounted to £5000. On 1 July the company paid its suppliers £27 000 and received £31 000 from its customers; thus trade creditors at 31 December 19X2 amounted to £3000 and trade debtors equalled £5000. The company's overdraft at the year end was

	£
Overdraft at 1 January 19X2	2 000
add Paid to suppliers	27 000
Paid for overheads	5 000
	34 000
less Received from customers	31 000
Overdraft at 31 December 19X2	£3 000

Depreciation is to be provided at 20 per cent per annum on a straight line basis. Assume that the appropriate price indices moved as follows:

Date	1 January	1 July	31 December
General price index	90	100	110
Stock price index	80	100	120
Fixed asset price index	95	100	105

Note that the stock price index increased by more than the rate of inflation while the fixed asset price index rose by less (i.e. the price of the fixed assets fell in real terms).

In order to see clearly how certain elements of CCA can be combined with a set of CPP accounts, it is helpful to prepare first the CPP accounts. These will appear as follows:

CPP accounts

Profit and loss account for 19X2	£(31 Dec)	£(31 Dec)	Workings
Sales, 36 000 x 110/100		£39 600	
less Opening stock,			
£6000 x 110/90	7 333		
Purchases,			
£30 000 x 110/100	33 000		
	40 333		
less Closing stock,			
£90 000 x 110/100	9 900	30 433	
Gross profit		9 167	
less Overheads,			
£5000 x 110/100	5 500		
Depreciation,			
£2400 x 110/90	2 933	8 433	
		734	
Gain on short-term monetary items	344		A1
Gain on long-term monetary items	889	1 233	A1
CPP profit for the year		£1 967	

Balance sheet as at 31 December 19X2

	£(*31 Dec*)	£(*31 Dec*)
Fixed assets		
Cost,		
£12 000 x 110/90	14 667	
less Accumulated		
depreciation,		
£2 400 x 110/90	2 933	11 734
Current assets		
Stock, £900 x 110/100	9 900	
Debtors	5 000	
Current liabilities	14 900	
Creditors	(3 000)	
Overdraft	(3 000)	8 900
		20 634
Debentures		4 000
		£16 634
Share capital,		
£12 000 x 110/90		14 667
Retained profits		1 967
		£16 634

CPP workings

A1 Loss on short-term monetary items is given by

		Actual £		Conversion factor	£(*31 Dec*)	
1 Jan	Opening balance		2 000	110/90		2 444
1 Jul	Sales	36 000		110/100	39 600	
	Purchases		30 000	110/100		33 000
	Overheads		5 000	110/100		5 500
31 Dec	Closing balance	1 000			1 344	
		£37 000	£37 000		£40 944	£40 944

Gain on short-term monetary items is £(31 Dec) (1344 − 1 000) = £(31 Dec) 344.
Gain on long-term monetary liabilities is

$$£(31\ Dec)\ 4000\left(\frac{110}{90} - 1\right) = £(31\ Dec)\ 889$$

Current cost adjustments

Four adjustments need to be calculated, the realised and unrealised real gains (or losses) on stock and fixed assets expressed in closing pounds.

(a) *Real realised gain on stock (the cost of sales adjustment)* Stock with a historical cost of £27 000 was sold on 1 July by which date the stock price index had moved to 100, i.e. the replacement cost at date of sale was:

Opening stock, £(1 Jan) 6 000 x 100/80	£(1 July)	7 500
1 July purchases	£(1 July)	21 000
	£(1 July)	28 500

These are 1 July pounds and have to be converted to year-end pounds;

£(1 July) 28 500 x 110/100	£(31 Dec)	31 350
Cost of goods sold per CPP profit and loss account	£(31 Dec)	30 433
Cost of sales adjustment	£(31 Dec)	917

(b) *Real realised loss on fixed assets (depreciation adjustment)*

	£(31 Dec)
Depreciation charge based on movement in specific prices, £2400 x 105/95	2 653
Depreciation charge per CPP accounts	2 933
Depreciation adjustment (loss) £(31 Dec)	280

Note:
(i) Depreciation is based on year-end prices.
(ii) The loss means that the cost of the asset consumed (deemed to be 20 % of the fixed assets) increased by less than the rate of inflation.

(c) *Real unrealised gain on stock*

		£(31 Dec)
Closing stock		
At replacement cost, £9 000 x 120/100		10 800
At adjusted historical cost £900 x 110/100		9 900
Real unrealised gain	£(31 Dec)	900

(d) *Real unrealised loss on fixed assets*

		£(31 Dec)
Net book value at 31 Dec		
At replacement cost 80% of £12 000 x 105/95		10 611
At adjusted historical cost (per CPP accounts), 80% of £12 000 x 110/90		11 734
Real unrealised loss[4]	£(31 Dec)	1 123

---

4 Since this is the first year in the life of the assets and as depreciation is based on year-end values, there is no backlog depreciation.

We are now in a position to present the accounts, which we will do in summarised form:

Profit and loss account

	£(31 Dec)	£(31 Dec)
Sales		39 600
less: Current cost of goods sold	31 350	
Overheads	500	
Depreciation	2 653	39 503
Current cost operating profit	£(31 Dec)	97

Statement of gains and losses

	£(31 Dec)	£(31 Dec)
Current cost operating profit		97
Gains/losses on assets		
Realised		
Gain on stock	917	
Loss on fixed assets	(280)	637
Unrealised		
Gain on stock	900	
Loss on fixed assets	(1123)	(223)
Gains on monetary items (per CPP accounts)		
Short term	344	
Long term	889	1223
	£(31 Dec)	1774

Balance sheet 31 December

	£(31 Dec)	£(31 Dec)
Fixed assets, net current replacement cost		10 611
Current assets		
Stock at replacement cost	10 800	
Debtors	5 800	
	15 800	
Current liabilities		
Creditors	(3 000)	
Overdraft	(3 000)	9 800
		20 411
Debentures		(4 000)
	£(31 Dec)	16 411
Share Capital		
Issued	12 000	
Inflation adjustment[5]	2 667	14 667
Reserves		1 744
	£(31 Dec)	16 411

---

5 In years other than the first, the inflation adjustment would be applied to the opening balance of shareholders' equity. In this case the inflation adjustment is £12 000 (110/90 − 1) = £2667.

A REAL ALTERNATIVE – MAKING CORPORATE REPORTS VALUABLE

Even a casual perusal of the earlier chapters of this book would lead the reader to conclude both that most accountants (both theoretical and practical) who have thought seriously about the issues agree that historical cost accounting is unhelpful and in periods of rapid price changes positively dangerous, while the current cost accounting path to reform has proved difficult to travel and may not bring us to the promised land. Perhaps we should approach the problem from another direction? Is there a real alternative? Some, but as yet very few, accountants believe that there is. For some years a number of theoreticians notably Professors Chambers in Australia and Sterling in the United States[6] have advocated the use of the net realisable value basis for asset valuation. More recently their proposals have received a powerful stimulus in the UK from the publication in 1988 of the report of a major research project undertaken by the Research Committee of the Institute of Chartered Accountants of Scotland, entitled *Making Corporate Reports Valuable*.[7] The report is extremely stimulating and challenging and is an important contribution to the debate on accounting reform. It succeeds in its attempts to challenge preconceived ideas and is revolutionary rather than evolutionary. The revolutionary nature of its proposals is reflected in the committee's decision to reject traditional terms such as profit and loss account, balance sheet and auditor which are replaced by phrases such as operations statement, assets and liabilities statement and independent assessor.

The report deals both with matters which could be addressed in the reasonably short term and those which could only be implemented in the longer term. We will not attempt to summarise the whole of the 108-page document but focus on three aspects; the desirability of providing more contextual information; the incorporation in financial statements of the company's market capitalisation and the longer-term proposals about a radically different form of financial reporting based on net realisable values.

More contextual information

The authors of *Making Corporate Reports Valuable* (which will from now on be referred to as *MCRV*) take a similar view to David Solomons (*see* p. 11) on the identification of user groups. In MCRV four users groups are recognised: equity investors, loan creditors, employees and business contacts. It is suggested that the fundamental information needs of these external users are:

(a) information on an entity's objectives and its performance towards achieving them;
(b) a comparison of an entity's total wealth now as against that at the previous reporting date and the reasons for the change;
(c) the entity's likely future status, performance and resources;
(d) the present and projected environment of the entity; and
(e) information on the ownership and control of the entity and on the background of its management.[8]

---

6 *See* R. J. Chambers, *Accounting, Evaluation and Economic Behaviour*, Prentice-Hall, NJ, 1966; R. J. Chambers, *Second Thoughts on Continuously Contemporary Accounting*, Abacus, September 1970; R. R. Sterling, *Theory of the Measurement of Enterprise Income*, University Press of Kansas, 1970.
7 *Op.cit.*
8 *Op. cit.*, Para. 9.9.

In order to satisfy these needs, *MCRV* advocates the provision of a substantial amount of structured descriptive data to accompany the quantitative data.

Market capitalisation

Equity shareholders are very interested in the price at which they could sell their shares but the aggregate figure, i.e. the share price multiplied by the number of shares in issue, or market capitalisation, is traditionally not thought to be of any relevance to statements about the financial success of the company. The conventional view is that the market price is a marginal price reflecting deals between the seller and purchaser of a small parcel of shares, and hence a poor guide to the value of the company as a whole, and is affected by changes in the market which do not relate specifically to the company concerned. In response to this traditional view *MCRV* makes an important empirical observation when it suggests that it is believed that there is only one case on record in which the premium on a successful bid for a company quoted on the London Stock Exchange was negative.[9] Thus, it is suggested that the market capitalisation provides an estimate of the value of the entity which is consistently at or below the true value. The report goes on to suggest that the underestimation of the true value is likely to be in the region of 15–20 per cent on the grounds that this range covers the average amount of takeover premiums and that such an error is likely to be far less than that derived from a comparison of true value with the balance sheet net worth based on the historical cost convention. Thus *MCRV* suggests that the market capitalisation figure should have a prominent place in the financial statements and that directors should be required to explain the reasons for significant changes between the differences between market capitalisation and the reported figure for net identifiable assets.

A net realisable value accounting model

MCRV argues that the two main criteria for selecting a basis for asset and liability valuation should be additivity and reality.[10] By additivity is meant the quality that when all the numbers in a statement are added together, the sum should have the same meaning as each of the numbers taken on their own; *MCRV* reminds us of the old adage of the undesirability of adding apples and pears. The meaning placed on reality is that numbers in the accounts should reflect as closely as is practical one or more economic facts with which most skilled observers would agree and not conjectures where there can justifiably be a considerable difference of opinion even amongst reasonable and skilled people.

In the view of *MCRV* both current replacement cost (the main element of current cost accounting) and net realisable value pass the additivity and reality tests, albeit with some difficulties.[11]

A number of reasons why NRV is preferred to current replacement are advanced of which the following are perhaps the most important.

(a) NRV is a value which is readily understandable by investors and other users of accounts. *MCRV* points to evidence that some external users believe that this is the

---

9 *Op. cit.*, Para. 6.16.
10 *Op. cit.*, Para. 6.4.
11 *Op. cit.*, Para. 6.11.

value which is actually disclosed by financial statements. Thus, it is suggested that the use of NRV would go some way to reducing the 'expectation gap' in financial reporting.[12]

(b) The use of current replacement cost still includes the making of 'arbitrary decisions' about such matters as depreciation (*see* page 84). NRV is in this context far more elegant and simple for there is no need to allocate costs to different accounting periods. Assets are simply valued by reference to the market place and their total value is the sum that would be obtained if all the assets were sold in an orderly fashion (i.e. not as a forced sale) – very additive and very realistic.

Of course the second of the two reasons given above can be turned round and used as a strong argument against NRV as a basis for valuation. An asset which is highly specific to the needs of a particular company may have a very low value in the market place irrespective of its value to the company.

MCRV's answer is to question the definition or rather the delineation of the asset to be valued. A highly specific asset may, in the market place, be worthless in isolation but have a value when combined with other assets. To return to the railway example (*see* page 499), the market value of a tunnel may be very low (depending primarily on its use for growing mushrooms or storing wine) but *MCRV* would argue that it is more meaningful to value the business unit of which the tunnel is a part.[13]

The question of whether the focus of asset valuation can be moved from the individual asset to the business unit is perhaps the key issue to be resolved if a practical and acceptable system of accounting based on NRVs is to be established.

MCRV's structure for financial systems

As part of its longer-term proposals, *MCRV* suggests that there should be four main statements:

(a) Assets and liabilities statement.
(b) Operations statement.
(c) Statement of changes in financial wealth.
(d) Distribution statement.

Assets and liabilities statement

This should show the entity's assets and liabilities at the end of the period, each stated at net realisable value. Trade creditors would normally be shown at their nominal value but, if the liabilities include securities which are traded, then that element could be included at market value.

For companies whose shares are traded, the statement would include its market capitalisation together with a statement from the directors explaining what they think are the main reasons for the difference, normally positive, between the market capitalisation and the total of the net identifiable assets.

---

12 *Op. cit.*, Para. 6.20(b).
13 *Op. cit.*, Para. 6.8.

A possible structure of an Assets and Liabilities Statement is:

Market value of assets (listed individually)		x
Debtors		x
Cash		x
		x
less Market value of long-term loans	x	
Creditors	x	
Deferred taxation	x	x
Net identifiable assets		x
Market capitalisation		x

Operations statement

The operations statement shows the financial wealth created by trading. It differs from a profit and loss account in the following ways:

(a)   No depreciation charge,

(b)   Stock would be shown at NRV,

(c)   Only exceptional and extraordinary items of a revenue nature would be included, exceptional or extraordinary gains or losses relating to fixed assets would be included in the Statement of Changes in Financial Wealth.

An operations statement might be constructed as follows:

Sales		x
less Opening stock at market value	x	
Purchases	x	
Closing stock at market value	x	
	x	
Operating costs	x	x
		x
add Dividend income		x
Income from unusual events		x
		x
less Taxation		x
Financial wealth added by operations		£x

Statement of changes in financial wealth

This statement would show the change in the wealth of the business analysed into the main components, for example, change due to operations and changes due to movements in the market value of assets and liabilities.

It might appear as follows:

Financial wealth added by operations		x
Increase in value of quoted investments		x
Reduction in debenture liability		x
Increase in value of stock (i.e. holding gain)		x
		x
less Decrease in value of plant	x	
Decrease in value of vehicles	x	x
Distributable change in financial wealth		x
less Distributions		x
		x
New share capital		x
Change In financial wealth		£x
Movement in market capitalisation		£xx

Perhaps one of the weaker aspects of the report is the *MCRV*'s treatment of changes in the general price level. It is not that the issue is ignored but more that its impact on the *MCRV*'s model is not explained clearly. In the case of the statement of changes in financial wealth it is suggested that the changes should be measured in terms of year-end results. It therefore appears that the changes reported should be the real changes, excluding fictitious gains due to inflation.

Distributions statement

This statement would articulate with the previous statement in that it starts with the distributable change in financial wealth for the year and then show the undistributable surpluses brought forward, from which any distributions made or proposed would be deducted. The statement could also include an inflation adjustment derived from the application of the retail price index to the value of shareholders' contributed capital at the start of the year; in addition an entity which wishes to maintain its operating capability in physical terms could make a further appropriation to maintain its asset portfolio.

The statement might be shown as follows:

Distributable change in financial wealth for the year		x
less Inflation adjustment	x	
Appropriation to maintain operating capability	x	x
		x
add Undistributed surpluses brought forward		x
less Dividends		x
Paid	x	
Proposed	x	x
Undistributed surpluses carried forward		£x

Additional statements

In addition to the above four main elements, *MCRV* advocates the publication of cash flow statements showing the inflow and outflow of cash analysed into its main components both historical for the year past and projected for, say, the next three years. Segmental reporting is also regarded as being of importance. Where the amounts are significant it is suggested that the statements should be split:

(a) by type of product;
(b) by manufacturing location;
(c) geographically;
(d) by currency.

In the longer term *MCRV* proposes the publication of much more descriptive information about such matters as innovation, the economic environment and staff resources.[14]

The longer-term proposals of *MCRV* are illustrated in Example 18.3.

EXAMPLE 18.3

Egghead Limited is a management consultancy business which occupies its own premises. It has a small computer services division which has for the last 15 months been engaged in the production of a suite of software under contract for a company in the furnishing industry.

Egghead's summarised historical cost balance sheets as at 1.1.19X2 and 31.12.19X2 and its profit and loss account for the year ended 31.12.19X2 are shown below:

Balance sheets

	1.1.19X2		31.12.19X2	
	£000	£000	£000	£000
Fixed assets				
Freehold property				
Cost	1 000		1 000	
Acc. depr.	200	800	220	780
Vehicles and equipment				
Cost	400		440	
Acc. depr.	250	150	300	140
Investments, cost		200		200
		1 150		1 120
Current assets				
Work in progress	30		310	
Trade debtors	100		200	
Balance at bank	10		110	
	140		620	
Current liabilities				
Trade creditors	50		70	
Proposed dividends	30		80	
	80	60	150	470
		1 210		1 590
10% Debentures		500		500
		£710		£1 090
Share capital		400		400
Unappropriated profits		310		690
		£710		£1 090

14 *Op. cit.*, Para. 7.44.

Profit and loss account, Year ended 31.12.19X2

	£000	£000
Fees		1 200
Increase in work in progress		280
		1 480
less		
Sundry expenses	900	
Depreciation		
Property	20	
Vehicles and equipment	50	
Debenture interest	50	1 020
		460
less Proposed dividend		80
Unappropriated profits for year		380
P and L account balance 1.1.19X2		310
P and L account balance 31.12.19X2		£690

A *Additional information*

1 The net realisable values of the fixed assets at 1.1.19X2 and 31.12.19X2 were as follows:

	1.1.19X2	31.12.19X2
	£000	£000
Freehold property	900	945
Vehicles and equipment	190	205
Investments	400	480

2 The only material work in progress relates to the computer services division's contract. The work done under the terms of the contract had a negligible value at 1.1.19X2 but it is estimated that the software developed under the terms of the contract could have been sold for £500 000 at 31.12.19X2.

3 The market value of the debentures were:

1.1.19X2	£400 000
31.12.19X2	£370 000

4 The shares of the company are traded on the USM. The market capitalisation figures were:

1.1.19X2	£3 000 000
31.12.19X2	£2 900 000

B *Taxation and changes in the general price levels will be ignored.*

We can now prepare the four main statements proposed by *MCRV*.

Assets and liabilities statement as at 31.12.19X2

	£000	£000
Market value of:		
Freehold property		945
Vehicles and equipment		205
Investments		480
Work completed by computer services division		500
Trade debtors		200
Balance at bank		110
		2 440
Less		
Market value of debentures	370	
Trade creditors	70	
Proposed dividend	80	520
Net identifiable assets		£1 920
Market capitalisation		£2 900

Notes

The directors would be required to comment on the possible reasons for the difference between the value at the net identifiable assets and the market capitalisation.

A case could be made for excluding proposed dividends from the above statement on the grounds that it is not a liability until approved by the shareholders.

Operations statement for the year ended 31.12.19X2

	£000	£000
Fees from services		1 200
Increase in value of work done by computer services division		500
		1 700
less		
Operating expenses	900	
Debenture interest	50	950
Wealth added by operations		£750

Note

Because the increase in the value of the contracts undertaken by the computer services division is due primarily to the work undertaken by that group during the year the increase in value has been included in the operations statement. If, in contrast, much of the work had been completed in 19X1 and the increase in value was due primarily to changes in the market value for such software, the increase of wealth would not be included in the operations statement but shown separately in the statement of changes in financial wealth.

Statement of changes in financial wealth for the year ended 31.12.19X2

	£000
Wealth added by operations	750
Increases in value of freehold property	45
Increase in value of investments	80
Decrease in value of debentures consequent upon	
an increase in interest rates	30
	905
less Decrease in value of vehicles and	
equipment (*see* note b)	25
Distributable change in wealth	880
less distribution	80
Change in financial wealth	£800
Change in market capitalisation	£(100)

(a) The directors would be required to comment on the reasons for the difference between the change in financial wealth and the change in market capitalisation.

(b) The fall in value of vehicles and equipment is found as follows:

	£000
NRV at 1.1.19X2	190
Cost of assets acquired during the year	40
	230
NRV at 31.12.19X2	205
	£25

Distribution statement for the year ended 31 December 19X2

	£000
Distributable change in financial wealth for the year	880
Undistributed surpluses brought forward (Note (a))	720
Surplus available for distribution	1600
less Proposed dividend	80
Undistributed surpluses carried forward (Note (b))	£1520

Notes

(a) The undistributed surpluses brought forward may		
be derived thus:	£000	£000
Assets, at NRV, at 1.1.19X2		
Freehold property		900
Vehicles and equipment		190
Investments		400
Trade debtors		100
Balance at bank		10
Carried forward		1600

	£000	£000
Brought forward		1600
less MV of debentures	400	
Trade creditors	50	
Proposed dividend	30	480
		1120
less Share capital		400
Undistributed surplus at 1.1.19X2		£720

(b) The articulation of the statements can be demonstrated
by showing how this figure is derived:

	£000
Net identifiable assets at 31.12.19X2, per the assets and liabilities statement	1920
less Share capital	400
Undistributed surplus at 31.12.19X2	£1520

In the example we have ignored the effects of changes in the general price level, the treatment of which we have already identified as a weakness in the report. Further thought is needed on ways of accounting for changes in the general price level within the *MCRV* model. In other respects the example does indicate the virtues of the approach. The statement of assets and liabilities is based on a clear and easily understandable principle. It indicates how much the assets would realise if sold in an orderly fashion. In contrast, a conventional balance sheet is, as we argued, vague in its concept and not readily understandable by users, especially laymen.

The *MCRV* operations statement reflects not only its fees and expenses but what for this company has been an important event, the success of the programme of work for the design of software. The profit and loss account on the other hand, fails to recognise the event and hence gives only a partial picture of what actually occurred during the year.

The obvious concern about the *MCRV* approach is its subjectivity. The NRV of individual assets cannot always be ascertained with reasonable confidence but the estimation of NRV of 'business units' which are probably unique is even more difficult. Two points can, however, be made in mitigation:

(a) The *MCRV* proposals which include the requirement for directors to provide systematic contextual information, including historical and projected cash flow statements, would enforce some discipline on those responsible for making the estimates. Wild guesses unsupported by reasoned arguments would be difficult to sustain in an *MCRV* system.

(b) The second point is related. The market would become suspicious of companies which habitually made wrong estimates. It may be that companies could for a year or two fool the market but, eventually, as chickens come home to roost so estimates are converted into actual cash flows. If that suggests that the market should place less reliance on one year's figures and in particular one year's 'bottom line' and take a longer view then that would be no bad thing. The UK securities market does tend to take a short-term view and moves which would reduce the tendency would help the economy.

The *MCRV* approach is fresh and imaginative and it seems to provide an excellent basis for further thought and experimentation. The ICAS published an annual report for a company, Melody Plc, based on the ideas in *MCRV* and it is hoped that other companies will be prepared to adopt and experiment with this approach.

THE ASB APPROACH

As we have seen, there exist several different current value systems which could be adopted in place of modified historical cost accounting. To understand the approach favoured by the ASB it is necessary to return briefly to FRS 3 Reporting Financial Performance and then to examine the discussion paper 'The Role of Valuation in Financial Reporting' issued in March 1993.

In Chapter 6, we saw how FRS 3 has introduced a new primary statement, the statement of total recognised Gains and Losses. This includes both the profit for the year and any unrealised surpluses relating to assets which have been revalued during the year. If all of a company's assets were revalued, this statement would be used to collect the holding gains and losses. Thus a framework is in place to accommodate the introduction of a current value system of accounting and the ASB has been accused in some quarters of trying to introduce a system of current cost accounting surreptitiously. Any such aim is firmly rebutted in the Third Annual Review of the Financial Reporting Council:[15]

> Some have seen the existing Discussion Paper and other ASB work as indicating a desire by the ASB to focus on the balance sheet at the expense of the profit and loss account or even as a covert move towards a system of current cost accounting. The ASB has no such intentions, as various passages in its existing publications clearly show.

When we turn to the discussion paper, we find that the envisaged approach of the ASB is much more modest. While recognising that the present version of modified historical cost accounting is clearly unsatisfactory,[16] it proposes to retain that system but to try and remove some anomalies. Thus it proposes an evolutionary approach involving more consistent revaluations of limited classes of assets for which supplementary information is already required by law and which are traded on a ready market. The relevant assets are:[17]

(a) Properties
(b) Quoted investments
(c) Stock of a commodity nature and long-term stock where a market of sufficient depth exists.

While Financial Reporting Standards requiring the regular revaluation of such assets would undoubtedly produce more relevant information in the financial statements; this approach is a long way short of the current value systems which have been discussed in this book.

---

15 Para. 3.22, The State of Financial Reporting, Third Annual Review, Financial Reporting Council, November 1993.
16 Para. 30, The Role of Valuation in Financial Reporting, ASB, March 1993.
17 *Op. cit.,* Para. 34.

CONCLUSION

Most married couples are only too aware that there is more than one way of perceiving and describing the facts. The same can be said of business. There is more than one way of telling a story.

At various stages in the debate on accounting reform the publication of financial statements giving equal prominence to accounts based on different bases for the valuation of assets and liabilities and concepts of capital, the so called multicolumn approach has been suggested. In hindsight it seems that the view that this approach would confuse users was too readily accepted; as it is, users have been pretty confused by the current cost accounting debate. If over the last few decades more effort had been devoted to explaining that there is more than one way of viewing the results and progress of a business enterprise and reporting thereon, we might now be in a better position.

It may be that in due course, the models presented earlier in this chapter will provide the basis for financial reporting which gives a broader perspective. Both the CCA/CPP and the *MCRV* models of financial reporting provide information which is relevant to the needs of users and there seems no reason, other than cost of producing the information for smaller companies, why they should both not appear in a company's published financial reports. In the meantime, despite the many weaknesses and limitations of historical cost accounts, recognised by the professional accounting bodies as well as by academic accountants, they continue to be regarded as the 'real' accounts. While this continues, it is difficult to argue against that old adage that an accountant is someone who prefers to be precisely wrong than approximately right.

RECOMMENDED READING

Accounting Standards Committee, *Accounting for the Effects of Changing Prices: a Handbook*, ASC, London, 1986.

W. T. Baxter, *Inflation Accounting*, Philip Allan, Deddington, 1984.

Institute of Chartered Accountants of Scotland, *Making Corporate Reports Valuable*, P. N. McMonnies (ed), Kogan Page, London, 1988.

D. R. Myddleton, *On a Cloth Untrue*, Woodhead-Faulkner, Cambridge, 1984.

D. Tweedie and G. Whittington, *The Debate on Inflation Accounting*, Cambridge University Press, Cambridge, 1984.

G. Whittington, *Inflation Accounting: an Introduction to the Debate*, Cambridge University Press, Cambridge, 1983.

APPENDIX I

Questions

Answers to questions with the prefix A are included in this textbook in Appendix II.

Answers to questions without a prefix are included in the Solutions Manual which is published separately.

Answers have been prepared by Brian Pain, Senior Lecturer in Accounting, the University of Luton, and John Blakemore, Visiting Lecturer in Accounting, the University of Luton.

1 Introduction

A1.1
(a) Who were considered to be the potential users of financial reports in *The Corporate Report*?
(8 marks)
(b) What do you consider to be their information needs? (8 marks)
(c) How would you expect a consideration of user needs to influence financial reporting?
(9 marks)

ACCA The Regulatory Framework of Accounting, December 1982 **(25 marks)**

A1.2 The Accounting Standards Committee has frequently been criticised for its failure to develop a 'conceptual framework'.

Required
(a) What is generally understood by the term a 'conceptual framework'? (4 marks)
(b) What advantage(s) might arise from using a 'conceptual framework'? (8 marks)
(c) What do you consider would be the difficulties in trying to develop a conceptual framework in the UK? (8 marks)

ACCA The Regulatory Framework of Accounting, December 1985 **(20 marks)**

1.3 *The Corporate Report* states that accounting information should be useful.

Required
(a) Identify the characteristics of useful information and discuss each briefly (10 marks)
(b) Explain whether or not you consider that identification of desirable characteristics helps to improve financial reporting. (6 marks)
(c) It has been suggested that corporate reports which possess these desirable characteristics sometimes recognise the economic substance of a transaction in preference to its legal form. Describe two examples of where this may occur. (4 marks)

ACCA The Regulatory Framework of Accounting, June 1983 **(20 marks)**

2 Sources of authority

A2.1 Your managing director has approached you saying that he is 'confused at all the different accounting bodies that have replaced the old Accounting Standards Committee'.

You are required to draft a memorandum to your managing director explaining the purpose, a description of the type of work and, where applicable, examples of the work to date of the following:
(a) Financial Reporting Council   (3 marks)
(b) Accounting Standards Board   (4 marks)
(c) Financial Reporting Review Panel   (5 marks)
(d) Urgent Issues Task Force   (3 marks)

CIMA Advanced Financial Accounting, May 1993   **(15 marks)**

A2.2 'It is fundamental to the understanding and interpretation of financial accounts that those who use them should be aware of the main assumptions on which they are based.'

Requirement
Explain how Statement of Standard Accounting Practice 2, Disclosure of accounting policies, seeks to achieve this understanding.

ICAEW Financial Accounting I, May 1987   **(15 marks)**

2.3 The Accounting Standards Board ('ASB') has been in existence for some two years now. In comparison with its predecessor, it is striving for greater uniformity in the preparation and presentation of financial statements.

   To what extent do you consider that the ASB is succeeding in this objective, and to what extent are its intentions good news for users of financial statements?

ICAEW Financial Accounting II, December 1992   **(12 marks)**

2.4 During the examination of the financial records of various company clients you find the following material items:

(1) The profit and loss account of Albatross Ltd for the year ended 30 June 1983 has charged therein £16 400 being general rates payable for the year commencing 1 April 1983, and £15 000 being rent paid for the quarter to 30 September 1983.
(2) Eagle Ltd has included in the work in progress valuation as on 31 July 1983, for the first time, a sum of £60 000, which represents apportioned overheads at 10% on direct costs. In the accounts for the year ended 31 July 1982, the work in progress has been stated at £450 000.
(3) In the accounts for the year ended 31 May 1983, Birdie Ltd has included in sales £40 000 which represents goods sent to customers on a sale or return basis.
(4) Underpar Ltd has stocks and work in progress in the balance sheet at cost on 31 August 1983, including apportioned overheads, amounting to £110 000. Information available indicates that sales have been falling rapidly in the last six months following the introduction to the market of a rival product of improved specification and lower price. The company has an issued share capital of £20 000 and a debit balance on reserves of £2500 as on 31 August 1983.

You are required to write short memoranda to the directors of each of the above companies explaining the fundamental accounting concepts involved and the adjustments, if any, to their accounts which you consider necessary.

ICAEW Financial Accounting I, November 1983   **(16 marks)**

2.5 'In recent years, there has been growing interest in, and efforts directed towards, the harmonisation of international accounting'. *Advanced Financial Accounting* by Taylor and Underdown (CIMA/Butterworth Heinemann).

You are required to explain this statement.

CIMA Advanced Financial Accounting, November 1993   **(15 marks)**

2.6 Before the introduction of accounting standards, accounting practices varied from enterprise to enterprise – there was inconsistency and occasionally practices were inappropriate. Intercompany and inter-period comparisons were difficult as enterprises changed accounting policies and resorted to, for example, 'window-dressing' and 'reserve accounting'.

Discuss the extent to which the publication of more than 20 accounting standards has overcome these problems. Illustrate your discussion by reference to specific accounting standards.

ICAEW Financial Accounting II, July 1993   **(12 marks)**

3 What is profit?

A3.1
(a) State what you understand by the term 'capital maintenance' and give examples of TWO capital maintenance concepts.   **(10 marks)**
(b) Outline the practical reasons for measuring and reporting profit.   **(10 marks)**

ACCA The Regulatory Framework of Accounting, December 1984   **(20 marks)**

A3.2
(a) Give a brief summary of the current value replacement cost accounting system (entry values).
                                                                                      (6 marks)
(b) Give a brief summary of the current value net realisable value accounting system (exit values)
                                                                                      (6 marks)
(c) To what extent do you consider it would be useful to prepare financial statements which used entry values for the profit and loss account and exit values for the balance sheet and why?
                                                                                      (8 marks)

ACCA Level 2 The Regulatory Framework of Accounting, December 1989   **(20 marks)**

3.3 Three unrelated companies, Tower plc (a public company), Book Ltd (a private company) and Holdings plc (a quoted investment company) have summarised balance sheets, as on 30th June 1985, as set out below with relevant additional information.

(a) *Tower plc*

	£m		£m
Share capital	2.0	Fixed assets	3.3
Share premium account	0.5		
Revaluation reserves	1.0	Net current assets	2.7
Profit and loss account	2.5		
	6.0		6.0

(1) A partial revaluation of fixed assets took place during the year with the following result:

	£m
Surplus on land	0.65
Surplus on buildings	0.35
Surplus on plant and machinery	0.10
Deficit on fixtures and fittings	(0.10)
	1.00

The directors consider that the value of the remaining fixed assets not revalued is equal to their net book amounts.

(2) Depreciation is provided at 2% on buildings, 15% on plant and machinery, and 20% on fixtures and fittings. All fixed assets are depreciated for the full year on the cost or revalued amounts.

(3) Fixed assets comprise:

	£m
Land	1.2
Buildings	0.8
Plant and machinery	0.8
Fixtures and fittings	0.3
Development costs	0.2
	3.3

(b) *Book Ltd – Current Cost Balance Sheet*

	£000		£000	£000
Share capital	45	Fixed assets		50
Current cost reserve	40	Investment in Worm Ltd		40
Retained profit	55	Current assets		
		Stock	10	
		Long-term work in progress	30	
			40	
		Cash	10	50
	140			140

(1) No provision has yet been made for the losses of the subsidiary, Worm Ltd. It is estimated that the net assets of Worm Ltd in which Book Ltd has an interest of 60% are £50 000.

(2) The current cost reserve comprises:

	£000
CCA adjustments passed through profit and loss account	13
Uplift of fixed assets to CCA values	27
	40

(3) Long-term work in progress includes a profit element of £6000 calculated accordance with SSAP 9.

(c) *Holdings plc*

	£ 000		£ 000	£ 000
Share capital	650	Fixed assets		
Share premium	325	Tangible		20
Reserves	4 380	Investments		5 647
		Current assets		
		Debtors	98	
		Investments	2 436	
		Cash	147	
			2 681	
		Less creditors falling due		
		within 1 year	1 793	888
				6 555
		Creditors falling due in		
		more than 1 year		(936)
		Provisions		(264)
	5 355			5 355

Reserves consist of:

	£000
Unrealised capital losses	(48)
Unrealised revenue profits	140
Unrealised revenue losses	(17)
Realised capital profits	2 890
Realised capital losses	(1 241)
Realised revenue profits	2 666
Realised revenue losses	(10)
	4 380

Requirements

(a) **State concisely for each of the three types of company mentioned, the principles for calculating distributable profits under the Companies Act 1980 (now part of the Companies Act 1985)**

(5 marks)

(b) **Calculate for each of the three companies the maximum legally distributable profits.**

(7 marks)

(c) **Discuss the reasons why it is not normally commercially or practically desirable to make the maximum distribution.**

(7 marks)

ICAEW Financial Accounting II, December 1985   **(19 marks)**

3.4 The balance sheet of Omega as at 30 September 1992 contained the following balances and notes:

		£000
Share capital		10 000
Reserves:		
Share premium	*Note 1*	1 000
Revaluation reserve	*Note 2*	1 780
Other Reserves:		
Merger reserve	*Note 3*	550
Profit and loss account – 1992	*Note 4*	1 940
Profit and loss account b/f		(200)
Capital and reserves		15 070
Liabilities		15 070
Total assets		30 140

Note 1 The share premium arose on the issue of shares on 1 October 1989.

Note 2 The revaluation reserve arose as a result of a revaluation of certain of the fixed assets on 1 October 1991. It comprises a gain of £2 000 000 on the revaluation of plant and machinery, which is the balance remaining after the transfer to the profit and loss account of £200 000 representing the depreciation on the revaluation surplus; and a loss of £220 000 arising from the revaluation of office premises. The directors propose to revalue the remaining fixed assets which currently appear at historic cost in a subsequent financial year.

Note 3 The merger reserve represented the premium of £1 450 000 on shares issued on the acquisition on 1 October 1991 of a subsidiary, Alpha plc, in accordance with the merger provisions of the Companies Act 1985 less goodwill of £900 000 arising on a separate transaction. The goodwill has an estimated useful economic life of 15 years.

Note 4 The profit and loss account balance is the balance after:
(i)   writing off the total acquisition goodwill of £400 000 arising on the acquisition on 1 October 1991 of an unincorporated business carried on by Beta Associates. The estimated useful economic life of the goodwill is 10 years.

(ii) Creating a provision of £1 200 000 representing a permanent diminution in the value of a subsidiary, Gamma plc.

(iii) The transfer of the £200 000 mentioned in Note 2 from the revaluation reserve to the profit and loss account representing the amount by which the total depreciation charge for the year exceeded the amount that would have been provided if the plant had not been revalued.

(iv) Crediting an exchange gain of £38 000 that arose on the translation of a long-term loan taken out in French francs on 1 October 1991. The loan was taken out to use in the United Kingdom because the interest rate was favourable at the date the loan was raised.

Required

(a) Calculate the amount of distributable profit for Omega on the basis that it is:
  (i) A public company.
  (ii) An investment company   (10 marks)

(b) Explain briefly:
  (i) The disclosure requirements relating to distributable profits in a single company and group context.
  (ii) The effect on the distributable profits of the holding company if the group has sufficient distributable profits in aggregate to make a distribution to the holding company's shareholders but the holding company itself has insufficient distributable profits.
  (iii) The effect on the distributable profits of the holding company if the holding company has sold one subsidiary company to another subsidiary for a consideration that exceeds the carrying value of the investment in the holding company's accounts.
  (iv) The effect on the distributable profits of the holding company if a subsidiary company which has a coterminous accounting period declares a dividend after the end of the holding company's year end   (10 marks)

ACCA Advanced Financial Accounting, December 1992   **(20 marks)**

4 Assets: tangible and intangible

A4.1 The managing director of your company has always been unhappy at depreciating the company's properties because he argues that these properties are in fact appreciating in value.

Recently he heard of another company which has investment properties and does not depreciate those properties.

You are required to write a report to your managing director explaining
(a) the consequence of not depreciating the company's existing properties;   (2 marks)
(b) the meaning of investment properties;   (5 marks)
(c) the accounting treatment of investment properties in published financial statements (8 marks)

CIMA Advanced Financial Accounting, May 1991   **(15 marks)**

A4.2 Your Managing Director has been reading the corporate annual reports of one of your competitors. She noticed that this competitor included a percentage of its selling, administration, research and development costs in its stock valuation whereas her own company excluded all such costs from its stock valuation.

You are required to write a memorandum to your Managing Director explaining the requirements of Statement of Standard Accounting Practice 9 in relation to the valuation of stock.

CIMA Advanced Financial Accounting, November 1992   **(15 marks)**

A4.3 During recent years there has been a significant amount of debate regarding the accounting treatment of intangible assets.

You are required
(a) to state briefly the current practice to account for intangible assets; (5 marks)
(b) to outline the main areas of concern regarding accounting for intangible assets (10 marks)

CIMA Advanced Financial Accounting, May 1993 **(15 marks)**

4.4 In accounting for physical fixed assets, the use of 'cost' as a valuation basis is well established.

You are required to outline the difficulties that arise in applying the cost principle, and to justify the solutions normally adopted, in cases where:

(a) physical fixed assets are acquired OTHERWISE THAN for a single cash payment (or on short-term credit) with IMMEDIATE transfer of the legal title to the assets; and (12 marks)
(b) more than one separately identifiable item of physical fixed assets is acquired in the same transaction for a global sum of money, or for other valuable consideration that cannot be precisely apportioned (4 marks)

ACCA Advanced Financial Accounting, June 1983 **(16 marks)**

4.5 Your Managing Director has heard about a building company which has capitalised its interest costs in the cost of its assets.

You are required to write a report to your Managing Director explaining
(a) the alternative accounting treatments of interest costs; (5 marks)
(b) the arguments for and against the capitalisation of interest costs. (10 marks)

CIMA Advanced Financial Accounting, May 1992 **(15 marks)**

4.6 Hifly Ltd hires out aeroplanes, on a full repairing and maintenance charter, to the major tour operators. The company is about to purchase three new 373s and two secondhand jumbo jets. The manufacturers' data and the company's own business plan for the next few years contain the following information:

Manufacturers' data:

Aeroplane model	*373*	*jumbo jet*
Flying time	50 000 hours	30 000 hours
Frequency of major overhaul (every)	500 hours	300 hours
Cost of major overhaul	$10 000	$12 500
Standard replacement of engine parts (every)	5 000 hours	3 000 hours
Cost of replacement engine parts	$7 500	$8 000
Cost of replacement engine	$224 875	$350 000
Number of engines	2	4
Current manufacturers' price	$9 199 750	$15 000 000
Current scrap value	$100 000	$150 000
Hifly Ltd business plan:		
(exchange rate used $1.75 to £1)		
Expected annual flying time on charter	2 500 hours	2 000 hours
Charge per flying hour	£950	£2 000

You are also told that, in addition to the regular servicing costs, replacement engines for both models are fitted after 10 000 hours' flying time. Both jumbo jets, which will cost $9 537 500 each, have already recorded 6 000 flying hours. The directors advise you that it is their intention to hire out all planes over the period of their recommended lives. They anticipate that all prices, maintenance and associated costs will increase by 10% per annum cumulatively.

Requirements

(a) **Define depreciation and state the factors that should be considered in asssessing depreciation, as set out in Statement of Standard Accounting Practice 12.**   (4 marks)

(b) **Discuss the factors which should be taken into consideration by the directors of Hifly Ltd in deciding the method of depreciation for the aeroplanes, giving your reasons for the choice of depreciation method.**   (8 marks)

(c) **Prepare a schedule showing the total annual depreciation for the aeroplanes for the first five years of their operation and state how you would deal with the maintenance expenditure.**
(7 marks)

ICAEW Financial Accounting I, May 1988   **(19 marks)**

4.7 Global plc, which prepares accounts to 31 January each year, operates in several different countries and has recently obtained government financial assistance both in the UK and abroad:

(1) A foreign government has granted £4m to cover the establishment of a new factory. The factory and associated plant installation were completed in November 1992 at a cost of £10m for the land and buildings (land element – £2m) and £5m for the plant. Asset lives were estimated at 50 years for the premises and 10 years for the plant; a full year's depreciation is charged in the year of acquisition.

The grant was dependent on an inspection by government officials and the company retaining ownership of the factory for the next five years. The grant was released by the foreign government on 27 March 1993 following their inspection in January 1993.

The country in which the factory is situated has had a turbulent history with frequent changes of government but has enjoyed a period of relative stability over the past three years. No previous governments have granted assistance to foreign companies.

(2) A local authority in the UK has provided a grant of £130 000 which covers the total initial establishment costs of a new training programme for company staff. The grant is dependent on the company expanding its existing training unit and increasing the number of trainees in direct production areas within the local factory by 20 per cent. The increased number of trainees would have to be sustained for at least three years.

The grant was received in January 1993. Expected costs of the complete programme are £300 000 of which £100 000, relating to initial establishment costs, has been incurred to date.

Actual and projected trainee numbers provided by the production director are:

	Years ending 31 January			
	1993	*1994*	*1995*	*1996*
Welding shop	9	10	9	10
Lathe area	7	9	11	11
Computer controlled machinery	11	14	13	14
Trainee general managers	3	2	2	2
	30	35	35	37

Requirement
Calculate the amounts which should be included in the financial statements for the year ended 31 January 1993, preparing all relevant notes in accordance with SSAP 4, Government grants.

ICAEW Financial Reporting II, May 1993   **(8 marks)**

4.8 On 1 January, 1984, Hideehigh Ltd was incorporated to acquire from a property development company a ready-made holiday complex on the North Wales coast.

The complex is divisible into three distinct areas: a freehold site and two leasehold sites. The leases expire on 25 December, 2 000, and 25 December, 2 080. The developer designated these sites Meg I, II and III, respectively.

A schedule of the properties acquired describes the properties as:

Property Description	Meg I	Meg II	Meg III	Total
6-Room timber constructed chalets	38	48	66	152
3-Storey brick built 'town houses'	64	32	–	96

Hideehigh Ltd intend to lease the chalets and town houses. They have been advised that the chalets, which have a life of 25 years, and the town houses, which have a life of 50 years, should be let on 15-year leases.

You are required to discuss how Hideehigh Ltd should treat the properties in their annual accounts.

ICAEW Financial Accounting I, May 1984   (13 marks)

4.9 You are required to answer the following in accordance with SSAP 9, *Stocks and work in progress:*

(a) **SSAP 9 requires stock to be valued at the lower of the two following amounts: cost or net realisable value. How would you arrive at the 'cost' of finished goods stock in a manufacturing company?**   (14 marks)

(b) **The following information relates to Unipoly plc, a manufacturer of can openers, for the year ended 31 May 1987.**
   You are required to calculate the cost of finished goods stock in accordance with SSAP 9.

	£
Direct materials cost of can opener per unit	1
Direct labour cost of can opener per unit	1
Direct expenses cost of can opener per unit	1
Production overheads per year	600 000
Administrative overheads per year	200 000
Selling overheads per year	300 000
Interest payments per year	100 000

There were 250 000 units in finished goods stock at the year end. You may assume that there was no finished goods stock at the start of the year and that there was no work in progress.
   The normal annual level of production is 750 000 can openers, but in the year ended 31 May 1987 only 450 000 were produced because of a labour dispute.   (6 marks)

ACCA Level 2 The Regulatory Framework of Accounting, December 1987   (20 marks)

4.10 The assistant accountant of Rolf Construction plc has been requested to prepare draft entries for the profit and loss account and balance sheet as at 31st March 1988 to record the four long-term contracts which the company is currently working on. All four contracts had commenced after 1 April 1987. The contract details are as follows:

	North Contract £000	South Contract £000	East Contract £000	West Contract £000
Cost incurred	2 400	1 500	380	7 000
Costs relating to the work certified	1 840	1 390	336	6 800
Certified value of work done	2 800	1 390	336	7 700
Attributable profit/(foreseeable loss)	700	(48)	(108)	640
Progress payments	2 230	1 480	44	6 600
Total contract price	4 000	10 000	5 000	8 000

The following additional information was available to him:

(i) The current practice would be to take the attributable profit less foreseeable losses to the profit and loss account and to report in the balance sheet the costs incurred plus attributable profits less foreseeable losses less progress payments received and receivable.
(ii) The proposed new company policy was to apply the following disclosure criteria:

Long-term contracts should be disclosed in the balance sheet as follows:

(a) The amount of long-term contracts, at costs incurred, net of amounts transferred to cost of sales, after deducting foreseeable losses and applicable payments on account should be classified as long-term contract balances and separately disclosed within stocks. The balance sheet note should disclose separately the balances of:
   (i) net cost less foreseeable losses; and
   (ii) applicable payments on account.
(b) The balance of payments on account (in excess of amounts recorded as turnover and offset against long-term contracts) should be classified as payments on account and separately disclosed within creditors.
(c) The amount by which recorded turnover is in excess of payments on account should be classified as 'amounts recoverable on contracts' and separately disclosed within debtors.
(d) The amount by which the provision or accrual for foreseeable losses exceeds the costs incurred (after transfers to cost of sales) should be disclosed within either provisions for liabilities and charges or creditors as appropriate. The amount need not be separately disclosed unless material to the financial statements.

The assistant accountant has applied the new policy and prepared the following draft entries for the profit and loss account and balance sheet:

Profit and loss account entries

	North	South	East	West	Total
	£000	*£000*	*£000*	*£000*	*£000*
Turnover	2 800	1 390	336	7 700	12 226
Costs	2 400	1 500	380	7 000	11 280
Profit/(loss)	400	(110)	(44)	700	946

Balance Sheet entries

Stocks	£822 000
Creditors	£64 000

Calculated as follows:

	North	South	East	West
	£000	*£000*	*£000*	*£000*
Costs incurred	2 400	1 500	380	7 000
Less: Cost of sales	1 840	1 390	336	6 800
	560	110	44	200
Less: Foreseeable losses	—	(48)	(108)	—
	560	62	(64)	200

Stocks	*£000*	*Creditors*	*£000*
North	560	*East*	64
South	62		
West	200		
	822		64

Required

(a) Review the draft entries for the profit and loss account and balance sheet and amend if necessary to comply with the company's policy. Please show workings. (16 marks)

(b) Briefly explain the criticisms that may be made by an analyst of the company's current and proposed policies for reporting long-term contracts in the balance sheet and profit and loss account in the light of the current debate. (9 marks)

ACCA Level 3 Advanced Financial Accounting, December 1988 (25 marks)

4.11 Amesbury plc produces and distributes computer-controlled machinery. As accountant for the company, you have been provided with the following information regarding the company's activities in researching and developing products in the year ended 31 October 1993:

(1) Expenditure on developing a new computerised tool for a long-established customer has amounted to £150 000. The work is now well advanced and the customer is likely to authorise the start of commercial production within the next 12 months. The customer is reimbursing Amesbury plc's costs plus a 10% mark-up. To date the company has received £70 000 having invoiced £100 000 for agreed work done.

(2) A review of the company's quality control procedures has been carried out at a cost of £100 000. It is considered that the new procedures will save a considerable amount of money in the testing and analysis of existing and new products.

(3) The development of Product M479 has reached an advanced stage. Costs in the year ended 31 October 1993 amounted to £400 000. In addition there has been expenditure on fixed assets required for the development of this product amounting to £120 000 of which £60 000 was incurred in the year ended 31 October 1992. The fixed assets have a five-year life with no residual value and are depreciated on the straight-line basis with a full year's depreciation in the year of acquisition.

Market research, costing £20 000, has been carried out and this indicates the product will be commercially viable although commercial production is unlikely to start until April 1994. The company expects that Product M479 will make a significant contribution to profit.

(4) Commercial production started on 1 June 1993 for Product A174. The costs of developing this product had been capitalised as follows:

Development expenditure capitalised as on 31 October 1992	200 000
Expenditure incurred in the year ended 31 October 1993	50 000
	250 000

The company has taken out a patent which will last for ten years. The associated legal and administrative expenses amounted to £10 000.

Actual and estimated sales for Product A174:

Year ended 31 October	£
1993	250 000
1994	750 000
1995	1 000 000
1996	500 000
1997	250 000

After 31 October 1996 the company's market share and profitability from the product are expected to diminish significantly due to the introduction of rival products by competitors.

(5) It is company policy to capitalise development expenditure wherever possible.

Requirement

Prepare all relevant extracts of the published financial statements for the year ended 31 October 1993 in accordance with current accounting standards and legislation, explaining your treatment of items (1) to (4).

Note: You are not required to prepare extracts of the cash flow statement or the directors' report.

ICAEW Financial Reporting, November 1993 **(15 marks)**

4.12 *'A case can be made for putting brands on to the balance sheet to disclose to shareholders and others the true value of the assets in the business.'* (Pizzey – CIMA *Student*, August, 1990)

You are required to discuss the arguments for and against including a value for brand names in the balance sheet.

CIMA Advanced Financial Accounting, May 1991 **(15 marks)**

5 Liabilities and related issues

A5.1 Spock, a well known accounting guru, recently stated: 'Published financial statements are now so complex that only professional accountants and investment analysts can possibly understand all the data provided. The average investor assesses a company's performance on the basis of the profit and loss account and earnings per share and either ignores or is bamboozled by movements in reserves. Accordingly I believe that, other than share issues, the only movement in shareholders' funds each year should be the transfer from profit and loss account. My conclusion is that with full disclosure, such an approach would aid the readers' understanding and be easier to regulate.'

Requirements
(a) **Identify four examples of reserve movements (other than share issues and transfers from profit and loss account) and in each case explain why such reserve movements are permitted by accounting standards.** **(10 marks)**
(b) **Set out the arguments for and against the conclusion reached by Spock.** **(8 marks)**

ICAEW Financial Accounting 11, July 1989 **(18 marks)**

A5.2 As group chief accountant, you have been asked to provide information to the board of directors of Ardtoe plc on the following outstanding matters relating to the draft accounts for the year ended 30 September 1993:

(1) The company's share capital during the year ended 30 September 1993 was:

	Ordinary shares of £1 each
On 1 October 1992	2 000 000
Bonus issue of one for ten on 31 March 1993	200 000
Rights issue of one for four on 31 July 1993	550 000
On 30 September 1993	2 750 000

The company made a rights issue of one for four ordinary shares at £1.75 on 31 July 1993 when the current market price of each share was £2.00.

The entire proceeds of the rights issue were used to acquire the share capital of a company whose net assets had a book value of £850 000 and a fair value of £950 000 at the date of acquisition.

The earnings per share reported for 1992 was 11.0p.
(2) Stock held in a warehouse at the year end was destroyed by a fire on 3 October 1993. The stock had a balance sheet value of £50 000 and was uninsured.
(3) The group has earnings before taxation of £450 000 and has an estimated corporation tax liability of £140 000 before taking account of an interim dividend of £220 000 and a final dividend of £275 000 paid on 1 April 1993 and 1 October 1993 respectively. Profits chargeable to corporation tax for the year were £402 000. Franked investment income of £50 000 was

received on 30 June 1993. Due to poor trading conditions the group expects to break even over the next few years and future dividend payments will be negligible.

(4) One of the company's subsidiaries has received a claim for substantial damages from a customer on 2 October 1993. One of the company's directors believes that a similar case recently heard in court would indicate that no damages are likely to be paid. The company has counter claimed.

Requirement

Prepare a memorandum for the board of directors of Ardtoe plc providing advice on the relevant accounting treatment of the situations in (1) to (4) above together with your calculations of the earnings per share for 1993 and 1992 and other relevant amounts to be included in the financial statements.

Note: Assume an ACT fraction of 1/3.

ICAEW Financial Reporting, November 1993   (15 marks)

5.3
(a) **How does SSAP 18 *Accounting for Contingencies* define a contingency?**   (3 marks)
(b) **What information should be disclosed in financial statements with regard to contingencies?**
                                                                                  (5 marks)
(c) **State, with reasons, how you would account for the following items:**

   (i) The directors of a company have discovered a painting in a cupboard and have sent it to an auction house, who have confirmed that it should sell for £1 million in the following month's auction.   (3 marks)
   (ii) A claim has been made against a company for injury suffered by a pedestrian in connection with building work by the company. Legal advisers have confirmed that the company will probably have to pay damages of £200 000 but that a claim can be made against the building sub-contractors for £100 000.   (3 marks)
   (iii) A company uses 'recourse factoring' whereby the company agrees with the factor to re-purchase any debts not paid to the factor within 90 days of the sales invoice date. In the year ended 30 June 1987 the factored credit sales of the company were £2 million, of which £1.8 million had been paid to the factor, £150 000 was unpaid but due within 90 days and £50 000 was unpaid for more than 90 days.   (3 marks)
   (iv) The manufacturer of a snooker table has received a letter from a professional snooker player, who was defeated in the final of a major snooker competition, threatening to sue the manufacturer for £1 million, being his estimate of his loss of earnings through failing to win the competition, on the grounds that the table was not level.   (3 marks)

ACCA The Regulatory Framework of Accounting, December 1988   (20 marks)

5.4 You are chief accountant of a company with UK trading subsidiaries. Your managing director wishes to improve his understanding of two issues which may affect the accounts for the year ending 31 December 1988.

Firstly, he wishes to understand the implications, if any, of SSAP 24 on the results for the year. The group pension scheme is a defined benefit scheme and annual cash contributions in the year to 31 December 1988 were expected to be £1 200 000. Only two quarters contributions have been paid and charged to the profit and loss account.

An actuarial valuation at 31 December 1987 has recently been received. This showed that the scheme was overfunded to the extent of £2.4 million and that the group would be able to cease contributions for the two financial years following that date and thereafter contribute at a reduced level of £960 000 per annum for a further 10 years. Thereafter the regular cost would be £1 million per annum. The average remaining service life of employees in the scheme is 12 years.

Secondly, he wishes to gain a greater understanding of the tax charge in the accounts. In particular he complains that, while the corporation tax rate has recently remained constant, the actual tax charge for the group as a percentage of profit (the effective rate) has moved above and below this rate with disconcerting frequency.

Requirement
Prepare a memorandum for your managing director

(i) comparing and contrasting the effect on the results for the year ending 31 December 1988 of adopting SSAP 24 with other currently available accounting treatments for the pension costs;

(9 marks)

(ii) identifying the reasons why accounting for taxation may result in an effective tax rate which differs from the corporation tax rate. (9 marks)

ICAEW Financial Accounting II, December 1988   **(18 marks)**

5.5 Court plc has a defined benefits pension scheme for all its employees. Based on actuarial advice the company has previously made contributions of £2 million per annum to the pension fund, being 10% of pensionable earnings. The average remaining service lives of the company's existing employees is ten years and pensionable earnings will continue at their present level.

An actuarial valuation of the fund as at 1 January 1991 has revealed a surplus of £3 million (ie the actuarial value of the pension fund's assets exceeds the actuarial value of the liabilities). The surplus has arisen solely because the investment performance of the pension fund has been better than anticipated. The actuary has suggested to the company the following funding options:

(a) Reduce contributions from 10% to 7.5% for the next ten years; or,
(b) Have a one year pension holiday and reduce contributions to 9% in the following nine years; or,
(c) Receive a refund of £3 million now and retain the 10% contribution.

All of these options can be assumed to comply with the requirements of the Taxes Acts (including Finance Act 1986) concerning pension fund surpluses.

In advance of a board meeting, the finance director of Court plc wishes to consider the impact of the various options on the accounts of the company and has asked you to prepare appropriate analyses building up to the average annual profit and loss account charge in accordance with SSAP 24 under each option for the next ten years. Also for each option the finance director wishes to know the balance sheet effect, if any.

Requirements
Note: In parts (i) and (ii), ignore taxation and the interest effect in respect of pension contributions advanced or deferred.

(i) **Calculate the average annual charge to the profit and loss account of Court plc in respect of pension costs for the ten years commencing 1 January 1991 under each of the above options (a), (b) and (c).**

For each option, (a), (b) and (c), detail the balance sheet effects of accounting for pension costs.
(6 marks)

(ii) **Assume that Court plc follows option (b) above with effect from 1 January 1991 and that a further actuarial valuation as at 1 January 1996 leads the actuary to recommend reducing the pension contribution to 8% for 1996 only (with continuing contributions at 9%); under these assumptions calculate the profit and loss account charge for pension costs in each of the fifteen years commencing 1 January 1991, and the balance sheet provision at the end of each of those fifteen years. The average remaining service lives of existing employees can be assumed to remain at ten years.**
(6 marks)

(iii) Set out, in note form, the practical accounting and presentational considerations, including taxation, which you would recommend the board of directors to take into account when deciding on an appropriate course of action in relation to the pension fund surplus as at 1 January 1991.   (6 marks)

ICAEW Financial Accounting II, December 1991   **(18 marks)**

5.6 The Secretary of the pension scheme for Park Industries plc has written to you as the scheme's auditors indicating that he wishes to observe current best practice in the annual report as recommended in SORP 1. He enclosed the following information on the scheme for the year ended 31st March 1986:

(1) Balances

	£000
Employer's contributions	1 246
Employees' contributions	642
Transfers from other schemes	230
Dividends received (net)	2 196
Interest received (net)	217
Pensions paid	1 261
Lump sum benefits	576
Transfers out including refunds	650
Expenses	124
Cash balances	2 164
Overdraft	27
Accruals	37
Creditors	74
Due from employers	44
Tax recoverable	116
Debtors	81
Balance of fund on 1st April 1985	55 978

(2) Investments

	31st March 1986	
	Cost	*Market Value*
	£000	*£000*
UK gilt-edged securities	3 600	4 380
UK listed securities		
Ordinary stocks	33 290	49 665
Loan stocks	1 400	650
Overseas listed securities	7 400	9 675
	45 690	64 370

Market value of investments on 31st March 1985 £54 327 000

On 31st March 1986 the scheme purchased 6% of the ordinary share capital of Field plc, a listed company, at a cost of £600 000, which is also to be taken as the market value. This purchase has not yet been paid for or recorded in the books of the scheme.

In the year ended 31st March 1986 investments costing £4 550 000 were sold for £14 068 000.

(3) The rate of income tax for the year was 30%.
(4) Audit and accountancy charges of £20 000 will be paid by Park Industries plc.

Requirements
(a) **Present the information provided in a form suitable for inclusion in the accounts of the pension scheme for Park Industries plc.** (10 marks)
(b) **Identify the separate elements of a pension scheme's annual report and outline the objectives of each of those elements.** (8 marks)

ICAEW Financial Accounting II, December 1986 (18 marks)

6 Financial statements: form and contents

A6.1 The Accounting Standards Board has issued Financial Reporting Standard 3 which has 'the aim of moving the emphasis from concentrating on a single performance indicator to highlighting a range of important components of financial performance.'

Discuss how users of financial statements may be presented with an information set which is designed to present clearly the key components of performance.

CIMA Advanced Financial Accounting, November 1992 (updated) (15 marks)

A6.2 You are the finance director of RST plc whose last year end was 31 December 1992. Your managing director has been reviewing the financial statements of a competitor, JKL plc, whose year end was 31 July 1993, and has asked you to clarify certain matters.

You are required to write a memorandum answering the following questions raised by your managing director:

(a) 'JKL plc's financial statements are presented in a completely different way to ours. Why?'
(6 marks)
(b) 'What constitutes Discontinued Operations?' (6 marks)
(c) 'Why is a Statement of Total Recognised Gains and Losses included?' (3 marks)

CIMA Advanced Financial Accounting, November 1993 (15 marks)

A6.3

MEMORANDUM

To: Chief Accountant   From: Chairman
21 May 1993

Subject: **Accounting Article**

I have recently read an article in an accountancy magazine which stated that it is the economic substance of a transaction that should be reflected in the financial statements of a company rather than its legal form.

Could you please explain, giving an example, what this article is referring to. Please clarify what the current position is on this matter with regard to financial reporting.

You are required to draft a reply to the Chairman's memorandum.

CIMA Advanced Financial Accounting, May 1993 (15 marks)

6.4 Brachol plc is preparing its accounts for the year ended 30 November 1992.

The following information is available from the previous year's balance sheet: At 30 November 1991 there were credit balances on the share premium account of £2 025 000 the revaluation reserve of £4 050 000 and the profit and loss account of £2 700 000.

During 1992 the following transactions occurred:

1. One million shares of £1 each were issued in exchange for net assets that had a fair value of £3 755 000.
2. A factory property that had been revalued from £500 000 to £1 310 000 in 1990 was sold for £2 525 000.
3. A fixed asset investment was revalued from £1 305 000 to £900 000.
4. There was a currency translation loss of £270 000 arising on foreign currency net investments.
5. A warehouse property was revalued from £1 000 000 to £1 540 000.

A prior period adjustment of £1 350 000 was required which had arisen from a change in accounting policy that had overstated the previous year's profit.

The profit and loss account for the year ended 30 November 1992 showed a profit attributable to members of the company of £810 000 and a dividend of £675 000.

Required
(a) (i) Draft a note showing the movements on reserves as at 30 November 1992.
    (ii) Draft a statement of total recognised gains and losses to show the net deduction from or addition to net assets as at 30 November 1992. (6 marks)
(b) Explain briefly
    (i) the purpose of the statement of total recognised gains and losses; and
    (ii) the extent to which a user of the accounts will be better able to make decisions by referring to a statement of total recognised gains and losses rather than the statement of movements on reserves that is produced to comply with the Companies Act 1985. (7 marks)
(c) Explain briefly
    (i) the nature of the adjustments that would be required to reconcile the profit on ordinary activities before tax to the historical cost profit; and
    (ii) the possible use that can be made of such information by a potential investor. (7 marks)
ACCA Advanced Financial Accounting, June 1993 (20 marks)

6.5 You are the financial director of Pilgrim plc, a listed company. Your new group managing director, appointed from one of Pilgrim plc's overseas subsidiaries, is reviewing the principal accounting policies and is having difficulty understanding the accounting treatment and disclosure of assets leased by Pilgrim plc as lessee, of which there are a substantial number (both finance and operating leases).

Requirement
Prepare a memorandum for your managing director explaining, in simple terms, the basics of accounting for leased assets in the accounts of listed companies (in full compliance with the relevant accounting standards and the Companies Acts). Your memorandum should be set out in sections as follows:

(a) Outline the factors which can influence the decision as to whether a particular lease is a finance lease or an operating lease. (4 marks)
(b) As an example, taking the following non-cancellable lease details:
    – fair value (as defined in SSAP 21): £100 000
    – lease payments: five annual payments in advance of £20 000 each
    – estimated residual value at the end of the lease: £26 750 of which £15 000 is guaranteed by Pilgrim plc as lessee

– interest rate implicit in the lease: 10%
demonstrate whether the lease falls to be considered as a finance lease or an operating lease under the provisions of SSAP 21, explaining the steps in reaching a conclusion. (4 marks)

(c) Explain briefly any circumstances in which a lessor and a lessee might classify a particular lease differently, i.e. the lessee might classify a lease as an operating lease whilst the lessor classifies the same lease as a finance lease or vice versa. (3 marks)

(d) Explain briefly any circumstances in which the requirements of SSAP 21 with regard to accounting for operating leases by lessees might result in charges to the profit and loss account different from the amounts payable for the period under the terms of a lease. (3 marks)

(e) Draft a concise accounting policy in respect of 'Leasing' (as a lessee only) suitable for inclusion in the published accounts of Pilgrim plc and comment on the key aspects of your policy to aid your managing director's understanding. (4 marks)

(f) List the other disclosures Pilgrim plc is required to give in its published accounts in respect of its financial transactions as a lessee. (3 marks)

Note: Ignore taxation

ICAEW Financial Accounting II, December 1992 **(21 marks)**

6.6 Queen Ltd manufactures 'Magic' and to improve efficiency has scrapped all its existing plant and replaced it as follows:

(1) On 1st December 1985 Queen Ltd agreed to rent an 'Imperial Wizard' from Deacon & Taylor at a cost of £1 500 per month payable in advance. The agreement is terminable at three months' notice by either party.

(2) On 1st June 1986 Queen Ltd entered into an agreement with May for the lease of a 'Gandalf'. Terms included:
    (a) neither party could cancel;
    (b) Queen Ltd is to have responsibility for maintenance;
    (c) 6 instalments of £7 500 are payable half yearly in advance.

    The cash price of a Gandalf on 1st June 1986 was £40 000 and the machine is considered to have a residual value of £5 000 at the end of a 5 year life. The rate of interest implicit in the lease is 5.0% semi-annually.

(3) A 'Merlin' was bought on 1st September 1986 from Mercury Ltd. The price of £120 000 is payable in 10 equal quarterly instalments starting 1st September 1986. A Merlin is expected to have negligible value at the end of its 12-year life.

Other than the above items no amounts were unpaid at 30th November 1986. Queen Ltd uses a straight line basis for depreciation from the date of purchase.

Requirements

(a) Show how the above should be reflected in the financial statements, including the notes thereto, of Queen Ltd at 30th November 1986 in accordance with SSAP 21. The accounting policy note is not required. (10 marks)

(b) Discuss and explain the rationale for the accounting treatments in the standard. (10 marks)

ICAEW Financial Accounting II, December 1986 **(20 marks)**

6.7 Holmes Ltd, which has a year end of 30 September, is considering the replacement of its now outdated mainframe computer on 1 October 1988. The replacement computer has a cost of £2 120 000 and its useful economic life is estimated at 7 years. After negotiations with a leasing company, Duff Ltd, and other financial institutions, the directors of Holmes Ltd, have identified three options available to them for consideration:

Option A

Enter a 4 year lease with Duff Ltd for total lease payments of £2 000 000 payable in four equal instalments, the first instalment being due on day 1 of the leasing period. Under this arrangement Duff Ltd would have responsibility for upkeep and maintenance and has negotiated a guaranteed repurchase by the manufacturer at the end of the lease term. The interest rate implicit in the lease is 10%.

Option B

Enter a 4 year lease with the same rental payment arrangements as Option A, but at the end of four years, commence a secondary rental period which provides for 3 annual payments of 60%, 40% and 20% respectively of annual rental payments in the primary period. Under the terms of this lease, Holmes Ltd would be responsible for the maintenance and upkeep. The interest rate implicit in the lease is 10.25%.

Option C

Purchase the new computer outright by issuing sufficient £100 debentures at a price of £55. The debentures would carry a coupon of 2% and would be redeemable at par, 7 years after the date of issue.

Requirements
(a) **With regard to Option A, demonstrate whether the arrangement should be treated as a finance or operating lease in the accounts of Holmes Ltd.**   (4 marks)
(b) **With regard to Option B, calculate the amounts to be shown in the profit and loss account of Holmes Ltd for each of the years ending 30 September 1989 and 1990. Also calculate the amounts to be disclosed in the balance sheet at 30 September 1989 and draft the related notes thereto.**   (6 marks)
(c) **Identify the principles underlying the treatment recommended in SSAP 21 with regard to the accounting for finance leases in the books of the lessor.**   (5 marks)
(d) **Describe and assess the alternative methods of accounting in the books of Holmes Ltd for the financing arrangements outlined in Option C.**   (5 marks)

ICAEW Financial Accounting II, July 1988   **(20 marks)**

6.8 The accounting profession tackled the accounting treatment of off-balance-sheet transactions with the introduction of SSAP 21, Accounting for leases and hire purchase contracts, in 1984. This clearly demonstrates the importance the accounting profession attaches to the principle of 'substance over form'.

Requirements
(a) **Define the term 'substance over form' and relate this to the provisions of SSAP 21.** (3 marks)
(b) **Discuss the main accounting issues raised by two other forms of off-balance-sheet transactions.**   (4 marks)
(c) **Briefly discuss the arguments for and against the adoption of 'substance over form' when preparing financial statements.**   (3 marks)

ICAEW Financial Reporting, November 1993   **(10 marks)**

7 Taxation

A7.1 How should you treat the following items when preparing financial statements in accordance with statements of standard accounting practice:

(i)   franked investment income,   (3 marks)
(ii) proposed dividends and the related advance corporation tax,   (2 marks)

(iii) recoverable advance corporation tax,   (2 marks)
(iv) irrecoverable advance corporation tax,   (2 marks)
(v) value added output tax on turnover for a VAT registered trader,   (2 marks)
(vi) irrecoverable value added input tax on a fixed asset, purchased by a VAT
     registered trader,   (2 marks)
(vii) the receipt and payment of VAT to the Customs and Excise?   (2 marks)

ACCA Level 2 The Regulatory Framework of Accounting, December 1985   **(15 marks)**

A7.2 In connection with SSAP 15 *Accounting for Deferred Taxation*:

(a) Write a description of accounting for deferred taxation which includes all of the main items in the Standard. The description should be appropriate for inclusion in the statement of accounting policies in a company's annual financial report, in accordance with SSAP 2 *Disclosure of Accounting Policies*.   (6 marks)
(b) Prepare an example of a note on deferred taxation which includes all of the main items in the Standard. The note should be appropriate for inclusion in a company's financial statements and you should use your own figures to illustrate your answer. (You need not show comparative figures and you may assume that the company is not part of a group of companies.) (8 marks)
(c) Do you consider that the liability method adopts a balance sheet rather than a profit and loss account perspective? Contrast this with the deferral method. State your reasons.   (6 marks)

ACCA Level 2 The Regulatory Framework of Accounting, June 1989   **(20 marks)**

7.3 Gourmet Ltd is a small family-controlled company in the catering trade which was incorporated in 1987. You are advised that the profit for the year ended 31 July 1989 amounted to £98 000 after including dividends received of £4 000 (gross) but before taxation and before an extraordinary profit of £56 000 arising on the disposal of property.

The directors advise you that in addition to the interim dividend of £20 000 paid on 1 March 1989 it is proposed to pay a final dividend of £75 000 on 1 December 1989.

Shortly after the financial year end a fire in the kitchens caused considerable damage to the company's premises. The directors have indicated that it may take some time before renovations can be completed and this is likely to have a significant adverse effect on the current year's results.

Requirement
Prepare a memorandum to the directors:
(i) **describing the general accounting treatment of, and necessary disclosure requirements for, corporation tax and advance corporation tax in a company's financial statements; and**
(ii) **drafting the appropriate taxation notes for inclusion in the financial statements of Gourmet Ltd for the year ended 31 July 1989.**

Note: Assume the rates of corporation tax and advance corporation tax to be 35% and 25/75 respectively. Ignore deferred taxation.

ICAEW Financial Accounting I, November 1989   **(10 marks)**

7.4 The draft accounts of Orchaos plc have been prepared as at 31 December 1992 and showed a profit of £28m.

The fixed assets had a net book value of £138.6m and consisted of offices, new plant and equipment. The offices had been acquired on 1 January 1992 under a 20 year lease for £30m. The new plant had been acquired on 1 January 1992 for £10m and the company had received a government grant of £2.5m which it has credited to the plant fixed asset account. The equipment had been acquired in earlier years at a cost of £130m and had a written-down value of £102.9m at 31 December 1992. The company planned to undertake substantial further investment in fixed assets in 1997.

Capital allowances of £35.4m have been allowed. The offices did not qualify for any tax allowances. The new plant had an estimated useful life of 25 years and qualified for a 25% writing-down allowance on the net cost.

The company prepared the following estimates for the four years ended 31 December 1996:

Year ended 31 December	Depreciation	Capital allowances
	£m	£m
1993	11.0	18.92
1994	19.8	12.32
1995	19.8	10.12
1996	17.6	14.84

Assume a corporation tax rate of 35%.

Required
(a) Explain
  (i)   the extent to which tax deferred or accelerated by the effect of timing differences should be accounted for; and
  (ii) the procedure for determining the amount to be quantified.   (6 marks)
(b) (i)   Prepare the balance sheet entry for Orchaos plc as at 31 December 1992 for deferred taxation to comply with the provisions of SSAP 15 'Accounting for Deferred Taxation'.
  (ii) Explain the effect on the deferred tax computation for Orchaos plc as at 31 December 1992 if the company has suffered its first loss following a year in which it had incurred substantial costs in relocating with the result that the accounts showed a loss adjusted for tax purposes of £28m.   (14 marks)
(c) Assuming that the new plant attracted a 25% writing-down allowance on the full cost of £10m:
  (i)   Explain how this would affect the calculation of deferred tax; and
  (ii) Calculate the tax effect of the timing difference as at 31 December 1992.   (4 marks)
(d) Critically discuss the statement that SSAP 15 Deferred Taxation does not necessarily result in the accounts of different companies in the same industry being comparable   (6 marks)

ACCA Advanced Financial Accounting, June 1993   (**30 marks**)

7.5 Partial plc was a company that manufactured replacement keys. It had started with the manufacture of replacement metal keys for antique boxes where the original keys had been lost and had become recognised as specialists within this field. Their expertise has since extended to the provision of electronic, as well as mechanical, entry devices. This has resulted in the need for an ongoing capital asset investment programme. The draft profit and loss account for the year ended 30 November 1990 showed a pre-tax profit of £375 000 and it was forecast that the profit for 1991 would increase by 20% to £450 000.

The following information was available concerning the company's fixed assets as at 30 November 1990:

	£
Gross cost of fixed assets	1 000 000
Accumulated depreciation	400 000
Capital allowances	525 000

The following forecast information was available as at 30 November 1990 relating to depreciation charges and capital allowances for the next five years based on the assumption that they go ahead with the capital investment programme.

Year ending	Depreciation charge	Capital allowances
	£	£
30.11.91	234 000	265 000
30.11.92	253 000	303 000
30.11.93	276 000	193 000
30.11.94	278 000	192 000
30.11.95	248 000	262 000

The forecast depreciation charge of £234 000 and capital allowance of £265 000 were amended in the accounts prepared for the year ended 30 November 1991 to £250 000 and £289 000 respectively.

The following forecast information was available as at 30 November 1991 relating to depreciation charges and capital allowances for the next five years:

Year ending	Depreciation charge	Capital allowances
	£	£
30.11.92	250 000	289 000
30.11.93	278 000	197 000
30.11.94	275 000	193 000
30.11.95	253 000	265 000
30.11.96	254 000	278 000

Assume a corporation tax rate of 35%.

Required

(a) (i) Explain why permanent differences are not treated in the same way as timing differences in calculating a deferred taxation provision; and

(ii) State the requirements set out in SSAP 15 'Accounting for Deferred Tax' relating to the disclosure of the deferred taxation provision in the balance sheet; and

(iii) Explain how the deferred tax provision should be calculated for inclusion in the balance sheet. (12 marks)

(b) (i) Prepare the balance sheet entry for Partial plc as at 30 November 1990 for deferred tax to comply with the provisions of SSAP 15 'Accounting for Deferred Tax'.)

(ii) Prepare the profit and loss account and balance sheet entries for deferred taxation for Partial plc for the year ended 30 November 1991 to comply with the provisions of SSAP 15 'Accounting for Deferred Tax'. (12 marks)

(c) Discuss how the revaluation of fixed assets on which capital allowances are received could be dealt with when calculating the deferred taxation provision. (6 marks)

CACA Advanced Financial Accounting, December 1991 (30 marks)

8 Business combinations and goodwill

A8.1 In connection with merger accounting:

(a) Under what circumstances may a business combination be accounted for as a merger? (6 marks)

(b) What are the differences between acquisition and merger accounting, as may be seen from a consolidated balance sheet? (6 marks)

(c) The balance sheet of Beta plc at 31 December was:

	£
Ordinary share capital (nominal £1)	200
Revaluation reserve	250
Profit and loss account	350
	800
Net assets (at fair values)	800

Alpha plc merges with Beta plc and Alpha plc issues 800 ordinary shares (nominal value 5p) to acquire 200 shares in Beta plc.

(i)   Calculate the merger reserve.

(ii) Under what circumstances could this merger reserve be regarded as realised and available for distribution to Alpha plc's shareholders?   (8 marks)

ACCA The Regulatory Framework of Accounting, June 1993   **(20 marks)**

A8.2 Mr Bruno is the managing director and the sole shareholder of your client, Carpenter Ltd, a relatively small engineering company. Mr Bruno is considering the potential acquisition of Tyson Ltd ('Tyson'), a company of similar size and activities which is extremely profitable.

Carpenter Ltd has cash in the bank which will be used to satisfy approximately 80% of the purchase price for Tyson. Mr Bruno is undecided whether to finance the additional 20% by bank borrowings or by the issue of new shares in Carpenter Ltd to the vendor of Tyson. The latter course of action would dilute Mr Bruno's holding to approximately 70% of the enlarged group.

Mr Bruno wishes to ascertain the accounting and related factors that he should take into account in assessing the alternative forms of consideration. He is particularly concerned that, on the basis of the latest statutory accounts of Tyson, the proposed purchase price would give rise to goodwill approximating 40% of the existing shareholders' funds of Carpenter Ltd.

Requirement
Write a report for Mr Bruno
(a) explaining the arguments for and against treating the goodwill that may arise from the proposed acquisition as an asset in consolidated accounts,   (8 marks)
(b) discussing the issues involved in the determination of the goodwill arising from the proposed acquisition, under both forms of consideration, and   (6 marks)
(c) identifying the other financial and business factors which he should take into account in deciding on which method to use for financing the acquisition.   (4 marks)

ICAEW Financial Accounting II, July 1988   **(18 marks)**

8.3 Barnes plc, a food processing company, is considering the acquisition of Ulyett plc, whose activities complement its own. The latest published balance sheets of both companies show that Barnes plc and Ulyett plc have net tangible assets of £100 million and £20 million respectively.

During the negotiations, both companies have commissioned reports on the market value of their patents, brands and other intangible assets, which are not included in either balance sheet. The values attributed in the case of each company were £10 million for the intangible assets.

The purchase consideration is likely to be approximately £35 million, raised either by a rights issue of ordinary shares, or by the issue at £75 each of £100 4% debentures redeemable at par in 5 years time.

Requirement
Prepare a memorandum for the board which:
(i)   presents arguments for and against the inclusion of intangible assets in the balance sheets of Barnes plc and Ulyett plc;   (11 marks)
(ii) contrasts the effects on the balance sheet and profit and loss account of Barnes plc of the alternative forms of finance proposed for the acquisition.   (8 marks)

ICAEW Financial Accounting II, December 1989   **(19 marks)**

8.4 Your client, Grange plc, is a company whose fast growth in recent years has been fuelled by a number of acquisitions of other companies, usually for shares. You are to give a talk at the company's annual accountants' conference entitled 'To what extent should companies be able to choose between merger and acquisition accounting in respect of a particular business combination?'

Requirement
In preparation for this you are required to prepare notes setting out:
(a) **the principal advantages and disadvantages of merger accounting when compared with traditional acquisition accounting;** (6 marks)
(b) **apart from the factors you have considered at (a) above, which aspects you would advise Grange plc to concentrate on, and why, when considering how to account for any particular business combination; include consideration as to how users of accounts view the results, i.e. group accounts produced adopting either merger or traditional acquisition accounting.** (9 marks)

Note: You should assume that all the relevant merger accounting criteria have been satisfied in any particular instance; you are not required to detail or explain these criteria.

ICAEW Financial Accounting II, July 1991 (**15 marks**)

8.5 On 1 January 1989 Fruit plc acquired all of the issued share capital of Vegetables plc in exchange for shares in Fruit plc.

Shares in both companies have a nominal value of £1 each and a market value at 1 January 1989 of £5 for a £1 Fruit plc share and £2.25 for a £1 Vegetables plc share. The agreed terms were 1 ordinary share in Fruit plc for every 2 ordinary shares in Vegetables plc.

At 31 December 1989 the register of members of Fruit plc was correct but no entries had been made in the books of accounts of either company to record the exchange.

At 1 January 1989 the balance sheet of Vegetables plc was as follows:

	£	£
Share capital		
Ordinary shares of £1 each		765 000
Retained earnings		447 525
		1 212 525
Capital employed		
Fixed assets		
Freehold premises		573 750
Plant and machinery at cost	316 965	
Less provision for depreciation	127 500	
		189 465
Quoted investments at cost		140 250
Net current assets		309 060
Capital employed		1 212 525

At 1 January 1989 the quoted investments had a market value of £318 750; the freehold premises a market value of £828 750; the plant and machinery (which had an expected unexpired useful life of four years) a market value of £300 000. Vegetables plc advised that it was their regular practice to invest surplus cash on a short-term basis in quoted investments. Draft accounts prepared for the two companies at the end of their financial year on 31 December 1989 showed the following:

Profit and Loss Accounts for the year ended 31 December 1989

	Fruit plc £	Vegetables plc £
Profit before depreciation	568 310	437 070
Depreciation for the year	91 290	40 035
Trading profit	477 020	397 035
Profit on sale of investments	–	138 465
Profit before tax	477 020	535 500
Taxation	119 255	149 940
Profit after tax	357 765	385 560

Balance Sheets as at 31 December 1989

	Fruit plc £	Vegetables plc £
Fixed assets		
Freehold premises	1 657 500	573 750
Plant and machinery at cost	653 055	316 965
Aggregate depreciation	(276 165)	(167 535)
Net current assets	249 390	874 905
	2 283 780	1 598 085
Represented by		
Share capital		
Ordinary shares of £1 each	1 275 000	765 000
Retained earnings	1 008 780	833 085
	2 283 780	1 598 085

Required
(a) **Prepare draft accounts for 1989 for the consolidation on the basis that:**
  (i) **Merger accounting is applied.**
  (ii) **Acquisition accounting is applied – assume a policy of amortisation over ten years for any goodwill that arises. (Ignore any deferred taxation implications.)** (12 marks)
(b) **Discuss the bases for computing the asset values and reserves in the financial statements that appear under the two alternatives.** (8 marks)

ACCA Level 3 Advanced Financial Accounting, June 1989 (**20 marks**)

9 Intercompany investments

A9.1 The accountancy profession has developed a range of techniques to measure and present the effects of one company owning shares in another company.

Briefly describe each of these techniques and how the resulting information might best be presented.

(The Companies Act 1985 disclosure requirements are NOT required.)

ACCA Level 2 The Regulatory Framework of Accounting, December 1986 (**20 marks**)

A9.2 You are group financial accountant of a diverse group of companies. The board of directors has instructed you to exclude from the consolidated financial statements the results of some loss-making subsidiaries as they believe inclusion will distort the performance of other more profitable subsidiaries.

You are required to write a memorandum to the board of directors explaining the circumstances when a subsidiary can be excluded and the accounting treatment of such excluded subsidiaries.

CIMA Advanced Financial Accounting, November 1993 (15 marks)

A9.3 Fair value is a concept underlying external financial reporting.

You are required
(a) to explain why fair value accounting is required; (4 marks)
(b) to explain how the fair value concept is applied; (5 marks)
(c) to list three areas of application of fair value accounting. (6 marks)

CIMA Advanced Financial Accounting, November 1991 (15 marks)

9.4 On 1 January 1990 Bailey plc paid £6 000 000 in cash for 90% of the issued share capital in Maitland Limited. This was Bailey plc's first investment and it has decided, as a matter of policy, not to exercise a dominant influence over any company in which it invests. However, companies in which Bailey plc's interest, direct or indirect, is more than 50% are to be regarded as subsidiaries and consolidated accounts are to be prepared where appropriate.

Draft balance sheets for Bailey plc and Maitland Ltd as at 30 June 1990 are as follows:

	Balance sheets as at 30 June 1990	
	Bailey plc	*Maitland Ltd*
	£ 000	£ 000
Fixed assets – tangible	7 000	6 500
– investment in Maitland Ltd	6 000	–
	13 000	6 500
Current assets		
Dividend due from Maitland Ltd	180	–
Owed by Maitland Ltd	140	–
Other current assets	3 000	1 000
Cash	860	500
	4 180	1 500
Current liabilities		
Dividend payable	–	200
Due to Bailey plc	–	140
Other	1 000	2 860
	(1 000)	(3 200)
Net current assets/(liabilities)	3 180	(1 700)
	16 180	4 800
Share capital (£1 Shares)	12 000	3 000
Capital reserves	2 000	–
Profit and loss account		
– brought forward	690	1 000
– for year	1 490	800
	2 180	1 800
	16 180	4 800

Maitland Ltd has proposed a dividend of £200 000 for the year out of post acquisition profits.

Bailey plc now has the possibility of entering a major joint venture with a third party and various 'financing' options have been put to it by its financial advisers. These are:

(i) Direct investment by Bailey plc in the third party company such that Bailey plc will own 50% of the third party. The investment can be either cash of £5 000 000 (the third party's net assets upon investment will be £10 000 000) or 3 500 000 shares of £1 each.

(ii) Investment by Maitland Ltd in the third party. Maitland Ltd will issue shares to acquire 50% of the third party. Maitland Ltd will need to issue 2 900 000 shares for the £5 000 000 investment.

(iii) A cash payment by Maitland Ltd of £5 000 000 for 50% of the equity in the third party.

It can be assumed that the investment, in whatever form it takes, occurs as at 30 June 1990. Investments in cash will be financed initially by way of overdraft.

The third party will be heavily capital intensive and will incur high borrowings in the early years. It is for this reason that Bailey plc has restricted its investment in the third party to 50%.

The board of Bailey plc is considering how to structure its investment in the third party and has asked for your advice on the financial and accounting implications.

Requirement
Explain the effect upon the individual company and the group accounts of the various financing options, quantifying the effects with reference to the individual company and the group balance sheets as at 30 June 1990.

Note: Ignore taxation.

ICAEW Financial Accounting II, July 1990   (18 marks)

9.5 You are given the following information:

Profit and loss accounts for the year ended 31 December 1990

	ABC Ltd £000	DEF Ltd £000	GHI Ltd £000
Turnover	3 000	1 600	1 000
Cost of sales	(2 000)	(900)	(550)
Gross profit	1 000	700	450
Investment income	9	–	–
Administration expenses	(300)	(200)	(150)
Selling and distribution costs	(200)	(150)	(100)
Profit on ordinary activities before taxation	509	350	200
Taxation	(150)	(100)	(50)
Profit on ordinary activities after taxation	359	250	150
Extraordinary items	(50)	(30)	(10)
	309	220	140
Dividends – paid	(50)	–	(30)
Dividends – proposed	(50)	(100)	(50)
Retained profit for current year	209	120	60
Retained profit at beginning of year	800	350	190
	1 009	470	250

Notes:
(1) ABC Ltd acquired a 30% interest in the ordinary shares (and voting power) of GHI Ltd on 1 January 1988. At that date the retained profits of GHI Ltd were £100 000.
(2) ABC Ltd acquired a 60% interest in the ordinary shares (and voting power) of DEF Ltd on 31 March 1990.
(3) It may be assumed that the profits of DEF Ltd accrue evenly over time.
(4) The investment income of £9 000 in the accounts of ABC Ltd represents a dividend received from GHI Ltd.
(5) The stock of GHI Ltd at 1 January 1990 contained £100 000 of goods which had been purchased from ABC Ltd. These items had cost ABC Ltd £50 000 to manufacture.

purchased from ABC Ltd. These items had cost ABC Ltd £50 000 to manufacture.

(6) The board of directors has decided to include the full year's turnover of DEF Ltd in the 1990 consolidated profit and loss account.

You are required

(a) to show in working schedule format the adjustments needed to produce the consolidated profit and loss account for the ABC Group for the year ended 31 December 1990;   (30 marks)

(b to explain the composition of the retained profit of the ABC Group for the year ended 31 December 1990 in terms of the amounts retained by ABC Ltd, DEF Ltd and GHI Ltd;

(5 marks)

(c) to prepare in a format suitable for inclusion in the annual report of the ABC Group the consolidated profit and loss account for the year ended 31 December 1990.   (5 marks)

CIMA Advanced Financial Accounting, November 1991   **(40 marks)**

9.6 Bold plc the holding company of the Bold Group acquired 25% of the ordinary shares of Face plc on 1 September 1990 for £54 000. Face plc carried on business as a property investment company. The draft accounts as at 31 August 1991 are as follows:

Profit and loss accounts for the year ended 31 August 1991

	Bold Group £000	Face plc £000
Sales	175	200
Profit before tax	88	60
Taxation	22	20
	66	40
Extraordinary profit on sale of property to Face plc	13	
	79	
Proposed dividends	61	
	18	40

Balance sheets as at 31 August 1991

	Bold Group £000	Face plc £000
Fixed assets		
Tangible fixed assets	135	200
Investment in Face plc	54	
Current assets		
Stock	72	210
Debtors	105	50
Current liabilities		
Creditors	(95)	(20)
Overdraft	(14)	(100)
Net current assets	68	140
	257	340
Ordinary shares of £1 each	135	50
Reserves	122	90
10% loan	–	200
	257	340

On 1 September 1990 Bold plc sold a property with a book value of £40 000 to Face plc at its market value of £60 000. Face plc obtained the funds to pay the £60 000 by raising a loan which is included in the 10% loan that appears in its balance sheet at 31 August 1991.

Required

(a) Prepare

(i) **the consolidated profit and loss account of the Bold Group for the year ended 31 August**

(ii) relevant notes to comply with the requirements of SSAP 1 'Accounting for Associated Companies'. (8 marks)

(b) Explain *two* defects of equity accounting and the remedies that you would propose to overcome these defects. Please illustrate your answer with the data from the Bold Group. (4 marks)

(c) If Face plc issued 30 000 ordinary shares, each of £1 par value, to a third party on 1 September 1991, for a cash consideration of £4 per share

(i) explain any matters to be taken into consideration in finalising the 1991 consolidated accounts; and

(ii) calculate the carrying value of the investment in Face plc in the consolidated balance sheet at 31 August 1992 and comment upon any related items. (8 marks)

ACCA Advanced Financial Accounting, June 1992 (20 marks)

9.7 The draft balance sheets of four companies showed the following position on 31 March 1988:

	Pick Ltd £	Axe Ltd £	Crow Ltd £	Bar Ltd £
Fixed assets	711 370	284 150	177 750	76 730
Investments	262 950	–	1 000	1 250
	974 320	284 150	178 750	77 980
Current assets				
Stock	284 160	168 330	62 040	91 030
Debtors	889 350	214 700	98 340	144 650
Cash in hand	2 740	300	750	1 910
	1 176 250	383 330	161 130	237 590
Current liabilities				
Bank overdraft	149 630	36 340	118 420	3 610
Creditors	683 210	195 510	117 690	84 380
Proposed dividend	75 000	15 000	2 500	50 000
	907 840	246 850	238 610	137 990
Net current assets/(liabilities)	268 410	136 480	(77 480)	99 600
	1 242 730	420 630	101 270	177 580
Financed by:				
Authorised and issued share capital	500 000	150 000	50 000	100 000
Share premium	65 450	–	–	–
Revenue reserve	677 280	270 630	51 270	77 580
	1 242 730	420 630	101 270	177 580

You are given the following additional information:

(1) Pick Ltd subscribed for 225 000 shares of 50p each in Axe Ltd and 30 000 shares of 50p each in Crow Ltd at par when they were incorporated in 1982. On 31 October 1987 Pick Ltd purchased 55 000 shares of £1 each in Bar Ltd at a cost of £2.19 per share.

(2) Bar Ltd made a profit available for distribution for the fifteen months ended 31 March 1988 of £155 760. The pattern of Bar Ltd's trade is such that one third of its annual profits arise in the last quarter of the calendar year and the balance of the profit is estimated to accrue evenly throughout the year. The first three months of 1988 showed no increase in profits over the corresponding period in 1987.

(3) For the year ended 31 March 1988 Axe Ltd made a profit available for distribution of £64 350 and Crow Ltd incurred a loss, after taxation, of £7 320.

(4) The final and only dividend from Bar Ltd is included in debtors in the accounts of Pick Ltd but no account of the dividends from Axe Ltd and Crow Ltd has been taken in Pick Ltd's accounts.

Requirement
Prepare the consolidated balance sheet of Pick Ltd and its subsidiaries for the year ended 31 March 1988, together with your consolidation schedules.

Note: Ignore advance corporation tax.

ICAEW Financial Accounting I, May 1988   (24 marks)

9.8 At 30 September 1988, Grace plc had a 75% subsidiary, Barlow Ltd, and also held 30% of the issued share capital of its associated company, Hornby Ltd. Their summarised balance sheets at that date were as follows:

	Grace plc £000	Barlow Ltd £000	Hornby Ltd £000
Investment at cost in:			
Barlow Ltd	450	–	–
Hornby Ltd	210	–	–
Other net assets	1 690	1 000	800
	2 350	1 000	800
Share capital (£1 shares)	100	100	50
Reserves	2 250	900	750
	2 350	1 000	800

You are also informed that:

(i) Grace plc acquired its investment in Barlow Ltd many years ago when the reserves of Barlow Ltd were £500 000. The reserves of Hornby Ltd were £650 000 when Grace plc bought its 30% holding on 1 October 1986. No changes have taken place in the share capital of either company since Grace plc made its investments.

(ii) Grace plc's accounting policy is to amortise goodwill arising on consolidation over 20 years.

(iii) The following transactions have taken place during the year to 30 September 1989:
  – On 1 April 1989 Grace plc acquired a further 25 000 £1 shares in Hornby Ltd for £705 000 in cash.
  – On 1 July 1989 Grace plc sold its entire interest in Barlow Ltd for £1 100 000 in cash. The tax arising on this transaction was £83 000.

(iv) The draft results of the individual companies in the period since 1 October 1988 were:

	Grace plc Year to 30 September 1989 £000	Barlow Ltd Year to 30 September 1989 £000	Hornby Ltd 6 months to 31 March 1989 £000	Hornby Ltd 6 months to 30 September 1989 £000
Turnover	4 000	5 400	2 500	3 000
Profit before tax	400	320	300	340
Tax	(140)	(112)	(105)	(119)
Profit after tax	260	208	195	221

Profits for Barlow Ltd accrue evenly throughout the year.

(v) The results for Grace plc and Hornby Ltd do not reflect the disposal of Barlow Ltd or the information below:
  – Grace plc's directors have now indicated that £70 000 of costs incurred and charged by Hornby Ltd in its draft results for the 6 month period to 30 September 1989 related to the rationalisation of Hornby Ltd's operations upon it becoming a subsidiary. These costs should be provided in the balance sheet at 31 March 1989.
  – Hornby Ltd has now decided to write off a debtor balance of £40 000 of which £30 000 had been outstanding since 31 March 1989.

– The rationalisation and bad debt costs referred to above are all allowable for taxation.
(vi) Grace plc is a regular supplier to Hornby Ltd, and makes a pre-tax profit of 20% on the sales. Sales invoiced by Grace plc to Hornby Ltd in the 6 month period to 30 September 1989 were £800 000. As a matter of policy Grace plc only eliminated intra-group profit when Hornby Ltd became a subsidiary; deferred tax on related timing differences is not required.

Hornby Ltd held the following amounts of stock at the prices invoiced by Grace plc:

	£000
At 1 April 1989	200
At 30 September 1989	450

Goods invoiced by Grace plc to Hornby Ltd in September 1989 at £150 000 were not reflected in Hornby Ltd's accounts at 30 September 1989 as they had not been delivered to Hornby Ltd.

Requirements
(a) **Prepare the consolidated balance sheet of Grace plc at 30 September 1989 and the consolidated profit and loss account for the year then ended. Where applicable, assume a tax rate of 35%.**

(21 marks)

(b) **Outline the shortcomings of consolidated financial statements.**

(3 marks)

ICAEW Financial Accounting II, December 1989 (**24 marks**)

9.9 The directors of Brompton plc are considering whether to dispose of a part or the whole of the company's shareholding in Doulidge Limited, one of the company's two subsidiaries.

The draft balance sheets as at 30 June 1988 of the holding company and the two subsidiaries, Chieftain Limited and Doulidge Limited are set out below:

	Brompton plc £000	Chieftain Ltd £000	Doulidge Ltd £000
Net tangible assets	3 360	2 250	2 500
Investments at cost:			
1 000 000 £1 ordinary shares in Chieftain Ltd	2 240		
1 500 000 £1 ordinary shares in Doulidge Ltd	2 900		
	8 500	2 250	2 500
Share capital			
£1 ordinary shares	5 600	1 000	1 500
Retained earnings	2 900	1 250	1 000
	8 500	2 250	2 500

Brompton plc acquired its shareholding in Chieftain Limited on 1 July 1986 when its retained earnings were £280 000 and in Doulidge Ltd on 1 August 1986 when its retained earnings were £560 000.

Budgeted profit and loss accounts have been prepared for the three companies for the year ended 30 June 1989. These show:

Budgeted Profit and Loss accounts for the year ended 30 June 1989

	Brompton plc £000	Chieftain Ltd £000	Doulidge Ltd £000
Profit from ordinary activities before tax	2 200	820	1 344
Tax	1 025	402	415
Profit from ordinary activities after tax	1 175	418	929

The directors have been considering four proposals:

(a) Dispose of 1 500 000 £1 ordinary shares in Doulidge Ltd on 1 July 1988 for £3 640 000.
(b) Dispose of 1 500 000 £1 ordinary shares in Doulidge Ltd on 1 January 1989 for £3 640 000. Profits accrue evenly through the year.

(c) Dispose of 600 000 £1 ordinary shares in Doulidge Ltd on 1 July 1988 for £1 300 000.
(d) Dispose of 1 350 000 £1 ordinary shares in Doulidge Ltd on 1 July 1988 for £3 400 000.

A trainee accountant has prepared draft consolidated profit and loss accounts to illustrate the result if the company disposes of its total shareholding of 1 500 000 £1 ordinary shares. His drafts are shown below:

(a) Draft consolidated profit and loss account for year ended 30 June 1989 on assumption that the 1 500 000 shares in Doulidge Ltd *are sold on 1 July 1988.*

	Brompton plc £000	Chieftain Ltd £000	Consolidated £000
Profit before tax	2 200	820	3 020
Tax	1 025	402	1 427
Profit after tax	1 175	418	1 593
Extraordinary profit on sale of shares Note (1)	740	–	740
	1 915	418	2 333
Retained profit brought forward	2 900	1 250	4 150
Retained profit carried forward	4 815	1 668	6 483

Note (1)	£000
Profit on sale of shares:	
Sales proceeds	3 640
Cost of investment	2 900
	740

(b) Draft consolidated profit and loss account for year ended 30 June 1989 on assumption that the 1 500 000 shares in Doulidge Ltd *are sold on 1 January 1989 for £3 640 000.*

	Brompton plc £000	Chieftain Ltd £000	Doulidge Ltd £000	Consolidated £000
Profit before tax	2 200	820	1 344	4 364
Tax	1 025	402	415	1 842
	1 175	418	929	2 522
Less: Post disposal profit				464.5
				2 057.5
Extraordinary profit	740	—	—	740
				2 797.5
Retained profit brought forward				4 150.0
Retained profit carried forward				6 947.5

Required
(a) **Review and correct the consolidated profit and loss accounts prepared by the trainee accountant and include the appropriate taxation charge of £222 000 on the extraordinary item.** (9 marks)
(b) **Write brief instructions to advise him how to prepare a consolidated profit and loss account for:**
    (i) **the disposal of the 600 000 shares on 1 July 1988;**
    (ii) **the disposal of the 1 350 000 shares on 1 July 1988.** (9 marks)
(c) **Critically comment on the above disposals.** (7 marks)

ACCA Level 3 Advanced Financial Accounting, June 1988 (25 marks)

9.10 Wiltshire plc's draft accounts for the year ended 30 June 1993 disclosed profit before tax of £20m, on turnover of £310m, and net assets of £140m. Wiltshire plc had made the following acquisitions during the year ended 30 June 1993, none of which has been accounted for in preparing the draft accounts referred to above:

(1) The shares in Nightingale Ltd not already owned by Wiltshire plc were acquired by Wiltshire plc on 1 January 1993 for £10m – satisfied by the issue of 4m ordinary £1 shares in Wiltshire plc with a market value on 1 January 1993 of £2.50 per share. 25% of Nightingale Ltd had been acquired by Wiltshire plc in 1979 for £3m (in cash) when Nightingale Ltd's net assets were £8m. Draft accounts for Nightingale Ltd, which has been treated as an associated undertaking by Wiltshire plc since 1979, for the year ended 30 June 1993 are:

Balance sheet	*£m*
Net assets	12
Share capital	1
Retained profits	11
	12
Profit and loss account	
Profit before tax	3
Taxation	(1)
Retained for the year	2

(2) The Adam partnership's trade, assets, liabilities and undertaking were acquired on 30 June 1993 for £1.4m (in cash). The value of the net tangible assets acquired was £0.5m. In arriving at the purchase consideration Wiltshire plc took into account the Adam partnership's budget for the six month period to 31 December 1993 which envisages losses of some £75 000.

(3) On 1 April 1993 shares to the value of £28.6m (11m ordinary £1 shares, market value £2.60) were issued in respect of the acquisition of the entire issued share capital of Massen Ltd, a company with net assets of £12.5m (comprising share capital of £8m and accumulated reserves of £4.5m) at 1 April 1993. The shares in Wiltshire plc were initially issued to the shareholders in Massen Ltd. They were then immediately offered by Wiltshire plc's merchant bankers to the existing shareholders in Wiltshire plc by way of a rights offer (in proportion to their existing shareholdings) which was fully taken up. The shareholders in Massen Ltd thereby received a cash consideration (of £28.6m) for their shares from Wiltshire plc's merchant bankers.

Requirement
Write a report to the directors of Wiltshire plc detailing and discussing their accounting and reporting considerations and requirements in respect of the three acquisitions and in each case describe and explain the impact that accounting for the acquisition will have on Wiltshire plc's consolidated accounts.

ICAEW Financial Accounting II, July 1993   (20 marks)

10 Overseas involvement

A10.1 'The requirement in SSAP20, Foreign currency translation, to reflect exchange movements affecting long-term monetary assets and liabilities in the profit and loss account of an individual company can unduly distort profits and impairs the presentation of a true and fair view.'

Discuss this assertion, considering possible alternative accounting treatments, illustrating your discussion by reference to Bengal Ltd whose only foreign currency transaction was to borrow $30 million on 1 January 1985 repayable in full no later than 1 January 1992. The interest rate payable by Bengal Ltd is fixed for the term of the loan. Bengal Ltd's financial year ends on 31 December each year and profits on ordinary activities (before exchange differences) have risen steadily from £2.5 million in 1985 to £6 million (estimated) in 1991. Exchange rates have moved as follows:

	$/£ exchange rate		
	As at 31 December	Average for year to 31 December	
1984	1.30	1.35	
1985	1.45	1.30	
1986	1.50	1.45	
1987	1.85	1.65	
1988	1.80	1.75	
1989	1.60	1.65	
1990	1.55	1.75	
1991	1.80 (at 16 December)	1.90 (estimated)	

ICAEW Financial Accounting II, December 1991 (13 marks)

A10.2. Your managing director has been studying the accounts of two similar groups with overseas subsidiaries. He is puzzled by the different notes on accounting policies relating to foreign exchange transactions which read as follows:

Company 1 *'Overseas assets and liabilities are translated at the closing rates of exchange. Results for the year are translated at the average rate of exchange. Gains and losses arising in translation are dealt with in accordance with SSAP 20.'*

Company 2 *'The accounts of overseas subsidiaries are translated using the temporal method applied in accordance with SSAP 20. Results for the year are translated using average rate.'*

You are required to write a report for your managing director
(a) **explaining the concepts on which the closing rate and temporal methods are based;** (6 marks)
(b) **discussing the factors which will be considered when a group is choosing between the closing rate and temporal methods.** (9 marks)

CIMA Advanced Financial Accounting, May 1991 (15 marks)

10.3 Groups of companies with overseas branches and subsidiaries have problems in determining the manner in which their results are included in the consolidated and parent company accounts.

Required
(a) **Explain the two alternative methods of foreign currency translation now in general use, and distinguish the circumstances in which each is appropriately used.** (19 marks)
(b) **Give your views on the appropriateness of the two alternative methods of translating the 'foreign currency' annual accounts of an overseas branch or subsidiary.** (6 marks)

ACCA Level 3 Advanced Financial Accounting, December 1987 (25 marks)

10.4 Peach plc has a wholly owned German subsidiary company, Bremen GmbH, that it set up to manufacture food colourings that would satisfy European health regulations.
Using the information provided in the question below for Peach plc and Bremen GmbH you are required to:
(a) **Prepare, using the closing rate method**
(i) **a consolidated balance sheet for Peach plc and its subsidiary Bremen GmbH as at 1 December 1991;**
(ii) **a consolidated profit and loss account for the year ended 30 November 1992;**
(iii) **a consolidated balance sheet as at 30 November 1992;**
(iv) **a statement of movement on the group reserves for inclusion in the consolidated balance sheet as at 30 November 1992.** (22 marks)

(b) **The decision as to whether to use the temporal or closing rate method has been described as subjective and critical.**

Explain briefly why there are these two methods of foreign currency translation and the reason for them being described as subjective and critical.   (8 marks)

                    (30 marks)

The balance sheets of Peach plc and Bremen GmbH as at 1 December 1991 and 30 November 1992 were as follows:

		Peach plc		Bremen GmbH	
		1991	1992	1991	1992
		£000	£000	000DM	000DM
Fixed assets					
Plant at cost		42 000	42 000	28 000	28 000
Aggregate depreciation		11 200	14 000	4 900	7 560
Net book value		30 800	28 000	23 100	20 440
Investment in Bremen GmbH		7 000	7 000		
Loan to Bremen GmbH		7 000	7 000		
Current Assets					
Stock	Note 1	23 800	25 200	14 000	18 200
Trade debtors		13 720	14 000	13 440	14 560
Current account –					
Bremen GmbH		1 792	2 100		
Cash		280	93 072	9 800	29 680
		39 592	134 372	37 240	62 440
Less creditors due within one year					
Trade creditors		2 800	3 360	2 520	2 800
Current account – Peach plc				4 480	4 200
		2 800	3 360	7 000	7 000
Net current assets		36 792	131 012	30 240	55 440
Assets less current liabilities		81 592	173 012	53 340	75 880
Creditors due after more than					
one year					
Borrowings	Note 2			7 000	7 778
Loan from Peach plc	Note 3			17 500	14 000
		81 592	173 012	28 840	54 102
Capital and reserves					
Called up share capital		70 000	70 000	28 000	28 000
Profit and loss account		11 592	103 012	840	26 102
		81 592	173 012	28 840	54 102

Note 1 Peach plc sold goods to Bremen GmbH and there were unrealised profits in the stock held by Bremen GmbH as follows:

At 1 December 1991 unrealised profit was £1 400 000

At 30 November 1992 unrealised profit was £1 680 000

Note 2 The borrowings consist of a loan of 35 000 000 francs raised by Bremen GmbH on 1 December 1990 and denominated in francs

Note 3 The loan from Peach plc to Bremen GmbH is regarded by the parent company as a part of its net investment and is denominated in £s.

Consolidated profit and loss account for 1992

The draft consolidated profit and loss account of the Peach Group for the year ended 30 November 1992 has been prepared to the operating profit level incorporating the results of Bremen GmbH using the closing rate as follows:

	£000	£000
Sales		311 220
Stock at 1.12.91	29 400	
Purchases	102 200	
	131 600	
Stock at 30.11.92	32 620	
	98 980	
Depreciation	4 130	
Other expenses	106 148	
Gain on current account with Bremen	(448)	
		208 810
Operating profit		102 410

Exchange rates have been as follows:

On date investment was made by Peach in Bremen	£1 = 4DM
On date loan was made by Peach to Bremen	£1 = 4DM
On date of purchasing the fixed assets	£1 = 3.616DM
On date of purchasing the stock held at 1.12.91	£1 = 2.701DM
At 1.12.91	£1 = 2.5DM
At 1.12.91	5 francs = 1DM
The historical rate applicable to the profit and loss account balance at 1.12.91	£1 = 3.0DM
At 30.11.92	£1 = 2.0DM
At 30.11.92	4.5 francs = 1DM

ACCA Advanced Financial Accounting, December 1992

10.5 Howard plc acquired 2 100 000 ordinary shares of Kroner 1 in Pau Ltd on 1 January 1985 when the reserves of Pau Ltd were Kr1 500 000 and the exchange rate was Kr10 to £1. Goodwill was eliminated against the consolidated reserves on 31 December 1985.

The profit and loss accounts of Howard plc and Pau Ltd for the year ended 31 December 1992 were as follows:

	Howard £000	Pau Kr000
Turnover	9 225	94 500
Cost of sales	6 027	63 000
Gross profit	3 198	31 500
Distribution cost	1 290	7 550
Administrative expenses	1 469	2 520
Depreciation	191	2 100
	248	19 330
Dividends from subsidiary	315	
	563	19 330
Tax	195	7 570
Profit on ordinary activities after tax	368	11 760
Dividends paid 30.6.92	183	4 200
Retained profit for the year	185	7 560

The balance sheets of Howard plc and Pau Ltd as at 31 December 1992 were as follows:

	Howard £000	Pau Kr000
Fixed assets		
Tangible assets	1 765	38 500
Investment in Pau Ltd	305	
Current assets		
Stock	2 245	3 675
Debtors	615	1 750
Cash	156	9 450
	3 016	14 875
Current liabilities		
Trade creditors	(2 245)	(4 375)
Creditors falling due after more than 1 year		
Loan	(1 230)	(8 680)
	1 611	40 320
Capital and reserves		
Share capital in £1 ordinary shares	600	
Share capital in Kr1 ordinary shares		3 500
Profit and loss account	1 011	36 820
	1 611	40 320

The tangible assets of Pau Ltd were acquired 1 January 1985 and are stated at cost less depreciation.

Stocks represent six months purchases and at 31 December 1991 the stock held by Pau Ltd amounted to Kr 4 760 000.

Exchange rates have been as follows:

	Kroner to £1
1 January 1985	10
30 June 1991	10.5
30 September 1991	10
31 December 1991	9.5
Average for 1992	8
30 June 1992	8
30 September 1992	7.5
31 December 1992	7

In determining the appropriate method of currency translation, it is established that the trade of Pau Ltd is more dependent on the economic environment of the investing company's currency than that of its own reporting currency.

Required
(a) Explain briefly how it would be established that the trade of Pau Ltd is more dependent on the economic environment of the investing company's currency than that of its own reporting currency. (4 marks)
(b) Prepare the consolidated profit and loss account for the year ended 31 December 1992 and a balance sheet as at that date, using the temporal method of translation. (22 marks)
(c) Calculate the amount to be included in the consolidated balance sheet of the Howard Group as at 31 December 1992 if Howard plc had sold goods to Pau Ltd on 30 September 1992 for £14 000 which had cost £10 000 and which remained unsold at 31 December 1992 using
  (i) the closing rate method;
  (ii) the temporal method. (4 marks)

ACCA Advanced Financial Accounting, June 1993 (30 marks)

10.6 One of the frequent criticisms of SSAP 20, Foreign currency translation, is that exchange differences on net investments in foreign enterprises, and on borrowings which are a hedge, never pass through the profit and loss account.

Discuss the validity of this criticism and suggest a possible solution to the perceived problem.

ICAEW Financial Accounting II, July 1993   (13 marks)

10.7

(a) Newton plc, to whom you are financial adviser, is preparing its financial statements for the year ended 31 March 1992. It has two wholly owned subsidiaries:
   - An Italian company, Darwin SpA, which it acquired a number of years ago at a cost of 500m Lira. Newton plc incorporates the financial statements of Darwin SpA in its consolidated financial statements using the closing rate method. During 1989, Newton plc borrowed 1 000m Lira (repayable in 1999) to provide a hedge against the investment, which was then considered to be worth in excess of 1 500m Lira. The net assets of Darwin SpA at 31 March 1991 were 1 200m Lira.
   - A German company, Hoyle GmbH which it set up on 1 June 1991 at a cost of Dm 25m. Newton plc is to incorporate Hoyle GmbH in its consolidated financial statements using the temporal method. The exchange loss for the period is £52 000. Newton plc partially financed the acquisition of the shares by borrowing Dm 20m repayable in 1997.

In addition, Newton plc has a 15% investment in a Japanese company, Gamow Inc, which it acquired in 1980 at a cost of Yen 220m, financed by means of a Yen loan of the same amount. At 31 March 1992 none of the loan had been repaid.

The relevant exchange rates were:

	£1 = Lira	£1 = Dm	£1 = Yen
31 March 1991	1 000	–	230
1 June 1991	–	3.7	–
31 March 1992	950	4.0	290
Average – period to 31 March 1992	960	3.8	260

(b) The directors of Newton plc have asked your advice in respect of the following.

   For sound commercial reasons Darwin SpA is to change its year end to 31 January with effect from 31 January 1993. The consolidated financial statements will hence forward include results for Darwin SpA drawn up for the period to 31 January. The directors wonder which 'closing exchange rate' to use for the purposes of the 31 March 1993 financial statements for the Newton plc group – that at 31 January 1993 or that at 31 March 1993.

Requirements

(a) **For the year ended 31 March 1992 calculate, in accordance with standard accounting practice, the exchange differences in respect of the investments/borrowings in (a) above and explain the treatment thereof in both the company and the consolidated financial statements for Newton plc.**   (11 marks)

(b) **Prepare a paper advising the directors of Newton plc as to the accounting considerations to be taken into account in connection with Darwin SpA's change of year end; advise the directors of any appropriate accounting treatments for the purposes of the consolidated financial statements.**   (10 marks)

Note: Ignore taxation

ICAEW Financial Accounting II, July 1992   (21 marks)

11 Expansion of the Annual Report

A11.1 In connection with Financial Reporting Standard 1 'Cash Flow Statements':

(a) List the FIVE headings in the statement, give an example of the information to be included under each heading and state why this information might be useful to a reader.   (10 marks)
(b) State the purposes of a cash flow statement and explain its advantages as compared to a funds-flow statement.   (10 marks)

ACCA The Regulatory Framework of Accounting, June 1993   (**20 marks**)

A11.2 The Managing Director of your company has heard that the Accounting Standards Board has issued its first Financial Reporting Standard, entitled *Cash Flow Statements*, and has asked you as the company's accountant to explain certain aspects of this new Standard.

You are required to write a report to your Managing Director on this Standard on *Cash Flow Statements*, summarising

(a) its stated objective;   (3 marks)
(b) the required format for such Statements;   (3 marks)
(c) the meaning of each of the following classifications of cash flows:
 (i) operating activities;
 (ii) investing activities;
 (iii) financing.   (9 marks)

CIMA Advanced Financial Accounting, May 1992   (**15 marks**)

11.3 The finance director of one of your clients, a public limited company, has recently attended an accounting conference. At the conference it was stated that an objective of producing financial statements is to provide information so that users can assess the amount, timing and uncertainty of future cash flows of an entity. Your client is not convinced that the introduction of FRS 1, Cash flow statements, will help achieve this objective, despite the intention of the standard that cash flow statements will provide information on liquidity, viability and financial adaptability.

Requirement
Write a letter to your client discussing whether FRS 1 will assist a user's understanding of the liquidity, viability and financial adaptability of an entity.

ICAEW Financial Reporting II, May 1993   (**10 marks**)

11.4 The draft balance sheets of Christie Ltd as on 30 September 1992 and 1991 are given below:

	30 September 1992 £	30 September 1991 £
Freehold property, at cost or valuation	225 000	186 700
Plant and machinery, at cost	194 300	190 200
Fixtures and fittings, at cost	94 800	89 200
9.5% Treasury stock (at par)	40 000	50 000
Stocks	129 300	112 500
Debtors	126 800	145 300
Bank	87 600	–
	897 800	773 900
Bank loan	–	5 000
Bank overdraft	–	48 800
Creditors	132 700	91 700
Corporation tax	38 700	42 500
Advance corporation tax	8 100	5 300
Proposed dividends	24 300	15 900
Depreciation on plant and machinery	58 800	41 500
Depreciation on fixtures and fittings	31 400	22 700
Mortgage	138 000	174 000
Issued share capital	250 000	200 000
Profit and loss account	153 700	126 500
Revaluation reserve	38 300	–
Hire purchase liability (capital element)	23 800	–
	897 800	773 900

You also obtain the following information:

(1) The mortgage was taken out in 1991 for a period of five years. Interest and capital repayments are made monthly and during the year ended 30 September 1992 net interest paid to the lender was £13 200.
(2) Plant and equipment costing £30 400 was purchased half way through the year under a hire purchase agreement. Hire purchase interest of £1 900 has been charged to the profit and loss account.
(3) Interest on the Treasury stock, part of which was sold on 18 September 1992 at book value, was received on 1 January and 1 July 1992.
(4) Machinery costing £26 300, which had been written down to £5 900, was sold for £3 700.
(5) The proposed dividend for the year ended 30 September 1991 was paid on 1 February 1992. Corporation tax and advance corporation tax relating to 1991 were paid on the due dates.
(6) The company negotiated a short-term bank loan of £7 500 on 1 August 1991. The loan was repaid by six equal monthly instalments and interest charged to the profit and loss account for the year ended 30 September 1992 was £575.

Requirement
Prepare the cash flow statement and supporting notes for Christie Ltd in accordance with FRS 1, Cash flow statements, for the year ended 30 September 1992.

ICAEW Financial Accounting I, November 1992   (18 marks)

11.5 Wimborne plc is the holding company of an international trading group. The draft profit and loss account and balance sheets of the Wimborne plc group are as follows:

Consolidated profit and loss account	*Year ended 30 September 1993*	
	Note	*£000*
Turnover		112 430
Cost of sales		(58 583)
Gross profit		53 847
Distribution costs and administrative expenses		(31 456)
Operating profit		22 391
Interest payable		(1 350)
Income from fixed assets investments		175
Exceptional item	1	(2 500)
Profit before tax		18 716
Tax	2	(6 750)
Profit after tax		11 966
Minority interests		(1 545)
Dividends		(1 800)
Retained profit for the year	3	8 621

Consolidated balance sheets	*Note*	*30 Sept 1993*	*30 Sept 1992*
		£000	*£000*
Fixed assets			
Tangible	4	25 700	22 430
Investments		3 400	6 900
Current assets			
Stocks		19 773	17 702
Debtors		12 470	12 358
Cash at bank and in hand	5	10 125	5 100
Creditors due within one year			
Trade creditors		(23 365)	(25 592)
Dividend payable to shareholders		(1 200)	(1 100)
Dividend payable to minority		(350)	(325)
Corporation tax		(6 250)	(4 750)
ACT		(120)	(79)
Creditors due after more than one year			
Loans from banks		(7 500)	(11 850)
Deferred taxation		(4 300)	(3 094)
		28 383	17 700
Capital and reserves			
Share capital		3 000	3 000
Reserves	3	20 283	11 300
Minority interests		5 100	3 400
		28 383	17 700

Notes:

(1) Exceptional item

This arose on the disposal of the group's 25% interest in Ringwood Ltd. Ringwood Ltd had cost £4.5m in 1985 and was disposed of in the year to 30 September 1993 for £2m.

(2) Tax

The tax charge is made up as follows:

	£000
Corporation tax	5 500
Deferred tax	1 206
Tax credit on dividends	44
	6 750

(3) Reserves

Movements on reserves in the year ended 30 September 1993 were as follows:

	£000
Reserves at 1 October 1992	11 300
Retained profit for the year	8 621
Exchange gain on translation	1 762
Revaluation of property	(1 400)
Reserves at 30 September 1993	20 283

The exchange gain is made up as follows:

Fixed assets	2 117
Stocks	205
Debtors	158
Cash	140
Loans	(476)
Other creditors	(124)
Minority interests	(258)
	1 762

(4) Fixed assets

The depreciation charge for the year ended 30 September 1993 was £3 197 000. Fixed asset additions were £5 750 000.

(5) Cash at bank and in hand

This comprises:

	1993	1992
	£000	£000
Six month term deposits	7 500	5 000
30-day money market deposit	2 000	–
Current balances	625	100
	10 125	5 100

Requirements

(a) Prepare the consolidated cash flow statement for the Wimborne plc group for the year ended 30 September 1993, in accordance with FRS 1. State clearly any assumptions you make and list any further information which would be helpful. (18 marks)

(b) Briefly explain why the definition in FRS 1 of cash and cash equivalents has come under criticism. (5 marks)

ICAEW Financial Accounting II, December 1993 (**23 marks**)

11.6 You are given the following information for the AZ Group:

1. *Group profit and loss account for the year ended 30 June 1992*

	£ million
Net profit before taxation	382
Share of associated undertakings' profits	183
	565
Interest	50
	515
Taxation (of which £49 million attributable to associated undertakings)	137
	378
Proposed dividend	58
Retained profit for year	320

Profits retained	£ million	
in parent and subsidiaries	306	
in associated undertakings	14	320

2. *Group Balance Sheet at 30 June 1992*

	1992 £ million	1992 £ million	1991 £ million	1991 £ million
Fixed assets				
Tangible fixed assets		3 334		2 579
Investments – associated undertakings		1 536		1 522
		4 870		4 101
Current assets				
Stocks	1 214		972	
Debtors	1 861		1 705	
Cash	30		54	
	3 105		2 731	
Creditors: amounts falling due within one year				
Creditors	(1 340)		(1 082)	
Bank overdrafts	(647)		(240)	
Taxation	(165)		(140)	
Proposed dividend	(58)		(44)	
	(2 210)		(1 506)	
Net current assets		895		1 225
		5 765		5 326
Creditors: amount falling due after more than one year				
Loan		(419)		(457)
Provisions for liabilities and charges				
Deferred taxation		(77)		(126)
		5 269		4 743
Capital and reserves				
Called-up share capital		3 427		3 343
Reserves		1 842		1 400
		5 269		4 743

3. During the year, in relation to its operating activities, the AZ Group received £1 520 million from its customers and made the following cash payments:

	£ million
To suppliers	430
To and on behalf of employees	326
Other	227

4. During the year the AZ Group acquired 100% of the ordinary share capital of TR Ltd. This purchase was financed by £525 million in cash and 84 million ordinary shares of £1 each with a market value of £235 million. The following figures related to TR Ltd at the date of acquisition:

	£million
Tangible fixed assets	486
Stock	214
Debtors	130
Bank and cash balances	5
Creditors	(104)
	731

	£million
Share capital	280
Reserves	451
	731

5. During the year, additions to the tangible fixed assets, excluding those on acquisition, amounted to £324 million and there were no disposals of fixed assets during the year. Depreciation of fixed assets for the year amounted to £55 million.
6. Dividends of £110 million were received from associated undertakings during the year.
7. Interest of £40 million was paid during the year.

You are required to prepare a cash flow statement, using the direct method, for the AZ Group for the year ended 30 June 1992, including the notes to the cash flow statement suggested by Financial Reporting Standard 1.

Note: All workings should be shown.

CIMA Advanced Financial Accounting, November 1992 (35 marks)

11.7 The Chairman of DEF Group plc has flown in for a board meeting to be held tomorrow to discuss the group's draft financial statements. Following his review of the profit and loss account and balance sheet, he has called into your consultancy office with a draft copy of the group's cash flow statement, as shown below. He has left the remaining cash flow statement notes on the aeroplane and cannot obtain a replacement set at short notice. He has raised certain questions with you.

DEF Group plc
Draft consolidated cash flow statement for the year ended 31 December 1992

	£m	£m
Net cash inflow from operating activities		111
Returns on investment and servicing of finance:		
Interest paid	(11)	
Interest element of finance lease rentals	(7)	
Dividends received from associated undertaking	12	
Dividends paid	(15)	(21)
Taxation:		
Taxation paid		(17)
Investing activities:		
Purchase of fixed assets	(62)	
Purchase of subsidiary undertaking	(30)	
Sale of trade investment	11	
Sale of plant and machinery	25	
Net cash outflow from investing activities		(56)
Net cash inflow before financing		17
Financing:		
Issue of ordinary share capital	10	
Capital element of finance lease rentals	(25)	
Net cash outflow from financing		(15)
Increase in cash and cash equivalents		2

Notes to the cash flow statement:

1. Reconciliation of operating profit to net cash inflow from operating activities:

	£m
Operating profit	88
Depreciation	12
Loss on sale of tangible fixed assets	10
Increase in creditors	16
Increase in stocks	(10)
Increase in debtors	(5)
Net cash inflow from operating activities	111

The Chairman has raised the following matters with you:

(i)   The statement shows the purchase of the subsidiary as only £30 million whereas DEF plc paid £33 million for the shares of the subsidiary.

(ii) DEF plc's dividends, as shown in the profit and loss account, amounted to £12 million yet the cash flow statement shows £15 million.

(iii) Why are the finance lease rental payments split between servicing of finance and financing?

(iv) In the statement there is a figure of £62 million for the purchase of fixed assets but in the balance sheet our fixed assets additions are £70 million.

(v)   There is no mention of the effect of exchange rates on the group's foreign currency borrowings.

(vi) The statement does not show the loan DEF plc received from one of its 100% owned subsidiaries.

(vii) According to the balance sheet, the bank balance has increased by £0.9 million. This disagrees with the cash flow statement which gives an increase of £2 million.

You are required
(a) to prepare a report for the chairman of the DEF Group plc
    (i) giving a brief possible explanation of each of the matters raised in (i) to (vii) above, and
              (20 marks)
    (ii) providing any other information regarding the cash flow statement which you believe would
       help the chairman; (10 marks)
(b) to discuss whether the direct method would produce more useful information than the indirect
    method which is being used. (5 marks)

CIMA Advanced Financial Accounting, November 1993 (35 marks)

11.8 Fogel Limited commenced trading as a carpet manufacturer on 1 November 1986. The accountant decided to produce a value added statement with the financial accounts for the year ended 31 October 1988.

The draft manufacturing and trading account for the year ended 31 October 1988 showed:

	£000	£000
Material in stock at 1 November 1987	47.0	
Purchases	470.0	
	517.0	
Material in stock at 31 October 1988	47.0	470.0
Direct labour		470.0
Overheads		
Material	117.5	
Labour	352.5	
Depreciation	235.0	705.0
		1 645.0
Add: Work in progress at 1 November 1987		
Material	117.5	
Labour	117.5	
Overheads	23.5	258.5
		1 903.5
Less: Work in progress at 31 October 1988		
Material	152.75	
Labour	152.75	
Overheads	47.00	352.5
		1 551.0
Sales		1 645.0
Finished goods in stock at 1 November 1987		
Material	235.0	
Labour	235.0	
Overheads	235.0	
	705.0	
Cost of production	1 551.0	
	2 256.0	
Less: Finished goods in stock at 31 October 1988		
Material	305.5	
Labour	305.5	
Overheads	235.0	
Cost of sales		846.0
		1 410.0
Profit		235.0

The trainee accountant submitted an initial draft of a value added statement to the accountant as follows:

	£000
Sales	1 645.00
Materials consumed	481.75
	1 163.25
Cost of sales	928.25
Profit	235.00
	1 163.25

The accountant returned the draft with the following comments:

'Thank you

Please note that the statement has no heading and you have not submitted your workings to support the materials consumed and cost of sales figures.

Please redraft the value added statement to show:

Sales
Materials
Value added
Labour
Depreciation
Retained profit.'

Required
(a) Explain how the materials consumed of £481 750, and cost of sales of £928 250 were calculated in the initial draft.
(5 marks)
(b) Prepare a statement of added value in the format suggested by the accountant. Explain clearly how each figure is arrived at.
(5 marks)
(c) Calculate the ratio of employee rewards to value added and discuss how the ratio can be used in financial incentive schemes and wage negotiations.
(7 marks)
(d) Comment on the usefulness of value added statements to users of financial reports with particular reference to differences between industries.
(8 marks)

ACCA Level 3 Advanced Financial Accounting, December 1988   (25 marks)

11.9 Pitted Prunes plc merged with Rosy Plums plc and changed its name to Pitted Rosy Plums plc in June, 1987. The figures included in the accounts for the year ended 31 December 1987 included the results of both companies from 1 January 1987.

The financial highlights printed in the annual report showed:

	1987 £000	1986 £000
Turnover		
Pitted Prunes plc	46 434	43 354
Rosy Plums plc	110 420	78 050
	156 854	121 404
Profit before taxation		
Pitted Prunes plc	4 336	4 171
Rosy Plums plc	2 019	1 144
	6 355	5 315
Shareholders' funds	38 061	35 772

	Pence per share	
Earnings per ordinary share	19.6	16.8
Dividends per ordinary share (net)	5.9	5.12

The five year review showed:

Year ended 31 December	Pitted Rosy Plums		Pitted Prunes			
	1987 £000	1986 £000 restated	1986 £000	1985 £000	1984 £000	1983 £000
Turnover	156 854	121 404	43 354	40 959	34 832	25 209
Percentage exported	52%	49%	44%	45%	44%	38%
Operating profit	8 437	6 476	4 174	3 137	2 607	1 569
Profit on ordinary activities before taxation	6 355	5 315	4 171	2 667	2 208	1 205
Profit on ordinary activities after taxation	4 538	3 940	3 040	2 072	1 836	952
Dividends:						
Preference	287	289	285	124	77	77
Ordinary	1 288	1 601	625	454	403	330
Shareholders' funds	38 061	35 772	15 470	13 529	10 066	8 590
Earnings per ordinary share	19.6p	16.8p	22.6p	16.0p	14.4p	7.1p
Dividends per ordinary share	8.1p	7.2p	7.2p	5.3p	4.7p	3.8p

Required

(a) Explain the current requirements for a company to produce a five year summary with its annual report and the circumstances in which it may be necessary to restate the actual figures.

(5 marks)

(b) Discuss how historical summaries may be of interest and use to an investor or potential investor.

(5 marks)

(c) Discuss the adequacy of the five year historical summary produced for Pitted Rosy Plums plc and the minimum content that you consider desirable.

(10 marks)

ACCA Level 3 Advanced Financial Accounting, December 1989

(20 marks)

12 Capital reorganisation, reduction and reconstruction

A12.1 In recent years several large listed companies have purchased their own ordinary shares.

You are required to summarise

(a) the accounting requirements for a public listed company when it purchases its own shares;

(9 marks)

(b) six advantages of a company purchasing its own shares.

(6 marks)

CIMA Advanced Financial Accounting, November 1991

(15 marks)

A12.2 The Companies Act 1985 permits companies to purchase their own shares. Chest Ltd and Nut Ltd are both private companies and hold minority shareholdings in each other. Relevant information for each company is as follows:

	Chest Ltd £		Nut Ltd £	
£1 ordinary called up share capital	3 000	Issued at a premium of 50p	2 000	Issued at a premium of £1
Share premium account	1 500		2 000	
Reserves – profit and loss account	500		4 000	
	5 000		8 000	
Number of shares owned in Nut Ltd by Chest Ltd		800		
Number of shares owned in Chest Ltd by Nut Ltd		1 200		

The majority shareholders of both companies have decided that the two companies will be arranged in a group structure. If possible, when creating the group structure, the shareholders wish to avoid making a permissible capital payment and the parent company should be chosen accordingly. It is proposed that a new issue of 800 shares by the prospective parent company should be made in order to help finance the purchase at a price of £1 each.

Requirements
(a) For Chest Ltd and Nut Ltd determine which company is to be the parent; produce the revised statement of shareholders' funds together with journal entries necessary to effect the group structure; and describe the procedures necessary to effect the plan.   (8 marks)
(b) Discuss the principal reasons why companies may wish to purchase their own shares and the reasons for the provisions in the Companies Act 1985.   (8 marks)

ICAEW Financial Accounting II, July 1986   **(16 marks)**

12.3 Metal Fasteners plc is a listed company that distributes metal fasteners to the automobile industry. During the 1980s the company has experienced severe competition from an increasing number of small entrepreneurs who have been marketing a small range of products on low margins. In 1986 an additional threat has been created by a major competitor's decision to sell fasteners at cost in an effort to increase its market share. The major competitor is a subsidiary of a large conglomerate and for this reason the competitor is able to finance its aggressive marketing policy.

As a result of the pressure on margins, the directors of Metal Fasteners plc have seen the price of the company's shares fall from 230p on 1 January 1986 to 150p on 31 December 1986. As a consequence, there has been severe criticism of the directors from a group of shareholders holding 30% of the issued share capital. As part of the review of the corporate strategy for the company, one of the directors has suggested that the company should consider buying out the 30% shareholding by means of one of the following three methods:

(i) Purchasing the 30% shareholding at 150p per share out of reserves.
(ii) Purchasing the 30% shareholding at 150p out of the proceeds of the issue of new shares to a major supplier of Metal Fasteners plc at a price of 185p. These new shares would be equal in number to the shares being redeemed.
(iii) Purchasing the 30% shareholding, half out of reserves and half from the issue of new shares to a major supplier of Metal Fasteners plc at a price of 185p. These new shares would be equal in number to the shares being redeemed.

The following extracts have been made from the financial accounts of Metal Fasteners plc as at 30 December 1986:

	£	£
Trading profit		9 020
Loan interest payable		(1 000)
Income from investments		480
		8 500
Tax on profit for the year		2 500
Profit after tax		6 000
Dividend		2 000
Balance carried forward		4 000

Capital and reserves		£
Ordinary shares of £1 each fully paid up		20 000
Share premium		5 000
Revenue reserves		5 500
Profit for year		4 000
Capital employed		34 500
Represented by:		
Fixed assets		18 000
Stock	16 200	
Debtors	12 500	
Investments	3 000	
Cash	5 000	
	36 700	
Creditors	10 200	
Net current assets		26 500
Total net assets		44 500
Debentures 10%		10 000
Capital employed		34 500

Note: An overdraft would cost the company 10% after tax for interest.

Required
(a) **For each of the three methods suggested above, calculate the effects on the capital and reserves of Metal Fasteners plc.**   (11 marks)
(b) **Briefly discuss the advantages and disadvantages of a company buying its own shares.**
                                                                                                      (8 marks)
(c) **Briefly discuss the implications of each of the above three methods and advise Metal Fasteners plc which you would recommend.**   (6 marks)

ACCA Level 3 Advanced Financial Accounting, December 1987   **(25 marks)**

12.4 High plc acquired 60% of the issued ordinary shares of Low plc on 1 December 1989 at which date Low plc had a debit balance on reserves of £2 230 000. The directors of High plc expected to turn the company into profit by 1991. However, the losses continued and the debit balance on reserves in Low plc increased to £2 787 500 on 30 November 1990 and £3 791 000 on 30 November 1991. It was resolved to seek court approval to write off the accumulated losses of Low plc and to write down the plant and machinery in Low plc by £1 784 000 against paid up capital on 30 November 1991.

The balance sheets of High plc and Low plc as at 30 November 1991 immediately before the reduction are set out below:

Balance sheets as at 30 November 1991

	High plc £	Low plc £
Freehold property	14 495 000	–
Leasehold property	–	1 226 500
Plant and machinery	7 805 000	5 463 500
Investment in Low plc	5 575 000	–
Current assets	8 920 000	6 467 000
Current liabilities	(4 237 000)	(5 798 000)
Net current asset	4 683 000	669 000
Capital employed	32 558 000	7 359 000
Share capital		
Ordinary shares of £1 each	27 875 000	11 150 000
Reserves	4 683 000	(3 791 000)
	32 558 000	7 359 000

Required
(a) **Prepare the balance sheets for High plc, Low plc and the consolidated balance sheet as at 1 December 1991 immediately after the capital reduction. Show workings.** (7 marks)
(b) **Prepare an analysis of the losses of Low plc for consolidation purposes at 30 November 1990 and 30 November 1991.** (3 marks)
(c) **Explain how the consolidated reserves would be calculated as at 30 November 1992 if, although when the reconstruction took place, the subsidiary was expected to be profitable, in the event it incurred losses but High plc continued its support.**
   Illustrate your answer on the assumption that High plc increased its reserves by £1 600 000 and Low plc decreased its reserves by £6 000 000. (4 marks)
(d) **Discuss the legal and commercial obligations of a holding company to support an insolvent subsidiary.** (6 marks)

ACCA Advanced Financial Accounting, December 1992 (20 marks)

12.5 Contemplation Limited is a company that carries on business as film processors. For the past few years it has been making losses due to the low price competition.
   The company's balance sheet as at 30 June 1988 was as follows:

	£000
Fixed assets	3 600
Net current assets	3 775
	7 375
Share capital:	
Ordinary shares of £1 each fully paid	10 000
8% cumulative preference shares of £1 each, fully paid	2 500
Reserves:	
Profit and loss balance	(8 625)
Debentures:	
11% Debentures redeemable 1995	3 500
	7 375

The company has changed its marketing strategy and is now aiming at the specialist portrait print market. It is expected that the company will earn annual profits after tax of £1 500 000 for the next five years – the figure is before an interest charge. Corporation tax is assumed to be at a rate of 35%.

The directors are proposing to reconstruct the company and have produced the following proposal for discussion:

(a) To cancel the existing ordinary shares.
(b) The 11% debentures are to be retired and the debenture holders issued in exchange with
   (i) £3 000 000 14% redeemable debentures 2010, and
   (ii) £2 000 000 ordinary shares of 25p each, fully paid up.
(c) The 8% cumulative preference shareholders to be issued with 2 000 000 ordinary shares of 25p each, fully paid up, in payment of the four years arrears of preference dividend.
(d) The existing ordinary shareholders will be issued with 3 500 000 ordinary shares of 25p each, fully paid up.

In the event of a liquidation, it is estimated that the net realisable value of the assets would be £3 100 000 for the fixed assets and £3 500 000 for the net current assets.

Required
(a) **Prepare a balance sheet as at 1 July 1988 after the reconstruction has been effected and describe the legal process required.** (6 marks)
(b) **Prepare computations to show the effect of the proposed reconstruction scheme on each of the debenture holders, preference shareholders and ordinary shareholders.** (8 marks)
(c) **Write a brief report to advise a shareholder who owns 10% of the issued ordinary share capital on whether to agree to the reconstruction as proposed. The shareholder has informed you that he feels the proposals are unfair.** (8 marks)
(d) **In your capacity as adviser to the shareholder, write a brief report to the directors suggesting any amendments you consider advisable.** (8 marks)

ACCA Level 3 Advanced Financial Accounting, June 1989 (30 marks)

12.6 Medical Equipment plc was incorporated in 1970 to assemble medical equipment used in hospitals. The directors of the company had a major shareholding and were all engaged full time in the operational management of the company. The company had experienced operating losses and the directors believed that profit improvement depended on reducing labour costs. They accordingly decided to automate the assembly process by investing in the development of an automatic machine known as 'AutoAssembler'

The 'Auto-Assembler' was tested and developed in 1990 and by 31 December 1990 development expenditure of £157 300 incurred in the development of the 'Auto-Assembler' has been capitalised. It was estimated that its operational use would result in cost savings of £130 000 per annum before tax and that it could be made operational in 1991 for a capital outlay of £75 000. The directors had been building up a short-term investment during 1989–1990 to cover this capital outlay.

The production engineer estimated that as a result of automation an additional £40 000 investment would be required for working capital to meet the additional cost of higher specification materials.

In December 1990 the manager of the bank informed the directors that he wanted the overdraft reduced to around £75 000 from its present level of £270 480.

The directors immediately approached Mr Jeremiah, a partner in the accounting firm of Hard Reality & Co. who were the company's auditors. They believed in the potential profitability of the new automated assembly process and advised Mr Jeremiah that they believed that they would be able to negotiate long-term loan finance to clear the overdraft. At the request of the accountants the company produced the following:

(i) draft accounts as at 31 December 1990
(ii) additional information on assets and liabilities.

Draft profit and loss account for the year ended 31 December 1990

	£	£
Sales		2 008 000
Cost of sales		
Materials	1 398 800	
Labour	300 000	
		1 698 800
Gross profit		309 200
Distribution costs		(213 200)
Administration expenses		(129 000)
Profit before interest and tax		(33 000)
Interest		(51 600)
Profit before tax		(84 600)

Draft balance sheet as at 31 December 1990

	£
Fixed assets	
Freehold land and buildings	312 000
Plant and machinery	197 600
Development cost of 'Auto-Assembler'	157 300
Current assets	
Stock	302 400
Investments	52 000
Debtors	169 000
Cash	2 600
	526 000
Current liabilities	
Creditors	(303 240)
Overdraft	(270 480)
	(573 720)
Non-current liabilities	
10% debentures	(208 000)
Capital employed	411 180
Capital and reserves	
Ordinary shares of £1 each	425 000
Share premium account	42 500
7% non-cumulative preference shares of £1 each	260 000
Profit and loss account	(316 320)
	411 180

Additional information on individual assets and liabilities as at 31 December 1990:

	Going concern values assuming 'Auto-Assembler' does NOT become operational	Going concern values assuming 'Auto-Assembler' DOES become operational	Values realisable on liquidation
	£	£	£
Freehold land and buildings	385 000	385 000	385 000
Plant and machinery	123 500	88 400	44 200
Stock	292 400	254 800	200 100
Debtors	149 000	149 000	119 840
Investments	52 000	52 000	81 000
Development costs	–	157 300	–

The creditors comprised:

	£
Preferential creditors	34 700
Loan interest accrued on debentures	10 400
Trade creditors	258 140
	303 240

Trade creditors allow 60 days' credit.

The debentures were secured on the freehold land and buildings and were redeemable at par in 1997.

Mr Jeremiah was not convinced that the directors would be able to arrange long-term loan finance to replace the overdraft and was of the opinion that a scheme of internal reconstruction would become necessary. He requested one of his staff to draft a brief report to explain to the directors feasible ways forward.

Required

(a) Prepare a balance sheet as at 31 December 1990 on the basis that the company ceased trading on that date and explain its significance for the relevant parties. (5 marks)

(b) (i) Explain briefly the purposes of a scheme for reconstruction as it would apply to equity and loan stockholders. (4 marks)

(ii) Propose a scheme for the capital reconstruction of Medical Equipment plc.
Show your calculation of the loss involved in the scheme; state what you would do with this loss; calculate the working capital requirements of the company; calculate the possible additional equity capital that might be required.
Note: The revised balance sheet after the implementation of the scheme is not required. (16 marks)

(iii) Explain briefly to the directors how the scheme will be fair to all relevant parties. (5 marks)

ACCA Advanced Financial Accounting, June 1992   (30 marks)

13 Interpretation of accounts

A13.1 You have recently been appointed chief accountant of Oakbrook plc, a computer manufacturer with a number of overseas subsidiaries which have accounted for approximately 15% of the group turnover in recent years. The group has grown partly by acquisition and partly by organic growth. During the same period it has also sold a number of non-core activities.

The most recent acquisitions occurred during 1985, when Oakbrook plc acquired, for a mixture of shares and cash, a 90% interest in a well established and successful software house to complement its existing business. In the same year Oakbrook plc also acquired for cash an advertising company to promote the combined businesses.

The only significant currency effects on the results of the group were experienced in 1986 when the pound strengthened by about 20% against the major trading currencies of the overseas subsidiaries.

1986 also saw the introduction of a new range of computer hardware by Oakbrook plc.

The financial information regarding the group is summarised in the table below:

	1987 £m	1986 £m	1985 £m	1984 £m	1983 £m
Turnover	131.0	109.6	124.3	105.3	106.1
Trading profit	6.0	4.8	3.3	1.9	1.3
Interest	0.6	0.9	0.7	0.2	0.2
Fixed assets	18.3	16.7	12.2	11.1	10.8
Net current assets	5.1	3.0	4.1	3.8	3.4
Shareholders' funds	15.9	10.7	7.2	12.7	12.1
Share capital (average during year)	2.0	2.0	1.5	1.0	1.0
Earnings per share (p)	35.1	22.3	30.0	36.2	25.7

Requirements
(a) Comment on and suggest explanations for the trends in:
    (i)   gearing and interest cover
    (ii) return on capital employed
    (iii) earnings per share
    (iv) net assets per share   (13 marks)
(b) Outline the benefits and shortcomings of five-year summaries as a basis for interpreting a group's financial performance   (5 marks)

ICAEW Financial Accounting II, December 1988   **(18 marks)**

A13.2
Required
(a) Describe the current requirements for the disclosure of segmental information in the annual report.   (7 marks)
(b) Discuss the advantages and disadvantages to the users and preparers of annual reports of disclosing segmental data classified by:
    (i) Industry groupings.
    (ii) Legal entities within the group structure.   (9 marks)
(c) Discuss the importance of the disclosure of extraordinary items to the users of the annual report in addition to the operating profit   (9 marks)

ACCA Level 3 Advanced Financial Accounting, June 1988   **(25 marks)**

13.3 RST plc is considering purchasing an interest in its competitor XYZ Ltd. The managing director of RST plc has obtained the three most recent profit and loss accounts and balance sheets of XYZ Ltd as shown below:

XYZ Ltd

Profit and loss accounts for years ended 31 December	1990	1991	1992
	£000	*£000*	*£000*
Turnover	18 000	18 900	19 845
Cost of sales	(10 440)	(10 340)	(11 890)
Gross profit	7 560	8 560	7 955
Distribution costs	(1 565)	(1 670)	(1 405)
Administrative expenses	(1 409)	(1 503)	(1 591)
Operating profit	4 586	5 387	4 959
Interest payable on bank overdraft	(104)	(215)	(450)
Interest payable on 12% debentures	(600)	(600)	(600)
Profit on ordinary activities before taxation	3 882	4 572	3 909
Taxation on ordinary activities	(1 380)	(2 000)	(1 838)
Profit on ordinary activities after taxation	2 502	2 572	2 071
Proposed dividend	(1 600)	(1 693)	(1 800)
Retained profit	902	879	271

XYZ Ltd

Balance sheets at 31 December	1990		1991		1992	
	£000	*£000*	*£000*	*£000*	*£000*	*£000*
Fixed assets						
Land and buildings	11 360		12 121		11 081	
Plant and machinery	8 896		9 020		9 130	
		20 356		21 141		20 211
Current assets						
Stock	1 775		2 663		3 995	
Trade debtors	1 440		2 260		3 164	
Cash	50		53		55	
	3 265		4 976		7 214	
Current liabilities						
Trade creditors	390		388		446	
Bank	1 300		2 300		3 400	
Taxation	897		1 420		1 195	
Proposed dividend	1 600		1 696		1 800	
	4 187		5 804		6 841	
Net current assets/ (liabilities)		(922)		(828)		373
12% debentures 1995–1998		(5 000)		(5 000)		(5 000)
		14 434		15 313		15 584
Share capital		8 000		8 000		8 000
Profit and loss account		6 434		7 313		7 584
		14 434		15 313		15 584

You are required to prepare a report for the managing director of RST plc commenting on the *financial position* of XYZ Ltd and highlighting any areas that require further investigation. (Marks will be awarded for ratios and other financial statistics where appropriate.)

CIMA Advanced Financial Accounting, May 1993 **(35 marks)**

13.4 The new managing director of Olympic Group Ltd, a company in the sports goods industry, has asked you, as auditor and financial adviser, to analyse and give your views on the relative profitability and liquidity of its two wholly-owned subsidiaries Walkers Ltd and Runners Ltd, whose activities are the manufacture and sale of sports equipment and sports clothing, respectively. There were no intercompany transactions.

The following information has been extracted from the summarised financial statements of each company for the two years ended 31st March 1986.

	Walkers Ltd		Runners Ltd	
	1986	*1985*	*1986*	*1985*
	£000	*£000*	*£000*	*£000*
Profit before tax	2.1	1.4	1.9	2.3
Turnover	45.2	38.1	17.0	14.0
Depreciation	0.5	0.4	0.5	0.3
Cost of sales	38.4	30.5	11.2	9.4
Other costs	4.2	5.8	3.4	2.0
Tangible fixed assets	8.3	9.2	3.5	2.5
Stock	9.3	10.2	1.8	2.3
Trade debtors	6.9	7.2	10.2	6.3
Trade creditors	8.5	8.2	3.2	2.2
Borrowings				
Overdraft	3.4	6.7	4.6	2.1
Long term	2.1	1.8	0.2	–
Capital and reserves	10.5	9.9	7.5	6.8

Requirement
Write a report to the managing director analysing the results of each company and commenting on any significant trends, using not more than four relevant ratios as illustrations.

ICAEW Financial Accounting II, July 1986   (**18 marks**)

13.5 Max plc and Emil plc are two large public groups operating broadly in the same industrial sector. In particular both produce beer and related drinks and retail these through a large number of both tied and non-tied licensed premises.

An institutional client of yours has asked you to compare the financial performance of the two groups from the point of view of a potential minority investor. You have obtained the following financial information:

Profit and loss accounts for the year ended 31 December	Max plc		Emil plc	
	1989 £m	1988 £m	1989 £m	1988 £m
Turnover	4 300	3 625	3 750	3 225
Operating Costs				
Raw materials consumables, duty	2 200	1 900	1 700	1 575
Staff costs				
– remuneration and social security	635	555	556	500
– pension costs	36	32	–	–
Depreciation				
– owned assets	159	124	110	91
– leased assets	–	–	5	4
Rentals				
– property	26	23	25	21
– plant and machinery	10	8	30	25
Auditors' remuneration	2	2	1	1
Other operating charges	800	690	850	620
Investment income	(7)	(4)	(19)	(15)
	(3 861)	(3 330)	(3 258)	(2 822)
Operating profit	439	295	492	403
Related companies	42	36	–	–
Property disposals	30	30	45	15
Interest payable	(151)	(109)	(50)	(32)
Interest receivable	27	47	10	12
Profit before tax	387	299	497	398
Tax	(97)	(81)	(157)	(132)
	290	218	340	266
Minority interest	(45)	(15)	(10)	(8)
Extraordinary items	12	(40)	25	25
Dividends – ordinary	(95)	(80)	(80)	(65)
– preference	(5)	–	(1)	(1)
Retained for year	157	83	274	217

Balance Sheets	Max plc		Emil plc	
As at 31 December	1989	1988	1989	1988
	£m	£m	£m	£m
Fixed assets				
Intangibles	–	–	100	80
Tangibles	2 475	2 400	2 900	2 700
Investments	175	310	300	230
	2 650	2 710	3 300	3 010
Current assets				
Stocks	950	975	305	275
Debtors	575	560	380	330
Investments	–	–	120	70
Cash	90	90	25	20
	1 615	1 625	830	695
Current liabilities				
– overdraft and loans	(225)	(150)	(60)	(51)
– other creditors	(966)	(826)	(780)	(799)
	424	649	(10)	(155)
Total assets less current liabilities	3 074	3 359	3 290	2 855
Creditors due after more than one year				
– loans	(1 100)	(1 315)	(585)	(245)
– others	(70)	(74)	(115)	(95)
Provisions for liabilities and charges	(55)	(48)	(10)	(20)
	1 849	1 922	2 580	2 495
Called up share capital	215	185	93	90
Share premium	185	115	155	120
Revaluation reserve	877	925	1 040	1 050
Capital reserves	2	80	–	–
Profit and loss account	520	377	1 242	1 205
	1 799	1 682	2 530	2 465
Minority interest	50	240	50	30
	1 849	1 922	2 580	2 495

Both Max plc and Emil plc state in their accounting policies that acquisitions qualifying as such under the provision of SSAP 23 will generally be accounted for as mergers but that each acquisition will be considered on its merits.

Merger relief will also be taken by both groups where available.

Requirements
(a) Calculate for both Max plc and Emil plc the principal analytical ratios which a potential investor would expect to consider.   (9 marks)
(b) Using these ratios and the other information available to you, prepare a report for your client which compares the position and performance of Max plc and Emil plc. Pay particular attention to the impact of the groups' accounting policies and comment on any seemingly inappropriate policies.

State clearly any assumptions you feel justified in making in preparing your report and highlight in the report the additional information you would require to further advise your client.   (14 marks)

ICAEW Financial Accounting II, July 1990   (23 marks)

13.6 Travis plc is a large grocery retailing and wholesaling organisation. It is presently drawing up its financial statements for the year ended 31 October 1993 and, mindful of the requirements of SSAP 25, has drafted the following segmental report:

Segment information

	Turnover		Profit before tax		Operating net assets	
	31.10.93	31.10.92	31.10.93	31.10.92	31.10.93	31.10.92
	£m	£m	£m	£m	£m	£m
By category						
Retailing:						
Food	5 650	6 126	300	295	2 925	2 964
Drinks	1 951	2 047	219	136	987	917
Consumables	115	106	8	5	86	82
Wholesaling:						
Warehousing	3 843	3 651	391	382	1 560	1 490
	11 559	11 930	918	818	5 558	5 453
By activity						
Retailing:						
Hypermarkets	6 235	6 608	465	314	3 120	3 040
Large shops	545	534	43	40	560	538
Small shops	936	1 137	19	82	318	385
Wholesaling:						
Warehousing	3 843	3 651	391	382	1 560	1 490
	11 559	11 930	918	818	5 558	5 453

Notes:

Head office and service costs of £53m (1992: £51m) have been allocated according to the relative contribution of each segment to the total of continuing operations.

The group's borrowing requirements are centrally managed and so interest expense of £475m (1992: £415m) has been apportioned on the basis of average net assets for each segment.

Operating net assets represent the group's net assets adjusted to exclude interest bearing operating assets and liabilities.

Businesses discontinued during the year contributed £450m (1992: £850m) to turnover and £38m (1992: £68m) to profit before tax.

Requirements
(a) **Discuss the objectives of segmental reporting in the context of each of the following user groups of financial statements:**
    (i) **the shareholder group**
    (ii) **the investment analyst group**
    (iii) **the lender/creditor group**
    (iv) **Government** (10 marks)
(b) **Critically assess the presentation of Travis plc's draft 'Segment information' report, considering in particular its helpfulness to users of financial statements and its compliance with the requirements of SSAP 25. Outline any ways in which the information might be presented more effectively or in which the treatment of items might be improved.** (11 marks)

ICAEW Financial Accounting II, December 1993 (**21 marks**)

14 The valuation of securities and businesses

A14.1 The valuation of unlisted shares is highly subjective, especially when the object is to fix a fair price for acquisition by the company or by the owner's fellow-shareholders.

You are required
(a) to set out the principal bases commonly used for valuing unlisted shares, distinguishing the situations in which such bases are most appropriate; and   (9 marks)
(b to evaluate critically the theoretical soundness of the said bases of valuation, and the extent to which they achieve approximate justice as between buyer and seller.   (7 marks)

ACCA Advanced Financial Accounting, Second paper, December 1983   **(16 marks)**

A14.2 Charles Moon, the managing director of your client Neptune plc, is negotiating with a view to Neptune plc acquiring the entire share capital of Sirius Group Ltd ('Sirius').

He has informed you that Sirius is the parent company of a diversified manufacturing group with overseas interests, and that he is considering making an offer at a price equivalent to the consolidated net assets disclosed by the most recent statutory accounts of Sirius as at 30 June 1987. He is also contemplating offering additional but deferred consideration based upon profits for the year ending 30 June 1988 as disclosed by the statutory accounts for that year.

Requirement
Prepare a report for Charles Moon to brief him on:
(a) four principal areas of accounting policy that could have a significant impact on the accounts of Sirius and thus on the total consideration to be paid;   (8 marks)
(b) the usefulness and limitations of using statutory accounts as the basis for determining the amounts of both the initial and the deferred consideration for Sirius.   (10 marks)

ICAEW Financial Accounting II, December 1987   **(18 marks)**

14.3 Look Ahead & Co were instructed to value as at 31 December 1992 a minority holding of 10 000 25p shares in Arbor Ltd held by D Dodd who is considering disposing of his shareholding.

Arbor Ltd is a private company with an issued share capital of £125 000. The shareholdings are as follows:

Shareholder	Shareholding
A Arny	61 250
B Brady	30 000
D Brady	20 000
E Brady	11 250
D Dodd	2 500

The following are extracts from the profit and loss accounts of Arbor Ltd for the four years ended 31 December 1992:

	1989 £000	1990 £000	1991 £000	1992 £000
Sales	4 200	5 600	8 470	11 700
Cost of sales	1 825	2 920	5 205	7 810
Gross profit	2 375	2 680	3 265	3 890
Administration expenses	900	1 000	1 200	1 400
Distribution costs	1 345	1 500	1 800	2 100
Profit before tax	130	180	265	390
Taxation	40	60	90	136
Profit after tax	90	120	175	254
Ordinary dividend	21.6	22.7	23.8	25.0

The following additional information is available:

The gross dividend yields on quoted companies operating in the same sector were 12% and the firm estimated that this yield should be increased to 18% to allow for lack of marketability.

Assume an income tax rate of 25%.

Required
(a) Discuss the relevance of dividends in the valuation of D Dodd's shareholding on the assumption that it is sold to his son W Dodd. Illustrate your answer from the data given in the question.

(4 marks)

(b) Explain briefly the factors that the firm would take into account when
   (i) estimating the future net dividends;
   (ii) estimating the investor's required gross yield.

(8 marks)

(c) Explain how the approach adopted by the firm when valuing a minority interest might be influenced by the size of the shareholding or its relative importance to the other shareholdings.

(8 marks)

ACCA Advanced Financial Accounting, June 1993

(20 marks)

14.4 One of your clients, Mr Sprouse, has approached you to advise on the purchase of 7 000 £1 ordinary shares in Spicey Limited, a private company engaged in wholesale confectionery.

The shares are being offered for sale by Mr Pearcey a shareholder in Spicey Limited who wishes to dispose of his interest and retire to Spain. Mr Pearcey is 64 and has worked as marketing manager for the company for the past 22 years. Mr Bassett, a director, is not interested in acquiring the shares.

Mr Pearcey has asked for £120 per share.

The profit and loss accounts of Spicey Limited for the years ended 31 March 1984–88 are shown below:

	1984	1985	1986	1987	1988
	£000	£000	£000	£000	£000
Turnover	5 772	9 113	8 749	12 825	15 376
Operating profit	215	1 723	673	725	848
Interest payable	94	192	185	159	234
Profit before tax	121	1 531	488	566	614
Tax	–	–	72	7	26
Profit after tax	121	1 531	416	559	588
Directors' remuneration	100	120	135	150	180

The following information has been obtained:

(i)   The remuneration paid to directors is made to the following: Mr Bassett £180 000;
      A more normal salary for his job specification would be £40 000.
(ii) The company operates from a warehouse that is owned by Tartan Limited a company of which Mr Bassett is the principal shareholder. The only charge made to the company by Tartan Limited is £12 000 to cover the cost of insurance on the premises.
(iii) Two comparable quoted companies are showing a return on net capital employed of 15% and 20% after tax. Their operations are similar except that they both pay a commercial rent for their premises of £50 000 per annum. Their respective price earnings ratios are 7 and 10.
(iv) Corporate tax rate is 35%.

The balance sheet of Spicey Limited as at 31 March 1988, is shown below:

Balance Sheet as at 31 March 1988

	£000	£000
Share capital		35
Revenue reserves		5 217
		5 252
Fixed assets		5 620
Current assets		
Stock	432	
Debtors	4 069	
Cash	–	
	4 501	
Current liabilities		
Creditors	3 796	
Bank overdraft	1 073	
	4 869	
Net assets		(368)
		5 252

The register of members shows that the shareholdings are held as follows:

	Ordinary shares of £1 each
Mr G. Bassett	21 000
Miss M. Bassett	6 000
J. Bassett (Junior)	1 000
M. Pearcey	7 000
	35 000

Required

(a) **Calculate the value of the shareholding on:**
  (i) **An earnings basis;**
  (ii) **A net asset basis.** (9 marks)

(b) **Comment on the relevance of these bases in this particular instance and offer whatever further advice you consider relevant.** (9 marks)

(c) **Write a brief report to advise Mr Sprouse on the offer.** (7 marks)

ACCA Level 3 Advanced Financial Accounting, December 1988 (**25 marks**)

14.5 You act in the capacity of financial adviser to a number of companies. One of them, Fig plc, whose managing director is not familiar with finance, has asked you to explain some financial terms which he does not understand and has also asked you to assist him in obtaining certain information. An extract of the letter received from the managing director of Fig plc is as follows:

'I should be grateful if you would briefly explain the following matters:

(1) For ordinary shares quoted in the *Financial Times*, the following particulars:

Company	Price	+ or –	Dividend Net	Cover	Yield Gross	P/E
x	x	x	x	x	x	x

(2) This extract from the quotations page of the *Financial Times*:
"Price/earnings ratios are calculated on 'net' distribution basis …; bracketed figures indicate 10 per cent or more difference if calculated on 'nil' distribution. Covers are based on 'maximum' distribution."

In addition could you please inform me where I might obtain the following information:
(a) daily share prices for any share quoted on The Stock Exchange, London.

(b) recent dividends and rights issues of UK listed companies.
(c) copies of the financial statements of my competitors, which include both public and private companies in the UK.'

Requirement
Draft a letter in reply.

ICAEW Financial Accounting II, December 1985 (17 marks)

14.6 The share capital of Expansive plc consisted as at 30 September 1989 of 1 000 000 50p A ordinary shares.

On 31 December 1989 the company acquired shares in Problem plc and by way of consideration issued 500 000 50p B ordinary shares. It was agreed that because Problem plc had been experiencing trading losses these B ordinary shares would not rank for dividend until the year ending 30 September 1991 at which date they would rank equally with the A ordinary shares.

On 1 October 1990 Expansive plc issued options to its directors granting them the right to subscribe for 270 000 A ordinary shares at 80p each between 1995 and 1997.

The following information was available:

Year ended	Profits after tax £	Price of 2½% Consols £
30.9.89	100 000	22
30.9.90	110 000	20
30.9.91	121 000	21

Assume corporation tax at 35%.

Required
(a) (i) Calculate the basic and fully diluted earnings per share for Expansive plc as at 30 September 1989; 30 September 1990 and 30 September 1991; and
   (ii) State clearly which figures would be disclosed in the profit and loss accounts prepared for each of the three years ending 30 September 1989, 1990, and 1991; and
   (iii) Comment critically on the procedure for calculating the earnings per share figure when the company has granted options giving the holders the right to subscribe for shares at fixed prices on specified future dates and on the relevance of the figure to the shareholders.
(15 marks)
(b) Explain why the need has arisen to disclose a fully diluted EPS figure and state the circumstances in which it need not be disclosed. (5 marks)

ACCA Advanced Financial Accounting, December 1991 (20 marks)

18 Accounting and price changes

A18.1
(a) What do you consider to be the main weaknesses of historical cost accounting when prices are rising? (10 marks)
(b) State TWO ways in which firms have adopted different accounting policies for specific items in historical cost accounts so that they partly reflect rising price levels. (4 marks)
(c) The stewardship approach of traditional accounting has been said to have been replaced by a user-orientated approach. Briefly discuss this assertion in relation to historical cost accounts.
(6 marks)

ACCA Level 2 The Regulatory Framework of Accounting, June 1988 (20 marks)

A18.2 In the ASC's handbook, Accounting for the Effect of Changing Prices, accountants are faced with a choice of systems of accounting when dealing with the effects of inflation.

Requirements
(a) Briefly describe the three factors which combine to make up these systems of accounting.

(3 marks)

(b) Explain the main advantages and disadvantages of two such systems.   (6 marks)

ICAEW Financial Reporting II, May 1993   **(9 marks)**

18.3
(a) Explain the primary objective of current purchasing power accounting and outline the basic technique.   (8 marks)
(b) What do you consider are the advantages and disadvantages of current purchasing power accounting as a method of adjusting financial statements for price level changes?   (12 marks)

ACCA Level 2 The Regulatory Framework of Accounting, December 1988   **(20 marks)**

18.4
(a) Provide a definition of the deprival value of an asset.   (2 marks)
(b) For a particular asset, suppose the three bases of valuation relevant to the calculation of its deprival value are (in thousands of pounds): £12, £10 and £8.
    Construct a matrix of columns and rows showing all the possible alternative situations and, in each case, indicate the appropriate deprival value.   (6 marks)
(c) Justify the use of deprival value as a method of asset valuation, using the matrix in (b) above to illustrate your answer.   (12 marks)

ACCA Level 2 The Regulatory Framework of Accounting, December 1988   **(20 marks)**

18.5 An assistant accountant of Changeling plc has been requested to prepare a profit and loss account using the CPP model for the year ended 31 March 1991. He has calculated the net operating profit for the year and the remaining entries are yet to be completed.
    The profit and loss accounts for the year ended 31 March 1991 are set out below, comprising the historic cost profit and loss account and partially completed CPP profit and loss account.

	Historic cost £000	Index factor	CPP units as at 31.3.91 000
Sales	6 500	2 000 / 1 875	6 933
Opening stock	700	2 000 / 1 700	824
Purchases	4 250	2 000 / 1 875	4 533
	4 950		5 357
Closing stock	(900)	2 000 / 1 937	(929)
	4 050		4 428

	Historic cost £000	Index factor	CPP units as at 31.3.91 000
Gross profit	2 450		2 505
Expenses	1 150	2 000 / 1 875	1 227
Depreciation:			
Original equipment	500	2 000 / 1 025	976
New equipment	50	2 000 / 1 813	55
Net operating profit	750		247
Tax	338		
Profit (loss) after tax	412		
Gain (loss) on net monetary assets	–		
Gain (loss) on long-term loans	–		
Net profit (loss) for year	412		
Dividends	187		
Retained profit (loss) for year	225		
Retained profit brought forward	750		
Retained profit carried forward	975		

Balance sheet as at 31 March 1990:

	Historic cost £000	Index factor	CPP units as at 31.3.90 000	Index factor	CPP units as at 31.3.91 000
Capital	2 500	1 750	4 605	2 000	5 263
Retained profit	750	950	1 142	1 750	1 305
	3 250		5 747		6 568
Fixed assets					
Equipment	5 000	1 750 / 1 025	8 537	2 000 / 1 750	9 757
Depreciation	(1 500)	1 750 / 1 025	(2 561)	2 000 / 1 750	(2 927)
Current assets					
Stock	700	1 750 / 1 700	721	2 000 / 1 750	824
Debtors	1 050	–	1 050	2 000 / 1 750	1 200
Current liabilities					
Trade creditors	(875)	–	(875)	2 000 / 1 750	(1 000)
Non-current liabilities					
Loan	(1 125)	–	(1 125)	2 000	(1 286)
	3 250		5 747	1 750	6 568

Balance sheet as at 31 March 1991:

	Historic cost £000	Index factor	CPP units as at 31.3.91 000
Capital	2 500	$\frac{2\ 000}{950}$	5 263
Retained profit	$\underline{975}$	–	$\underline{1\ 142}$
	$\underline{\underline{3\ 475}}$		$\underline{\underline{6\ 405}}$
Fixed assets			
Equipment	5 000	$\frac{2\ 000}{1\ 025}$	9 757
Depreciation	(2 000)	$\frac{2\ 000}{1\ 025}$	(3 903)
New equipment	500	$\frac{2\ 000}{1\ 813}$	552
Depreciation	(50)	$\frac{2\ 000}{1\ 813}$	(55)
Current assets			
Stock	900	$\frac{2\ 000}{1\ 938}$	929
Debtors	1 150	–	1 150
Current liabilities			
Trade creditors	(400)	–	(400)
Non-current liabilities			
Loan	$\underline{(1\ 625)}$	–	$\underline{(1\ 625)}$
	$\underline{\underline{3\ 475}}$		$\underline{\underline{6\ 405}}$

Assume that inflation index increased evenly throughout the year ended 31 March 1991.

Required
(a) **Calculate the retained profit (loss) for the year using the CPP Model for the year ended 31 March 1991.**   (5 marks)
(b) **Explain what the method of indexing is attempting to deal with and discuss the process from the viewpoint of both the entity and the proprietors.**   (5 marks)
(c) **Write a brief report to the principal shareholder of Changeling Ltd who holds 20% of the issued share capital on the management of the company commenting on profitability, liquidity and financial structure.**   (10 marks)

ACCA Advanced Financial Accounting, December 1991   **(20 marks)**

18.6 The accountant of Newsprint plc has produced three sets of accounts for the year ended 31 December 1988 using the historic cost, replacement cost with specific index adjustments and current purchasing power with general price index adjustments.
   The historic and replacement cost accounts are set out below:

Profit and Loss Accounts for the year ended 31 December 1988

	Historic cost £	Historic cost £	Specific index	Replacement cost £	Replacement cost £
Sales		357 500	–		357 500
Opening stock	41 250		240/200	49 500	
Purchases	178 750		–	178 750	
	220 000			228 250	
Closing stock	71 500			71 500	
Cost of sales		148 500			156 750
Gross profit		209 000			200 750
Wages	17 875			17 875	
Establishment and other charges	71 500			71 500	
Depreciation					
Fixtures	5 500		160/140	6 286	
Lease	5 500		220/160	7 563	
		100 375			103 224
Net profit		108 625	*Operating profit*		97 526

Balance Sheets as at 31 December 1988

	Historic cost £	Historic cost £	Specific index	Replacement cost £	Replacement cost £
Fixed assets					
Leasehold					
Premises	55 000		220/160	75 625	
Amortisation	5 500	49 500		7 563	68 062
Fixtures	55 000		160/140	62 857	
Depreciation	5 500	49 500		6 286	56 571
Current assets					
Stock		71 500	280/240		83 416
Cash		55 825	–		55 825
		226 325			263 874
Share capital					
Ordinary shares		90 200			90 200
Profit and loss account		108 625			97 526
					11 099[1]
					37 549[2]
Loan		27 500			27 500
		226 325			263 874

Note 1

Stock	8 250
Fixtures	786
Lease	2 063
	11 099

Note 2

Closing Stock	
$(71\ 500 \times {}^{280}/_{240} - 71\ 500)$	11 916
Fixtures	
$(49\ 500 \times {}^{160}/_{140} - 49\ 500)$	7 071
Lease	
$(49\ 500 \times {}^{220}/_{160} - 49\ 500)$	18 562
	37 549

The historic and current purchasing power accounts are set out below:

Profit and Loss Accounts for the year ended 31 December 1988

	Historic cost		General index	£CPP	£CPP
	£	£			
Sales		357 500	160/130		440 000
Opening stock	41 250		160/100	66 000	
Purchases	178 750		160/130	220 000	
	220 000			286 000	
Closing stock	71 500		160/130	88 000	
Cost of sales		148 500			198 000
Gross profit		209 000			242 000
Wages	17 875		160/130	22 000	
Establishment and other charges	71 500		160/130	88 000	
Depreciation					
Fixtures	5 500		160/100	8 800	
Lease	5 500		160/100	8 800	
		100 375			127 600
Net profit		108 625	Operating profit		114 400

Balance Sheets as at 31 December 1988

	Historic cost		General index	£CPP	£CPP
Fixed assets	£	£			
Leasehold premises	55 000		160/100	88 000	
Amortisation	5 500	49 500	160/100	8 800	79 200
Fixtures	55 000		160/100	88 000	
Depreciation	5 500	49 500	160/100	8 800	79 200
Current assets					
Stock		71 500	160/130		88 000
Cash		55 825	–		55 825
		226 325			302 225
Share capital					
Ordinary shares		90 200	160/100		144 320
Profit and loss account		108 625			114 400
					16 005[3]
Loan		27 500			27 500
		226 325			302 225

Note 3

Loan	
(27 500 x 160/100 – 27 500)	16 500
Purchases	
(178 750 x 160/130 – 178 750)	41 250
Fixtures	
(55 000 x 160/100 – 55 000)	33 000
Lease	
(55 000 x 160/100 – 55 000)	33 000
Expenses	
(89 375 x 160/130 – 89 375)	20 625
Cash	
(76 450 x 160/100 – 76 450)	(45 870)
Sales	
(357 500 x 160/130 – 357 500)	(82 500)

Required
(a) **Explain briefly what the following amounts relate to and why they are in the balance sheets:**
  (i) in the replacement cost model
    £11 099
    £37 549;
  (ii) in the current purchasing power model
    £16 005. (6 marks)
(b) **Explain the case for and against the replacement cost model.** (8 marks)
(c) **Consider the implication of the replacement cost model figures for 1988 to the management of Newsprint plc.** (8 marks)
(d) **Explain to a shareholder why the historic cost net profit is different from the CPP operating profit using the data in the question to illustrate your answer and explain which figure is to be regarded as the base for calculating earnings per share under each model.** (8 marks)

ACCA Level 3 Advanced Financial Accounting, June 1989 (30 marks)

18.7 The Paraffin Supply Company Limited acquired freehold land as a depot for its delivery vans and started business on 1 January 1986. It collected sufficient paraffin from a wholesaler each day to satisfy known orders. The wholesaler was paid in cash and the customers paid cash on delivery. The opening balance sheet at 1 January 1986 showed the following:

Balance Sheet of Paraffin Supply Company Limited as at 1 January 1986

	£
Freehold land for use as garage premises	100 000
Delivery vehicles	96 000
	196 000
Financed by: Share capital	150 000
Long-term loan	46 000
	196 000

The company traded for 2 years until 31 December 1987. All profits had been retained in the business. There were no creditors, debtors or stocks. At 31 December 1987 the directors were considering whether to cease trading at 31 December 1988.

The accountant produced the following estimated accounts for the year ended 31 December 1988 with the 1986 and 1987 actual comparative figures:

Profit and Loss Accounts for the years ended 31 December

	1986	1987	1988
	£	£	£
Sales	140 000	184 000	248 000
Less: Purchases	70 000	90 000	124 000
Administration expenses	21 400	22 000	27 500
Selling expenses	21 000	30 000	42 500
Depreciation	24 000	24 000	24 000
	3 600	18 000	30 000

	1986	1987	1988
Return on equity	$\frac{3\,600}{150\,000} \times 100$	$\frac{18\,000}{153\,600} \times 100$	$\frac{30\,000}{171\,600} \times 100$
	=2.4%	=11.7%	=17.5%

In preparing the accounts the following conventions and policies had been followed:

(a) The capital maintenance concept is that capital will be maintained if the cost of assets representing the initial monetary investment is recovered against operations.

(b) The concept of profit is that profit for the year is regarded as any gains arising during the year which may be distributed while maintaining the amount of the shareholders' interest in the company at the beginning of the year.

(c) The measurement unit used is the medium of exchange.

(d) Depreciation of delivery vans is over 4 years using the straight-line method.

The directors had recently attended a seminar on the treatment of inflation in financial reports and they required the profits to be calculated using the general purchasing power income model and the replacement cost model.

The accountant obtained the following information to allow him to redraft the profit and loss account using these two models:

(a) The retail price index was as follows:

1 January 1986	100
31 December 1986	110
31 December 1987	120
31 December 1988 (Estimated)	130

(b) The replacement cost of the assets was:

	Garage premises £	Delivery vehicles £
31 December 1986	120 000	102 000
31 December 1987	130 000	115 000
31 December 1988 (Estimated)	141 000	128 000

Required

(a) (i) Prepare the profit and loss account for the year ended 31 December 1988 using the general purchasing power income model and explain the following:

The concept of capital maintenance used.
The concept of profit used.
The measurement unit used. (8 marks)

(ii) Mention four criteria for selecting an appropriate unit of measurement for financial reporting and briefly discuss whether the general purchasing power income model satisfies these criteria. (8 marks)

(b) (i) Prepare the profit and loss account for the year ended 31 December 1988 using the replacement cost model to show reported income on the assumption that backlog depreciation is not deducted in arriving at this reported income and explain the following:

The concept of capital maintenance used.
The concept of profit used.
The measurement unit used. (5 marks)

(ii) Discuss the arguments for and against excluding backlog depreciation when calculating the reported income. (4 marks)

ACCA Level 3 Advanced Financial Accounting, December 1988 (25 marks)

18.8 (A) The Bureau Limited is a company that is being incorporated to organise and manage a computer bureau operation. The directors are considering whether to finance the company by equity or equity and loan.

They estimate that the company will require £5 000 000 and that the rate of return on capital employed, calculated on the basis of profit before interest and tax to capital employed, could range from 10% to 20% as follows:

A return on capital employed of 20% if the company is able to obtain a contract with the government for processing monthly statistics, or

A return on capital employed of 15% if it is able to obtain a contract with a major commercial organisation for routine processing of the weekly payroll, or

A return on capital employed of 10% if it is only able to obtain a series of small contracts.

Required

(a) Calculate the earnings per share on the basis of the three possible rates of return on capital employed assuming that:

(i) The company is financed wholly by equity of £1 ordinary shares. Assume corporation tax at 30%.

(ii) The company is financed half by ordinary shares of £1 each issued at par and half by 10% loan stock. Assume corporation tax at 30%. (5 marks)

(b) Explain how the shareholders of Bureau Limited would be advantaged or disadvantaged by introducing a 50% gearing. (5 marks)

(B) Three proposals have been suggested to record the effect of gearing when accounts are prepared on an inflation accounting basis. These are:

(i) If current cost adjustments have been made to calculate a current operating profit, a gearing adjustment is allowed to abate the operating adjustments in the gearing proportion to derive a current cost operating profit.*

(ii) In addition to the abatement of the operating adjustments, required in part (i) above, an additional entry is to be made to recognise the proportion of the unrealised revaluation surpluses arising in the year that may be regarded as being financed by borrowing.

(iii) A gearing adjustment may be made to reflect the effect of general price changes on the net borrowings and net monetary assets other than those included in monetary working capital.

Required

Discuss whether each of the above three proposals has a logical reason to support it and why there is difficulty in agreeing on a standard treatment to record the effect of gearing. (15 marks)

ACCA Level 3 Advanced Financial Accounting, June 1988 (25 marks)

---

* There appears to be an error in the official version of this question. In the opinion of the authors, it should read:

'If current cost adjustments have been made to calculate a current cost operating profit, a gearing adjustment is allowed to abate the operating adjustments in the gearing proportion to derive a current cost profit attributable to the shareholders.'

APPENDIX II

Answers

Appendix 2 gives answers to those questions in Appendix 1 which are marked with the prefix A.

Answers have been prepared by Brian Pain, Senior Lecturer in Accounting, University of Luton, and John Blakemore, Visiting Lecturer in Accounting, University of Luton.

1 Introduction

1.1 *The Corporate Report*

(a) The following groups were considered to be potential users of financial reports:

(i) The equity investor group, including existing and potential shareholders and holders of convertible securities, etc.

(ii) The loan creditor group, including existing and potential holders of debentures and loan stock, and providers of short-term secured and unsecured loans and finance.

(iii) The employee group, including existing, potential and past employees.

(iv) The analyst–adviser group, including financial analysts, journalists and providers of advisory services.

(v) The business contact group, including customers, suppliers and competitors.

(vi) The government, including tax authorities.

(vii) The public, including special interest groups and political parties.

(b) The information needs of the above groups may be summarised as follows:

(i) **Equity investor group**
Information is required to help make trading decisions regarding securities including decisions on the taking up of rights issues and the acceptance of takeover proposals. Existing shareholders may also need information relevant to resolutions on which they will be asked to vote, including the election of directors.

(ii) **Loan creditors**
They will need to decide whether a loan should be advanced and, if so, on what terms. Once a loan is made, the creditors will want to monitor the progress of the company to allow them to invoke any provisions of the loan agreement which might appear appropriate or take other action, for example, providing against doubtful debts.

(iii) **Employees**
This group (current and prospective) will need information to assist them in wage and other negotiations, e.g. on redundancies and conditions of service.

(iv) **Analyst–advisers**
Their information needs are the same as the group which they are advising, for example the equity investors or employees. However, it is presumed that this group could deal with more sophisticated and detailed information than the members of the groups whom they are advising.

(v) **Business contacts**
The information needs of customers and suppliers cover the question of whether to trade with the company. Customers will be particularly interested in the prospect of continuity of supply while suppliers will be concerned both with the prospect of future orders and the risk

associated with the granting of credit. Competitors and business rivals will be interested in information both as potential investors (or takeover bidders) and to promote their own efficiency by making economic comparisons.

(vi)   **The government**

As the representatives of the public (*see* below), the government requires information in order to levy taxes and to assess the effects of its economic policies, e.g. the Inspector of Taxes and Customs and Excise.

(vii) **The public**

The public has a right to receive information about the impact on the community of the operations or organisations which control substantial resources, e.g. 'green' organisations.

SUMMARY

Whilst there are differences in the needs of the various groups, many of the groups are interested in both past and future profitability and in the related question of the future survival of the entity.

(c)   Financial accounts are of no value unless they provide information which helps the users to make decisions. Thus, it might be expected that a consideration of user needs has a significant influence on financial accounting. It therefore follows that those responsible for the regulation of accounting practice should first identify the various uses of accounts and assess their needs for information.

The needs of users as determined by the above procedure should be the main factor influencing the development of regulations on financial reporting. This is not to suggest, however, that the accountant should not attempt to educate the user groups if he/she believes that the models used for decision making could be improved.

Whilst the needs of users are an important influence, accounting legislators must also consider the cost of producing information as well as the conflicting needs of the different interest groups.

1.2   Conceptual framework

(a)   A 'conceptual framework' in relation to financial reporting is the theoretical principles which underpin both the development of new reporting practices and the evaluation of existing ones. The conceptual framework will determine what fiscal information is to be reported, how it should be measured and how the information should ultimately be disclosed to the user.

(b)   Advantages which would arise from the development of a conceptual framework include:

(i)   Avoidance of the current 'fire-fighting' approach prevalent in the UK, in relation to standard setting.

(ii)   Development of an agreed conceptual framework would prevent the current problem where different standards re-visit the same theoretical issues and develop dissimilar solutions. For example, inconsistencies currently exist in UK accounting standards due to conflicts between several of the accounting concepts e.g. substance *versus* form, matching *versus* prudence etc.

(iii) Avoidance of political interference and lobbying in the standard setting process. The current brand accounting debate is a case in point. The ASB have made no definitive pronouncements on brand accounting because of significant ideological differences between the main parties involved. Thus a stand-off has been reached. If a conceptual framework existed the problem could be equivocally resolved by reference to this framework.

(iv)   Certain UK standards focus on the balance sheet as opposed to the profit and loss account and vice versa e.g. SSAP 12 defines the depreciation calculation to comply with the accruals concept in relation to the profit and loss account. The NBV (net book value) on the balance sheet is of little use. This type of problem would be clarified by the development of a conceptual framework.

(c)   The difficulties in trying to develop a conceptual framework include:

(i)   There are many distinct user groups of financial statements each with different needs. It is unlikely that a single accounting model can be devised to meet all their needs.

(ii)   Following on from the above point, any framework would require widespread agreement for it to be effective. Given the diversity of interest groups and the complexity and sophistication of the current accounting environment, such agreement is extremely unlikely.

(iii)   To develop such a framework will be a costly and time-consuming process, the funding of which may be difficult to obtain.

2 Sources of authority

2.1 Accounting bodies

COMMENT

Students should read *Accountancy Age* for comments on this area as developments are reported and commented on.

To: Managing Director   From: Chief Accountant

Subject: Current Accounting Bodies   Date: 1994

(a) Financial Reporting Council (FRC)

This body determines broad policy and direction. Its members will come from a variety of relevant backgrounds, e.g. not just the accounting profession and it has an 'overseeing' function.

(b) Accounting Standards Board (ASB)

This board is 'subsidiary' to the above council. The nine members are appointed by the FRC. The ASB issues the standards (FRSs) and will, if necessary, issue using a two thirds majority. Since its constitution there has been a flow of standards i.e. FRS 1 to FRS 5. The ASB has continually been in touch with the commercial community and has encouraged feedback.

(c) Financial Reporting Review Panel (FRRP)

This panel is 'subsidiary' to the above council. It reviews apparent departures from accounting requirements. It specifically reviews problems regarding distortion of the true and fair view. It can use the sanction of the court to force companies to publish revised accounts. It reviews complaints regarding items appearing in annual accounts. Since its inception, it has forced companies to revise their accounts. The FRRP has acted on several problems, with the forcing of Trafalgar House PLC (market value March 1994 £1 billion) to revise their accounts, as their most 'visible victory'.

(d) Urgent Issues Task Force (UITF)

The task force is a committee of the ASB and its role is to rule on urgent or emerging issues where the accounting treatment is unsatisfactory or unclear. The issue will be one of principle where an expedient ruling is considered important.

Its decisions are published as abstracts which have the support of the ASB. The UITF have announced that they will communicate with interested parties, but will act unilaterally if necessary.

2.2 Disclosure of accounting policies

The main points to include are:

(i)   The purpose of SSAP 2 is to assist the understanding of financial statements by improving the quality of information disclosed.

(ii)   This is achieved by ensuring policies used by companies in preparing their accounts are appropriately and clearly disclosed.

(iii)   SSAP 2 ensures that the fundamental accounting concepts used by companies are consistent, namely:

- going concern
- prudence
- accruals
- consistency.

(iv)   The fact that these concepts have been adopted need not be disclosed since it is assumed that every company follows such concepts. Only deviation from these concepts requires disclosure.

(v)   Subjectivity still remains, however, since different assessments of prudence and materiality, for example, will be exercised by different companies.

(vi)   SSAP 2 recognises that within different industries different accounting practices are required. Accounting bases, as referred to in SSAP 2, are the methods of applying the fundamental concepts.

(vii)   Accounting bases are methods for determining which revenues and costs for the period should be recognised and which items of material value should be stated in the balance sheet.

(viii)   Accounting bases should be fair and consistently applied.

(ix)   SSAP 2 Para 13 suggests some accounting areas where bases should be adopted. These include:

- depreciation
- stock valuation
- treatment of intangibles
- deferred taxation
- consolidation policies.

(x)   SSAP 2 requires that accounting policies are consistently applied each year.

(xi)   Accounting policies are the specific accounting bases adopted by the company which are best suited to present its results and financial position fairly.

(xii)   Since different companies adopt differing policies, full disclosure of policies followed is required to allow proper interpretation of the accounts.

(xii)   Therefore, through the methodology of applying accounting concepts, bases and policies, and their disclosure – as required by SSAP 2 – readers of accounts can be made aware of the main assumptions in the preparation of accounts.

3.1 Profit

(a)   'Capital' may be defined as a stock of wealth as measured at a particular point of time. In the context of financial corporate reporting, 'capital maintenance' means the formulation of a set of rules whereby 'profit' is only reported if the capital at the end of the period is at least equal to opening capital.

Hence, capital maintenance may be regarded as a benchmark or test used for the measurement of profit. The relationship between capital and profit (or income) can be best described by quoting Sir John Hicks who wrote that income is 'the maximum value which [a man] can consume during a week and still expect to be as well off at the end of the week as he was at the beginning'.

There is, however, one major problem, in theory as well as practice, in that there is more than one way of measuring wealth and hence capital. In traditional accounting, capital is measured by reference to the amount invested by the owners of an enterprise while the various alternative accounting systems can be described in terms of the different views that may be taken of capital maintenance. Two examples of these different approaches are:

(i)   **The current purchasing power (CCP) approach**
Capital is measured by reference to the purchasing power of owners' equity. Hence a profit is recognised only if the purchasing power of owners' equity at the end of the period is at least equal

to the purchasing power at the beginning. Purchasing power is measured by reference to the price changes faced by the shareholders as consumers rather than those which relate specifically to the assets used by the business and hence the adjustments are made using a broadly based index of retail prices.

(ii) **Operating capability approach**

In sharp contrast to the CPP method is the operating capability approach. In this case capital is measured by reference to the company's ability to maintain its level of output. It is not possible in any but the most simple of enterprises to measure future output directly and hence proxy methods must be used. The best known proxy is the method which underlies current cost accounting (CCA) which uses net assets as an approximation for operating capability. With CCA a profit is reported only if the company retains sufficient funds to replace the assets which have been consumed by operations.

(b) The practical reasons for measuring and reporting profit may be summarised as follows:

(i) **Consumption**

It follows from what was said above that the measurement of profit allows the owners of an enterprise to decide how much can be withdrawn from the business for consumption without reducing its substance and hence the opportunities for future consumption. In addition, the information will be of value to other groups, notably employees, who may have a legitimate interest in sharing in the success of the enterprise.

(ii) **Stewardship**

To the extent that owners invest funds in an enterprise which is managed by others, the reporting of profit provides an indication of the success or otherwise of the managers over the period.

(iii) **Prediction**

The reporting of past profits might give some indication of the prospects of future profits.

(iv) **Taxation**

Since it is the policy of most governments that the capacity of business enterprise to pay tax is related to profits, the measurement of profit is required for the purpose of levying tax.

(v) **Investment and borrowing**

The reporting of profit provides information which helps investors and creditors make judgements about the security of investments and loans and, in the case of investors, the price which they should pay for shares.

(vi) **Governmental purposes**

Governments require information about business profitability in order to assist them frame their economic policies both as they relate to specific industries and to the economy as a whole.

3.2 Current value accounting

(a) Replacement cost is the price which must be paid to replace an asset used or given up in exchange for another asset. This approach puts forward the idea that it is the replacement cost which should be used to calculate charges for consumption and gains or losses on disposal. This accounting system results in assets being valued at the balance sheet date by reference to the price which would have to be paid at that date to purchase a similar asset in a similar condition.

This model results in two types of gain, an operating and a holding gain on non-monetary assets. An operating gain is the difference between the selling price obtained for an asset and its replacement cost. Holding gains, which may be realised or unrealised, arise from increases in replacement cost over the period for which an asset is held. This system therefore adopts a method of income determination which reflects changes in capital both at the point of realisation of assets and, before realised, in the process of holding assets over time.

(b) Under net realisable value (NRV) accounting, asset values are based on exit or net realisable values. This value is taken to be the value of disposing of the asset in an orderly manner in its existing state. It is therefore valued on an opportunity cost basis. Under the exit model, income in the period is the sum of:

- distributions made in the period, plus
- the change in net realisable value in an entity's net assets over the period.

(c) The answer to this question must be that as a method of preparing financial statements, combining entry and exit value for profit and loss account and balance sheet respectively would produce extremely confusing and ultimately inaccurate financial statements. The statements would not balance, since the entry value retained profit or loss would not correspond to the exit value increase or decrease in capital.

4 Assets: tangible and intangible

4.1 Depreciation

COMMENT

There are many companies which are not depreciating their properties, at the time of writing Brewers are defending their decisions not to depreciate. Tesco and Sainsbury (early 1994) have decided to depreciate their stores after mounting pressure.

(a) The company will not be complying with company law and SSAP 12(R)
The company will have to rely on the true and fair override available, if it is to avoid depreciating its property.

(b) SSAP 19 regulates investment properties. Those properties held at arm's length are considered investment properties. The criteria in SSAP 19 are:
(i) Construction and development work have been completed
(ii) A property owned and occupied by a company for its own purpose is not an investment property
(iii) A property let to and occupied by another group company is not an investment property in its own or the group's accounts.

(c) In the fixed assets analysis, investment properties are shown separately. They are included in the balance sheet at open market value and are not depreciated (unless held on a lease with 20 years or less to run). The revaluation reserve arising is also shown separately. Where investment properties are significant in the balance sheet, the properties are annually revalued by employed staff and at least every 5 years by outside valuers. Where the revaluation reserve goes into deficit, SSAP 19 requires the profit and loss account to be charged with the deficit.

4.2 Stock and SSAP 9

COMMENT

Although this area appears well regulated, students should read the financial press for any problem that may 'surface'. Examples of the latter are Alexon, Dash and Spring Ram (1992–1993).

To: Managing Director   From: Chief Accountant

Subject: Stock and valuation methods

(a) SSAP 9(R) regulates stock and long-term contracts.

(b) The SSAP requires stock to consist of (i) raw materials (ii) direct labour (iii) appropriate production overheads (iv) other overheads if attributable to the present location and condition of the stock.

(c) For selling, administration and research and development to be included in the stock valuation, there need to be very strong reasons:

Selling:	The competitor has kept precise records and can show that expenses incurred relate to the particular stock (Para. 48). Firm sales contracts must exist for the stocks in question.
Administration:	The administration costs must be related to production, for example, the accounts department paying direct production wages (Para. 53, SSAP 9).
Research and Development:	Firstly the company must have looked at the criteria in the SSAP 13(R). Again it must have kept precise records and be very confident that the auditors will agree to the method of valuation (Para. 17, SSAP 13). There is a contract to carry out design and development work as well as the manufacture of products.

4.3 Intangible assets

COMMENT

Intangibles are now competing with inflation accounting – a definitive answer is not on the horizon!

(a) Intangible assets are disclosed under fixed assets in the balance sheet, and include goodwill, brands, patents and trademarks.

Companies disclose their purchased intangibles and generally do not disclose their non-purchased intangibles. The preferred practice is for the intangibles to be capitalised and amortised over their economic lives.

Companies are allowed to write off acquired goodwill (SSAP 22(R) directly to reserves. The latter can be share premium (with permission of the court) and profit and loss account (Saatchi and Saatchi used the share premium account to write off goodwill).

(b) Areas of concern

(i) Assessing original economic life and subsequent reviews. Consider the ferry company Townsend Thorenson after the Zeebrugge ferry disaster (1987) – the name was dropped.

(ii) Quite often the cost is also a subjective problem where other assets were purchased along with any intangibles.

(iii) Many companies have sought outside help in assessing the value and economic life of an intangible, but there is limited expertise in this area.

(iv) There is frequently a lack of openness when disclosing intangibles in the balance sheet and similarly with the associated charge in the profit and loss account for the year (i.e. amount amortised).

5 Liabilities and related issues

5.1 Spock

(a) Reserve accounting is when adjustments are made to reserves solely through balance sheet entries. This type of accounting is not generally permitted since the annual profit and loss account should reflect all transactions relevant to the period. However, there are situations where reserve accounting should be adopted. This is because the reflection of the movement through the profit and loss account would not be 'true and fair', as the movement does not relate exclusively to the accounting period in question, or represent an unrealised item.

(i) **Movements in revaluation reserves**
When assets are revalued, surpluses or deficits are taken directly to the revaluation reserve for a number of reasons:

- they are not realised profits or losses
- surpluses cannot be distributed
- movements in asset values do not necessarily relate to the accounting period under review.
Similarly, movements in investment properties are taken to an investment revaluation reserve (SSAP 19).

(ii) **Goodwill**
Goodwill arises when a premium is paid on the acquisition of a company. SSAP 22 states that such 'purchased goodwill' should be written off directly to reserves because:
- The goodwill relates to the accumulation over a number of years by another company.
- It is not a real asset with which any related amortisation could easily be matched with future revenues.
- Prudence would suggest immediate write-off rather than matching amortisation with possible future revenues.
- Immediate write-off of purchased goodwill is consistent with the treatment of non-purchased goodwill – which is not normally reflected in a company's balance sheet as an asset.

(iii) **Prior year adjustments**
As the term suggests, these relate to transactions occurring in a prior year. Hence, it would be inappropriate to reflect them through a later period's profit and loss account (FRS 3).
Only fundamental errors or material changes to accounting policy may be adjusted by way of a prior year adjustment.

(iv) **Foreign exchange differences**
When companies hold overseas assets, SSAP 20 allows such assets to be translated into sterling at the currency rate ruling at the balance sheet date (the net investment method). This method should be used when the overseas subsidiary is not dependent on the parent and activities are unrelated. Fluctuations in the value of the currency will result in a movement in the 'value' of the investment. SSAP 20 states that such year-on-year fluctuations should be taken directly to reserves because:

- The results of the holding company's trading operations would be distorted since this method of translation is used by companies with unrelated activities.
- Exchange differences cannot be realised.
- The differences arise due to accounting treatment and not actual cashflows.

Similarly, if the investment is being financed by long-term loans or inter-company deferred trading balances exchange differences on these transactions – to be consistent – should also be taken direct to reserves.

(b)   Spock is supporting the 'all-inclusive' concept of accounting for the movement in reserves. This requires that all reserve movements, except capital issues, are reflected through the profit and loss account. The advantages of such an application would be:

(i)   To allow shareholders to easily identify the movements in reserves in one statement.
(ii)   Through appropriate disclosure, an improved understanding of why the movements have occurred.
(iii)   Limits the extent of confusion which could result if notes on the movements were spread throughout the financial statements.

There are disadvantages through the adoption of such a policy – some of them related to problems outlined in section (a) above.

(i)   Movements may not relate to the period in question, for example, prior year adjustments and purchased goodwill.
(ii)   Movements may relate to trading activities not common to the group – such as the inclusion of exchange differences on overseas subsidiaries.
(iii)   Gains realised are not profits, for example, revaluation surpluses.
(iv)   Not all movements relate to distributable profits therefore making it difficult to ascertain the true level of distributable profits.

FRS 3, however, requires the adoption of the all-inclusive concept although, as we have seen, other SSAPs require the adjustment of certain transactions to be taken directly to reserves.

COMMENT

This is a pre-FRS 3 question and the answer above is a short post-FRS 3 answer.

FRS 3 changes the presentation of the revenue results quite dramatically. The following additional statements force the company to adopt an all inclusive approach:

(a)   Statement of total recognised gains and losses e.g. revaluation surplus, foreign currency gains, prior year adjustment(s) *along with* the profit for the financial year.

(b)   Note of historical cost profits and losses. This note formally explains differences between historical cost and alternative bases e.g. historical cost depreciation charge and depreciation charge based on the revalued amount.

(c)   Reconciliation of movements in shareholders' funds, including:
    (i)   Year's pre-dividend profit or loss
    (ii)   Dividends paid and proposed
    (iii)   Other recognised gains/losses (per (a) above)
    (iv)   Share capital movements (par and premium)
    (v)   Goodwill adjustments

    The above movements then reconcile with the opening and closing shareholders' funds.

5.2   Ardtoe plc

Note: Earnings per share (EPS) questions are popular with examiners and can pose technical or time constraint problems. This question is in the latter category.

Weighted Average Computation (required by SSAP 3)

(1)   1 Oct 92–31 Jul 93 10/12 x 2 200 000 x 2.00/1.95 (W1)   1 880 342
       Rights issue shares 500 000
       31 Jul 93–30 Sept 93 2/12 x 2750 000   458 333
       Number of shares (1993)   2 338 675

In the case of a bonus issue, the opening number of shares is adjusted (by the increase), irrespective of the date of issue in the year (SSAP 3, Para. 36).

W1. With a rights issue it is necessary to adjust the number of shares before the issue to reflect the 'bonus' element. The adjustment made is equal to:

$$\frac{\text{Actual cum rights price prior to issue}}{\text{Theoretical ex-rights price (TERPS)}}$$

TERPS will be:

2 200 x £2.00 =	4 400.0	
550 x £1.75 =	962.5	
2 750	5 362.5	
£5 362.5 / 2750 =	£1.95	

The EPS in previous years needs to be adjusted for the bonus issue and the rights issue.
EPS for 1992:

11.0p x (Rights) 1.95/2.00 x (Bonus) 2 000/2 200 = 9.75p

(2)   This is a non-adjusting post-balance sheet event, as defined by SSAP 17. It is subjective whether the loss is material. In the context of the question, it would appear to be material (i.e. approx. 10% of the pre-tax earnings), and so disclosure, by way of a note, is required of the nature of the event and an estimate of the financial effect.

A suitable note would be thus:

On 3 October 1993, stock held in the company's warehouse was destroyed by fire. The stock was uninsured and valued in the balance sheet at £50 000.

(3)	Operating Profit		450 000
	Investment Income		50 000
	Profit before tax		500 000
	Tax on Profit		(204 550)
	(Corp. Tax 140 000 + ACT w/o 52 050 + ACT FII		12 500 (50 000 x 25%)
	(see Appendix A below)		
	Post tax profits		295 450
	Dividends: Paid Interim	220 000	
	Proposed Final	275 000	
			(495 000)
	Retained Loss		(199 550)
	EPS (1993):		
	Net £295450/Shares 2 338 675		12.63p
	Nil (295 450 + ACT w/o 52 050 / 2 338 675		14.86p

Both NIL and NET must be disclosed, as the difference is material (SSAP 3, Para. 9).

(4)   This item is a contingency, since it does relate to a condition which existed at the balance sheet date (SSAP 18, Para. 14).

If the item is considered to be material legal advice is required by the company before approval of the accounts.

The company should accrue for the estimated legal expenses.

Any disclosure will depend on the legal advice, e.g. **Remote** – no disclosure; **Probable** – provide in full. (It is assumed the letter arrived on 2 October 1993, but the matter related to a condition that existed prior to the year end 30 September 1993.)

APPENDIX A

Summary of CT61 returns

QUARTER	Franked Payment	Franked Inv. Income	Net	ACT Paid	
Qtr 1 31 Dec '92	n/a	n/a	n/a	n/a	
Qtr 2 31 Mar '93	n/a	n/a	n/a	n/a	
Qtr 3 30 Jun '93	293 333	(50 000)	243 333	60 833	(25% x 243 333)
Qtr 4 30 Sept '93	n/a	n/a	n/a	n/a	
Payable	366 667	n/a	366 667	91 667	(25% x 366 667)
Taxable Profits				402 000	
Liability				140 000	

Maximum recovery of ACT will be (402 000 × 25%) 100 500.[4]

Recovery of ACT paid	[1]	(60 883)
Recovery of ACT payable	[2]	(39 617)

ACT Irrecoverable will be (91 667 (due on final dividend) less 39 617 (recoverable brought forward) £52 050.[3]

[1] The ACT paid in the CT61 return for the quarter ended 30 June 1993 is all recoverable against the corporation tax liability.

[2] This is the ACT payable on the final dividend which can be recovered against the current year's corporation tax liability.

[3] This is the ACT payable on the final dividend which cannot be recovered against the current year's corporation tax liability. It is assumed that recovery will not be possible in the next year or against previous tax charges.

[4] The maximum ACT set off against the corporation tax liability is restricted to the profits chargeable to corporation tax multiplied by the basic rate of tax (here 25% taken from the ACT fraction of 1/3 = 25/75).

6 Financial Statements: form and contents

6.1 FRS3

Students should obtain several sets of published accounts and compare the published profit and loss accounts.

The profit and loss account prior to FRS3 showed the results of the entity but gave little analysis of how the entity had created the profit figures. Thus, users of accounts focused on the profit figure to the exclusion of all else.

FRS3 was introduced to provide users with a range of components of financial performance to assist them in understanding the entity's results. A layered format to the profit and loss account has been adopted so that operations are analysed between continuing operations, newly acquired operations and discontinued operations. The aim is to enable users to analyse the impact of operations that have ceased, or of new operations that have been acquired, and so assist users to better assess the future performance of the entity.

FRS3 has also reduced the scope for manipulation by redefining extraordinary items as extremely rare and so almost all transactions will be included in ordinary profit. Certain classes of exceptional items are also to be disclosed separately on the face of the profit and loss account.

A new primary statement, the 'Statement of total recognised gains and losses', has been introduced by FRS3. This shows users not only the profit in the year but all other gains and losses, such as those arising from retranslations of foreign currency transactions, which have been recognised in the year and are attributable to the shareholders. Further supplementary statements are required by FRS3, for example a note on historical cost profits and losses and a reconciliation of movements in shareholders' funds.

The aim in providing the additional information is to give users further insight into the components of performance and therefore enable them to use a range of measures to analyse the results and assess the entity's future potential.

6.2 RST plc

COMMENT

Students should review published accounts pre- and post-FRS3 and assess the impact of the standard.

MEMORANDUM

To: Managing Director
From: Chief Accountant   Date: 30 October 1993
Subject: Review of financial statements of JKL plc

(a) For accounting periods ending on or after 22 June 1993, Financial Reporting Standard No. 3 (FRS3) 'Reporting financial performance' is effective. This standard brought about a number of changes to the format of the profit and loss account and introduced a new primary statement, the 'Statement of total recognised gains and losses', together with a number of additional notes to the accounts.

Post-FRS3 annual profit and loss accounts now disclose information relating to continuing, discontinued and acquired operations, which was not required pre-FRS3.

(b) Discontinued operations are those which the entity has sold or terminated and satisfy all of the following:
  (i) The sale or termination is completed in the period or the earlier of three months after the period end and the date the financial statements are approved.
  (ii) If a termination, the activity has permanently ceased.
  (iii) The sale or termination is material to the entity's operations and is a material reduction in operating facilities due to the withdrawal from a market or material reduction in turnover in continuing markets.
  (iv) The assets, liabilities, results and operations are separately identifiable physically, operationally and for financial reporting purposes.

(c) This is a new primary statement introduced by FRS3. In it are shown the gains and losses recognised in the period which are attributable to shareholders. So, as well as the profit (loss) for the financial year shown in the profit and loss account, other gains and losses, such as revaluation surpluses and foreign currency transaction differences are included. The figure derived reflects the net gain or loss recognised by the entity over the period covered by the statement. Previously the user had to 'know where to look' when establishing a complete overview of gains and losses for a period.

6.3 Substance over form

COMMENT

Students should be aware that this is a 'growth area' and preparers face problems deciding how to disclose a variety of transactions.

Traditionally, all transactions were straightforward and quite easy to account for.

In recent years accounting techniques have not kept abreast of the increasing number of financial instruments. The latter have become quite sophisticated and pose many problems for the regulators to solve (comparable to the traditional gamekeeper and poacher relationship). Many companies found they could present more favourable results by not disclosing a transaction/situation in the annual accounts. Adverse comment could be avoided by controlling the degree of disclosure.

Consequently transactions have been entered into or specifically arranged so that their legal nature was such that companies could avoid disclosure of the transaction.

An example of the above is that of leasing. A leased asset is not the property of the lessee! The lessee has total control of the leased asset during the life of the lease, and these transactions were not disclosed until the introduction of SSAP 21.

SSAP 21 requires leased assets (i.e. assuming they meet certain criteria) to be disclosed in the balance sheet and the profit and loss account and the cash flow statement. The leased asset will appear as a fixed asset (BS), a liability (BS), depreciation on the asset (PL), interest on the loan (PL), a source of finance on signing the lease (Cash Flow) and repayment of finance as the lease instalments are paid (CF).

Current position
FRS 5: 'Reporting the substance of transactions', has recently been issued (Spring 1994), and deals with off-balance sheet financing. Under its requirements, companies will have to ensure that financial statements report the substance of the transactions, not just the legal form.

7.1 Accounting for taxation

(i) Franked investment comprises the amount of a qualifying distribution received from another UK resident company with the addition of the related tax credit. The gross amount should be included as income with the related tax being shown as part of the taxation charge for the year (gross amount = distribution received + tax credit).

(ii) Proposed dividends and the related ACT should be shown as a current liability in the balance sheet under the heading 'creditors: amounts falling due within one year'. If the ACT is regarded as recoverable it should also be shown as either a deduction from the deferred tax liability or a deferred asset within current assets. If the ACT is regarded as irrecoverable it should be included as part of the tax charge upon the company to be deducted in arriving at profits after tax.

(iii) As noted in (ii) above, recoverable ACT should be shown as either a deferred asset or as a deduction from the deferred tax account.

(iv) As noted in (ii) above, irrecoverable ACT should be treated as part of the company's taxation charge for the year.

(v) Turnover shown in the profit and loss account should exclude VAT on taxable outputs. Output VAT is a liability and must ultimately be paid over to Customs and Excise. Output VAT, net of input VAT for the same period, which has not been remitted to Customs and Excise at the period end should be shown as a current liability under the heading of 'other creditors including taxation and social security' on the balance sheet.

(vi) Irrecoverable VAT on the purchase of a fixed asset should be included as part of the cost of the fixed asset and capitalised in the balance sheet.

(vii) VAT received on sales is a liability. VAT paid on purchases is a recoverable amount and therefore an asset. Over a period of trading a business will net off the difference between output VAT (sales) and input VAT (purchases) and show the balance as either a debtor or creditor. When the cash is received or paid the debtor or creditor is extinguished.

7.2 SSAP 15 (revised)

(a) Deferred taxation is provided on the liability method on all timing differences to the extent that they are expected to reverse in the future and are not to be replaced by fresh timing differences, calculated at the rate at which it is estimated that tax will be payable. Advance Corporation Tax which is expected to be recoverable in the future is deducted from the deferred taxation balance. The amount of unprovided deferred tax is shown in a note to the accounts, analysed into its major components. No provision is to be made for taxation on chargeable gains arising from property disposals where any liability will be postponed indefinitely by rollover relief.

(b)   **Extract from the notes to the financial statements as at 30 June 199X**

Deferred taxation

Deferred taxation provided in the accounts and the amounts not provided are as follows:

	Provided £000	Not provided £000
Capital allowances in advance of depreciation	23	74
Other differences in recognising revenue and expense items in other periods for taxation purposes	2	–
	25	74
Taxation on valuation surplus	12	30
	37	104
Less: advance corporation tax	(6)	
	31	104

(c)   Under the liability method of calculating deferred tax, provisions are calculated at the rate at which it is estimated that tax will be paid (or recovered) when the timing differences reverse. Usually the current tax rate is used as the best estimate, unless changes in tax rates are known in advance. As a result, deferred tax provisions are revised to reflect changes in tax rates. Thus the tax charge or credit for the period may include adjustments of accounting estimates relating to prior periods. Thus the deferred tax provision represents the best estimate of the amount which would be payable or recoverable if the relevant timing differences reversed. Therefore, whilst the P & L figure may contain an adjusted figure for deferred tax, the balance sheet will show the amount payable if the differences reversed i.e. the liability method adopts essentially a balance sheet perspective.

8 Business combinations and goodwill

8.1 Merger accounting

COMMENT

This area is now well regulated and there appear to be few problems at the time of writing (Spring 1994).

(a)   According to the law:
  (i)   The acquirer must use equity
  (ii)   The acquirer must acquire 90% of the target company's equity
  (iii)   The offer must be made to all holders of the target company's equity
  (iv)   The acquirer must not hold more than 20%, before making the offer
  (v)   The offer should be a share swap but an element of non-equity is allowed
  (vi)   The element of cash is restricted to 10% of the nominal value of the shares, issued by the acquirer.

(b)   The major differences between the balance sheets are (ABS – Acquisition balance sheet; MBS – Merger balance sheet):
  (i)   The fixed assets are revalued to fair value in the ABS, but can be left at book value in the MBS. In practice companies revalue in both instances – to establish a consistent approach within the group.
  (ii)   The ABS will have goodwill, either positive or negative arising on the acquisition of the subsidiary. The MBS will not have goodwill, but instead differences arising from the transaction/merger will be accounted for within the reserves. The goodwill arising from the acquisition can be capitalised and amortised or written off through the reserves.

(iii) In acquisition accounting the new shares issued to acquire the new subsidiary will generate share premium (subject to SI 3I – CA 1985 'Merger Relief'). Merger accounting will ordinarily involve an adjustment to consolidated reserves.

(c) (i) Calculation of the merger reserve:

Note the market value of Alpha plc's ordinary shares is not given.

Nominal value of Alpha's new shares (800 @ 5p)	£40
Fair value of Alpha's new shares (assumed to equal the fair value of Beta's net assets)	£800
Difference = Merger reserve	£760

(ii) If the subsidiary's shares were sold for more than the £800, then the £760 merger reserve would now become realised. The realised merger reserve could now be transferred to the profit and loss account, for distribution purposes.

COMMENT

The appendix to the standard (paragraph 44) refers to the situation where the subsidiary pays a dividend to the holding company out of pre-acquisition profits. It may be necessary for the dividend to be credited to the investment and so reduce the value of the investment. In this circumstance it may be that an equivalent amount of merger reserve should be treated as realised. SSAP 23 offers no answer, merely stating that no legal ruling has yet been made on this point. It should also be noted that the UITF have not had to pronounce on this. (See introduction to UITF, paragraph 6 [May 1992].)

8.2 Mr Bruno

(a) The report should include the following comments:

Goodwill is an amount created when acquiring a business when the purchase price is higher than the fair value of the net assets of the business. This premium reflects the value of items such as managerial ability and customer base.

If purchased goodwill is treated as an asset then it is capitalised and written off over its useful life. This treatment would be consistent with other fixed assets and the charge for consumption of the asset is matched with the benefits accruing over the estimated useful life. However, the determination of the useful life of goodwill is extremely difficult in practice.

The practice recommended by SSAP 22 Accounting for goodwill is to write off goodwill immediately to reserves. This approach does not distort group EPS or return on capital employed ratios since there is no charge for depreciation or an increase to capital employed caused by the inclusion of intangible assets. However, when many significant acquisitions take place over a short period of time, a company's reserves are liable to be heavily depleted (i.e. by the write-offs).

(b) If the consideration is to be 80% cash then acquisition accounting must be used. Goodwill is therefore calculated as the difference between the consideration and the fair value of the separable net assets.

Separable net assets are taken to be identifiable assets and liabilities which are capable of being disposed of or discharged separately without necessarily disposing of a business of the undertaking.

Assessing the fair value of the separable net assets can be difficult and in July 1990, ED53 'Fair value in the context of acquisition accounting', was issued to suggest possible methods of achieving a consistent valuation.

Two main methods can be used in assessing fair values:

(i) by considering how much the acquirer would have been prepared to pay for the individual item if it had been acquired directly, rather than as a package of assets;
or

(ii) by considering how much the acquirer would have adjusted the consideration had the relevant item (e.g. tax losses) not existed.

Both these methods allow for a starting point and aggregation to determine the fair value. Book values cannot be used since they are of no relevance to fair, realistic or current values.

ED53 allows up to six months of 'hindsight' after the acquisition to determine and adjust fair values.

The above provisions concern the determination of the fair value of what is to be acquired. However, it is also necessary to determine the fair value of the consideration. ED53 outlines how to assess the fair value of the consideration and it depends on whether the offer is to be in securities (shares, loan stock etc), monetary items or non-monetary items (assets etc.).

The valuation of the consideration under each option is:

Securities
Based on market price at the date the acquisition becomes unconditional and averaged for recent, short-term fluctuations. Where securities are unlisted, estimated values should be calculated based on price/earnings ratios.

Monetary items
Based on amount paid or payable.

Non-monetary items
Based on realisable value or replacement cost.

For the acquisition in Tyson, 80% is in cash – i.e. monetary item – which is fixed and offers no difficulty in assessing its fair value.

The remaining 20% was either by way of a share issue or financed by way of a loan. The fair value of the share issue would follow the guidelines, as stated for securities above. The fair value of the loan is a monetary item and is easy to identify, but may be augmented by interest paid or accrued if the loan had been arranged prior to the acquisition date.

(c)   **Business considerations**

- loan capital increases gearing and interest charges
- this may be acceptable if current gearing is low
- reduces potential for future borrowing
- issuing shares dilutes ownership
- 70% holding is below level required to pass special resolutions
- difficulty in valuing shares.

9 Intercompany investments

9.1 Methods of consolidation

There are a number of techniques which have been developed by the accountancy profession to measure and present the effects of one company owning shares in another company. The application of a particular technique depends whether the shares in the owned company are treated as:

- an investment
- an associated company
- a subsidiary.

Where the holding in the owned company is not substantial and the holding company has no significant influence or control over the investee company this situation should be treated as an investment.

In such a situation a decision must be made as to whether the holding is long or short term. If the holding is for the long term it should be shown as a fixed asset at cost. A short-term investment should be included in current assets and valued at the lower of cost and net realisable value.

Companies Act 1989 introduced the term 'participating interest'. A participating interest in an undertaking (known as the associated undertaking) is deemed to mean an interest in the shares of the undertaking which is held for the long term, for the purpose of securing a contribution to the activities of the investing company. This is achieved by the exercise of control or influence arising from that interest. The CA 1989 includes a presumption that once a holding exceeds 20% it becomes a participating interest and should be accounted for using the equity method of accounting.

The investing group's share of the profit before tax of the associated undertaking should be included in its consolidated financial statements. The group taxation charge should likewise include any taxation attributable to the profits of the associated company. The effect on the consolidated balance sheet is the total of:

(a) the investing group's share of the net assets other than goodwill of the associated undertakings stated, where possible, after attributing fair values to the net assets at the time of acquisition of the interest in the associated companies; and

(b) the investing group's share of any goodwill in the associated companies' own financial statements, together with;

(c) the premium paid (or discount) on the acquisition of the interests in the associated companies in so far as it has not already been written off or amortised.

A company becomes a subsidiary undertaking where the parent company:

(i)   has a majority of the voting rights; or
(ii)   is a member and can appoint or remove a majority of the board; or
(iii) is a member and controls alone a majority of the voting rights by agreement with other members; or
(iv)   has the right to exercise a dominant influence through the memorandum and articles
(v)   has a participating interest and either actually exercises a dominant influence over it, or manages both on a unified basis.

Under the acquisition method in the consolidated accounts, the investment should be replaced by the underlying separable assets and liabilities of the subsidiary at their fair values, representing their 'cost' to the group. Any difference between the cost of the investment and the sum of the values of the separable assets and liabilities is recorded as goodwill. Pre-acquisition profits of the subsidiary are no longer available for distribution and the results of this new subsidiary are only brought into the consolidated profit and loss account from the date of acquisition.

There is a second type of accounting which can be used in the parent–subsidiary relationship called merger accounting. The conditions for this type of accounting are very detailed and provisions introduced by the CA 1989 will, to some extent, restrict the ability of UK companies to apply merger accounting. The significant conditions are that:

(a) at least 90% of the nominal value of the relevant shares in the acquired undertaking must be held by or on behalf of the parent company and its subsidiaries; and

(b) not more than 10% of the nominal value of the considerations should be in the form of cash.

The investment in the subsidiary is stated at the nominal value of shares issued in consideration. Any difference between the nominal value of the issued shares and the nominal value of their acquired shares is taken to reserves. There is no revaluation of assets to the fair value and no goodwill (SSAP 23, Para. 18, allows latitude, i.e. 'it is not necessary to adjust the carrying values of the assets').

9.2 Subsidiary include/exclude

COMMENT

Students should note that this has always been a subjective area. The current FRS2 clarifies the situation, along with the discussion papers preceding its publication.

MEMORANDUM

To: Board of Directors   From: Chief Accountant
Re: Exclusion of subsidiaries

   The Financial Reporting Standard 2 regulates this area as well as the Companies Act 1985
   The Companies Act 1985 makes it a little more difficult to exclude a subsidiary than the early
   regulations (i.e. Company law and SSAP 14)
   The Act permits or requires the exclusion of subsidiaries in a number of specified circumstances.
   FRS2 elaborates on the conditions for exclusion and is more prescriptive than the Act.
A subsidiary should be excluded in the following circumstances:

(a)   The investment in the subsidiary is held exclusively with a view to resale (and the subsidiary was
      not previously consolidated) [reference paragraph 25b].
(b)   There are 'severe long term restrictions', which hinder the rights of the parent company [reference
      paragraph 25a].
(c)   The activities of the subsidiary are so different that to include its results would distort the true
      and fair view. It is considered that this reason will rarely be used! [reference 25c].

Accounting for excluded subsidiaries
Investments held for resale: [paragraph 29]. Here the investment is shown in the current assets at the
lower of the cost and net realisable value.
   Severe long term restrictions: [paragraph 27]. Each subsidiary is considered individually.
   Normally the subsidiary will be shown as a fixed asset – investment at the carrying value when the
restrictions occurred. No accrual should be made by the parent for the subsidiary's profits. Where
significant influence is still held, the subsidiary should be treated as an associate and the equity method
should be used (see FRS2, paragraph 27 for the detail).
   Different activities: [paragraph 30]. The equity method should be used.

Note:
The Companies Act 1985 permits exclusion where:

(i)   Inclusion is not material.
(ii)   The information cannot be obtained without disproportionate expense or undue delay.
(iii)   Severe long-term restrictions exist.
(iv)   The interest is held exclusively for subsequent resale.

FRS2 requires exclusion in (iii) and (iv). The FRS only deals with material items so exclusion in (i) is
implied. Exclusion in (ii) is not accepted by FRS2 for any material items.
   Both the Act and FRS2 require exclusion where the subsidiary's activities are so different from those of
the rest of the group as to distort the true and fair view.

9.3   Fair value

COMMENT

FRS2 fair value paragraphs 38, 50, 51. This is another subjective area that has provided the preparers of
accounts with many problems.

(a)   'Fair value' appears in SSAP 1(R), SSAP 21, SSAP 22(R), SSAP 23 and FRS2. SSAP 22 defines fair
      value as 'the amount for which an asset (or liability) could be exchanged in an arm's length
      transaction'.
         Fair value is used when considering the non-tangible elements within an acquisition, i.e.
      consideration = net tangible assets + intangible assets. The group accounts will use fair value to
      establish 'cost to the group'. The latter is required for SSAP 12(R) purposes – the group should
      depreciate 'the cost of the group' not the original cost to the newly acquired group member subsidiary.

The fair value concept had to be incorporated in the accounting requirements, otherwise the resultant goodwill would not have reflected the negotiated values and the depreciation charge would not have been based on the 'true' cost to the group (and so not conforming with SSAP 12(R)).

(b)   The application of the fair value concept is subjective in many instances where consideration is exchanged for a collection of tangible assets. Attributing fair values in most cases becomes, therefore, highly subjective.

The fair value of the consideration, if shares, will be the market price of those shares. There is a problem where the consideration is based on future profits.

The acquirer will use a variety of methods – consistently applied – to establish the fair value of the assets and liabilities acquired within the subsidiary. These will range from the internal and external sources, e.g. valuers to theoretical profits generated times a multiple, e.g. valuation of hotels in the Queens Moat Group.

(c)   Three areas of where fair value accounting is applied:
   (i)   Acquiring a subsidiary (FRS2 and SSAP 22/23).
   (ii)   Acquiring an investment in an associated/related company (SSAP 1/22).
   (iii) Deciding if a lease meets one of the SSAP 21 criteria, to be treated as a finance lease (i.e. present value of the lease payments exceed 90% of the leased asset's fair value).

10 Overseas involvement

10.1 SSAP 20

COMMENT

This is a highly subjective area and preparers face continual problems establishing fair values, especially in an ever changing economy (i.e. moving from boom to recession).

SSAP 20 requires, at the individual company stage, all exchange gains and losses to be reported as part of the profit or loss for the year. Paragraphs 9 and 10 of the standard explain the rationale for this treatment as it applies to long-term monetary items. In particular paragraph 10 states that in order to show a true and fair view, exchange differences on such items should be included in the profit and loss account in accordance with the accruals concept.

The standard requires both gains and losses to be shown in the profit and loss account except where there are doubts as to the convertibility of the currency. Under those circumstances it may be necessary to restrict the gains recognised in the profit and loss account on the grounds of prudence (Paragraph 11).

The Companies Acts permit only profits released at the balance sheet date to be included in the profit and loss account. The inclusion of exchange gains on unsettled long-term monetary items in the profit and loss will therefore require the 'True and fair override' to be invoked.

Appendix 1 shows the effect on Bengal Ltd's profit and loss account of the exchange differences arising on the loan. The exchange differences are material to the profit on ordinary activities. This could be misleading given that the gains and losses are unrealised. Adopting a prudent approach would allow the inclusion of losses but exclude gains. Yet SSAP 20 requires symmetry of treatment and in so doing emphasises the accruals concept over prudence.

In the calculation of distributable profits, it is necessary to exclude such unrealised gains even though they are included in the profit and loss account. There is no doubt this will *not* help the user's understanding of the financial statements.

An alternative treatment would be to show exchange differences as a movement in reserves and therefore under FRS3, they would appear in the statement of total recognised gains and losses. As noted above, it would be prudent to include losses in the profit and loss account but to reflect profits as a reserve movement. This approach would, of course, lose the symmetry of treatment deemed necessary by SSAP 20.

Appendix 1 to Question 10.1

The loan would originally be translated at a rate of \$1.30/£1.00 (31 December 1984 exchange rate approximates to 1 January 1985 rate) £30 million @ \$1.30/£1.00 = £23.077 million.

Sterling equivalent of loan (£m)

31 Dec	Exchange rate	(\$/£)	Gain/(Loss)
1984	(1.30)	(23 077)	—
1985	1.45	20 690	2.387
1986	1.50	20 000	0.690
1987	1.85	16 216	3.784
1988	1.80	16 667	(0.451)
1989	1.60	18 750	(2.083)
1990	1.55	19 355	(0.605)
1991	1.80	16 667	2.688
(16 Dec)			

Profit and loss extracts for the years ended . . .

	1985	1986	1987	1988	1989	1990	1991 (16 Dec est.)
	£M	£M	£M	£M	£M	£M	£M
Operating profit	2.500	3.083	3.667	4.250	4.833	5.417	6.000
Other interest (Receivable/Payable)*	2.387	0.690	3.784	(0.451)	(2.083)	(0.605)	2.688
Profit on ordinary activities before tax	4.887	3.773	7.451	3.799	2.750	4.812	8.688

[* Paragraph 68, SSAP 20]

10.2 Foreign currency

COMMENT

Students should appreciate there are considerable practical problems in reporting foreign currency transactions/situations. Several major plcs have found their trading results severely distorted by foreign currency accounting requirements (not to mention Polly Peck).

(a) The closing rate method is otherwise referred to in SSAP 20 as the net investment. It recognises that a company's investment in a foreign subsidiary is in the net worth of that subsidiary rather than in its individual assets and liabilities; the subsidiary is not dependent on the investing company in its day-to-day operations. The investing company is, therefore, only interested in the dividends it will receive, as the net investment will only be realised on the sale or liquidation of the foreign subsidiary.

However the investing company may be undertaking transactions in foreign currencies through the medium of a foreign subsidiary in such a way that the subsidiary has very little autonomy. In such circumstances, it is appropriate for the financial statements to record the transactions as if they had been undertaken by the investing company directly. It is in such circumstances that the temporal method is considered more appropriate.

(b) SSAP 20 requires that the closing rate method should normally be used when preparing group accounts which include a company and its foreign enterprises. However, where the trade of the foreign enterprise is more dependent on the economic environment of the investing company's currency than of its own reporting currency, SSAP 20 requires the use of the temporal method.

A number of factors should be considered when determining whether the foreign currency enterprise is dependent on the investing company's currency. Paragraph 23 of SSAP 20 identifies four factors in particular:

(i) The extent to which the cash flows of the enterprise have a direct impact upon those of the investing company.

(ii) The extent to which the functioning of the enterprise is dependent directly upon the investing company.

(iii) The currency in which the majority of the trading transactions are denominated.

(iv) The major currency to which the operation is exposed in its financial structure.

Paragraph 24 gives examples of when the temporal method may be appropriate. These are where the foreign enterprise:

(i) acts as a selling agency receiving stocks of goods from the investing company and remitting the proceeds back to the company;

(ii) produces raw materials or manufactures parts or sub-assemblies which are then shipped to the investing company for inclusion in its own products.

(iii) is located overseas for tax, exchange control or similar reasons to act as a means of raising finance for other companies in the group.

It is not necessary to use the same method for all foreign enterprises in a group, but rather the circumstances of each enterprise should be considered and the appropriate method employed. However, once chosen, the translation method should be applied consistently from period to period unless its relationship with the investing company changes.

11 Expansion of the annual report

11.1 FRS1 Cash Flow Statements

COMMENT

Students can establish the wisdom of FRS1 by comparing the old funds flow statement with the new cash flow statement.

(a) The five headings in a FRS1 cash flow statement are:

(i) Operating activities
(ii) Returns on investments, servicing of finance
(iii) Taxation
(iv) Investing activities
(v) Financing activities

Examples of (i) will include the operating profit, adjusted for depreciation and working capital movements. The reader can now look at the cash generated or absorbed by the operating activities. The latter will reflect the management decisions in the day-to-day running of the business.

(ii) This will include interest paid/received and dividends paid/received. The reader can assess the relationships between the latter items and with the operating activities cash flow. It should be noted that the items in this section are highly objective and not open to abuse through cynical subjective decisions by the preparers.

(iii) This will include corporation tax, advance corporation tax and overseas tax paid. The reader can now assess the difference between provisions and payments and relationships between profits (in cash form) and tax burden (in cash form).

(iv) This will include the purchase/sale of fixed assets. The reader is informed of the management decision regarding the allocation of funds for future economic benefits and any attempts to fund that allocation by disposal opportunities.

(v) This will include any movements of cash regarding capital, e.g. ordinary shares, preference shares and debentures. The reader can assess the means of financing the company has adopted e.g. equity only, debt only, mix of either. The reader can see very quickly matched transactions e.g. debt repaid, new borrowings.

(b)   Purposes of a cash flow statement:
    (i)   An alternative to profit and loss and balance sheet, focusing on cash movements.
    (ii)   The headings are areas of specific interest.
    (iii)   The headings within the profit and loss account and balance sheet are problem areas due to accruals affecting various figures in a material way e.g. debtors, creditors, taxation, fixed assets and dividends.
    (iv)   The movement between opening and closing cash balances is formally explained.

SSAP 10 Funds flow statement
    (i)   The cash flow statement is prescribed (funds flow was not)
    (ii)   The working capital section in funds flow was distorted by accruals, and does not feature in the cash flow.
    (iii)   The servicing of finance provides a clear picture in cash flow that was not obviously apparent in funds flow.
    (iv)   All fixed assets aspects are together in cash flow and not separated, as in funds flow.

11.2 FRS1

COMMENT

Companies are complying with the requirement to use a standardised format.
(a)   Its stated objective is:
    (i)   To require reporting entities to report on a standard basis cash generation and absorption.
    (ii)   To require a primary financial statement analysing cash funds, under standard headings.
    (iii)   To assist users assess an entity's liquidity, viability and financial adaptability.

(b)   The required format:
Net cash inflow from operating activities
Returns of investments, servicing of finance
    Interest received
    Interest paid
    Dividends paid (received)
Net cash flow from returns on investments and servicing of finance
Taxation
UK corporation tax paid
Investing activities
    Purchase/sale of tangible fixed assets
    Purchase/sale of subsidiary undertaking
Net cash outflow from investing activities
Net cash inflow/outflow before financing
Financing
    Issue of ordinary share capital (redemption)
    Proceeds of long-term borrowing (repayment)
Net cash inflow/(outflow) from financing
Increase in cash and cash equivalents.

(c)   (i)   Operating Activities
    The cash flow from the above will represent that generated from trading activities excluding non-trading items. The standard items all represent the entity's trading decisions, i.e. cash received from customers, cash paid to suppliers.
    (ii)   Investing Activities
    This section focuses on the acquisition and disposal of fixed assets, i.e. intangible, tangible and investments. The reader can then compare the net 'fixed asset' situation's relationship with the other cash flows in the statement.

(iii) Financing
The items appearing in this section all relate to long-term capital. The financing section reveals movements in ordinary and preference shares, various types of borrowings, including lease finance.

12 Capital reorganisation, reduction and reconstruction

12.1 Purchase of own shares

COMMENT

This is not a popular topic and consists of a series of rules. Several major plcs have taken advantage of the company law and redeemed their shares without recourse to the courts.

(a) Accounting requirements
  (i) The redeemed share must have been fully paid in the first instance.
  (ii) There are strict rules regarding the maintenance of capital levels.
  (iii) Shares purchased, with no *new* shares issued – here a transfer must be made out of distributable profits, equalling the par value of the redeemed shares. This maintains the capital levels.
  (iv) Shares purchased, with new shares issued – here the transfer will be the difference between the par value redeemed and the proceeds of the fresh issue. Again the capital level is maintained.
  (v) Where the redemption is at a premium, the latter is charged to distributable profits. Where the redeemed share was originally issued at a premium, the original premium (assuming it remains in the share premium) is matched to the outgoing premium, with any excess of the latter being charged to the distributable profit.
  (vi) The share purchase must not result in just redeemable shares remaining as the company's capital.

(b) Six advantages (and more)
  (i) The available earnings are enhanced (in most circumstances).
  (ii) The share price will increase (assuming there is no change in the price/earnings ratio).
  (iii) A minority/dissident shareholder can be simply dealt with, without recourse to the courts.
  (iv) Small shareholders can be removed from the share register – reducing costs.
  (v) ACT will be reduced, maybe reducing the ACT irrecoverable written off.
  (vi) Staff shareholders are easier to manage, without recourse to the courts.
  (vii) Fewer shareholders may simplify the politics within the company.
  (viii) With fewer shareholders, take-over bids may be easier to defend against.
  (ix) Surplus capital can be returned, where the company's original operations are drawing to a close (TV franchise company).

12.2 Chest Ltd and Nut Ltd

(a) Different schemes are possible in divising a group structure; this solution is only one of a number of alternative options.

Parent company
The choice of parent company depends on the financial strength of the company, its capital structure – if there is cheap prior capital, for example – and the amount of reserves. In this question, the shareholders also wish that no reduction of capital by way of a permissible capital payment (PCP) is made. Insufficient information is given to make a decisive choice but Nut Ltd appears a strong, large company and with suitable reserves to purchase shares without making a PCP.

Value of Nut's shares:

	£
Asset value	8 000
No of shares	2 000
Price per share	4
Funds required to buy Chest's stake in Nut:	
Number of shares held by Chest	800 shares
Payment required @ £4 per share	3200

Therefore Nut's reserves of £4000 are sufficient to fund this repurchase and no PCP is required. Since the purchase is being made at £4 per share – and the original issue was made at £2 – Chest is making a profit of £1600 on the transaction. Chest's net worth increases to:

	£
Original net assets	5 000
Profit on repurchase by Nut	1 600
	6 600
Share value (3000 shares)	£2.20

Nut already holds 1200 shares in Chest and to form a 100% subsidiary Nut needs to buy the remaining 1800 shares at £2.20 at a total cost of £3960. This will be partially funded by the issue of 800 new £1 shares at par.

The journal entries to record these transactions are:

	Dr £	Cr £
1. Share capital	800	
Profit and loss account – share premium	2 400	
Bank – paid to Chest		3 200

Being Nut's repurchase of own shares
for Chest's holding.

	Dr £	Cr £
2. Investments – Chest Ltd	3 960	
Bank – paid to Chest		3 960

Being purchase of remaining shares (i.e. 1800)
in Chest at £2.20 each.

	Dr £	Cr £
3. Bank – received from Nut	3 200	
Investments – Nut Ltd		1 600
Gain on investment disposal		1 600

Being Chest's profit on sale
of Nut shares.

	Dr £	Cr £
4. Bank	800	
Share capital		800

Being issue of 800 shares at
par by Nut Ltd.

The revised statement of shareholders funds is:

Nut Ltd

	£
Share capital	2 000
Share premium	2 000
Reserves	1 600
	5 600

Notes

1.   Reserves

	£
Opening reserves	4 000
Repurchase of shares – Journal 2	(2 400)
Revised reserves	1 600

2.   Share values

It has been assumed that share values based on net assets value approximates to market value for the relevant sized holdings.

(b)   Until the Companies Act 1981, a UK company could not normally purchase its own shares. A company may decide to purchase its own shares in order to:

(i)   Distribute surplus cash other than by way of a dividend.

This would be an option when a company with cash resources wishes to make a distribution to shareholders but poor results would prohibit a large dividend or if such a dividend could not be maintained in future periods.

(ii)   Provide a readily available market for shares.

For private companies the main advantage of purchasing its own shares may be to overcome the disadvantages inherent in the lack of a readily available market for the shares. Thus individuals may be more willing to invest in private companies, malcontent shareholders and retiring directors may be bought out and the existence of these purchasing powers helps to popularise employee share schemes.

(iii)   Reduce the scope of ownership

Having the option to buy its own shares reduces the risk of a predator building up a large stake of a target company. Shareholders can sell their shares to the company rather than be forced to sell their stake externally, diluting ownership and possibly disadvantaging remaining shareholders.

(iv)   Gain redeemable shares at low value

A company which has issued redeemable shares can buy them back from the holder before the redemption date if the price is low, thus saving itself money – a practice which has always been possible in the case of debentures.

(v)   Acquire an alternative to company reconstructions.

A court order required under company reconstructions is not required for purchase of own shares.

Companies Act provisions

Sections 159–177 contain the requirements for companies to purchase their own shares. These provisions ensure, for public companies, that permanent capital is not reduced and that only a certain amount of capital – a permissible capital payment – may be made in respect of private companies.

The legal provisions protect shareholders and creditors who may be disadvantaged by the proposed scheme. Section 176 permits any shareholder who did not vote in favour of the special resolution for the re-purchase, and any creditor to apply to the court for its cancellation. The court may confirm or cancel the resolution or adjourn the proceedings to arrange for the purchase of the dissentient member's shares or the protection of the creditor.

13 Interpretation of accounts

13.1 Oakbrook plc

(a)   Summary of ratios

	1987	1986	1985	1984	1983
Gearing[1]	32.1%	45.7%	55.8%	14.8%	14.8%
Interest cover[2]	10	5.3	4.7	9.5	6.5
ROCE[3]	25.6%	24.4%	20.2%	12.8%	9.2%
EPS (per question)	£0.351	£0.223	£0.300	£0.362	£0.257
Net assets per share[4]	£7.95	£5.35	£4.80	£12.70	£12.10

(i)   **Gearing and interest cover**

Gearing
- low until 1985 when it peaks at 55.8% to reduce substantially by 1987
- the increase in 1985 is likely to be a result of increased borrowings and minority interest as a result of acquisitions during the year
- gearing is based on shareholders' funds which decreased in 1985 which is likely to be have been caused by goodwill write-offs after the acquisition
- gearing falls after 1985 as borrowings are re-paid and no further takeovers occur
- fixed assets and shareholders' funds have substantially increased in 1986 causing gearing to fall, which is possibly due to revaluations
- gains on the sale of non-core business would have also improved gearing.

Interest cover
- cover falls after the acquisitions in 1985 but recovers during 1986 to reach a five-year high in 1987
- interest on borrowings for acquisitions in 1985 is the cause of reduced interest cover in the year
- increasing profitability and repayment of the borrowings in 1986/87 allows the ratio to improve during these years.

(ii)   **Return on capital employed**
- ROCE is low in 1983 but increases every year to 1987
- after large increases from 1983 to 1986, the level of increase drops in 1987
- the 1983–84 increase is due to profitability increases in 1984
- as a result of acquisitions, a large increase in trading profit occurred in 1985, improving ROCE
- ROCE continues to increase after 1985 as profitability increases, even though capital employed has significantly increased due to revaluations
- profitability has increased in 1986 despite a drop in turnover, perhaps due to the sale of low profitability non-core businesses which have been sold off during the year
- if currency gains are reflected through the profit and loss account, and not directly through reserves, this would also improve the company's profitability

---

[1] Long-term liabilities divided by (long-term liabilities + equity)
Long-term liabilities 7.5 ((18.3 + 5.1) – 15.9)
Equity/shareholders' funds 15.9 (per question)

$$\frac{7.5}{7.5 + 15.9}$$

[2] Trading profit divided by interest

$6.0 \div 0.6$

[3] Trading profit divided by fixed assets and net current assets i.e. $6.00 \div (18.3 + 5.1)$

[4] Net assets divided by number of shares

$15.9 \div 2$ (assume shares are £1)

- the increases to ROCE tail off in 1987, as the improvements to profitability achieved through acquisition are not repeated.

(iii) **Earnings per share**
- EPS are volatile throughout the five-year period, peaking in 1984
- acquisitions in 1985 partly financed by a share issue has diluted EPS, hence the fall from 1984
- EPS is calculated after deducting minority interests and therefore as these increase due to acquisitions, EPS falls
- without having further details it is difficult to ascertain why EPS continues to fall in 1986. It is possible that the issue of shares was a contributory factor
- EPS rises sharply in 1987, reflecting the profitability of the company and unaffected by deferred tax differences if these had been resolved in 1986.

(iv) **Net assets per share**
- this ratio is stable in 1983/84 but falls substantially in 1985, gradually rising thereafter
- the small improvement between 1983 and 1984 reflects stable trading conditions and increasing profitability
- a sharp fall in net assets occurs in 1985 when borrowings increase and goodwill is written off, two factors adversely affecting net assets per share
- net assets increase from 1986 due to revaluations and the sale of non-core activities, allowing repayment of borrowings and favourably affecting net assets per share.

(b) **Five year summaries**
Benefits
- simplified and concise information for presentation to the users of accounts
- where a significant event has occurred between three and five years earlier this would not be ascertained in a standard set of accounts but can be identified in a long-term summary
- it is easier to identify and analyse trends of key ratios from five-year summaries, than the normal two years given in financial statements.

Shortcomings
- inability to determine or ascertain changes in accounting policies and how these have affected a company's performance
- no standard of disclosure or presentation
- no account is taken of inflation and the effect on changing prices and the real value of money
- summaries become meaningless where businesses have radically changed the nature of their business in the period under review.

13.2 Segmental reporting

(a) The current requirements for the disclosure of segmental information in the annual report stem from three sources:

(i) The Companies Act (1985)
(ii) Stock Exchange requirements
(iii) SSAP 25

(i) The Companies Act required that:
If in the course of the financial year the company had carried on business of two or more classes that, in the directors' opinion, differ substantially from each other, there shall be stated in respect of each class:
- turnover attributable to the class
- profit or loss before taxation attributable to the class.

There is a further requirement to disclose the turnover attributable to differing geographical market segments. The disclosure requirements relate only to material amounts.

(ii)   The Stock Exchange requires that:
Listed companies provide in their annual report a geographical analysis of both turnover and contribution to trading results of those trading operations outside the United Kingdom.

(iii)   SSAP 25 applies to:
- plcs or holding companies with a plc subsidiary
- banking and insurance companies or groups
- private companies which exceed the criteria for defining a medium sized company under the Companies Act multiplied by 10.

SSAP 25 requires that for each of its reported classes of business and each geographical segment a company must disclose:
- turnover
- results
- net assets.

A class of business is a distinguishable component of an entity that provides a separate product or service or a separate group of related products or services.

A geographical segment is a geographical area comprising an individual country or group of countries in which an entity operates, or to which it supplies products or services.

(b) (i) Users

Advantages
- Facilitates comparison of similar industry segments within different diversified companies.
- Allows users to identify profitable and/or loss-making segments.
- Allows users to determine if the industry segment is performing favourably or otherwise compared to non-diversified companies in the same industry.
- Improves users' ability to predict future earnings and dividends.

Disadvantages
- Major problem is classification of industry classes. Different companies may classify business segments on a different basis.
- A segment's performance may be distorted by transfer pricing.

(b) (i) Preparers

Advantages
- Encourages internal management responsibility
- May lead to more efficient management of shareholders' resources.

Disadvantages
- Additional costs involved
- May disclose potentially useful information to competitors and/or corporate raiders
- Short-termism encouraged as poor results for a segment are revealed.

(ii) Users

Advantages
- Will make the structure of the company clearer. May reveal the ultimate owner. This type of reporting would have been valuable in the recent collapse of large companies e.g. Polly Peck, Maxwell Communications Corporation.

Disadvantages
- May distort the users' impression of the company as economic reality might not conform to legal form.

(c)   There are essentially two schools of thought to the reporting of income:
- the all inclusive concept (prescribed by FRS3)
- the current operating performance concept.

Under the all inclusive concept net profit/loss would include all transactions which effect the net worth of the entity. The arguments put forward to support this approach include:

1. The omission of certain charges or credits may lead to manipulation of profits over a period.
2. A profit or loss which includes all amounts is more understandable to users of accounts.

The adoption of the 'all inclusive' concept has led to the disclosure of any non-recurring items in the accounts, to allow users to make their own judgements on the effect of these items on the financial statements.

The second approach is known as the current operating performance concept. This would mean that extraordinary or prior period transactions should be excluded from the current operating profit or loss. Arguments in favour of this method include the following:

1. The operating profit is an important figure to the users of financial statements. Whilst sophisticated users of financial statements would be able to determine what was extraordinary or not under the all inclusive concept it could prove misleading to the less sophisticated user. Separate disclosure of such items using standard rules would remove this problem.
2. Removing non-recurring items from operating profit allows more meaningful comparison of a company's results over time.

The approach prescribed by the superseded SSAP 6, whilst a compromise, favoured the current operating performance concept. It defined those items which could be disclosed because of their size both within (exceptional) and outside (extraordinary) trading profit. This approach was adopted because of the importance users of accounts attached to operating profit. The past performance of a company is used as an indicator of future performance and the exclusion of non-recurring items makes this projection easier for the users of accounts.

It is interesting to note that one of the Urgent Issues Task Force's pronouncements concerned this matter. It further clarified SSAP 6 by ensuring that costs relating to restructuring or reorganising business activities should be disclosed as exceptional items not as extraordinary items unless they stem directly from a separate extraordinary event or transaction. This measure was designed to counter-act the practice of manipulating annual results by including such costs as non-recurring.

14 The valuation of securities and businesses

14.1 Valuation of shares

COMMENT

Students should structure their answers ensuring that there are sections on: (a) Dividend Basis, (b) Asset Basis; (c) Earnings Basis, in a comprehensive answer.

(a) If non-pecuniary benefits are ignored, then the benefit to an owner from the possession of any assets is the cash (and hence consumption opportunities) which will be generated over time. If we assume that immediate cash flows are of more value than future cash flows of the same nominal amount and that the 'cost' of delaying the receipt of cash can be measured by a reference to a 'discount' rate then, if risk is ignored, the basic valuation model for any asset is of the form:

$$V = \sum_{i=1}^{n} \frac{C_i}{(1+k)^i} + \frac{P_n}{(1+k)^n} \qquad \text{Equation (A)}$$

Where V is the current value, C_i, the cash inflow generated by that asset in year i (assumed to be received in full at the end of each year), P_n the price for which the asset will be sold at the end of n years and k the discount rate (assumed for simplicity to be constant over time although the possibility that it may change has to be recognised, in which case a modified formula would be used).

When the asset is sold it may be assumed that its price will depend on the cash the asset will generate in the future and hence equation (A) may be rewritten as follows:

$$V = \sum_{i=1} \frac{C_i}{(1+k)^i}$$

Equation (B)

In other words the value of an asset is the present value of the cash flows that will accrue to its owner. If we interpret the discount rate as the required post-tax rate of return desired by the owner, or potential owner, the above formula can be regarded as providing the theoretical foundation which underlies the valuation of shares.

The principal bases commonly used for valuing unlisted shares will be discussed below, but before doing so it will be helpful to comment on the derivation of the required post-tax rate of return. The minimum level which potential purchasers would require is the rate of return that could be earned on a 'risk free' investment. A holding in unlisted securities is not risk free and hence an adjustment must be made to take this into account. In practice this is usually done by increasing the required rate of return, although this approach has been attacked on theoretical grounds, because, *inter alia*, risk may not necessarily vary with time. The usual approach is to start with the rate of return earned on listed shares in businesses which are similar to that of the companies whose shares are the subject of the analysis. The rate of return on the listed security will include a premium for risk based on the market's perception of risks attaching to the activities of the business. When valuing an unlisted share it is customary to use a higher rate of return than is observed in the case of the listed company to take account of the greater risk that is usually associated with smaller companies and the reduced marketability which is a feature of unlisted shares.

The principal bases of valuation may be analysed between those which focus on dividends, earnings and asset values.

Dividend models

Dividend valuation methods are usually applied to the validation of holdings which constitute only a small proportion of the shares of a company. In such circumstances, the owner of the shares will not be able to influence the dividend policy and hence will need to estimate the dividends that will be received.

The basic model has already been introduced – Equation B. However, that model requires estimates to be made of all future dividends and hence in practice a number of simplifying assumptions will be made. The most common of these simplified approaches include the following:

(i)   **Dividends capitalisation basis**
If the dividend is expected to be constant then Equation B can be simplified to the form

$$V = \frac{D}{r}$$

i.e. the value of the share is the expected constant dividend divided by the required rate of return. This method is usually employed in the valuation of preference shares.

(ii)   **Dividends net present value basis**
The method exemplified by Equation B is modified by only including estimates of dividends for a limited period or planning horizon of, say, 5 years, and estimating the present value of dividends to be received after that period. The valuation mode then becomes:

$$V = \sum_{i=1}^{t} \frac{D_i}{(1+k)^i} + \frac{P_t}{(1+k)^t}$$

Where D_i is the expected dividend in year i, t the length of the planning expressed in years and P_t the estimated present value of dividends receivable after time t.

Earnings models

If the parcel of shares which is being valued is sufficiently large as to allow the owner to exercise significant control over the size of dividends, the valuation will focus on earnings rather than dividends. This is because the owner will be able to influence, or actually decide, the way in which earnings are distributed. If the earnings approach is used, the dividend models described above can be used with earnings substituted for dividends.

The earnings approach is only wholly relevant when the shares concerned constitute over 50% of the total shares in issue but may be used for smaller but still substantial holdings (say, over 20%) depending on the extent to which the owner can influence distribution policy.

Asset valuation models

These models can be applied on the going concern or liquidation bases. In either case the valuer estimates the value of each asset and then deducts the liabilities to give the residual value of owners' equity. If the going concern basis is used it is usually necessary to include in the asset a figure for goodwill. Goodwill is sometimes valued by use of an arbitrary formula, e.g. x years' purchase of the average profit over the last 3 years which, superficially at least, makes the asset valuation model attractive because it does not appear to depend on estimates of future earnings. This benefit is, however, illusory in that goodwill only exists if the business can in the future earn a greater than normal return on its tangible assets, and the magnitude of goodwill depends on the size of the future profits.

It is suggested that since some estimate has to be made of future earnings and/or dividends the dividend or earning valuation models described above are to be preferred to the going concern asset valuation model.

The asset valuation approach using the break up value of the asset (i.e. the amounts for which they could be sold in the current condition) is extremely useful when assessing the risk of an investment. Its purpose is to show the amount that would be obtained if all the assets were sold and hence provides a lower limit to the price which the purchaser would be prepared to pay.

The asset valuation models are concerned with the value of the business as a whole and hence are of greater relevance in the valuation of large parcels of shares. The break-up value is, however, of interest to the potential owner of a small parcel of shares in that it provides an estimate of how much he would receive if the assets were sold and all debts discharged.

In general, the value of a parcel of shares which give the shareholder control of the company will be proportionally higher than the value of a smaller holding. In this context, it should be noted that 50% of the voting shares affords control but that full control is only obtained at the 75% level. It should also be noted that potential purchasers might be prepared to pay a higher price than might otherwise be the case for a small parcel of shares which would take their holding above the 50% or 75% levels.

(b)   The theoretical basis for the various valuation methods was discussed in Para. (a).

Standard economic theory suggests that so long as both the potential buyer and seller have equal access to information (which is not to say they would make the same forecasts based upon that information) then the methods described above would achieve 'approximate justice' between the two parties. Thus a deal would only be struck if there was a gap between the minimum price which the seller would accept and the maximum price which the buyer would pay. However, when dealing with transactions between the company and one of the shareholders or between shareholders it is likely that one of the parties would have more information than the other. This would certainly be the case if the company purchased its own shares from a shareholder who was not also a director of the company. It is for this reason that many companies include in their articles a clause establishing some form of arbitration (often by the auditor) when one shareholder wishes to purchase shares from a fellow member.

14.2   Neptune plc

(a)(i)   **Goodwill**

Under the terms of SSAP 22 (revised) the preferred treatment of goodwill is to write it off immediately against reserves. However the SSAP also allows goodwill to be capitalised and amortised over its useful economic life. If Sirius adopts the latter approach then net assets may be considerably higher than if the goodwill was immediately written off. Conversely however reported profits will be lower as a result of the annual amortisation. Ratios such as EPS and ROCE will be materially affected.

(ii) **Depreciation**

The choice of depreciation rates are at the management's discretion. This could lead to significantly inflated asset values and reported profit levels if an unrealistic depreciation policy has been chosen. Whilst this may not be a significant problem in the UK where there is a reasonably strict accounting regime, the company does have foreign subsidiaries whose depreciation policies must be carefully scrutinised.

(iii) **Research and development**

SSAP 13 (revised) allows development expenditure to be deferred only if it satisfies a number of criteria. However some companies choose to write off development expenditure irrespective of whether it meets the deferral criteria laid down by SSAP 13. Clearly differing R&D policies can have a significant impact on net assets and profitability.

(iv) **Revaluation of fixed assets**

There is no generally accepted accounting treatment concerning the revaluation of fixed assets, with the exception of investment properties. On a similar basis as goodwill and R&D, differing revaluation approaches may result in significantly different financial statements. A policy to revalue the assets regularly will result in higher net assets, although there will be a higher annual depreciation charge. Conversely a policy to show fixed assets at historic cost will result in lower net assets but higher annual profits. This may be very important for future financial statements of Neptune. If Sirius maintain their assets at historical cost then on consolidation, if the acquisition method is used, this will increase goodwill and thus ultimately decrease Neptune's assets, as goodwill is amortised.

(b) **Usefulness**

- Statements will have been audited and if a clean audit report was given will show a true and fair view of the state of the company's affairs.
- Will have been prepared on a consistent basis so trends can be established.
- Various accounting ratios can be calculated from the financial statements to give useful information regarding liquidity, profitability, return on capital employed etc.
- Accounting policies will be disclosed so that a reconciliation between Sirius and Neptune's reported results can be made.
- Financial statements will report annual profits, which although subject to fluctuations as a result of differing accounting policies, do provide the best means of valuing the company.

Limitations

- May have been prepared under historic cost convention so asset valuations of limited use if out of date.
- As illustrated in part (a) accounting policies can have a significant effect on a company's reported results.
- Balance sheet gives no indication of a company's net worth. This is because:
- Debtors/stock realisable values are likely to be considered less than book value.
- There may have been profit smoothing through the use of provisions which in turn affects the book values of figures in the financial statements.
- There may be redundant/out-of-date assets shown on Sirius Group's balance sheets which will be of no use to Neptune and must be written off. This can be discovered only from physical inspection and not from the financial statements.
- The main purpose of financial statements is to report on the fiscal management of the company to its owners. Investment decisions are not part of this process and this must be kept in mind if they are to be used in predicting future results.

18 Accounting and price changes

18.1 Historical cost accounting and rising prices

(a) The limitations of historical accounting covered in detail in the main text as well as the effect of changing prices and alternative accounting conventions. There is little point in repeating these ideas verbatim for the purpose of this solution (and later solutions to theoretical questions on this topic) therefore only a brief outline is given here.

Limitations of historical cost accounting include:

(i) Depreciation charged on historically costed assets is only an arbitrary amount based on out-of-date values and estimated useful economic lives.

(ii) Depreciation does not consider what is actually required to replace those assets at today's prices.

(iii) Profit will not reflect the actual 'costs' of trading – which include the replacement of assets at some point in time.

(iv) By not accounting for inflation there is no assurance that the company is maintaining its capital base.

(v) Overstating profits by under-charging depreciation based on historical cost – and charging cost of sales at historical cost values of stock and not current cost – can lead to the depletion of a company's capital through high tax charges and distributions.

(vi) Whilst historical accounting provides a consistent basis for companies to prepare accounts, inflation affects different products and markets – and hence companies – to different degrees.

(vii) Historical accounting makes it difficult for shareholders and analysts to assess the real performance and ability of directors since changes to current market conditions are not accounted for in the historical valuation basis.

(viii) The true valuation of companies is difficult to assess under historical cost rules.

(ix) Interpretation of accounts over a period of time is difficult since each year relates to different purchasing powers.

(x) Key ratios, such as return on capital employed, are inflated under historical rules since profit is overstated (as outlined above) and capital employed reduced since assets are undervalued compared to current costs. Therefore companies investing in new assets, leading to increased efficiencies and profits, will be penalised under such ratio analysis due to higher capital employed, effectively stated at current cost.

(b) Under legislation, companies may revalue the following components:
  • fixed assets
  • investment properties
  • investments
  • stock.

(c) Directors are entrusted with running the business owned by the shareholders. Therefore, the directors hold a stewardship role, responsible to the shareholders who are informed of the company's progress through the publication of accounts. On the basis of these accounts, shareholders should be able to assess the ability of directors and decide whether a change in management is necessary.

However, as stated in (a) above, historical cost accounts do not lead to a true indication of a company's performance or future potential if capital is not being maintained. Furthermore, the actual assessment of performance through ratios such as return on capital are meaningless if profits are overstated, capital undervalued and when assets are valued under a mixture of conventions.

Alternative conventions to allow for changes in prices and purchasing power and giving the user more realistic information on company performance and valuation are open to adoption by companies. However, despite these user-oriented needs, the accountancy profession has failed to deliver these through the inception of an acceptable and mandatory application of current cost accounting.

18.2 Price changes

COMMENT

It should be appreciated that there is currently no solution to the problem of accounting for price changes.

(a) **Three factors**

(i) The capital maintenance concept. The choice is between financial or operating capital maintenance, that is, the value in money terms of the entity's ability to produce goods.

(ii) The method of valuing assets. Either historic cost – the cost when originally acquired, or current cost – generally net replacement cost.

(iii) Unit of measurement – this may be nominal pounds or units of current purchasing power.

(b) (i) **Historic cost accounting**

Advantages
- Relatively objective
- Easy to understand
- Compatible with concepts
- Used for assessing tax liabilities
- Based on actual events

Disadvantages
- Changing prices mean asset values are out of date
- Assets acquired at different times will be valued at different price levels
- Overstates real profits

(ii) **Current purchasing power accounting**

Advantages
- Gives a better indication of 'real' profit trend
- Easy to apply indices

Disadvantages
- Uses a general index which may not represent price changes experienced by the entity
- Asset values are frequently meaningless (the use of a specific index is too arbitrary)

(iii) **Current cost accounting**

Advantages
- Balance sheet values reflect current value of the entity
- Profits only stated after operating capability maintained
- Provides users with balance sheet values they want and can use

Disadvantages
- Uses subjective values
- Costs of preparation
- Difficult to understand adjustments

INDEX